The Americas, Atlantic, Caribbean and P

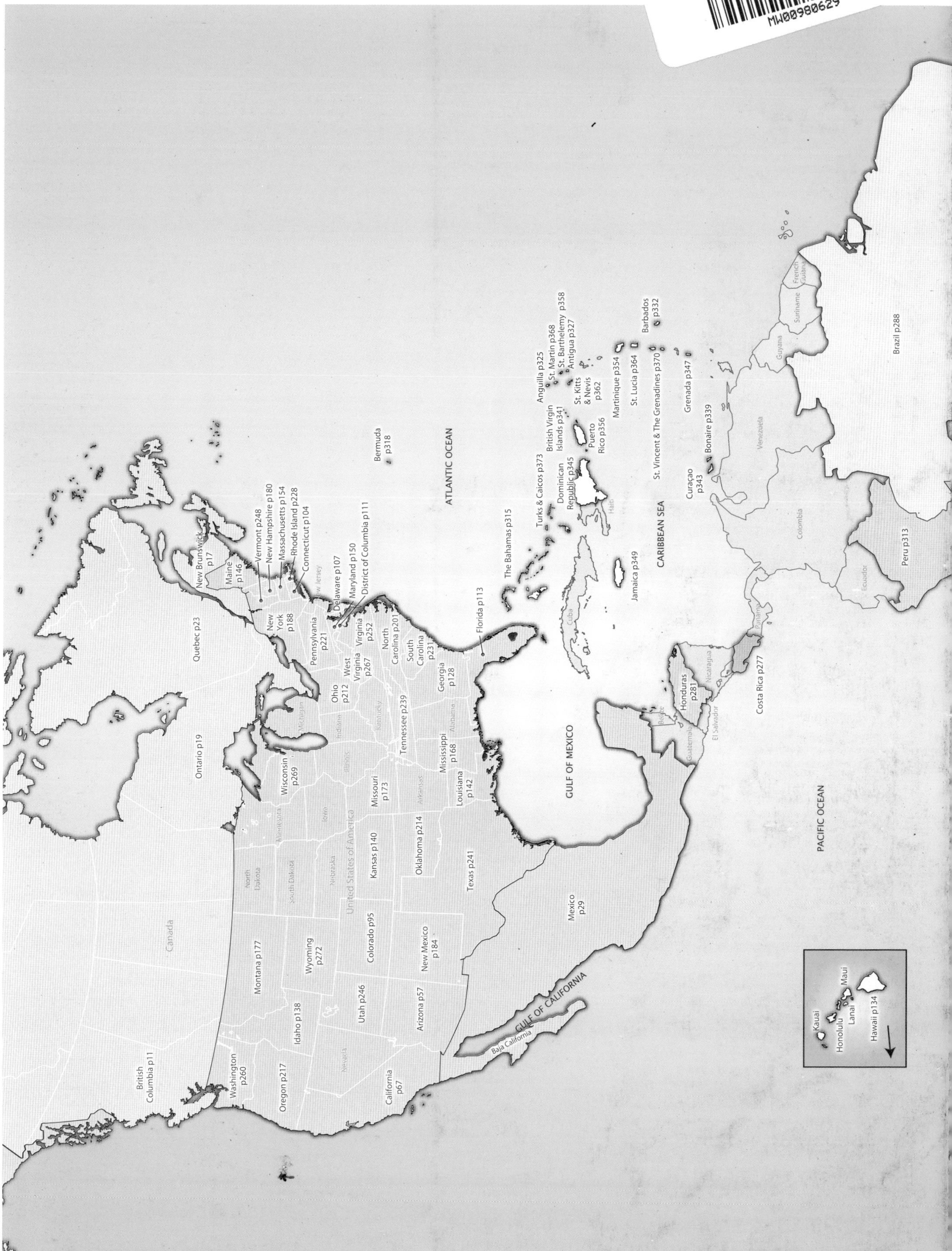

ATLANTIC OCEAN
CARIBBEAN SEA
GULF OF MEXICO
PACIFIC OCEAN
GULF OF CALIFORNIA
Baja California
Canada
British Columbia p11
Ontario p19
Quebec p23
New Brunswick p17
Maine p146
Vermont p248
New Hampshire p180
Massachusetts p154
Rhode Island p228
Connecticut p104
New Jersey
New York p188
Pennsylvania p221
Delaware p107
Maryland p150
District of Columbia p111
Virginia p252
West Virginia p267
North Carolina p201
South Carolina p231
Georgia p128
Florida p113
Ohio p212
Michigan
Indiana
Kentucky
Tennessee p239
Alabama
Mississippi p168
Wisconsin p269
Illinois
Minnesota
Iowa
Missouri p173
Arkansas
Louisiana p142
North Dakota
South Dakota
Nebraska
Kansas p140
Oklahoma p214
Texas p241
United States of America
Montana p177
Wyoming p272
Colorado p95
New Mexico p184
Idaho p138
Utah p246
Arizona p57
Washington p260
Oregon p217
Nevada
California p67
Mexico p29
Bermuda p318
The Bahamas p315
Turks & Caicos p373
Cuba
Jamaica p349
Haiti
Dominican Republic p345
Puerto Rico p356
British Virgin Islands p341
Anguilla p325
St. Martin p368
St. Barthelemy p358
Antigua p327
St. Kitts & Nevis p362
Martinique p354
St. Lucia p364
Barbados p332
St. Vincent & The Grenadines p370
Grenada p347
Bonaire p339
Curaçao p343
Belize
Guatemala
El Salvador
Honduras p281
Nicaragua
Costa Rica p277
Panama
Colombia
Venezuela
Guyana
Suriname
French Guiana
Ecuador
Peru p313
Brazil p288
Kauai
Honolulu
Maui
Lanai
Hawaii p134

How to use this Guide

To find a hotel by location:

- Use the **map** at the front of this Guide to identify the country you wish to search.
- Turn to the relevant **country / state / regional section** where properties are featured alphabetically by location.
- Alternatively, turn to the **title page** of the state / country required where you will find a map. The location of each property appears in red with a number corresponding to the page on which the property entry is published.

To find a property by its name or the name of its nearest town look in the indexes on pages 417-424.

The indexes also list recommended properties by their amenities such as swimming pool, golf, etc.

Once you have made your choice please contact the property directly. The majority of prices throughout the Guide refer to "room" rate, **not** "per person" rate. In addition, some prices are subject to state taxes. Rates are correct at the time of going to press but should always be checked with the property before you make your reservation. When making a booking please mention that Condé Nast Johansens was your source of reference.

We occasionally receive letters from guests who have been charged for accommodation booked in advance but later canceled. Readers should be aware that by making a reservation with a property, either by telephone, e-mail or in writing, they are entering into a legal contract. A hotelier under certain circumstances is entitled to make a charge for accommodation when guests fail to arrive, even if notice of the cancellation is given.

All Guides are available from bookstores or by calling Freephone 0800 269397 (U.K.) or 1 800 564 7518 (U.S.), by using the Order Form on page 431 or at our on-line Bookstore at www.johansens.com

Contents

Introduction

Andrew Warren, Managing Director, Condé Nast Johansens Ltd.

On behalf of the Condé Nast Johansens team of Inspectors, I am proud to present to you our Recommendations for 2007.

We all feel sure that you will enjoy visiting these wonderful hotels, inns, resorts and spas and that you will appreciate the hospitality that they have to offer.

Our 310 Recommendations have been chosen as much for their excellence of service and cuisine as for their unique style, diverse character and exceptional location. This edition features Canada for the first time as well as new wonderful locations in both South and North America, the Atlantic, Caribbean and the Pacific.

We value your comments, as they help us both to compile a better Guide each year and to select nominees for our Annual Awards. You may wish to complete a Guest Survey Report printed at the back of this Guide or join our e-Club at www.johansens.com to complete electronic Guest Survey Reports, participate in prize drawings, receive our monthly newsletter and create a custom portfolio of favorite Recommendations on-line. You can also submit award nominations and view Special Offers from our Recommendations at www.johansens.com

The hotels, inns, resorts and spas that we recommend take great pride in being selected by Condé Nast Johansens, so please remember to mention us when you make your reservation and again when you arrive!

The Condé Nast Johansens Promise

Condé Nast Johansens is the most comprehensive illustrated reference to annually inspected, independently owned accommodation and meetings venues throughout Great Britain, Continental Europe, the Mediterranean, the Americas, Atlantic, Caribbean and Pacific.

It is our objective to maintain the trust of Guide users by recommending by annual inspection a careful choice of accommodation offering quality, excellent service and value for money.

Our team of more than 50 dedicated Regional Inspectors visit thousands of hotels, country houses, inns, resorts and spas throughout the world to select only the very best for recommendation in the 2007 editions of our Guides.

No property can appear unless it meets our exacting standards.

Condé Nast Johansens Guides

Recommending only the finest hotels in the world

As well as this Guide, Condé Nast Johansens also publish the following titles:

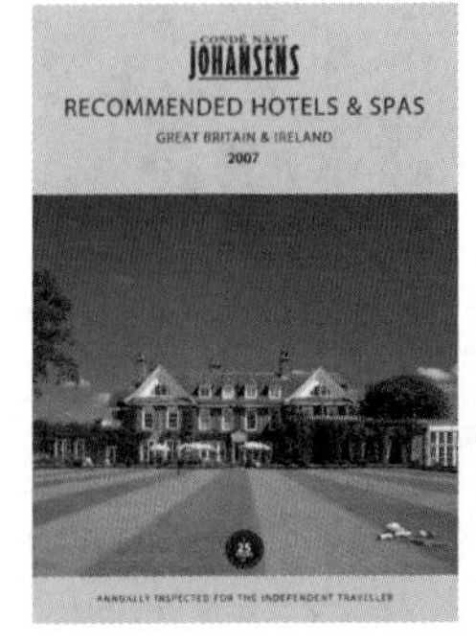

Recommended Hotels & Spas, Great Britain & Ireland

Unique and luxurious hotels, town houses, castles and manor houses chosen for their superior standards and individual character.

Recommended Country Houses, Small Hotels, Inns & Restaurants Great Britain & Ireland

Small and often intimate properties that include old coaching inns, hunting lodges and manors. The emphasis is on personal service and high levels of comfort.

Recommended Hotels & Spas Europe & The Mediterranean

A wonderful choice of properties including châteaux, resorts, charming countryside hotels and stylish city hotels.

To order Guides please complete the Order Form on page 431, call FREEPHONE 1 800 564 7518 or visit our on-line bookstore at www.johansens.com

Condé Nast Johansens

6-8 Old Bond Street, London W1S 4PH, U.K. Tel: +44 20 7499 9080 Fax: +44 20 7152 3565 E-mail: info@johansens.com www.johansens.com

V.P. & Publishing Director: Lesley J. O'Malley-Keyes
Assistant to Publishing Director: Julia Ott
Regional Inspectors: Terri Bisignano, Brooke Burns, Felipe Candiota, Mollie Christensen, Carol Clark, Griselda Contreras, Tiffany Dowd, Suzy Farmer, Anna Lucia Fernandez, Dana Halliday, Michael Kelly, Kerry Kerr, Maggie Kerr, Renata Medeiros, Cheryl Murphy, Roberto Prata, Pablo Pries, Arianna Rossell, Freda Rothermel, Sue Stafford, Sasha Travers

Production Manager: Kevin Bradbrook
Production Editor: Laura Kerry
Senior Designer: Michael Tompsett
Marketing Promotions Executive: Charlie Bibby
Client Services Director: Fiona Patrick

Managing Director: Andrew Warren

Condé Nast Johansens Ltd. is part of The Condé Nast Publications Ltd.

ISBN 1-903665-31-0

Printed in England by St. Ives plc
Color origination by Wyndeham Icon

Distributed in the UK and Europe by Portfolio, Greenford (bookstores).
In North America by Casemate Publishing, Havertown (bookstores).

The King and I

2006 Awards For Excellence

Recipients of Condé Nast Johansens 2006 Americas Awards for Excellence

The Condé Nast Johansens 2006 Awards for Excellence were presented at Hotel Plaza Athenee in New York City in January 2006. Properties were selected for an award by reader nominations and by our team of hotel Inspectors

Most Excellent Boutique Hotel in Mexico

Hacienda Xcanatun - Casa de Piedra

Yucatán, Mexico, p56

Most Excellent Spa Hotel in Mexico

Grand Velas All Suites & Spa Resort

Nayarit, Mexico, p48

Most Excellent Resort in Mexico

One & Only Palmilla

Baja California Sur, Mexico, p34

Most Excellent Romantic Hideaway in the Atlantic, Caribbean & Pacific Islands

Yasawa Island Resort

Fiji Islands, p388

Most Excellent Resort in the Atlantic, Caribbean & Pacific Islands

Ladera

St. Lucia, Caribbean, p365

Most Excellent Spa Hotel in the Atlantic, Caribbean & Pacific Islands

Cambridge Beaches

Bermuda, Atlantic, p322

Most Excellent Spa Hotel in Central & South America

Praia do Forte Eco Resort & Thalasso Spa

Bahia, Brazil, p292

Most Excellent Eco Resort in Central & South America

The Lodge at Pico Bonito

Atlántida, Honduras, p282

2006 Awards For Excellence

Recipients of Condé Nast Johansens 2006 Americas Awards for Excellence

Most Excellent Boutique Hotel in Central & South America

Hotel Marina All Suites

Rio de Janeiro, Brazil, p304

Most Excellent Spa Hotel in the U.S.A.

Hotel Hana-Maui and Honua Spa

Hawaii, U.S.A., p137

Most Excellent Hotel in the U.S.A.

Hotel Bel-Air

California, U.S.A., p78

Most Excellent Boutique Hotel in the U.S.A.

Nine Zero Hotel

Massachusetts, U.S.A., p159

Most Excellent Inn in the U.S.A.

Post Ranch Inn

California, U.S.A., p69

Most Excellent Service in the U.S.A.

The Hay Adams

District of Columbia, U.S.A., p112

Most Excellent Golf Resort in the U.S.A.

The Sanctuary at Kiawah Island Golf Resort

South Carolina, U.S.A., p236

Most Excellent Ranch in the U.S.A.

Triple Creek Ranch

Montana, U.S.A., p179

Most Excellent Resort in the U.S.A.

Elk Mountain Resort

Colorado, U.S.A., p100

Condé Nast Johansens Preferred Partner for

HOSPITALITY RECRUITMENT

CANADA - BRITISH COLUMBIA

Hotel location shown in red with page number

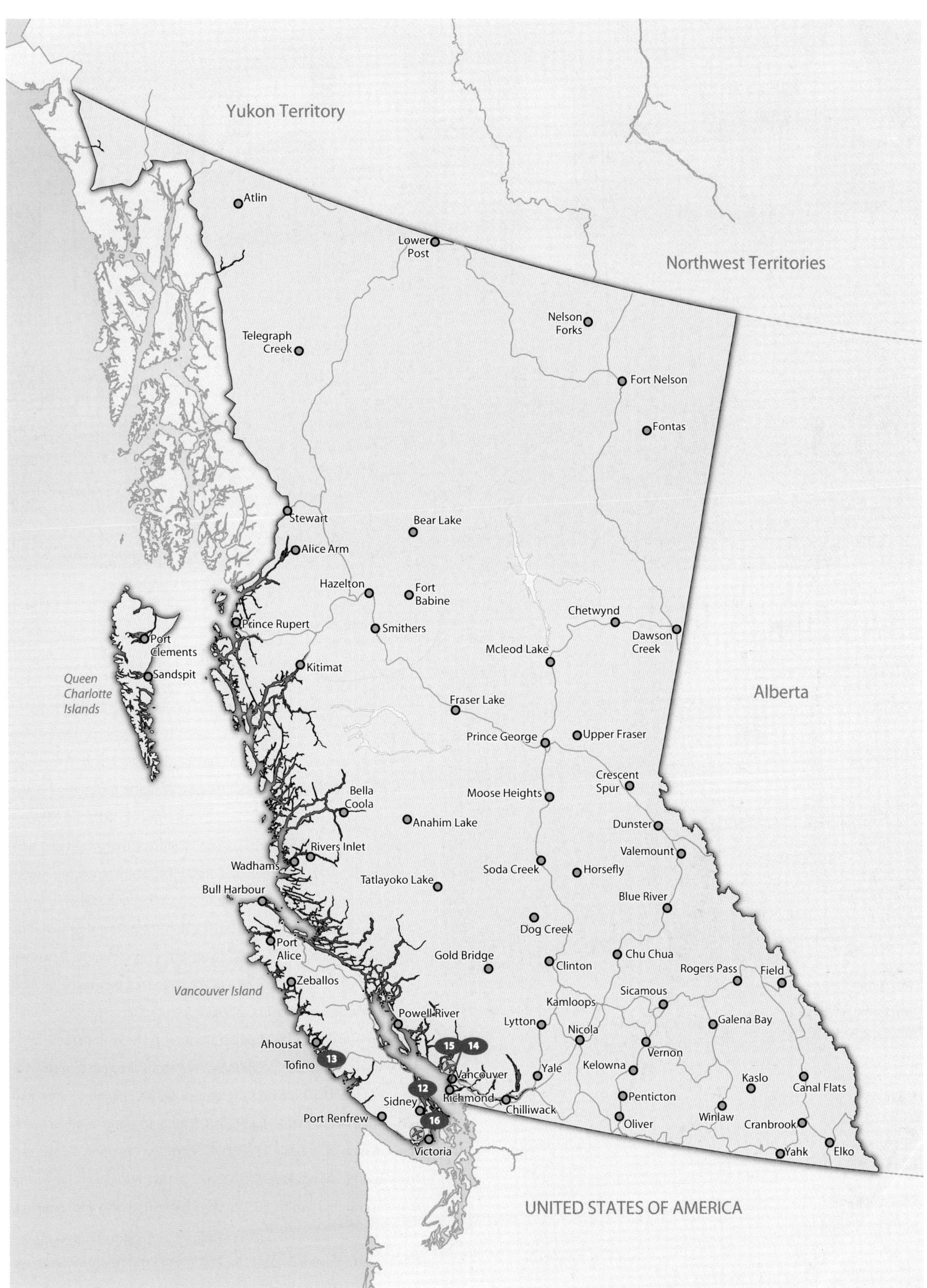

Hastings House Country Estate

160 UPPER GANGES ROAD, SALT SPRING ISLAND, BRITISH COLUMBIA V8K 2S2

The Hastings House Country Estate is a graceful and intimate resort set along 22 acres of rolling lawns, gardens and forests overlooking picturesque Ganges Harbour on quaint Salt Spring Island. The stately 11th-century, Sussex-style Manor House is central to the Estate and was built in 1940 using natural stone and native woods. There are 18 guest suites situated in 6 carefully maintained buildings. Each suite has a cozy fireplace, English country antiques, luxury bedding, sumptuous fabrics and local artwork. Guests of the Estate enjoy full English breakfast in the Manor House and afternoon tea in the Living Room. Revitalize in the Spa or enjoy a good book in the small library of the Manor House. Described as one of the top 10 dining rooms in North America, the cuisine, created by European-trained Chef Marcel Kauer, features Salt Spring Island lamb, fresh local seafood and the freshest produce and herbs from the Estate's gardens and orchards. His daily menus are complemented by an award-winning wine cellar offering the best of British Columbia wines and gems from around the world. Salt Spring Island is a vibrant arts community and is easily accessible by ferry or seaplane. Guests can enjoy biking, sailing, kayaking, tennis, garden, art studio and winery tours, the Farmers Market on Saturdays, gallery-hopping and shopping.

Our inspector loved: *Dinner at the Estate with its home-grown herbs and fresh local seafood.*

Directions: Reached by car-ferry from Vancouver or Victoria or by seaplane from Vancouver, Victoria or Seattle.

Web: www.johansens.com/hastingshouse
E-mail: info@hastingshouse.com
Tel: +1 250 537 2362
Fax: +1 250 537 5333
U.S./Canada Toll Free: 1 800 661 9255

Price Guide:
rooms C$525-C$910

THE WICKANINNISH INN

BOX 250, TOFINO, BRITISH COLUMBIA V0R 2Z0

The Wickaninnish Inn, located on Vancouver Island's beautifully rugged west coast in Tofino, sits on an expansive stretch of Chesterman Beach, at the gateway to the Pacific Rim National Park Reserve and Clayoquot Sound. Surrounded on 3 sides by ocean, the 75 spacious guests rooms and suites feature magnificent floor-to-ceiling picture windows with ocean views, private balconies, fireplaces, deep soaker tubs, binoculars to enjoy the incredible view, private bar, C.D. clock radio, writing desk, microwave, coffee maker and cozy down duvets. The setting is very romantic and the inn provides rain slickers and boots to all guests for exploring the rainforest or beach. Complementing the rustic décor are magnificent pieces of local art, which adorn the inn throughout. Guests can enjoy relaxing treatments in the Ancient Cedars Spa, and the Pointe Restaurant features incredible 240° views of the open Pacific Ocean and panoramic vistas of the adjacent beach and coastline. Its West Coast Canadian gourmet cuisine features fresh coastal foods and fine wines of the Pacific Northwest. The inn is available for groups and the Salal Room is ideal for executive meetings and retreats. In nearby Tofino, guests can visit local art galleries, fish for salmon, whale or bird watch, sea kayak or surf the magnificent waves.

Our inspector loved: *Dining at the restaurant with its spectacular views.*

Directions: Located on the west side of Vancouver Island, approx. 3 hours from Nanaimo and 4½ hours from Victoria. Air charters are available from Vancouver, Victoria and Seattle. 50 minutes from Vancouver Intl. Airport. Pacific Rim Navigator's luxury shuttle service can be arranged to and from the Tofino Long Beach Airport.

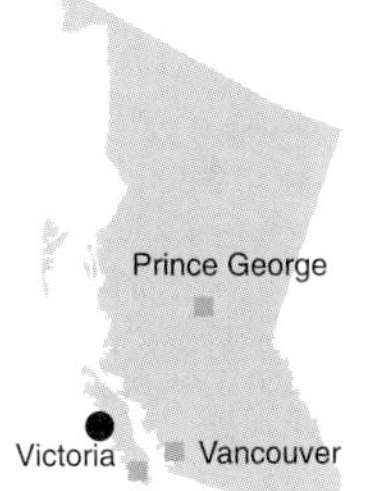

Web: www.johansens.com/wickaninnish
E-mail: info@wickinn.com
Tel: +1 250 725 3100
Fax: +1 250 725 3110
U.S./Canada Toll Free: 1 800 333 4604

Price Guide:
rooms C$260-C$640
suites C$380-C$1,500

The Sutton Place Hotel Vancouver

845 Burrard Street, Vancouver, British Columbia V6Z 2K6

The Sutton Place Hotel Vancouver brings a touch of Europe to Vancouver with its luxurious and grand setting. Centrally located downtown, the hotel boasts 47 Executive and Grand bedroom suites and 350 guest rooms. Rated 5 Diamond by AAA 17 years in a row, the level of service and attention to detail is evident in all areas of the hotel. Each guest room and suite has luxurious amenities including plush bathrobes, high-speed Internet access, web T.V., 27" flat-screen televisions and D.V.D./C.D. players. Known as one of Vancouver's premier business hotels, the hotel also offers La Grande Résidence, featuring terraced apartments, which are available for extended stays. Guests can savor the innovative French continental cuisine of Fleuri Restaurant, where Executive Chef Raman Anand showcases his classical cooking with house specialties on an ever-changing menu. The European health, beauty and fitness center at the Vida Wellness Spa can provide spiritual health with its vast array of services and treatments. A favorite for entertainment industry professionals, the Gerard Lounge is reminiscent of an English club with tapestries, leather chairs and a cozy fireplace and is perfect for cocktails and light bistro fare. Stanley Park, Granville Island, the historic Orpheum Theater, GM Place, and the chic boutiques on Robson Street are all within walking distance.

Our inspector loved: *The Chocoholic Bar, all-you-can-eat chocolate buffet.*

Directions: Vancouver International Airport is 12km/8 miles away; approximately a 30-minute drive from the hotel.

Web: www.johansens.com/suttonplacebc
E-mail: res_vancouver@suttonplace.com
Tel: +1 604 682 5511
Fax: +1 604 682 5513
U.S./Canada Toll Free: 1 866 3SUTTON

Price Guide: (room only)
rooms C$169-C$350
suites C$350-C$500

 397    300       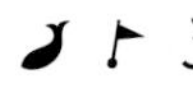 SPA 

Wedgewood Hotel & Spa

845 HORNBY STREET, VANCOUVER, BRITISH COLUMBIA V6Z 1V1

This world-class boutique hotel has long been Vancouver's best kept secret since its opening in 1984. Located in a chic downtown area, this intimate and romantic hotel exudes elegance and charm. Beautiful personal touches by the hands-on owner, Eleni Skalbania, can be seen throughout, from the fresh flowers to the rich upholstered furniture and Murano Venetian crystal fixtures. The high level of service ensures the perfect romantic city getaway. Each of the beautifully appointed rooms has a spacious balcony, fine linens and duvets. The expansive Penthouse Suites are unrivaled with fireplaces, wet-bars, Jacuzzi tubs in luxurious spa bathrooms and scenic garden terraces - favourite suites for visiting celebrities! The suites overlooking Hornby Street have views of the Robson Square gardens, and rooms on the other side of the hotel have beautiful Vancouver city or scenic mountain views. Spa treatments and services are available at the new Wedgewood Hotel Spa. Executive Chef Lee Parsons brings his unique style of modern French cuisine to the table at Bacchus Restaurant & Piano Lounge, with its inviting fireplace, bar and lounge. Bacchus has quickly become one of Vancouver's most popular places to have lunch, dinner, a sumptuous weekend brunch or afternoon tea. Conveniently located steps from cosmopolitan Robson Street where high-end shopping and designer boutiques are found.

Our inspector loved: *Dining fireside at Bacchus restaurant.*

Directions: 30 minutes north of Vancouver International Airport. Follow Grant McConachie Way over the Arthur Laing Bridge. From the bridge take Granville Street north and proceed over the Granville Street Bridge. Exit onto Seymour and follow it to Smythe, turn left, then turn right onto Hornby Street to the hotel.

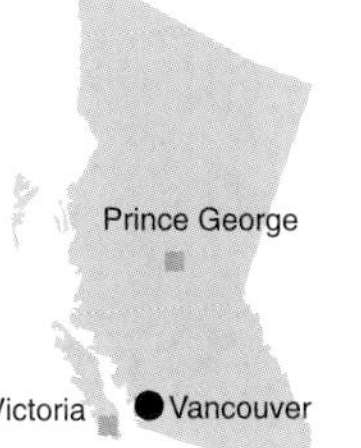

Web: www.johansens.com/wedgewoodbc
E-mail: info@wedgewoodhotel.com
Tel: +1 604 689 7777
Fax: +1 604 608 5348
U.S./Canada Toll Free: 1 800 663 0666

Price Guide:
rooms C$169-C$350

 83   100        SPA

Villa Marco Polo Inn

1524 SHASTA PLACE, VICTORIA, BRITISH COLUMBIA V8S 1X9

Directions: 1½ hours by Ferry from Vancouver - Victoria (Tsawwassen-Swartz Bay). 35 minutes by sea plane from Vancouver. 40 minutes by air from Seattle to Victoria International Airport.

Web: www.johansens.com/villamarcopolo
E-mail: enquire@villamarcopolo.com
Tel: +1 250 370 1524
Fax: +1 250 370 1624
U.S./Canada Toll Free: 1 877 601 1524

Price Guide:
suites C$165–C$325

Located in Victoria's elegant Rockland quarter, Villa Marco Polo Inn has classical architecture and design, an Italianate garden and 4 beautifully appointed suites. The inn resembles an Italian Renaissance mansion, and was built in 1923 as a gift to a young bride. Today it remains popular for special vacations, weddings and honeymoons. The suites: Silk Road, Zanzibar, Alexandria and Persia feature double soaker tubs, romantic fireplaces, fine linens, hardwood floors with Persian carpets and comfortable beds. Delicate fresh flowers fill the rooms, which are tastefully decorated with antiques and fine art from proprietors Eliza Livingston's and Clarke Bingham's personal family collections. Gourmet breakfasts, created from locally grown produce, are served in the dining room or in the sunny Italian Orangerie; vegan, gluten-free or vegetarian meals are available upon request. In the afternoons, guests can enjoy tea and sherry in the serene setting of the garden or in front of the fire in the wood-paneled library. The Villa is located minutes from downtown Victoria and the city's beautiful Inner Harbour. Innkeeper Liam Morton can arrange en-suite spa services, and activities such as whale watching, sailing, paddling, tours of local vineyards and the Gulf Islands, float plane tours and carriage tours. Craigdarroch Castle and the beautiful park-like gardens of Government House are a short walk away.

Our inspector loved: *Having tea in the inn's wood-paneled library.*

Canada - New Brunswick

Hotel location shown in red with page number

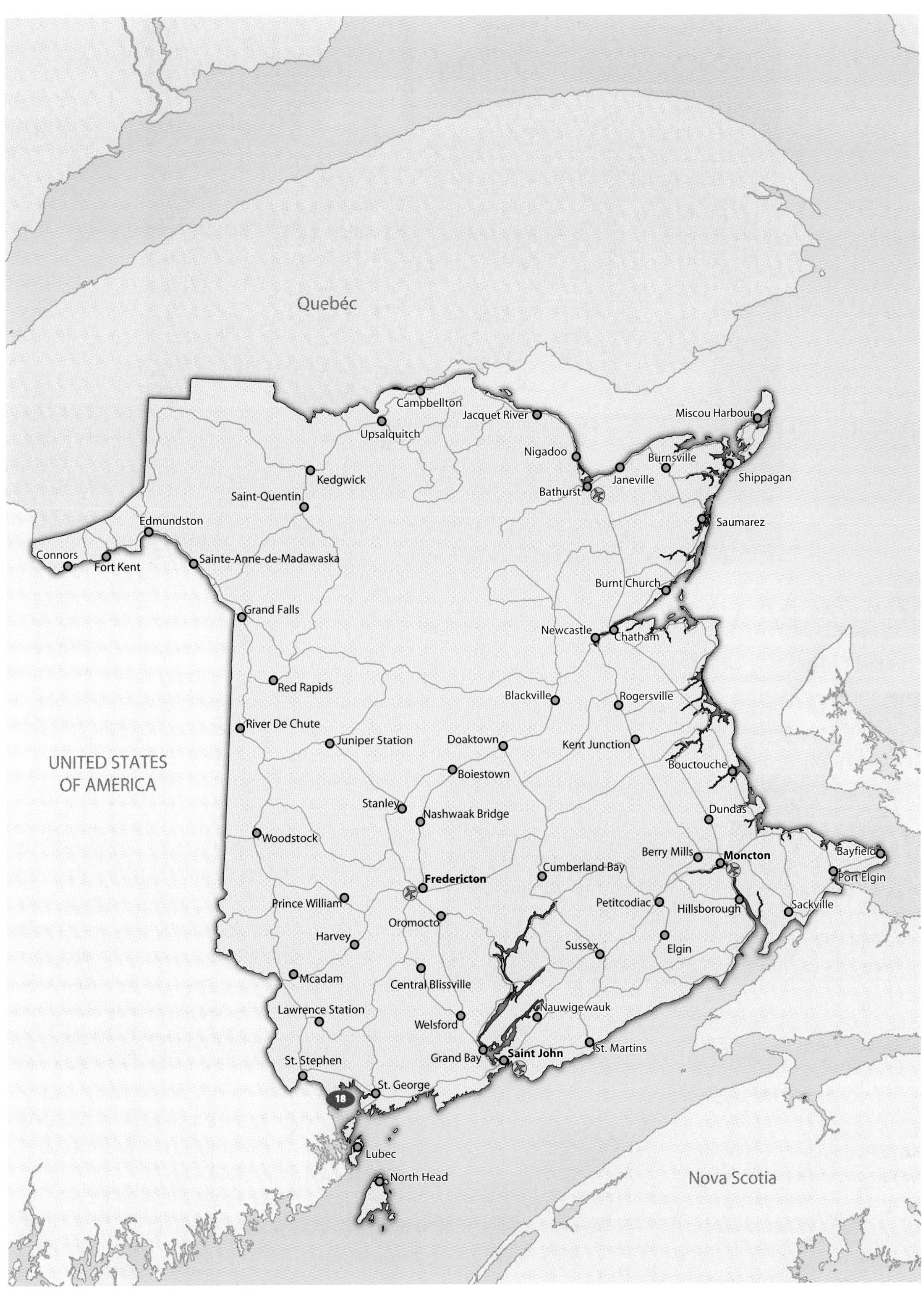

KINGSBRAE ARMS

219 KING STREET, ST. ANDREWS BY-THE-SEA, NEW BRUNSWICK E5B 1Y1

This private enclave on the Atlantic has welcomed international guests since 1897. The historic house and gardens are reserved exclusively for dinner and resident guests. This is the only Relais & Chateaux, Mobil 4-Star hotel and restaurant in the Canadian Maritimes. The inn has twice earned the Andrew Harper Grand Hideaway Award of the Year. Dinner at Kingsbrae Arms is an unforgettable experience. Guests gather for cocktails in the library overlooking the sea and are then served an exquisite multi-course tasting menu in the dining room set with crystal and candlelight. Chef Marc Latulippe works with an array of fresh seafood, game, fowl, and meats enhanced by organic produce from his own garden. As a slow food advocate, Marc presents his "cuisine du terroir et de la marée" simply and bursting with flavor. The extensive, Wine Spectator award-winning list has been assembled to complement the fare. Upstairs, 8 suites and 2 rooms are luxuriously appointed with marble bathrooms, deep soaking tubs, and sweeping views of gardens and sea. In-room massage services are available using hot lava rock therapies.

Our inspector loved: *This exquisite, luxurious country house with its fine restaurant.*

Directions: From New England, take I-95 to Bangor ME then Route 9 east to Calais ME. St. Andrews by-the-Sea is 20 minutes beyond the International Bridge, exit 25 off Canada Highway 1.

Web: www.johansens.com/kingsbraearms
E-mail: reservations@kingsbrae.com
Tel: +1 506 529 1897
Fax: +1 506 529 1197
U.S./Canada Toll Free: 1 877 529 1897

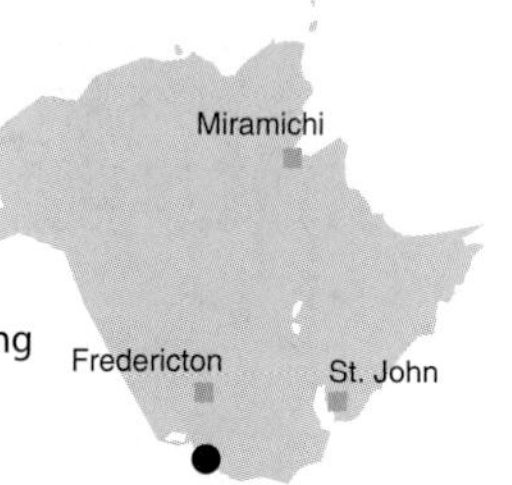

Price Guide: (including full breakfast and tasting menu dinners, double occupancy)
rooms U.S.$575-U.S.$700
suites U.S.$800-U.S.$1,000 dinner only: U.S.$85-U.S.$125

Canada - Ontario

Hotel location shown in red with page number

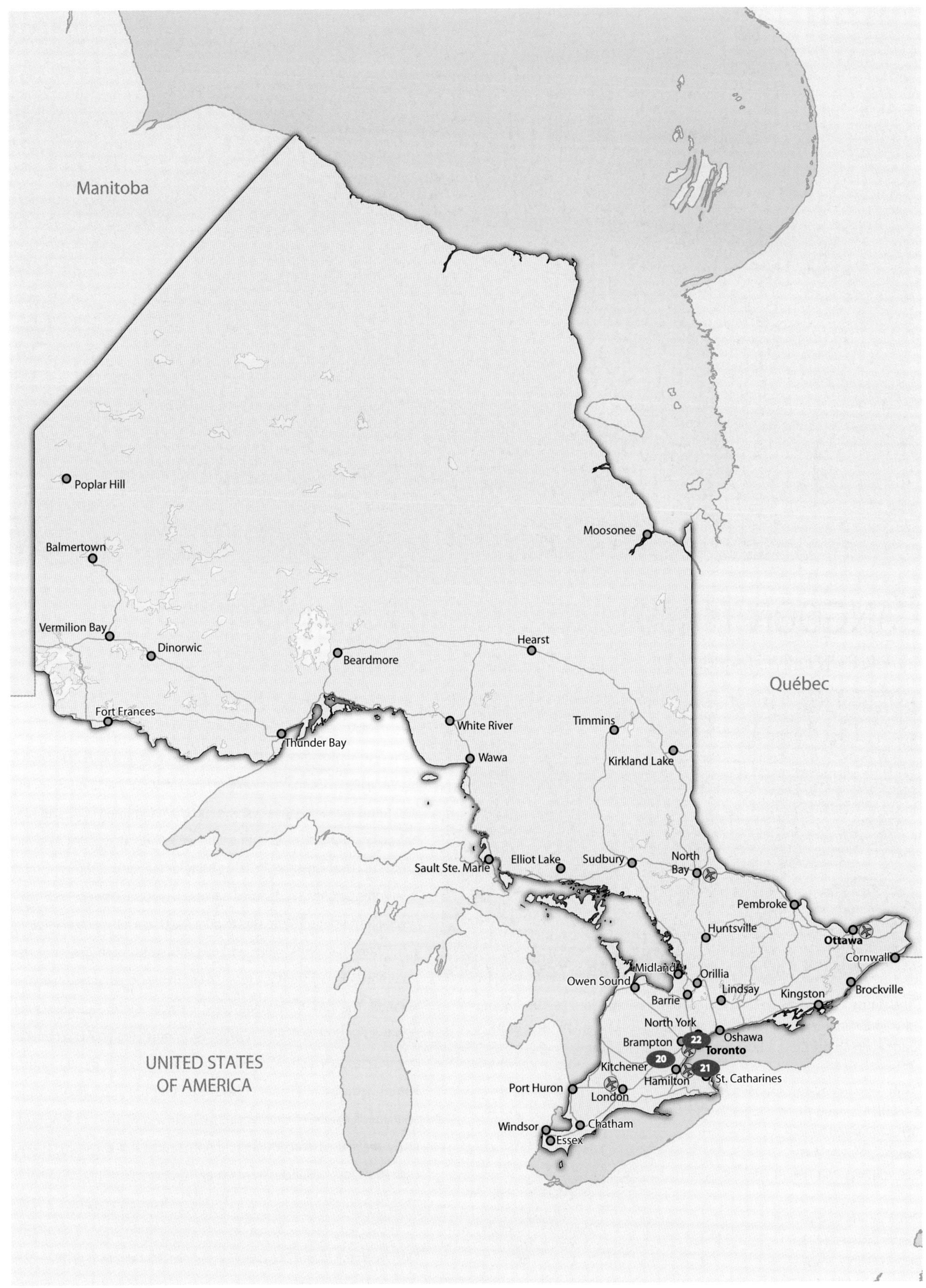

LANGDON HALL COUNTRY HOUSE HOTEL & SPA

1 LANGDON DRIVE, CAMBRIDGE, ONTARIO N3H 4R8

Directions: Take Highway 401 to Cambridge and take exit 275. Turn south onto Fountain Street and then right onto Blair Road. Langdon Drive is the fourth road on the right. 1 hour from Toronto area by car.

Web: www.johansens.com/langdonhall
E-mail: reservations@langdonhall.ca
Tel: +1 519 740 2100
Fax: +1 519 740 8161
U.S./Canada Toll Free: 1 800 268 1898

Price Guide: (room only)
rooms C$240-C$420
suites C$459-C$629

Langdon Hall Country House & Spa is the beautifully restored summertime estate of Eugene Langdon Wilks, the great-grandson of John Jacob Astor, the owner of the Waldorf Astoria and American real estate magnet. Opened as a luxury hotel in 1989, the 53 guest rooms and suites are well-appointed and many are furnished with exquisite antiques, private terraces and sitting areas with cozy wood-burning fireplaces. The elegant main house is the centerpiece of the estate and is surrounded by landscaped lawns, beautiful flower, herb and vegetable gardens. The Spa at Langdon Hall has a full menu of relaxing spa treatments and services and is available for both guests of the hotel and visitors. Afternoon tea is served in the Conservatory or on the veranda. The AAA 5 Diamond rated restaurant with Executive Chef Jonathan Gushue at the helm, offers exceptional regional and classical cuisine perfectly complemented by wines selected by the hotel's Sommelier Sylvain Brissonnet. The restaurant has also won the Wine Spectator's Award of Excellence 2 years in a row. The outdoor pool, finely manicured croquet lawn, tennis courts and expansive hiking trails allow for an all-inclusive getaway. Toronto is just 1 hour away, and the Niagara Falls wine region and attractions are also nearby.

Our inspector loved: *The peaceful and beautiful estate, and afternoon tea in the Conservatory.*

Riverbend Inn & Vineyard

16104 NIAGARA RIVER PARKWAY, NIAGARA-ON-THE-LAKE, ONTARIO L0S 1J0

Situated in a stately 1860's Georgian mansion, which has been home to a school, to the disabled and even an art gallery during various periods since its construction, Riverbend Inn & Vineyard was purchased and completely restored by the Wiens family in 2002 to create an elegant country inn. 21 rooms and suites are decorated in authentic Georgian style with rich, warm colors. All rooms have fireplaces and some feature private balconies and the building's original hardwood flooring. Along with fine antique furnishings and amenities, in-room services including massage therapy, reflexology, esthetic treatments, hair and make-up services are available to enrich your stay. The 1890s salon bar, with its marble pillars and roaring fire, is a popular gathering place for locals and visitors. Guests can sample fresh, creative country cuisine in the 26-seat dining room or spend a summer afternoon enjoying a bottle of the Estate wine on the 40-seat vineyard patio. The inn's unique location within its own working Chardonnay and Merlot vineyards overlooking the Niagara River, make it an idyllic retreat. Manicured lawns and gardens offer plenty of space for exploring and breathtaking river views; guests can also venture out on foot or rent bicycles to discover more of the region. The Shaw Festival Theatre is also nearby.

Our inspector loved: *Enjoying the sun on the beautiful patio overlooking the vineyard.*

Directions: From the Niagara River Parkway turn onto John Street. The entrance is on the left.

Web: www.johansens.com/riverbend
E-mail: fd@riverbendinn.ca
Tel: +1 905 468 8866
Fax: +1 905 468 8829
U.S./Canada Toll Free: 1 888 955 5553

Price Guide: (room only)
rooms C$160-C$325
suites C$260-C$370

Windsor Arms

18 St. Thomas Street, Toronto, Ontario M5S 3E7

Originally constructed in 1927 to mirror the University of Toronto's signature Victorian buildings, the hotel has undergone an extensive renovation to preserve the historical characteristics and update its facilities. Re-opened in 1999, the result has combined Old World charm with modern luxury. Custom mahogany furnishings based on 1920's French styles adorn the hotel, and guest rooms and suites feature cozy fireplaces, bathrooms with limestone floors and walls, 320-thread count Frette bed linens and state-of-the-art entertainment systems. The 2-floor Windsor Arms Hotel Spa, with its philosophy of "intimate privacy," is designed to provide the ultimate pampering experience with a full menu of treatments, fireside swimming pool, steam rooms, sauna and special spa cuisine. A full-service salon and separate barber shop are also on-site, and personal training services are available in the fitness center or in guests' rooms. The 3-story Courtyard Café serves excellent cuisine in one of Toronto's most impressive dining rooms, with dramatic David Bierk paintings, huge chandeliers and a grand piano. Club 22 offers lighter fare and an exclusive collection of fine Cognacs, Ports and Scotches. Afternoon and high tea can be savored in the French-style Tea Room with original 1927 fireplace, overlooking a tree-lined street. Exclusive boutique shopping is nearby.

Our inspector loved: *The great history and extraordinary dining room.*

Directions: Located in the heart of downtown Toronto's Bloor-Yorkville shopping district, take the Q.E.W. into Toronto to the Gardiner Expressway. St. Thomas Street is located off 11A near the Queens Park, a short distance from Toronto International Airport.

Web: www.johansens.com/windsorarms
E-mail: reserve@windsorarmshotel.com
Tel: +1 416 971 9666
Fax: +1 416 921 9121
U.S./Canada Toll Free: 1 877 999 2767

Price Guide: (including Continental breakfast)
rooms C$275-C$295
suites C$325-C$2,000

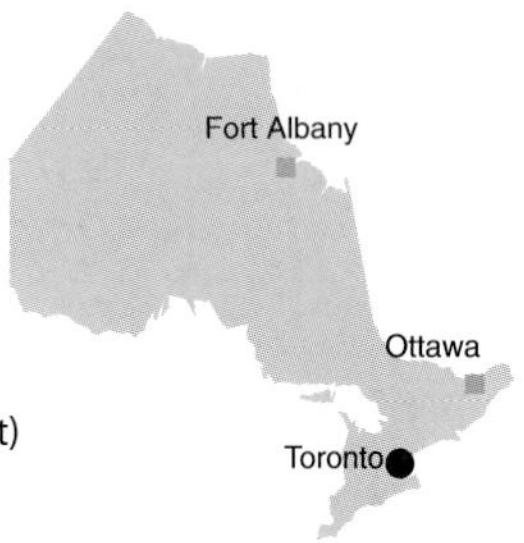

CANADA - QUÉBEC

Hotel location shown in red with page number

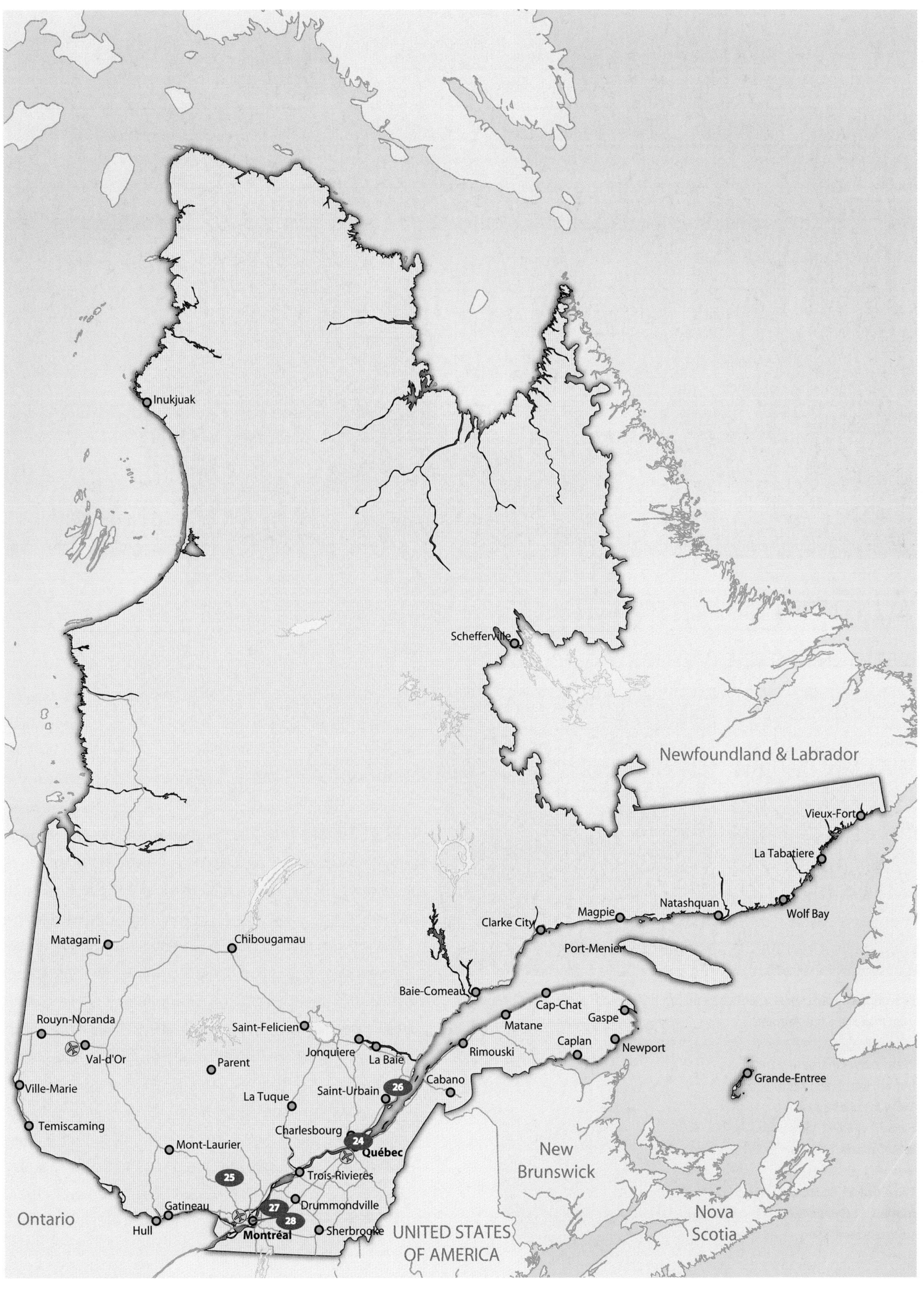

Auberge Saint-Antoine

RELAIS & CHÂTEAUX

8, Rue Saint-Antoine, Québec City, Québec G1K 4C9

Directions: From boulevard Champlain or Charest, continue to rue Dalhousie, then take rue Saint-Antoine.

Web: www.johansens.com/saintantoine
E-mail: info@saint-antoine.com
Tel: +1 418 692 2211
Fax: +1 418 692 1177
U.S./Canada Toll Free: 1 888 692 2211

Price Guide: (room only, excluding tax)
rooms C$139-C$379
suites C$259-C$549

Built on one of Québec City's richest archeological sites, the Auberge integrates 3 historic buildings of the 18th and 19th centuries as well as a wharf and battery structure, which date back to the end of the 17th century. There are a wealth of artifacts and testimonies of 3 centuries of Québec's history beautifully displayed throughout. Each of the 6 floors is dedicated to one of the site's previous owners and their period in history. In the corridor of each floor, a text presents a short biography of the previous owner to whom it is dedicated and objets d'art from that period are displayed both in the corridor and rooms of that floor. The Auberge has 26 original rooms all with their own theme, and an additional 68 new rooms of contemporary design, which have heated bathroom floors, no-fog mirrors, deep soaking tubs and some also have a fireplace and terrace. There is a 94-seat auditorium ideal for a meeting. In 2004 the Auberge opened its restaurant, Panache, where guests can enjoy a view of the St. Lawrence River. Voted one of Canada's 10 best new restaurants by enRoute magazine in 2005. The menu is traditional French Canadian cuisine with a twist. Located in the heart of one of the most historically rich areas in Canada, close to the Place Royale, this hotel offers a most suitable base from which to explore Québec City.

Our inspector loved: *So much about this hotel, from the unique display of artifacts to the "cookies for the road" given to departing guests.*

Hôtel Quintessence

3004 Chemin de la Chapelle, Mont-Tremblant, Québec J8E 1E1

The historic definition of "Quintessence" is the "fifth element " in addition to earth, air, fire and water. "The Quintessential things of life" are what Quintessence, the first boutique hotel in Mont-Tremblant, strives to provide its guests, allowing them to experience a lasting sense of wellbeing. In the heart of the Laurentian Mountains, at the foot of Mont-Tremblant, on the shores of Lac Tremblant, this unique area is a year-round destination that enjoys a multitude of outdoor activities including down-hill and cross-country skiing, sledding, golf, mountain biking, tennis and fishing. There are many dining and shopping opportunities, cultural events and music festivals. The suites are luxuriously decorated and have oversized bathrooms, wood-burning fireplaces and stunning lake views. Outdoors, guests can enjoy the infinity pool and hot tubs, which all look out to the same beautiful lake view. There are many places to relax in the 3 acres of landscaped grounds featuring the Garden of the Five Senses and boardwalk by the lake. Q Restaurant and Wine Bar is a great dining experience. Traditional specialties using local ingredients are complemented by fresh organic herbs grown in the hotel gardens. There is a 5,000 bottle capacity wine cellar located in a secluded turret with tasting rooms where connoisseurs can experience some of the world's finest wines.

Directions: Hotel Quintessence is located 130km northwest of Montréal. It is easily accessible year-round by car, limousine or helicopter. Less than 30 minutes from Mont-Tremblant International Airport and 90 minutes from Montréal-Pierre Elliott Trudeau International Airport (Montréal-Trudeau).

Québec City

Montréal

Web: www.johansens.com/quintessence
E-mail: info@hotelQuintessence.com
Tel: +1 819 425 3400
Fax: +1 819 425 3480
U.S./Canada Toll Free: 1 866 425 3400

Price Guide:
suites C$339-C$1,789

Our inspector loved: *The infinity pool overlooking the lake and mountains.*

La Pinsonnière

RELAIS & CHATEAUX

124 SAINT-RAPHAËL, LA MALBAIE, QUÉBEC G5A 1X9

Perched on a hill in the charming village of Cap-à-l'Aigle with stunning views of the St. Lawrence River, La Pinsonnière blends naturally into the beauty of the Charlevoix region of Québec. Formerly the home of Senator Marc Drouin, this family-run inn has recently undergone extensive renovation, including the enlargement of several rooms to create luxurious guest rooms with spa bathrooms, fireplaces, down bedding, Frette bathrobes and slippers, and wireless high-speed Internet. Some rooms also have L.C.D. televisions and private balconies with spectacular river views. The gardens are colorful and there is a wonderful terrace where guests can enjoy a cocktail before dinner or a light lunch. The restaurant offers menus featuring creative cuisine and many local products. Daily tours of the multiple Wine Spectator award-winning wine cellar with its 12,000 bottles and 750 labels are available. An art gallery, a nature trail and beach are located on-site; nearby outdoor activities include fishing, whale watching, golf, skiing and snowmobiling. For those wishing to just relax, there is a small spa, sauna and indoor pool. The excellent staff at this intimate property are also happy to accommodate special events and requests such as picnics, gala dinners and wine tasting sessions.

Our inspector loved: *The views from almost everywhere on the property.*

Directions: Located 90 miles northeast of Québec City. Take Highway 138 (toward Sainte-Anne de Beaupré) to Cap-à-l'Aigle.

Web: www.johansens.com/lapinsonniere
E-mail: pinsonniere@relaischateaux.com
Tel: +1 418 665 4431
Fax: +1 418 665 7156
U.S./Canada Toll Free: 1 800 387 4431

Price Guide: (room only, excluding tax)
rooms C$300-C$500
suite C$650-C$750

HÔTEL NELLIGAN

106 RUE SAINT-PAUL OUEST, MONTRÉAL, QUÉBEC H2Y 1Z3

This boutique hotel mingles contemporary décor with the warmth and charm of Old Montréal. Rooms are furnished with high quality, custom linens and drapery, dark wood furniture and many have fireplaces; suites are spacious with luxurious bathrooms. Passages of Emile Nelligan's most beautiful poems are transcribed on the walls, immersing guests in Québec culture. The elegant ground floor consists of an efficient check-in and full concierge service, a library with fireplace, a garden atrium serving both breakfast and afternoon tea and a bar-salon with welcoming leather and rattan furniture. Verses Restaurant is one of Old Montréal's hippest new restaurants, with contemporary French cuisine underscored by Québec's finest fresh produce. The menu features specialties such as marinated duck breast, Québec lamb and rack of deer. Large windows open onto rue Saint-Paul, allowing natural light to enhance the rich décor, 10ft. mirrors and an impressive glass wine cellar. Enjoy a pre-dinner drink in Verses Bar; martinis are their specialty, made with fresh juices in frosted cocktail shakers and served in over-sized martini glasses in the bar or on the rooftop terrace. Restaurants, shops and historical landmarks are within walking distance, and during the week, a complimentary shuttle service to major downtown business centers is available.

Our inspector loved: *The loft suites with large bathrooms and Jacuzzis.*

 63  120       

Directions: Located in Old Montréal, a 20-minute drive from Montréal-Trudeau International Airport (Y.U.L.).

Québec City

Montréal

Web: www.johansens.com/nelligan
E-mail: info@hotelnelligan.com
Tel: +1 514 788 2040
Fax: +1 514 788 2041
U.S./Canada Toll Free: 1 877 788 2040

Price Guide:
rooms from C$280
suites from C$350

Le Place d'Armes Hôtel & Suites

55 Rue Saint-Jacques Ouest, Montréal, Québec H2Y 3X2

Old Montréal's first boutique hotel combines classic urban chic with the 19th-century architecture of the 3 historic buildings that comprise Le Place d'Armes. Rooms have high ceilings, exposed brickwork and a contemporary, comfortable feel. The bathrooms are large and luxurious with spacious rain showers and deep soaking tubs. The lobby and lounges are filled with fresh flowers and apples, as well as comfortable seating, a flat-screen T.V. and a fireplace. Guests are offered several dining options: Restaurant Aix Cuisine du Terroir, devoted to the enjoyment of local Québec cooking, has an elaborate menu with seasonal variations. Suite 701 serves great martinis and creative cuisine to trendy Montréalers and visitors in a chic gourmet bar/lounge setting. There is also a roof-top terrace which serves lunch, dinner and cocktails during the summer. Rainspa, featuring Montréal's only hammam, is a must. The traditional Middle Eastern steam bath, along with many body and facial treatments, make the Rainspa a great experience for guests. Le Place d'Armes' location amid Montreal's finest restaurants and quaint shops and just steps from Notre Dame Basilica, the Old Port and Palais des Congrès makes this a good choice for either a business or leisure visit. Shuttle services to major downtown business centers are available.

Our inspector loved: *The beautifully designed bathrooms with their large rain showers and luxuriously deep tubs.*

Directions: Located in Old Montréal, a 20 minute drive from Montréal-Trudeau International Airport (Y.U.L.).

Web: www.johansens.com/hotelplacedarmes
E-mail: info@hotelplacedarmes.com
Tel: +1 514 842 1887
Fax: +1 514 842 6469
U.S./Canada Toll Free: 1 888 450 1887

Price Guide:
rooms from C$280
suites from C$365

SPA

Mexico

Hotel location shown in red with page number

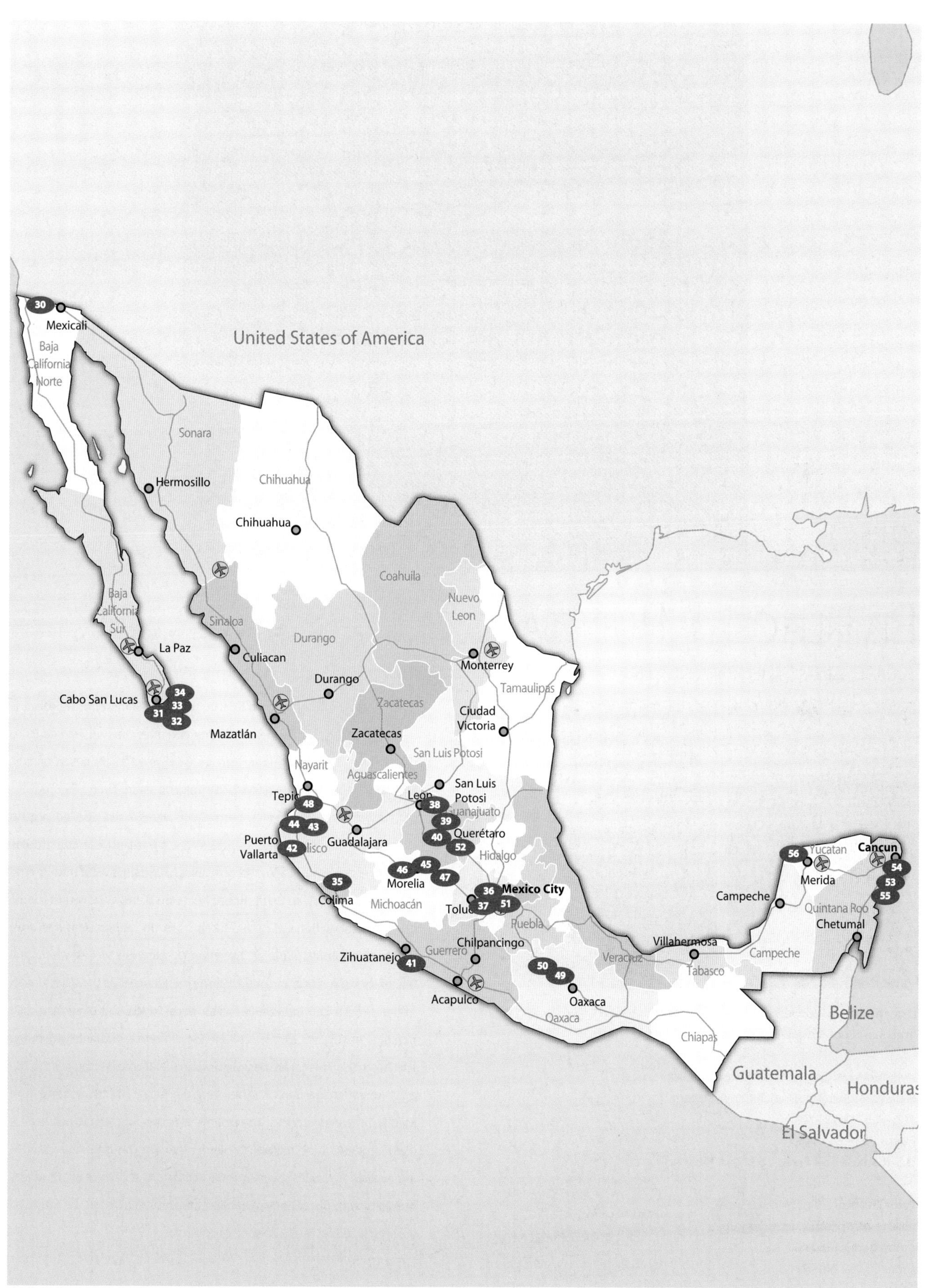

RANCHO LA PUERTA

TECATE, BAJA CALIFORNIA NORTE

Founded in 1940, Rancho La Puerta, meaning "Ranch of the Door," is now a sophisticated wellness resort named after the two arching oaks, the "door," to the original campsite. Privately owned, the resort creates a balanced program of mind/body/spirit in each 7-day, Saturday to Saturday stay. Beautifully set on 3,000 acres of unspoiled nature preserve at a 1,800 ft. altitude, there are gyms and exercise studios located in the resort's valley. Forty miles of hiking trails wind through the wilderness, which lead up to Mount Kuchumaa at 3,885 ft. Guest rooms are decorated with hand-carved furniture, crafts and artwork with cozy fireplaces and private patios. Each weekly program includes an equal mix of exercise, relaxation, meditation and massage. At the Villas Health Center, guests can indulge in facials, body wraps and other heavenly personal treatments. Cuisine at Rancho La Puerta is primarily vegetarian and fresh daily menus are based on what is available nearby or from the organic ranch garden. Recipes feature Baja California Norte and Mediterranean influences. The resort's very own homemade olive oil is used in many of the recipes. Cooking classes and nutrition workshops are available weekly. The year-round climate is a perfect blend of low humidity with distant ocean cooling breezes. Wildlife can be found all around including over 120 species of birds.

Directions: 1 hour south-east of San Diego by car. Drivers will collect guests from San Diego International Airport at scheduled times.

Web: www.johansens.com/rancholapuerta
E-mail: reservations@rancholapuerta.com
Tel: +1 877 440 7778
Fax: +1 858 764 5560
U.S./Canada Toll Free: 1 800 443 7565

Price Guide: (per person per week, minimum 2 people, excluding tax)
rooms $2,535-$3,840
suites $3,030-$3,835

Our inspector loved: *The focus on health and renewal.*

       SPA

Esperanza

KM. 7 CARRETERA TRANSPENINSULAR, PUNTA BALLENA, CABO SAN LUCAS, BAJA CALIFORNIA SUR 23410

Situated atop the bluffs of Punta Ballena overlooking 2 private coves on the Sea of Cortez, this Cabo San Lucas resort offers 56 suites on 17 acres. The resort, opened in 2002 as part of the exclusive Auberge Resorts collection, features the latest in technology and amenities combined with Mexican culture and traditional Baja style. Each spacious room offers oceanfront views, open outdoor terraces and handcrafted furnishings with local, original artwork. The Luxury Suites also offer full kitchens, private outdoor pools, butler service and airport transfers, with chefs available for in-suite dining. The Restaurant at Esperanza, which includes both indoor and outdoor dining with dramatic beachfront views, offers regional cuisine and an expansive wine and tequila menu, while the Palapa Grill and newly-opened TAPAS restaurant serves lighter fare. The full-service Spa at Esperanza incorporates the elements of water, light, and desert into its services and provides guests with a variety of pampering, restorative and wellness treatments. La Galeria, an open-air art gallery, promotes prominent Mexican and Latin American artists and sculptors. Esperanza has a private beach with beach services and a full fitness center. Poolside service includes complimentary snacks and hand and foot massages. Guests will find championship-level golf courses, sport fishing, and horseback riding nearby.

Our inspector loved: *The view from the hammocks on the open terraces.*

Directions: From San Jose del Cabo (S.J.D.) International Airport take the highway to Cabo San Lucas. The resort is at the 7km. marker, a 30-minute drive from the airport. The resort is 10 minutes from Cabo San Lucas and 30 minutes from San Jose del Cabo.

Web: www.johansens.com/esperanza
E-mail: info@esperanzaresort.com
Tel: +52 624 145 6400
Fax: +52 624 145 6499
U.S./Canada Toll Free: 1 866 311 2226

Price Guide:
rooms $475-$1,500
suites $2,500-$6,000

Marquis Los Cabos

LOTE 74, KM. 21.5 CARRETERA TRANSPENINSULAR, FRACCIONAMIENTO CABO REAL, LOS CABOS, BAJA CALIFORNIA SUR 23400

Marquis Los Cabos Beach, Golf, Spa & Casitas Resort is a family-owned property with contemporary Mexican décor, lush landscaping and incredible views. Considered one of the smaller resorts of the region with 237 rooms, Marquis Los Cabos offers the ultimate in luxury and service. Upon entering the lobby, the stunning infinity pool appears to fall into the Sea of Cortés, with the water cascading dramatically down 36 feet to a spectacular pool. Each of the resort suites has lovely ocean views from the private balconies or terraces, hydrotherapy tubs, Bulgari toiletries, frette bed linens, down comforters, original oil paintings and beautiful bathroom floor tiles with eye-catching turquoise accents. There is an impressive art collection throughout the resort. Those who prefer to hear the waves while they sleep can stay in one of 28 beachside casitas, each with private pool. Choose to lounge on the pristine, white sand beach or relax in the resort's full-service spa, one of the largest in Latin America. There are 3 outstanding restaurants including the Five Diamond Award-winning Canto del Mar. The resort is situated between Cabo San Lucas, a town known for its colorful nightlife and restaurants, and San José del Cabo, a quaint area for shopping. Championship golfing, surfing, and whale watching can be arranged nearby.

Our inspector loved: *The stunning view of the Sea of Cortés from the main lobby with the dramatic waterfall.*

Directions: From Los Cabos International Airport (S.J.D.), take the highway to Cabo San Lucas to the 21.5 Km marker.

Web: www.johansens.com/marquisloscabos
E-mail: reservations@marquisloscabos.com
Tel: +52 624 144 2000
Fax: +52 624 144 2001
U.S./Canada Toll Free: 1 877 238 9399

Price Guide:
junior suites U.S.$465-U.S.$550
suites U.S.$825-U.S.$1,090

CASA NATALIA

BLVD. MIJARES 4, SAN JOSE DEL CABO, BAJA CALIFORNIA SUR 23400

A European-style boutique hotel, Casa Natalia nestles amidst palm trees and tropical bougainvillea in the heart of historic San José del Cabo. Owners, Nathalie and Loïc Tenoux, were inspired by the natural beauty of the region and worked with a famed Mexican architect to create an environment that reflected the spectacular deserts, mountains, seas and skies in its hand-plastered walls, wood-beams, tropical flowers and waterfalls. Each guest room is individually named and decorated, combining local artwork, striking contemporary furnishings and earthy colors. The overall ambience is one of comfortable elegance, with extra special touches of luxury, such as the in-room spa service and complimentary breakfast served on guests' private terraces. Sliding glass doors open onto private balconies, which feature hammocks and views across the courtyard, pool or neighboring tropical estuary. At night, open flame braziers light up the outdoors and guests can enjoy dinner and cocktails al fresco. Owner, Loic Tenoux, serves innovative Mexican-Euro cuisine in the Mi Cocina restaurant accompanied by fine wines, tequilas and martinis. The charming town of San José del Cabo awaits discovery along with the stunning local beaches. Golf, fishing, horse riding, sailing, safaris and whalewatching can also be organized. A complimentary shuttle to the beach club is available.

Our inspector loved: *Dining at Mi Cocina among the towering palm trees.*

16 13

Directions: From S.J.D. Airport take the highway to San José then follow signs to downtown.

Monterrey
Cabo San Lucas
Cancun
Mexico City
Zihuatanejo

Web: www.johansens.com/casanatalia
E-mail: casa.natalia@casanatalia.com
Tel: +52 624 14671 00
Fax: +52 624 14251 10
U.S./Canada Toll Free: 1 888 277 3814

Price Guide: (excluding 13% tax and 10% service charge per room per night)
deluxe rooms U.S.$230–U.S.$385
spa suites U.S.$350-U.S.$525

One & Only Palmilla

KM 7.5 CARRETERA TRANSPENINSULAR, SAN JOSE DEL CABO, BAJA CALIFORNIA SUR 23400

This is the ultimate in luxury and style: beautiful and tranquil, situated on the southernmost tip of the Baja Peninsula where Pacific waters merge with the Sea of Cortez to a backdrop of mountainous desert terrain. From pristine beaches, gray whales can be seen rising beyond the crashing surf. One & Only Palmilla, winner of Condé Nast Traveler Best Latin American Resort 2004 and 2005, reflects Mexico's vibrant culture and artistry, palm trees, fountains, bird of paradise and other tropical blooms shade, color and highlight the whitewashed buildings with contrasting red-tiled roofs. Founded in 1956 by Don Abelardo Rodriguez, son of the President of Mexico, the resort stands on 250 acres of a 900-acre estate that includes a Jack Nicklaus signature golf course. A $90 million investment, 3 years ago, has raised it to the highest of vacational ranks. Guest rooms are superb, with cool décor, exquisite furnishings and the finest of linens, accessories and facilities; all have panoramic sea views. Guests have a choice of several restaurants: a particular favorite is "C" run by celebrity Chef Charlie Trotter of Chicago. It has a number of private and intimate dining areas and wonderful collection of glasswork. The palapa-style Agua serves gourmet Mediterranean cuisine. Facilities include a spa, 2 infinity-edge pools, children's pool and play area.

Our inspector loved: *The spacious rooms with remarkable ocean views.*

Directions: San Jose del Cabo (S.J.D.) International Airport take the Highway to Cabo San Lucas and the resort is at the 7.5 km marker.

Web: www.johansens.com/oneandonlypalmilla
E-mail: reservations@oneandonlypalmilla.com
Tel: +52 624 146 7000
Fax: +52 624 146 7001
U.S./Canada Toll Free: 1 888 691 8081

Price Guide: (room only, excluding tax)
rooms U.S.$575-U.S.$1,000
suites U.S.$1,300-U.S.$2,100

SPA

Hacienda de San Antonio

MUNICIPIO DE COMALA, COLIMA, COLIMA 28450

An architectural phoenix, Hacienda de San Antonio withstood both volcanic eruption and revolution. Through extensive renovations in 1978 and 1988, this stately 19th-century hacienda was restored to greatness. Interiors reflect brilliant color, furnishings of grand scale and craftsmanship of the indigenous people of Mexico. Of particular note are Highland Maya textiles, primitive Colonial antiques and hand-painted frescoes and armoires. The 25 spacious bedrooms feature tiled baths, oversized beds, fireplaces and French doors. From the rooftop terrace, guests can enjoy dramatic views of the surrounding mountains and volcanoes. There is much to see and do at Hacienda de San Antonio: meander through the formal gardens, an area that also features a 105-ft. pool, tennis court, outdoor dining area and amphitheater. Explore the property, dotted with lakes, on horseback or mountain bike and do not miss the dramatic volcanic rock aqueduct that channels water around the estate. For sightseeing excursions to historic Colima, a car and driver are at guests' disposal. The hacienda is the centerpiece of a 5,000-acre working ranch, which produces organically raised meat, produce and coffee. Dining is truly an experience!

Our inspector loved: *The spectacular views of the surroundings and the volcano from the Hacienda's gardens and lakes.*

Directions: From Colima Airport the Hacienda is 28km, a 35-minute drive.

Web: www.johansens.com/sanantonio
E-mail: reservations@haciendadesanantonio.com
Tel: +52 312 314 9554
Fax: +52 312 313 4254
U.S./Canada Toll Free: 1 866 516 2611

Price Guide:
(excluding tax and service charge)
suites U.S.$800-U.S.$1,800

Casa Vieja

EUGENIO SUE 45 (COLONIA POLANCO), MEXICO DISTRITO FEDERAL 11560

This exquisite mansion, once home to and still owned by television journalist and broadcaster Lolita Ayala, Casa Vieja has been transformed into a boutique hotel. The interior designer traveled throughout Mexico to gather furniture, textiles, paintings, statuary, chandeliers and rugs reflecting vibrant aspects of Meixco' Mexican culture. Walls are vividly hand-painted by artisans. In each room, the full-size refrigerator is illustrated with motifs portraying famed artists such as Frida Kahlo and Diego Rivera. Treasures from the proprietor's personal art collection are on display for guests to enjoy. 10 suites include a 2-bedroom, 2-bathroom presidential suite, master suites with living room, and 1-bedroom junior suites. There is a casual roof terrace restaurant bar, and an adjoining formal salon serving traditional and modern cuisine by award-winning Chef Ignacio Mondragon, who is happy to prepare special requests according to the wishes of the guest. The service at Casa Vieja is highly personalized, and a concierge can arrange elite tours and private visits to museums and places of interest in Mexico City. The hotel is located on a quiet residential street in the upscale Polanco district, close to important tourist attractions and shopping areas.

Our inspector loved: *The superb personal attention, daily valet-style wake-up call with orange juice, coffee and newspaper.*

Directions: 30 minutes from Mexico City International Airport.

Web: www.johansens.com/casavieja
E-mail: sales@casavieja.com
Tel: +52 55 52 82 0067
Fax: +52 55 52 81 3780

Price Guide:
suites U.S.$325-U.S.$950

Casa Limon

RIO LERMA 103, BARRIO DE SANTA MARÍA, MALINALCO, ESTADO DE MEXICO 524040

Situated a short drive from the center of a peaceful little town, and surrounded by a beautiful mountain range, Casa Limon offers guests a serene, elegant and very private retreat. It caters only for adults, who will revel in the warmth, comfort and harmony of its atmosphere and ambience. It is a vacation venue of very modern and stylish design both outside and in. Furniture, furnishings and décor are simplistically cool and contemporary, and potted plants and colorful flower arrangements are displayed throughout. The ultra modern, but welcoming atmosphere, continues into the spacious state-of-the-art, romantic suites and bedrooms, all of which feature every amenity and a terrace on which to relax and enjoy the picturesque garden, pool and countryside views or to enjoy breakfast, a snack or a cool drink served by an extremely attentive staff. Dining is an experience to be savored in the terrace restaurant, which is shaded by a stick-slatted roof and 2 impressive, 60-year-old plum trees. Chef Leonel Garcia creates excellent international cuisine using the finest local produce, complemented by an extensive wine list. For total relaxation the spa offers a range of therapies and treatment programs. Golf and riding nearby.

Our inspector loved: *The sophisticated pool area.*

Directions: 100km from Mexico City.

Web: www.johansens.com/casalimon
E-mail: leonel@casalimon.com
Tel: +52 714 147 0256
Fax: +52 714 147 0619

Price Guide:
rooms $150
suites $180

Quinta Las Acacias

PASEO DE LA PRESA 168, GUANAJUATO, GUANAJUATO 36000

Quinta Las Acacias evokes the atmosphere of former times in Mexico, and its striking façade is a testament to the French architecture that once dominated the city of Guanajuato. The interior of the property has retained the characteristics of the original building and is adorned with wood and marble floors and period furniture with oriental rugs. Standard suites are individually appointed with brass, wicker and wooden furnishings combining past pleasures with contemporary facilities. The Mexican suites with Jacuzzis are bedecked with arts and curio from the country and guests will admire the terraces covered in flowers and verdant plants. The balcony by the Master Suite affords magnificent views across Florencio Antillon Park and the room has been designed in an opulent European style. Master chef, Pedro Garcia, has combined authentic family recipes with international favorites and the result is a gourmet menu that appeals to all palates; breakfast is renowned as the finest in the city. Nearby attractions include the Diego Rivera Museum, the historic town center and Jardin de la Union. Ceramic collectors should peruse Gorky, Capelo and Santa Rosa.

Our inspector loved: *The home from home ambience.*

Directions: 45 minutes from El Bajio Airport.

Web: www.johansens.com/acacias
E-mail: quintalasacacias@prodigy.net.mx
Tel: +52 473 731 1517
Fax: +52 473 731 1862
U.S./Canada Toll Free: 1 888 497 4129

Price Guide:
rooms U.S.$228-U.S.$245
suites U.S.$280-U.S.$300

Dos Casas

CALLE QUEBRADA 101, SAN MIGUEL DE ALLENDE, GUANAJUATO 37700

This elegant, modern boutique hotel offers a romantic atmosphere and exclusive personal service in an intimate 6-room setting. True to its name, its size, layout and service give Dos Casas the feel of a spacious, exquisitely furnished home. Built in traditional San Miguel de Allende Colonial style, the minimalist architecture lends the building clean lines and a breezy air. To maintain privacy and exclusivity, the main entrance is kept closed to all but Dos Casas guests. Upon arrival, guests are greeted with a glass of wine or a margarita at a small bar near the entrance. All guest rooms have views of San Miguel de Allende, while the Master Suites have views of the city and feature a sauna, Jacuzzi and private terrace. For breakfast, guests can enjoy homemade breads, jams and Chiapas coffee on the hotel's terrace overlooking the city. The comfortable lounge is a great place to relax, as is the outdoor Jacuzzi. There is also a business center and charming gardens. The hotel is located 3 blocks from the main square in San Miguel de Allende.

Our inspector loved: *The modern architecture, and personal service.*

Directions: 1 hour 15 minutes from Leon airport; 1 hour from Queretaro.

Web: www.johansens.com/doscasas
E-mail: info@livingdoscasas.com
Tel: +52 415 154 4073
Fax: +52 415 154 4958

Price Guide:
deluxe rooms U.S.$230
suites U.S.$290
master suites U.S.$330

La Puertecita Boutique Hotel

SANTO DOMINGO 75 COL. LOS ARCOS, SAN MIGUEL DE ALLENDE, GUANAJUATO 37740

This beautiful boutique hotel is set within a tranquil private park surrounded by gardens, waterfalls and flowering trees. With a unique family atmosphere it is an ideal place to unwind and enjoy the beautiful views of San Miguel de Allende. Colonial architecture is perfectly combined with sculpted stone-framed windows, colorful and comfortable furnishings and a traditional Mexican atmosphere that is warm and welcoming. Elegant guest rooms and suites have stunning domed brick Boveda ceilings and are exquisitely appointed with Colonial-style furniture. Some rooms have private patios, fireplaces and garden baths. Fine dining in the acclaimed restaurant offers delicious traditional Mexican dishes and is reputed to be one of the best in the area. Al fresco meals, by the pool or on private patios, are delightful. For a private celebration for 4-6 people, "La Palapa" treehouse is idyllically surrounded by trees and has a spectacular view of a 300-year-old aqueduct. 2 pools are available (1 heated), as well as a Jacuzzi, water luge and well-equipped fitness area. Private golf and tennis can be arranged nearby and there are many mountain biking trails in the area. The center of San Miguel de Allende, with its pretty Colonial architecture and breathtaking mountainous surroundings, is a short walk away.

Our inspector loved: *The beautiful view, the gardens, and the excellent service.*

Directions: 1 hour and 20 minutes from Leon Airport and 1 hour from Queretaro Airport.

Web: www.johansens.com/lapuertecita
E-mail: lapuertecita@lapuertecita.com
Tel: +52 415 152 5011
Fax: +52 415 152 5505

Price Guide: (room only)
rooms U.S.$200-U.S.$270
suites U.S.$295-U.S.$324

Villa del Sol

PLAYA LA ROPA, P.O. BOX 84, ZIHUATANEJO, GUERRERO 40880

Cross a little Hispanic charm with an incredible amount of natural beauty and the result is the Villa del Sol. Set like a pearl on the Pacific shoreline of Mexico at Ixtapa-Zihuatanejo, the Hotel Villa del Sol lives up to its name with dazzling sunshine, idyllic beaches and magnificent groves of flourishing palm trees that simply blanket the area in a haze of green. The rooms are expansive and stunning using designs and colors that hark back to the days of the ancient civilizations that populated the area. Those wishing to indulge in an afternoon siesta must choose one of the numerous little nooks and crannies where you can doze in comfort on a swinging chair or in a hammock. Dinner is a mélange of flavors, with dishes drawing on irresistible Mexican tastes and using fresh seafood straight from the Pacific. There are innumerable leisure activities at the Villa del Sol, with water sports widely available, including everything from sailing to snorkeling. For something a little more cultural, take to the cobblestone streets of Zihuatanejo and explore the fascinating surrounds with its art gallery and interesting shops. A small but fully-equipped spa is available.

Our inspector loved: *The suites, and the pool near the beach.*

Directions: The hotel is 15 minutes from Ixtapa-Zihuatanejo International Airport. The airport has direct and non-stop services from Los Angeles, Houston, Phoenix, San Francisco and Mexico City.

Monterrey
Cabo San Lucas
Cancun
Mexico City
Zihuatanejo

Web: www.johansens.com/villadelsol
E-mail: reservation@hotelvilladelsol.net
Tel: +52 755 555 5500
Fax: +52 755 554 2758
U.S./Canada Toll Free: 1 888 389 2645

Price Guide: (room only)
rooms U.S.$430–U.S.$480
suites U.S.$700–U.S.$1,500

MEXICO - JALISCO (PUERTA VALLARTA / COSTA ALEGRE)

Las Alamandas Resort

CARRETERA BARRA DE NAVIDAD - PUERTO VALLARTA KM 83.5, COL. QUEMARO, JALISCO 48850

A perfect paradise for those seeking beauty, romance and privacy, Las Almandas is surrounded by 1,500 acres of tropical gardens, breathtaking blue lagoons and endless white sandy beaches. With a maximum of 30 guests in the hotel, there is an extremely high standard of individual care and hospitality. Lovely colorful décor is in a traditional Mexican style with stunning fabrics and elegant design complemented by hand-painted artefacts and Mexican folk art. Pale yellow paths with stone mosaics wind through deliciously fragrant flowers to the bedrooms, which have oversized bathrooms with private outdoor showers and spacious terraces overlooking the Pacific Ocean. There is a choice of 2 excellent restaurants, all of which serve unique dishes featuring freshly caught fish, free range meat and many organic fruits and vegetables from the hotel's garden. Owner, Isabel Goldsmith, has spearheaded many projects to preserve the Mexican coastline and bird lovers will appreciate the bird sanctuary within the grounds, which is home to more than 100 species of wild birds. Leisure activities include swimming, tennis, horse riding, mountain biking, fishing, snorkeling and hiking. Boats are available for rental, and there is a superb, fully-equipped gym and an extensive range of massage and salon services.

Our inspector loved: *The nearby lake and river where guests enjoy horse-back riding, and savoring a private dinner on one of the exclusive beaches.*

Directions: The hotel is located in the Costa Alegre, between Puerto Vallarta and Manzanillo, through the Federal Highway No. 200.

Web: www.johansens.com/lasalamandas
E-mail: infoalamandas@aol.com
Tel: +52 322 285 5500
Fax: +52 322 285 5027
U.S./Canada Toll Free: 1 888 882 9616

Price Guide: (excluding breakfast)
suites U.S.$460-U.S.$1,990

Casa Velas Hotel Boutique

PELICANOS 311, FRACC. MARINA VALLARTA, PUERTO VALLARTA, JALISCO 48354

Enjoying a privileged position in Puerto Vallerta, this hotel is well known for its secluded location and sense of intimacy. Visitors will appreciate the high standard of personal service as well as the welcoming atmosphere that emanates from every corner. Traditional Mexican-style textures and colors are stunning and enhance the luxurious interiors that make it a perfect choice for a relaxing, refined vacation. The Grand Spa offers special treatments that are the ultimate in relaxation. The hotel is surrounded by world-class Marina Vallarta golf course, designed by Joe Fingers, as well as 2 artificial turf tennis courts and a state-of-the-art gym. Only a few steps away are the secluded beaches of the area. A private ocean-front beach club has a comfortable lounge area and a superb restaurant, which serves Oriental specialties. For gourmet dining, guests will delight in the sumptuous Mexican fare served in the elegant Elmiliano restaurant in the main hotel. Spacious suites have a private splash pool or Jacuzzi (the Presidential Suite has both!) and are tastefully appointed with superb style and luxurious bathrooms. There are many opportunities to indulge in the activities provided by the hotel or guests can lie back with a book at the poolside, surrounded by palm trees and tropical gardens.

Our inspector loved: *The excellent service and personlized attention to each guest.*

Directions: 10 minutes from Puerto Vallarta International Airport.

Web: www.johansens.com/casavelas
E-mail: reservations1@velasresorts.com
Tel: +52 322 226 9585
Fax: +52 322 226 6699
U.S./Canada Toll Free: 1 800 8352 778
Mexico Toll Free: 1 800 3263 200

Price Guide: (all inclusive, per person)
suites $320-$3,500

 80    130    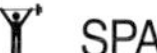  SPA   

HACIENDA SAN ANGEL

MIRAMAR 336, COL. CENTRO PUERTO VALLARTA, JALISCO 48300

Once owned by the actor Richard Burton and his wife Susan, the Hacienda has been beautifully restored. Each of the 9 elegant suites is individually decorated with exquisite antiques and original art, bed linens are of the finest quality, with touches such as Venetian lace and goosedown pillows, and the overall atmosphere is quiet, romantic and luxurious. The Hacienda comprises 5 Mexican villas. 4 are joined together by a path that winds through a terraced garden filled with tropical plants, flowers, statues and a charming fountain; each has 3 or 4 rooms. Las Campanas villa is particularly private and has a king-size bed, fireplace, salon, dining room, kitchenette and several terraces, one of which has a private hot tub. The combination of architecture and décor creates so many special places that make it unique and enchanting, from the terraces, secluded palapas, rooftop areas and sun decks. Breakfast is served on each suite's terrace, and snacks by the pool or in the Jacuzzi can be enjoyed while savoring the spectacular view of the Bay of Banderas. In the 1960s the town became famous when Elizabeth Taylor and Richard Burton filmed Tennessee Williams' "The Night of the Iguana," and subsequently, reporters from all over the world began writing about its beauty. Puerto Vallarta offers a wide range of attractions including golf, whale watching and eco-tourism.

Directions: 15 minutes from Puerto Vallarta International Airport. Situated in the center of Puerto Vallarta.

Web: www.johansens.com/sanangel
E-mail: info@haciendasanangel.com
Tel: +52 322 222 2692
Fax: +52 322 223 1941
U.S./Canada Toll Free: 1 415 738 8220

Price Guide: (excluding taxes)
rooms U.S.$230-U.S.$625

Our inspector loved: *Having dinner on a private terrace.*

Hotel Los Juaninos

MORELOS SUR 39, CENTRO, MORELIA, MICHOACÁN 58000

Once the Episcopal Palace in the capital of Michoacán state, this magnificent pink limestone building has been restored to its former grandeur and transports guests on a journey back through time. The romantic design of the hotel fuses Mexican colonial architecture with art nouveau, neo-classical and gothic elements. This eclectic style continues inside incorporating stately corridors, majestic staircases and elegant furniture with contemporary design features such as the high-tech elevator. Each bedroom has a high ceiling and is individually appointed with unique original doors, windows, bathroom woodwork and European-style tubs. Some of the rooms afford wonderful views of the cathedral and downtown Morelia, an attribute shared by the restaurant, La Azotea, where guests delight in savoring the best of Mexican haute cuisine. The hotel bar boasts an extensive selection of wines and liquors but its specialty are the unusual cocktails known as "remedies". For business meetings the hotel offers a unique art nouveau-style boardroom with Internet access and secretarial support. The city of Morelia is steeped in history with colonial structures such as cathedrals, convents and El Aceducto. There are many arts and crafts available to buy, and the area has been designated a UNESCO world heritage site.

Our inspector loved: *The contrast between the contemporary and Colonial architecture.*

 30  40   

Directions: 25km from Morelia International Airport.

Web: www.johansens.com/juaninos
E-mail: juaninos@hoteljuaninos.com.mx
Tel: +52 443 312 00 36
Fax: +52 443 312 00 36

Price Guide: (room only, excluding tax)
rooms U.S.$180
suites U.S.$220-U.S.$320

MEXICO - MICHOACÁN (MORELIA)

Hotel Virrey de Mendoza

AV. MADERO PTE. 310, CENTRO HISTÓRICO, MORELIA, MICHOACÁN 58000

Housed in a building that since 1595 has witnessed many memorable events in Mexican history, this hotel has a reputation of being one of the most beautiful in the country, dating back to its opening in 1938. Retaining the magnificence of its former Colonial atmosphere, the patio, with its exquisite features covered by a majestic glass window, provides a stunning and singular touch. The comfortable and elegant rooms, suites and Virreynal Suite are distinctively decorated with priceless antiques. Some have balconies overlooking either the Main Square, Cathedral or Avenida Madero, and all have well-equipped bathrooms. The Del Virrey Restaurant serves breakfast, lunch and dinner, and offers traditional Michoacán food and international haute cuisine. Hotel Virrey de Mendoza is located in the most magical and atmospheric part of the city, the heart of Morelia's historic downtown, designated by Unesco as a World Heritage Artistic Site. Facing the Main Square and 1 block from the Cathedral, the museums, antiques, restaurants and busy nightlife are all within walking distance.

Our inspector loved: *The individually decorated guest rooms, and the centuries-old castle ambience.*

Directions: The hotel is situated 45 minutes from the airport.

Web: www.johansens.com/hotelvirrey
E-mail: hvirrey@prodigy.net.mx
Tel: +52 44 33 12 06 33
Fax: +52 44 33 12 67 19
U.S./Canada Toll Free: 1 800 45 02000

Price Guide:
rooms $190-$230
suites $250-$370

Villa Montaña Hotel & Spa

Patzimba 201, Vista Bella, Morelia, Michoacán 58090

Nestled in the picturesque Santa Maria hills, with stunning views over the city of Morelia, Villa Montaña offers guests a serene and tranquil private retreat. Each cottage-like room and suite enjoys a secluded setting amongst sub-tropical gardens interconnected by paths and patios adorned with statues and exotic plants. In the bedrooms, exquisite colonial antiques combine with traditional Michoacán crafts, even the majestic fireplaces are works of art. Each room has every modern convenience and the en-suite bathrooms provide shower tubs, fine toiletries and luxurious robes. The elegant yet casual dining area serves an innovative menu that is a fusion of contemporary international and Mexican cuisine. The restaurant's specialty is roasted cornish rock hen with black truffle, and there is an extensive wine list to complement every dish. Health facilities include a gym, heated pool and tennis court; the newly constructed Spa features modern facilities, services and treatments to harmonize health and enhance beauty. Business clients will benefit from the full-service conference center and smaller meeting rooms, whilst the enchanting hilltop setting provides a wonderful backdrop for an unforgettable wedding day. Visitors to the area can explore nearby towns with hidden chapels, historic sites and even pyramids or shop for fabulous local ceramics, fabrics and furniture.

***Our inspector loved:** The elegant Spa; it is simply amazing.*

Directions: 10 minutes from downtown historic center. 45 minutes from Morelia International Airport.

Web: www.johansens.com/montana
E-mail: res@villamontana.com.mx
Tel: +52 443 314 02 31
Fax: +52 443 315 14 23
Mexico Toll Free: 01 800 96 331 00

Monterrey
Cabo San Lucas
Cancun
Mexico City
Zihuatanejo

Price Guide: (room only)
rooms U.S.$236
suites U.S.$323-U.S.$547

Grand Velas All Suites & Spa Resort

AV. COCOTEROS 98 SUR, NUEVO VALLARTA, NAYARIT 63735

Directions: Grand Velas is located in Nuevo Vallarta, just 15 minutes (10 miles) north of the Puerto Vallarta International Airport.

Web: www.johansens.com/grandvelas
E-mail: reservas@grandvelas.com
Tel: +52 322 226 8000
Fax: +52 322 297 2005
U.S./Canada Toll Free: 1 877 398 2784

Price Guide: (all inclusive)
rooms U.S.$450-U.S.$4,500

The only all-inclusive AAA 5 Diamond rated resort in Puerto Vallarta, Grand Velas is artfully constructed in a crescent shape, allowing every suite an ocean view. This beach-front resort is a blend of the traditional and contemporary. The décor expresses a new take on original Mexican design, utilizing indigenous materials from native villages and the Asian tropics. Handmade carvings and engravings adorn the walls and the use of rich, natural hues creates a warm and inviting ambience. The spacious state-of-the-art suites are dressed with unusual teak, bamboo and wicker furnishings. Guests are afforded every conceivable amenity, including a 29" television with Internet access. Visitors can choose from a wealth of activities: the waters of the Pacific are perfect for an abundance of water sports, while land pursuits include golf, tennis and fitness. The spa has an extensive range of therapies and an indoor treatment area. Guests can also take classes in pottery, dance and Spanish. The entertainment continues into the evening with shows by the resident magician and performances in the outdoor theater. There are 5 restaurants: the casual Azul, offering international cuisine; fine Mexican food in the Frida; the exquisite Italian Lucca; Selva del Mar, a snack bar with a variety of appetizers; and the new specialty Piaf, which serves French cuisine.

Our inspector loved: *The infinity Jacuzzi.*

Casa Oaxaca

CALLE GARCÍA VIGIL 407, CENTRO, OAXACA, OAXACA 68000

Located in the center of the beautiful ancient city of Oaxaca, declared part of the world's cultural heritage by UNESCO, Casa Oaxaca is a traditional colonial house that perfectly combines Old World charm with the comfort and convenience of modern living. The cozy atmosphere of a traditional family home makes this hotel an ideal venue for a serene, relaxing getaway. Open spiral staircases are stunning against white and earth tone walls, complemented by designer armchairs and amazing Mexican pieces of art. A picturesque garden has a heavenly "Temazcal" steam bath, where herbs, used for centuries by the indigenous Mexican people, cure and balance the body, mind and spirit. Aromatherapy massages, facials, yoga and pedicures and manicures with reflexology can be arranged. Tempting classic, seasonal Oaxacan dishes are lovingly created, by appointment only, in the hotel's superb restaurant, which has a quiet, intimate ambience. Oaxaca is a wonderful city with plenty to offer: there are stunning churches, outstanding museums and many archaeological sites to explore. The city itself has 6 markets worth visiting that display local handicraft and unique food items. For many, the best way to enjoy this city is simply to stroll down its narrow streets or sit on one of the benches in a plaza and enjoy the glorious sun. Tour guides and transportation can be organized.

Our inspector loved: *The individual Mexican décor in each room.*

Directions: 15 minutes from Oaxaca Airport. A transfer from the airport can be arranged.

Web: www.johansens.com/oaxaca
E-mail: reservaciones@casaoaxaca.com
Tel: +52 951 514 4173
Fax: +52 951516 4412

Price Guide:
rooms U.S.$180-U.S.$300
suites U.S.$380

HACIENDA LOS LAURELES - SPA

HIDALGO 21, SAN FELIPE DEL AGUA, OAXACA, OAXACA 68020

The Hacienda Los Laureles - Spa hotel in Oaxaca city, built in1855, is a delightful refuge, nestling amidst aging Laureles and colorful gardens in the heart of this provincial district and not far from the ruins of San Felipe del Agua. There are just 23 bedrooms and suites in the hotel, and each has a distinct Mexican flavor. Cool whitewashed walls, terracotta floors and wrought-iron furniture lend a rustic authenticity, which is combined with warm woods and bold Mexican fabrics to create a welcoming and informal atmosphere. The restaurant and bar features an exciting and varied selection of cuisine – both traditional Mexican and more modern international dishes, and whether they be taken inside the restaurant or on the cool terracotta terrace, the setting is charming. The views from the hotel swimming pool are idyllic, looking way over the mountains, and tempt guests to relax with a long drink rather than take too many energetic lengths, although the exercise conscious will enjoy the runner's track and gym. The pre-Hispanic ritual of the adobe "Temazcal" or indigenous steam bath is also practiced here and is a must for the well-being and relaxation of even the most well-traveled guest. History lovers will also appreciate that the city of Oaxaca has a rich cultural heritage and the archeological zone of Monte Alban is nearby.

***Our inspector loved:** The beautiful gardens, and the personal attention.*

Directions: Located just outside of the center of Oaxaca City. 10km from the airport.

Web: www.johansens.com/laureles
E-mail: bookings@hotelhaciendaloslaureles.com
Tel: +52 951 501 5300
Fax: +52 951 501 5301 or +52 951 520 0890

Price Guide:
rooms (room only) U.S.$230-U.S.$250
suites (including breakfast) U.S.$350
special Sunday - Thursday rates from U.S.$160

LA QUINTA LUNA

3 SUR 702, SAN PEDRO CHOLULA, PUEBLA 72760

Situated in the oldest city of the American Continent, Cholula, on the outskirts of Puebla, La Quinta Luna is a 17th-century mansion which was completely restored between 1996-1998 by the family who still reside here and run the hotel. They have created a beautiful contrast between the building's classical Colonial architecture and the colorful contemporary Mexican art that adorns its walls. The 7 luxurious rooms are housed within thick walls and tall bearned cellings and overlook the central patio and fountain. There are 3 standard rooms, 1 junior suite with chimney and 1 with a kitchen, 1 master suite that includes a chimney, Jacuzzi and living area and a presidential suite in a private area with terrace, Jacuzzi, living room, chimney and separate bedroom. Meals may be served by the patio, which during the evening, is the perfect spot for a romantic candle-lit dinner. The Lobby and Restaurant are located where an old chapel once stood, and there is a carved stone of Colonial origin and a beam which dates back to 1736. The menu offers Mexican dishes, from traditional to new, as well as international cuisine. There is also a Library within the hotel containing 3,000 books, and guests may borrow them by prior arrangement. Nearby places of interest include Puebla, Tonanzintla, a Colonial church built by indigenous people in the 16th century and various archaeological sites.

Our inspector loved: *The personal attention by the owners.*

Directions: Huejotzingo Airport is 20 minutes from the hotel.

Web: www.johansens.com/quintaluna
E-mail: reservaciones@laquintaluna.com
Tel: +52 222 247 8915
Fax: +52 222 247 8916

Monterrey
Cabo San Lucas
Cancun
Mexico City
Zihuatanejo

Price Guide:
standard U.S.$145
junior suite U.S.$170
master suite U.S.$190
presidential suite U.S.$290

La Casa de la Marquesa

MADERO 41, QUERÉTARO, CENTRO HISTÓRICO 7600

Considered an architectural jewel of Colonial Mexico, La Casa de la Marquesa has 25 beautifully decorated suites adorned with fine antiques and exquisite art from all over the world. It is now a family-owned hotel but was originally built as a palace and private residence in 1756. It was re-opened in 1995 after much restoration of the fresco-painted walls, beautiful arches and even a small private chapel. The suites maintain a comfortable yet rich ambience and are decorated with antiques, Persian rugs, and original oil paintings. The hotel hosts 2 restaurants: the Comedor de la Marquesa restaurant, which provides delectable international and Mexican cuisine in a perfect charming setting. The less formal bistro-style café is located in the Casa Azul, which offers traditional Mexican food. A popular place to enjoy evening cocktails is the "Don Porfirio Bar." While staying at the hotel, guests can peruse the hotel's antique shop or art gallery or simply relax with a soothing massage. The hotel is situated in the heart of colonial Santiago de Querétaro where one can tour the beautiful churches and museums of the city including the Church of San Francisco and the Regional Museum, a former monastery.

Our inspector loved: *The antique architecture.*

Directions: 140 miles north of Mexico city. 5 miles from Querétaro Airport.

Web: www.johansens.com/marquesa
E-mail: marquesa@abanet.net
Tel: +52 442 212 0092
Fax: +52 442 212 0098
Mexico Toll Free: 01 800 401 7100

Price Guide:
rooms U.S.$135
suites U.S.$195-U.S.$245

Royal Hideaway Playacar

LOTE HOTELERO NO. 6, MZA 6 FRACC., PLAYACAR, PLAYA DEL CARMEN, QUINTANA ROO 77710

Set on a beautiful stretch of beach on the Yucatán Peninsula, Royal Hideaway Playacar is an all-inclusive, adults-only resort. This Spanish-Mexican colonial-style property is a favorite with couples and has a wide range of activities, dining and nightly entertainment. The 200 spacious rooms have garden or ocean views and are spread into 11 luxurious villas surrounding a central courtyard. The rooms, including 2 Presidential Suites, have furnished private terraces or balconies and elegant marble bathrooms with relaxing hydromassage tubs. The villa's private concierge can co-ordinate a multitude of activities, meals and invigorating treatments at the Royal Hideaway Playacar Spa. There are 3 swimming pools, one featuring a cascading infinity edge pool. The 3 relaxation pools, set in secluded locations, are paired with cool-water spa tubs and spacious sundecks. For energetic guests, the pool attendant can arrange scuba clinics, snorkeling, kayaking, sailing, and windsurfing. There are 6 restaurants to choose from including Mexican-Caribbean, Pan-Asian and Italian. The Club Royal Dinner Theater is a great way to enjoy an evening of entertainment. The hotel is 5 minutes from Playa del Carmen, a popular area for its white sand beaches, gentle surf, and laid back atmosphere. The "people ferry" to Cozumel is a short trip for snorkeling or diving on Cozumel's world-famous reefs.

Directions: The resort is 45 minutes from Cancun International Airport.

Web: www.johansens.com/royalhidewaway
E-mail: services@mx.occidentalhotels.com
Tel: +52 984 873 4500
Fax: +52 984 873 4507
U.S./Canada Toll Free: 1 800 999 9182

Price Guide: (per person, all inclusive)
rooms U.S.$373-U.S.$595

Our inspector loved: *The activities available with the all-inclusive plan.*

 200   220   13      SPA  

Ceiba del Mar Spa Resort

Preferred BOUTIQUE

COSTERA NORTE LTE. 1, S.M. 10, MZ. 26, PUERTO MORELOS, QUINTANA ROO 77580

Set on a stretch of pristine beach along the Caribbean coast of Mexico's Yucatan Peninsula, Ceiba del Mar Resort is secluded, yet is within a 15-minute seaside walk of the charming seaport town of Puerto Morelos. A recent renovation has expanded the resort to include 88 guest rooms, spacious master suites and terrace-topped penthouses with dazzling views of the sea, stars and sunrise. Interiors are quietly exquisite with a soothing sensation of space and innovative touches. The great Maya Reef forms a natural breakwater just ½km off shore, keeping the crystalline water calm for swimming. Teeming with tropical sealife, the reef also offers spectacular snorkeling and scuba. The vast swimming pool features a congenial swim-up bar. 2 restaurants, one on the beach with a rooftop bar, serve a variety of Mexican and international cuisine. Alternatively, the palapa-topped pagoda at the end of a long wooden pier is a lovely choice for candle-lit dinners and even weddings. The Spa at Ceiba del Mar is famous for its holistic treatments and revitalizing aromatherapy with indigenous Maya elements. The region's fascinating fusion of ancient Maya, Spanish Colonial, Yucatecan, Caribbean, and contemporary Mexican cultures is reflected in the architecture, folkdance, cuisine, décor, and personality of the resort.

Our inspector loved: *The private and peaceful atmosphere; a place for complete relaxation.*

Directions: Ceiba del Mar Resort is located 25km south of Cancun International Airport and 3km north of the coastal town, Puerto Morelos.

Web: www.johansens.com/ceibademar
E-mail: reserve@ceibadelmar.com
Tel: +52 998 872 8060
Fax: +52 998 872 8061
U.S./Canada Toll Free: 1 877 545 6221

Price Guide: (excluding 17% tax and service charge)
rooms $370-$530
suites $700-$1,250

88 100 SPA

Casa Nalum

SIAN KA'AN BIOSPHERE RESERVE, QUINTANA ROO

Casa Nalum is a private villa located inside the biosphere reserve of Sian Ka'an, the ideal setting to experience the seclusion of nature. With only 3 rooms including a master bedroom, this all-inclusive villa has a beautiful open-air common area that expands into a deck with gorgeous views of the Mexican Caribbean waters. A scenic lagoon is located behind the main house where guests are taken by private boat to explore ancient Mayan canals. The location offers complete peace and relaxation, and the welcoming staff includes a maid, cook, butler and gardener to accommodate every need, from a special drink to snorkeling equipment to planning aerial tours of the reserve. The house combines eco design with all the modern comforts of home and has cool and classic Caribbean décor. The villa includes a huge cinema screen with DVD player, table games and wireless Internet access. Dining is a wonderful experience with its exciting fusion of Mexican and European flavors. Guests can choose to dine in the formal dining room or al fresco on one of the terraces overlooking the sea. A relaxing Swedish massage is included for all adults. Guests can tour the Sian Ka'an Biosphere Reserve, UNESCO World Heritage site, which has 23 known archaeological sites. It covers 1.3 million acres and comprises one third of the Caribbean coast of Mexico.

Our inspector loved: *The elegant yet simplicistic architecture and décor.*

Directions: 25 minutes from Tulum. 2 hours from Cancun International Airport.

Web: www.johansens.com/casanalum
E-mail: info@nalum.com
Tel: +52 984 806 4905

Price Guide: (all inclusive, 4-night minimum stay)
rooms U.S.$9,800-U.S.$17,000 per week

HACIENDA XCANATUN - CASA DE PIEDRA

CARRETERA MÉRIDA-PROGRESO, KM 12, MÉRIDA, YUCATÁN 97302

Set in 9 acres of exquisite gardens, this former 18th-century sisal plantation, with gleaming polished stone and marble floors, 18ft beamed ceilings and luxurious furnishings offers privacy, 5-star cuisine and attentive service. All of the spacious, romantic suites feature carved cedar doors, hand-crafted Caribbean colonial furnishings, antiques and original oil paintings. Each has a private veranda or balcony strung with hammocks. Skylit marble-wrapped bathrooms are fitted with a hydrotherapy tub/shower or hand-crafted stone tub filled by a waterfall. Breakfast may be taken on the dining terrace or in suite. Unique international-Caribbean cuisine and Yucatecan specialties are served in Casa de Piedra, the former threshing room, with a multi-national wine list that must be sampled! Live music, Thursday - Sunday. Stress reducing, detoxifying massages, body-wraps and ancient Mayan healing treatments are offered in the full service spa. 2 freshwater swimming pools are situated in the garden. Private meetings, weddings and parties are accommodated in the family chapel with on-site planners. This is the only Yucatecan hacienda to receive the AAA 4-Diamond rating, plus the Star Diamond Award from the American Academy of Hospitality Sciences.

Our inspector loved: *The unique and tranquil ambience throughout the hacienda and gardens.*

Directions: From Mérida, take Montejo Avenue north and follow the signs to Progreso. Turn right at the pedestrian overpass at Km 12 of the Progreso Highway (Mexico 261). From Cancun, follow the signs to Progreso (Mexico 261) when approaching the outskirts of Mérida.

Web: www.johansens.com/xcanatun
E-mail: hacienda@xcanatun.com
Tel: +52 999 941 0273
Fax: +52 999 941 0319
U.S./Canada Toll Free: 1 888 883 3633

Price Guide:
suites U.S.$235-U.S.$310

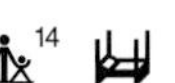

ARIZONA

Hotel location shown in red with page number

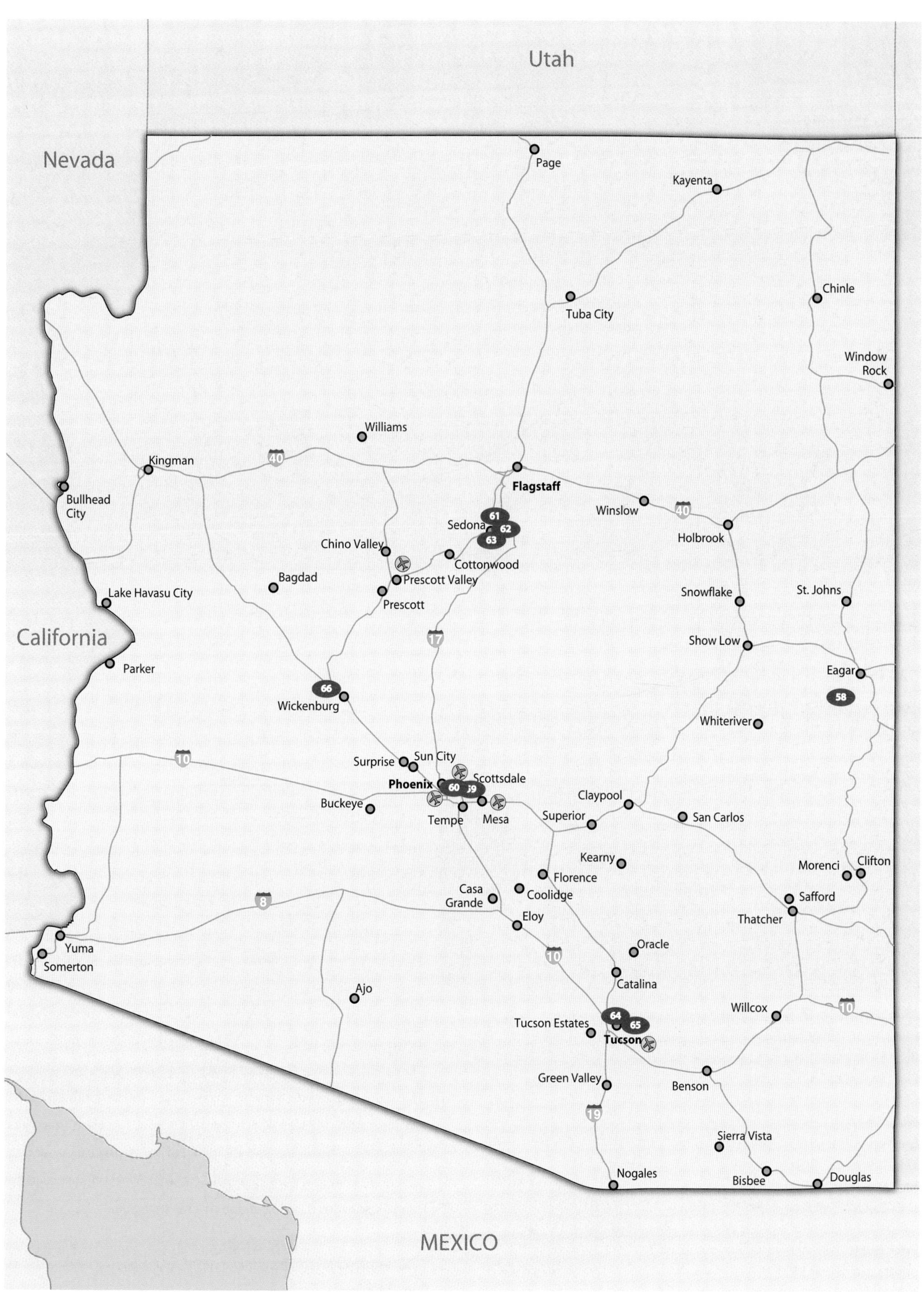

Hidden Meadow Ranch

620 COUNTRY ROAD 1325, GREER, ARIZONA 85927

Embraced by 2 million acres of spectacular Apache-Sitgreaves National Forests and shaded by towering aspen and ponderosa pine trees, this acclaimed retreat within Arizona's White Mountains is a luxurious and peaceful vacation venue with a staff dedicated to the comfort and relaxation of their guests. Far from the nearest highway and 10 miles north of the quaint town of Greer, the 150 acres of the ranch are a haven for wildlife such as elk, deer, turkey, antelope, bald eagles and the occasional black bear. 8,500ft. above sea level, the rhythms of the ranch are governed by the seasons: cool summers, falls framed by golden leaf glows, snowy, sunshine-filled winters and spring fields of purple iris. The well-appointed log cabins have living/dining areas with wood-burning fireplaces, downstairs master bedrooms, separate powder rooms and bathrooms with custom soaking tubs and loft bedroom/sitting areas. Pet-friendly cabins with attached dog runs are available. Meals include full mountain breakfasts, picnic lunches and 4-course gourmet dinners in the casually elegant Ranch House. Cookout breakfasts, margarita wagon rides, barbecues and campfire picnics are regularly arranged. There are a range of warm and cold weather activities on-site or nearby, and a supervised Ranch Roundup children's program.

Our inspector loved: *The luxurious cabins set among 50 acres of meadows and National Forest.*

Directions: From Phoenix take Highway 87 north. In Payson head east on Highway 260 to Show Low then take Highway 60 for approximately 30 miles. Phoenix International Sky Harbor is the nearest major airport and commuter flights are available to Show Low Airport.

Web: www.johansens.com/hiddenmeadow
E-mail: information@hiddenmeadow.com
Tel: +1 928 333 1000
Fax: +1 928 333 1010
U.S./Canada Toll Free: 1 866 333 4080

Price Guide: (all inclusive, double occupancy) private cabin from $500

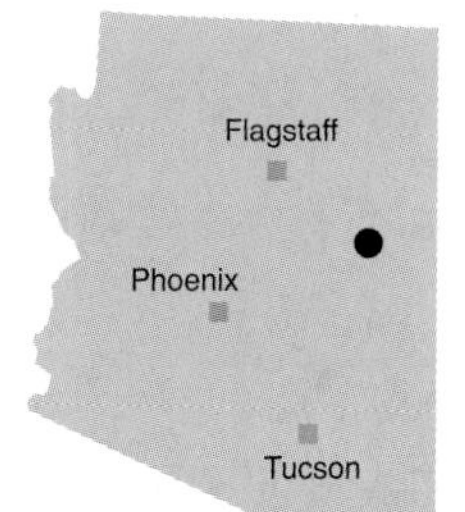

The Hermosa Inn

5532 NORTH PALO CRISTI ROAD, PARADISE VALLEY, ARIZONA 85253

Built as a home and studio by locally famed cowboy artist, Lon Megargee, this charming and unique, luxury boutique hotel stands serenely in an affluent, quiet neighborhood of Paradise Valley. The Hermosa is surrounded by attractive, private homes that front a beautiful desert landscape, exclusive shopping and hiking trails are nearby. The atmosphere is relaxed and peaceful, and the décor is authentic, elegant Southwestern. The artist's work is prominently displayed throughout the rooms and on secluded patio areas; all are comfortably furnished to the highest standard. An unusual feature is the wonderful beehive fireplaces, which are located throughout the hotel. Owners Fred and Jennifer Unger are proud of the appealing and welcoming ambience and their staff offers impressive and attentive individual service. Each guest room is fitted with refined furnishings and every comfort of home. Eating in the stylish restaurant and on the patio, which is regularly voted the No. 1 dining spot in Phoenix, is an experience to be savored. The award-winning American cuisine is superb, and the views of the "Praying Monk" on Camelback Mountain are spectacular. Elegant meeting and dining spaces are available, and private entertaining can be arranged in the underground wine cellar.

Our inspector loved: *Eating outside on the beautiful patio with a spectacular view of Camelback Mountain.*

Directions: From Sky Harbor International Airport head north on 44th Street then turn left on Stanford and right on North Palo Cristi Road.

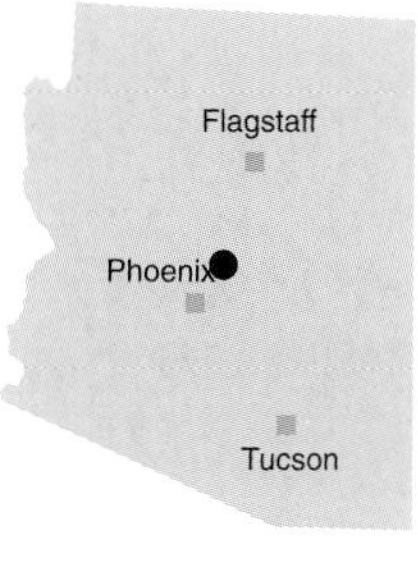

Web: www.johansens.com/hermosa
E-mail: reservations@hermosainn.com
Tel: +1 602 955 8614
Fax: +1 602 955 8299
U.S./Canada Toll Free: 1 800 241 1210

Price Guide:
rooms $199-$349
suites $429-$689

Sanctuary on Camelback Mountain

5700 EAST MCDONALD DRIVE, SCOTTSDALE, ARIZONA 85253

Directions: 8 miles north of Phoenix Sky Harbor Airport.

Web: www.johansens.com/sanctuarycamelback
E-mail: info@sanctuaryaz.com
Tel: +1 480 948 2100
Fax: +1 480 483 7314
U.S./Canada Toll Free: 1 800 245 2051

Price Guide:
casita rooms $225-$690
casita suites $325-$815

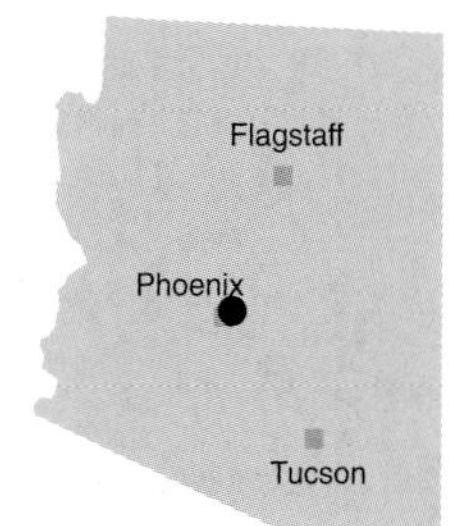

Perched atop Camelback Mountain, the Sanctuary offers 98 newly remodeled Mountain and Spa casitas. Everything about the resort complements the spectacular setting surrounded in nature's colors, which change from morning golden sand yellow to evening purples and pinks. The Mountain casitas feature modern furnishings, spacious bathrooms with oversized tubs, fine linens and unusual touches such as silk throws and a velvet sandbag that informs housekeeping when you are in residence. Some also have wood-burning fireplaces and outdoor terraces. The Spa casitas are surrounded by the infinity-edge pool and intimate spa. Some have outdoor soaking tubs and lava-rock fireplaces. Sanctuary Spa provides Asian-inspired treatments in 14 indoor and outdoor treatment rooms, a meditation garden, reflecting pond and Watsu pool. Guests can also enjoy the state-of-the-art fitness center and movement studio featuring Pilates, meditation and yoga. Outdoor activities include tennis, hiking and biking, and golf and shopping are close by. The sophisticated "elements" restaurant offers breathtaking views of Paradise Valley and fine American cuisine with Asian accents. The adjoining "jade bar" has both indoor and outdoor seating with a fire bowl to warm cool desert evenings. There is an extensive wine cellar and delectable cocktails conceived by the Sanctuary's "mixologists".

Our inspector loved: *The changing lights of the mountain views.*

Amara Creekside Resort

310 NORTH HIGHWAY 89A, SEDONA, ARIZONA 86336

Peacefully set on the banks of Oak Creek with spectacular views of the red rocks of Sedona, this eco-friendly 100-room romantic resort is a tranquil escape. Each of the sleek and urbane rooms in this AAA 4-Diamond resort has a minimalist, contemporary style with rich fabrics, high ceilings and comfortable furnishings including Mascioni Italian bedding. Further enhancing its calm ambience are the de luxe amenities by Aveda, ergonomic chairs, majestic views and the ever-changing color of the red rocks. Rooms have walk-in closets, mini bars, comfortable mattresses, D.V.D. players with complimentary movies and WiFi access. In-keeping with the philosophy of renewing the mind, body and spirit, the Serenity Spa offers massage and body treatments in the new treatment room or in the privacy of one's room. At night, visitors can star-gaze from the salt-water pool. Gallery at Oak Creek is the resort's signature 4 Diamond restaurant offering an eclectic menu and a balancing wine list. Guests dine al fresco on the patio by the fire pit where sunsets are spectacular. Room service is also available. The resort is ideal for weddings and can accommodate up to 200 people with over 11,000 square feet of meeting and event space. The resort is 5 minutes from the restaurants, shops and galleries of uptown Sedona, known as an artists' mecca and minutes away from the best hiking trails in Sedona.

Directions: From Phoenix travel north on I-17 for 114 miles. Take exit 298 and turn left on Highway 179 then right on 89A.

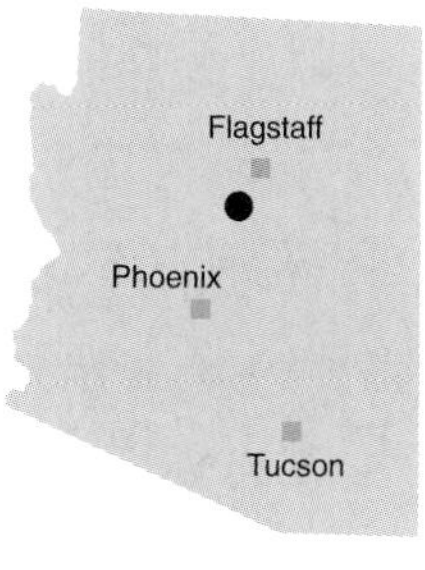

Flagstaff
Phoenix
Tucson

Web: www.johansens.com/amaracreekside
E-mail: info@amararesort.com
Tel: +1 928 282 4828
Fax: +1 928 282 4825
U.S./Canada Toll Free: 1 866 455 6610

Price Guide:
rooms $150-$485

Our inspector loved: *Dining in the Gallery at Oak Creek.*

L'Auberge de Sedona

301 L'AUBERGE LANE, SEDONA, ARIZONA 86336

Directions: Take I-17 north from Phoenix for approximately 90 miles then Route 179. Go west to Sedona and turn right onto 89A. Turn right immediately at L'Auberge Lane and follow the road for approximately 200 ft. The hotel is on the right.

Web: www.johansens.com/laubergedesedona
E-mail: info@lauberge.com
Tel: +1 928 282 1661
Fax: +1 928 282 2885
U.S./Canada Toll Free: +1 800 474 8114

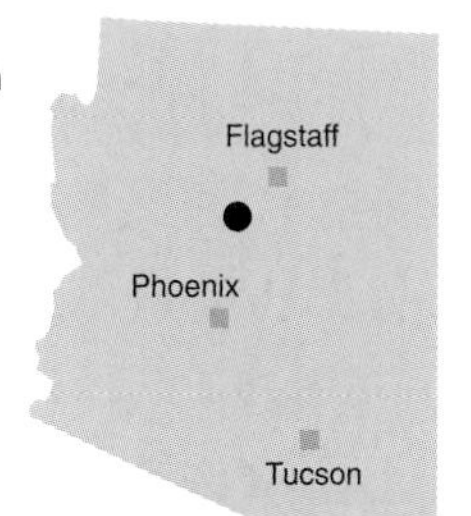

Price Guide: (room only)
rooms $175–$350
suites$225–$800

The Red Rock country of Arizona is home to a charming country European retreat set within 11 acres of striking grounds. Guests can stay in the 31 cottages, the 21-room lodge or the private 4-suite Creek House where sumptuous furnishings create a comfortable and welcoming ambience. The spacious lobby in the lodge is dominated by an impressive fireplace and these are also omnipresent in the beautifully-appointed cottages. Gourmet fare is served in the restaurant, which affords stunning views across Oak Creek. Artisan's brunches are held on the first Sunday of every month, mid-May through mid-October, where guests can indulge in continental pastries and create their own flavors at the omelet and waffle stations while enjoying the company of local artists. Dining al fresco is also available creek side under a canopy of trees in the gardens. The new L'Auberge Spa offers 4 indoor treatment rooms and outdoor creek side cabanas that are prefect for romantic couples' massages. 5 modern function rooms can be hired for meetings or events, and a plethora of team-building activities can be arranged such as a ropes course, tai chi, mountain biking, rock climbing, trout fishing, white-water rafting and tours of the Grand Canyon.

Our inspector loved: *The new spa that enhances guests' experience at this truly relaxing destination.*

Sedona Rouge Hotel & Spa

2250 West Highway 89A, Sedona, Arizona 86336

Surrounded by landscaped gardens, secluded courtyards with carved stone columns and the stunning Red Rock country vistas of Arizona, this new city boutique hotel has gained a reputation as a relaxing and stylish retreat with a comfortable and exotic ambience. The opulent, modern décor features intricate and rich textures reminiscent of Andalucía, Spain, while cascading fountains and delicate ironwork balconies enhance the welcoming exterior. Each of the cool, attractive guest rooms has an individual and tranquil charm with fine linens, a spacious bathroom, exquisite imported furniture and every amenity. Some have a fireplace, private garden or patio. The rooftop terrace enjoys a 360° panoramic viewpoint and is the perfect location to lounge in the shade or chat over a cool drink. The Spa at Sedona Rouge features seasonal custom treatments, indoor and outdoor whirlpools, yoga classes, a spa boutique, a tranquil room and gardens. There are 6 Spa Guest Rooms and a Spa Suite located in the Spa and include soaking tubs in the living areas. In the west wing, Reds restaurant serves an imaginative menu of American cuisine. 2 golf courses are within easy reach, and riding and jeep tours to the Grand Canyon can be arranged.

Our inspector loved: *The view of the Red Rocks of Sedona from the rooftop terrace.*

Directions: The nearest airport is Sky Harbor International. From Phoenix take I-17 north and exit 287 west on 260. Turn right on Highway 89A to Sedona.

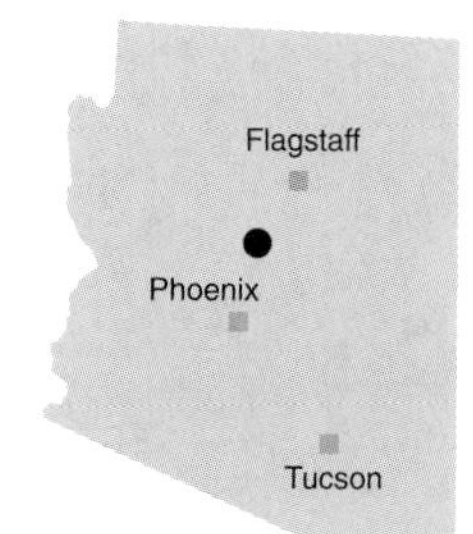

Web: www.johansens.com/sedonarouge
E-mail: info@sedonarouge.com
Tel: +1 928 203 4111
Fax: +1 928 203 9094
U.S./Canada Toll Free: 1 866 312 4111

Price Guide: (room only)
rooms $185-$300
suites $240-$380

ARIZONA INN

2200 EAST ELM STREET, TUCSON, ARIZONA 85719

More than 75 years of family ownership have earned this beautiful Mediterranean-style inn a place on the National Register of Historic Places and a host of awards including a Zagat Survey of U.S. Hotels, Resorts and Spas rating as one of the "Top 100 hotels in the U.S." and a position on Condé Nast Traveler's Gold List of the highest-rated hotels and resorts around the world. Situated in a residential area close to Tucson city center, Arizona Inn is surrounded by 14 acres of immaculate lawns, mature trees, flowerbeds, hedged private patios and water features. The inn combines modern comfort with antique charm and is as eclectic in décor as it is cosmopolitan in service and clientele. Little has changed since opening in the 1930s, when owner and Arizona Congresswoman Isabella Greenway welcomed guests such as Eleanor Roosevelt and John D. Rockefeller Jr. Today's men and women of distinction and of the entertainment world return time and again to enjoy their favorites among the 86 individually and luxuriously decorated rooms and suites, or 2 large private villas. International cuisine is enjoyed in the elegant restaurant and afternoon tea is served in a quiet library decorated with family heirlooms. There are tennis courts and a 60-foot outdoor swimming pool framed with tiled porches, exercise room and rose-covered walkway.

Our inspector loved: *The beautiful historic neighborhood, and the library.*

Directions: From Tucson International Airport take I-10 north and head east on Speedway Boulevard. Head north on Campbell then turn into East Elm Street.

Web: www.johansens.com/arizonainn
E-mail: reservations@arizonainn.com
Tel: +1 520 325 1541
Fax: +1 520 881 5830
U.S./Canada Toll Free: 1 800 933 1093

Price Guide: (room only)
rooms $159-$280
suites $250-$499

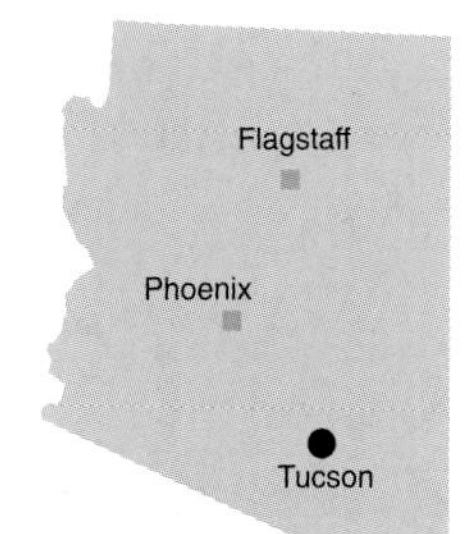

Tanque Verde Ranch

14301 EAST SPEEDWAY BOULEVARD, TUCSON, ARIZONA 85748

Established in 1868, Tanque Verde Ranch is a 4-star quality resort, recognized as the last luxurious outpost of the Old West. Located on 640 acres in the spectacular, lush desert foothills of the Rincon Mountains, surrounded by the Saguaro National Park and adjacent to Coronado National Forest, the ranch offers breathtaking mountain and desert views. The scenic, tranquil beauty coupled with an energy of various activities, make this a rejuvenating and unforgettable experience. The 74 authentically decorated rooms and suites are fully air conditioned, most with fireplaces and patios. Rates include 3 delicious meals a day and all of the scheduled ranch activities, including horseback riding, tennis, hiking, mountain biking, nature programs, a children's program and more. 3 sparkling pools, 2 whirlpool spas and 2 saunas provide the perfect way to relax after a long day in the saddle. Soothing massages and luxurious body treatments, spa pedicures and manicures may be arranged on-site in La Sonora Spa. Relax on the veranda, watching the fabulous Arizona sunset; enjoy a festive outdoor barbecue and a scenic breakfast ride to the Old Homestead – the magic of the American West is waiting for you here. Resort quality facilities in the beautiful setting of a historic ranch make Tanque Verde a unique and special experience.

Our inspector loved: *The serene desert setting at the base of the Rincon Mountains.*

Directions: 30 minutes from Tucson Airport. Go east on Valencia, then turn north on Houghton Road. Turn east on Speedway Boulevard and go all the way to the dead end where the ranch driveway begins.

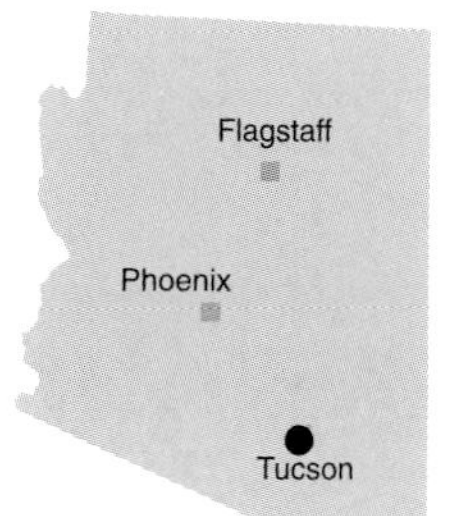

Web: www.johansens.com/tanqueverde
E-mail: dude@tvgr.com
Tel: +1 520 296 6275
Fax: +1 520 721 9427
U.S./Canada Toll Free: 1 800 234 3833

Price Guide: (includes 3 meals per day and scheduled activities.Double occupancy, excluding tax and service charge.)
rooms $325–$560 suites $390–$640

RANCHO DE LOS CABALLEROS

1551 SOUTH VULTURE MINE ROAD, WICKENBURG, ARIZONA 85390

Set in Wickenburg, this full-service ranch, enveloped in 20,000 acres of desert cactus plants and blooming flowers, is the epitome of South Western allure. Each of the rooms and suites of this family-owned property has been carefully decorated with handcrafted furniture, Mexican tiling and fabrics, and there is an abundance of activities available. Trap and skeet shooting, golf on the 18-hole course, jeep rides, hiking through challenging trails, hot-air ballooning and nature horseback rides through the Sonoran Desert Uplands. Groups of all ages will savor the awe-inspiring flora and fauna of Arizona, and with 300 species of birds in the area, ornithologists are invited to enjoy bird watching with the resident naturalist. At dusk, guests may head down to the South Yucca Flats for a cookout with a cowboy and enjoy steaks, chicken or ribs barbecued over an open mesquite fire. Residents of the Spanish Empire, Yavapai Indians and the gold miners of 1862 have all left their vestiges in historic Wickenburg, and the area also boasts Vulture Mountain and national forests, making it a pleasure to explore. The brand new Los Caballeros Spa offers a variety of de-stressing massages, nourishing body wraps and facials designed for dramatic results and even luxurious spa manicures and pedicures by the fire. Events can be organized at the 4,500ft.² Palo Verde conference center.

Our inspector loved: *The serene setting in the high desert.*

Directions: From Phoenix Sky Harbor International Airport head towards I-10 and go north on I-17 to State Road 74. Travel 30 miles to U.S. Route 60 then turn right, then left onto Vulture Mine Road.

Web: www.johansens.com/caballeros
E-mail: home@sunc.com
Tel: +1 928 684 5484
Fax: +1 928 684 9565
U.S./Canada Toll Free: 1 800 684 5030

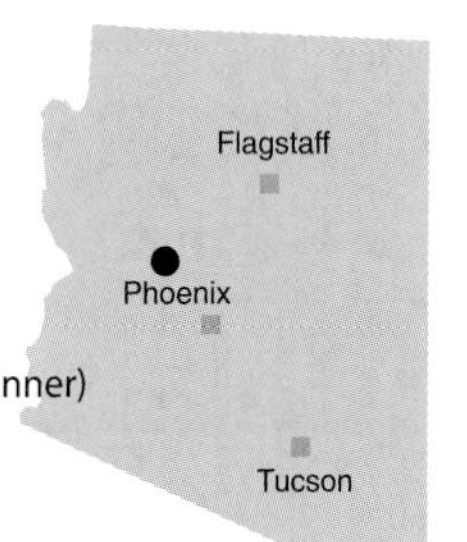

Price Guide: (including breakfast, lunch and dinner)
rooms $270-$530
suites $370-$600

CALIFORNIA

Hotel location shown in red with page number

The Carlton Hotel

6005 El Camino Real, Atascadero, California 93422

Directions: The hotel is midway between San Francisco and Los Angeles. The nearest airport is San Luis Obispo Airport.

Web: www.johansens.com/carltoncalifornia
E-mail: info@the-carlton.com
Tel: +1 805 461 5100
Fax: +1 805 461 5116
U.S./Canada Toll Free: 1 877 204 9830

Price Guide: (room only)
rooms $155-$310
suites $375-$455

This elegant and historic luxury California hotel has a warm and intimate feel and its exceptional, elegant décor has been featured in Architectural Digest. The owners have carefully preserved the character of the property and integrated luxurious touches including handmade ironwork on the staircase and hand-selected designer glass fixtures. Guests feel at home with the personal service and warm family hospitality. Guest rooms are tastefully designed with all the comfort and amenities of a fine residence. Located in downtown Atascadero, the restaurant offers fine and casual dining, a gourmet bakery, 2 lounges and wine bar. The Carlton Restaurant & Grill, the hotel's upscale fun restaurant with a high energy bar and lounge, serves drinks and specialty appetizers as well as the full menu. The Sushi Bar is also a guest favorite. The inviting Lounge and Wine Bar with open fireplace and relaxing atmosphere, serves cocktails, light fare and afternoon tea. The diVINE Piano Lounge is another comfortable spot to enjoy a beverage or meal from any menu. Perfectly located for exploring California's central coast, home to California's fastest growing wine region, and beautiful, pristine beaches. Guests can drive north to visit Hearst Castle, south to the charming town and historic mission of San Luis Obispo or sample award-winning wines at the area's numerous wineries.

***Our inspector loved:** The great selection of sushi served in the restaurant.*

Post Ranch Inn

HIGHWAY 1, P.O. BOX 219, BIG SUR, CALIFORNIA 93920

Like a jewel in its setting, Post Ranch Inn sits amid the unparalleled beauty of Big Sur's rugged coastline, rolling mountains and towering redwoods. An architectural marvel, Post Ranch Inn is in harmony with nature. Luxurious redwood and stone accommodations provide stunning panoramas of the blue Pacific while stilted tree houses enjoy mountain vistas. Each room is appointed with a wood-burning fireplace, slate spa tub, organic-cotton linens, massage table and private terrace. Awarded Condé Nast Johansens Most Excellent Inn in the U.S.A. 2006, Post Ranch Inn offers a world-class amenity package attuned to natural surroundings. Bask in the infinity pool or heated lap pool. Take a guided nature walk or yoga class. Harmonize the body and soul with luxurious spa treatments. An extensive activities program introduces guests to the treasures of Big Sur, and the inn provides Lexus S.U.V. shuttles for sightseeing adventures. Dining is a distinct pleasure: the award-winning Sierra Mar Restaurant prepares superb cuisine, has a world-class wine cellar and boasts spectacular views.

Our inspector loved: *The breathtaking natural beauty and rustic elegance of this cliff-side property.*

Directions: The resort is approximately 45 minutes from Monterey Peninsula Airport. 2 hours from San Jose Airport and 3 hours from San Francisco Airport.

Sacramento
San Francisco
Los Angeles
San Diego

Web: www.johansens.com/postranchinn
E-mail: reservations@postranchinn.com
Tel: +1 831 667 2200
Fax: +1 831 667 2512
U.S./Canada Toll Free: 1 800 527 2200

Price Guide:
rooms $550-$1,385
suites $1,175-$2,400

U.S.A. - CALIFORNIA (BIG SUR)

Ventana Inn and Spa

HIGHWAY 1, BIG SUR, CALIFORNIA 93920

Snuggly nestled on a gently sloping wooded hillside overlooking Big Sur's rugged coastline, the enchanting Ventana Inn and Spa provides unforgettable luxury, unique architecture, world-class dining and spectacular spa treatments. With a serene, romantic atmosphere, this hotel is ideal for those wishing to get away from the stresses of everyday life. Newly decorated rooms are simply stunning with wood paneling, open fireplaces and plenty of space. Décor is tasteful and perfectly in harmony with the beautiful furniture and fine linens. Many rooms have their own balconies with sweeping vistas of the Pacific Ocean and the green and gold flowered hills of the surrounding countryside. Some rooms benefit from private decks with Jacuzzi tubs and hammocks. Each meal in the restaurant is a memorable one: outstanding cuisine is fresh, simple and delicious. A fantastic spa offers complimentary yoga as well as a large variety of holistic treatments to relax and rejuvenate the soul. The hotel is situated in 243 acres of meadows and hills, making it ideal for those who enjoy the outdoors. Guests will be spoiled for choice of what to do; miles of untouched natural surroundings offer a unique opportunity for guests to explore the woods, coast and meadows.

Our inspector loved: *The photo safari led by artist David Gubernick; guests can capture the beauty of Big Sur with their own 16x24 archival print!*

Directions: Monterey Peninsula Airport is 45 minutes from the inn on Highway 1.

Web: www.johansens.com/ventana
E-mail: reservations@ventanainn.com
Tel: +1 831 667 2331
Fax: +1 831 667 2419
U.S./Canada Toll Free: 1 800 628 6500

Price Guide:
rooms $400-$650
suites $600-$2,000

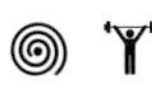

L'AUBERGE CARMEL

MONTE VERDE AT SEVENTH, CARMEL-BY-THE-SEA, CALIFORNIA 93921

Set in a romantic location, in the heart of the quaint village of Carmel-by-the-Sea, a short walk from Carmel's main beach, this European-style inn is the ideal getaway for the discerning gourmand. Built in 1929, the inn has undergone major renovation work, which has transformed the entrance, guest rooms and landscaped courtyard. Bedrooms are well appointed and individually decorated and have every modern comfort with generous bathrooms and flat-screen TVs. Warm jewel tones and fine fabrics complement the charm of the inn's architecture, and the floor heating creates a welcoming feel. A truly memorable gastronomic experience awaits guests: a sumptuous French country Continental breakfast is served each morning and the 12-table restaurant, ruled by head chef Walter Manzke, creates gastronomic delights that will please the most discerning palate. The underground wine cellar houses a 4,500-bottle wine collection, including great worldwide wines, notably from Monterey County, California and France. The picturesque Carmel-by-the-Sea has always been a magnet for artists, writers and travelers, and its interesting art galleries, fine restaurants, excellent shopping and famous beach provide the perfect surroundings for a relaxing break. The location and mild climate throughout the year make this an ideal base from which to explore the Northern Californian coast.

Our inspector loved: *The restaurant, which is not to be missed!*

Directions: From Highway 1 take Ocean Avenue exit to Carmel then follow Ocean Avenue through the village. Turn left at Monte Verde and the inn is a half block on the left-hand side. Monterey Airport is a 20-minute drive from the property.

Sacramento
San Francisco
Los Angeles
San Diego

Web: www.johansens.com/laubergecarmel
E-mail: reservations@laubergecarmel.com
Tel: +1 831 624 8578
Fax: +1 831 626 1018

Price Guide: (excluding $20 service fee)
rooms $295-$500

TRADEWINDS CARMEL

MISSION STREET AT THIRD AVENUE, CARMEL-BY-THE-SEA, CALIFORNIA 93921

Nestled on a quiet, tree-lined residential street, this luxury boutique hotel has a peaceful, zen-like quality that guarantees a tranquil, relaxing stay. Tradewinds' guest rooms provide ultimate comfort in opulent surroundings and most have been styled with an Asian influence complemented by authentic wooden furnishings produced in Bali and China. Inspiring views of the lush courtyard, Point Lobos and Carmel Bay can be enjoyed from bedroom balconies. King and queen rooms have magnificent beds enveloped with 100% Egyptian cotton linens and stylish, custom marble bathrooms; most king rooms boast whirlpool tubs. King suites offer the utmost privacy and are situated in the View Wing, which offers spectacular views across the Pacific Ocean. Originally built when the village was primarily an artist colony, it is not surprising to learn that there are many art galleries in the area, in addition to great shopping, renowned wineries and world-class restaurants. Carmel Beach, with its mile of pristine white sand, is a short walk away. Alternatively, guests may wish to take a short drive along the scenic route of world famous Pebble Beach or the breathtaking Big Sur Coast. Hiking, cycling, kayaking and wine tasting can all be arranged or relax in the meditation garden with the soothing sounds of the waterfall. This is a non-smoking inn.

Our inspector loved: *The character shaped by designer, Charles Gruwell.*

Directions: Monterey Peninsula Airport is a 20-minute drive from the inn.

Web: www.johansens.com/tradewinds
E-mail: reservations@tradewindscarmel.com
Tel: +1 831 624 2776
Fax: +1 831 624 0634
U.S./Canada Toll Free: 1 800 624 6665

Price Guide:
rooms $250-$550

THE CARTER HOUSE INNS

301 L STREET, EUREKA, CALIFORNIA 95501

Comprising of 4 beautifully renovated buildings, this establishment is the jewel of the historic district of Eureka. The charming seaport on the California coastline overflows with unusual boutiques, museums, galleries, antique shops and places to eat. Visitors are never short of things to do! At the Carter House Inns the warmest of welcomes awaits guests and the hospitable staff are attentive but never intrusive. Tasteful interior design incorporates sumptuous fabrics, original artwork and antique furnishings. In each one of the luxurious bedrooms aspects of a bygone era combine with contemporary in-room entertainment centers to create a stylish and comfortable environment. Large windows allow the rooms to be bathed in natural daylight and bouquets of fresh flowers add splashes of vibrant color. At the hotel's Restaurant 301, dishes are created using local ingredients such as freshly caught Kumamoto oysters from Humboldt Bay and produce from the property's own garden. In the grounds over 300 varieties of herbs, fruit and vegetables are grown and each afternoon guests are invited to collect ingredients for the evening's menu. The surrounding area is home to a myriad of recreational activities and other interesting visits include Redwood National Park and the Sequoia Park and Zoo.

Our inspector loved: *The menu and wine list on offer at the Restaurant 301, a gastronomic delight.*

Directions: The Carter House is located less than 15 miles from Arcata Airport.

Web: www.johansens.com/carterhouse
E-mail: reserve@carterhouse.com
Tel: +1 707 444 8062
Fax: +1 707 444 8067
U.S./Canada Toll Free: 1 800 404 1390

Price Guide:
rooms $175–$275
suites $275–$650

THE GAIGE HOUSE

13540 ARNOLD DRIVE, GLEN ELLEN, CALIFORNIA 95442

Nestled in the beautiful Sonoma Valley, within the charming village of Glen Ellen, the award-winning Gaige House is only a short distance from downtown Sonoma. The property offers luxurious accommodation in a calm and peaceful environment. Most of the individually designed rooms enjoy elegant fireplaces, outside decks, air conditioning and sumptuous designer linens. Particularly outstanding are the new spa suites with immense windows affording views over the glorious Calabazas Creek. Another exceptional feature is the Gaige Suite bathroom, which boasts an enormous 2-person shower and a wrap-around deck overlooking the delightful verdant gardens. The heated pool is set in the lawn at the rear of the estate and new health facilities include a spa room and whirlpool. Guests can relax with a pampering massage either in-room or poolside. The monumental breakfasts are created by chef Charles Holmes who brings his artistic flair and unique style to the dishes; consisting of 2 or 3 courses the cuisine is light yet extremely satisfying. Sonoma Valley is part of the famous Napa wine country and there are plenty of wine tasting tours available for visitors. For recreation, there is hiking and cycling, and there are many quality restaurants in the surrounding area.

Our inspector loved: *The new spa suites along the creek, which feature 2,500 pound granite soaking tubs.*

Directions: San Francisco Airport is 1 hour and 20 minutes away.

Web: www.johansens.com/gaige
E-mail: gaige@sprynet.com
Tel: +1 707 935 0237
Fax: +1 707 935 6411
U.S./Canada Toll Free: 1 800 935 0237

Price Guide: (breakfast $15)
rooms $175-$375
suites $395-$595

The Grape Leaf Inn

539 JOHNSON STREET, HEALDSBURG, CALIFORNIA 95448

Located in the heart of the northern Sonoma wine country, the 106-year-old Grape Leaf Inn has been welcoming guests for over 2 decades. The inn's 12 distinct beautifully appointed rooms offer fresh flowers, fine fabrics, thick towels and down bedding. Many accommodations feature generous 2-person spa tub/showers, king beds and private fireplaces; one room boasts a 2-person steam shower and Japanese soaking tub. A 10-acre vineyard property with 3 charmingly renovated cottages has recently been added to the inn, affording guests the opportunity to experience authentic vineyard living. Surrounded by 80-year-old Zinfandel vines, the cottages offer some of the most spectacular views in wine country. Each cottage has its own private outdoor hot tub set amongst the vines, and one cottage features its own 100-year-old wine cellar. Breakfasts at the inn are a multi-course gourmet affair, prepared using the freshest locally grown produce and served on fine china with crisp pristine linens. After a day of relaxation or wine-hopping among the more than 120 wineries within 20 minutes of the inn, visitors can step behind the secret bookcase and enjoy complementary tastings of outstanding Sonoma County wines and cheeses in the cellar "Speakeasy" before dining out at a local restaurant.

Our inspector loved: *The fabulous wine cellar ("Speakeasy") where guests can enjoy local wines every evening.*

Directions: 1 hour and 30 minutes from San Francisco and Oakland Airports.

Web: www.johansens.com/grapeleaf
E-mail: info@grapeleafinn.com
Tel: +1 707 433 8140
Fax: +1 707 433 3140
U.S./Canada Toll Free: 1 866 732 9131

Sacramento
San Francisco
Los Angeles
San Diego

Price Guide:
rooms $225-$395
vineyard cottages $425-$790

The Kenwood Inn and Spa

10400 SONOMA HIGHWAY, KENWOOD, CALIFORNIA 95452

Directions: The inn is 1 hour and 45 minutes from San Francisco Airport.

Web: www.johansens.com/kenwoodinn
E-mail: info@kenwoodinn.com
Tel: +1 707 833 1293
Fax: +1 707 833 1247
U.S./Canada Toll Free: 1 800 353 6966

Price Guide:
rooms $350
suites $700

Situated on a hillside in Sonoma's Valley of the Moon and overlooking 2,000 acres of vineyard, The Kenwood Inn and Spa has all the character of a sultry Mediterranean villa. The property offers 30 opulent rooms centered around 3 private courtyards. Each suite is perfectly appointed for total comfort with wood burning fireplaces, feather beds and sumptuous fabrics accentuating the warm, romantic mood of the premises. A complimentary 3-course breakfast can be enjoyed in the secluded courtyard or in the dining room. The property has full spa facilities consisting of 12 suites in 4 buildings that encircle an impressive salt-water pool. The estate also boasts the first Caudalíe vinothérapie center in the U.S.A. where treatments are based on the extracts of vine and grape seeds combined with organic essential oils to restore and rejuvenate. These therapies are expertly administered in the barrel bath cabin and terrace, which afford stunning views over the vine-covered hills. Located only 45 minutes from San Francisco, Sonoma Valley is best known for its award-winning wines and wineries, however it is also home to numerous small farms, unique historical sites, wonderful shops and boutiques and fabulous restaurants.

Our inspector loved: *Dinner at The Kenwood Inn, which is not to missed!*

     SPA  

Estancia La Jolla Hotel & Spa

9700 NORTH TORREY PINES ROAD, LA JOLLA, CALIFORNIA 92037

Set on almost 10 acres on the bluff of La Jolla, Estancia La Jolla Hotel & Spa is an adobe-style luxury hotel, spa and executive learning retreat. The well-appointed rooms include one Presidential Suite and have attractive marble baths, a luxurious selection of guest amenities and lovely patios or balconies with views of lush courtyards. The surrounding fragrant gardens showcase many native California plantings and are enhanced by fountains, flamenco guitar music, outdoor fireplaces and picturesque pathways. There are 2 restaurants offering traditional California and Spanish fusion cuisine; the casual-chic Adobe el Restaurante and the Mustangs & Burros where guests dine al fresco or indoors while listening to live music. The Bodega Wine Bar serves some of California's finest wines. The Library and Garden Suite are also available for private dining. The Spa at Estancia La Jolla is a full-service spa with an array of organic treatments. With 9 luxurious indoor and outdoor treatment rooms, guests can rejuvenate while surrounded by serene gardens and balmy ocean breezes. The state-of-the-art Learning Retreat is a certified I.A.C.C. conference center with 25,000 sq. ft. of meeting facilities. The hotel is conveniently located near the University of California at San Diego and is minutes from world-class shopping, famous beaches, golf courses and major attractions.

***Our inspector loved:** Adobe el Restaurante overlooking the courtyard.*

 210         SPA 

Directions: The nearest airport is San Diego International.

Web: www.johansens.com/estancialajolla
E-mail: reservations@estancialajolla.com
Tel: +1 858 202 3389
Fax: +1 858 202 3399
U.S./Canada Toll Free: 1 877 4 ESTANCIA

Price Guide: (room only)
rooms $229-$359
suites $520-$1,400

Hotel Bel-Air

701 STONE CANYON ROAD, LOS ANGELES, CALIFORNIA 90077

Located only 2 miles from Beverly Hills, this Mobil 5-star rated sanctuary is the essence of sophistication. The pink stucco structure, intimate courtyard areas and iron terraces reflect the elegant past and a stylish ambience. Enveloped by 12 acres of verdant gardens, the hotel offers 91 rooms, including 39 suites; all are individually appointed (some suites are even customized for longstanding guests) and have private entrances from the lush gardens or fountain courtyards. Following a multi-million dollar renovation, the bathrooms include double marble sinks, large showers and spacious bathtubs. Some feature tiled patios, wood-burning fireplaces and Jacuzzis, and complimentary tea and cakes are served in each room upon arrival. A popular venue for private parties and weddings, Swan Lake and the front lawn are picturesque settings and there is function space in the Garden Room and the Pavilion Room. Accommodating up to 45 delegates, the recently-opened Palm Room boasts a plasma monitor, pocket doors to create breakouts, 2 fireplaces and a private patio with fountain. Enjoy exquisite meals served in the restaurant or al fresco on the terrace, before adjourning to the award-winning wood-paneled bar. Complimentary transportation to Beverly Hills, Westwood and Century City can be arranged 7 days a week.

Directions: Los Angeles Airport is 20-35 minutes from the hotel.

Web: www.johansens.com/belair
E-mail: sales@hotelbelair.com
Tel: +1 310 472 1211
Fax: +1 310 909 1611
U.S./Canada Toll Free: 1 800 648 4097

Price Guide: (room only)
rooms $395-$600
suites $800-$3,700

Our inspector loved: *The sense of seclusion and superior service.*

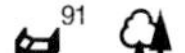         

The Fess Parker Wine Country Inn

2860 Grand Avenue, Los Olivos, California 93441

A model of class, comfort and quality, this is an elegant getaway that has been awarded many accolades. A Victorian-style inn, The Fess Parker Wine Country Inn is situated deep in the sunny wine country just north of Santa Barbara. Built and owned by former actor Fess Parker, who played Davy Crocket in Disney's King of the Wild Frontier television series from 1954-1956, there is something for everyone: quiet and romantic, small and quaint and a multi-facility resort with a spa. The individually designed and decorated guest rooms have been lovingly furnished and have every facility and amenity to please the most discerning traveler including air conditioning, fireplaces, pristine bathrooms, voicemail, high-speed Internet and twice-daily maid service. The inn boasts one of the finest restaurants in the region, The Wine Cask Restaurant, where service is impeccable and cuisine is prepared by renowned executive chef Troy Tolbert; the wine list is extensive. There is a heated swimming pool, Jacuzzi and beautiful outdoor areas for sampling wine from Mr. Parker's vineyards and enjoying the central coast's beautiful weather. Some evenings there is live music, and there are excellent restaurants and shopping in Los Olivos. Numerous leisure and sporting activities are nearby.

Our inspector loved: *Spa Vigne: the blissful 80-minute facial is spectacular.*

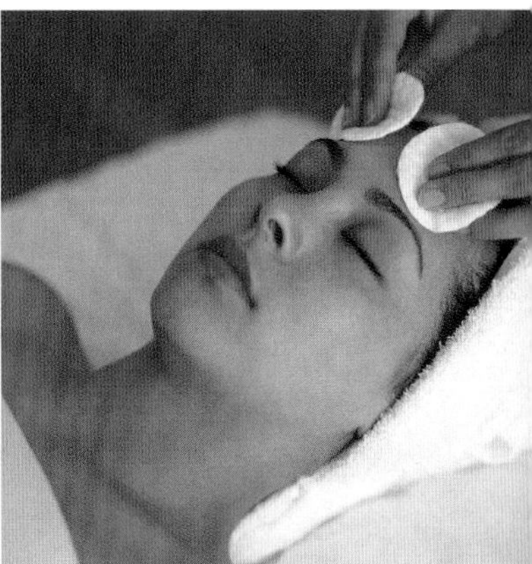

Directions: Santa Barbara Airport is approximately a 45-minute drive from the inn.

Web: www.johansens.com/fessparker
E-mail: reservations@fessparker.com
Tel: +1 805 688 7788
Fax: +1 805 688 1942
U.S./Canada Toll Free: 1 800 466 2455

Price Guide:
rooms $265-$365
suites $290-$450

           SPA

The Stanford Inn By The Sea

COAST HIGHWAY ONE & COMPTCHE-UKIAH ROAD, MENDOCINO, CALIFORNIA 95460

A relaxing retreat on the rugged California coastline, The Stanford Inn By The Sea rests comfortably between lush forest and the majestic Pacific Ocean. The Eden-like grounds, which surround the property, are stunning and consist of flower, herb and vegetable gardens. In fact, the inn is a family home and certified organic farm, the products of which are utilized to create fantastic gourmet vegetarian and vegan cuisine in the highly acclaimed Ravens restaurant. Guests will not be disappointed with the exquisite overnight accommodation the property offers: all of the rooms and suites boast pine and redwood paneling, a roaring log fire, king or queen four-poster or sleigh beds and are embellished with plants, antiques and works of art. The Stanford Inn is a tranquil oasis where visitors can enjoy a relaxing massage or private yoga session. The pool, spa and sauna are situated in one of the greenhouses and are encircled by lush vegetation and tropical plants but for more energetic pursuits, the beautiful town of Mendocino offers a myriad of activities including golfing and surfing as well as many excellent shopping and dining options. Mountain bikes may be hired from the hotel and canoeing and kayaking at the on-site canoe-kayak livery, Catch a Canoe & Bicycles, too! organizes trips along the unspoiled Big River. There is also a fitness center and yoga classes available.

***Our inspector loved:** Ravens: a culinary treat even for non-vegetarians!*

Directions: 3 hours and 30 minutes from Oakland or San Francisco Airport.

Web: www.johansens.com/stanford
E-mail: info@stanfordinn.com
Tel: +1 707 937 5615
Fax: +1 707 937 0305
U.S./Canada Toll Free: 1 800 331 8884

Price Guide:
rooms $265-$325
suites $395-$465

Mill Valley Inn

165 THROCKMORTON AVENUE, MILL VALLEY, CALIFORNIA 94941

30 minutes north of San Francisco and set in a unique location at the foot of Mount Tamalpais, surrounded by redwood trees, this romantic hideaway combines the quaint charm of a historic Californian mill town with the sophisticated air of a modern European hotel. With a modern, Tuscany-style ambience the 25 distinctive bedrooms, including 2 cottages built along a creek, offer an eclectic style and king or queen-sized beds. All reflect a respect for nature and incorporate furnishings handcrafted in Northern California. Breakfast is served on the splendid flower-filled Sun Terrace and includes fresh fruit, local pastries and espresso drinks. An evening wine and cheese reception is also served on the Sun Terrace during the afternoon. Mill Valley, with its bustling plaza surrounded by shops, boutiques, cafés and fine restaurants is within easy walking distance. Just outside the town, enjoy the beauty of Northern California, which includes San Francisco Bay, miles of hiking and biking trails, Muir Woods National Park, Muir Beach and Mount Tamalpais. Napa Valley is a 50-minute drive away. A must is a scenic drive along the coast on the famed Highway One. Conference facilities are available; the Terrace Room offers space for small meetings and presentations.

Our inspector loved: *The tranquil creek view rooms.*

Directions: A 45-minute drive from San Francisco Airport. From the airport take Highway 280 and exit at 19th Avenue. Go over the Golden Gate Bridge and exit at Tiburon/East Blithedale. Turn left into East Blithedale and continue for 2 miles, turn left onto Throckmorton. The hotel is on the left.

Web: www.johansens.com/millvalleyinn
E-mail: millvalleyinn@jdvhospitality.com
Tel: +1 415 389 6608
Fax: +1 415 389 5051
U.S./Canada Toll Free: 1 800 595 2100

Price Guide:
rooms $169–$309
rooms $309–$409

 25   12      

Old Monterey Inn

500 MARTIN STREET, MONTEREY, CALIFORNIA 93940

Steeped in the history of the city in which it resides, Old Monterey Inn is reminiscent of the days of pioneers and the infamous Californian Golf Rush and it is this timeless elegance that is present throughout the charming boutique property. Much of the original stonework of the manor remains and inside the rooms have been lovingly restored to their former glory with the 10 guest rooms evoking the romance of a bygone era. Featherbeds, aromatic candles and lined silk robes add to the sense of true decadence while Patti Valletta, and her gracious staff, pride themselves on a warm yet unobtrusive level of service. Antiques adorn every pocket and corner of the public rooms and it is this attention to detail that invites guests to explore the Tudor manor and revel in the property's historic past. Breakfasts may be served in the garden, dining room or simply in bed and tempting afternoon treats include freshly-baked cookies served with tea and coffee. Wine and hors d'oeuvres tease the palate in the evenings and there is a splendid choice of restaurants nearby. The Monterey Peninsula has much to offer its visitors including a choice of golf courses, wineries, coastal activities and a fascinating aquarium. The charming Carmel-by-the-Sea is only minutes away.

Our inspector loved: *The new spa suites, which boast garden views, fireplaces and freestanding spa tub.*

Directions: Monterey Peninsula Airport is a 20-minute drive from the inn.

Web: www.johansens.com/oldmontereyinn
E-mail: omi@oldmontereyinn.com
Tel: +1 831 375 8284
Fax: +1 831 375 6730
U.S./Canada Toll Free: 1 800 350 2344

Price Guide:
rooms $270-$350
suites $390-$450

1801 First Inn

1801 FIRST STREET, NAPA, CALIFORNIA 94559

Built in 1903 by architect William Corlett, 1801 First is an elegant boutique bed and breakfast property in the heart of Napa downtown. Décor is stylish with colors inspired by nature to create a most relaxing mood. Accommodations comprise 5 spacious suites, 2 cozy cottages and the Carriage House. All of the well-appointed guest rooms enjoy luxurious beds, sateen linens, baths with large soaking tubs or Jacuzzis and thick sumptuous bathrobes. After a restful night's sleep visitors are treated to a gourmet 3-course breakfast, prepared by the in-house chef, which can be served in-room or on intimate tables for 2 in the dining room. In the evening, wine, often including tastings from local wineries, and hors d'oeuvres provide great pre-dinner indulgences. A variety of in-room spa treatments are on offer, from an invigorating morning massage to late night therapy complete with candles, music and wine. The local area offers a plethora of activities including golfing, hiking, biking, ballooning, wine tasting and touring. This is an ideal base from which to explore the wonderful boutiques and restaurants of Napa, with the Opera House, the Wine Train, Copia (the Center for Food, Wine and The Arts) and numerous local wineries.

Our inspector loved: *The incredible breakfast and afternoon appetizers prepared by 1801's private chef.*

Directions: San Francisco Airport is approximately 1 hour and 30 minutes from the inn.

Sacramento
San Francisco
Los Angeles
San Diego

Web: www.johansens.com/1801inn
E-mail: info@1801first.com
Tel: +1 707 224 3739
Fax: +1 707 224 3932
U.S./Canada Toll Free: 1 800 518 0146

Price Guide: (excluding tax)
rooms $275-$425

Milliken Creek Inn & Spa

1815 SILVERADO TRAIL, NAPA, CALIFORNIA 94558

Located on the quiet banks of the Napa River, this intimate and elegant inn is nothing short of magical. The estate has a lively history dating back to 1857 when the main building served as a stagecoach stop during the days of the California gold rush. A multi-million dollar renovation in 2000 transformed the property to create the exceptional luxury inn that stands today. One of the most notable attributes is the amazing attention to detail given to the appointment of the suites. Drawing from exotic Indian and Thai influences, the décor of the rooms enhances the placid beauty of the property. Everything from the decadent mini-chocolate torte that welcomes guests to their rooms to the linens, towels and French spa, has been impeccably chosen. Guests at Milliken Creek enjoy amenities such as Magic Hour, a wine and gourmet cheese reception that features live piano music, a complimentary breakfast, served wherever requested on the property, and a luxury spa that caters solely to guests. The rustic Napa Valley is most famous for its vineyards but the area also offers terrific shopping, fine dining and other outdoor pursuits such as hot-air ballooning, golfing, fishing and hiking.

Our inspector loved: *The new spa; a great addition to this wonderful inn.*

Directions: 1 hour and 30 minutes from San Francisco Airport.

Web: www.johansens.com/milliken
E-mail: info@millikencreekinn.com
Tel: +1 707 255 1197
Fax: +1 707 255 3112
U.S./Canada Toll Free: 1 800 809 2986

Price Guide:
rooms $325-$800

CHÂTEAU DU SUREAU & SPA

48688 VICTORIA LANE, OAKHURST, CALIFORNIA 93644

Situated in a nature lover's paradise, with a backdrop of Yosemite National Park, Chateau du Sureau is a stunning inn. Recipient of some of the hotel industry's highest accolades within 11 years, including the American Automobile Association's Five Diamond Award and a number of culinary awards, this is a romantic haven where guests immediately relax in the warm and luxurious ambience. There are only 10 guest rooms and each is immaculately designed and appointed to incorporate a sense of traditional luxury and style, whilst providing every modern convenience. The carefully chosen soft furnishings complement beautiful antique pieces and encourage guests to indulge in lazy days spent reading and enjoying the comfort of indoors. Over the kitchen door one finds the quotation from Oscar Wilde, "I have the simplest of tastes, I only want the best," and this is reflected in the award-winning restaurant, Erna's Elderberry House, where an French country estate ambience has been created. The experience is quite sublime, due to the culinary talent of head chef James Overbaugh and exceptional wine list. The restaurant's 2 and 3-day cooking courses can be arranged. Surrounding Oakhurst plays host to some of the best hiking, river rafting and rock climbing.

Our inspector loved: *The great new full-service spa.*

Directions: Fresno Airport is a 45-minute drive from the chateau.

Web: www.johansens.com/chateausureau
E-mail: chateau@chateausureau.com
Tel: +1 559 683 6860
Fax: +1 559 683 0800

Price Guide:
rooms $375-$575
suites $2,800

The Villa Toscana

4230 BUENA VISTA, PASO ROBLES, CALIFORNIA 93446

Nestled in the rolling hills of the Martin & Weyrich vineyards of Paso Robles, in the heart of the central coast of California, as its name implies, The Villa Toscana resembles a beautiful Tuscan villa in the Italian countryside. There are 8 luxury suites, each named after one of their award-winning wines. 2 separate, private residences, the spectacular 3,000 sq. ft. Winemakers Residence and the charming 1,200 sq. ft. cottage Casa Dolcetto, provide wonderful, tranquil and romantic settings to relax for a change of pace, celebrate a special occasion or a romantic getaway. In the evening, Chef prepares complimentary hors d'oeuvres for a nightly wine tasting that guests can savor while strolling through the immaculate gardens and imported fountains. It is very apparent that attention to detail is a high priority for the owners. Guests may enjoy a lavish breakfast en suite or in the elegant bistro, dining on the patio at sunrise or inside around the cozy fireplace. Paso Robles is known for its terrific wines and agreeable climate, a wonderful place from which to explore the surrounding area. Visit historic Hearst Castle, located 40 minutes away, or take a picnic to Lake Nacimiento. For those interested in wine tasting, there are a number of nearby vineyards that have tasting rooms. Golf, horseback riding and llama riding are nearby.

***Our inspector loved:** The fantastic vineyard views and incredibly romantic atmosphere.*

Directions: The Villa Toscana is located 1.5 miles off of Highway 101 in Paso Robles at Highway 46 east and Buena Vista Drive. San Luis Obispo Airport is the nearest airport.

Web: www.johansens.com/villatoscana
E-mail: myvillatoscana@martinweyrich.com
Tel: +1 805 238 5600
Fax: +1 805 238 5605

Price Guide:
rooms $355-$445
suites $515-$2,600

THE INN AT RANCHO SANTA FE

5951 LINEA DEL CIELO, RANCHO SANTA FE, CALIFORNIA 92067

This charming inn is set amidst 20 acres of beautifully landscaped grounds in the center of the exclusive upscale residential community of Rancho Santa Fe, 20 miles north of San Diego and 6 miles east of Del Mar and the ocean. Designed in 1924 by Lilian Rice, one of the first female architects in California, the inn is a unique example of Spanish colonial revival style. The 87 charmingly decorated guest rooms, including 14 suites and several individual Spanish-tiled cottages with up to 3 bedrooms, are dotted around the gardens, surrounding the original main building with its richly appointed lounge and cozy bar. Also in the main building is the restaurant, which is extremely popular among residents and non-residents alike and serves Rancho Cuisine celebrating the history and harvest of Southern California in a romantic courtyard setting. Alternatively, there is the Poolside Bistro Garden Cafe and Spa. The spa includes 3 tennis courts, heated swimming pool, Jacuzzi, croquet lawn and a fitness room, whilst several first-class golf clubs are within easy reach. Box seats and turf club passes are offered during the thoroughbred racing season. Numerous boutiques, galleries and excellent restaurants can be found on the doorstep, and the rose garden and sprawling lawns are the perfect scene for unforgettable weddings. Conference and banqueting facilities are available as well as WiFi access.

Our inspector loved: *The romantic ambience, and great guest service.*

Directions: From I-5, exit at Lomas Santa Fe. Driving east, Lomas Santa Fe Drive becomes Linea Del Cielo after approx 2 miles. Continue for another 2 miles to the inn.

Sacramento
San Francisco
Los Angeles
San Diego

Web: www.johansens.com/ranchosantafe
E-mail: reservations@theinnatrsf.com
Tel: +1 858 756 1131
Fax: +1 858 759 1604
U.S./Canada Toll Free: 1 800 843 4661

Price Guide: (room only)
rooms $210-$295
suites $425–$755

TOWER23 HOTEL

723 FELSPAR, SAN DIEGO, CALIFORNIA 92109

Tower23 Hotel has a beautiful beach hotel atmosphere in both architecture and design. Its 44 sleek, modernist rooms are divided into 3 types: Spirit, Sky, and Surf Pads and 2 distinctive suite categories: Sanctuary and Sweet. Each features a signature serenity bed, step-in rain shower, plush bathrobes by Boca Terry, Egyptian cotton bath towels, flat screen T.V., executive work desk, WiFi (throughout the hotel and even at the beach) and customized bar and nutrition centers. The fresh design schemes include private balconies or patios, high-end amenities and teak furnishings. Massage and spa services are available en suite. The Tower Deck is located on the second floor and is reserved for hotel guests and their guests only. In the evenings, it is the ultimate place to watch the spectacular sunsets while lounging on a teak chaise. The indoor and outdoor oceanfront restaurant, JRDN Surf: Sky: Spirit, is a contemporary steak and seafood restaurant, which serves breakfast, lunch and dinner. The hotel boasts spectacular views of Pacific Beach's Crystal Pier and the Pacific Ocean. Activities include surfing, jet skiing, whale-watching and beach cruising. The exclusive resort community of La Jolla is just north of the hotel, while downtown San Diego, the airport, and major business centers are minutes away. Belmont Amusement Park, Seaworld and San Diego Zoo are also nearby.

Our inspector loved: *Enjoying the view from the restaurant patio.*

Directions: From San Diego Intl. Airport take I-5 north to Grand Avenue exit and follow signs to Garnet. Head west to Mission Boulevard and turn right, then left onto Felspar Street. The hotel is on the left.

Web: www.johansens.com/tower23
E-mail: Reserve23@t23hotel.com
Tel: +1 858 270 2323
Fax: +1 858 274 2333
U.S./Canada Toll Free: 1 866 TOWER23

Price Guide: (room only)
spirit/sky/surf pad $359/$379/$439

U.S.A. - CALIFORNIA (SAN FRANCISCO BAY AREA)

Inn Above Tide

30 EL PORTAL, SAUSALITO, CALIFORNIA 94965

There can be few more spectacular settings than this relaxing retreat situated on the waters of San Francisco Bay. The inn claims, "There are hundreds of hotels around San Francisco Bay. There is, however, only one on it." This gives an indication of how important the surrounding water is to the style of the hotel. There are 29 rooms and suites, each carefully and luxuriously designed with private decks on the bay. Waves lap just below guests' feet creating an immediate sense of calm and romanticism. Designed in a boutique style, gentle, muted colors are used throughout and evoke a serenity that is instantly relaxing. Many of the bedrooms have fireplaces, which in winter provide wonderful coziness as one watches otters playing in the cold waters outside. Service is friendly yet unobtrusive, and privacy is well-respected. Generous breakfasts can be served in a guest room, private deck or in the drawing room; during sunset, guests can enjoy cheese and wine while watching the sun set over the hills. The concierge will happily arrange dinner reservations and spa treatments.

Our inspector loved: *The serene, romantic ambience, and unbeatable views.*

Directions: San Francisco and Oakland Airports are a 30/45-minute drive from the inn.

Web: www.johansens.com/innabovetide
E-mail: stay@innabovetide.com
Tel: +1 415 332 9535
Fax: +1 415 332 9535
U.S./Canada Toll Free: 1 800 893 8433

Price Guide:
rooms $270-$945

29 12

The Union Street Inn

2229 UNION STREET, SAN FRANCISCO, CALIFORNIA 94123

Directions: From San Francisco International Airport take Freeway 101 north to San Francisco. Exit at Vanness Avenue then turn left into Union Street. The inn is located in the Cow Hollow district.

Web: www.johansens.com/unionstreetsf
E-mail: innkeeper@unionstreetinn.com
Tel: +1 415 346 0424
Fax: +1 415 922 8046

Price Guide:
rooms $189-$289

Imagine taking afternoon tea in an English cottage garden, surrounded by a wealth of colors from magnificent potted plants and aromas of roses, lavender, sage and rosemary while only being a short stroll from the most fashionable shopping and dining district of San Francisco. This becomes possible while staying at The Union Street Inn. The owners of this elegant Edwardian home pride themselves on offering guests the ultimate hospitality experience and place enormous emphasis on pampering and relaxation. All of the spacious bedrooms are individually decorated with antique furniture, rich fabrics and exquisite artwork and finished with fresh fruit, flowers and chocolates to create a romantic, cozy atmosphere. In particular, the Carriage House is extremely quiet and private with a bubbling Jacuzzi in the center of the room, ideal for a honeymoon couple. Guests will not be disappointed by the extensive gourmet menu. The full breakfast changes daily and includes mouth-watering specialties such as chicken and apple sausages and spinach frittata. A lavish cheese, wine and hors d'oeuvres menu is available at other times. The inn is a perfect retreat in the heart of the city, with San Francisco Bay, the Golden Gate Bridge and San Francisco International Airport all within easy reach. Wireless Internet access is available.

***Our inspector loved:** The beautiful courtyard garden, and outstanding hospitality.*

Harbor View Inn

28 West Cabrillo Boulevard, Santa Barbara, California 93101

This ocean-front hotel lies across the white sands of West Beach and the historic Stearn's Wharf, and is just a short stroll from Santa Barbara's downtown boutiques and attractions. Casually elegant and inviting, Harbor View Inn can be simultaneously romantic and family friendly. The spacious and well-appointed rooms and 13 luxury suites all have a private patio or balcony, as well as facilities such as toweling robes, refrigerators, coffee makers and daily newspapers delivered to the door. Dual line telephones feature dataports and voicemail. Eladio's Restaurant and Bar offers traditional Italian fare as well as wonderful panoramic views, and is open for breakfast, lunch, dinner and weekend brunch. The heated fountain patio is an ideal place to relax, enjoy a great meal and people watch. Cocktails are also served and there is a bar with an extensive list of regional and international wines. The Harbor View Inn's impressive location is ideal for guests interested in water sports such as kayaking, surfing and swimming.

Our inspector loved: *The stunning new ocean-view suites with beautiful mosaic bathrooms.*

Directions: 11 miles from Santa Barbara Airport. 2½ hours from L.A.X. in Los Angeles.

Web: www.johansens.com/harborview
E-mail: sylvie@harborviewinnsb.com
Tel: +1 805 963 0780
Fax: +1 805 963 7967
U.S./Canada Toll Free: 1 800 755 0222

Price Guide: (room only)
rooms $165-$425
suites $255-$795

THE SANTA YNEZ INN

3627 SAGUNTO STREET, SANTA YNEZ, CALIFORNIA 93460-0628

Describing itself as Victorian elegance in the Wine country, The Santa Ynez Inn is a charming property, which exudes the grace of a bygone era and combines 19th-century architecture with contemporary facilities. The 14 rooms and junior suites are individually appointed with antiques, frette linens on the spacious beds, fireplaces and whirlpool marble baths. Private balconies and patios afford a panoramic vista of the Santa Ynez Valley. Gourmet treats are complemented by fine wines from the inn's well-stocked cellar and served in the elegant parlor area. Flower essence energy massages and sage and warm stone treatments are available in the spa and the fitness suite features cardio-vascular machines and weights. Guests can relax in the heated whirlpool or enjoy the sundeck before indulging in a wine tasting tour in one of the many nearby wineries. Outdoor activities abound and these include glider rides above the valley, golf at the Rancho San Marcos, horseback riding in Rancho Oso's superb mountain setting, hiking and eagle watching. Events may be held in the parlor room, which accommodates 60 guests reception-style and the Library which seats 12. The lawns and gardens are ideal for weddings, receptions and executive functions.

Our inspector loved: *The wonderful European spa tubs.*

Directions: The inn is 50 minutes from Santa Barbara Airport.

Web: www.johansens.com/santaynez
E-mail: info@santaynezinn.com
Tel: +1 805 688 5588
Fax: +1 805 686 4294
U.S./Canada Toll Free: 1 800 643 5774

Price Guide:
rooms $275-$365
suites $445

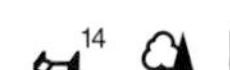

Ledson Hotel & Harmony Restaurant

480 FIRST STREET EAST, SONOMA, CALIFORNIA 95476

Blending into the rustic background of Sonoma sits this charming Old World-style hotel, a concept of Sonoma farmer and winemaker Steve Ledson. Situated on the historic Sonoma Plaza, the property is elegant, romantic and well appointed. 6 bedrooms occupy the upper floor, and each has its own tasteful design. No attention to detail has been spared from the intricately designed wood flooring to the fine linens and crystal fixtures in the bathrooms, creating lavish and comfortable accommodation. The impressive décor continues throughout the hotel: the Harmony Restaurant spans the ground floor and incorporates cool marble and warm hand-carved wood. Exquisite, mouth-watering cuisine, focusing on fresh, local ingredients, is highlighted by an extensive international wine list. Inside the stylish wine bar and restaurant guests are warmed by a crackling fire whilst outside, the sidewalk tables are enveloped by the relaxing sound of live music. Ledson Winery & Vineyards is located in the nearby town of Kenwood. The winery specializes in small lots of handcrafted wines, boasting over 30 different varietals and encompasses 6 magnificent tasting bars, glorious picnic grounds, a gourmet market and clothing boutique.

Our inspector loved: *The hotel's restaurant, the Harmony Restaurant, which offers outstanding food, wine and music.*

Directions: The hotel is 1 hour and 15 minutes north of San Francisco Airport.

Sacramento
San Francisco
Los Angeles
San Diego

Web: www.johansens.com/ledsonhotel
E-mail: info@ledsonhotel.com
Tel: +1 707 996 9779
Fax: +1 707 996 9776

Price Guide: (room only, excluding tax)
room $350-$395

Meadowood

900 MEADOWOOD LANE, ST. HELENA, CALIFORNIA 94574

RELAIS & CHATEAUX

Meadowood is an elegant private estate nestled in over 250 acres in the beautiful Napa Valley. It is a center for social, cultural and viticultural life, and as soon as one leaves the highway, there is an overwhelming sense of tranquility and relaxation. The grounds create a magnificent backdrop for both relaxing weekend retreats and extravagant country parties. The clubhouse commands a masterful position overlooking the lawns, which in summer play host to croquet games. Most guests rooms have fireplaces and their own private decks from which to savor the surroundings. The staff at Meadowood takes great pride in their exceptional levels of service and successfully achieves to combine informality with unobtrusiveness. Guests may choose where to take breakfast, whether in their room, on the deck or even as a picnic to take out into the countryside. The Restaurant, or the more informal Grill, serves a careful balance of fresh flavors with tempting colors and aromas. The Health Spa boasts some of the most up-to-date fitness equipment and a personal trainer can be hired. An extensive range of invigorating treatments and massages are available. St. Helena and the surrounding valley have some breathtaking vineyards, a delightful selection of shops, museums and art galleries.

Our inspector loved: *The terrific sense of seclusion on this verdant estate in the heart of the wine country.*

Directions: San Francisco Airport is a 1 hour and 45-minute drive from Meadowood.

Web: www.johansens.com/meadowood
E-mail: reservations@meadowood.com
Tel: +1 707 963 3646
Fax: +1 707 963 3532
U.S./Canada Toll Free: 1 800 458 8080

Price Guide:
rooms $500-$920
suites $675-$4,300

       SPA    

Colorado

Hotel location shown in red with page number

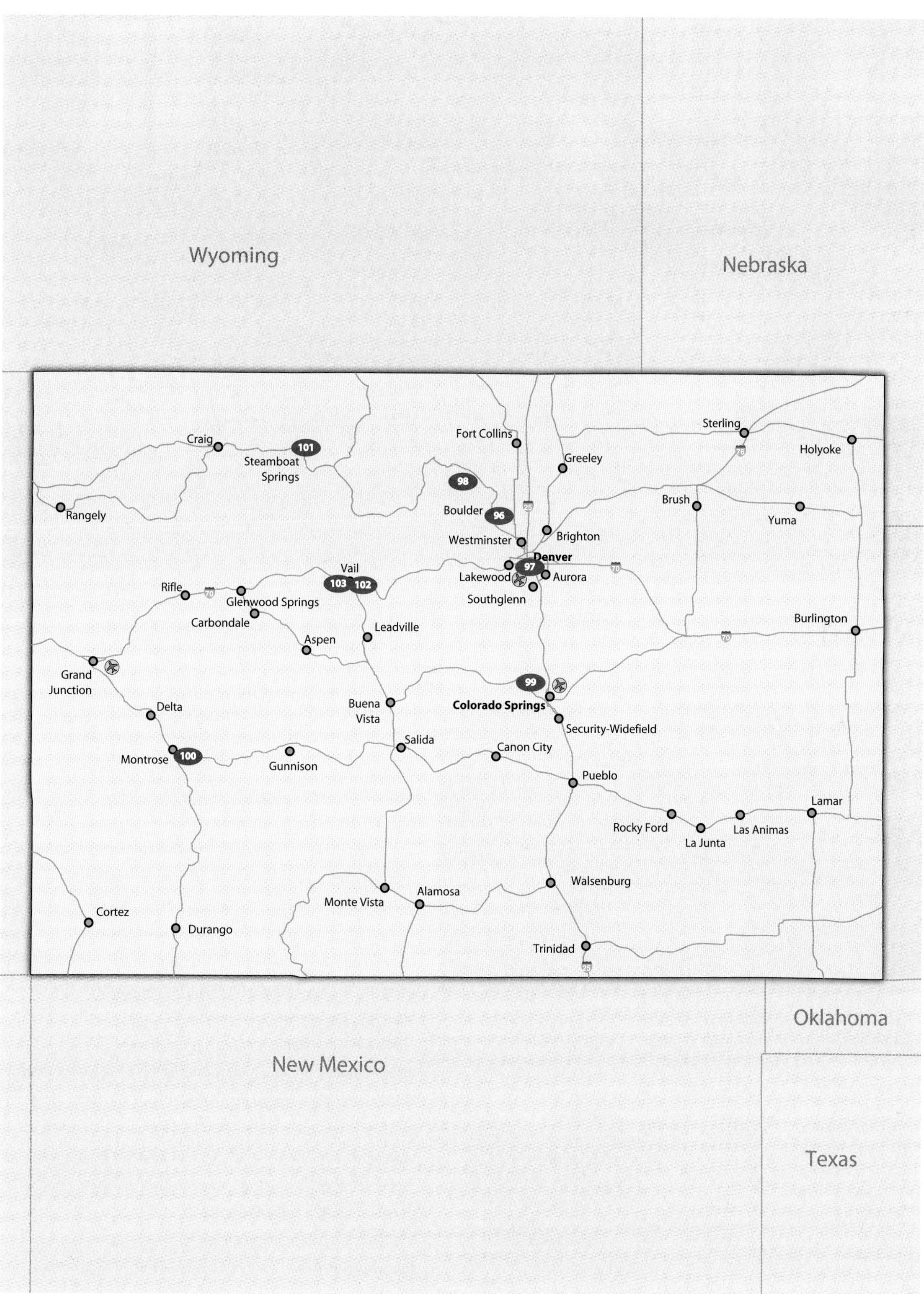

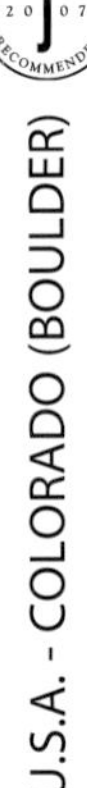

THE BRADLEY BOULDER INN

2040 16TH STREET, BOULDER, COLORADO 80302

Set in a residential and picturesque neighborhood of downtown Boulder, Colorado, The Bradley Boulder Inn is a contemporary-style inn with 12 exquisite guest rooms, a lovely retreat for a romantic getaway or short business stay. Each of the comfortable, stylish rooms has a private bath and amenities such as Jacuzzi tub, mountain view from a balcony, cozy fireplace, luxury fine linens, Aveda bath amenities, flat-screen TV and DVD movies. A sumptuous breakfast is provided each morning in the dining room, and in the evenings guests can gather around the artwork in the magnificent Great Room for complimentary wine and cheese. The stunning art collection is provided by some of Boulder's top galleries, shown in changing rotation throughout the year. The inn has become a popular place for business travelers due to its central location, wireless Internet access and business center and meeting facilities. Before exploring the area, guests can enjoy homemade cookies and bottled water, a treat for guests on the go. Located near the University of Colorado and just one block from the international shopping, street entertainers and popular restaurants of Boulder's Pearl Street Mall. Fitness enthusiasts can explore mountain trails and famous bike paths or work out at the nearby health club.

Our inspector loved: *The Great Room with its shining wood floors, crackling fire and stunning original artwork.*

Directions: The Inn is approximately a 45-minute drive from Denver International Airport (D.I.A.). From the airport take I-70 west to I-270 north and exit for Boulder/Fort Collins north to Highway 36 West. Once in Boulder, turn left on Pearl Street then right onto 16th Street.

Web: www.johansens.com/bradleyboulderinn
E-mail: reservations@thebradleyboulder.com
Tel: +1 303 545 5200
Fax: +1 303 440 6740
U.S./Canada Toll Free: 1 800 858 5811

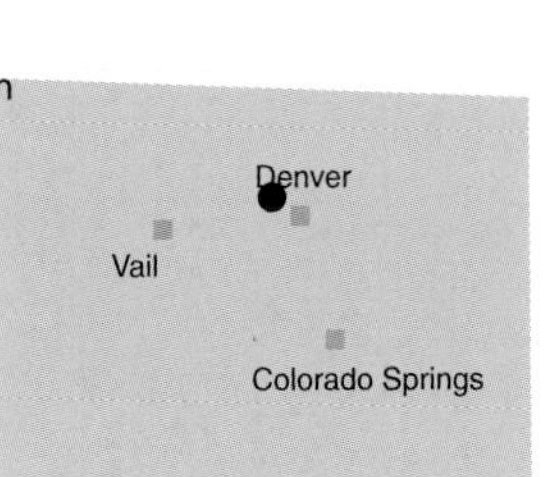

Price Guide:
rooms $145-$200

Castle Marne Bed & Breakfast Inn

1572 RACE STREET, DENVER, COLORADO 80206

Historic Castle Marne, a Victorian home transformed into an elegant bed and breakfast inn, holds the honor of a 2005 nomination from Condé Nast Johansens for Most Outstanding Small Inn of North America. Many vestiges of the castle's past are scattered throughout the rooms such as hand-rubbed woods, family heirlooms and ornate fireplaces. Following a careful restoration, original features dominate the interior, which is enhanced by Rococo gilt mirrors and fine antiques. The individually decorated bedrooms are stylish and display nuances of the period. Guests are made to feel extremely welcome by the friendly and hospitable owners. The comfortable parlor is ideal for reclining and reading a book beside the beautifully carved fireplace. Special private 6-course candlelight dinners can be arranged. Guests indulge in delicious breakfasts and afternoon tea. House specialties include stuffed tomato with egg and spinach purée topped with parmesan and Jack cheeses and the home-baked cakes and scones at teatime are a delight to the palate. There are many museums and historic sites clustered around the area. Other attractions include the zoo, botanical gardens or perusing the shops at "Cherry Creek." A Denver Airport shuttle drop-off and pick-up at the door can be arranged.

Our inspector loved: *The surprise of the tree-top level private decks with hot tubs that adjoin several of the rooms.*

Directions: From DIA take Pena Boulevard to I-70 west then exit at Colorado Boulevard. Turn left and travel south then take a right onto 17th Avenue west. Turn left onto York Street and drive south 2 blocks. Turn right onto 16th Avenue and travel 4 blocks. Turn left onto Race Street. Free parking available.

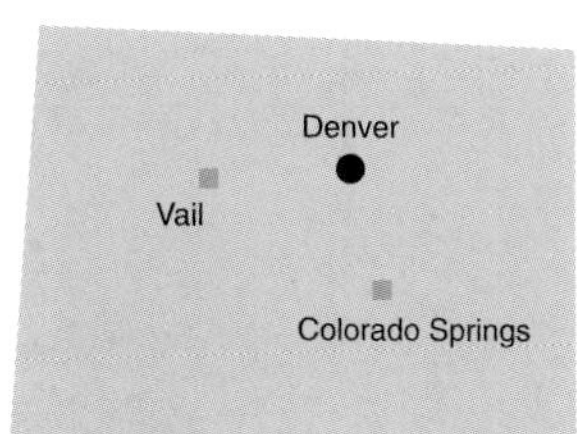

Web: www.johansens.com/castlemarne
E-mail: info@castlemarne.com
Tel: +1 303 331 0621
Fax: +1 303 331 0623
U.S./Canada Toll Free: 1 800 926 2763

Price Guide:
rooms $105–$260

Taharaa Mountain Lodge

P.O. BOX 2586, ESTES PARK, COLORADO 80517

Custom-built in 1997 out of log and stone on a high plateau in the Rocky Mountains, the Taharaa Mountain Lodge is a luxurious hotel with breathtaking panoramic views and delightful interiors. Built with comfort and enjoyment in mind, yet to maximize the impact of the mountains surrounding it, the hotel offers stunning large windows, crackling fires and striking wood and stone work throughout the interior. Restful rooms are complemented by tasteful western and eclectic international furnishings that were hand selected by the owners during their travels throughout the world. Each bedroom has its own unique theme and benefits from a fireplace and private deck. Breakfast in the morning is an absolute pleasure, served in the Dining Room or on the adjacent deck. Guests can relax in the fresh, clean air surrounded by pine trees, whilst taking in the spectacular view over the valley, which continually reinforces the thrill of being in the Rockys. Set only 4 miles from Rocky Mountain National Park and Roosevelt National Forest, the lodge is perfect for wildlife watching, fishing, biking, golf, horse riding, climbing, river rafting, hiking and a host of other exciting outdoor adventures. The hotel has an excellent solarium and outdoor spa with scenic views.

Our inspector loved: *The new rooms and fantastic new spa area.*

Directions: From Denver take Highway 36 to Estes Park. Continue 4 miles south on Highway 7, past Fish Creek Road and mile marker 4.

Web: www.johansens.com/taharaa
E-mail: info@taharaa.com
Tel: +1 970 577 0098
Fax: +1 970 577 0819
U.S./Canada Toll Free: 1 800 597 0098

Price Guide:
rooms $150-$185
suites $180-$330

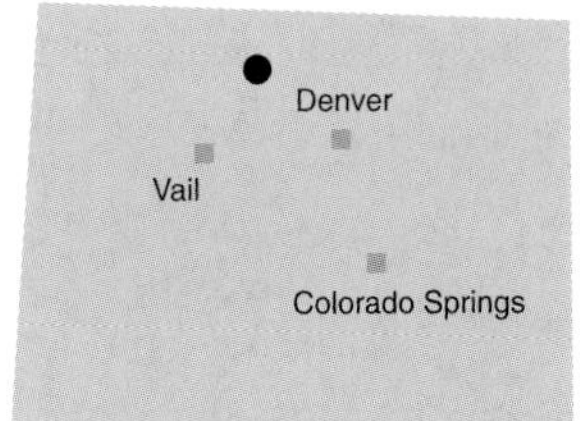

THE CLIFF HOUSE AT PIKES PEAK

306 CAÑON AVENUE, MANITOU SPRINGS, COLORADO 80829

Built in 1874 as a boarding house, the Cliff House is Colorado's second oldest operating hotel and was originally a key stop on the stagecoach trail. In the last couple of years it has been the subject of a $10-million refurbishment program and is now a characterful hotel that pays tribute to its heritage, yet offers guests the very latest in modern comforts and luxury. There are 55 rooms and suites, each individually designed, including the wonderful "Celebrity" suites that reflect their previous inhabitants, including Clark Gable, Teddy Roosevelt, Henry Ford and Buffalo Bill Cody. The hotel has gained wide renown for its gourmet dining and outstanding friendly service and is a very romantic getaway within an hour's drive of Denver. The menu is based on Colorado ingredients and traditional French cuisine, enhanced by some modern international twists. The hotel's Colorado Experience Coordinator will tailor a package of fantastic adventures to make this a memorable Rocky Mountain escape. The Pikes Peak Cog railway goes to the 14,100 feet summit and there are numerous trails, hikes, rock climbs and jeep tours. The Garden of the Gods is fascinating, as are the cliff dwellings of the native Americans. Don't miss the world's highest suspension bridge at Royal Gorge Park.

Our inspector loved: *The celebrity-themed rooms, especially the "Clark Gable Suite".*

Directions: Colorado Springs Airport is approximately a 15-minute drive. From Colorado Springs west on US24. 10 minutes to Manitou Springs, exit south through the town to Cañon Avenue.

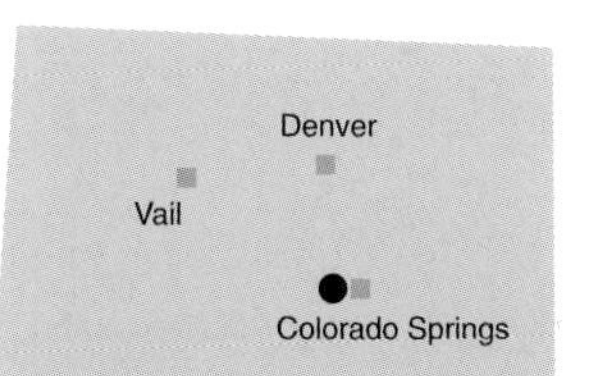

Web: www.johansens.com/thecliffhouse
E-mail: info@thecliffhouse.com
Tel: +1 719 685 3000
Fax: +1 719 685 3913
U.S./Canada Toll Free: 1 888 212 7000

Price Guide:
rooms $145–$189
suites $199–$475

Elk Mountain Resort

97 ELK WALK, MONTROSE, COLORADO 81401

Directions: Montrose Airport is a 25-minute drive from the property. Telluride is 50 minutes away.

Web: www.johansens.com/elkmountain
E-mail: reservations@elkmountainresort.com
Tel: +1 970 252 4900
Fax: +1 970 252 4913
U.S./Canada Toll Free: 1 877 355 9255

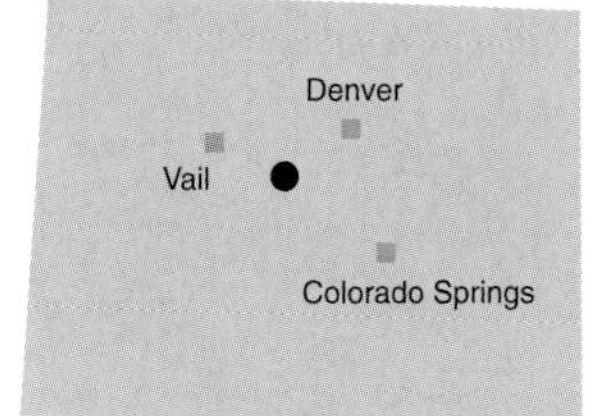

Price Guide: (room only)
deluxe lodge rooms $275-$325
3-bedroom cottages $1,500-$1,800

Providing an air of luxurious seclusion, Elk Mountain Resort is simultaneously many things: a hidden romantic getaway, a gourmand's treasure, a spa retreat and a nature lover's paradise. The architecture blends into the natural surrounding environment, and the pseudo-rustic exteriors of rough hewn log buildings conceal plush interiors. Guests can choose to stay in one of the many independent cottages throughout the property or the main lodge building. All of the accommodation are impeccably appointed and furnished. Each fixture, piece of furniture, painting and linen has been carefully chosen; a philosophy that also extends to the staff. The service at the resort possesses an integrity that provides guests with an exceptional experience. Dinner at the Tarragon restaurant is to be savored, as are selections from the impressive wine list. Numerous activities are available such as fishing, shooting, horse riding, a rock climbing wall and spa treatments. The Montrose area is a beautiful part of Colorado and is close to Telluride, which has fantastic skiing, shopping and restaurants. The resort is next to 60,000 acres of national forest and provides an excellent opportunity for hiking.

***Our inspector loved:** Playing James Bond for a day at the Valhalla Shooting Club.*

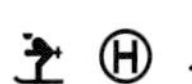

Vista Verde Guest Ranch

P.O. BOX 770465, STEAMBOAT SPRINGS, COLORADO 80477

Nestled deep in the Rocky Mountains, Vista Verde is a truly unique ranch experience for all seasons. The 500-acre property offers accommodation in secluded, spacious log cabins or de luxe lodge rooms. Each cabin has a private hot tub on the deck to relax in while enjoying the panorama of the national forest. In summer the crisp air and clear skies invite you to rise early, enjoy a breakfast of fresh berries, pastries and eggs, and then try your hand at relaxing. Fishing, hot air ballooning, hiking, white water rafting, kayaking, as well as horse riding, with or without instruction, are among the many activities with which to fill each day. In the evening enjoy a drink on the deck or cool off under the water of the fountain deck. As the sun sets, a gourmet dinner is served in the main lodge, or on some evenings there is an informal cookout. In fall, the rivers run lower, the elk move back in and the aspens prepare for a magical color extravaganza. A winter ranch experience is a must! Guests can sleigh ride, cross-country and downhill ski, dog sled, ice climb or horse ride, before they return to après ski at the parlor, dip into their own hot tub, and then enjoy a gourmet dinner.

Our inspector loved: *Fine dining in the rustic lodge followed by songs around a crackling outdoor fire topped off with a soak in a private hot tub under the starlit mountain sky.*

Directions: Fly into Hayden Airport for transfer to ranch or drive from Denver Airport (approximately 4 hours).

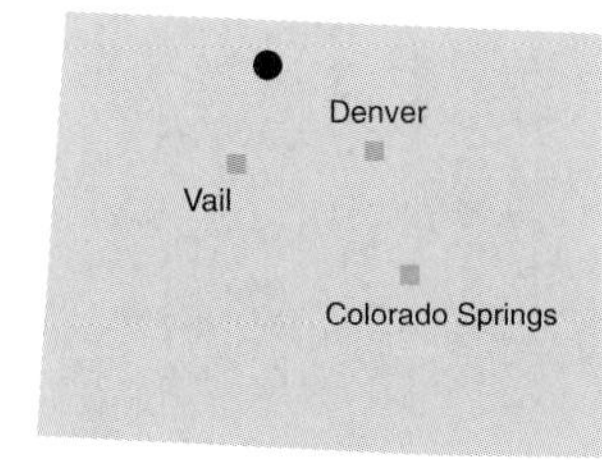

Web: www.johansens.com/vistaverderanch
E-mail: reservations@vistaverde.com
Tel: +1 970 879 3858
Fax: +1 970 879 6814
U.S./Canada Toll Free: 1 800 526 7433

Price Guide: (per person, including activities and meals)
cabins $300–$450

The Tivoli Lodge at Vail

386 HANSON RANCH ROAD, VAIL, COLORADO 81657

Directions: Take I-70 west from Denver (D.I.A.) to exit 176. Travel east on Frontage Road and turn right on Vail Valley Drive, then right on Hanson Ranch Road.

Web: www.johansens.com/tivoli
E-mail: reservations@tivolilodge.com
Tel: +1 970 476 5615
Fax: +1 970 476 6601
U.S./Canada Toll Free: 1 800 451 4756

Price Guide:
rooms $300-$1,700

Nestled in the heart of Vail Village is the recently rebuilt, family-owned Tivoli Lodge that has been known for years for providing friendly, caring personal service. The new European-style architecture blends into the surrounding natural environment with unobstructed views of Vail Mountain and is within steps of Vail's Vista Bahn and Riva Bahn ski lifts. The luxurious and spacious lobby offers stunning mountain views and is reminiscent of one's living room with over-sized chairs, leather sofas, floor to ceiling stone fireplace and small wine bar. Guests enjoy the complimentary daily Tivoli breakfast. There are 62 over-sized guest rooms offering a choice of mountain or village views, many with fireplaces, and the Peter Seibert Suite with panoramic views of the mountains. All are appointed with the finest linens and a mini-refrigerator. Large soaking bathtubs and separate walk-in showers are featured in the mountain view rooms. The entire hotel has complimentary wireless Internet access. Other amenities include meeting rooms, fully-equipped fitness room, two outdoor hot tubs, underground parking and ski storage. Within a short walk, guests can take advantage of hiking, biking trails and Vail Village with shops, restaurants, galleries, and the Ford amphitheater.

Our inspector loved: *The thoughtful attention to artistic detail evident throughout this newly recreated Vail landmark.*

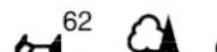

Vail Mountain Lodge & Spa

352 East Meadow Drive, Vail, Colorado 81657

Beautifully situated on Gore Creek, Vail Mountain Lodge & Spa captures the charm of rustic camps of yesterday's Yellowstone. Its 27 spacious rooms offer a comfortable and relaxing atmosphere after a long day on the slopes or at the popular Athletic Club. Many of the luxurious rooms and suites have cozy fireplaces, soaking tubs and expansive views of Vail Mountain and Gore Creek. Terra Bistro, featuring innovative cuisine in a stylish atmosphere, is a local favorite perfect for a romantic dinner for two or group dining. The menu highlights seasonal ingredients influenced by Southwest, Mediterranean and Asian cultures. The Bistro also offers one of the most extensive wine lists in the area. The on-site Vail Athletic Club is an 18,000 square foot gym with state-of-the-art equipment, Vail's only full-size indoor climbing wall, and a wide variety of classes. The Spa at Vail Mountain Lodge is a relaxing way to rejuvenate, with holistic treatments including massages and facials designed to be therapeutic rather than superficial. The Lodge is just a few steps across the bridge from the heart of the village and a short walk from the local ski slopes. Offering the quintessential Vail experience, the Lodge has become the "hot spot" for Hollywood celebrities to hang out, lounge in the solarium or sip martinis in the fabulous lobby.

Our inspector loved: *The heated bathroom floors - a comforting way to start your day before heading to the slopes.*

Directions: From Denver (D.I.A.), take I-70 west to the main Vail village exit. Travel east on Frontage Road and turn right on East Meadow Drive. Vail Mountain Lodge is approximately 2 hours by car from Denver International Airport.

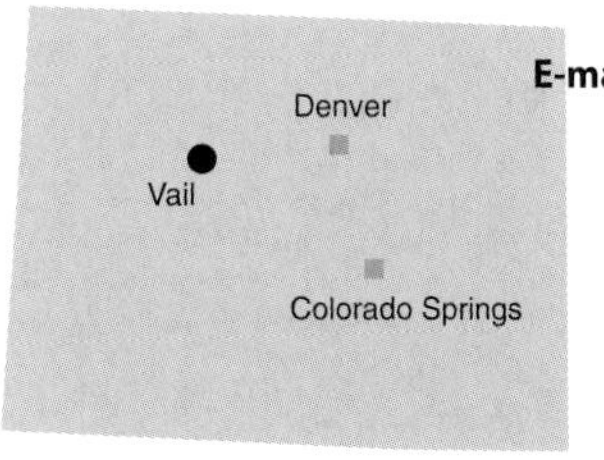

Denver
Vail
Colorado Springs

Web: www.johansens.com/vailmountain
E-mail: reservations@vailmountainlodge.com
Tel: +1 970 476 0700
Fax: +1 970 476 6451
U.S./Canada Toll Free: 1 866 476 0700

Price Guide:
rooms $149-765
condos $235-$2,450

Connecticut

Hotel location shown in red with page number

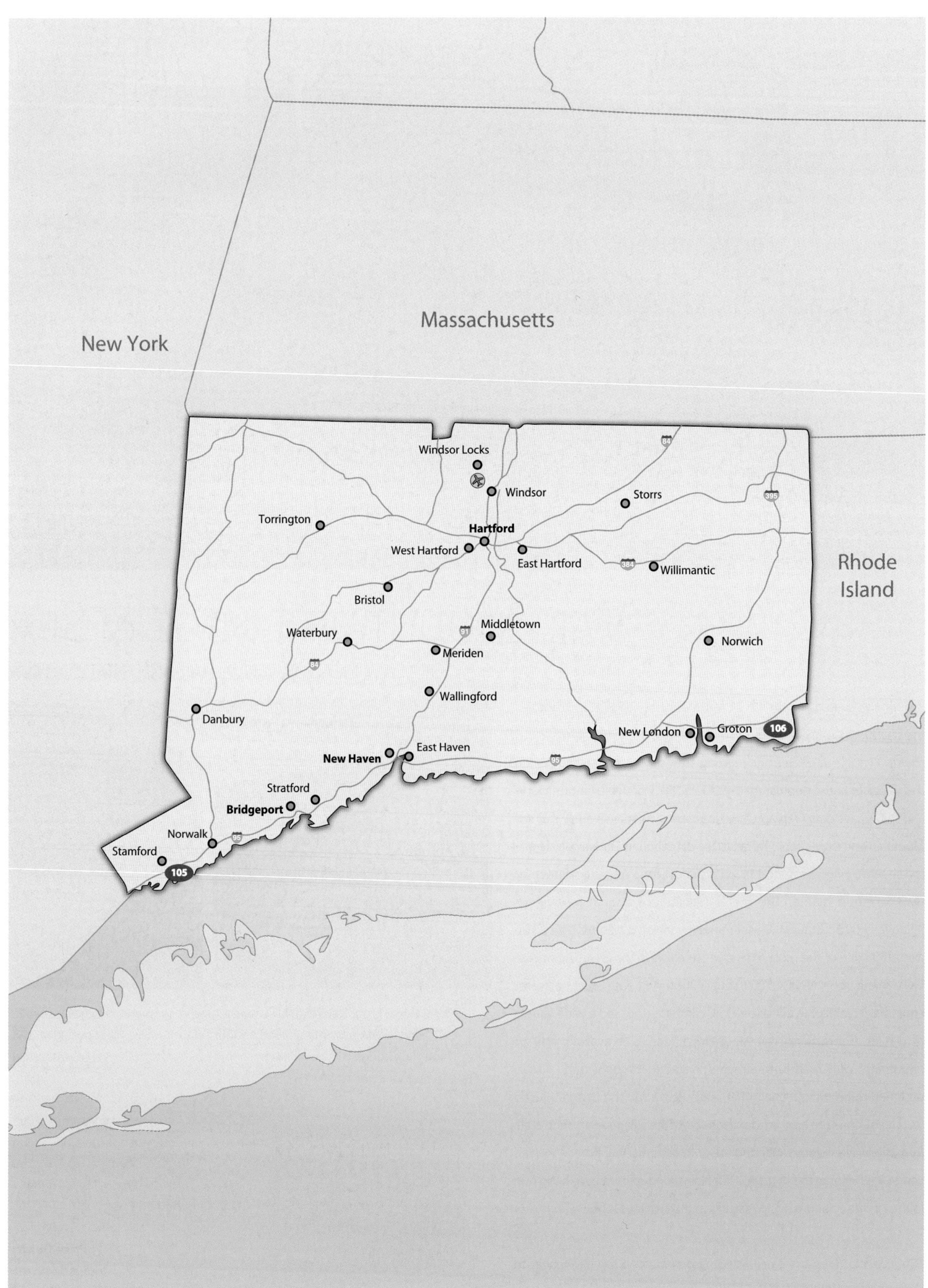

Delamar Greenwich Harbor

500 Steamboat Road, Greenwich, Connecticut 06830

Situated in a spectacular waterfront location on Greenwich Harbor, this new luxury hotel is built in the style of a beautiful Tuscan villa, with an authentic terracotta-tiled roof and soft yellow stucco walls. Inside, lush fabrics, subtle colors and distinctive Mediterranean furnishings abound, and the walls are adorned with original paintings and artworks, many of which come from a renowned private collection in Greenwich. The 74 bedrooms and 8 suites are beautifully decorated with exquisite Italian linens by Fili D'oro and Frette and are equipped with modern amenities, including C.D. and D.V.D. players, flat-screen television, 2-line telephones, fax and high-speed Internet access. The suites have fireplaces and large balconies overlooking the harbor. Culinary delights and fine wines can be sampled at the waterfront L'Escale, which serves a Provençal menu focusing on seafood and Mediterranean cuisine, and offers a room service menu 7 days a week. Banqueting and meeting facilities, including state-of-the-art audio-visual equipment, can cater for up to 200 guests. There is a fully-equipped fitness suite, and the hotel has its own private dock, which berths yachts up to 160'. The city's main shopping area, restaurants and galleries are a few steps away, and the Metro-North train station is close by.

Our inspector loved: *Having dinner at L'Escale Restaurant and Bar on the harbor-front terrace.*

Directions: Exit 3 off I-95. 20 minutes from White Plains Airport, 15 minutes from La Guardia, 15 minutes from Westchester and 60 minutes from J.F. Kennedy.

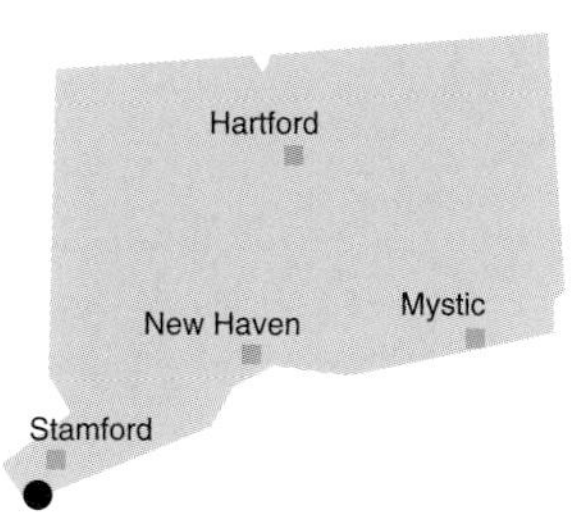

Web: www.johansens.com/delamar
E-mail: info@thedelamar.com
Tel: +1 203 661 9800
Fax: +1 203 661 2513
U.S./Canada Toll Free: 1 866 335 2627

Price Guide: (room only)
rooms from $299
suites $650-$1,500

82 200

The Inn at Stonington

60 WATER STREET, STONINGTON, CONNECTICUT 06378

Idyllically located on the waterfront of Stonington Borough, The Inn at Stonington is a delightful haven for anyone wishing to escape the hustle and bustle of modern life. Stonington Borough has retained much of its 17th and 18th-century flavor and is one of the last true New England seaside villages, home to the Stonington fishing fleet. The Inn has 18 beautifully appointed, individually decorated guest rooms with fireplaces. Common rooms and many of the guest rooms afford views of Fisher's Island and Stonington Harbor where lobster boats, scallop boats and yachtsmen can be seen everyday. Guests enjoy Anachini bed linens and large luxuriously equipped bathrooms with Jacuzzis and frette robes. An extended Continental breakfast is served daily and each evening the Inn invites guests to participate in a wine and cheese hour. Stroll the quiet, tree-lined streets of the village and sample the 4 fantastic local restaurants, which are all within walking distance. Exploring the specialty and antique shops, some of the finest in New England, is a must.

Our inspector loved: *The artwork found throughout the inn created by local maritime artists.*

Directions: Approximately 45 miles from T.F. Green Airport in Warwick. 70 minutes from Bradley Airport in Hartford.

Web: www.johansens.com/stonington
E-mail: innkeeper@innatstonington.com
Tel: +1 860 535 2000
Fax: +1 860 535 8193

Price Guide:
rooms $135-$440

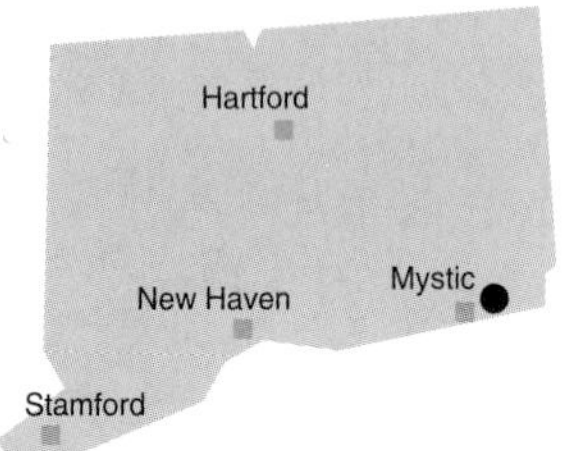

Delaware

Hotel location shown in red with page number

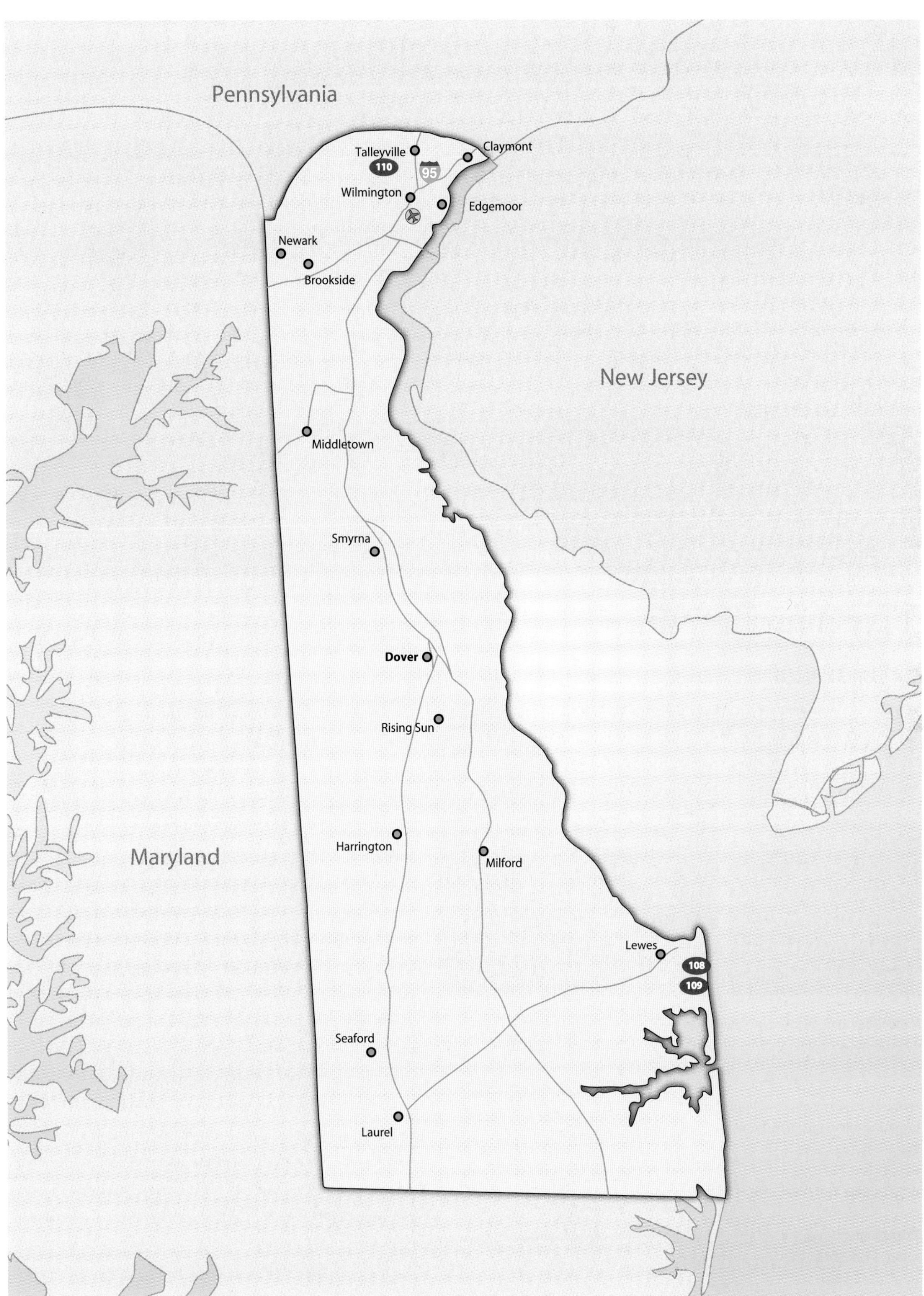

THE BELLMOOR

SIX CHRISTIAN STREET, REHOBOTH BEACH, DELAWARE 19971

Directions: Take Rehoboth Beach, exit 1A. Continue 1.1 miles to the traffic light at 2nd St./Bayard Avenue then turn right. Continue 300 feet and turn right at Christian Street. The Bellmoor is on the left.

Web: www.johansens.com/thebellmoor
E-mail: info@thebellmoor.com
Tel: +1 302 227 5800
Fax: +1 302 227 0323
U.S./Canada Toll Free: 1 800 425 2355

Price Guide:
rooms $125-$345
suites $195-$645

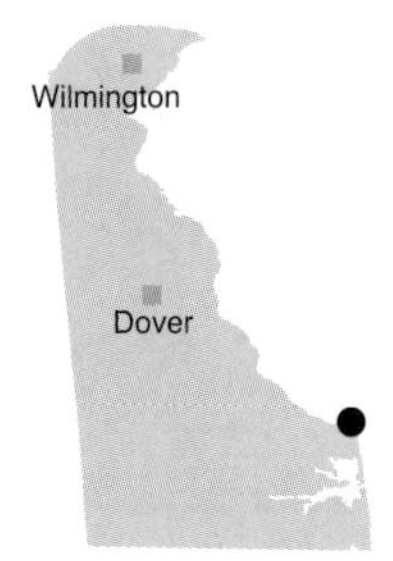

The Bellmoor in Rehoboth Beach, Delaware is a warm and residential inn that combines old-fashioned hospitality with first-class accommodations. Its 78 rooms and suites make the perfect seaside setting to relax and rejuvenate. The inn's comfortable guest rooms range from garden and deluxe rooms to the generously sized Bellmoor Club Suites, accessible only by private elevator key, which occupy the entire fourth floor. After a long day at the beach, cozy up next to the in-room fireplace, soak in the Ultra Masseur hydrotherapy tub or enjoy a drink from the wet bar. The Bellmoor Club Library serves snacks and beverages and is a wonderful place to read a favorite book nestled by the fire. Start your day with the complimentary country breakfast served each morning, and in the afternoon enjoy cookies and tea served in a beautiful garden setting. In the evenings, the concierge can arrange many fine dining options, all very close to the inn. The full-service Spa at The Bellmoor offers over 40 different services to refresh and invigorate the mind, body and spirit. The inn is only a two-minute walk from the beach and is just off the main street of town. Rehoboth Beach is a quaint and stylish beach community with tax-free shopping and several interesting shops, galleries, coffee houses and restaurants.

***Our inspector loved:** The lovely rooms, tranquil garden area, and full-service spa.*

       SPA   

Boardwalk Plaza Hotel

OLIVE AVENUE & THE BOARDWALK, REHOBOTH BEACH, DELAWARE 19971

Built in 1990 and equipped with every modern amenity, the Boardwalk Plaza Hotel transports guests back to Victorian times and the service afforded by the attentive staff is one reminiscent of bygone years. Upon walking through the lobby, guests are welcomed by lively parrots, caged or not! Set in Delaware's premier resort town of Rehoboth Beach, the accommodation comprises a varied selection of rooms and suites, all of which have T1 Internet access and are bedecked with interesting antiques or fine period reproductions. The friendly owners have collected many pieces over the years to enhance the rooms and recreate the elegance and authentic character of the Victorian age. Victoria's Restaurant is situated adjacent to the thriving boardwalk, with a view of the Atlantic from every table, and here, diners may sample an array of tasty dishes made with fresh produce such as local fish, shellfish and Black Angus beef. Rehoboth Beach is a particularly convivial area with special events and festivals throughout the year. Other activities within the area include boating, fishing, kayaking, antiquing, sales, tax-free shopping and simply lazing on the beach.

Our inspector loved: *The smiling, attentive staff, and the prime beachfront location.*

Directions: From Route 1 south, turn left onto Route 1A, which becomes Rehoboth Avenue, then left onto 1st Street and right onto Olive Avenue to The Boardwalk. Boardwalk Plaza Hotel is on the right.

Web: www.johansens.com/boardwalkplaza
E-mail: reservations@boardwalkplaza.com
Tel: +1 302 227 7169
Fax: +1 302 227 0561
U.S./Canada Toll Free: 1 800 332 3224

Price Guide: (room only)
rooms $129–$509

 84  100    

INN AT MONTCHANIN VILLAGE

ROUTE 100 & KIRK ROAD, MONTCHANIN, DELAWARE 19710

Montchanin is a charming 19th-century hamlet in the Brandywine Valley that is very proud of its history. In the heart of this quaint village is The Inn at Montchanin, a lovingly restored, family-run hotel that is listed on the National Register of Historic Places and retains a whimsical atmosphere of colonial splendor. Quiet and romantic, its immaculately decorated rooms are brimming with beautiful antiques and period reproductions, yet have all the conveniences of a modern hotel. Exquisite bedrooms are spacious, stunningly individually decorated with an emphasis on total luxury and comfort, including frette linens and turn down service. Painstaking attention to detail creates a gracious, restful ambience. All the rooms have a wet bar, handsome bathroom, every possible amenity, and fresh flowers. Most rooms benefit from a beautiful landscaped private courtyard; some rooms have fireplaces. Krazy Kat's Restaurant, which was once the blacksmith's shop, has fun, wacky décor and a cozy ambience. It serves the most mouth-watering international cuisine. The Brandywine Valley has a lot to offer with many world-renowned museums and gardens such as Longwood Gardens, Winterthur Museum a Country Estate, Brandywine River Museum and Hagley Museum and Library.

Our inspector loved: *The beautiful gardens and first-class restaurant.*

Directions: 4 miles northwest of Wilmington. 25 miles from Philadelphia Airport.

Web: www.johansens.com/montchanin
E-mail: inn@montchanin.com
Tel: +1 302 888 2133
Fax: +1 302 888 0389
U.S./Canada Toll Free: 1 800 269 2473

Price Guide: (room only)
rooms $179-$229
suites $269-$379

28 40 NR HP

District of Columbia

Hotel location shown in red with page number

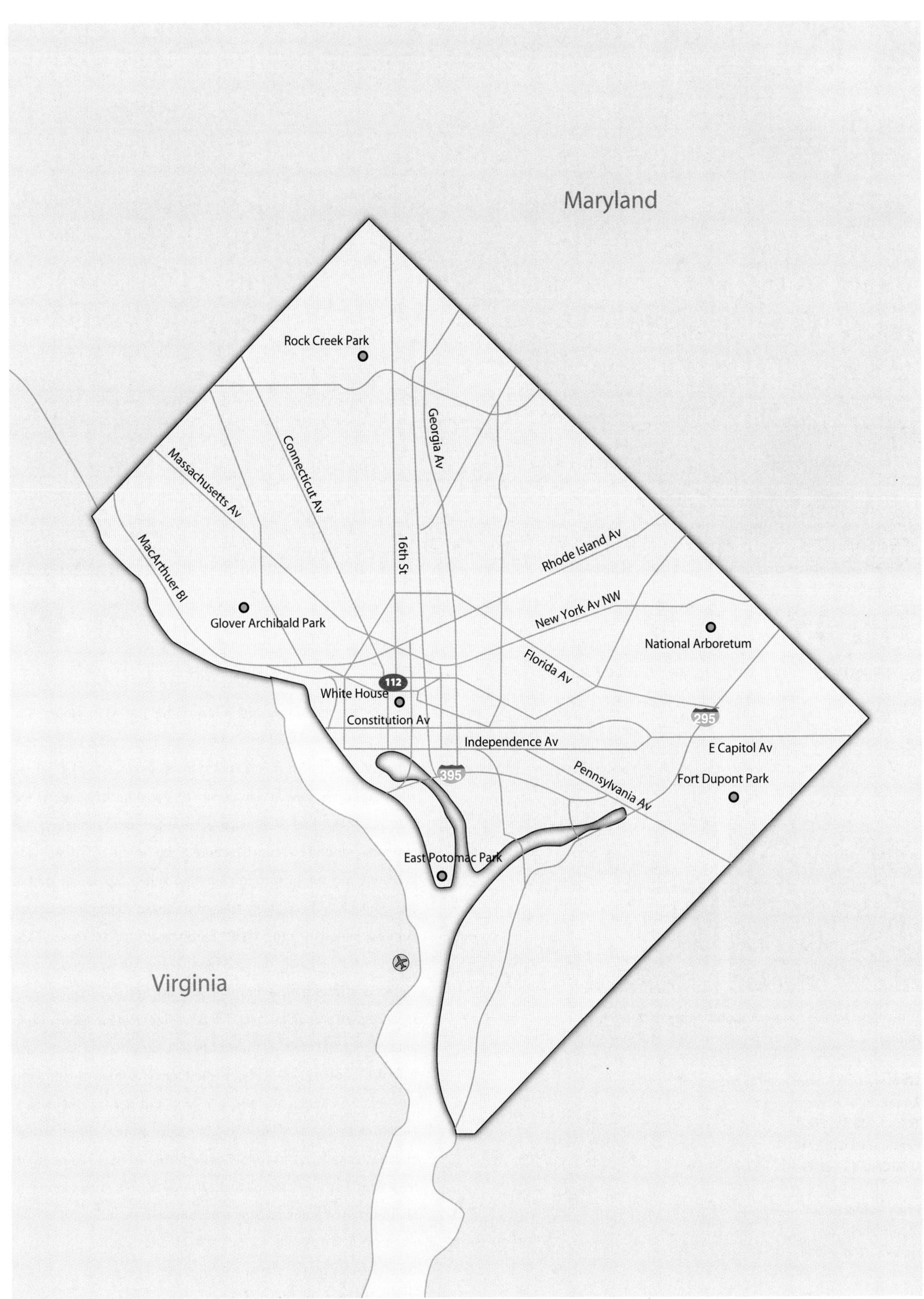

U.S.A. - DISTRICT OF COLUMBIA (WASHINGTON)

THE HAY ADAMS

SIXTEENTH & H. STREETS N.W., WASHINGTON D.C. 20006

Directions: Ronald Reagan National Airport is a 15-minute drive from The Hay Adams.

Web: www.johansens.com/hayadams
E-mail: info@hayadams.com
Tel: +1 202 638 6600
Fax: +1 202 638 2716
U.S./Canada Toll Free: 1 800 424 5054

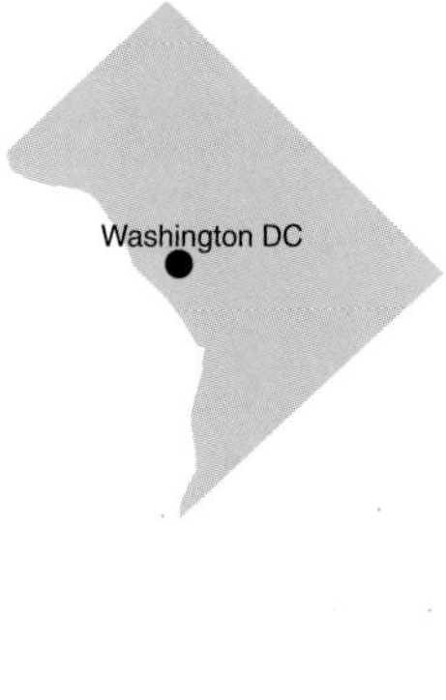

Price Guide: (room only)
rooms $425-$925
suites $1,200-$6,000

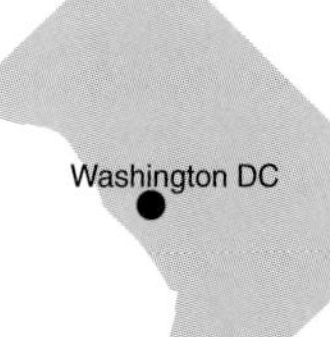

Located just across Lafayette Square from The White House, The Hay Adams has retained its popularity and importance in the social life of Washington. It is well known for its warm, attentive service and impeccable style. Italian Renaissance architecture reflects the elegance of the interior with subtle, traditional furnishings and eye-catching antiques complemented by neutral tones and contemporary furniture. Upon entering, guests will be amazed at the opulent lobby with its beautiful ornate ceiling, mahogany-colored paneling and classic European color schemes. Each bedroom is individually designed to an exceptionally high standard with a common theme throughout: plush sofas, canopied beds, large pillows; and uniquely detailed ceilings create a distinguished atmosphere that matches the equally remarkable views. Some have Baronial fireplaces. The Lafayette restaurant is flooded with light and features Chippendale-style chairs, and crystal chandeliers. Superb cuisine is served here together with an impressive selection of wines. For a light meal or delicious midnight snack, retreat to Off the Record bar. Enjoy a stroll to the nearby Washington Monument, Smithsonian Museum or Connecticut Avenue for shopping.

Our inspector loved: *The Hay Adams, where nothing is overlooked but the White House.*

 145  50      

FLORIDA

Hotel location shown in red with page number

U.S.A. - FLORIDA (COCONUT GROVE)

GROVE ISLE HOTEL & SPA

NOBLE HOUSE HOTELS & RESORTS

FOUR GROVE ISLE DRIVE, COCONUT GROVE, FLORIDA 33133

This private 20-acre gated island sanctuary offers a peaceful and secure respite. The calm, secluded atmosphere of this island oasis belies its location just 5 minutes from the world-class shopping and abundant outdoor cafés of Coconut Grove. Lush gardens, views of Biscayne Bay, original artwork and guests sipping martinis by the pool as yachts dock at the marina below, create the ambience of a private luxury residence. Accommodations feature Italian marble bathrooms, iron four-poster beds, terracotta tiling and balconies with views of the bay and the edged shoreline of Miami. BALEENmiami, the fine dining restaurant, serves Euro-Asian fare amid candle-lit elegance and a whimsical monkey motif. Alternately, opt for "Dining on the Rocks" to enjoy BALEENmiami's cuisine in a tropical oceanfront setting or choose the Palapa Bar for lighter poolside fare. Island-style cuisine is served on the open-air loggia or guests may dine in the comfort of their own rooms. For recreation, Grove Isle offers a beautiful pool overlooking the bay, a life-size chess set on the ship's deck, the first ever Patrick McEnroe Tennis Center featuring 12 lit tennis courts, a scenic waterside jogging path, fitness center and marina. The new 6000ft.^{2} SpaTerre offers exotic Balinese spa treatments and Thai body rituals, a private couple's Zen steam room, outdoor yoga deck, Watsu pool and full-service salon.

Our inspector loved: *The spectacular views while dining waterside.*

Directions: The resort is 5 minutes from Coconut Grove and a short drive from Miami's South Beach.

Web: www.johansens.com/groveisle
E-mail: reservations@groveisle.com
Tel: +1 305 858 8300
Fax: +1 305 858 5908
U.S./Canada Toll Free: 1 800 884 7683

Price Guide: (room only)
rooms $259-$689
suites $429-$859

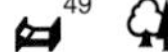
49 250

SPA

The Shores Resort & Spa

2637 South Atlantic Avenue, Daytona Beach Shores, Florida 32118

The Shores Resort & Spa, Daytona's only AAA 4 Diamond award winner, is a playful yet provocative beachfront resort offering guest a surprising Daytona Beach experience. A spirited retreat, and the only hip, luxury boutique resort along Florida's Atlantic coast north of South Beach, The Shores encourages relaxation whether lounging under a private cabana or relishing in a milk and honey body wrap at SpaTerre. Unparalleled luxury emanates from the well-appointed guest rooms with four-poster beds and upgraded linens with stunning water views and hi-tech features such as 42-inch plasma flat-screen T.V.s and high-speed Internet. A beautifully landscaped oasis in the heart of dynamic and iconic Daytona Beach, The Shores offers the only beachfront fine dining in the area. Enjoy a candle-lit ambience or al fresco seating at Baleen, which serves fresh seafood, artfully prepared. Baleen's terrace overlooks a beachfront pool deck and charming Tiki Bar, complete with sand and fire pits. Pampering awaits at SpaTerre, where exotic treatments, including massages and nail and skin therapies, provide a cross-cultural spa experience with a wet room featuring Vichy shower and private steam room. There is also a state-of-the-art fitness center. The picturesque setting and modern amenities create a productive and stimulating environment for corporate and social events.

Directions: 10 miles from Daytona International Airport. From I-95 take exit 256 and head towards Port Orange. Follow 421 west over the causeway to Atlantic Avenue then turn left onto AIA and head north for 3 miles.

Web: www.johansens.com/shoresresort
E-mail: reservations@shoresresort.com
Tel: +1 386 767 7350
Fax: +1 386 760 3651
U.S./Canada Toll Free: 1 866 934 SHORES

Price Guide: (room only)
rooms $159-$489
suites $699-$1,500

Our inspector loved: *Dining by the beach at Baleen restaurant.*

 212    740        SPA 

Fisher Island Hotel & Resort

ONE FISHER ISLAND DRIVE, FISHER ISLAND, FLORIDA 33109

Originally built in the 1920s by William and Rosamund Vanderbilt as their impressive winter estate, Fisher Island is now home to the world-class Fisher Island Hotel & Spa. There are 62 elegant suites, villas, and cottages that make up part of the historical Vanderbilt Mansion, each with sitting rooms, private patios and hot tubs. Some rooms overlook the Atlantic Ocean or are adjacent to the private Beach Club. With 216 beautiful acres, guests of the hotel receive a complimentary golf cart for use during their stay. There are several superb dining options available on the island from gourmet cuisine to casual grilles. The Garwood Lounge, located inside the Vanderbilt Mansion is the perfect setting for cocktails at the piano bar. Golfers will enjoy a round at the par 35 championship 9-hole golf course, while tennis enthusiasts will enjoy a match at the resort's first-class tennis facility with its 18 lighted Har-Tru clay, grass and hard courts. There is a 22,000 sq. ft. Spa Internazionale with Fitness Center and Salon di Bellezza open daily. Fisher Island is only accessible by air or a 7-minute ferry ride to the island, and is minutes from the exclusive shopping and cultural activities of Miami Beach, 20 minutes from the Bal Harbour Shops and 15 minutes from the charming Coconut Grove.

Our inspector loved: *The charming ocean-side private Beach Club available only to guests and residents of Fisher Island.*

Directions: 20 minutes from Miami International Airport.

Web: www.johansens.com/fisherisland
E-mail: reservations@fisherislandclub.net
Tel: +1 305 535 6000
Fax: +1 305 535 6003
U.S./Canada Toll Free: 1 800 537 3708

Price Guide: (room only)
suites $500-$2,200

Jupiter Beach Resort & Spa

5 NORTH A1A, JUPITER, FLORIDA 33477-5190

Jupiter Beach Resort & Spa is a boutique beach hotel located on the northern tip of Palm Beach County on the Atlantic Ocean. The intimate nature of this elegant Caribbean-style resort offers more of a private club feel than a hotel. The luxurious guest rooms are spacious with island-style décor and rich dark tropical woods. The Penthouse Suites have breathtaking views of the ocean and are beautifully decorated with designer furnishings. A visit to the spa to indulge in an island wrap or sugar massage is a treat after a day on the expansive private beach. Afterwards, enjoy a relaxing cup of tea or a warm Belgian chocolate shot at the Spa's Tea Bar before dinner. There are 3 on-site restaurants including the elegant Sinclairs Ocean Grill, the resort's signature Palm Beach restaurant where guest dine in a tropical atmosphere, the Sandbar, which serves casual fare at the beach or by the pool and the Sinclairs Lounge, which provides weekend entertainment. Private cabanas and chairs are exclusively for guests. Other sporty recreation nearby include snorkeling, fishing, riverboat tours, and boat rentals. There are several golf courses nearby that offer exclusive privileges to hotel guests. The affluent Jupiter Island is adjacent to the resort. World-class shopping, dining and entertainment are just 20 miles away in downtown West Palm Beach.

Directions: 20 minutes from Palm Beach International Airport off I-95, 1 hour from Fort Lauderdale International Airport and 90 minutes from Miami International Airport.

Tallahassee
Orlando
Miami

Web: www.johansens.com/jupiterbeachresort
E-mail: reservations@jupiterbeachresort.com
Tel: +1 561 746 2511
Fax: +1 561 744 1741
U.S./Canada Toll Free: 1 800 228 8810

Price Guide: (room only)
rooms $199-$399
suites $269-$1,500

Our inspector loved: *The spacious rooms and incredibly comfy pillows.*

U.S.A. - FLORIDA (KEY WEST)

Ocean Key Resort

ZERO DUVAL STREET, KEY WEST, FLORIDA 33040

Ocean Key Resort & Spa is a luxury resort located in the historic and vibrant town of Key West. The resort overlooks the Gulf of Mexico and is adjacent to the famous Mallory Square. In keeping with the tropical feel of Key West, all of the island-style suites are appointed with bold and colorful fabrics, hand-painted furniture and unique local artwork. Many rooms have beautiful views from the oceanfront balconies. Hot Tin Roof is the resort's oceanfront restaurant serving gourmet dining and a creative menu of Latin, Caribbean and South Florida flavors. Chef Kevin Montoya creates a one-of-a-kind experience and is celebrated for his delectable "conch-fusion" cuisine. For more casual fare, guests can choose to dine at the pool, at the Sunset Pier or in the comfort of their guest room. Spa Terre provides a relaxing retreat and specializes in exotic Balinese spa treatments and Thai body rituals. Flowers and spices are used to enhance each spa experience specifically for their healing properties. The resort provides ample activities for everyone including romantic sunset catamaran sails, fishing charters through the resort's marina, kayaking, parasailing and jet ski rentals. A trip to Key West is not complete without a tour of the Ernest Hemingway House or the Key West Aquarium. Charming shops are located steps from the resort.

Our inspector loved: *Dining with a view at Hot Tin Roof.*

Directions: Fly directly into Key West International Airport from Miami.

Web: www.johansens.com/oceankey
E-mail: contactus@oceankey.com
Tel: +1 305 296 7701
Fax: +1 305 292 7685
U.S./Canada Toll Free: 1 800 328 9815

Price Guide:
rooms $249-$609
suites $299-$1,139

Simonton Court Historic Inn & Cottages

320 SIMONTON STREET, KEY WEST, FLORIDA 33040

Located in 2 acres of lush tropical gardens, this elegant collection of cottages, manor house and town house is positively idyllic for rest and relaxation at the very most southern point of the USA. Formerly a cigar factory, this collection of elegant buildings has gradually become the benchmark for attentive service in the most picturesque of settings. Vast tropical palms shade the 4 swimming pools and hot-tub and gentle sea breezes caress the verandas, whilst a series of pretty brick paths connect the various buildings by twinkling night-lights. Guests may choose to stay in one of the 6 enchanting and beautifully restored factory workers' cottages that boast the very latest in luxurious amenities yet still retain the period charm of their 1880 origins. These make the most wonderful hideaway for privacy-seekers although the suites and guest bedrooms in the main house are breathtakingly appointed and many have private sun-decks or porches, king-size beds and Jacuzzis. The sunset over Key West is a well-fabled sight and Simonton Court is just 3 blocks walk away from the top spot from which to view. Similarly Duval Street is just a stone's throw away, the home of many wonderful boutiques and fashionable pubs.

Our inspector loved: *The tropical gardens.*

Directions: Take US Highway 1 to Key West and then follow Roosevelt Boulevard to Truman Avenue. Turn right on Simonton Street and continue to Eaton Street. Turn left just past the Eaton Street intersection.

Web: www.johansens.com/simontoncourt
E-mail: simontoncourt@aol.com
Tel: +1 305 294 6386
Fax: +1 305 293 8446
U.S./Canada Toll Free: 1 800 944 2687

Price Guide: (room only)
rooms $145–$399
cottages $279–$429

Sunset Key Guest Cottages

245 FRONT STREET, KEY WEST, FLORIDA 33040

Sunset Key is a 27-acre luxury island with a resort and a residential community located just 500 yards from historic "Old Town" Key West. Sunset Key Guest Cottages are accessible only by launch, which runs 24 hours a day from The Westin Key West Resort & Marina. This car free island makes for the most tranquil vacation with its spectacular views of the Gulf of Mexico, fresh ocean air and colorful tropical blooms. Each of the luxurious 1, 2 and 3-bedroom cottages is nestled around tropical foliage and has either an ocean or garden view, wraparound veranda with Adirondack chairs, living room, dining area and an equipped and pre-stocked kitchen. Breakfast baskets are served to guests on their cottage porch each morning with a newspaper. Latitudes Beach Cafe offers an upscale yet casual setting, with al fresco beachfront dining. For a more intimate dinner experience guests may request the Private Chef Service and have dinner prepared in their cottage. There is an abundance of activities from exploring the museums and bars of Old Key West to just about any water activity you can imagine including deep-sea fishing. There is also the option to just relax and enjoy a game of tennis or stroll along the white sandy beach.

Our inspector loved: *The privacy of this tropical island so close to the festivities Key West is so well known for.*

Directions: Sunset Key is located approximately 10 minutes from Key West International Airport. Take a taxi from the airport to The Westin Key West Resort & Marina then a boat to the island.

Web: www.johansens.com/sunsetkey
E-mail: rebecca.hysell@westinkeywestresort.com
Tel: +1 305 292 5300
Fax: +1 305 292 5395
U.S./Canada Toll Free: 1 888 477 7SUN

Tallahassee
Orlando
Miami

Price Guide:
1-bedroom cottage $595-$1,170
2-bedroom cottage $675-$1,865
3-bedroom cottage $975-$2,225

MARCO BEACH OCEAN RESORT

480 SOUTH COLLIER BOULEVARD, MARCO ISLAND, FLORIDA 34145

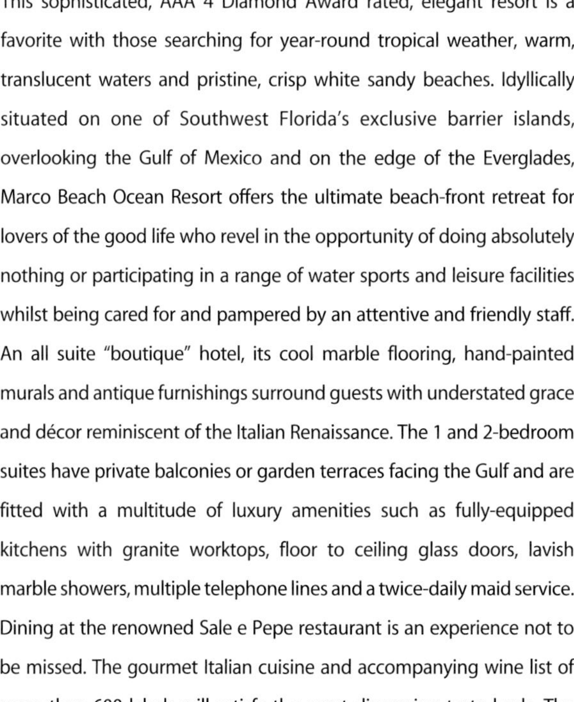

This sophisticated, AAA 4 Diamond Award rated, elegant resort is a favorite with those searching for year-round tropical weather, warm, translucent waters and pristine, crisp white sandy beaches. Idyllically situated on one of Southwest Florida's exclusive barrier islands, overlooking the Gulf of Mexico and on the edge of the Everglades, Marco Beach Ocean Resort offers the ultimate beach-front retreat for lovers of the good life who revel in the opportunity of doing absolutely nothing or participating in a range of water sports and leisure facilities whilst being cared for and pampered by an attentive and friendly staff. An all suite "boutique" hotel, its cool marble flooring, hand-painted murals and antique furnishings surround guests with understated grace and décor reminiscent of the Italian Renaissance. The 1 and 2-bedroom suites have private balconies or garden terraces facing the Gulf and are fitted with a multitude of luxury amenities such as fully-equipped kitchens with granite worktops, floor to ceiling glass doors, lavish marble showers, multiple telephone lines and a twice-daily maid service. Dining at the renowned Sale e Pepe restaurant is an experience not to be missed. The gourmet Italian cuisine and accompanying wine list of more than 600 labels will satisfy the most discerning taste buds. The flourishing city of Naples, with its stylish shopping, is within easy reach.

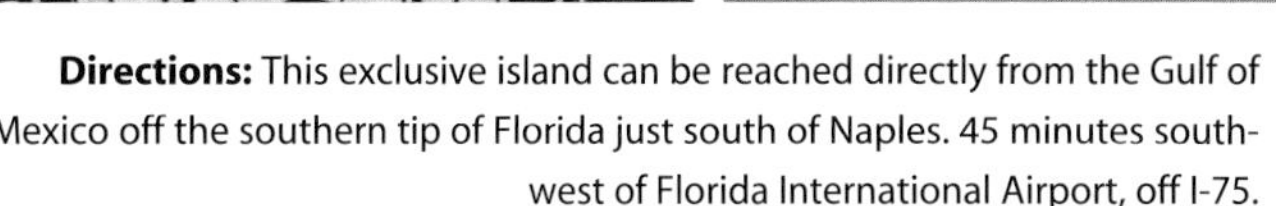

Directions: This exclusive island can be reached directly from the Gulf of Mexico off the southern tip of Florida just south of Naples. 45 minutes south-west of Florida International Airport, off I-75.

Web: www.johansens.com/marcobeach
E-mail: reservations@marcobeachoceanresort.com
Tel: +1 239 393 1400
Fax: +1 239 393 1401
U.S./Canada Toll Free: 1 800 260 5089

Price Guide: (room only)
1-bedroom suites $169-$599
2-bedroom suites $270-$1,200

Our inspector loved: *The décor, ambience, and Sale e Pepe's wine list.*

99   100        SPA   

Hotel Victor

1144 OCEAN DRIVE, MIAMI BEACH, FLORIDA 33139

Set in the heart of the art deco district of Miami Beach's colorful South Beach, Hotel Victor is the epitome of glamour and style. The vibe is hip yet elegant, and all 88 vibrant rooms have spectacular views of the ocean or South Beach, custom furniture and sensual designer fabrics. Open bathrooms feature oversized soaking tubs, rain showers, luxurious amenities, 350-count Fili d'Oro Egyptian cotton linens, L.C.D. T.V.s, D.V.D. and C.D. players, WiFi and indulgent Big Bars. The Penthouse, a favorite for local V.I.P.s and celebrities, occupies the entire 8th floor and has its own private entrance, gourmet kitchen, rain shower, infinity edge tub and outdoor entertainment areas with hot tubs and incredible 360° views. Dining at VIX is considered a provocative experience: the dining room features a rare jellyfish tank, original artwork, chic lighting and fashionable décor where Executive Chef James Wierzelewski brings his perfectly spiced and culturally inspired cuisine to the table. A resident D.J. spins the most in-vogue tunes around the hotel and pool terrace. Spa V is perfect for pampering with its fitness room, Cool Down Room and signature Turkish-style Hamman. Vibe Managers can arrange reservations at the area's hottest nightclubs and restaurants, and beach lovers will enjoy the white sand steps from the hotel.

Our inspector loved: *The Very Victor Suite overlooking Ocean Drive.*

Directions: 20 minutes from Miami International Airport.

Web: www.johansens.com/hotelvictor
E-mail: treynolds@hotelvictorsouthbeach.com
Tel: +1 305 428 1234
Fax: +1 305 421 6281

Price Guide: (room only)
rooms $300-$5,000
suites $900-$10,000

       SPA  

NOBLE HOUSE HOTELS & RESORTS

LaPlaya Beach & Golf Resort

9891 Gulf Shore Drive, Naples, Florida 34108

This is the place for sun worshippers and all who like the attractions of year-round sub-tropical weather, warm turquoise waters and sugar-white sandy beaches. LaPlaya is a casually elegant boutique beachfront resort for all lovers of the good life with the opportunity to indulge in doing absolutely nothing or participating in a range of water sports, leisure activities or swinging a club over a challenging 18-hole par 72 golf course. Situated on Vanderbilt Beach this award-winning resort has everything for everybody. It revolves around a magnificent meandering pool complex and has an interior that is equally stunning. French doors attractively span the width of the first floor, and the elegant main lobby is adorned with crystal chandeliers and plush cane and wicker furnishings. The lounge features an impressive number of wines, and bedrooms reflect a classical Florida style; oversized and luxuriously appointed, each is decorated in fresh greens and warm yellows, have bamboo-patterned bedcovers, four poster beds, a balcony and superb ocean views. An evening in Baleen, the resort's signature restaurant, begins indoors and ends on the long shoreline terrace. Local fish with Asian flavors dominate the menu. Adjacent to the fitness center is a fully-equipped 4,500 sq. ft. spa featuring 1920s décor.

Our inspector loved: *The huge private balconies overlooking the beach and bay.*

Directions: 30 minutes from south-west Florida International Airport (Ft. Myers). From the airport take I-75 south to exit 111. Head west then cross Highway 41 and turn left after the bridge onto Gulf Shore Drive.

Tallahassee
Orlando
Miami

Web: www.johansens.com/laplaya
E-mail: sales@laplayaresort.com
Tel: +1 239 597 3123
Fax: +1 239 597 8283
U.S./Canada Toll Free: 1 800 237 6883

Price Guide: (room only)
rooms $189-$849
suites $805-$2,600

Portofino Bay Hotel

LOEWS HOTELS

5601 UNIVERSAL BOULEVARD, ORLANDO, FLORIDA 32819

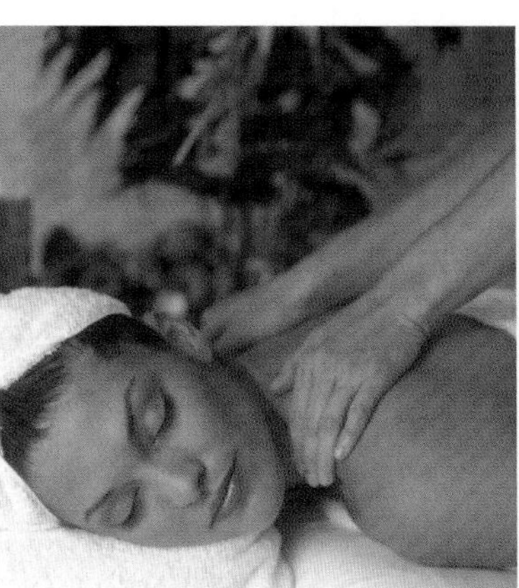

Situated within Universal Orlando Resort, this magnificent Italian-style hotel has its guests almost believing they are staying in the beautiful fishing village of Portofino on the Italian Riviera. This magical illusion is created by the sunwashed stucco buildings and cobblestone streets alongside the authentic harbor piazza, viewed from the hotel's Bay View guest rooms. Elegant Italian style pervades the hotel where furnishings are complemented by many marble features. A variety of accommodations are available; every guest room has a desk area, dual voice lines, data port, voice mail and high-speed internet access. A standard room sleeps up to 5 persons while suites provide an adjoining room specifically designed for children or an ideal space for business meetings and entertaining. 8 restaurants and lounges offer an extensive choice of cuisine in diverse atmospheres, from family-friendly to intimate cafes. There are 3 themed swimming pools, bocce ball courts and Mandara Spa, which boasts 14 treatment rooms, saunas and a hair salon; alternatively there are specialty shops and an art gallery for window-shopping. Guests enjoy the special benefit of bypassing the regular attraction lines at Universal Studios and Universal's Islands of Adventure plus complimentary transportation by water taxi and priority restaurant seating within the parks and Universal CityWalk.

Our inspector loved: *The Gelateria, and the theme park benefits.*

Directions: A 20-minute drive from Orlando International Airport. Take the north exit from the airport to Highway 528 west (Beeline Expressway) to I-4 east, exit for Universal Studios.

Web: www.johansens.com/portofinobay
Tel: +1 407 503 1000
Fax: +1 407 503 1010
U.S./Canada Toll Free: 1 888 823 4466

Price Guide: (room only)
rooms $269-$499
suites $519-$2,500

750 1380 SPA

THE LODGE & CLUB AT PONTE VEDRA BEACH

607 PONTE VEDRA BOULEVARD, PONTE VEDRA BEACH, FLORIDA 32082

Framed by palm trees and white beaches, The Lodge & Club at Ponte Vedra Beach sparkles as one of Florida's most elegant oceanfront resorts. Located midway between Jacksonville and St. Augustine, this Mediterranean-styled resort reflects romantic charm and uncompromising service. The Lodge & Club is a member of the prestigious Preferred Hotels & Resorts Worldwide and is a recipient of Condé Nast Traveler's Gold List Award. Each of 66 luxurious guest rooms and suites overlook the Atlantic and are richly appointed, as are the spacious bathrooms, many with oversized Jacuzzi tubs. From triple-sheet luxury to full-length terry robes, sheer comfort is guaranteed. The Lodge & Club's beautiful wide beach and colorful umbrellas provide a spectacular playground for all ages. Additional recreational pleasures include 3 heated pools, sailing and biking. A 12,500 sq. ft. fitness center, steam room, sauna, Jacuzzi and massage services are provided for guests' enjoyment. The resort's sophisticated style is best represented by its diversified dining experiences. 2 charming restaurants feature formal and informal settings with extraordinary ocean views.

Our inspector loved: *The oversized luxurious bathrooms, and romantic atmosphere.*

Directions: Located directly on the ocean. Exit I-95 at Butler Boulevard east and travel 13 miles. Exit at AIA south and travel 3 miles to Corona Road. The Lodge is 1 mile further on. 35 minutes from Jacksonville International Airport.

Web: www.johansens.com/ponteverdrabeach
E-mail: reservations@pvresorts.com
Tel: +1 904 273 9500
Fax: +1 904 273 0210
U.S./Canada Toll Free: 1 800 243 4304

Price Guide: (room only)
rooms $260-$460
suites $360-$560

WATERCOLOR INN AND RESORT

34 GOLDENROD CIRCLE, SANTA ROSA BEACH, FLORIDA 32459

Directions: Located in the Florida Panhandle on the Gulf of Mexico, between the resort towns of Destin and Seaside. Take exit 331 off I-10 south to Highway 98 east. Turn south onto 30A to WaterColor.

Web: www.johansens.com/watercolor
E-mail: info@watercolorreservations.com
Tel: +1 850 534 5000
Fax: +1 850 534 5001
U.S./Canada Toll Free: 1 866 426 2656

Price Guide:
rooms $365-$480
suites $525-$730
vacation homes $410-$1,750

A more delightful and picturesque setting for this sunshine retreat would be hard to find. Covering 499 acres it nestles between the sandy shores of Florida's fabled Emerald Coast and the banks of a 220-acre dune lake bordered by pine forests and part of the Grayton Beach State Park. Embraced by wind-sculptured oak groves, palmettos and sea grasses, the inn is surrounded by a maze of pathways and parks that meander from the Gulf of Mexico to the lake around brick-lined streets, water gardens, unique shops, and attractive vacation rental houses and cottages. With the intimacy and hospitality of a traditional Southern grand hotel the inn offers magnificent David Rockwell-designed architecture, superb service and luxurious accommodation. Each of the spacious guest rooms has a king-size bed and sofa sleeper, huge walk-in shower, and beach views from a private balcony. There are also 150 beautifully appointed, fully equipped vacation homes, with 1-6 bedrooms, available. The Fish Out of Water restaurant is a venue of casual elegance, and takes an imaginative approach to traditional ways of preparing and serving excellent cuisine. The BaitHouse, and The Beach Club, with its pool deck and grill, are great alternative dining choices. Water, beach and lake sports, fishing, canoeing and kayaking can be arranged. Enjoy the spa or golf at the resort's own course.

Our inspector loved: *The powder-white sand beach and clear gulf water.*

LOEWS HOTELS

Don CeSar Beach Resort

3400 GULF BOULEVARD, ST. PETE BEACH, FLORIDA 33706

Affectionately referred to as a grand dame of sunny Florida and widely known as the Pink Palace because of its flamingo-pink façade, Don CeSar sprawls long and high on the edge of a sugar-white beach on the island of St. Pete Beach, on the Gulf of Mexico. This internationally renowned Mediterranean-style castle was built in 1928 and was recently enhanced by a $23 million investment. Accented by Moorish bell towers and imperial turrets, it stands proudly against the bluest of skies offering casually elegant, luxurious accommodation. The resort has every amenity, comfort and leisure activity a visitor could wish for as well as superb dining and a variety of spa facilities including 2 swimming pools. The interior emulates European elegance with rich and refined English carpets, Italian crystal chandeliers, French candelabras, fountains, polished mahogany and vibrant upholsteries. The beautifully decorated European-styled guest rooms, 40 spacious suites and 2 penthouses boast panoramic sea views; each is lavishly furnished with custom made pieces and every home-away-from-home comfort. Dining is a delight with a choice of restaurants ranging from the Maritana Grille, which serves creative New American cuisine, to the poolside Beachcomber Grill with its salads and burgers.

Our inspector loved: *The old fashioned ice-cream parlor, and the beautiful beach.*

Directions: 35 minutes from Tampa International Airport. 30 minutes from St. Petersburg/Clearwater International Airport. I-275 to exit 17.

Web: www.johansens.com/doncesar
E-mail: doncesarinfo@loewshotels.com
Tel: +1 727 360 1881
Fax: +1 727 367 3609
U.S./Canada Toll Free: 1 800 282 1116

Price Guide: (room only)
rooms $184-$359
suites $299-$2,284

277 350 SPA NR HP

GEORGIA

Hotel location shown in red with page number

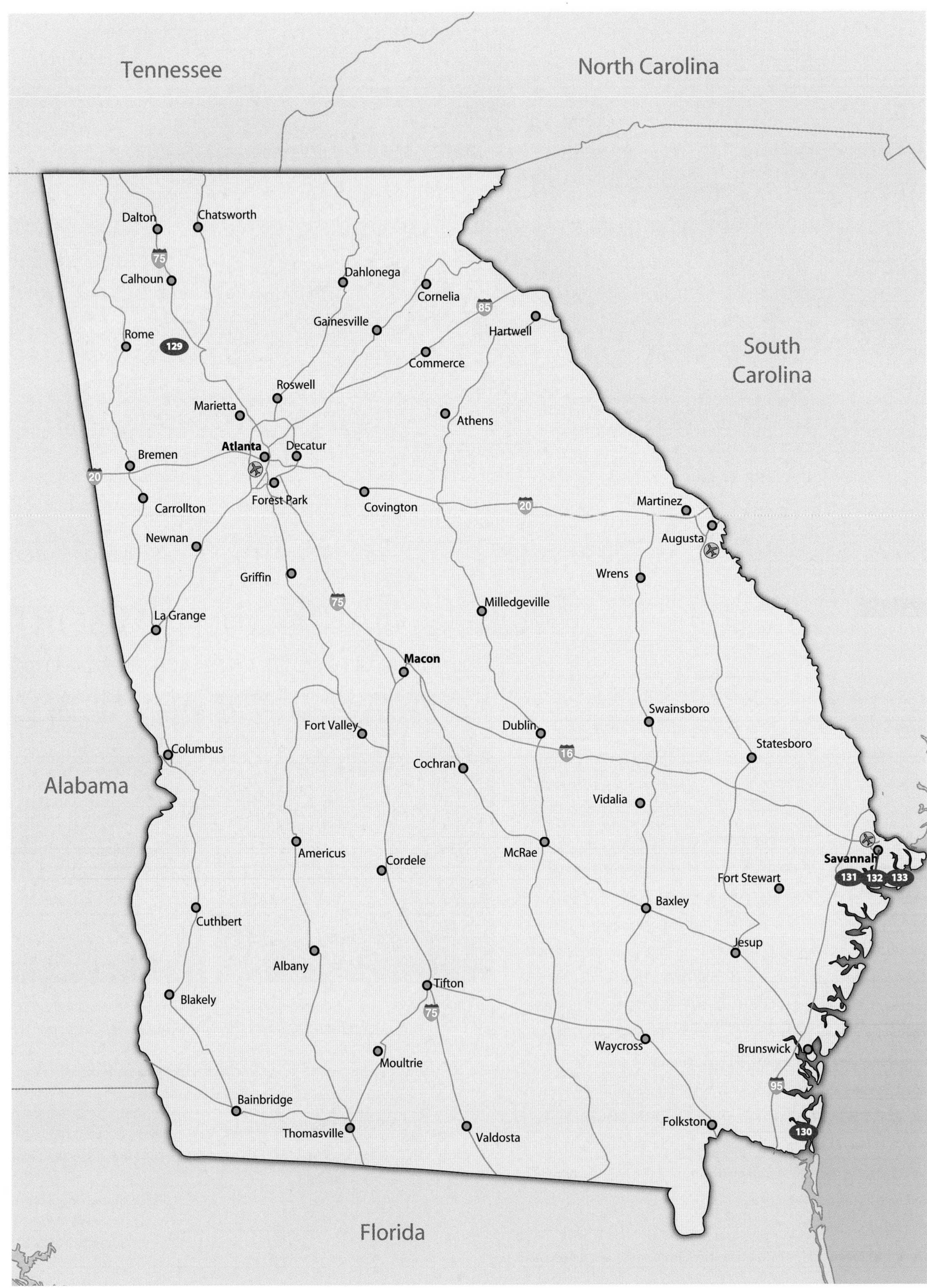

Barnsley Gardens Resort

597 BARNSLEY GARDENS ROAD, ADAIRSVILLE, GEORGIA 30103

33 charming cottages, housing 70 luxurious suites, built to resemble a 19th-century, English-style village, are nestled in 1,300 acres of lush gardens and historic land in the foothills of the beautiful Blue Ridge Mountains. This luxurious resort is 75 miles north of Atlanta where guests can relax, unwind and recuperate in hospitable Southern style. Dominated by the ruins of the Italian-style manor's historic mansion, which was destroyed by a tornado in 1906, the original ornamental gardens have been stunningly restored and feature more than 150 types of roses. All the cozy, gabled, fretted and shingled cottages edge tree-lined walkways and are decorated with warmth and comfort in mind. Each suite features antique and fine furnishings, a wood-burning fireplace, king-size sleigh or four-poster bed and period-inspired bathrooms with a cast-iron ball and claw foot tub. There are also 2-line telephones, high-speed Internet access and satellite television. Guests have a choice of 3 excellent dining areas: enjoy Southern cuisine in Rice House, the Woodlands Grill steakhouse or German beer and sausages in the Beer Garden. Activities include golf on the Jim Fazio-designed 18-hole championship course, a sporting clay shooting ground developed by the British School of Shooting, lake fly fishing, riding stables, mountain bike trails, canoeing, kayaking and a full-service spa.

Our inspector loved: *The abundance of activities to enjoy.*

Directions: Take I-75 north to exit 306 and travel approximately 2.2 miles on Highway 140. Turn left at Hall Station Road and travel south for approximately 5.5 miles. Hall Station Road intersects with Barnsley Gardens Road. Turn right onto Barnsley Gardens Road and travel 2.5 miles to the resort.

Web: www.johansens.com/barnsleygardens
E-mail: reservations@barnsleyresort.com
Tel: +1 770 773 7480
Fax: +1 770 877 9155
U.S./Canada Toll Free: 1 877 773 2447

Price Guide:
rooms $285-$390
suites $285-$390

Greyfield Inn

CUMBERLAND ISLAND, GEORGIA

Cumberland Island is the largest and most southern of Georgia's 120-mile long coastal archipelago. It was the 19th-century retreat of steel baron Thomas Carnegie and his wife Lucy, who, in 1901, built Greyfield as a wedding gift for their daughter, Margaret Ricketson. Converted to an inn during 1962 by her daughter, Lucy Ferguson, and family – who oversee the daily operation – Greyfield Inn exudes the welcoming atmosphere and charm of a family home. This white mansion of gracious elegance retains the original furnishings from the turn of the century alongside the added luxury of contemporary amenities. Many of the furnishings are treasured heirlooms, and family portraits and photographs adorn the walls. Guests can relax in the Baronial living room, with fireplace, in the cozy bar, well-stocked library, on the shady veranda and, of course, in the exquisite bedrooms with fabulous views. Greyfield Inn is the only overnight accommodation on an island the size of Manhattan and is reached solely by ferry. Surrounded by a 17-mile long protected national seashore of pristine beaches and ancient oaks there is an abundance of wildlife including deer, wild horses, bobcats, boar, alligators and 230 species of birds. Rates include ferry transportation, breakfast, lunch, a gourmet dinner, a conducted wilderness drive and the use of bicycles, kayaks and fishing equipment

Our inspector loved: *Feeling like part of the family.*

Directions: A car service is available from Jacksonville Airport, which is a 30-minute drive north.

Web: www.johansens.com/greyfieldinn
E-mail: seashore@greyfieldinn.com
Tel: +1 904 261 6408
Fax: +1 904 321 0666
U.S./Canada Toll Free: 1 866 410 8052

Price Guide: (including round-trip ferry service, 3 meals per day and various trips)
rooms $350-$495
suites $450-$575

THE BALLASTONE

14 EAST OGLETHORPE AVENUE, SAVANNAH, GEORGIA 31401-3707

The charm and grace of The Ballastone, a historic mansion situated in the heart of Savannah, is unsurpassed. Located amidst beautiful landscaped squares and tree-shaded avenues, this genteel bed and breakfast offers ultra luxurious accommodation with all modern amenities. Discreet southern hospitality and friendly staff ensure guests feel at home with the warmest of welcomes. The sitting room is intimate and cozy with a remarkable antique harp and marble fireplace. Stunning bedrooms are themed according to the history of Savannah with opulent fabrics, gorgeous beds, exquisite antiques and sumptuous color schemes. Most rooms have sitting areas and some open out onto the courtyard garden. A full Southern breakfast is served on crisp white tablecloths either in the garden overlooking the city, in the tearoom or in the bar. Afternoon tea is delightful and pre-dinner hors d'oeuvres leave guests wondering whether they should leave the hotel for dinner at all! Savannah's Historic District is home to one of the most valuable collections of 18th and 19th-century architecture. Enjoy exploring the quaint cobbled streets, impeccably kept gardens and stately mansions where more than 1,400 buildings have been beautifully restored to their original splendor. A personal driver can take guests shopping, and there are romantic antique carriage rides to any of the fine restaurants nearby.

Our inspector loved: *The elegant décor depicting Savannah's history.*

Directions: Take I-16 to Savannah. Proceed until the Interstate merges into Mongtomery Street. Continue to Oglethorpe Avenue. Turn right onto Oglethorpe Avenue. Pass Bull Street to Drayton Street. Make a u-turn onto the opposite side of Oglethorpe Avenue. The hotel is in the middle of the block.

Atlanta
Augusta
Savannah

Web: www.johansens.com/ballastone
E-mail: inn@ballastone.com
Tel: +1 912 236 1484
Fax: +1 912 236 4626
U.S./Canada Toll Free: 1 800 822 4553

Price Guide: (including tea and hors d'oeuvres)
rooms $215-$355
suites $395

Eliza Thompson House

5 WEST JONES STREET, SAVANNAH, GEORGIA 31401

The Eliza Thompson House, built in 1847, offers a delightful fusion of past and present times with traditions and customs of the last century and the comforts and amenities of today. Set on a quiet residential street, the house is one of the oldest inns in the heart of Savannah's historical district and is an architectural landmark. Meticulous restoration work has resulted in the superb interior, enhanced by heart pine floors and antique furnishings. Guests may stay in either the 12 stately rooms in the main house or in the Carriage House, which boasts a further 13 rooms. All the bedrooms are furnished in an exquisite style with en-suite facilities, have color televisions and complimentary high speed wireless Internet access. The soft bathrobes and make-up mirrors are thoughtful extras. The deluxe continental breakfast, served buffet style in the courtyard, features a hot entrée and delicious side dishes. Other delightful traditions include an afternoon wine and cheese reception and evening dessert and coffee. Guests may relax in the beautifully landscaped courtyard, where the air is scented with southern fragrances and the gentle sound of the Ivan Bailey fountain may be heard. Savannah is a wonderful town to explore with many antique shops, museums and old churches nearby.

Our inspector loved: *The peaceful courtyard with the soft sound of the fountain - the perfect spot to breakfast or read a book.*

Directions: Travel east on I-16, towards Savannah. Exit at Montgomery Street, turn right at traffic lights on Liberty Street. Turn right on Whitaker Street and left onto Jones Street.

Web: www.johansens.com/elizathompsonhouse
E-mail: innkeeper@elizathompsonhouse.com
Tel: +1 912 236 3620
Fax: +1 912 238 1920
U.S./Canada Toll Free: 1 800 348 9378

Price Guide:
rooms $189–$369

The Gastonian

220 East Gaston Street, Savannah, Georgia 31401

In the heart of Savannah's beautiful Historic District exists a landmark to Southern grandeur: The Gastonian. Built in 1868, the dual mansions reflect an elegant private residential atmosphere and are synonymous with gracious hospitality. Quiet and romantic, The Gastonian features a formal side garden with tiered fountain as well as a secluded walled garden with goldfish pool. Each luxurious guest room includes a working fireplace and private bath, whirlpool or claw-foot soaking tub. All rooms are elegantly appointed and offer nightly turndown service as well as 24-hour concierge availability. As an honored guest of The Gastonian, the incredible gourmet breakfast can be delivered to the bedroom on a silver tray. Reflect on the pleasures of the day over afternoon tea or wine with hors d'oeuvres. Each evening, enjoy homemade desserts, coffee and cordials in the candle-lit ambience of the front parlor. The staff is efficient, discreet and attentive.

Our inspector loved: *Taking breakfast in the kitchen with the chef. A real treat!*

Directions: Take I-95 to I-16 east. Exit 167B (Montgomery Street), right on Liberty, right on Bull then left on Gaston. The hotel is at the corner of Gaston and Lincoln.

Web: www.johansens.com/gastonian
E-mail: innkeeper@gastonian.com
Tel: +1 912 232 2869
Fax: +1 912 232 0710
U.S./Canada Toll Free: 1 800 322 6603

Price Guide:
rooms $215-$415

HAWAII

Hotel location shown in red with page number

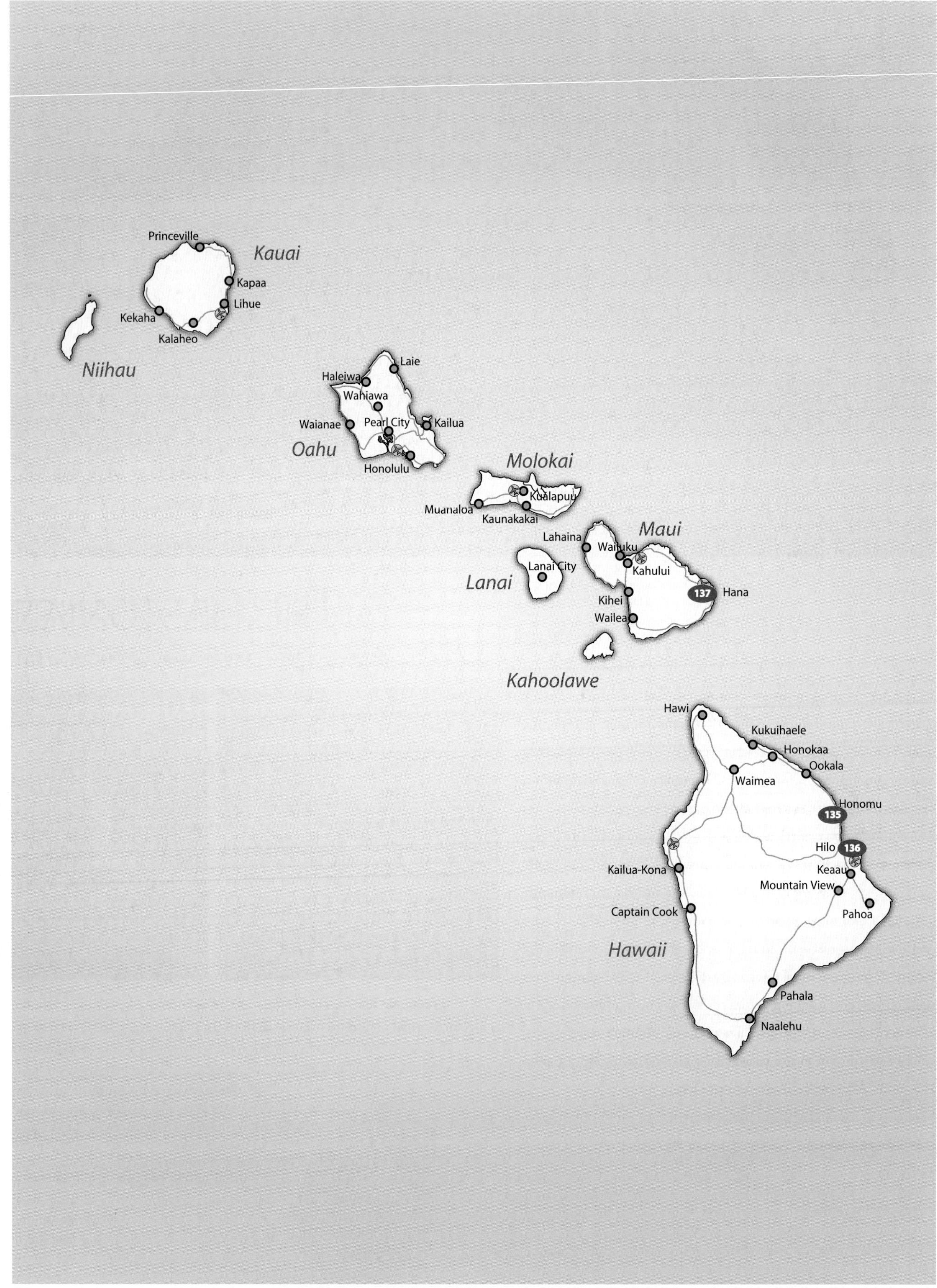

The Palms Cliff House

28-3514 MAMALAHOA HIGHWAY 19, P.O. BOX 189, HONOMU, HAWAII 96728-0189

Perched at cliff's edge 100 feet above the ocean, The Palms Cliff House has the enviable position of being set within acres of its own tranquil estate, yet only a 15-minute drive from the restaurants, museums, and shops of Hilo. Celebrated in song and in hula, the inn has quickly become one of Hawaii's most gracious locations since opening in 2001. Guests will find themselves captivated by the stunning setting of this charming inn where each of the 8 guest suites is carefully decorated in a unique tropical style. The views of the ocean below are truly spectacular, with whales and Spinner dolphins taking their regular morning frolic in the waters of Pohakumanu Bay whilst hovering tropical birds fill the sky. The suites are cool, elegant, and large. The Grande Suites have 2-person sunken Jacuzzis, large seated marble showers and gas fireplaces. The full gourmet breakfasts are exquisite; fresh produce from the fruit and nut orchards bring the tropics to your table. Quiche, crêpes, and omelets are just a few of the delights that will be on offer each morning.

Our inspector loved: *The magnificent views and splendid detail.*

Directions: From Hilo take Highway 19 north to Honomu. After the 13-mile marker turn right at The Palms Cliff House sign.

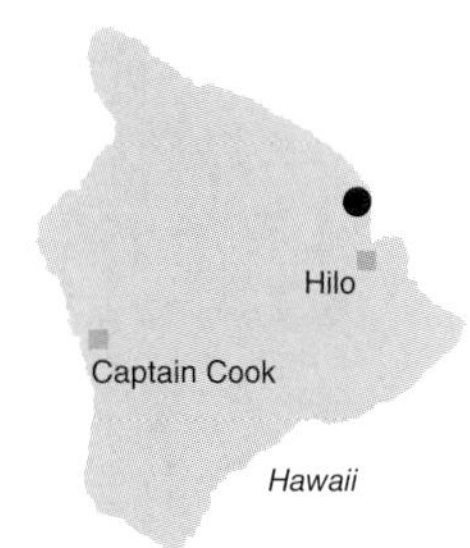

Web: www.johansens.com/palmscliff
E-mail: information@palmscliffhouse.com
Tel: +1 808 963 6076
Fax: +1 808 963 6316
U.S./Canada Toll Free: 1 866 963 6076

Price Guide:
suites $175-$375

Shipman House

131 KA'IULANI STREET, HILO, HAWAII 96720

Built in 1899 and one of the few remaining Victorian mansions on the Island of Hawaii, the Shipman House has been owned by the same family for over 100 years. "Willie" Shipman bought the house for his beloved wife and 7 children, and his great-granddaughter offers guests today the same levels of hospitality that have always been a part of life here. Perched high on a ridge overlooking a deep canyon, the house is surrounded by 5.5 acres of tropical gardens with streams, waterfalls and exotic stands of palm and bamboo. The recently refurbished bedrooms have a distinct air of Hawaiian charm, and are carefully decorated with traditional custom quilts and fabrics. Names such as "Auntie Carrie's Room" and "Flossie's" are a gentle reminder that this really is the family home where Barbara Ann Andersen played as a child. All bathrooms have large bath tubs, custom-made bath accessories and delicate cotton kimonos. Breakfast is served on the lanai, and makes a celebration of local ingredients serving homemade macadamia nut granola, exotic juices, fruit breads and muffins. Self-guided tours of the house are fascinating and the house library and concert grand piano are also available to all guests, for a little light relaxation. WiFi access is available.

Our inspector loved: *The inn's family history, its location in downtown Hilo, and Hawaii's volcanoes and waterfalls.*

Directions: From Highway 19 in Hilo take Waianuenue Avenue. Take the fifth right turning into Kaiulani Street. The hotel is right across the bridge.

Web: www.johansens.com/shipman
E-mail: innkeeper@hilo-hawaii.com
Tel: +1 808 934 8002
Fax: +1 808 934 8002
U.S./Canada Toll Free: 1 800 627 8447

Price Guide: (excluding tax)
rooms $209-$229

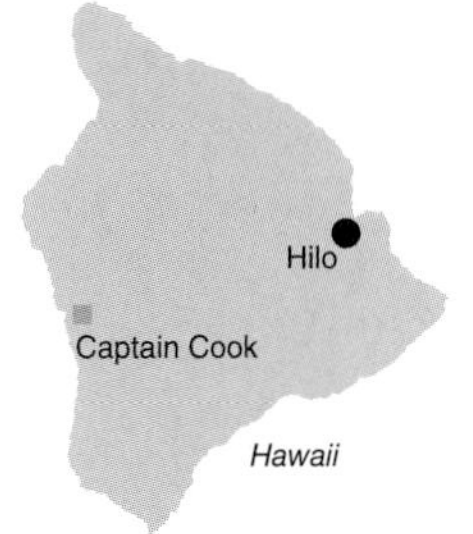

Hotel Hana-Maui and Honua Spa

5031 Hana Highway, Hana, Maui, Hawaii 96713

If splendid seclusion is your desire, Hotel Hana-Maui is your destination. Winner of the Condé Nast Johansens Most Excellent Spa Hotel 2006, this plantation-style resort of understated elegance reflects hospitality as pervasive as the surrounding dramatic vistas. The storied town of Hána is separated from the rest of civilization by a 2-hour drive. The winding road is breathtaking, with cascading waterfalls, bountiful fruit trees and banks of wild ginger. It is a small wonder Hána-Maui is a historic hideaway for the rich-and-famous. Luxury accommodations in the AAA 4-Diamond resort include bungalow-style Bay Cottage suites with patios and Sea Ranch cottages with dramatic ocean and mountain views. All have huge tiled baths with private pocket gardens. Small touches such as welcome baskets in each room and furniture made from recycled wood from Chinese rickshaws give a casually elegant ambience. Enjoy the ultimate in nurturing at the Honua Spa, where an extensive treatment menu emphasizes traditional healing and native plants. Resort activities abound, such as horseback riding, yoga, tennis and hiking. Cultural workshops acquaint guests with the art of lei making and hula dancing. Tantalizing cuisine is served with innovative flair.

Our inspector loved: *The view from the watsu pool, and the natural spacious grandeur of the resort.*

Directions: Hana Airport is 3 miles from the hotel. Alternatively fly to Kahului Airport and take the famous scenic drive along the Hana Highway.

Molokai
Kaunakakai
Kahului
Maui

Web: www.johansens.com/hanamaui
E-mail: reservations@hotelhanamaui.com
Tel: +1 808 248 8211
Fax: +1 808 248 7202
U.S./Canada Toll Free: 1 800 321 HANA

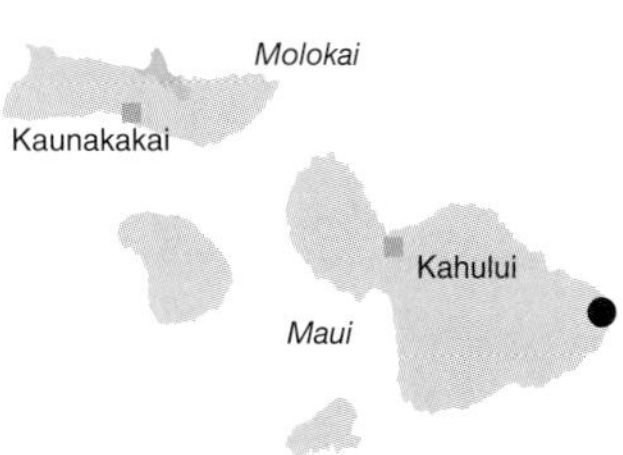

Price Guide: (room only)
rooms $475-$4,500

IDAHO

Hotel location shown in red with page number

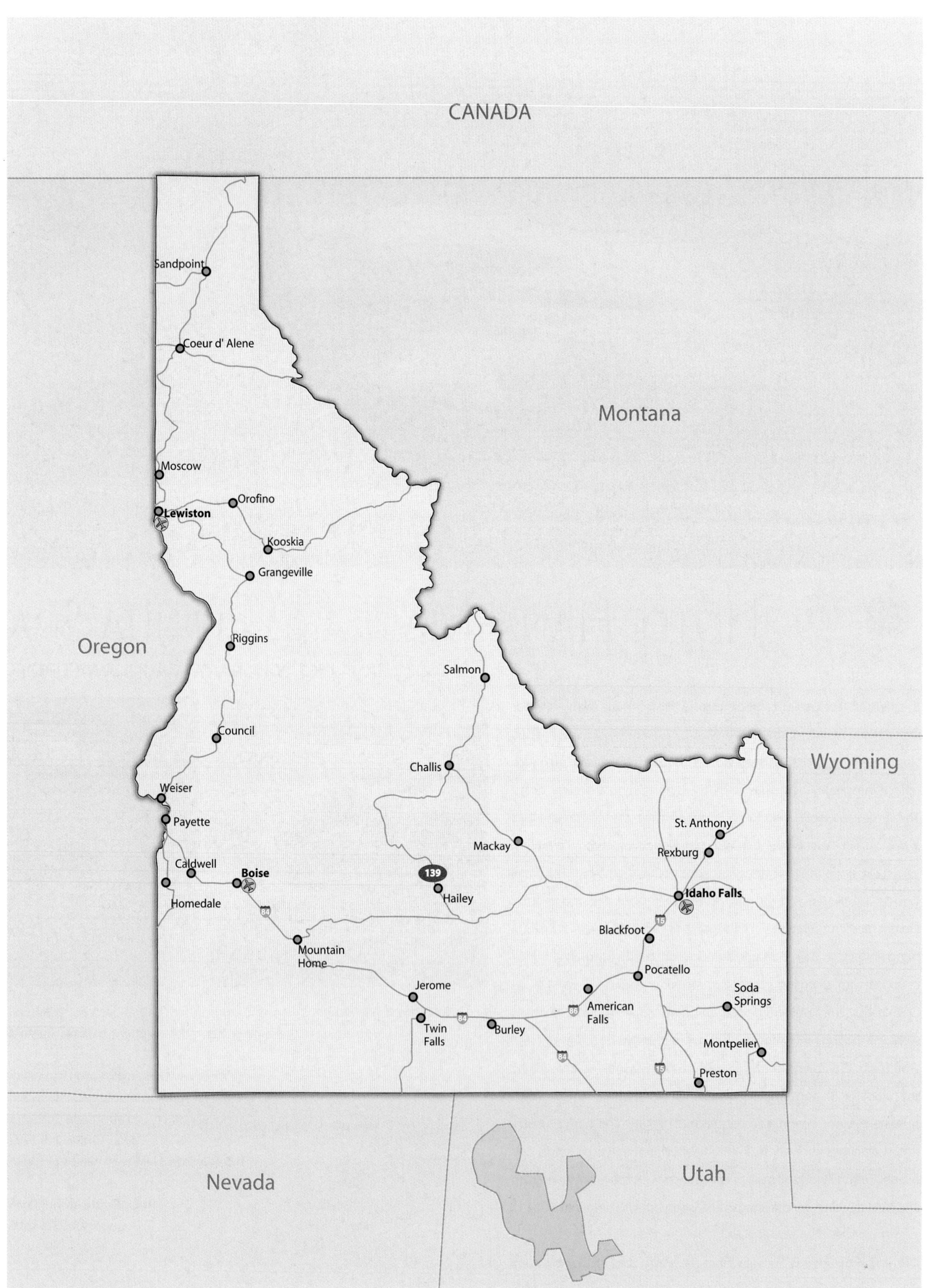

Knob Hill Inn

960 NORTH MAIN STREET, P.O. BOX 800, KETCHUM, IDAHO 83340

Knob Hill Inn is an Austrian-style inn set in the heart of Hemingway country in Ketchum, Idaho. This 26-room bed and breakfast is centrally located and ideal for guests who enjoy both winter skiing at Sun Valley or summer-type activities. The inn is located in America's first destination ski resort with views of the world-famous Bald Mountain, the majestic Sawtooths and the Boulder Mountain ranges. Most of the charming rooms have fireplaces, dressing rooms, marble bathrooms with oversized tub and separate shower. In addition, each room has glass doors that open onto a balcony with breathtaking views of the spectacular mountain peaks. A cozy and warming fireplace is central in the lobby. Each morning, guests are treated to a buffet of fresh pastries, breads and muffins and daily entrees to order, while each afternoon, Knob Hill Café offers Austrian-style Konditorei, which includes espresso and pastries, a glass of wine or cup of tea. Other amenities include landscaped gardens, an exercise room, ski and golf storage, indoor/outdoor swimming pool, sauna and a small group meeting facility. High-speed wireless Internet access is available at no charge. Guests can also partake in mountain biking, horse riding, hunting, fishing, canoeing, rafting and skiing. The inn is within walking distance of downtown Ketchum and close to all amenities at Sun Valley.

Directions: From Hailey Airport the hotel is 12 miles north on Highway 75, 2 blocks after the Warm Springs turn off on the right.

Lewiston
Boise
Idaho Falls

Web: www.johansens.com/knobhillinn
E-mail: khi@knobhillinn.com
Tel: +1 208 726 8010
Fax: +1 208 726 2712
U.S./Canada Toll Free: 1 800 526 8010

Price Guide:
rooms $250-$325
suites $400-$500

Our inspector loved: *The breathtaking mountain views.*

Kansas

Hotel location shown in red with page number

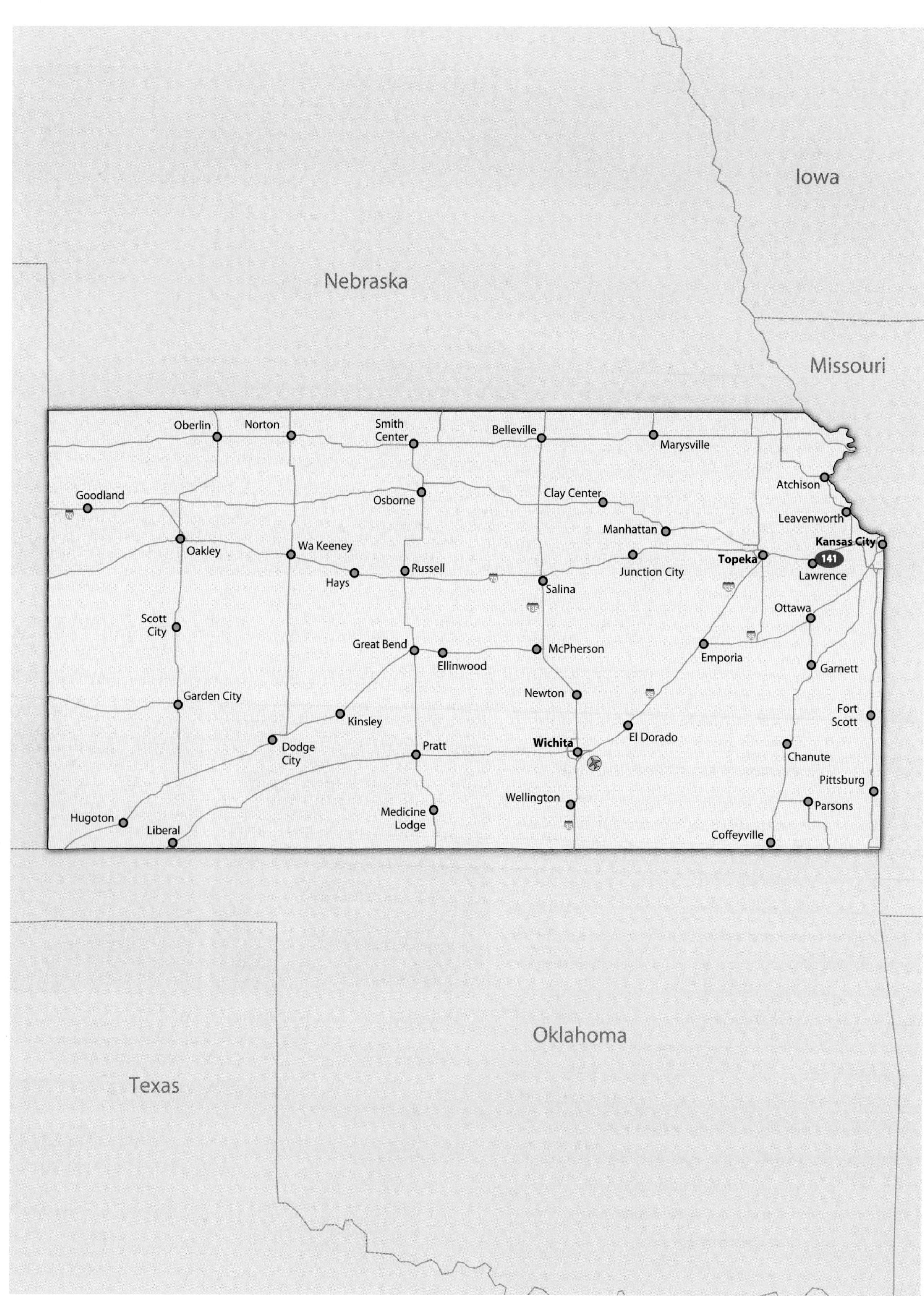

The Eldridge Hotel

701 MASSACHUSETTS, LAWRENCE, KANSAS 66044

As a member of Historic Hotels of America and on the National Register of Historic Places, The Eldridge Hotel was originally built as temporary quarters for settlers who came to Kansas from Boston and other areas in the early 1800s, and initially named the Free State Hotel to emphasize that Kansas should come into the Union as a free state. Over the years it was rebuilt as The Hotel Eldridge, which stood until 1925. Since then, it has been restored to its grandeur and is now a 48-room luxury boutique hotel. Combining history with hospitality, the original Victorian style has been updated with black leather chairs, hardwood furnishings along with black and white photographs for a contemporary feel. Suites are spacious with beautiful furnishings , cozy living areas with sofa beds and modern amenities including wireless Internet, refrigerator and pod coffee makers. The Honeymoon Suite is perfect for a weekend getaway or romantic escape, has a flat-screen L.C.D. television and a luxurious two-person shower. TEN offers casual and hearty fare as well as a sumptuous Sunday brunch and The Jayhawker Bar, popular for its jazz nights, has an open layout with a beautiful granite bar and extensive wine list. The hotel is centrally located in Lawrence's historic downtown area surrounded by an array of shops, galleries, dining and entertainment venues.

Our inspector loved: *The history: preserved with integrity and care.*

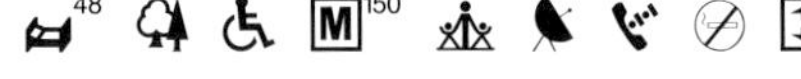

Directions: Take exit 204 off of I-70. Turn south onto U.S.40/North 3rd Street, which becomes Massachusetts Street. The Eldridge Hotel is located on the southwest corner of Massachusetts and 7th Street. 1 hour from Kansas City International Airport (MCI).

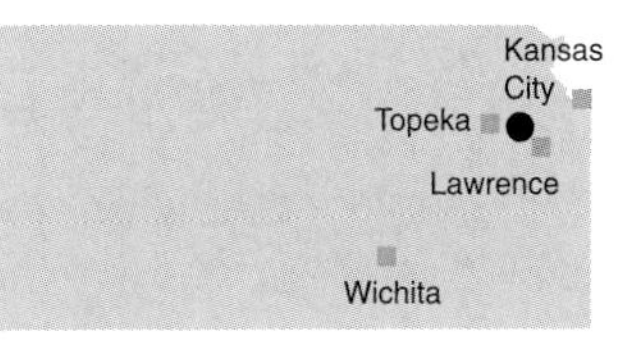

Web: www.johansens.com/eldridge
E-mail: info@eldridgehotel.com
Tel: +1 785 749 5011
Fax: +1 785 749 4512
U.S./Canada Toll Free: 1 800 527 0909

Price Guide: (room only)
suites $149-$295

Louisiana

Hotel location shown in red with page number

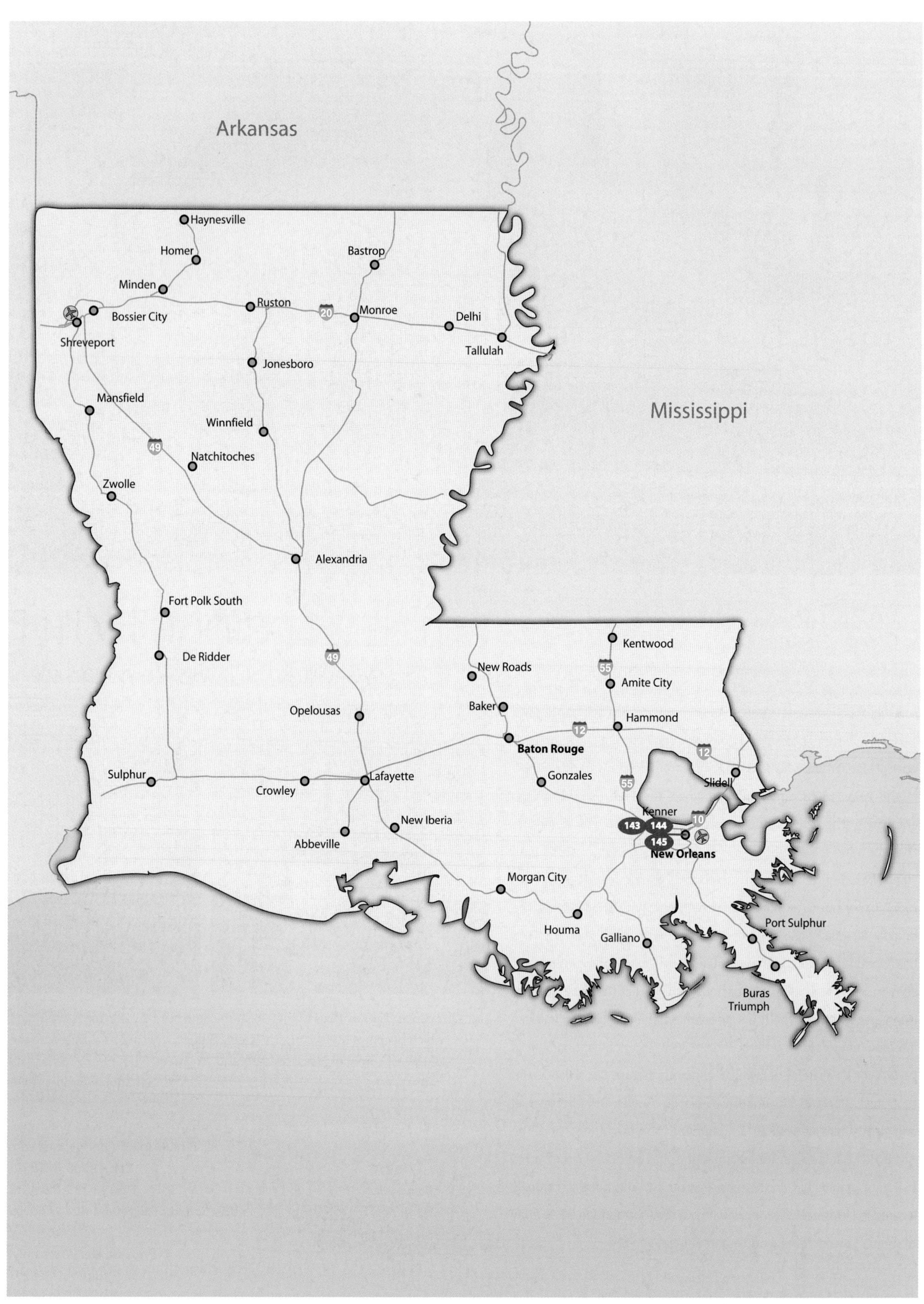

Hotel Maison de Ville

727 RUE TOULOUSE, NEW ORLEANS, LOUISIANA 70130

Situated in the heart of the Vieux Carre, the French Quarter that so typifies New Orleans, is this wonderfully preserved and charming building. Its character is totally of the period when New Orleans was a French colony and America still a British colony, with high elegant ceilings and pretty ensconced courtyards. The bedrooms, recently carefully refurbished, can be found either in the main building or within the Audubon Cottages, so named after the naturalist John James Audubon, who created many of his masterpieces here. Each has its own unique charm and style and in both the main house and the cottages the utmost care has been taken to restore everything to historical accuracy. Original paintings, antiques and individual décor feature in all of the bedrooms and the twice-daily housekeeping service ensures an unflinching attention to detail. The Bistro Restaurant enjoys a wide reputation for its innovative cuisine and unpretentious atmosphere and has been included in Condé Nast's Top 100 Restaurants. The heart of New Orleans remains just outside the front door and has a relaxed and infectious ambience. There are numerous antique stores to visit, as well as wonderful restaurants exuding the buzz and attractions of the sidewalk.

Our inspector loved: *This carefully preserved jewel in the heart of the French Quarter.*

Directions: From I-10, eastbound towards the central business district, take Orleans Avenue exit. Turn left at the traffic lights and make a u-turn at the "N. Rampart via Toulouse Street and French Quarter" sign. Cross over N. Rampart onto Toulouse Street then cross over Bourbon Street. The hotel is on the left. The nearest airport is Louis Armstrong Intl.

Shreveport
Baton Rouge
New Orleans

Web: www.johansens.com/maisondeville
E-mail: courtney.abercrombie@ihrco.com
Tel: +1 504 561 5858
Fax: +1 504 528 9939
U.S./Canada Toll Free: 1 800 634 1600

Price Guide: rooms $249–$399
cottages $279–$699

The Lafayette Hotel

600 ST. CHARLES AVENUE, NEW ORLEANS, LOUISIANA 70130

Directions: Take Poydras Street or Superdome exit from I-10. Take Poydras Street past the Superdome to St. Charles Avenue. Turn right and the hotel is on the left.

Web: www.johansens.com/lafayette
E-mail: reservations@neworleansfinehotels.com
Tel: +1 504 524 4441
Fax: +1 504 962 5537
U.S./Canada Toll Free: 1 800 272 4583

Price Guide: (room only)
rooms $159-$499
suites $229-$799

This stately and refined hotel lies on the St. Charles streetcar line in the center of the city and possesses the ambience of a historic gentleman's club. A recent cosmetic renovation has resulted in luxurious carpets and new paintwork throughout, as well as the addition of a tea room. Old World furnishings are complemented by elegant drapes and the trademarks of the building's heritage are now lovingly restored to their former glory. The original French doors and wrought iron balconies are now as beautiful as they were in their heyday and magnificent four-poster beds, relaxing ottomans and plush easy chairs are very much in evidence. Each bedroom and suite is individually decorated and filled with thoughtful touches such as French-milled soaps and thick Terry bathrobes; suites feature wet bars, refrigerators and V.C.R.s and some have whirlpool baths. Enjoy gourmet cuisine in the hotel restaurant before exploring the surrounding area: in a superb location, the Central Business District, the hotel is a convenient base from which to discover the French Quarter, Superdrome, riverfront and the uptown garden district's mansions and shopping.

Our inspector loved: *The lovely foyer; feels like stepping back in time to the roaring 1920s.*

The St. James Hotel

330 Magazine Street, New Orleans, Louisiana 70130

In-keeping with the period when New Orleans was a colony of France, charm and elegance are the hallmarks of this downtown boutique hotel located in the Banks Arcade, a 19th-century landmark once the center of the Caribbean sugar and coffee trade. The hotel is just a few blocks from where it first opened its doors to guests in the mid-1800s, and is within easy walking distance of the French Quarter famed for its antique and specialty shops, the Superdome and Convention Center. It has spacious, comfortable rooms, a host of original features and 2 pretty courtyards. Complete restoration has reintroduced an attractive New Orleans' Creole-Caribbean influence in each of the guest rooms in order to celebrate the area's connection with exquisite West Indies décor. All rooms offer special touches such as marble bathrooms, goosedown feather beds, a coffee maker, 3 telephones, voicemail and Internet access. Residents can enjoy dining in the highly acclaimed, informal Cuvee Restaurant, which specializes in innovative, Nouveau Orleans gourmet cuisine attractively presented and attentively served. Alternatively, there are a variety of excellent restaurants in the neighborhood. For outdoor relaxation there is a lounging pool in a lush courtyard setting surrounded by rooftop terraces. Business facilities include a high-tech, flexible conference room.

Our inspector loved: *The hidden courtyards including one with a playpool.*

Directions: From Louis Armstrong Intl. Airport take I-10 east towards New Orleans then take exit 234B on the left toward Poydras Street/Superdome. Go straight ahead onto Poydas then left onto Camp Street. Turn right onto Gravier Street then right onto Magazine Street. The hotel is on the left.

Shreveport
Baton Rouge
New Orleans

Web: www.johansens.com/stjamesno
E-mail: reservations@neworleansfinehotels.com
Tel: +1 504 304 4000
Fax: +1 504 304 4444
U.S./Canada Toll Free: 1 800 272 4583

Price Guide: (room only)
rooms $149-$350
suites $179-$500

Maine

Hotel location shown in red with page number

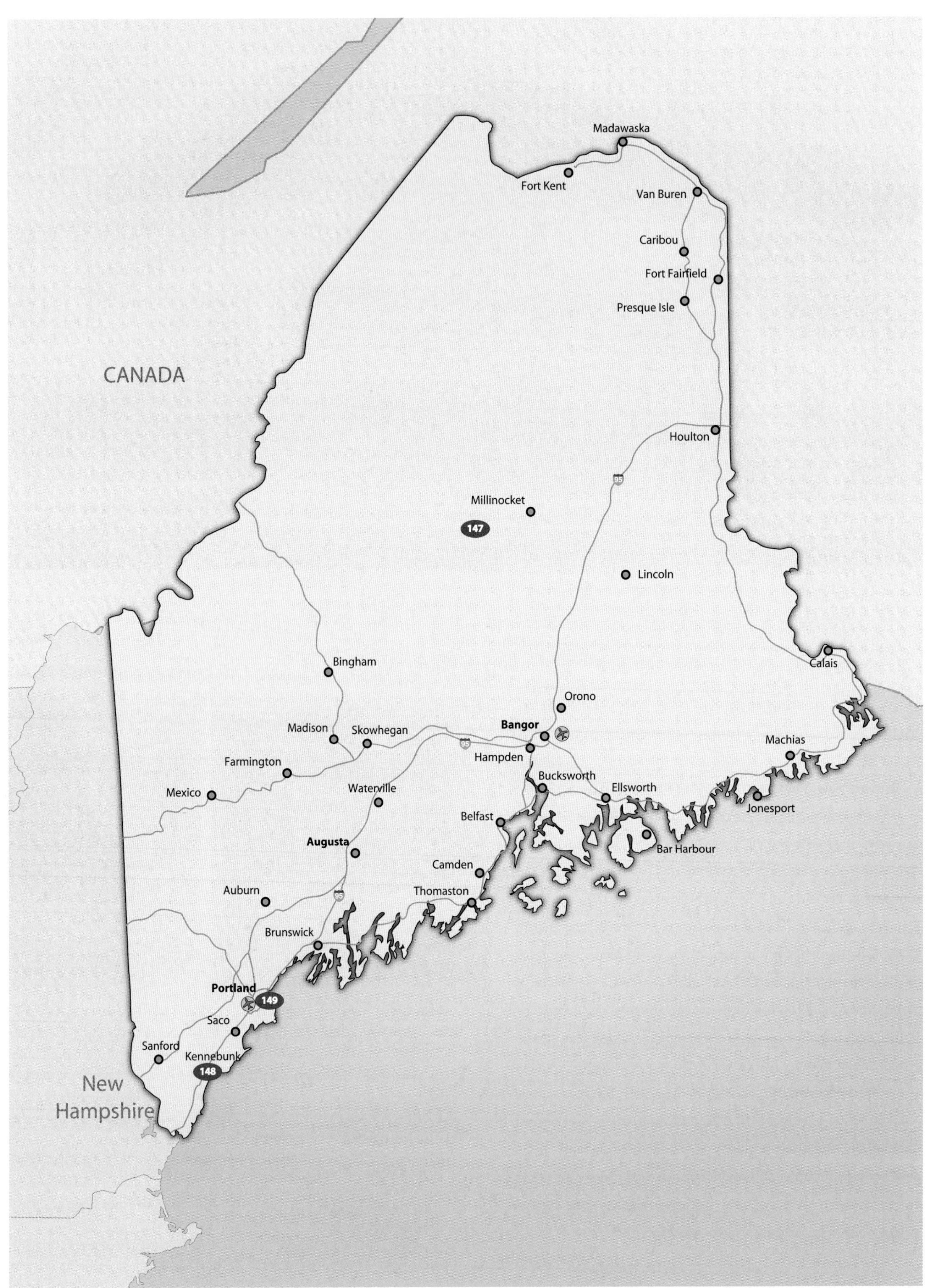

The Lodge At Moosehead Lake

LILY BAY ROAD, P.O. BOX 1167, GREENVILLE, MAINE 04441

In the small town of Greenville, within the northern reaches of Maine, The Lodge at Moosehead Lake can be found on a 40-mile lake. Perched gracefully atop a rise on 7 manicured acres with beautifully landscaped gardens and overlooking the broad waters of Moosehead Lake, with direct access to its shores, this award-winning inn with spectacular lake views, sensational sunsets, peaceful atmosphere, warm hospitality and pampered service, is the ideal retreat. This exquisite and stately Colonial property was built in 1917 and abounds with elegance, sophistication and comfort. Revel in the ever-changing vista across Moosehead Lake that is both stunning by day and magical by moonlight. This ultra private lodge is filled with unique imports, rich custom designer fabrics and bespoke furnishings. Meticulous in every conceivable detail, this luxury inn is a timeless masterpiece that captures the very essence of Maine. Every effort has been taken to provide guests with the optimum of luxury and comfort. The Lakeview Dining Room is simply magical in an enchanting setting. During your visit experience a privately guided moose safari or fly-fishing on a mountain stream. 2004 Grand Award Winner in the Andrew Harper's Hideaway Report Listing to the World's Top 24 Captivating Hideaway Hotels and Resorts, and inland Maine's only AAA 4 Diamond lodging establishment.

Our inspector loved: *The unique lake view location, and charming hosts.*

Directions: Take I-95 north to Newport then Route 7 north, then Route 23 north to Route 15 north.

Presque Isle
Augusta
Portland

Web: www.johansens.com/lodgeatmooseheadlake
E-mail: innkeeper@lodgeatmooseheadlake.com
Tel: +1 207 695 4400
Fax: +1 207 695 2281
U.S./Canada Toll Free: 1 800 825 6977

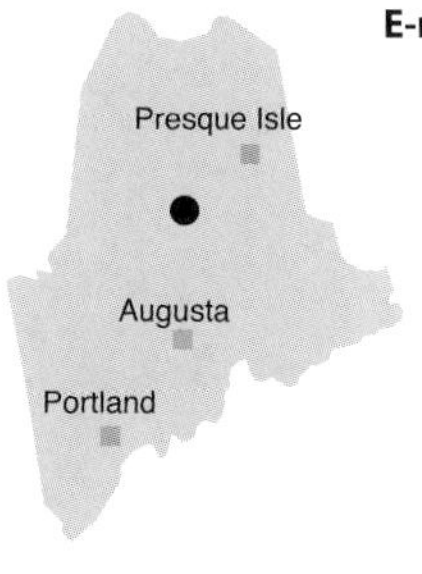

Price Guide:
rooms $205–$375
suites $350–$475

The White Barn Inn

37 BEACH AVENUE, KENNEBUNKPORT, MAINE 04043

Since welcoming its first travelers in the 1800s, the award-winning White Barn Inn has earned an envious reputation for a wonderfully relaxing atmosphere, charm, luxury, attentive service and superb cuisine. The restaurant, set in 2 restored barns dating from the 1860s, is one of only 3 in New England that has received the AAA 5-Diamond Award and now also boasts a Mobil 5 Star rating. Ranked among the Top 25 North American Small Hotels, the inn is situated within close proximity of Kennebunkport's multitude of fine shops, art galleries and attractions that include former President Bush's summer home overlooking the Atlantic Ocean at Walker's Point. Kennebunk beach is ¼-mile walk from the more secluded Parsons beach and Goose Rocks beach. The interior is beautifully decorated and furnished; guest rooms are the epitome of luxury and comfort. Each has every amenity from flatscreen plasma T.V.s to voice mail and fresh flowers. Some have a fireplace, steam shower, whirlpool bath and private deck looking out to manicured grounds. There are also fully-equipped waterfront cottages close by with private marina clubhouse alongside the inn's 44-ft. Hinkley Talaria jet cruiser, which can be chartered for coastal tours. Guests may enjoy the outdoor heated pool, canoeing, cycling and full service spa with treatment suites, skin services, Kohler sok tub and swiss shower.

Our inspector loved: *The Hinckley Talaria available for private charter.*

Directions: 62 miles from Boston Airport. 19 miles from Portland Airport. Take I-95 north to Maine turnpike then Route 35 to Kennebunkport.

Web: www.johansens.com/whitebarninn
E-mail: innkeeper@thewhitebarninn.com
Tel: +1 207 967 2321
Fax: +1 207 967 1100

Price Guide:
rooms $345-$565
suites $620-$850
waterfront cottages $620-$1,290

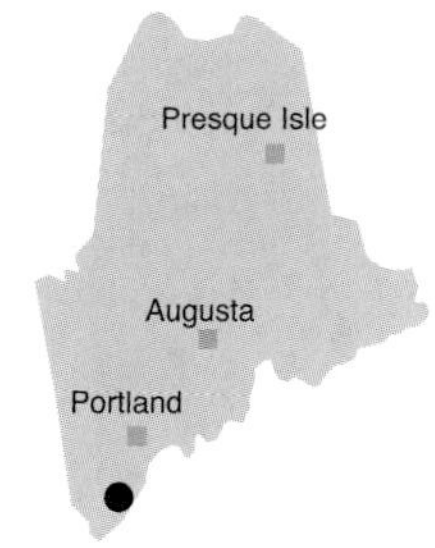

Portland Harbor Hotel

468 FORE STREET, PORTLAND, MAINE 04101

Experience Old World charm and exceptional service at Portland's only AAA 4 Diamond rated hotel. Located in the heart of the Old Port, Portland Harbor Hotel is just 1 block from the Portland waterfront, one of America's 60 Best Public Places. Enjoy views of the city skyline or the hotel's lush garden from the well-appointed guest rooms. Each room is distinctive with custom-made his and her armoires. Luxury bathrooms include granite surround and an enclosed shower or soaking tub. Pampering touches such as high-thread count bed linens, feather pillows and comforters, and plush towels and robes make each room a retreat, while attentive service from the professionally certified concierge assures each guest's stay is delightfully memorable. Lovingly restored shops and restaurants reflect the charm of the Old Port Victorian district, within easy walking distance from the hotel. Portland's vibrant waterfront is a must-see, with cobblestone streets, historic landmarks and full-service marinas on both sides of the harbor. Reflect on the day's experiences over a candle-lit dinner at the award-winning Eve's restaurant overlooking the hotel garden.

Our inspector loved: *The downtown location, close to the harbor, quaint shops and cobbled streets.*

Directions: The hotel is 10 minutes from Portland International Airport.

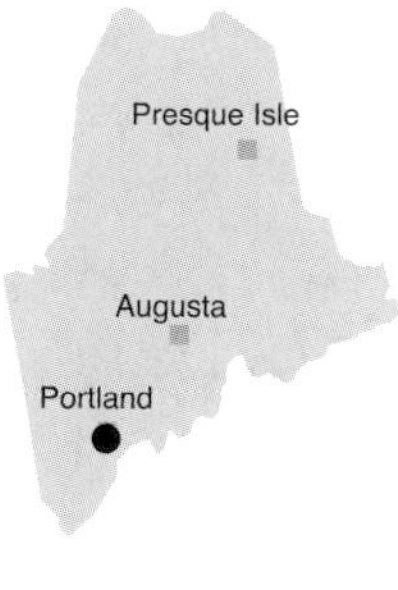

Presque Isle
Augusta
Portland

Web: www.johansens.com/portlandharbor
E-mail: vip@harthotels.com
Tel: +1 207 775 9090
Fax: +1 207 775 9990
U.S./Canada Toll Free: 1 888 798 9090

Price Guide: (room only)
rooms $199-$299
suites $279-$379

      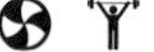

MARYLAND

Hotel location shown in red with page number

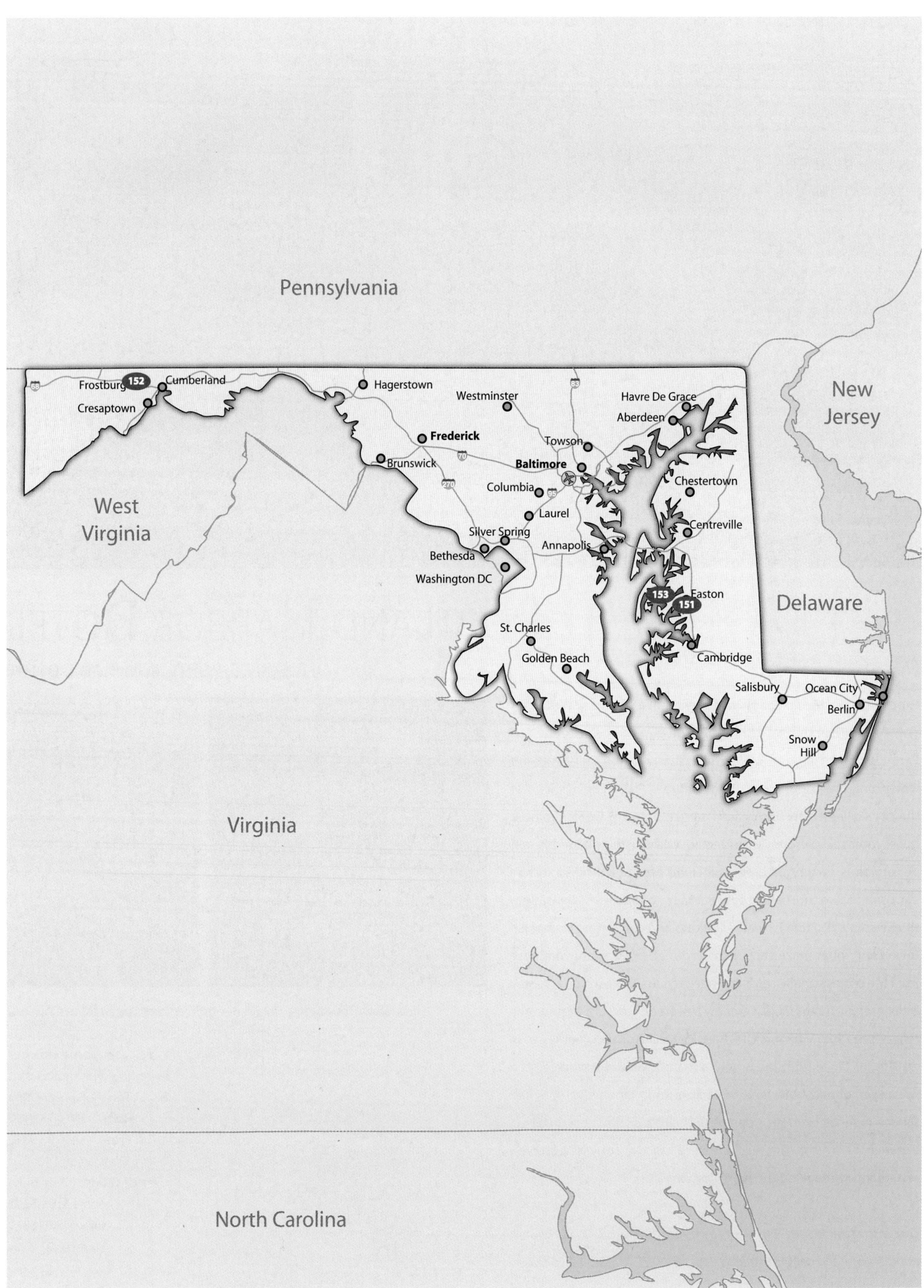

Inn at 202 Dover

202 E. Dover Street, Easton, Maryland 21601

Immerse yourself in elegance in this circa 1874 inn that has recently been carefully restored to its original grandeur. It is a shining example of Colonial-Revival architecture and features five luxury accommodations, including four elegant suites and an ensuite Victorian guest room. The owners created a one-of-a-kind look that is elegant and welcoming. Guest quarters have been carefully decorated with antiques and authentic reproduction, and feature fine linens, beautiful fabrics, and special touches from the owners' own collection. Modern conveniences include state-of-the-art air-jet tubs, steam showers and an elevator. The dining room serves a full gourmet breakfast daily. The gardens, designed by N.Y.C. landscape architect Eileen Imber feature a park-like setting and include a cutting garden, a potager, a pergola and other outdoor gathering areas, perfect for entertaining or quiet reflection. Situated one block from historic downtown Easton, the inn is a short walk to boutiques, art galleries, restaurants, museums, and the Avalon Theater. The quaint waterfront town of St. Michaels as well as the Chesapeake Bay and its tributaries - unparalleled for sailing, canoeing, kayaking and fishing - are only minutes away.

Our inspector loved: *Looking up at the stars through the domed ceiling of the conservatory.*

Directions: $1\frac{1}{2}$ hours from both Reagan National Airport and Baltimore-Washington Airport. A 2-hour drive from Philadelphia and 3 hours from N.Y.C.

Web: www.johansens.com/innat202dover
E-mail: info@innat202dover.com
Tel: +1 410 819 8007
Fax: +1 410 819 3368
U.S./Canada Toll Free: 1 866 450 7600

Price Guide:
rooms $375-$400
suites $425-$475

Savage River Lodge

1600 MT. AETNA ROAD, FROSTBURG, MARYLAND 21532

Directions: Take I-68 to Finzel and exit 29 south at Beall School Road. Travel 1 mile to the T-intersection then turn right. The lodge is then signposted.

Web: www.johansens.com/savageriver
E-mail: info@savageriverlodge.com
Tel: +1 301 689 3200
Fax: +1 301 689 2746

Price Guide: (room only)
rooms $190-$210

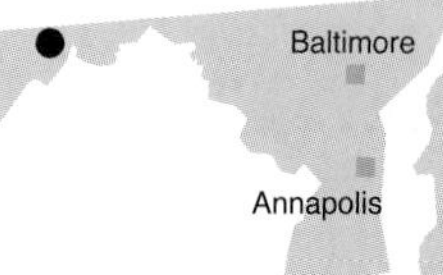

Rustic lodge, log cabins, luxurious comfort, porches with rocking chairs, gourmet dining, excellent service, on a mountain side encircled by 700 acres of forest teeming with grouse, wild turkey, white tailed deer, beaver and black bear - if that is what you want from a vacation then this is it. To relax in supreme comfort and enjoy, or action pack every day and enjoy! Nestling in 42 private acres, Savage River Lodge offers a unique opportunity to retreat and revel in the abundance that nature provides, claim owners Jan Russell and Mike Dreisbach. Scattered along a tree-lined road are 18 cabins with every solace from overstuffed furniture to down comforters on queen-size beds, to gas fireplaces and oversized soaking tubs. Telephone but no television. The lodge itself is for relaxing with friends, or a place in which to just curl up by the fire or window with a book. Dining is casual with an open view into the kitchen. Continental breakfast is delivered to cabins in a picnic basket. The main emphasis is on the outdoors with every activity available to guests nearby, from fishing, canoeing, kayaking and white water rafting to skiing, riding, clay shooting, mountain biking and golf.

***Our inspector loved:** The privacy of the luxurious cabins, the excellent cuisine, and extensive list of outdoor activities to choose from.*

Five Gables Inn & Spa

209 North Talbot Street, St. Michaels, Maryland 21663

Set in a picturesque village near the Chesapeake Bay, Five Gables Inn & Spa has 20 beautiful rooms located in 4 carefully renovated 19th-century homes. The Inn's charming setting is ideal for a weekend getaway or romantic escape. The main building features 8 well-appointed guest rooms. Directly across the street is the original inn where 2 historic homes were joined together and comprise 6 rooms and suites. The Green House opened this year and has 5 suites and 1 guest room. Many of the original details from 1860 remain. All rooms have cozy down duvets, luxury linens, private baths with whirlpool tubs, Aveda bath amenities, seasonal gas log fireplaces, air conditioning, cable T.V. with V.C.R. and C.D. players, and many feature porches. The Inn provides a splendid Continental breakfast as well as afternoon refreshments. Guests may relax the mind, body and spirit at the spa, which offers an array of treatments including body wraps, hot-stone massage and Aveda facials. The Inn is only a 40-minute drive from the famous Chesapeake Bay Bridge. In St. Michaels, guests can enjoy fresh local blue crab at one of the waterfront crab houses or browse the charming boutiques and antique shops.

Our inspector loved: *The lovely use of color throughout the inn.*

Directions: 2 hours by car from Baltimore, Washington D.C. or Philadelphia.

Web: www.johansens.com/fivegables
E-mail: info@fivegables.com
Tel: +1 410 745 0100
Fax: +1 410 745 2903
U.S./Canada Toll Free: 1 877 466 0100

Price Guide: (excluding tax)
rooms $150-$335
suites $275-$425

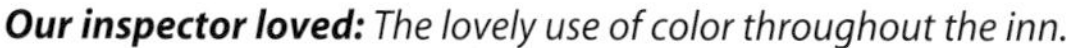

Massachusetts

Hotel location shown in red with page number

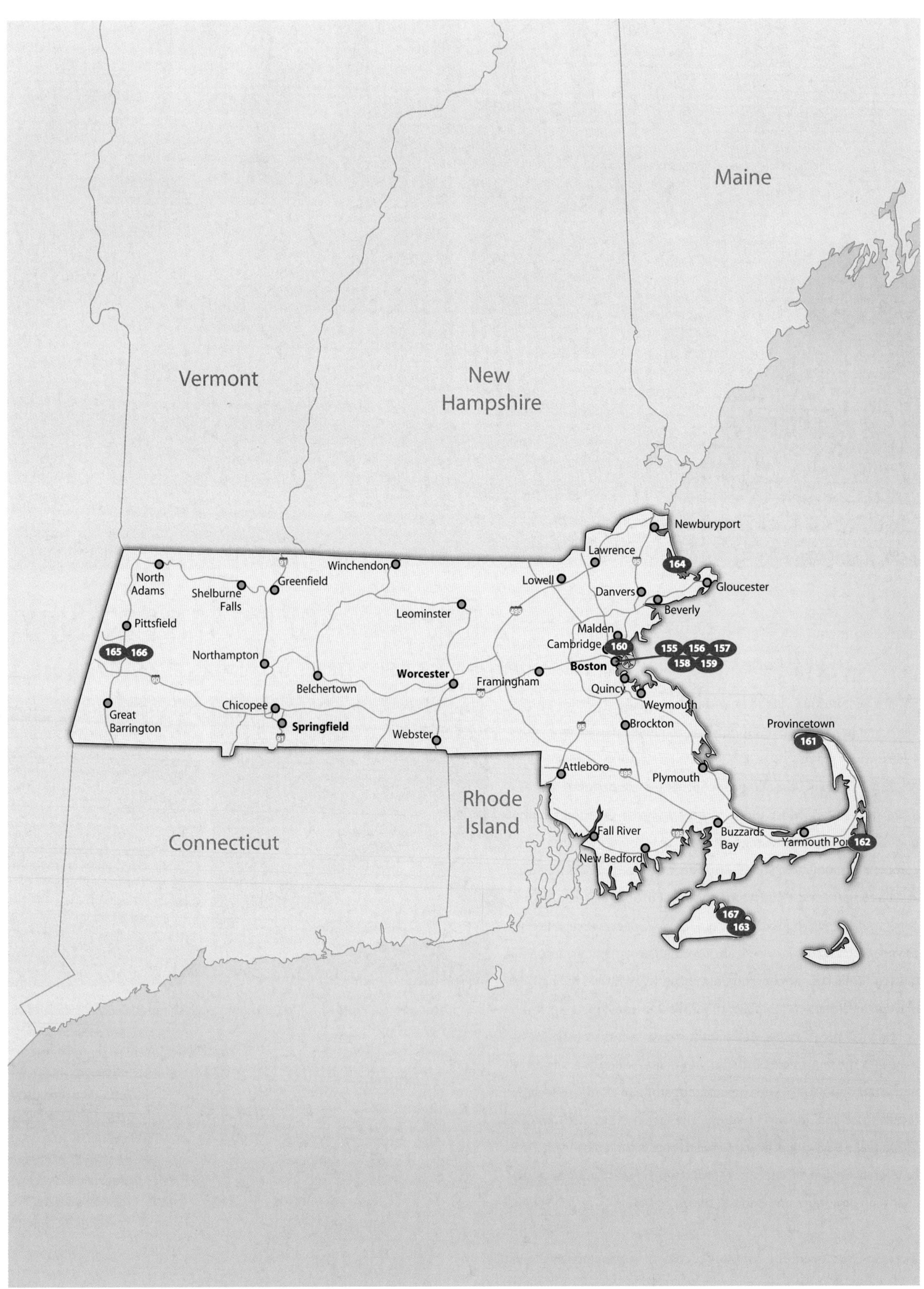

The Charles Street Inn

94 Charles Street, Boston, Massachusetts 02114

This charming European-style luxury inn is conveniently situated in the heart of Boston's Beacon Hill, only a few short blocks from the Boston Public Garden. The elegant brownstone façade features small, decorative windows and 2 beautiful overhanging bedroom bow windows. Originally built in 1860 as a model home, the inn has been extensively renovated to preserve and enhance its original style alongside the best in 20th-century facilities and amenities. The 9 beautifully inspired and distinct guest rooms are decorated in exquisite Victorian style, and are named after famous Boston writers or artists. The rooms have romantic king or queen-size four-poster or canopy beds, Frette linens, authentic period pieces, original working 1860 fireplace with complimentary fire logs, Turkish carpets, a chenille throw, European antique armoires, lamps and chairs as well as other luxurious textiles. Each room has a deluxe private bathroom with air-jet whirlpool tub, kitchenette with sub-zero refrigerator, 2-line phone with voice mail, fax, D.S.L. wireless Internet access, Bose C.D./radio, cable T.V., V.C.R., D.V.D. player, safe, minibar and coffeemaker. The romantic Elegant Seduction Package includes chocolate covered strawberries, chilled champagne and fresh flowers. Owners Sally Deane and Louise Venden provide warm and personalized service and serve an excellent breakfast.

Directions: Leave I-93 at Storrow Drive exit and follow signs to Charles Street/Government Center.

Web: www.johansens.com/charlesstreetinn
E-mail: info@charlesstreetinn.com
Tel: +1 617 314 8900
Fax: +1 617 371 0009
U.S./Canada Toll Free: 1 877 772 8900

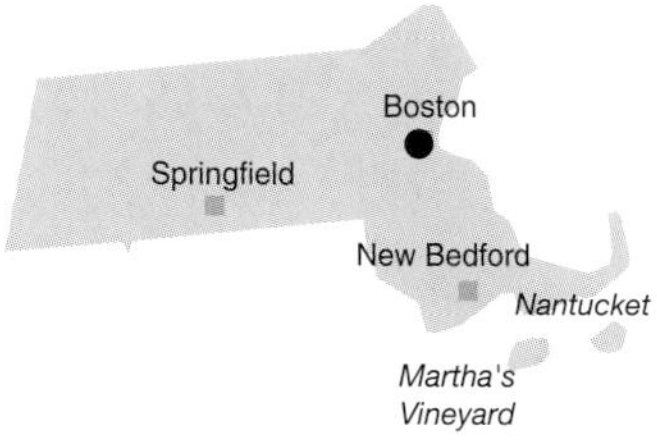

Boston
Springfield
New Bedford
Nantucket
Martha's Vineyard

Price Guide:
rooms $225-$525

Our inspector loved: *The spacious bathrooms with whirlpool tubs.*

Clarendon Square Inn

198 WEST BROOKLINE STREET, BOSTON, MASSACHUSETTS 02118

Stylish, comfortable and quaint, the ultra-chic, 3-bedroom Clarendon Square Inn is located in Boston's popular South End in an elegant and quiet district lined with 19th-century townhouses. The charming hosts provide the warmest of welcomes at this recently restored 1850's merchant home, which incorporates many of the traditional brownstone features with modern touches to create an interior décor focused on style and sophistication. With all the amenities of a luxury hotel, this boutique inn boasts rich architecture, ultra-hip design and great attention to detail. Luxurious and spacious guest rooms are located on private floors and have attractive queen-size beds, fine soaps and linens and lavishly restored interior finishes. For additional relaxation, guests can soak in the inn's rooftop hot tub with an unusual view of the Boston skyline. There is also a beautiful and unique koi and goldfish pond in the Japanese water garden. A sumptuous continental breakfast is served in the elegant dining room each morning and is a perfect way to start the day before exploring all that Boston has to offer. Clarendon Square Inn is conveniently located a few minutes' walk from Copley Square, the fashionable Newbury Street shopping and the Boston Common. The inn is also close to the city's subway.

Our inspector loved: *The stylish décor including Morano glass lighting.*

Directions: Located in Boston's South End, a 15-minute drive from Logan International Airport in South End.

Web: www.johansens.com/clarendonsquare
E-mail: stay@clarendonsquare.com
Tel: +1 617 536 2229
Fax: +1 617 536 2993 ext. 3

Price Guide:
rooms $125-$445

Hotel Commonwealth

500 COMMONWEALTH AVENUE, BOSTON, MASSACHUSETTS 02215

Hotel Commonwealth, located on historic Commonwealth Avenue in Boston, fuses traditional and modern styles. Completed in 2003, the exterior blends into the Federalist, Victorian and neo-classical architectural designs of the Avenue, whilst inside a beautiful staircase leads into a vibrant lobby with rich colors, grand floral designs and eclectic furnishings. Each of the 150 bedrooms is a generous size and elegantly decorated: frette bed linens, yellow washed walls and custom furnishings complement the oversized writing desks, high-speed Internet access and wireless telephones for business guests, and a complimentary library of classic films on DVD provides unusual in-room entertainment. Great Bay, the hotel's signature restaurant, offers a fresh approach to the locally caught seafood, and is created by an award-winning team. Alternatively, the recently opened Eastern Standard, provides outdoor dining within the heart of Kenmore Square; the perfect location for people watching. Not only is the hotel close to Boston's most vibrant nightlife, it is just minutes from the Museum of Fine Arts, Boston University, the Back Bay and the Charles River Esplanade.

Our inspector loved: *Late night dining and music at the new Foundation Lounge.*

Directions: From Logan Airport take Route 1-A through the Sumner Tunnel then follow signs onto Expressway North. Take the Back Bay/Storrow Drive exit and follow signs onto Storrow Drive, exit at Kenmore. At the first set of lights turn right. At the second set of lights make a u-turn. The hotel is on the right.

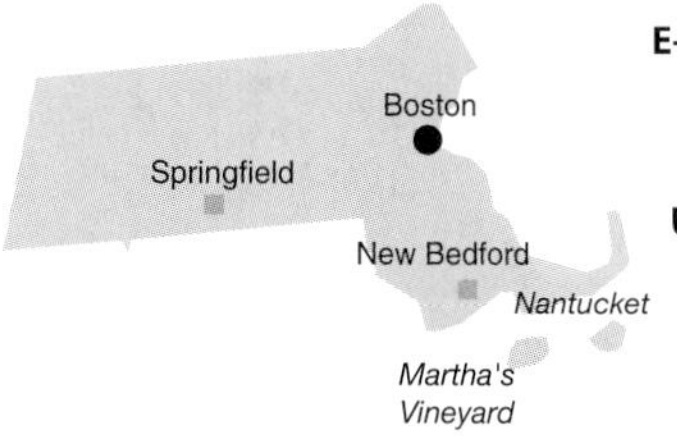

Boston
Springfield
New Bedford
Nantucket
Martha's Vineyard

Web: www.johansens.com/commonwealth
E-mail: sales@hotelcommonwealth.com
Tel: +1 617 933 5000
Fax: +1 617 266 6888
U.S./Canada Toll Free: 1 866 784 4000

Price Guide: (room only)
rooms $245-$465
suites $285-485

The Lenox

61 EXETER STREET AT BOYLSTON, BOSTON, MASSACHUSETTS 02116

Directions: 1 block from Massachusetts Turnpike Exit 22, Copley Square. There is a shuttle service from the hotel to Logan International Airport.

Web: www.johansens.com/lenox
E-mail: info@lenoxhotel.com
Tel: +1 617 536 5300
Fax: +1 617 267 1237
U.S./Canada Toll Free: 1 800 225 7676

Price Guide: (room only)
rooms $199–$429
suites $495–$695

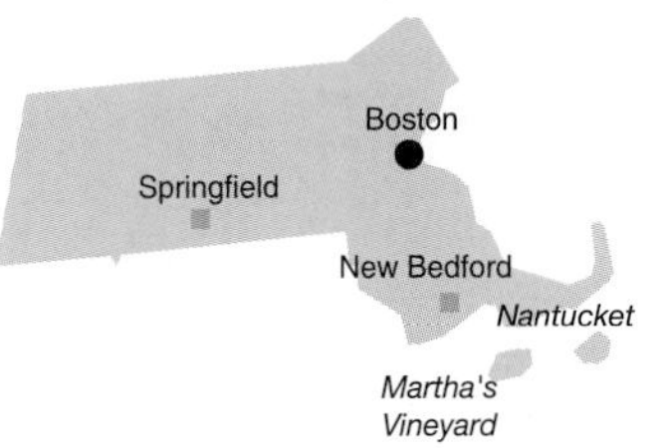

Since opening in 1900, The Lenox has been synonymous with grace, style and luxury; a Who's Who of the famous - from opera singer Enrico Caruso and former President George Bush to film stars Judy Garland, John Travolta and Kenneth Branagh - have arrived at its terracotta brick exterior and entered the lavish interior. Sympathetic modernization has taken place over the past century and today this AAA 4 Diamond recipient and Historic Hotel of America is the epitome of personal attention, understated elegance and the quiet, intimate atmosphere of a boutique-style establishment. At the corner of Boylston and Exeter Streets in Copley Square, The Lenox is within walking distance of Boston's business district, attractions and finest shops. All guest rooms and suites blend Old World charm with 21st-century amenities, such as complimentary wireless Internet access, and are equipped with the luxuries expected from a hotel of this caliber (along with a few unexpected surprises, such as working fireplaces in 12 of the guest rooms). Robert Fathman, acclaimed 4-star chef, holds court with eclectic American cuisine in the fine dining restaurant, Azure, whilst Solas, an Irish pub, offers more casual dinners and lunches. There is a fully-equipped fitness center, business center and valet parking.

Our inspector loved: *The warm hospitality throughout this family-owned hotel.*

Nine Zero Hotel

90 Tremont Street, Boston, Massachusetts 02108

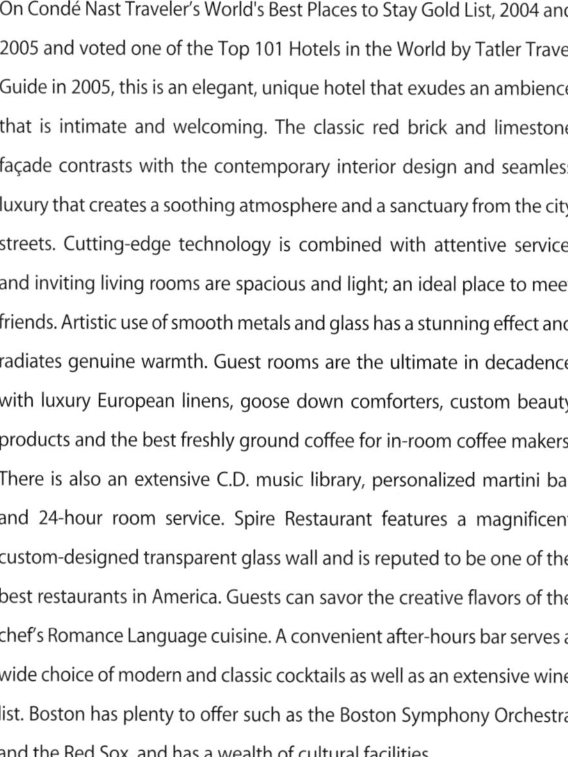

On Condé Nast Traveler's World's Best Places to Stay Gold List, 2004 and 2005 and voted one of the Top 101 Hotels in the World by Tatler Travel Guide in 2005, this is an elegant, unique hotel that exudes an ambience that is intimate and welcoming. The classic red brick and limestone façade contrasts with the contemporary interior design and seamless luxury that creates a soothing atmosphere and a sanctuary from the city streets. Cutting-edge technology is combined with attentive service, and inviting living rooms are spacious and light; an ideal place to meet friends. Artistic use of smooth metals and glass has a stunning effect and radiates genuine warmth. Guest rooms are the ultimate in decadence with luxury European linens, goose down comforters, custom beauty products and the best freshly ground coffee for in-room coffee makers. There is also an extensive C.D. music library, personalized martini bar and 24-hour room service. Spire Restaurant features a magnificent custom-designed transparent glass wall and is reputed to be one of the best restaurants in America. Guests can savor the creative flavors of the chef's Romance Language cuisine. A convenient after-hours bar serves a wide choice of modern and classic cocktails as well as an extensive wine list. Boston has plenty to offer such as the Boston Symphony Orchestra and the Red Sox, and has a wealth of cultural facilities.

Our inspector loved: *Lunch at Spire Restaurant.*

Directions: 15 minutes from Logan Airport. From the airport follow signs to Summer Tunnel/Boston then signs to Storrow Drive west. Take the first exit on the left and follow signs to Government Center/Downtown. Bear left then merge right onto Cambridge Street. After 9 blocks turn left onto Bosworth St.

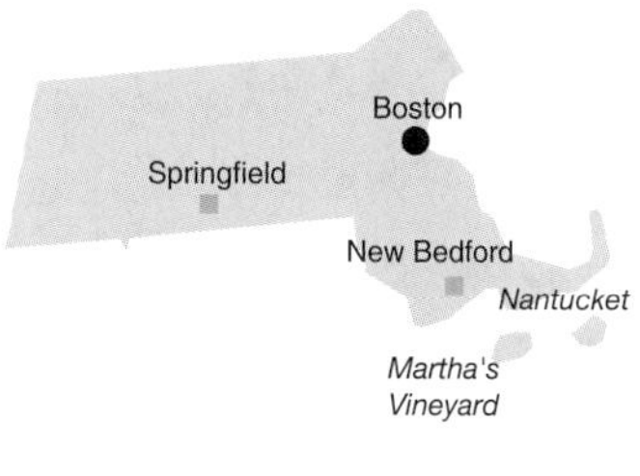

Boston
Springfield
New Bedford
Nantucket
Martha's Vineyard

Web: www.johansens.com/ninezero
E-mail: info@ninezerohotel.com
Tel: +1 617 772 5800
Fax: +1 617 772 5810
U.S./Canada Toll Free: 1 866 906 9090

Price Guide: (room only)
rooms $249-$449
suites $450-$5,000

Hotel Marlowe

25 Edwin H. Land Boulevard, Cambridge, Massachusetts 02141

Overlooking Boston's marvelous skyline, Hotel Marlowe is a vibrant hotel with rich décor, textured fabrics and boutique-style setting. Each of the 236 accommodations, including 14 suites, have rich colors of gold, crimson and deep blue with whimsical detail, animal print carpeting, plush velvet fabrics and high-end finishes. All rooms and suites have Frette bed linens, down comforters, C.D. stereos, free WiFi access, "Forgot It? We've Got It!" essential travel items and Aveda bath amenities. Mind, Body, Spa in-room exercise programs are available for yoga, Pilates and core strengthening or guests can use the fitness room. In-room spa treatments are available including massage, facials and hand and foot treatments. Bambara, the lively American brasserie adjacent to the hotel, features American and New England-style cuisine. For lighter fare, the central bar serves tapas-style food, a selection of fine international wines and creative cocktails overlooking the park, the Charles River and downtown Boston. Families and pets are welcome. The Very Important Pet amenity includes a lunch box full of tasty complimentary treats for returning guest pets. This is a great location for private events and weddings, conveniently located near M.I.T., Harvard University and Downtown Boston.

Our inspector loved: *The Pampered Pet Package for guests who travel with their cats or dogs.*

Directions: 15 minutes from Boston's Logan International Airport (B.O.S.).

Web: www.johansens.com/marlowe
E-mail: info@hotelmarlowe.com
Tel: +1 617 868 8000
Fax: +1 617 868 8001
U.S./Canada Toll Free: 1 800 825 7040

Price Guide:
rooms $199-$429
suites $249-$509

The Crowne Pointe Historic Inn & Spa

82 BRADFORD STREET, PROVINCETOWN, CAPE COD, MASSACHUSETTS 02657

Located at the tip of Cape Cod, in Provincetown, The Crowne Pointe is a beautifully renovated 19th-century mansion with other historic carriage houses. Given the AAA 4-Diamond Award, the inn is also a Member of the Historic Hotels of America. Each spacious guest room is decorated in Victorian elegance and luxury with classic colors, antiques, graceful moldings and hardwood floors. Room amenities include cable T.V. with V.C.R./D.V.D., C.D. players, oversized bath towels, 250 thread count linens, down comforters, Internet access including WiFi in the common areas, pima cotton bathrobes, and a "Heavenly Bed" premium mattress. Savor gourmet handmade chocolates, and in the afternoon, the innkeepers invite all to gather for the free wine and cheese social. The Bistro, recipient of the Wine Spectator's Award of Excellence 2006, and hotel bar create exquisite gourmet cuisine and offer carefully selected labels from the inn's own wine cellar. The Asian-inspired Shui Spa, located in a serene place on the inn's grounds, has its own meditation garden. This modern facility has an extensive menu of treatments and is surrounded by a 4,000 gallon Koi pond. Provincetown is a culturally diverse area and has flawless beaches, shopping, nightclubs, water sports, art galleries and museums. Local activities include dune tours, sightseeing by airplane, bike rentals, boating and kayaking.

Directions: The hotel offers a complimentary ferry and airport pick-up service from Provincetown Harbor and Airport.

Web: www.johansens.com/crownepointe
E-mail: welcome@crownepointe.com
Tel: +1 508 487 6767
Fax: +1 508 487 5554
U.S./Canada Toll Free: 1 877 276 9631

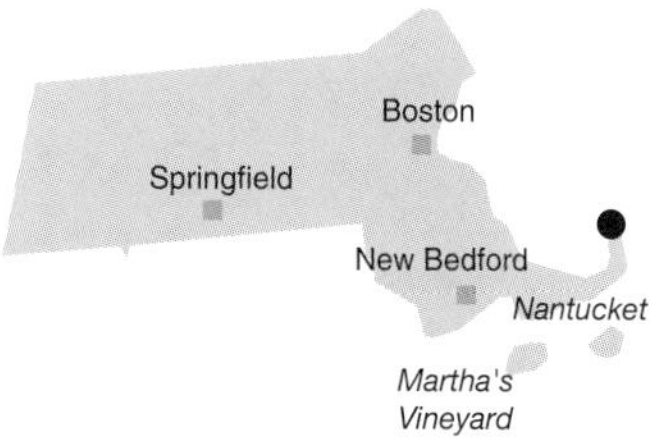

Boston
Springfield
New Bedford
Nantucket
Martha's Vineyard

Price Guide:
rooms $100-$469

Our inspector loved: *The relaxing atmosphere at the Shui Spa.*

Wequassett Inn Resort and Golf Club

On Pleasant Bay, Chatham, Cape Cod, Massachusetts 02633

Combining old fashioned elegance with modern-day comforts, Wequassett Inn in Chatham comprises 22 historic buildings dating back to 1740. Pleasant Bay and the Atlantic Ocean envelope the grounds and the magnificent views add to the overall sense of complete seclusion. The charming guest rooms, many of which have been recently renovated, feature fine linens, fluffy towels and soft country-style fabrics and all offer a deck, patio or balcony. Private decks leading from the cottages overlook the seasonal gardens and encourage guests to explore the meandering paths that traverse the glorious grounds. 4 distinct dining options include the informal LiBAYtion, a beachfront bar offering the best water views for cocktails and light fare under a fashionable pergola, the Outer Bar and Grille for sophisticated yet casual dining and the relaxed lounge-style Thoreau's for an evening with cocktails, fine wines and delicious dishes. Exceptional cuisine is served in Twenty-Eight Atlantic, decorated in an eclectic fashion with Shaker décor, nautical etchings and exquisite chandeliers. Private dinners for up to 200 can be held in the state-of-the-art Pavilion while the canopied Garden Terrace, a wraparound farmer's porch, and the garden reception room are ideal spaces for breakouts. The versatile Cape Villa conference rooms are suitable for groups of 10 to 220.

Our inspector loved: *The views of Pleasant Bay and the Atlantic Ocean.*

Directions: From Boston take Route 3 south to Cape Cod then Route 6 east to exit 11. Turn left onto Pleasant Bay Road.

Web: www.johansens.com/wequassett
E-mail: info@wequassett.com
Tel: +1 508 432 5400
Fax: +1 508 430 3131
U.S./Canada Toll Free: 1 800 225 7125

Price Guide: (room only, excluding tax)
rooms $275-$1,500

 104   220      

THE CHARLOTTE INN

27 SOUTH SUMMER STREET, EDGARTOWN, MASSACHUSETTS 02539

Ideally situated a short walk from the vibrant and historic Edgartown, The Charlotte Inn is an elegant and tranquil hotel nestled amongst chestnut and linden trees. This grand house was originally built for a wealthy merchant in 1864 and in recent years has been sympathetically restored to recreate the ambience of a bygone era. A collection of 19th-century oil paintings lines the walls of the lobby and there are antique pieces still in use including grandfather clocks, umbrellas and hat stands. Each of the bedrooms has been individually designed, yet remains in-keeping with its Victorian heritage featuring mahogany furniture, leather bound books and silver dressing table sets, while goose-down bedding and European drapes ensure absolute comfort for discerning guest. The inn's restaurant serves some of the finest cuisine in the area with a menu that cleverly creates a union between the area's regional favorites; the freshest locally grown herbs and some of New England's finest fish. The candle-lit conservatory dining room provides a romantic atmosphere, and on summer nights guests may dine on the ivy-clad terrace. Service is carefully attentive yet unobtrusive and is one of the many factors that encourages guests to return to this delightful inn year after year.

Our inspector loved: *The magnificent Carriage House with its antiques and super outlook over the courtyard.*

Directions: Take a ferry or plane to Martha's Vineyard. The inn is a short distance from the airport and ferry terminals.

Boston
Springfield
New Bedford
Nantucket
Martha's Vineyard

Web: www.johansens.com/charlotte
E-mail: charlotteinn@aol.com
Tel: +1 508 627 4151
Fax: +1 508 627 4652

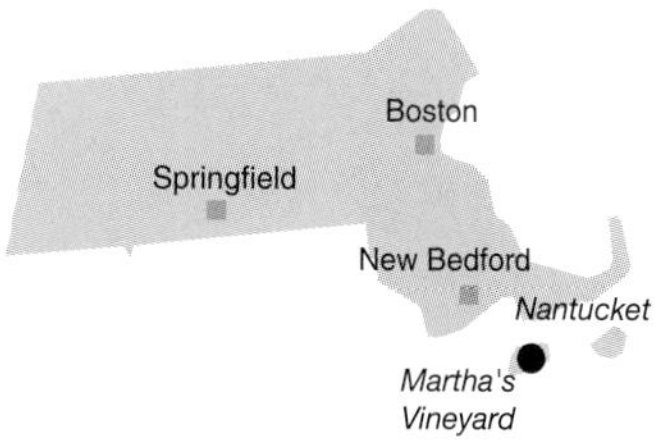

Price Guide:
rooms $295-$695
suites $550-$895

The Inn at Castle Hill

280 ARGILLA ROAD, IPSWICH, MASSACHUSETTS 01938

This luxuriously restored sanctuary is quietly nestled at the foot of Castle Hill. Its secluded setting, in the heart of the Crane Estate, is the ideal location for retreat and relaxation. Friendly staff create a warm and welcoming atmosphere where guests can enjoy the simple pleasures of life amidst the glorious countryside of Boston's North Shore. Individually appointed bedrooms are cozy and comfortable with stunning views over the salt marshes, sand dunes and beyond to the ocean. To maintain the serenity of the hotel no radios or televisions are allowed. Hearty breakfasts are sumptuous and picnic lunches are simple, light and nourishing. Afternoon tea is taken on the wraparound veranda, which benefits from spectacular views, and guests may enjoy a full cocktail and wine service. Explore the surrounding rolling hills, woodlands, meadows and miles of sandy beaches; Crane Beach has been voted one of the best in the area. Outdoor pursuits include kayaking, fishing, whale watching, hiking and cycling. There are many interesting museums in Salem, which is well known for its infamous 17th-century witch trials, and Rockport's residing artists display their works of art in galleries and on stalls. The Crane Estate is a designated conservation area containing historical buildings, a wildlife refuge and rare maritime forest. All proceeds from the inn contribute to the conservation efforts of the area.

Our inspector loved: *Relaxing on the porch rocking chairs.*

Directions: Follow Mass turnpike east to exit 14 then take Routes 95 and 128. After the tolls stay on the left and follow the signs to Route 95 north, Portsmouth. Merge onto 95/128 north and take exit 45. Follow 128 Gloucester and continue north on Route 128 to exit 15.

Web: www.johansens.com/castlehill
E-mail: theinn@ttor.org
Tel: +1 978 412 2555
Fax: +1 978 412 2556

Price Guide:
rooms $115-$385

Blantyre

16 BLANTYRE ROAD, P.O. BOX 995, LENOX, MASSACHUSETTS 01240

Built in 1902 and modeled after an ancestral home in Scotland, Blantyre is an exquisite manor house hotel located in the beautiful Berkshires. Offering the atmosphere of a private estate, the exquisite décor is highlighted by beautiful leaded glass windows, richly burnished woods and luxurious fabrics. There are 25 impeccably designed guest rooms and suites with romantic four-poster beds, unique furnishings and spacious marble bathrooms with soaking tubs. In the Main House, guests can relax in comfortable and inviting plush chairs and enjoy the fresh flowers in the sun-lit music room. Period pieces and treasured heirlooms are a focal point of the main floor's Baronial Main Hall. Dining is a highlight with unparalleled French cuisine served in an elegant candle-lit, music-filled setting and there is an impressive wine collection of more than 1,600 vintages. "the potting shed" spa offers a variety of treatments including hot stone therapy and massage, alternatively, enjoy a game of croquet, tennis, ice skating, cross-country skiing and snowshoeing available on the property. Golf and fishing are available nearby. Beautifully prepared picnic baskets are perfect for a summer's day in the hotel grounds or an afternoon at nearby Tanglewood, the open-air music venue featuring the Boston Symphony Orchestra, the Boston Pops and the Jazz Festival.

Our inspector loved: *Savoring a glass of red wine in the Music Room.*

Directions: 2½ hours by car from Boston's Logan International Airport. 3 hours by car from New York City.

Web: www.johansens.com/blantyre
E-mail: welcome@blantyre.com
Tel: +1 413 637 3556
Fax: +1 413 637 4282

Boston
Springfield
New Bedford
Nantucket
Martha's Vineyard

Price Guide:(excluding 9% service charge and 9.7% tax)
rooms $525-$775
suites $575-$1,650

CRANWELL RESORT, SPA & GOLF CLUB

55 LEE ROAD, ROUTE 20, LENOX, MASSACHUSETTS 01240

In the heart of the Berkshires, surrounded by 380 acres, this historic Gilded Age mansion offers exceptional accommodation, fine dining, all modern amenities and unforgettable service. Winner of the AAA Four Diamond Award for Excellence for the fourth consecutive year, Cranwell has been carefully renovated to preserve its original 19th-century grandeur and is a member of the Historic Hotels of America. The beautifully decorated bedrooms have been designed with comfort in mind and feature breathtaking views. 3 restaurants offer a variety of delicious cuisine created by the highly acclaimed culinary team. Views of the picturesque golf course can be enjoyed whilst dining in Sloane's Tavern, an intimate candle-lit meal for two may be taken in the Wyndhurst Restaurant or in the Music Room. The 35,000 ft.^{2} Spa, which is one of the largest resort spas in the northeast, consists of 16 treatment rooms with over 50 services available such as massage therapies, facial treatments and healing wraps. With a glorious mountain backdrop, the panoramic 18-hole championship golf course with G.P.S. equipped golf carts and driving range provide a real challenge. Spacious rooms for conferences and weddings are available in this memorable, delightful setting.

Our inspector loved: *This sophisticated resort close to Tanglewood for music lovers.*

Directions: The nearest airport is Bradley International. From the airport take Route 91 north to the Mass Turnpike (I-90) exit 14. Take exit 2 and turn right onto Route 20 west. Cranwell is on Route 20, on the right after 3.5 miles.

Web: www.johansens.com/cranwell
E-mail: info@cranwell.com
Tel: +1 413 637 1364
Fax: +1 413 637 4364
U.S./Canada Toll Free: 1 800 272 6935

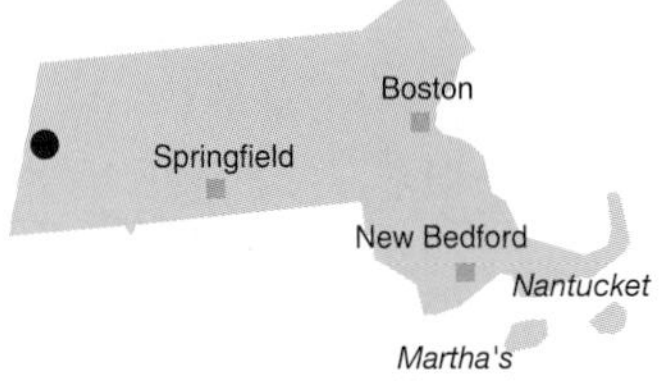

Price Guide: (room only)
rooms $225-$375
suites $275-$1,100

Winnetu Oceanside Resort

31 DUNES ROAD, EDGARTOWN, MASSACHUSETTS 02539

Overlooking South Beach in Edgartown, Winnetu Oceanside Resort is set on 11 acres that blend into the natural beauty of Martha's Vineyard. This welcoming resort features suites with kitchenettes and outdoor decks or patios, with WiFi connection throughout, or private townhouses and single-family homes available for rent. Enjoy delicious, fine-dining, with an emphasis on fresh, local seafood and the new Winnetu Wellness Cuisine, at the Resort's on-site Lure restaurant, complete with spectacular ocean views through large French windows. The Lure Kid's Club offers a special family dining option. Lighter takeout is available at the poolside, as well as at The Winnetu General Store. The new Island Adventure & Wellness Center opened in May 2006 and allows guests to create a healthy, integrated vacation experience with a range of classes and activities from yoga, Pilates, aquatics, strength training and stretching to power walks, bicycle hikes, jogging and therapeutic massage. The Center features a 1,200ft. studio, workout area with free weights, Paramount circuit training and cardio equipment, and personal trainers who can provide customized fitness programs. Life-size lawn chess, grocery delivery, a Teen Program and a free Children's Day Program in season are also available. To unwind in the evening, enjoy a sunset water taxi cruise from the resort into Edgartown.

Our inspector loved: *The great water view location, and life-size chess set.*

Directions: There are frequent ferries from Cape Cod or direct flights from Boston, New York, Philadelphia, Providence, and Washington D.C. The Winnetu also operates a V.I.P. ferry/transfer service from New Bedford, Massachusetts to the Resort.

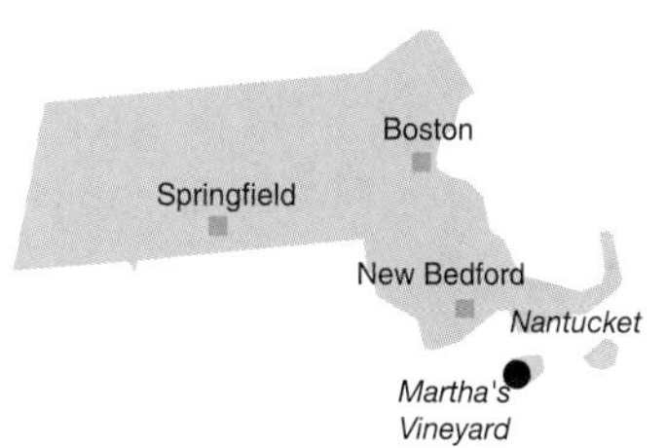

Web: www.johansens.com/winnetu
E-mail: reservations@winnetu.com
Tel: +1 978 443 1733
Fax: +1 978 443 0479

Price Guide: (room only)
suites $195-$2,185
weekly: homes $1,450-$9,250

Mississippi

Hotel location shown in red with page number

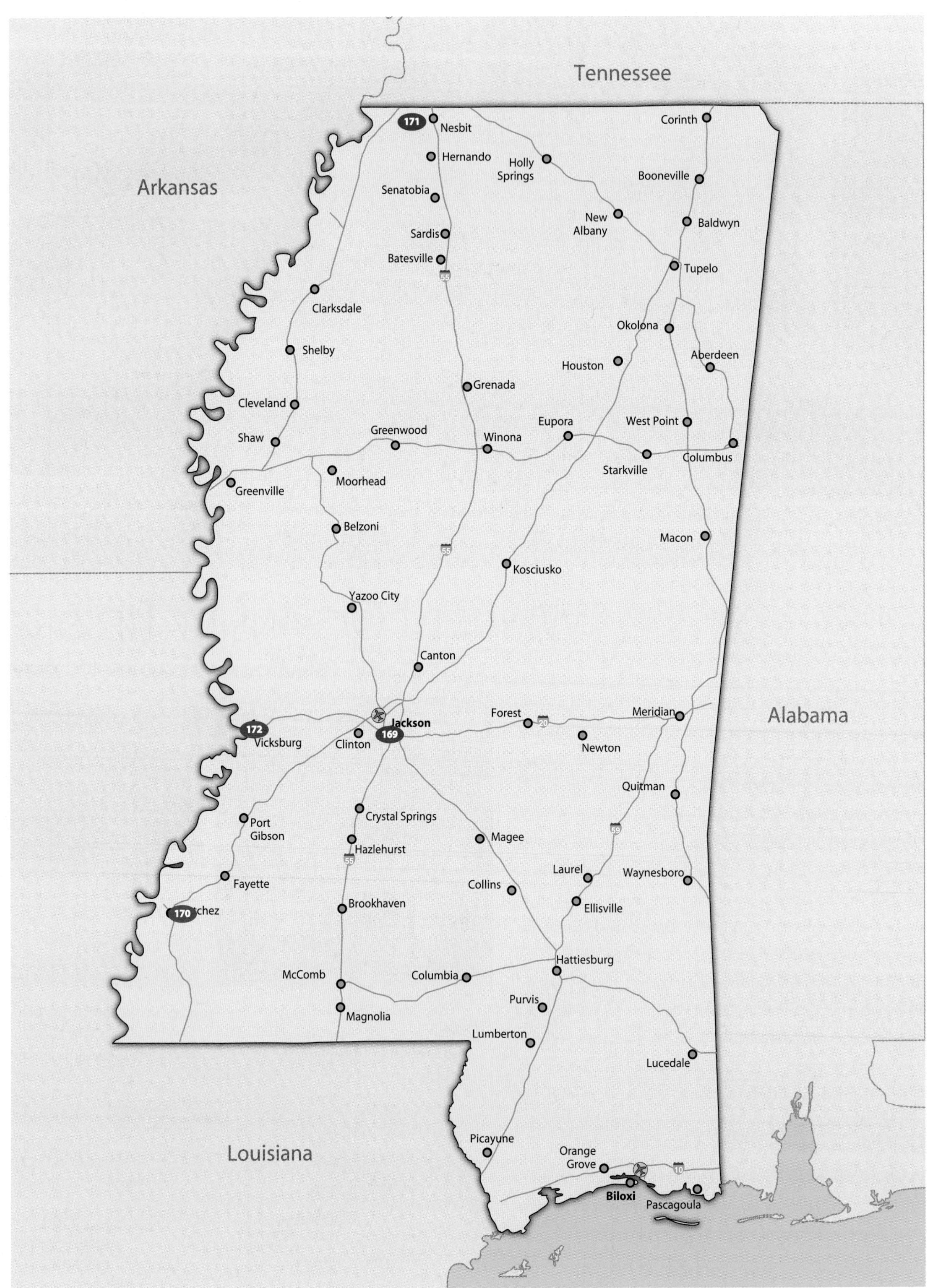

Fairview Inn & Restaurant

734 FAIRVIEW STREET, JACKSON, MISSISSIPPI 39202

This gracious pillared white house with its sweeping driveway and beautifully landscaped gardens is reminiscent of George Washington's Mount Vernon residence. Situated in the exclusive Belhaven District of Jackson, it is a grand Colonial Revival house listed in the National Register of Historic Places. From the moment guests step into the traditional hallway, the charm and luxurious atmosphere of this property are apparent, with reception rooms to left and right, sparkling chandeliers and polished wooden floors scattered with antique rugs. The Simmons family has owned the house since 1930; there are old family portraits, photographs and crests tracing the history of the family name. The house has 3 luxurious bedrooms and 15 opulent suites. All incorporate the original characteristics of 1908 when the house was built combined with every accessory and comfort that today's visitor expects. 2 of the suites are very private and have their own entrances and car parking. There is a large, elegant dining room where co-owner Carol Simmons and her executive chef serve excellent gourmet meals. The hotel is close to the center of Jackson and its historic attractions, art galleries, museums and theaters.

Our inspector loved: *The charming residential ambience.*

Directions: From I-55 exit at 98A into Woodrow Wilson Drive. Turn left at the first set of traffic lights into North State Street and Fairview Street is the first left after the second set of traffic lights.

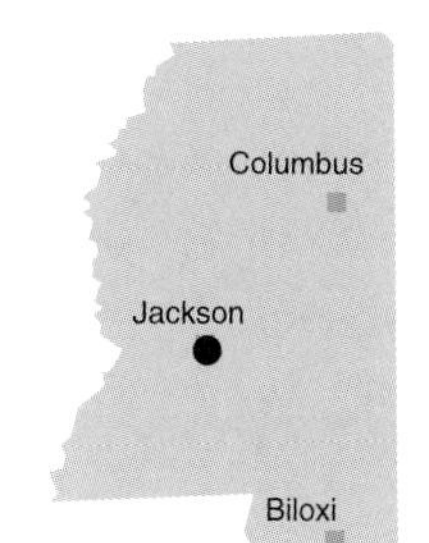

Web: www.johansens.com/fairviewinn
E-mail: fairview@fairviewinn.com
Tel: +1 601 948 3429
Fax: +1 601 948 1203
U.S./Canada Toll Free: 1 888 948 1908

Price Guide:
rooms $115–$165
suites $165–$350

18 100 NR HP

Monmouth Plantation

36 MELROSE AVENUE, NATCHEZ, MISSISSIPPI 39120

This is truly one of the grand old ladies of the South, lovingly restored by owners Ron and Lani Riches to her full glory when built in 1818, and offers complete luxury alongside great Southern hospitality. Listed as a historic landmark, the hotel has won numerous accolades including 4 Diamonds by AAA, recognition by Condé Nast Traveler's Gold List, Travel and Leisure's World's Best and recently nominated for a Condé Nast Johansens Award for Excellence. Many distinguished guests have visited this magnificent estate of 26 immaculate acres with rose garden, ponds and walking trails. Each of the well-appointed rooms and suites has its own personality and charm. Every modern comfort has been considered without compromising the building's architecture resulting in a perfect blend of comfort and Southern splendor. A 5-course dinner is served by candlelight each evening, and the chef plans daily menus to incorporate traditional favorites and regional ingredients. The district of Natchez is 5 minutes away with its carriage rides, antique shops and air of pre-Civil War elegance and many antebellum homes are open all year for tours including Monmouth. During Spring and Fall Pilgrimages hostesses dress in antebellum costumes in the historic mansions. In May, enjoy the Natchez Music Festival and a Symphony of Gardens, in August the Great River Road Food festival and in October the Balloon Race Weekend.

Directions: From Highway 61 pass 4 sets of traffic lights then turn left onto Junkin Street. Pass another set of traffic lights then take a right turn at John A. Quitman Parkway. Monmouth Plantation is on the left.

Web: www.johansens.com/monmouthplantation
E-mail: luxury@monmouthplantation.com
Tel: +1 601 442 5852
Fax: +1 601 446 7762
U.S./Canada Toll Free: 1 800 828 4531

Price Guide: (dinner $48)
rooms $170–$385

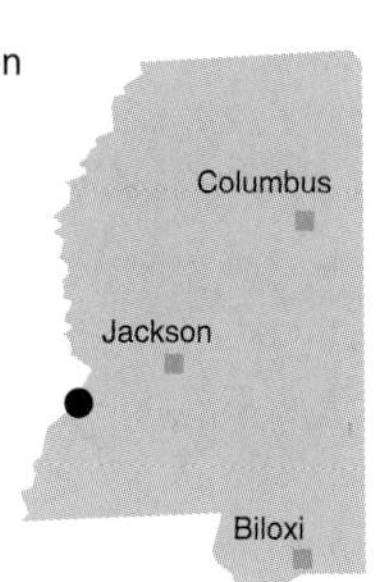

Our inspector loved: *The attention to detail, and beautiful grounds.*

Bonne Terre Country Inn

4715 CHURCH ROAD WEST, NESBIT, MISSISSIPPI 38651

Set in a quiet, romantic location surrounded by 120 wooded acres of Mississippi highlands, yet only 20 minutes from downtown Memphis, this elegant inn is the perfect retreat from the stresses of daily life. The décor is simply impeccable, and the tastefully, individually decorated guest rooms have sumptuous beds and are filled with fine art and French and English antiques. Fresh flowers, whirlpool tubs and fireplaces complete the feeling of utter luxury and relaxation. The 4 downstairs guest rooms have access to a quaint Southern porch, while the balconies of the rooms upstairs provide stunning views of the magnificent grounds that include 2 lakes and a swimming pool. Guests may start the day with a full country breakfast served on the indoor veranda of the Café overlooking one of the beautiful lakes, and in the evenings, innovative, seasonal French country cuisine, complemented by fine wines from an extensive selection, is served in the hotel's sophisticated, intimate restaurant. Accommodating up to 250 guests, the 2 function rooms are available for meetings, corporate dinners or private parties, while the hotel's perfectly landscaped grounds provide a stunning backdrop for outdoor functions. Enjoy fishing on Bonne Terre's 2 lakes or take a walk along the numerous paths and scenic hiking trails. Memphis and its various attractions are only 20 minutes away by car.

Our inspector loved: *The tranquil surroundings, and the friendly staff.*

Directions: From I-55 take exit 287 (Church Road). Go west by turning on to Church Road. Bonne Terre is located after 4.4 miles on the left-hand side of the road.

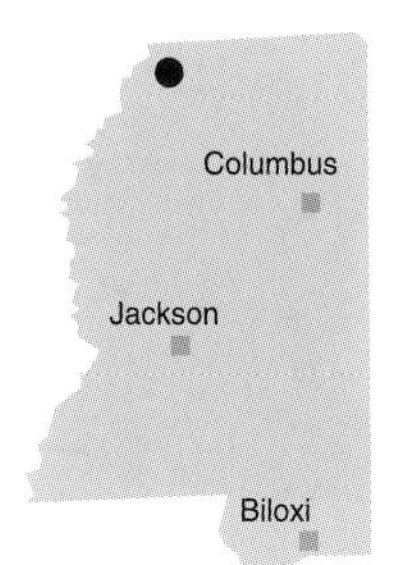

Web: www.johansens.com/bonneterre
E-mail: info@bonneterre.com
Tel: +1 662 781 5100
Fax: +1 662 781 5466

Price Guide:
rooms $160-$260
suites $260-$475

CHATEAU ON THE LAKE

415 NORTH STATE HIGHWAY 265, BRANSON, MISSOURI 65616

This spectacular resort is located a few minutes from Branson, the famous live entertainment capital. Surrounded by lush woodland and overlooking the Ozark Mountains and Table Rock Lake, nature lovers will savor the spectacular scenery and enjoy the peace and seclusion. From all areas of the hotel the views are breathtaking, and the veranda is one of the most inviting places to linger with a drink and enjoy watching the world go by. The guest rooms are carefully appointed and spacious with air-conditioning and state-of-the-art technology, and the staff is delightfully courteous, friendly and helpful, whilst remaining professional and unobtrusive. The new $6 million Spa Chateau provides a haven of relaxation and a range of progressive and luxurious treatments. The resort's restaurant offerings include the award-winning Chateau Grill and the more casual Atrium Café. The hotel's fully-serviced marina offers an unrivaled selection of water sports including boating, water-skiing and fishing. Families will benefit from Crawdaddies Kid's club, with its fun-filled children's program, which is open daily, in season, for both indoor and outdoor activities.

Our inspector loved: *The panoramic hilltop view of the sunrise and sunset - delightful and so relaxing!*

Directions: Springfield - Branson Airport is a 55-minute drive from the hotel.

Web: www.johansens.com/chateaulake
E-mail: chateau.reservations@jqh.com
Tel: +1 417 334 1161
Fax: +1 417 339 5566
U.S./Canada Toll Free: 1 888 333 LAKE (5253)

Price Guide: (room only)
rooms $129-$259
suites $199-$319

301 550 SPA

The Raphael Hotel

325 WARD PARKWAY, KANSAS CITY, MISSOURI 64112

The Raphael is a one-of-a-kind boutique hotel. Designed with the distinguished styles of Europe's finest small hotels, its stunning architecture offers a unique Kansas City experience with a relaxing atmosphere, intimacy and highly individualized service. Currently being renovated to an extremely high standard of comfort, it has all the latest modern luxuries but still captures an Old World style with beautiful furnishings and distinctive charm. A weekly rotating dinner menu at the romantic restaurant offers exciting "creative continental" and "new American" cuisine complemented by an exceptional list of international wines. The delicious food, together with friendly service, is a true asset to the city's excellent reputation for fine dining. Guests will love the intimate ambience of the Raphael Lounge with its fantastic piano bar and live entertainment during many evenings. Kansas City's elegant "little" hotel overlooks the Country Club Plaza, a 15-block district of Spanish architecture with fountains, sculptures and courtyards. The area features upscale shopping and dining, and is centrally located to the river walk, art galleries, musems and music venues featuring famous K.C. jazz.

Our inspector loved: *The relaxing, elegant accommodations in the heart of the Country Club Plaza.*

Directions: From I-35 south take south west trafficway exit 1A. After approx. 3 miles turn left onto Roanoke Parkway and follow it onto 47th Street, then turn right onto Broadway. Follow Broadway through the plaza then left onto Ward Parkway. The hotel is on the right.

Web: www.johansens.com/raphael
E-mail: information@raphaelkc.com
Tel: +1 816 756 3800
Fax: +1 816 802 2131
U.S./Canada Toll Free: 1 800 821 5343

Price Guide: (room only)
rooms $134-$184
suites $185-$200

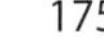

Big Cedar Lodge

612 DEVIL'S POOL ROAD, RIDGEDALE, MISSOURI 65739

Big Cedar Lodge is a breathtaking wilderness resort named after the sparkling spring-fed pool situated on its vast grounds. Surrounded by 800 acres of wilderness, nature trails and the magnificent wooded hillsides of the Ozarks with a ridge-side view of Table Rock Lake, this rustic retreat offers a tranquil setting in which to relax and enjoy the superb recreational facilities available. Modern luxury blends effortlessly with natural countryside. Some interiors feature vaulted wooden ceilings, handcrafted furniture, stone fireplaces and sumptuous fabrics, and the accommodations are extremely flexible. The private Knotty Pine Cottages and log cabins nestle within leafy cedar glades, and rooms are decorated in an Adirondack style with an atmosphere of coziness and comfort. There are 4 swimming pools as well as a superb fitness center complete with a fully-qualified and experienced personal trainer. Golf enthusiasts will enjoy the Jack Nicklaus signature course, which is situated just south of Branson. Activities include fishing, boating, canoeing, carriage rides and a very popular Kids' Club. Cuisine at Big Cedar Lodge celebrates the diverse and rich gastronomic traditions of the area and the lodge's 4 restaurants provide anything from home baked breads to smoked meats and fresh trout.

Our inspector loved: *The refreshing and invigorating natural beauty.*

Directions: From Springfield-Branson Aiport, Big Cedar Lodge is 50 miles south, off U.S. 65. Private planes fly to Graham Clark Airport, 7 miles from the property.

Web: www.johansens.com/bigcedar
E-mail: bigcedar@big-cedar.com
Tel: +1 417 335 2777
Fax: +1 417 335 2340

Price Guide: (room only)
rooms $135-$335
suites $169-$1,699

Montana

Hotel location shown in red with page number

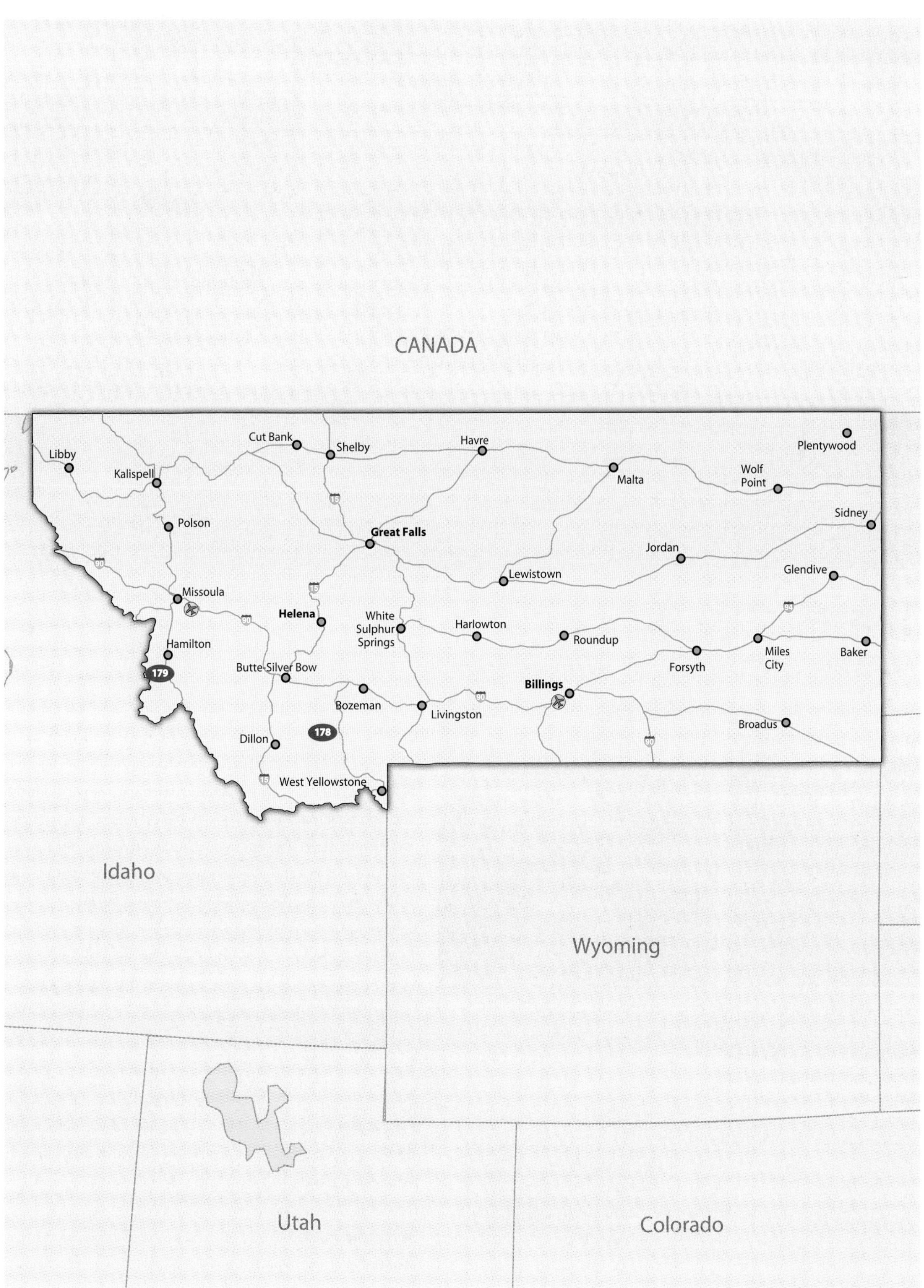

The Big EZ Lodge

7000 BEAVER CREEK ROAD, BIG SKY, MONTANA 59716

Directions: Bozeman Montana Airport is 1-hour drive from the Lodge.

Web: www.johansens.com/bigez
E-mail: jharrison@bigezlodge.com
Tel: +1 406 995 7000
Fax: +1 406 995 7007
U.S./Canada Toll Free: 1 877 244 3299

Price Guide: (room only)
rooms $325-$645
suites $900-$1,650

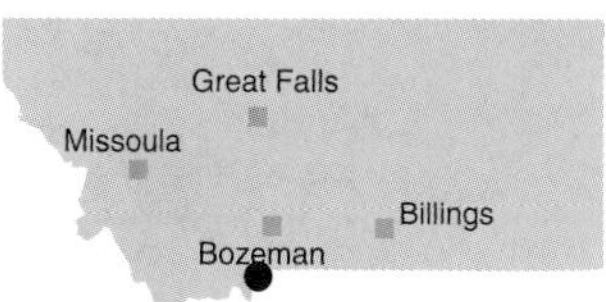

Situated with Yellowstone Park as a backdrop, The Big EZ Lodge is a stunning retreat that has sympathetically blended modern luxury with western rustic charm. The Montana Range, visible from the front of the hotel, instantly creates a sense of peace and wellbeing, and the stunning architecture of the hotel itself is evidence of the style and attention to detail apparent throughout the property. Large public rooms are decked with antlers and furs to evoke a sense of oasis in the wilderness and vast wooden beams and roaring log fires are mixed with leather and animal skin to create a stylish yet warm ambience. Large walk-in showers and deep bathtubs offer total relaxation, whilst every modern amenity is available for guests. The dining room takes great pride in its varying cuisine that features organic herbs from the hotel's own gardens; wild game is a house specialty. Yellowstone National Park is a sport enthusiast's paradise and guests can choose from an array of activities available at the hotel. Trout fishing, horse riding, skiing and snow shoeing are all popular winter sports, whilst hiking is the perfect way to make the most of the stunning surrounding scenery.

Our inspector loved: *The Lonestar Suite's triple shower head steam shower.*

Triple Creek Ranch

5551 West Fork Road, Darby, Montana 59829

Taking its name from the three creeks that border the property, Triple Creek is a spectacular ranch-style hideaway deep in the Montana Mountains. The setting is simply breathtaking, surrounded by some of the most beautiful wilderness playing host to a wide variety of wildlife. The snow-covered peaks are awe-inspiring in winter, whilst the babbling creeks in springtime ensure that a stay here in any season will have a its own special delights. Alpine and cross-country skiing are popular activities during the colder months, and in springtime fly fishing on the Bitterroot River provides a chance to admire the stunning surroundings. Accommodation is provided in a series of traditional log cabins throughout the grounds, each carefully designed and decorated to take advantage of the great outdoors from blazing log fires to outdoor hot tubs. Dining in the candle-lit dining room is a particular treat; the rooftop lounge offers a more informal menu with breathtaking views over the West Fork of the Bitterroot River. Alternatively, the kind and attentive staff will deliver meals to guests' cabins or prepare a picnic to take on a hiking adventure.

Our inspector loved: *Waking up to elk in the front of my cottage!*

Directions: The lodge is a 1 hour and 30-minute drive from the Missoula, Montana International Airport.

Web: www.johansens.com/triplecreek
E-mail: tcr@bitterroot.net
Tel: +1 406 821 4600
Fax: +1 406 821 4666
U.S./Canada Toll Free: 1 800 654 2943

Price Guide: (all inclusive)
rooms $650-$1,095

New Hampshire

Hotel location shown in red with page number

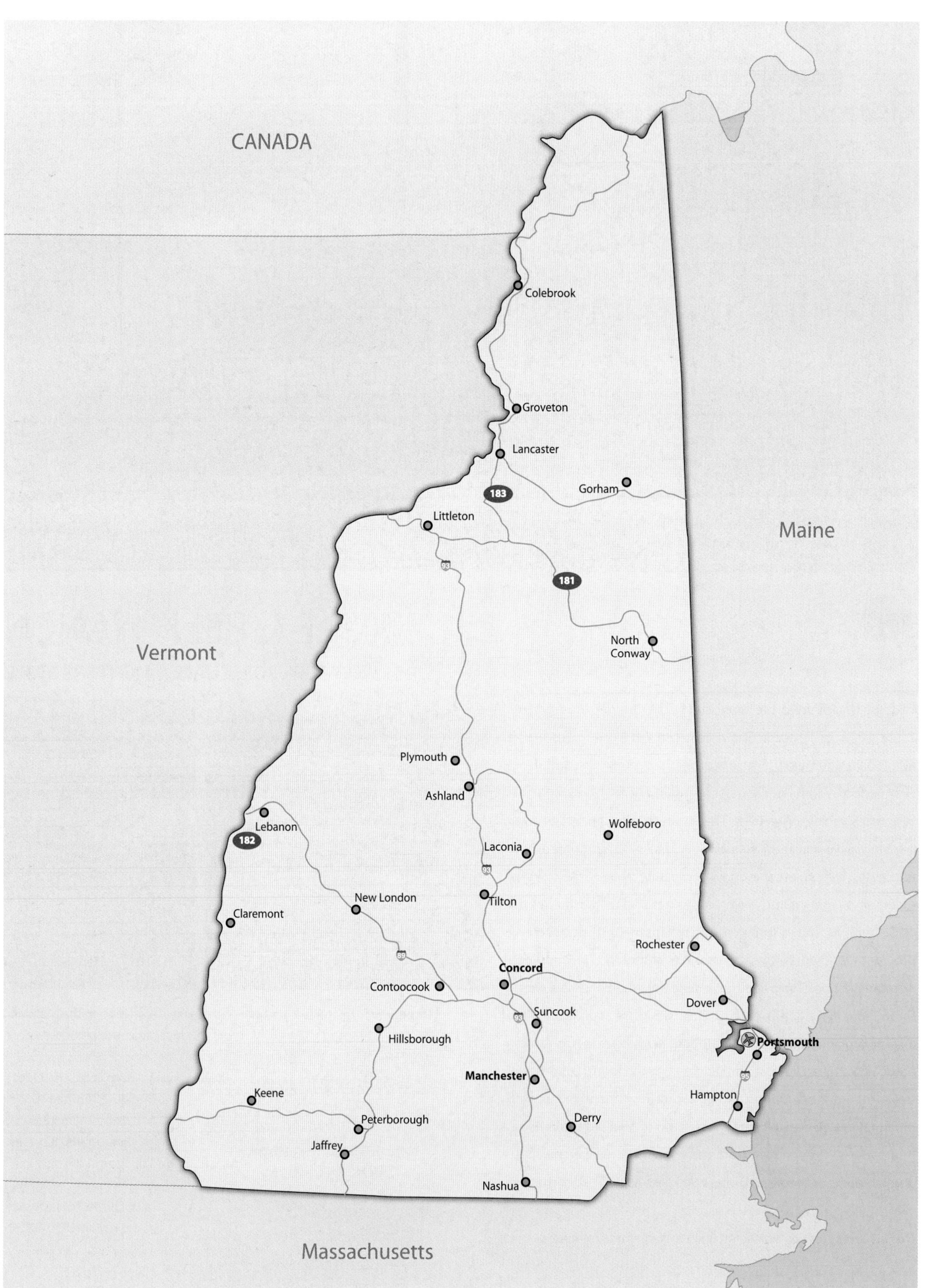

THE WENTWORTH

JACKSON VILLAGE, NEW HAMPSHIRE 03846

In the picturesque White Mountains of New Hampshire this elegant, romantic property nestles at the foot of Mount Washington. The owner/manager since 1991, Fritz Koeppel, places enormous emphasis on the total comfort, relaxation and enjoyment of his guests. Of the 51 guest rooms, 21 have so far been renovated and now have comfortable sitting areas, fireplace and either a Jacuzzi or outdoor hot-tub, as well as all the usual amenities visitors expect form such a high-quality establishment. It is these rooms that Condé Nast Johansens recommend for 2007. All of the rooms enjoy panoramic views of either the Wildcat River, Wentworth golf course or Jackson village. The dining experience is pleasurable and memorable as chefs at The Wentworth Dining Room lovingly prepare dishes using only the finest New England ingredients. The restaurant has been awarded an AAA 4 Diamond rating and the accompanying wine list, a Wine Spectator Award of Excellence. Visitors can choose from an abundance of recreational activities including golf, tennis, croquet, badminton, volleyball and billiards. The Wildcat River provides opportunities for white water rafting and canoeing or for more relaxed water pursuits there is a heated outdoor pool. The area is a renowned ski resort and in winter guests can try ice-skating or take a wonderful sleigh ride.

Directions: From Route 16 cross the Jackson Covered Bridge into Jackson Village. The resort is in the center of town.

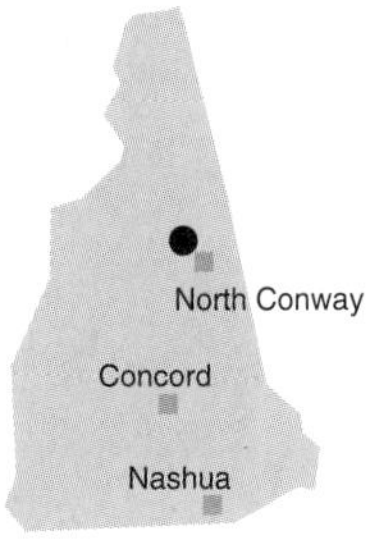

Web: www.johansens.com/wentworth
E-mail: info@thewentworth.com
Tel: +1 603 383 9700
Fax: +1 603 383 4265
U.S./Canada Toll Free: 1 800 637 0013

North Conway
Concord
Nashua

Price Guide:
rooms $124.20-$178.20
suites $234-$307.80

Our inspector loved: *The deep Jacuzzi tubs, surrounded by mirrors.*

Home Hill

RELAIS & CHATEAUX

703 RIVER ROAD, PLAINFIELD, NEW HAMPSHIRE 03781

This elegant French-inspired retreat lies in historic Plainfield, New Hampshire and was built in 1818, on the original site of a Georgian mansion that was burned to the ground in 1763. Today it is a tranquil hotel that has been carefully and sympathetically designed to offer guests every modern day comfort without sacrificing any of its delightful Victorian charm. There are 3 guest rooms and a 2-bedroom suite in the main house and a further 5 guest rooms and 1 suite in the nearby Carriage House. The extremely romantic may enjoy staying in La Piscine, a private cottage with poolside terrace used only in summer months. Open fireplaces and elegant drapes convey an expensive sense of luxury and heritage, with each of the main rooms named after local artists or residents such as Isadora Duncan and Maxfield Parrish, and country antiques and queen-sized beds are to be found throughout. In the warmer months, the inn is a delightful country retreat with putting green and tennis court as well as colorful bike trails and fishing rights. Guests can play at a private golf course nearby. In the winter the owners put down cross-country ski trails in the surrounding 25 acres and skating and downhill skiing are available close by. The welcome awaiting guests' return is first class with fires blazing in the library lounge.

Our inspector loved: *The beautiful French-inspired décor and excellent restaurant.*

Directions: 2 hours from Boston north on I-93. Follow I-93 to I-89 north to West Lebanon exit 20 (south) to Route 12A for 3 miles then turn right onto River Road.

Web: www.johansens.com/homehill
E-mail: homehillinn@relaischateaux.com
Tel: +1 603 675 6165
Fax: +1 603 675 5220

Price Guide: (excluding tax and service charge)
rooms $295-$495

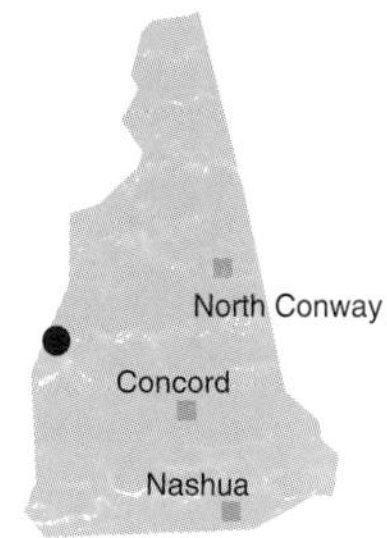

Mountain View, The Grand Resort & Spa

MOUNTAIN VIEW ROAD, WHITEFIELD, NEW HAMPSHIRE 03598

A 2-year, $20 million restoration has seen Mountain View transformed into an ultimate resort of legendary charm matched only by its stunning location. Recipient of the AAA 4-Diamond Award and the Best of New Hampshire 2006, the hotel stands within 1,800 acres, in the heart of the White Mountains. Its tradition of hospitality dates back to 1865, and today retains its grandeur yet offers intimate guest areas, from the veranda, with its breathtaking views, to the lobby complete with baby grand piano, the Dodge Parlor and Eisenhower Library, named in honor of the former presidential visitor. The spacious rooms and suites display custom-made mahogany furnishings and sumptuous feather beds. Garden vistas can be appreciated from every room, and there is also individual climate control, cable T.V.s and telephones with dedicated data ports. There are several dining options available: The Maples offers a sophisticated atmosphere whereas Stage Coach Tavern is more casual, and al fresco dining can be enjoyed along with poolside selections from the Country Club. Perched high within the Colonial Revival observation tower is the Spa at Mountain View with its comprehensive menu of services and treatments derived from Asian, European, Middle Eastern and Native American traditions. Other activities include golf on the 100-year-old course, snowshoeing and sleigh rides.

Directions: Just 4 miles from Mount Washington Regional Airport. From Manchester Airport (M.H.T.) take I-293 north to I-93 north, exit 35.

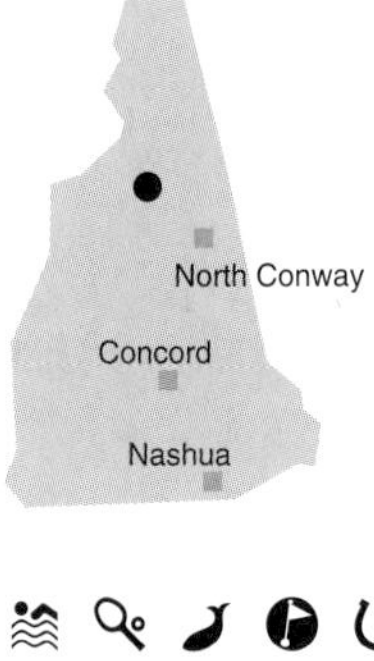

Web: www.johansens.com/mountainview
E-mail: info@mountainviewgrand.com
Tel: +1 603 837 2100
Fax: +1 603 837 8884
U.S./Canada Toll Free: 1 800 438 3843

North Conway
Concord
Nashua

Price Guide: (room only)
rooms $259-$559
suites $499-$3,000

Our inspector loved: *The mountain vistas from the elegant front porch.*

New Mexico

Hotel location shown in red with page number

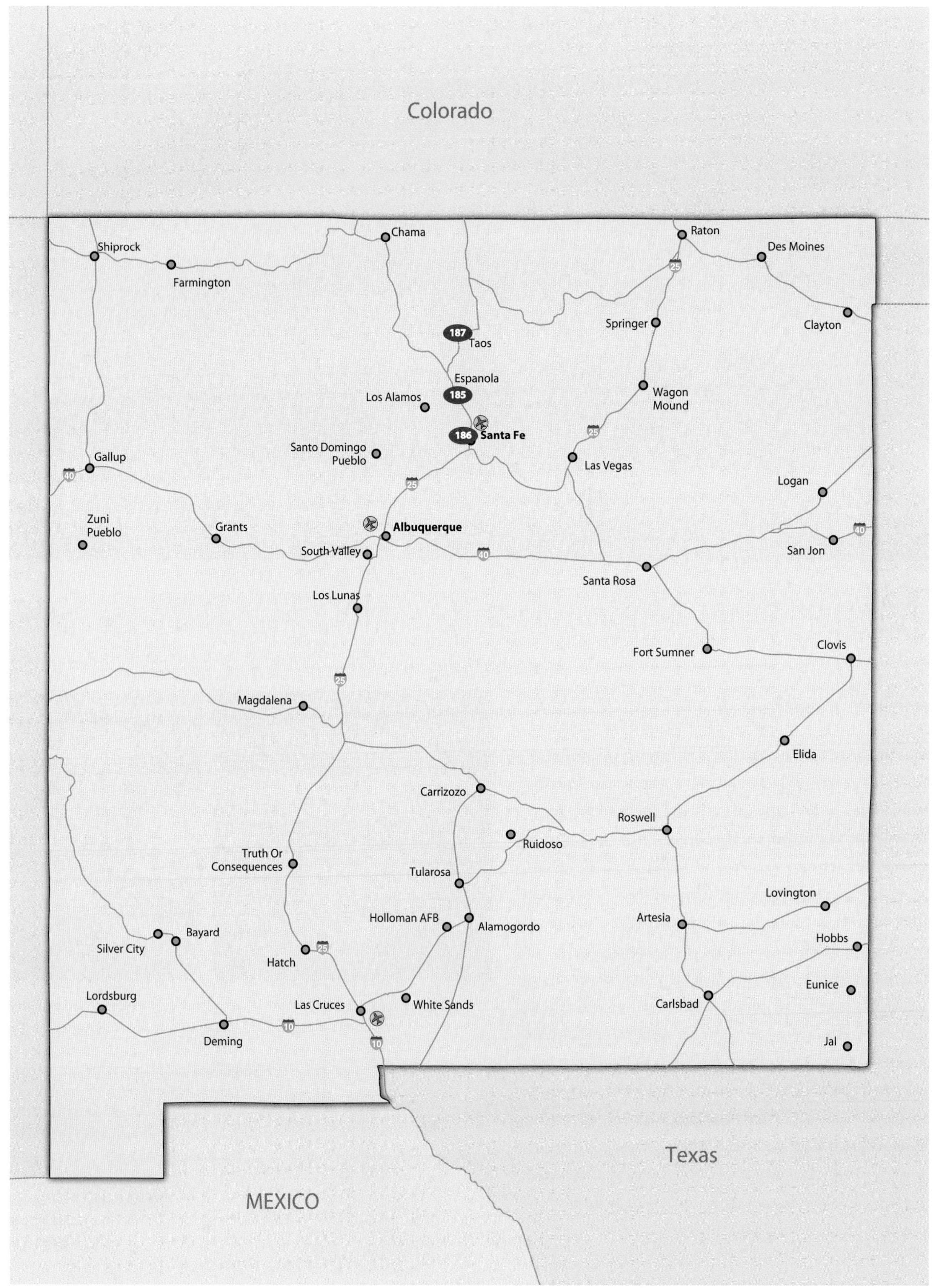

Rancho de San Juan

P.O. BOX 4140, HIGHWAY 285, ESPAÑOLA, NEW MEXICO 87533

Situated between Taos and Santa Fe, in 225 acres of rustic, rural northern New Mexico with outstanding views of the Jemez Mountains, Ojo Caliente River Valley and the renowned foothills of Georgia O'Keefe. Amidst this astonishing natural beauty stands Rancho de San Juan, a Spanish hacienda with wildflower-filled courtyards. Public rooms are adorned with the owners' private art and antique collections and feature exposed beams and cool tiled flooring enhancing relaxation and comfort. Many bedrooms feature kiva fireplaces and all benefit from private terraces that overlook glorious views. Each accommodation is decorated with eclectic furnishings, Egyptian cotton sheets, Frette bath towels and Aveda toileteries. Internet access is available in all rooms. A highlight is the highly acclaimed cuisine: rated the number one restaurant in New Mexico by Zagat Survey 2000-2004 and recipient of the Wine Spectator's Award for Excellence for 5 consecutive years, dining is a gourmet delight with custom-designed porcelain and family sterling silver. The weekly changing à la carte menu uses traditional Norteño ingredients to create classic meals combined with worldwide flavors. A diverse range of seasonal activities can be organized nearby, including white water rafting and hiking trails. Alternatively, enjoy a massage in the privacy of one's guest room or terrace.

Our inspector loved: *The sense of privacy, and exquisite gourmet dining.*

Directions: Located on Highway 285 between Española and Ojo Caliente, 3.5 miles north of Highways 84 and 285.

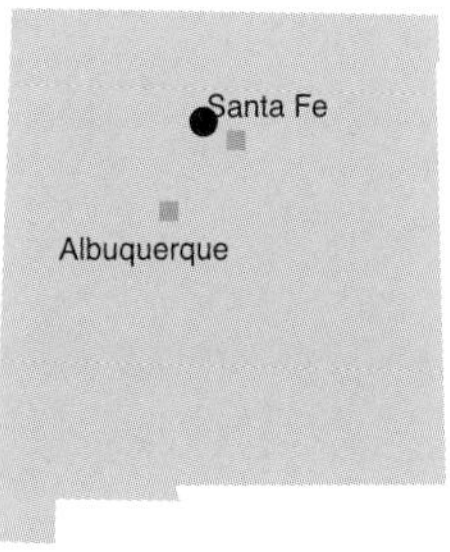

Santa Fe
Albuquerque

Web: www.johansens.com/ranchosanjuan
E-mail: ranchosj@cybermesa.com
Tel: +1 505 753 6818
Fax: +1 505 753 6818

Price Guide: (breakfast $7.50-$17.50, excluding tax)
rooms $295
suites $395-$550

Inn and Spa at Loretto

Noble House Hotels & Resorts

211 OLD SANTA FE TRAIL, SANTA FE, NEW MEXICO 87501

Directions: From Albuquerque Intl. Airport take I-25 north for 63 miles and exit at St. Francis Dive (exit 282). After 4 miles turn right on West Alameda to Old Santa Fe Trail. Turn left on Old Santa Fe Trail and the hotel is on the right.

Web: www.johansens.com/innatloretto
E-mail: reservations@innatloretto.com
Tel: +1 505 988 5531
Fax: +1 505 984 7968
U.S./Canada Toll Free: 1 800 727 5531

Price Guide: (room only)
rooms $252-$490
suites $499-$3,000

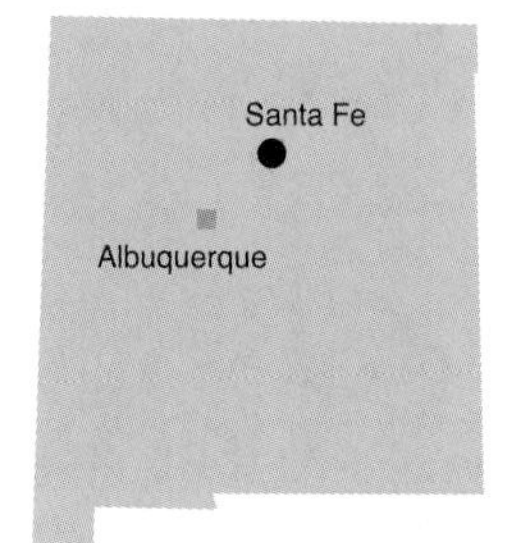

This is a modern and artful retreat built of traditional adobe located at the end of the historic Old Santa Fe Trail overlooking the picturesque Sangre de Cristo Mountains. Capturing the essence of Santa Fe, this luxury inn is ideal for romantic or family getaways and was designed to create the look and feel of the ancient Pueblo civilization. Throughout the inn, craftsmanship created by local Santa Fe artisans can be found from the handcrafted doors, canales, windows and light fixtures. Each guest room has distinct Santa Fe décor with native art, earthy fabrics and beautifully hand-carved furnishings, both historic and modern in comfort. Kiva fireplaces create a warm setting in some of the Pueblo-style guest suites. The art galleries and sculpture garden showcase some of the area's finest works. The luxurious SpaTerre is a cross-cultural spa with Indonesian, Thai and Balinese influences. Many of the herbs, minerals and elements used in the spa have been harvested from the surrounding area to create the most authentic and natural experience. Baleen is the hotel's critically acclaimed restaurant. Executive Chef John Cox blends international and local flavors to create a weekly-changing eclectic menu of Native American and Northern New Mexico cuisine. Ideally located near the historic Plaza and Santa Fe's Old Santa Fe Trail.

Our inspector loved: *Swimming in the outdoor pool surrounded by the intriguing sculpture garden after a visit to the famed Loretto Chapel.*

134

300

SPA

The Leading Small Hotels of the World

El Monte Sagrado Living Resort & Spa

317 KIT CARSON ROAD, TAOS, NEW MEXICO 87571

Tucked away in the shadow of the Sangre de Cristo Mountains and surrounded by Pueblo-style architecture, Taos has long been considered a place of artistic and spiritual inspiration and a hiking and skiing lover's paradise. The day-to-day tableau of the nearby plaza displays an exotic blend of cultures including the indigenous Native Americans, early Spanish and English speaking settlers. The Sacred Circle, an area set aside for quiet events or contemplation, forms the heart of this unusual compound and sets the theme of celebrating, embracing and respecting nature and local traditions. The Biolarium is a holistically designed structure, and the Spa offers specialized treatments, facials and massage therapies. Each of the Treasure of Taos casitas is uniquely designed and furnished using the skills of local artists and craftsman. The Native American Suites feature kiva-style fireplaces, stone tiles and stained wood furnishings and the lavishly appointed Global Suites offer total immersion in international art and culture. Awarded the Wine Spectator's Award of Excellence 2005, there are eclectic and diverse dining options. The Anaconda Bar often provides live entertainment and features a 1,100 gallon salt-water aquarium and a giant anaconda sculpture. Listed in Condé Nast Traveler's Gold List Top 50 Resorts in the U.S. 2006 and the Reader's Choice for 2005.

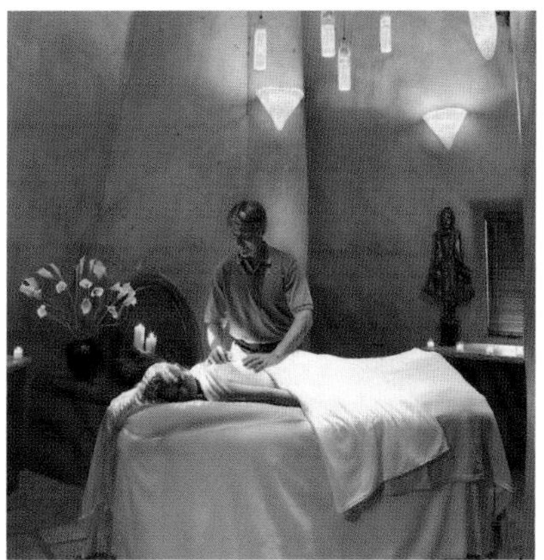

Directions: From Albuquerque Sunport follow signs to I-25. Take N.M.-599 north to U.S.84 to exit 285 then N.M. 68 for approximately 42 miles to Taos.

Web: www.johansens.com/elmontesagrado
E-mail: info@elmontesagrado.com
Tel: +1 505 758 3502
Fax: +1 505 737 2985
U.S./Canada Toll Free: 1 800 828 TAOS

Price Guide: (room only)
rooms $199-$399
suites $449-$699

Our inspector loved: *The Sacred Circle for quiet meditation.*

The Sagamore

110 SAGAMORE ROAD, BOLTON LANDING, NEW YORK 12814

Set on a private island at Bolton Landing, The Sagamore overlooks the calm waters of Lake George and its majestic backdrop is dominated by the Adirondack Mountains. Guests can choose from rooms or suites in the main historic property or the 7 lodges scattered around the lake and onto The Hermitage. The property prides itself on culinary excellence, and with 6 distinct dining options, even the most refined gastronome is certain to be pleased with the dishes on offer. The Morgan, a replica of a 19th-century tour vessel, is ideal for lunch and dinner cruises; informal dining is available in the Club Grill. The Veranda offers a most eclectic mix of afternoon tea, tapas and sushi while Mister Brown's Pub or the Sagamore Dining room add to the many venue choices. Meetings can be held in the 26,000 sq. ft. conference space. Spa treatments, including traditional rituals with herbs, oils and gemstones, are available for those wishing to be pampered while golf enthusiasts can tee off at the 18-hole course. Outdoor pursuits include sailing instruction at Offshore Sailing School, tennis in the championship center, kayaking, parasailing, scuba diving, fishing, and boating.

Our inspector loved: *The beautiful glass-enclosed porch with period furnishings overlooking Lake George.*

Directions: From Albany Airport take the Northway, Highway 87 north to exit 22. Take Route 9A and continue 10 miles to Bolton Landing. The hotel is signposted off to the right.

Web: www.johansens.com/sagamore
E-mail: reserve@thesagamore.com
Tel: +1 518 644 9400
Fax: +1 518 644 2851
U.S./Canada Toll Free: 1 800 358 3585

Price Guide: (room only)
rooms $180-$450
suites $285-$750
condo $499-$855

Mansion on Delaware

414 DELAWARE AVENUE, BUFFALO, NEW YORK 14202

Mansion on Delaware is, without doubt, a Buffalo landmark with international status. Dating back to 1869 when it was built as a private residence at an estimated cost of $200,000, it has earned a colorful history yet stood vacant for 25 years until 1998. A 3-year, multi-million dollar restoration elevated the hotel to sought-after status with high-style design, butler service and grand luxury. This sanctuary has received numerous awards for culinary quality, design, preservation and personal service. Upon entering through the Second Empire mahogany doors the pampering begins: greeted by a butler upon arrival, a whirlpool bath with complimentary bath salts will be prepared and a nightly turn-down service, including a sweet treat and bottled water, awaits at the end of the day. Butlers will mix the perfect beverage, press guests' attire and organize free downtown transportation or helipad access. There are 28 exquisitely decorated guest rooms, including 3 parlor suites. Each is impeccably appointed, has every modern amenity and a high level of comfort. 24-hour in-room dining and excellent business facilities are available. 5 minutes from Canada's border, between the Allentown Art and Antique District and the Theater District, and within walking distance of some of Buffalo's best shops and restaurants.

Our inspector loved: *This architectural treasure in the heart of downtown; a culturally rich neighborhood.*

Directions: From I-90 (N.Y. Thruway) take exit 51 west (Route 33 west) to 33 west Goodell Street exit. Goodell Street turns into Edward Street. Turn left onto Delaware Avenue and the hotel is on the immediate right (on the corner of Delaware and Edward).

Web: www.johansens.com/mansionondelaware
E-mail: info@mansionondelaware.com
Tel: +1 716 886 3300
Fax: +1 716 883 3923

Price Guide:
rooms $169-$298
suites $375

The Roycroft Inn

40 South Grove Street, East Aurora, New York 14052

Directions: Take New York south (Route 90) and exit 54 to Route 400. Exit at Route 20A/East Aurora then turn right for the exit onto Route 20A, which becomes Main Street. Continue through the village and turn left onto South Grove Street. The inn is on the left.

Web: www.johansens.com/roycroftinn
E-mail: info@roycroftinn.com
Tel: +1 716 652 5552
Fax: +1 716 655 5345
U.S./Canada Toll Free: 1 877 652 5552

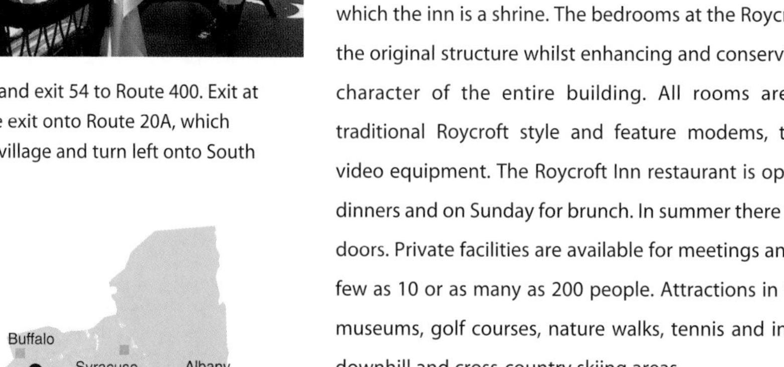

Price Guide:
rooms $150-$175
suites $145-$230

The Roycroft Inn is in every sense an American National Landmark. It was founded over a hundred years ago by the philosopher and writer Elbert Hubbard to provide congenial accommodation for devotees of the local Arts and Craft movement. His influence and memory live on at the Roycroft, thanks largely to the Margaret L. Wendt Foundation, which enabled the inn to be renovated and reopened in 1995 in a style worthy of the founder's highest beliefs and aspirations. The décor and furniture are either original or authentic reproduction examples of the celebrated movement to which the inn is a shrine. The bedrooms at the Roycroft conform to the original structure whilst enhancing and conserving the historic character of the entire building. All rooms are furnished in traditional Roycroft style and feature modems, televisions and video equipment. The Roycroft Inn restaurant is open for lunches, dinners and on Sunday for brunch. In summer there is dining out of doors. Private facilities are available for meetings and parties for as few as 10 or as many as 200 people. Attractions in the locality are museums, golf courses, nature walks, tennis and in season, many downhill and cross-country skiing areas.

Our inspector loved: *The beautiful woodwork and Mission-style, a home from home.*

WHITEFACE LODGE

7 WHITEFACE INN LANE, LAKE PLACID, NEW YORK 12946

The brainchild of former Olympian and developer Joe Barile, this all-suite resort, created in the style of the Adirondack Great Camps, opened in 2005. Blending rustic elegance with contemporary luxury and exceptional service, this is a world-class resort with a welcoming atmosphere. Suites feature jetted tubs, cast-iron gas fireplaces and L.C.D. high-definition T.V.s. Contemporary American cuisine, prepared from fresh, local organic ingredients and native North American fish and game, is served in the fine dining restaurant, Kanu, and the more casual Kanu Bistro. Gourmands and aspiring chefs will enjoy the Kanu exhibition kitchen and cooking classes. The Canoe Club boasts a private beach and offers traditional camp activities such as canoeing, kayaking, volleyball, badminton, croquet, bocci ball, horseshoes and ping pong. Other on-site facilities include an indoor/outdoor heated pool, fitness center, games room, year-round ice skating rink, 10-pin bowling alley, platform tennis and surround-sound theater. There is also hiking, mountain biking, snowshoe and cross-country ski trails. Winter sport facilities are not available on-site but sure to be found in the nearby 2-time Olympic village of Lake Placid. The Whiteface Lodge Spa, the East Coast's only 24-hour spa, offers treatments in its Spa Suites or in guests' own rooms. The 24-hour concierge service will help arrange any activity.

Our inspector loved: *The outstanding service, and abundance of activities.*

Directions: From I-87, take Exit 30 onto US-9 north. Make a slight left onto NY-73 north and continue for approximately 28 miles. Bear left onto Old Military Road/CR-35 then turn right onto Caroline Road/CR-35A. Turn right onto NY-86/Saranac Avenue then left onto Whiteface Inn Lane.

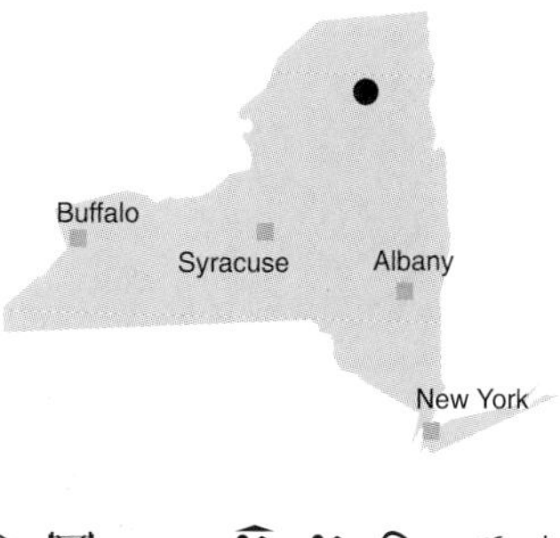

Buffalo
Syracuse
Albany
New York

Web: www.johansens.com/whiteface
E-mail: info@thewhitefacelodge.com
Tel: +1 518 523 0500
Fax: +1 518 523 0559
U.S./Canada Toll Free: 1 800 903 4045

Price Guide:
suites $300-$1500

HOTEL PLAZA ATHÉNÉE

37 EAST 64TH STREET, NEW YORK, NEW YORK 10021

Directions: 12 miles from La Guardia Airport, 16 miles from J.F.K. and 23 miles from Newark Liberty Airport.

Web: www.johansens.com/athenee
E-mail: res@plaza-athenee.com
Tel: +1 212 734 9100
Fax: +1 212 772 0958
U.S./Canada Toll Free: 1 800 447 8800

Price Guide: (room only)
rooms $580-$825
suites $1,335-$4,100

Voted "One of the Top Hotels in New York City" Gold List, by Condé Nast Traveler 2006, Hotel Plaza Athenee sets an exceptional standard for luxurious accommodation and professional service. Conveniently and fashionably situated on the East Side of Manhattan, Central Park, Madison Avenue shopping, museums and business areas are a short walk away. Nestled among a line of town houses on a quiet tree-lined street, a European influence pervades the interior. Reminiscent of an elegant home, rooms have recently been refubished with Asian silks and soothing earth tones. Each of the 115 rooms and 35 suites, has high-speed Internet access, and complimentary services include: 24-hour concierge, tea and coffee at 5.30-7pm, use of the fitness center and Internet access in the bar. Some suites have a sweeping view over the rooftops of Manhattan from a private balcony and atrium terrace. Modern American cuisine is served in Arabelle, a romantic gold-domed room with lovely murano glass. Enjoy an after-dinner drink in the exotic Bar Seine, where a fusion of Moroccan, African, European and Asian art are complemented by animal print fabrics and leather flooring. Relieve the stress of planning a vacation schedule and allow the concierge to arrange a myriad of activities in the exciting "Big Apple".

Our inspector loved: *The impeccable attention to detail and service.*

The Inn at Irving Place

56 IRVING PLACE, NEW YORK, NEW YORK 10003

Rated one of the top ten hotels in the world by the London Times and the most romantic hotel in New York by Time Out, The Inn at Irving Place is definitely an impressive venue to visit and a peaceful respite from the bustling city. Built in 1834, in the heart of New York's historic Gramercy Park, surrounded by tree-lined streets and landmark architecture, this unique hotel has been carefully renovated to reflect the timeless elegance of a bygone era. Luxurious furnishings and beautiful antiques adorn the 11 immaculate bedrooms, which are reminiscent of Edith Wharton's New York. They all have modern comforts such as Internet access and climate control and the junior suites boast extremely comfortable sitting rooms. A delicious breakfast can be served in bed or in the famous Lady Mendl's Tea Salon, renowned for its idyllic setting and fine teas. Your hosts will be happy to recommend one of the many excellent restaurants nearby and for health enthusiasts, there is a fitness club a few minutes away. Guests can shop at Greenwich Village, visit museums in the area or simply explore the historic neighborhood, which is full of surprises.

Our inspector loved: *High tea in Lady Mendl's Tea Salon.*

Directions: Located on Irving Place between 17th and 18th Streets.

Web: www.johansens.com/irvingplace
E-mail: innatirving@aol.com
Tel: +1 212 533 4600
Fax: +1 212 533 4611
U.S./Canada Toll Free: 1 800 685 1447

Price Guide:
rooms $415-$625

Castle On The Hudson

400 BENEDICT AVENUE, TARRYTOWN, NEW YORK 10591

Directions: Take I-87 to Tappan Zee Bridge and take exit 9 to Benedict. For more detailed directions please visit the Castle's website.

Web: www.johansens.com/hudson
E-mail: info@castleonthehudson.com
Tel: +1 914 631 1980
Fax: +1 914 631 4612
U.S./Canada Toll Free: 1 800 616 4487

Price Guide: (room only)
rooms $330-$430
suites $500-$800

This sumptuous medieval-style castle was built during the turn of the 20th century by New York writer, businessman and socialite, Howard Carroll, in order to flaunt his wealth. Following his death, the castle was converted into an opulent hotel offering traditional, warm hospitality and impeccable service. The stunning interior creates a comfortable atmosphere of sheer luxury and each of the individually appointed bedrooms and bathrooms has been lavished with rich fabrics, ornate artworks, antiques and beautiful wooden furniture. The magnificent Tower Suites are the ultimate in style with four-poster beds, wood-burning fireplaces, marble bathrooms, turret alcoves and panoramic vistas over the hillside, Hudson River and Manhattan. Dining at the hotel is sublime: there are 3 different rooms, each with their own unique ambience, in which to enjoy the creative and mouth-watering gourmet dishes prepared by the superb chefs, accompanied by fine wines. The spectacular outdoor terrace is perfect for a romantic al fresco meal and cocktails. Guests can enjoy a stroll around the picturesque landscaped gardens, which feature a bocce court, tennis court and heated swimming pool. The pool complex features a giant outdoor Jacuzzi and bar. There are also numerous activities nearby such as horse riding, hiking and mountain biking as well as scenic drives around the area.

Our inspector loved: *The beautiful gardens, and New York City skyline.*

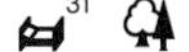

THE LODGE AT TURNING STONE

5218 PATRICK ROAD, VERONA, NEW YORK 13478

The Lodge at Turning Stone has become, without doubt, a Verona landmark. It is stylishly modern in design, elegant and attractive. A luxury boutique hotel that surrounds its guests with sophistication and comfort, providing a personal and attentive service that many regular guests report as unsurpassable. It is a peaceful and welcoming haven; a sanctuary for relaxation and pampering. At its heart is the magnificent Great Room, with its open fire, luxury seating, lavish furnishings, superb décor and interesting artwork – a superb venue in which to relax and enjoy stunning views before taking a memorable gourmet dinner in the elegant Wildflowers restaurant, whose kitchen team are accomplished in creating traditional continental dishes prepared to exact preferences. Guest suites are lavishly furnished and impeccably appointed with every modern amenity and comfort, each with wonderful balcony views over 2 of the country's finest and most challenging, Scottish-style, 18-hole landscaped golf courses. The expansive Presidential Suite is the ultimate accommodation: an opulent retreat with 3 bedrooms, a mini spa, kitchen and deluxe media center. More pampering is on offer at the high-tech health club and spa. For more casual enjoyment there is a large indoor heated pool, an expansive casino and a wide array of restaurants to choose from.

Our inspector loved: *The amazing Presidential Suite.*

 98        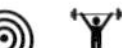   SPA

Directions: From the North and South take Route 81 to Syracuse and then the New York State Thruway (I-90) East to Exit 33 (Verona). Travel to the stoplight and turn left onto Route 365. Take the next left into Turning Stone Resort and Casino.

Web: www.johansens.com/turningstone
E-mail: info@turningstone.com
Tel: +1 315 361 8525
Fax: +1 315 361 8686
U.S./Canada Toll Free: 1 877 784 8375

Price Guide:
suites $199-$3,000

The Baker House 1650

181 MAIN STREET, EAST HAMPTON, NEW YORK 11937

East Hampton's charming Baker House 1650 exudes elegance and will delight visitors in search of an exclusive hideaway with a romantic ambience. The beautifully appointed mansion will appeal to Brits and Anglophiles alike with its wood craftwork derived from medieval English architecture and the Colonial revival staircase that leads up to 5 cozy bedrooms. Wood burning fireplaces and William Morris wallpaper contrast with the flat-screen T.V.s and state-of-the-art cable and D.V.D. players whilst the bathrooms are enhanced by whirlpools and L'Occitane products. The attractive surrounds are bedecked with flowering perennials and shrubs, delicately scented herbs and English gardens with outdoor terraces for al fresco dining, a 200-year-old wisteria and vine-covered walls. The new outdoor infinity-edge pool, with teak chaises for sunbathing, is delightfully relaxing and the Baker Spa, featuring a lap pool, massage area, 2 steam showers and a sauna, is the ideal retreat after a lunchtime stroll. In the summer, guests receive coveted East Hampton Village beach parking passes, as well as beach towels, umbrellas and chairs. Pastimes include cycling, fishing and jet skiing but for those seeking a more leisurely pace, the ample boutiques, antique shops and farmers' markets, not to mention the large retail outlets on Main Street, are worth a visit.

Our inspector loved: *The Baker Spa within this historic house.*

Directions: J.F.K. Airport is approximately a $2^1/_2$-hour drive from the property.

Web: www.johansens.com/bakerhouse
E-mail: info@bakerhouse1650.com
Tel: +1 631 324 4081
Fax: +1 631 329 5931

Price Guide: (excluding tax)
rooms $250-$795

     SPA     

The Mill House Inn

31 NORTH MAIN STREET, EAST HAMPTON, NEW YORK 11937

The Mill House Inn is a quiet and romantic getaway built in 1790 and located in East Hampton, which was named America's Most Beautiful Village by National Geographic. The inn is surrounded by spectacular ocean beaches, pristine bays and picturesque country roads and is a tranquil venue to relax and escape from the worries of everyday life. Warm, inviting interiors create a relaxed ambience that is friendly and welcoming whilst the attention to detail combined with old-fashioned hospitality truly makes each visit a memorable one. The well-appointed rooms are individually decorated with fine quality linens, lofty featherbeds, gas fireplaces and whirlpool tubs. The spacious suites have 6-foot serenity air baths, double marble showers and private decks. Guests can enjoy spectacular sunsets and starry skies from the front porch, which overlooks the historic Old Hook Windmill. The unforgettable breakfast features imaginative dishes such as crawfish and Andouille omelette or 5-cheese frittata to savor at a leisurely pace. The eastern end of Long Island is a fisherman's playground, a vintner's paradise and an artist's inspiration. Terrific restaurants, upmarket boutiques, art galleries and many outdoor activities are on offer in East Hampton. Explore the farmers' market in Amagansett, the wineries in Bridgehampton or simply indulge in the solitude of the lush gardens.

Directions: J.F.K. Airport is a 2½-hour drive from the inn.

Web: www.johansens.com/millhouse
E-mail: innkeeper@millhouseinn.com
Tel: +1 631 324 9766
Fax: +1 631 324 9793

Price Guide:
rooms $200-$600
suites $350-$1,400

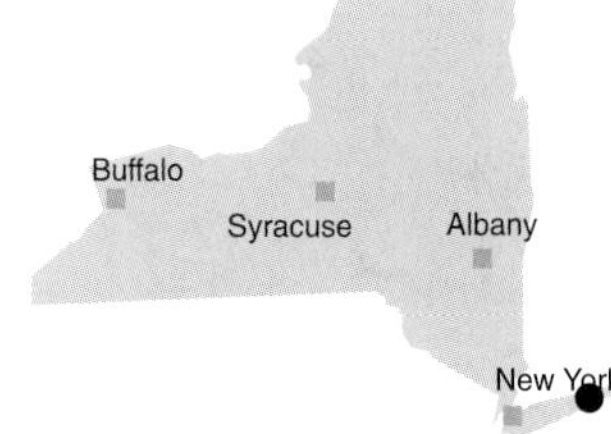

Our inspector loved: *The breakfast - simply remarkable!*

Ballantyne Resort

10000 BALLANTYNE COMMONS PARKWAY, CHARLOTTE, NORTH CAROLINA 28277

Part of Starwood Hotels & Resorts, The Luxury Collection, Ballantyne Resort stands in the heart of south Charlotte. An impressive porte cochere entrance welcomes guests into an expansive lobby and intimate bar. Enjoy the view from the 2-story Palladian window overlooking the 18th fairway of the championship golf course, selected one of the Great Golf Resorts of the World by P.G.A. Magazine. Decorated by the owner's wife, this AAA 4-Diamond resort features custom-made English furniture, fine fabrics and original paintings by Tom Vieth depicting renowned sites in Charlotte. Guest rooms and suites offer every modern amenity such as "Luxury Collection" beds, 300-thread-count Egyptian cotton sheets, marble baths and high-speed wireless Internet access. The Grill Room provides new menus in a classic setting and the Veranda Bar offers specialty drinks and light fare with live entertainment. The spa has more than 80 treatments including detoxifying wraps and full salon services. Golf enthusiasts can enjoy on-site instruction at the Dana Rader Golf School, consistently ranked as one of Golf Magazine's Top 25 Schools. Extensive fitness and leisure facilities include a state-of-the-art health club with K.M.X. Lab, indoor grotto pool and wave pools. There is also over 20,000 sq. ft. of elegant event space and a 40,000 sq. ft. lodge retreat with 35 guest rooms.

Directions: Take I-485 to exit 61, then Route 521.

Web: www.johansens.com/ballantyneresort
E-mail: info@ballantyneresort.com
Tel: +1 704 248 4000
Fax: +1 704 248 4005
U.S./Canada Toll Free: 1 866 248 4824

Price Guide:
rooms $180-$399
suites $400-$1200

Our inspector loved: *The balcony overlooking the 18th green.*

The Sanderling Resort & Spa

1461 DUCK ROAD, DUCK, NORTH CAROLINA 27949

Breathtaking views surround The Sanderling. The Outer Banks' only true resort, The Sanderling touches the shores of both the Atlantic Ocean and Currituck Sound. Miles of unspoiled beaches provide serenity which, like the ocean waves, insure your inevitable return. Relax at The Sanderling Spa, with its beautiful backdrop of the tranquil waters of Currituck Sound making the experience complete. The full menu of services include massage, body, skin and nail care treatments, many of them created uniquely for The Spa. The Sanderling's luxurious lodging reflects classic Outer Banks architecture. Each of 3 distinctive 2-story inns is decorated with a rare collection of fine wildlife art and sculptures, and each building offers private porches, most with ocean or sound views. 4 oceanside cottages and 1 ocean-front cottage are also available. The Sanderling affords 3 dining options, assuring a memorable meal for every palate. Dine casually among nautical artifacts in a restored 1899 U.S. Lifesaving Station or play the epicure in the formal dining room, where spectacular views of Currituck Sound complement fine cuisine. Just 5 miles from the charming village of Duck and adjacent to the 3,400-acre Pine Island Audubon Sanctuary, this is a true departure from the ordinary.

Our inspector loved: *This extremely relaxing place on the beach with beautiful views, great food, and the sea is incredible.*

Directions: The nearest commercial airport is Norfolk, V.A. 75 miles from the resort. Private transportation is available through Sea Air. Fly from Norfolk direct to Pine Island, 3 miles from the resort.

Web: www.johansens.com/sanderling
E-mail: reservations@thesanderling.com
Tel: +1 252 261 4111
Fax: +1 252 261 1638
U.S./Canada Toll Free: 1 800 701 4111

Raleigh
Charlotte
Wilmington

Price Guide: (room only)
rooms $256-$414
suites $330-$1,045

 96    100       SPA 

Inn at Half Mile Farm

P.O. BOX 2769, 214 HALF MILE DRIVE, HIGHLANDS, NORTH CAROLINA 28741

Tucked away on the outskirts of town, this lovely rambling inn is a paradise for nature lovers and those who hanker for fresh mountain air, forests, ponds, streams and the great outdoor life. There's hiking, fly-fishing, lake canoeing, white water rafting and just about every mountain activity. All can be arranged by a friendly and helpful staff. Originally a mid-19th-century farmhouse the inn is surrounded by beautiful grounds which feature a lake, swimming pool and an abundance of wild flowers and deep greenery, all of which can be viewed and enjoyed from comfortable whicker rocking chairs on the shaded porch. Sit and watch the sun rise and set over the mountain peaks while enjoying an early morning coffee or an evening complimentary wine and hors d'oeuvres. Tennessee fieldstone fireplaces, soft sofas, polished pine floors, local wood decorations and Rattan stick furniture in the breakfast room are particularly attractive features of the 4 guest rooms in the main house and those surrounding a colorful courtyard and fountain. All 23 rooms are spacious, individually decorated and have every comfort and amenity. Soft muted tones and locally crafted beds, tables and lights provide a calm, relaxing rustic atmosphere. Most rooms have decks and jetted tubs with king suites boasting fireplaces and sitting areas.

Our inspector loved: *The light and airy rooms.*

Directions: From Highlands take NC 64 west. After 1 mile turn right onto Mirror Lake Road and bear right onto Hicks Road. The inn is 1/2 mile further on the right.

Web: www.johansens.com/halfmilefarm
E-mail: stay@halfmilefarm.com
Tel: +1 828 526 8170
Fax: +1 828 526 2625
U.S./Canada Toll Free: 1 800 946 6822

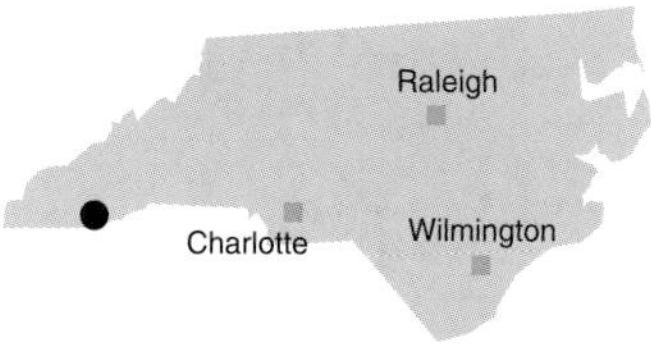

Raleigh
Charlotte
Wilmington

Price Guide:
rooms $220–$950

Preferred BOUTIQUE

Old Edwards Inn and Spa

445 Main Street, Highlands, North Carolina 28741

Recently the subject of an extensive refurbishment program, this is the ultimate luxurious getaway in the heart of the Blue Ridge Mountains. The inn has the ambience and romance of a historic building whilst offering every conceivable modern amenity. Highlands is a delightful and welcoming community, and Old Edwards Inn forms an integral part of the town. Upon arrival, guests are offered valet parking followed by champagne. Wide plasma TV and elegant frette linens set the scene for the bedrooms, whilst the bathrooms all have underfloor heating, raindancing showers and Bulgari amenities. Each of the guest rooms is individually decorated and there is a twice-daily maid service. Madison's Restaurant and Wine Garden serves Carolina High Country cuisine with a stunning backdrop of the wine garden; guests may dine al fresco. The spa is unrivaled in the Carolina mountains and features some of the most exotic and contemporary treatments from around the world. The entire area has heated limestone flooring and fine antique pieces, complete with 8 individual treatment rooms including the Rainforest Rejuvenation room. The "Farm", located nearby, is a superb venue for meetings and social events, and remains in-keeping with the style of the inn. An Executive Conference and Fitness Center opened in 2006.

***Our inspector loved:** The first-class accommodation complete with spa in the lovely picturesque Highlands.*

Directions: The nearest airport is Asheville, North Carolina. Located on the corner of Main and South Streets in downtown Highlands.

Web: www.johansens.com/oldedwards
E-mail: info@oldedwardsinn.com
Tel: +1 828 526 8008
Fax: +1 828 526 8301
U.S./Canada Toll Free: 1 866 526 8008

Price Guide:
rooms $255-$315
suites $275-$995
cottages $1,800-$2,400

THE AERIE INN

509 POLLOCK STREET, NEW BERN, NORTH CAROLINA 28562

This delightful Victorian villa, circa 1880, is the favorite year-round spot for travelers to enjoy Eastern North Carolina and truly understand that "North Carolina Begins Here." An inviting welcome pervades the inn, and the parlor, with its period furniture and cozy fireplace, has guests chatting eagerly over cheese and wine in the evening. Each of the bedrooms has its own distinct style, with names carefully chosen; for instance the popular "Magnolia Room," with its corner whirlpool bath, is so-called for the large magnolia tree located outside and also pays tribute to the beautiful white blossoms which embody North Carolina's Southern traditions of grace and sophistication. The décor is very much in-keeping with the heritage of the building, whilst a warmth and modern-day comfort is evident throughout. The inn serves an excellent gourmet breakfast, and the early evening appetizers are rapidly becoming legendary. A gentle stroll downtown takes guests to a fine selection of New Bern's excellent restaurants, as well as the Tryon Palace Historic Sites and Gardens and the many "Firsts" of New Bern. The Aerie is just 1 block from numerous tourist sites including the birthplace of Pepsi Cola and is just 2 blocks from the water.

Our inspector loved: *This beautiful Victorian inn set in a great location. Expect to come away with some new friends!*

Directions: Follow U.S. 17 or U.S. 70 to New Bern and follow signs to Tryon Palace and Historic Downtown New Bern. The Aerie Inn is 1 block east of Tryon Palace.

Web: www.johansens.com/aerieinn
E-mail: aerieinn@aol.com
Tel: +1 252 636 5553
Fax: +1 252 514 2157
U.S./Canada Toll Free: 1 800 849 5553

Price Guide:
rooms$109-$159
suites $139-$159

The Fearrington House

2000 FEARRINGTON VILLAGE CENTER, PITTSBORO, NORTH CAROLINA 27312

Tucked away on 1,400 acres of farmland, this friendly and welcoming country inn and restaurant was opened in 1986 by R.B. and Jenny Fitch. It forms the hub of the charming village of Fearrington, which was once a working dairy farm owned by the Fearrington family. Many of the original buildings now house quaint shops, cafés, the inn and The Fearrington House Restaurant. There are 33 exquisitely decorated bedrooms and suites; some offer fireplaces, Jacuzzis and canopied beds. Excellent service and sophisticated classic cuisine are the hallmark of the elegant restaurant, where Chef Graham Fox, Averey's Young British Chef of the Year 1999, creates an enticing blend of European and American flavors. Graham also runs the popular Cooking School. The only establishment in North Carolina to receive the AAA's prestigious 5 Diamond Award as well as Exxon Mobil's 5 Star Award, The Fearrington House has also won 29 Zagat Points and the Wine Spectator's Best of Award of Excellence. For a more casual dining experience, guests may walk or cycle to the village's Deli or the Market Café. A Swimming and Croquet Club is nearby, whilst the numerous gardens of Fearrington are worth exploring, including "Jenny's Garden," with its water sculpture centerpiece, and the herb garden, which is used for the restaurant.

Our inspector loved: *The beautiful rooms and grounds as well as attention to every detail. Prepare to be treated like royalty!*

Directions: Located south of Chapel Hill on US15-501. 40 minutes from Raleigh-Durham International Airport.

Raleigh
Charlotte
Wilmington

Web: www.johansens.com/fearrington
E-mail: fhouse@fearrington.com
Tel: +1 919 542 2121
Fax: +1 919 542 4202
U.S./Canada Toll Free: 1 800 277 0130

Price Guide:
rooms $240-$310
suites $390-$490

The Siena Hotel

1505 E. FRANKLIN STREET, CHAPEL HILL, NORTH CAROLINA 27514

Named after a small, beautiful Italian town cradled in the northern hills of Tuscany, The Siena Hotel embodies the spirit of Italy in the heart of North Carolina. A personalized check-in service surrounded by authentic marble is surpassed only by the sight and aroma of roses grown in the gardens. The décor is luxurious, with grand European antiques, elaborate furnishings, rich textured fabrics, majestic columns, warm colors and soft lighting. The hallways and rooms are a picture of grandeur reflected by the beautiful artwork together with the hotel's overall ambience, floral aromas and excellent service. Based on a Tuscan villa, The Siena is considered by many to be North Carolina's finest luxury boutique hotel and has been a AAA 4 Diamond holder since 1989. Each of the 68 guest rooms and 12 suites is individually appointed with rich fabrics and elaborate artwork; they have magnificent marble bathrooms, the latest technology, including high-speed Internet access, and lovely additional touches such as a nightly turndown service, Belgian Siena chocolates, soft bathrobes and European toiletries. Exceptional cuisine can be enjoyed in Il Palio, the only AAA 4 Diamond Italian restaurant in the State.

Our inspector loved: *Feeling as if you are in Italy.*

Directions: 15 miles from Raleigh-Durham International Airport on I-40 west

Web: www.johansens.com/siena
E-mail: stravers@sienahotel.com
Tel: +1 919 929 4000
Fax: +1 919 968 8527
U.S./Canada Toll Free: 1 800 223 7379

Price Guide:
rooms $185–$285
suites $230–$350

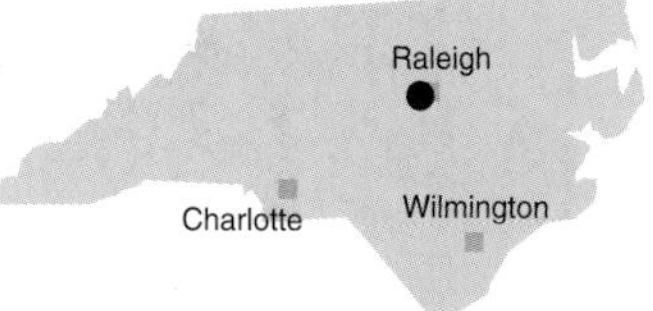

Pine Crest Inn and Restaurant

85 PINE CREST LANE, TRYON, NORTH CAROLINA 28782

Tucked away in the foothills of the Blue Ridge Mountains, this traditional English-style inn was once a favorite of F. Scott Fitzgerald and Ernest Hemingway. Today, the Inn is listed on the National Register of Historic Places and features 30 rooms, luxurious suites, and intimate cottages nestled among year-round flowering gardens. Accommodations are varied with individual character, private baths, and most have fireplaces and whirlpool tubs, creating a charming atmosphere of casual elegance where the Caudle Family have created a peaceful "home away from home" ambience. Fine dining is reason alone to visit the Inn; a sumptuous, made-to-order breakfast voted "Best in the Southeast" is served complimentary each morning. The extensive dinner menu offers gourmet American cuisine that embraces the bounty of fresh seasonal ingredients that highlight the efforts of local farmers and food artisans. Guests enjoy an extensive selection of spirits and a Wine Spectator award-winning wine cellar with fine vintages from around the world. The Conference Center is fully equipped for corporate retreats, training sessions and group meetings, while the meticulously landscaped 10-acre grounds invite guests to celebrate weddings, receptions, or family reunions. Waterfall and hiking trails, golf, tennis, horseback riding, and quaint small towns with unending antique shopping are all nearby.

Our inspector loved: *The range of rooms and country cottages available.*

Directions: From I-26, exit 67 to Tryon. Follow Route 108/176 to Tryon. Turn left into New Market Road. Follow signs to the inn.

Web: www.johansens.com/pinecrestinn
E-mail: johansens@pinecrestinn.com
Tel: +1 828 859 9135
Fax: +1 828 859 9136
U.S./Canada Toll Free: 1 800 633 3001

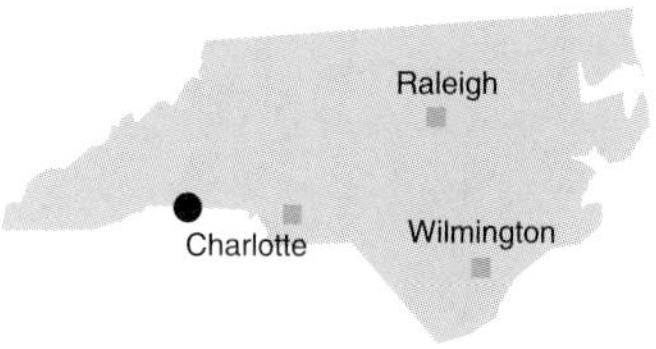

Raleigh
Charlotte
Wilmington

Price Guide:
rooms \$89–\$199
suites \$179–\$349
cottages \$139-\$559

Ohio

Hotel location shown in red with page number

U.S.A. - OHIO (CINCINNATI)

The Cincinnatian Hotel

601 VINE STREET, CINCINNATI, OHIO 45202-2433

The Cincinnatian Hotel was designed as a "Grand Hotel" in the 19th century and today is a great testament to the era. Built in 1882, this luxurious hotel stands in the heart of downtown Cincinnati amidst upscale shops and restaurants, 1 block from Fountain Square. Recipient of Mobil 4 Star and AAA 4 Diamond awards, this cosmopolitan hotel offers 146 guest rooms, including 7 suites. Lavish décor and amenities including whirlpools, fireplaces, balconies, tailored upholstery, luxurious linens, soft terrycloth robes and Roman tubs make the guest rooms truly elegant. All rooms include twice daily maid service and evening turndown, complimentary newspapers, coffee and free high-speed and wireless Internet access throughout the bedrooms, restaurant and lounge. The opulent décor reflects a European style and displays magnificent collections of art. The Palace Restaurant serves an exciting, eclectic, ever-changing menu; first-class American fine dining, and after-dinner drinks may be taken in the relaxing haven of the Cricket Lounge. Lighter meals are served here and its nightlife is legendary: solo piano on weekdays and live jazz trip is played during the weekend. For art lovers the hotel is near the Aronoff Center of Arts and Contemporary Art Center. For the health conscious, state-of-the-art fitness facilities with cardio theater equipment are available.

Our inspector loved: *Taking afternoon tea in the Cricket Lounge.*

Directions: From Cincinnati-Northern Kentucky Intl. Airport take 275 east to 75/71 north. Follow 75 north signs across the bridge over the Ohio River. Take the Fifth Street exit just after crossing the bridge into Ohio. Turn left onto Vine Street and left onto Sixth Street; the hotel is on the corner of Sixth and Vine.

Web: www.johansens.com/cincinnatian
E-mail: info@cincinnatianhotel.com
Tel: +1 513 381 3000
Fax: +1 513 651 0256
U.S./Canada Toll Free: 1 800 942 9000

Price Guide: (room only)
rooms $225-$295
suites $315-$1,500

U.S.A. - OREGON (ASHLAND)

THE WINCHESTER INN & RESTAURANT

35 SOUTH SECOND STREET, ASHLAND, OREGON 97520

This old 3-story inn, with large windows and attractive roof peaks, stands in downtown Ashland; an intimate lodging where guests can relax or take a stroll to the nearby shops, restaurants and attractions. Owned, restored, refurbished and managed since 1983 by Laurie and Michael Gibbs, the hotel has expanded from the original 1886 Victorian family house and today's 4 buildings and famed restaurant are surrounded by an award-winning, English cottage-style garden. The ambience, décor, furnishings and comfort of the rooms and suites, together with the attention to detail throughout the property, will appeal to the most discerning visitor. The Main House has 7 enchanting Victorian guest rooms and 1 suite. The Heritage House next door features 3 suites and 4 bedrooms. The Carriage House offers 2 suites and the Larkspur Cottage, a short brick-lined walk away, has 2 very private suites. The crowning touch of the inn is the food; exquisite meals are served in the elegant Main House restaurant with the kitchen team using organically grown local products whenever possible. Seasonal menus feature fresh morels in the spring, Chinook salmon in summer, fruits and berries in the fall and chanterelles and trout in winter alongside an extensive wine list awarded the Wine Spectator Award of Excellence.

Our inspector loved: *The inn's new wine tours, which include a progressive lunch at beautiful local Oregon vineyards.*

Directions: Located 15 minutes south of Medford.

Web: www.johansens.com/winchester
E-mail: Innkeeper@WinchesterInn.com
Tel: +1 541 488 1113
Fax: +1 541 488 4604
U.S./Canada Toll Free: 1 800 972 4991

Price Guide: (room only)
rooms $135-$175
suites $185-$250

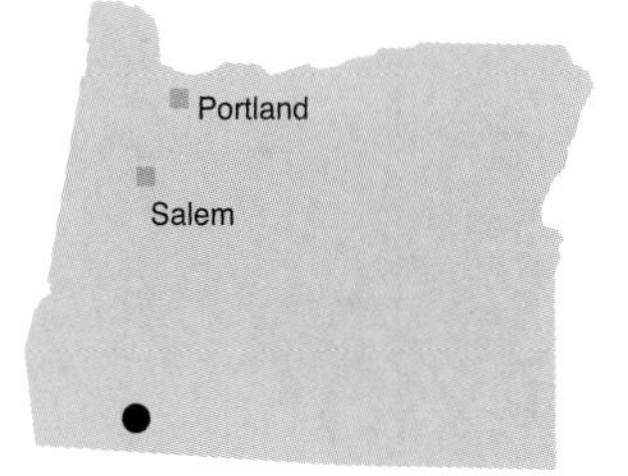

The Benson Hotel

309 SOUTHWEST BROADWAY, PORTLAND, OREGON 97205

This prestigious, grand hotel is ideally situated for shopping, sightseeing, the theater and absorbing the culture and atmosphere of Portland's vibrant downtown. With its high ceilings, stately and spacious rooms, elegant furnishings, rich curtains and fabrics, sumptuous carpets, huge chandeliers and highly polished woodwork, a special quality is projected alongside modern luxury in a classic setting. No task is too small for the staff who provide personal, discreet and excellent service. Each guest room and suite offers comfort, a restful ambience and every feature expected from a hotel rated with the distinguished AAA 4 Diamond Award. Taupe and black window treatments, velvet throw pillows, plush bathrobes, Nintendo games and movies, wireless Internet and more. Some suites feature a grand piano, an open fireplace, French doors and Jacuzzi. The Penthouse Suites on the exclusive 14th floor, have superb views of downtown and beyond. Elegant décor and soft lighting create an intimate dining ambience in the London Grill where Executive Chef Xavier Bauser and his team produce cuisine featuring traditional favorites and bold, innovative creations. The London Grill serves one of the most extensive wine lists in the Northwest with more than 6,000 bottles. Extensive business, private dining, conference and banquet facilities are available.

Our inspector loved: *The Wine Cellar of the London Grill.*

Directions: A 25-minute drive from Portland Airport.

Web: www.johansens.com/benson
E-mail: reservations@bensonhotel.com
Tel: +1 503 228 2000
Fax: +1 503 471 3920
U.S./Canada Toll Free: 1 888 523 6766

Price Guide: (room only)
rooms $139-$239
suites $214-$900

The Heathman Hotel

1001 S.W. BROADWAY, PORTLAND, OREGON 97205

This vibrant city hotel successfully combines its Old World atmosphere with a modern twist, and though it has 150 rooms it is full of intimate charm. This is partly due to the warm décor of the Lobby and Tea Court Lounge and the absence of a "check in" desk. A multi-million dollar renovation on all guest rooms and suites has just been completed to implement the first ever "Art of Sleep Bed Menu" offering each guest the opportunity to choose from 3 mattress types: Tempur Pedic, European Pillow Top or European Feather Bed. The "personal concierge" system assigns each guest an individual who will provide a seamless, personal service. The concept encourages interaction between guest and staff, achieving a sense of intimacy one might expect at a smaller hotel. The bedrooms feature French press coffee and tea, C.D. alarm clock radios, a turndown service and high-speed Internet access. The beautiful Mezzanine holds curated art exhibits and looks down over the art deco Lobby and Lounge, where jazz artists play most nights. Pacific Northwest cuisine is served in the award-winning Heathman Restaurant whose executive chef, Phillipe Boulot, has been honored as "Best Chef in the Northwest." Portland has fantastic restaurants, galleries, music and theater and the surrounding area features mountains, vineyards and a stunning coastline.

Directions: Portland Airport is a 30-minute drive from the hotel in downtown Portland.

Web: www.johansens.com/heathman
E-mail: reservations@heathmanhotel.com
Tel: +1 503 241 4100
Fax: +1 503 790 7110
U.S./Canada Toll Free: 1 800 551 0011

Price Guide: (room only)
rooms $189-$269
suites $229-$1,200

Our inspector loved: *The French press coffee in the rooms.*

PENNSYLVANIA

Hotel location shown in red with page number

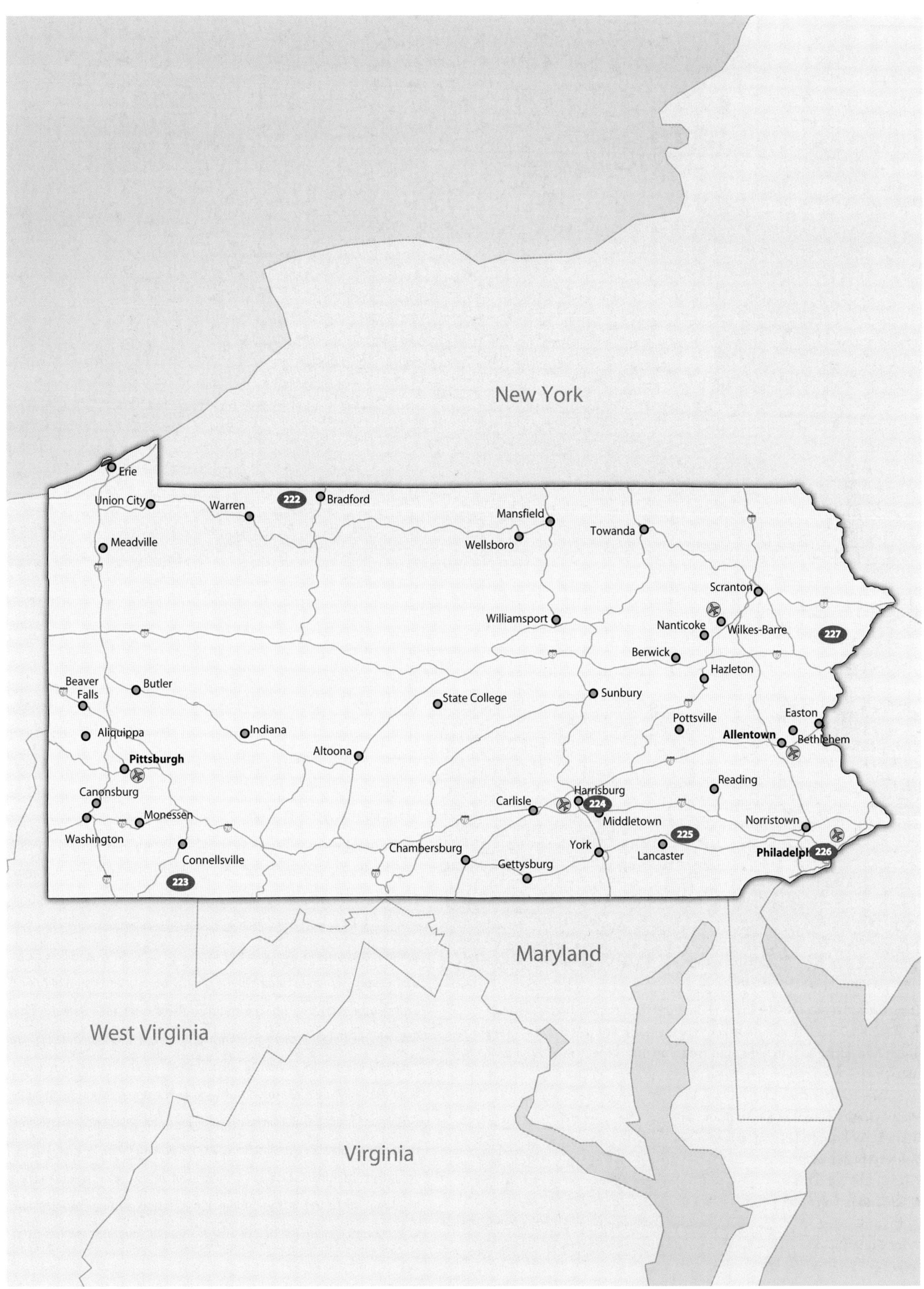

GLENDORN

1000 GLENDORN DRIVE, BRADFORD, PENNSYLVANIA 16701

Glendorn is a remarkable country retreat nestled next to the Allegheny National Forest, Pennsylvania. This family-owned estate, with 1,280 acres complete with running streams and private lakes, offers high levels of luxury, fine dining, comfort and tranquility. A variety of accommodations include a main lodge with 2 master suites and 2 luxury guest rooms; all have views of wild fields and woodlands. The centerpiece of the lodge is the great room with a magnificent cut-stone fireplace surrounded by antique furnishings and original family heirlooms from the 1930s. The cottage-style cabins offer seclusion and privacy; each one is unique with sumptuous furnishings and fireplaces, many boast screened porches. The dining room, with cathedral ceiling and redwood beams, offers a multi-course dinner each evening by a roaring fire. Fine wines selected from the award-winning wine list, are carefully paired to enhance each course. In the summer months, breakfast and lunch are served alfresco on the porch overlooking Fuller Brook and the heated swimming pool. Enjoy an Orvis endorsed fishing guide through clear trout streams and 3 private lakes. Year-round fly-fishing instruction is also available. Miles of untouched manicured trails are ideal for hiking in the spring, summer and autumn months and cross-country skiing and snow shoeing are enjoyed during the winter.

Our inspector loved: *The world-class service.*

Directions: Take Route 219 south to Bradford then the Forman Street exit. Turn left on Davis Street and turn right at the traffic light. At the end of Main Street turn left, then turn right onto West Corydon Street. Travel approx. 4 1/2 miles.

Web: www.johansens.com/glendorn
E-mail: glendorn@relaischateaux.com
Tel: +1 814 362 6511
Fax: +1 814 368 9923
U.S./Canada Toll Free: 1 800 843 8568

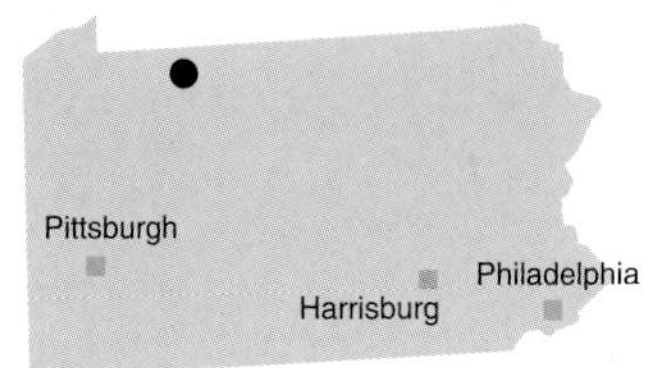

Price Guide:
rooms $495-$795

Nemacolin Woodlands

1001 Lafayette Drive, Farmington, Pennsylvania 15437

Beautifully situated in the Laurel Highland Mountains of Southwestern Pennsylvania, Nemacolin Woodlands is a spectacular destination that breaks new ground in resort travel. Set within an impressive 2,800 acres of stunning landscape, it boasts luxurious accommodations and an infinite variety of activities that in the property's own words, "will exceed what you've come to expect from a resort." There are multiple types of accommodations available; each has its own distinct character and offers first-class service and hospitality. Chateau LaFayette is inspired by the classic European hotels, town homes and luxury homes are ideal for families, the delightful Tudor-style Lodge has been designed in the style of a mountain hideaway, and the Frank Lloyd Wright-inspired Falling Rock is a study in luxury with complimentary 24-hour personal butler service. 14 restaurants include fine French, modern American, Italian and casual dining fare. There are two 18-hole championship golf courses and a state-of-the-art golf learning center, as well as a staggering variety of outdoor pursuits including equestrian trails, a shooting academy, rock climbing wall and snow sports to enjoy. The award-winning Woodlands Spa offers over 60 treatments ranging from Ayurveda to Reiki.

Directions: Located approximately 70 miles from Pittsburgh. Take I-76 (south) to Washington, Pennsylvania then take I-70 (east) to New Stanton and follow 119 south to 40 east into Farmington. The resort entrance is on the left.

Web: www.johansens.com/nemacolin
E-mail: birds.of.a.feather@nemacolin.com
Tel: +1 724 329 8555
Fax: +1 724 329 6947
U.S./Canada Toll Free: 1 800 422 2736

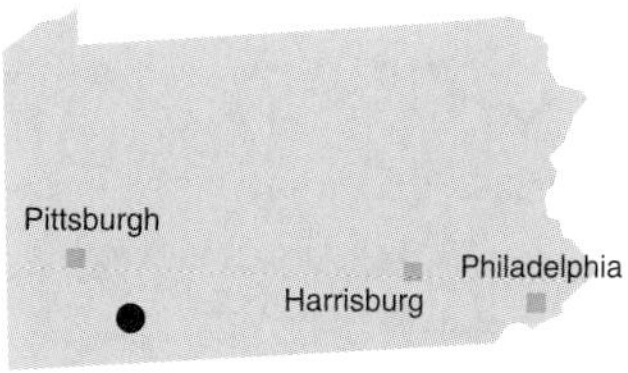

Price Guide: (room only)
rooms $200-$600
suites $300-$3,000

Our inspector loved: *The magnificent spa.*

 335  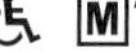 720       SPA     

THE HERSHEY HOTEL & SPA

100 HOTEL ROAD, HERSHEY, PENNSYLVANIA 17033

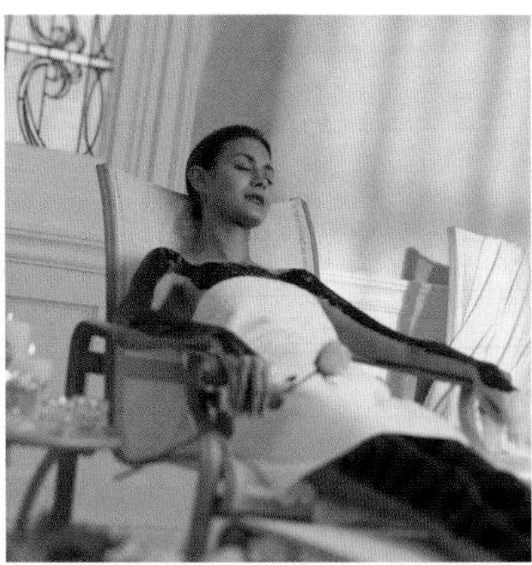

Directions: Located in central Pennsylvania, near Harrisburg. Easily accessed via Route 322. Only 90 minutes from Baltimore, 2 hours from Washington, D.C. and Philadelphia and 3 hours from New York City.

Web: www.johansens.com/hershey
E-mail: info@hersheyPA.com
Tel: +1 717 533 2171
Fax: +1 717 534 3165
U.S./Canada Toll Free: 1 800 HERSHEY

Price Guide: (room only)
rooms $289-$409
suites $305-$1,800

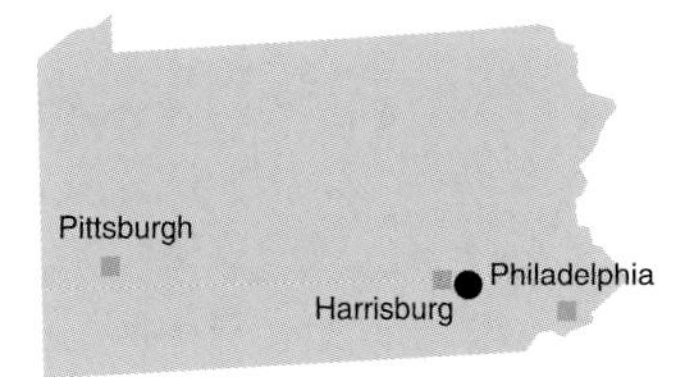

Dramatically situated on a hilltop overlooking the town of Hershey, this grand hotel is an award-winning national landmark known for its elegance, exemplary service and luxurious accommodations. Built in the 1930s, it was described by world traveler Lowell Thomas as, "a palace that out-palaces the palaces of the Maharajahs of India". The hotel today is a member of the Historic Hotels of America and has amenities to satisfy the most demanding tastes including The Chocolate Spa that features signature chocolate and Cuban themed treatments. Displays of wonderful old photographs line the corridors and each guest room features an original work of art. Panoramic views of the gardens, the lush green town of Hershey below, and the surrounding mountains, complete this world-class experience. Guests will enjoy gourmet cuisine at the spectacular AAA 4 Diamond-rated Circular Dining Room; more casual fare is served at The Fountain Café. Chocolate pastries and specialty coffees are served in The Cocoa Beanery; cocktails and chocolate martinis are served by the open fire in the Iberian Lounge. Guests have access to nearby Hershey Country Club and its two 18-hole golf courses.

Our inspector loved: *The rich history of this hotel, and the unique offerings at The Chocolate Spa.*

Leola Village Inn & Suites

38 DEBORAH DRIVE, ROUTE 23, LEOLA, PENNSYLVANIA 17540

Here is a place apart. A delightful "old" retreat where time appears to stand still, yet there is every modern amenity. Situated in the heart of Pennsylvania Dutch Country, and surrounded by lush farmland, Leola Village Inn and Suites is rich in history and architectural integrity. It comprises beautifully authentic, carefully restored Dutch Country homes and workplaces that have achieved recognition by the National Trust for Historic Preservation. Several of the buildings date back to 1873 and the lobby was once a tobacco barn. No two guest rooms or suites are alike. Each is larger than a standard hotel room, extremely comfortable and contains selected period and reproduction furniture. Every home-away-from-home luxury is on hand, from 27-inch television, D.V.D. player and 2-line speaker telephone with voicemail to king or queen-size bed, down comforters, Amish quilt, ultra-soft bathrobes and kitchenettes. Executive Suites have a fully-equipped kitchen and dining area. Located in the village is an outdoor pool, Destinations Hair Studio and Day Spa that features the Art of Shaving Products for men and a licensed barber. In addition, there are specialty shops and services including a popular wine bar and the restaurant, Mazzi, which offers a lavish Italian influenced menu and room service.

Our inspector loved: *The warm and friendly service, elegant rooms, and quaint village making this property a true gem.*

Directions: From Pennsylvania or New York: from the PA turnpike take Morgantown exit 298 and head west on Route 23 for 15 miles to Leola. Leola Village Inn is on the left in the center of town, in the heart of Armish Country.

Web: www.johansens.com/leolavillage
E-mail: jallen@leolavillage.com
Tel: +1 717 656 7002
Fax: +1 717 656 7648
U.S./Canada Toll Free: 1 877 669 5094

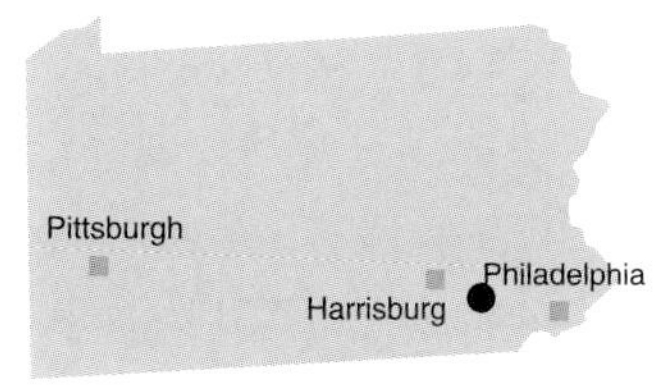

Price Guide:
rooms $160-$200
suites $189-$1,000

Rittenhouse 1715, A Boutique Hotel

1715 RITTENHOUSE SQUARE, PHILADELPHIA, PENNSYLVANIA 19103

Rittenhouse 1715 (formerly the Rittenhouse Square Bed & Breakfast) embraces its fresh, innovative look with a distinct new name. This traditional 19th-century carriage house in the fashionable Rittenhouse Square district of downtown Philadelphia has been restored and combined with the neighboring 18th-century Georgian town house to make it one of Philadelphia's most exclusive and luxurious boutique hotel accommodations. An intimate, comfortable retreat that exudes style, sophistication and charm, the hotel features fine furnishings, exquisite artwork and careful attention to detail. 16 individually designed guest rooms and suites are delightfully decorated with designer fabrics and furnished with antiques. All rooms feature marble bathrooms, plush robes, triple sheeting with fine European linens, 37" plasma T.V.s and nightly turndown service. A lovely complimentary Continental breakfast is served in the Parisian-style café and an evening wine reception is held in the newly decorated drawing room each day. The hotel also offers a 24-hour concierge service, wireless Internet access throughout the building, 2 computer workstations, fax and copier services, and is within walking distance of many of the city's leading restaurants, cafés, museums, historical attractions and shops.

Our inspector loved: *The evening wine receptions held in the newly decorated drawing room.*

Directions: Between Locust and Spruce Streets, between 17th and 18th Streets.

Web: www.johansens.com/rittenhouse
E-mail: reservations@rittenhouse1715.com
Tel: +1 215 546 6500
Fax: +1 215 546 8787
U.S./Canada Toll Free: 1 877 791 6500

Price Guide: (room only)
rooms from $240
junior suites from $290

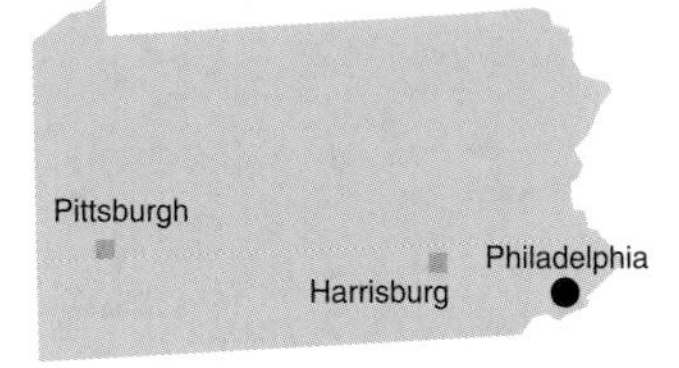

Skytop Lodge

One Skytop, Skytop, Pennsylvania 18357

Inspired by nature and enveloped in 5,500 acres of pristine forest, Skytop Lodge is an awe-inspiring holiday retreat with year-round, action-packed activities as well as plenty of quiet places to relax, admire the breathtaking views and let the worries of the world melt away. Accommodations are extremely flexible and range from spacious standard rooms to lovely streamside cottages ideal for families. Each room is decorated with care and reflects the abundance of fresh air and stunning surroundings. Guests can savor the delicious tastes of American cuisine in the historical main lodge or lakeside restaurant with splendid lake views, which serves outstanding Continental dishes complemented by a wide range of fine wines. A variety of activities can be arranged: during winter, sledding and skiing is superb and there is also a huge weather protected skating rink nearby and in the summer months guests will love the lake, with boating, fishing, canoeing and other watersports offered. The forests have many nature trails to explore or there is mountain biking, kayaking, tennis, golf, swimming (to mention only a few) as well as a spa and health club. Theme weekends can be organized and there is even a club for young people.

Our inspector loved: *The porch with rockers overlooking the mountains!*

Directions: On Route 390 north, approx. 3 miles from Canadensis. 45 miles from Allentown-Bethlehem-Easton Airport. 40 miles from Wilkes-Barre-Scranton Airport. Airport limousine/van transfers are available from an outside vendor.

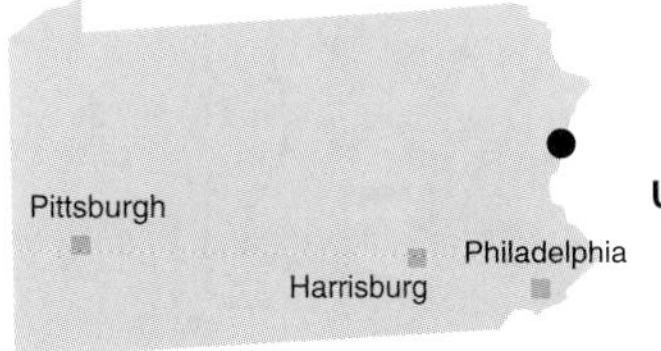

Web: www.johansens.com/skytop
E-mail: reservations@skytop.com
Tel: +1 570 595 8905
Fax: +1 570 595 7285
U.S./Canada Toll Free: 1 800 345 7759

Price Guide: (double occupancy, incl. breakfast, lunch and dinner, excl. taxes and gratuities) rooms $230-$675 suites $575-$1,000

The Inn at Palmetto Bluff

The Leading Small Hotels of the World

476 MOUNT PELIA ROAD, BLUFFTON, SOUTH CAROLINA 29910

Capturing the essence of Southern hospitality in South Carolina's Lowcountry, The Inn at Palmetto Bluff is one of the region's premier new golf resorts. This graceful and romantic 50-room cottage Inn offers luxury accommodations, exquisite dining and an abundance of activities. The private and spacious hideaway feel is the perfect setting for a romantic escape or golf getaway. Each of the well-appointed rooms has beautiful water views, vaulted ceilings, pine floors, luxury linens, wireless high-speed Internet, D.V.D./C.D. players, plasma televisions and cozy fireplaces. Guests can choose from the exceptional fine dining at the River House Dining Room with its signature South Carolina Lowcountry dishes, the more casual May River Grille or Buffalo's. After a day of golf at the 18-hole Jack Nicklaus Signature May River Golf Club, guests can relax in the acclaimed full-service Spa at Palmetto Bluff, set beside serene waterways, lush gardens and moss-laden oak trees. The charming and romantic ambience makes the Inn an idyllic location for weddings, special events and family breaks. In addition to golf, guests can explore the pristine wilderness that surrounds the Inn by bicycle, canoe or kayak on the internal waterways, fish, take a nature walk or exercise in the Fitness Center with heated lap pool. The Inn is just minutes from Savannah and Hilton Head Island.

Our inspector loved: *The Old South charm, and first-class rooms.*

Directions: The Inn is 30 minutes from Savannah Airport. Take I-95 north to Exit 8; turn right on 278 East to 170, then left on S.C. 46.

Web: www.johansens.com/palmettobluff
E-mail: reservations@palmettobluffresort.com
Tel: +1 843 706 6500
Fax: +1 843 706 6550
U.S./Canada Toll Free: 1 866 706 6565

Price Guide: (room only)
rooms $450-$800

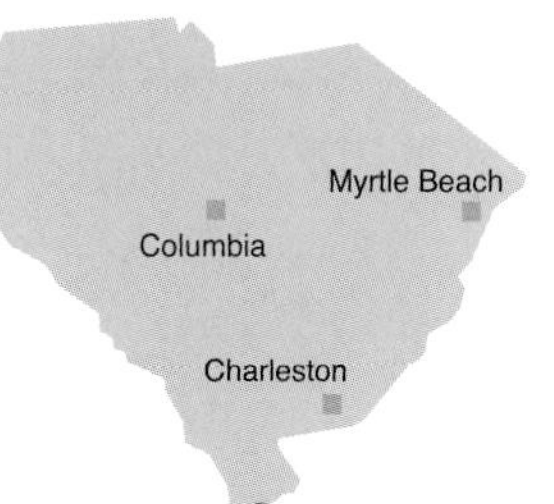

The Boardwalk Inn at Wild Dunes Resort

5757 PALM BOULEVARD, ISLE OF PALMS, SOUTH CAROLINA 29451

The Boardwalk Inn is an impeccable 4 Diamond hotel set in the heart of Wild Dunes Resort, just steps away from the beach and exciting recreational centers. A wonderful combination of elegant Charleston architecture and informal island style, this hotel overlooks the Grand Pavilion and exudes Old World charm and luxury at its finest. Each guest room and suite is spacious and comfortable. Rich, colorful fabrics complement the light, airy atmosphere and there is high-speed Internet access, in-room dining and a minibar. There are 3 restaurants in the resort. Sea Island Grill offers dazzling fresh seafood dishes and is famous for its tender and perfectly prepared lobster, accompanied by a fine chardonnay. Pasta dishes and Lowcountry specials are served in the fun Edgar's on the Links. Alternatively, snacks, pizza and groceries can be bought at Dunes Deli and Pizzeria. Outdoor facilities available to adults and children alike are superb: there are 2 award-winning golf courses, tennis courts, water sports, a marina and beautifully landscaped tropical pool complex as well as a fitness center, which includes wellness programs such as yoga, pilates and cycling. Guests can also explore the miles of unspoiled beaches and preserved natural habitats surrounding the resort. Boardwalk Inn is not far from Charleston, where there is shopping, museums and entertainment for people of all ages.

Our inspector loved: *The view of the ocean from a spectacular guest room.*

Directions: Take I-26 east to I-526 east toward Mount Pleasant and exit for Highway 17. Turn Left. From Highway north or south, turn east on 517, the Isle of Palms connector. Cross the connector then turn left on Highway 703. Follow Palm Boulevard to 41st Avenue and Wild Dunes is on the left.

Web: www.johansens.com/boardwalk
E-mail: reservations@wilddunes.com
Tel: +1 843 886 6000
Fax: +1 843 886 2916
U.S./Canada Toll Free: 1 877 221 0901

Price Guide: (room only)
rooms $120-450
suites $170-875

U.S.A. - SOUTH CAROLINA (CHARLESTON)

CHARLESTON HARBOR RESORT & MARINA

20 PATRIOTS POINT ROAD, CHARLESTON, SOUTH CAROLINA 29464

Set on the shore of Patriots Point, home of the World War II aircraft carrier U.S.S. Yorktown, and across the harbor from downtown Charleston, this resort offers an uncommon blend of unique low country culture, exciting downtown revelry and resort-style pampering. It includes a full-service marina and a stunning 18-hole championship golf course that meanders along the Atlantic coast. With 459 slips, the marina ranks as South Carolina's largest pleasure boat refuge with concierge service extended to all marina guests. In return, the marina launches sailboat charters, romantic dinner cruises and fishing trips for land-based guests. Rooms and suites have private balconies or juliette terraces with sweeping views of the water, city skyline or the historic Fort Sumter. All are equipped with work desks, Internet access, T.V.s and air conditioning. The Grille restaurant menu has an international focus, and drinks are served at the beachfront Tiki Bar or the Reel Bar, decorated with antique fishing reels from the 1920s. The harbor-side pool and private beach make ideal settings for oyster roasts and island-style theme parties. Other leisure activities range from tennis to nature trails, children's programs, volleyball and Eco-tours.

Our inspector loved: *The great city and harbor views.*

Directions: Charleston International Airport is 11 miles away.

Web: www.johansens.com/charlestonharbor
E-mail: reservations@charlestonharborresort.com
Tel: +1 843 856 0028
Fax: +1 843 856 8333
U.S./Canada Toll Free: 1 888 856 0028

Price Guide: (room only)
rooms $129-$300
suites $225-$995

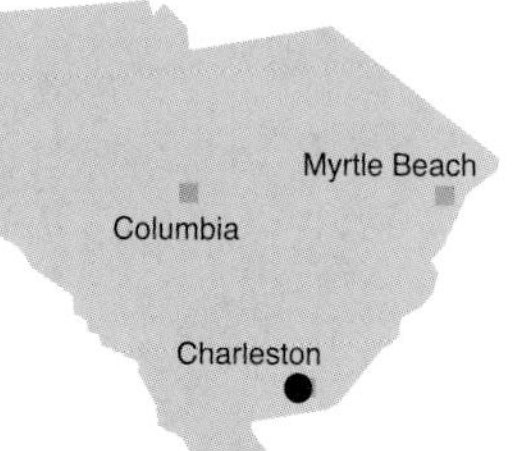

WOODLANDS RESORT & INN

125 PARSONS ROAD, SUMMERVILLE, SOUTH CAROLINA 29483

This elegant inn is situated in the historic district of Summerville, just 30 minutes from Charleston. Opened in 1995 the resort's 42-acre setting boasts a Day Spa, The Pavilion conference facility, 2 clay tennis courts, a heated swimming pool, croquet lawn and Wedding Garden. Upon entering the Inn's columned veranda and grand doorway, guests are greeted by helpful staff and luxurious furnishings, which reflect an English, Indian and Jamaican influence. Each of the 18 handsomely appointed guest rooms is tucked away in a variety of areas within this restored 1906 mansion; the top-floor guest rooms are whimsical, inviting havens, and a cozy guest cottage is a short stroll away at the end of a shaded path. All guest rooms have been decorated in rich colors and patterns, and have Bose C.D. players, monogrammed robes, fresh roses and Aveda pampering products. Woodlands is the only resort of its kind in the Southeastern United States to have received the AAA Five Diamond and Mobil Five-Star Awards for both the Inn and Dining Room. Afternoon tea or cocktails can be enjoyed in the Inn's airy parlors, and in the evenings guests gather for dinner and savor the international and regional delicacies of the formal Dining Room's New American menus.

Our inspector loved: *The elegance and security of this outstanding inn.*

Directions: From I-26 take exit 199A to Summerville.

Web: www.johansens.com/woodlandssc
E-mail: reservations@woodlandsinn.com
Tel: +1 843 875 2600
Fax: +1 843 875 2603
U.S./Canada Toll Free: 1 800 774 9999

Price Guide:
rooms $250-$295
suites $305-$650
cottage $850

The Sanctuary at Kiawah Island Golf Resort

ONE SANCTUARY BEACH DRIVE, KIAWAH ISLAND, SOUTH CAROLINA 29455

The shores of Kiawah Island, off South Carolina, are home to a luxurious ocean-front hideaway for the discerning traveler. Just 30 minutes from the historic streets of Charleston, The Sanctuary at Kiawah Island Golf Resort features 255 guest rooms and suites, the majority of which offer ocean views. Custom-made furniture and luxurious fabrics add to the unflinching attention to detail in this grand yet inviting property. Guests can enjoy a round of golf at the 5 championship courses including Pete Dye's Ocean Course host of the 2007 Senior PGA and 2012 PGA Championships, or play tennis on the 23 clay or 5 hard courts before relaxing in one of the 12 treatment rooms in the garden-themed spa. Treatments are based on Kiawah's natural assets such as the ocean and marsh and a sauna, steam room, whirlpool and beauty salon as well as a fitness center complement the holistic offerings. The Ocean Room restaurant seats 110 and the private wine room and spacious ocean view terrace add a sense of grandeur while casual dining can be enjoyed in the Jasmine Porch. The intimate martini bar and grand lobby bar are ideal for mingling and enjoying a beverage. Meeting and conference space covers 18,000 sq. ft. which includes a grand ballroom and an executive boardroom.

Our inspector loved: *The elegance and attention to detail throughout the resort, and the view of the ocean.*

Directions: Charleston International Airport is 45 minutes from Kiawah. Private and corporate jets can use the area's executive airport which is 15 minutes away.

Web: www.johansens.com/sanctuary
E-mail: reservations@thesanctuary.com
Tel: +1 843 768 6000
Fax: +1 843 768 5150
U.S./Canada Toll Free: 1 877 683 1234

Price Guide: (room only)
rooms $299-$4,500

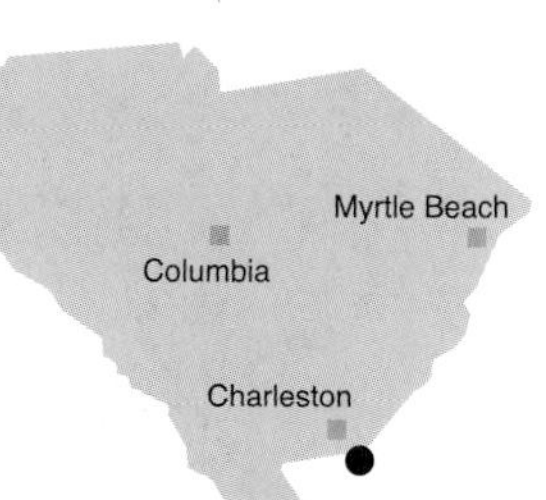

Litchfield Plantation

KINGS RIVER ROAD, BOX 290, PAWLEYS ISLAND, SOUTH CAROLINA 29585

Dramatically situated in the heart of a former rice plantation, Litchfield Plantation is a beautifully preserved country inn. Visitors are immediately struck by the magic of the location, as the quarter-mile avenue to the main house is flanked by century-old oak trees which form an enchanting tunnel to this languid South Carolina hideaway. Guests can stay in the luxurious suites within the main house or choose the seclusion of one of the many villas dotted around the 600-acre estate. These gorgeously designed and individually decorated retreats benefit from spacious lounges and huge bathrooms, some with Jacuzzi tubs. The Carriage House, an attractive low country-style building is the venue for excellent continental cuisine complemented by seasonal specialties, prepared by cordon bleu chefs. 2 tennis courts are available on the estate, whilst the large heated pool has excellent views of the rice fields. Guests can relax at the 3-story beach house, moor their yachts at the marina, or take trips along the coast. The region attracts golf fanatics and the inn has 10 of South Carolina's most celebrated golf courses at its doorstep. Deep sea and sport fishing, trips to historic Charleston and river cruises are also available to visitors.

Our inspector loved: *Feeling as if you have been transported into the 1700s. The drive onto the plantation will take your breath away.*

Directions: From Charleston, take Highway 17 north for approximately 70 miles. Turn left into Waverly Road; at the Stop sign turn right into Kings River Road, the entrance is 1 mile on left.

Myrtle Beach
Columbia
Charleston

Web: www.johansens.com/litchfieldplantation
E-mail: vacation@litchfieldplantation.com
Tel: +1 843 237 9121
Fax: +1 843 237 1688
U.S./Canada Toll Free: 1 800 869 1410

Price Guide: (room only)
rooms from $215
suites $240–$620

U.S.A. - TEXAS (AUSTIN)

The Mansion at Judges' Hill

1900 RIO GRANDE, AUSTIN, TEXAS 78705

This restored 19th-century mansion offers a serene and refined atmosphere reminiscent of a bygone era. Although situated deep within the heart of Austin, just minutes from downtown, the mansion is set in a secluded location away from day to day noise and distraction. Bedrooms have been decorated in a classic design with splashes of bright colors and unique touches of style. Each has a C.D. stereo, 2 or more multi-line telephones, high-speed Internet access and a computer and D.V.D. player are available upon request. Exquisite mosaic tile and marble floors feature in the bathrooms and public rooms display magnificent chandeliers. Local game and vegetables and seafood flown in from the Gulf of Mexico, combine to make East and West Coast specialties on the menu. Modern American cuisine, prepared with classic French influence, is served by the highly-acclaimed chef. Chef will also prepare personally chosen menus for weddings, meetings and conferences for up to 300 people in the new elegantly appointed ballroom and conference center. Professional staff will help organize events and exclusive use of the property can be arranged. The 1900 bar is the perfect place for a cocktail after a full day in Austin. Downtown shops and museums are a short distance away.

Our inspector loved: *Taking breakfast on the beautiful balcony outside the Celebrity Suite.*

Directions: From I-35 exit at MLK Boulevard to the right and proceed to Rio Grande Boulevard. Austin Bergstrom Airport is a 25-minute drive.

Web: www.johansens.com/judgeshill
E-mail: lisa@judgeshill.com
Tel: +1 512 495 1800
Fax: +1 512 691 4461
U.S./Canada Toll Free: 1 800 311 1619

Price Guide: (room only)
rooms $139-$395
suites $169-$395

The Inn on Lake Granbury

205 West Doyle Street, Granbury, Texas 76048

This private oasis, on approximately 2 acres of landscaped gardens and scenic lakefront views, provides a tranquil environment to renew your vitality. Cozy up to fire pits, relax by the flagstone pool or bask at the soothing waterfall with tanning ledge. The Inn on Lake Granbury offers upscale amenities, comfort and personal service – all within short walking distance to the historic town square of Granbury, voted the Best Small Town in Texas. Each guest room at the inn is luxurious and unique; some have stone fireplaces, sitting areas and outside porches. All have private baths, feathered beds, fine linens and guest robes. The inn and guest rooms are equipped with high-speed Internet and WiFi. Recreational options abound on the scenic Lake Granbury: water-skiing, kayaking and fishing to name a few. Downtown offers fine dining options and Broadway plays and musicals. Horseback riding, golf and an exotic wildlife refuge are a short drive from the Inn on Lake Granbury. With its spacious conference room and grounds, this is the idyllic setting for a corporate retreat, business meeting, family reunion or wedding.

Our inspector loved: *The lake views from the beautifully landscaped pool area.*

Directions: The inn is 1 hour and 30 minutes from D.F.W. Airport (west). 45 minutes from Ft. Worth and 1 hour 45 minutes from Dallas.

Web: www.johansens.com/lakegranbury
E-mail: info@innonlakegranbury.com
Tel: +1 817 573 0046
Fax: +1 817 573 0047
U.S./Canada Toll Free: 1 877 573 0046

Price Guide:
rooms $165-$245
suites $295-$345

7 M 50

THE HAVANA RIVERWALK INN

1015 NAVARRO, SAN ANTONIO, TEXAS 78205

Directions: On the northern end of the San Antonio Riverwalk, Downtown, between Convent and St. Mary's. The San Antonio Airport is a 15-minute drive from the hotel.

Web: www.johansens.com/havanariverwalkinn
E-mail: reservations@havanariverwalkinn.com
Tel: +1 210 222 2008
Fax: +1 210 222 2717

Price Guide: (room only)
rooms $129–$220

This unique inn was built in 1914 as a residence hotel and today retains its air of vintage-style and elegance. All of the beautiful 27 air-conditioned rooms have wooden floors, sisal rugs and down comforters, whilst some include elaborate four-poster beds. The European antiques are wonderful, as are the fresh flowers, thick robes and bottled water - thoughtful finishing touches which add that little bit of extra comfort. As well as luxurious surroundings there are up-to-the-minute facilities such as cable television and data ports. Within the charming décor and atmosphere of the inn, which has been awarded a Condé Nast Gold Reserve, it is easy to feel that you are in another country, an ambience that is enhanced by music in the public areas. Enjoy Club Cohiba - A Latin Bar & Tapas Grille offering extraordinary cuisine that features a blend of Spanish, Cuban and South American influences. A 5-course "pre-fixe" menu is eclectic and available every weekend. Special event facilities can accommodate up to 200 people and include the Riverwalk Arbor, Rooftop Terrace and Club Cohiba. The Riverwalk has many shops and restaurants to enjoy and is especially attractive at night. Nearby places of interest include downtown San Antonio, Sea World and the Alamo.

Our inspector loved: *Suite 300, affectionately called the "Oh My God" room because that's what everyone says upon entering.*

The Chaska House

716 West Main Street, Waxahachie, Texas 75165

An intimate bed and breakfast, the revival-style Chaska House was built in 1900 and was recently meticulously restored by owners Louis and Linda Brown, who opened the inn in 1993. The result is an elegant setting that combines historic charm with modern conveniences. With its warm Texas hospitality, Chaska House is an ideal getaway for couples as well as family and friends. The house is filled with rich colors, opulent fabrics and a remarkable blend of original architecture and interior design. Each of the large and beautifully appointed rooms is named after a famous author and styled accordingly, such as the Margaret Mitchell room featuring "Gone with the Wind" décor and the Teddy Roosevelt room designed to reflect White House elegance with a chic ranch twist. Ernest Hemingway's Key West residence is recreated a few steps away in Hemingway's Retreat, two guest cottages adjacent to the main inn. The rooms boast extraordinary king and queen beds, luxury linens, fine art and antiques and interesting memorabilia. The tiled bathrooms have glass showers, claw-foot tubs, whirlpools-for-two and fluffy towels. Waxahachie is a charming, historic town just minutes from downtown Dallas. Guests can stroll the short distance to wonderful restaurants and shopping or visit the historic courthouse that author James Michener referred to as a "fairytale palace."

Our inspector loved: *The fantastic antiques and bathrooms.*

Directions: From Dallas-Fort Worth (D.F.W.) Airport, exit south and take SH183 east to Dallas. Take I-35 east, south from Dallas, travel 30 miles to exit 401B (Bus. 287) and follow signs into town. The inn is 1.8 miles on the left, 40 miles from D.F.W.

Dallas
San Antonio
Houston

Web: www.johansens.com/chaskahouse
E-mail: chaskabb@sbcglobal.net
Tel: +1 972 937 3390
Fax: +1 972 937 1780
U.S./Canada Toll Free: 1 800 931 3390

Price Guide:
rooms $165-$235

VERMONT

Hotel location shown in red with page number

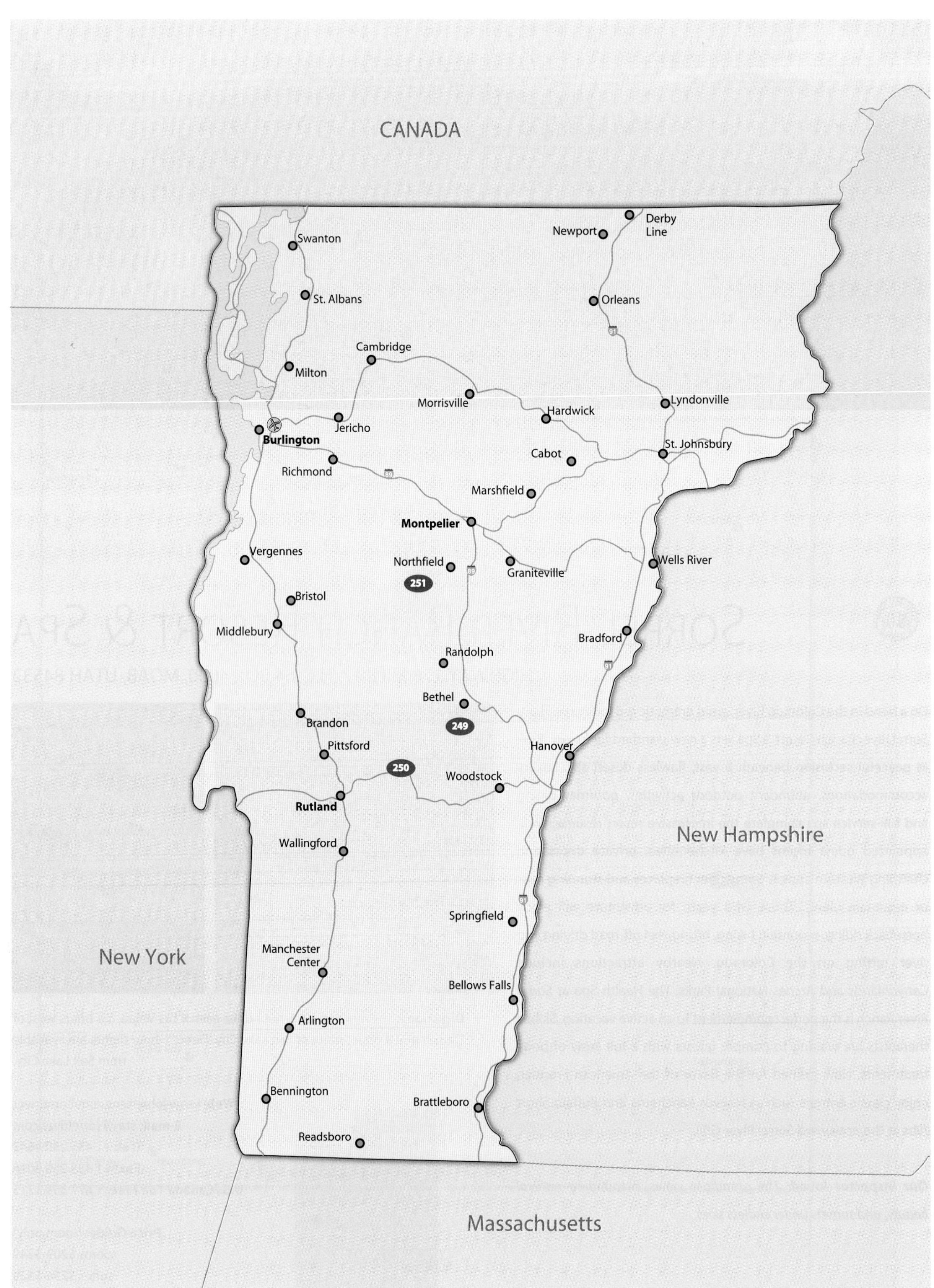

Twin Farms

P.O. BOX 115, BARNARD, VERMONT 05031

Twin Farms is an exclusive yet unpretentious country estate offering understated elegance and graceful hospitality since 1993. There are 20 distinctive guest cottages and suites located on 300 acres of picturesque rolling hills, meadows, orchards and ponds. Previously the summer residence of the Twigg-Smith family of Hawaii, Twin Farms has maintained the prestigious Mobil 5-Star Award since 1997. With a 19th-century farmhouse feel, the original 1795 Main House has beautiful southern views and 4 large private suites. There are 2 suites in the Lodge, 4 suites in Farmhouse at Copper Hill and 10 wood and stone free-standing cottages sprinkled about the estate. The owner's collection of fine contemporary art adorns the rooms and the unique furnishings are custom-crafted or antique. There is a pub, fitness center and rejuvenating, full-service Out of the Woods Spa. Dining is unparalleled at Twin Farms with Head Chef Neil Wigglesworth offering seasonal cuisine using the freshest of estate-grown herbs and vegetables. Guests dine on Chef's choices for both lunch and dinner as there is never a menu, however guests' dietary preferences are taken into account before preparation. Twin Farms is 10 miles north of Woodstock, Vermont, and seasonal activities include downhill and cross-country skiing, ice skating, hiking, canoeing and horseback riding.

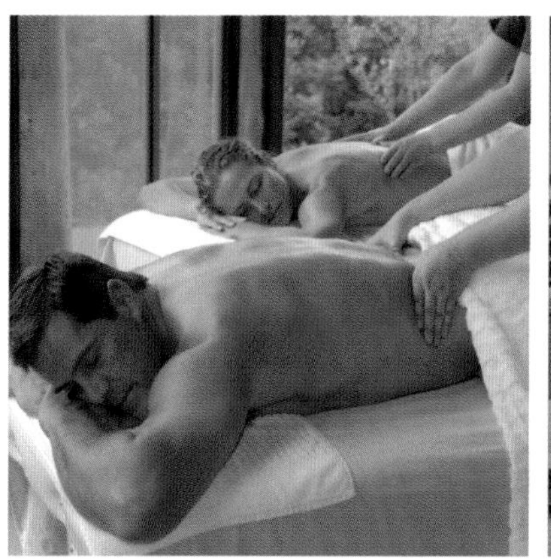

Directions: A 3-hour drive from Boston and 2 hours from Manchester Boston Regional Airport.

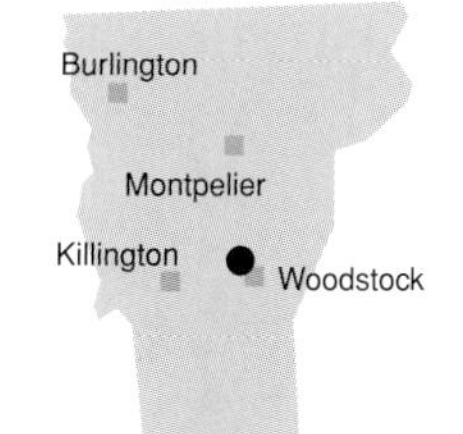

Web: www.johansens.com/twinfarms
E-mail: info@twinfarms.com
Tel: +1 802 234 9999
Fax: +1 802 234 9990
U.S./Canada Toll Free: 1 800 894 6327

Price Guide: (including all meals and on-site activities)
suites $1,100-$2,750

Our inspector loved: *The artwork by Milton Avery and Roy Lichtenstein.*

Mountain Top Inn & Resort

195 MOUNTAIN TOP ROAD, CHITTENDEN, VERMONT 05737

Directions: Take Route 7, then Route 4. Turn left onto Meadowlake Drive and follow the road to the very top.

Web: www.johansens.com/mountaintopinn
E-mail: stay@mountaintopinn.com
Tel: +1 802 483 2311
Fax: +1 802 483 6373
U.S./Canada Toll Free: 1 800 445 2100

Price Guide:
rooms $150–$545

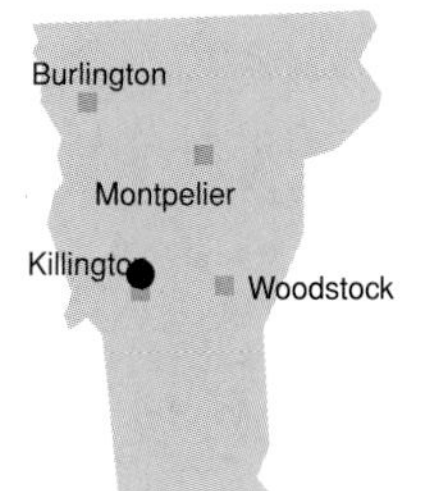

An idyllic retreat in the tradition of a classic mountain lodge, the Mountain Top Inn & Resort is Vermont's quintessential four-season resort, a short drive from Killington and Rutland. Set on 350 acres in the lush Green Mountains with sweeping views of a pristine recreational lake and infinite expanse of National Forest, the Resort offers Luxury and Classic Lodge Rooms and Suites, "pet friendly" mountain cabins and private chalets. With outdoor adventures for both couples and families, there is something for everyone. Catering to the experienced horseman and the novice rider, the Equestrian Center comes alive from spring through fall offering guided and custom-trail rides and lessons for all levels. The private beach is ideal for kayaking, scenic boat rides and swimming. Tennis, croquet, shuffleboard, fly-fishing, clay-bird shooting, hiking and mountain biking are on-site. In winter, the Resort is a magical wonderland in the snow. The renowned Nordic Ski & Snowshoe Center, one of the oldest in the U.S., offers 80km of groomed and back-country trails and skating lanes for skiers of all levels; horse-drawn sleigh rides, dog sledding, ice skating, and sledding are also available. Enjoy exceptional innovative cuisine served in the rustically elegant Dining Room or casual bistro fare in the Tavern, all complemented by a Wine Spectator award-winning wine list.

Our inspector loved: *The sheer beauty every season, for every experience.*

34 M 75

The Pitcher Inn

275 Main Street, P.O. Box 347, Warren, Vermont 05674

The Pitcher Inn is a delightful 11-room and suite inn located in the heart of Vermont's Green Mountains, at the foot of Sugarbush Resort, that has been welcoming guests since the early 1850s. Each charming Vermont-themed room is located in the main house or in the adjacent barn and features original art, memorabilia and antiques creating a comforting atmosphere with special luxurious touches. All rooms have air-climate control, a 3-line telephone with D.S.L. data port, WiFi access, C.D. player and T.V. with V.H.S. player, private bath with Jacuzzi tub and floor heating. Some rooms have steam showers and most have cozy and romantic wood-burning fireplaces with king beds. For the ultimate in relaxation, visit the Alta Day Spa for complete pampering with an array of spa and beauty treatments. Chef Sue Schickler's seasonal menus highlight some of Vermont's freshest ingredients including lamb, quail, rabbit, organic vegetables, artisanal cheeses and seafood. The Main Dining Room offers à la carte menus while Tracks, the inn's lounge, offers more casual bites. Wake up to sumptuous baked goods made fresh each morning and in the afternoon, enjoy tea and afternoon cocktails in the Library. Nearby alpine skiing, sleigh rides, maple sugaring and farmer's market complete the Vermont experience.

Our inspector loved: *The Hayloft Suite atop the old barn decorated in simple and beautiful Vermont style.*

Directions: 3.5 hours by car from Boston; 2.5 hours from Montreal.

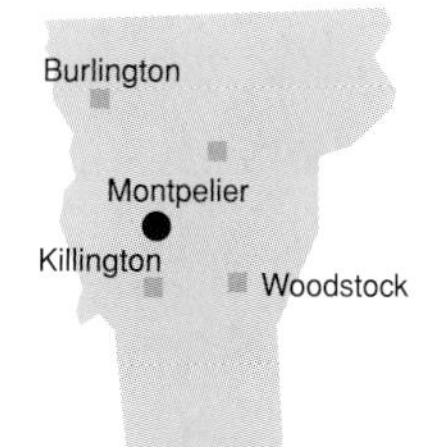

Web: www.johansens.com/pitcherinn
E-mail: info@pitcherinn.com
Tel: +1 802 496 6350
Fax: +1 802 496 6354

Price Guide:
rooms $350-$600
suites $700

200 South Street Inn

200 SOUTH STREET, CHARLOTTESVILLE, VIRGINIA 22901

Directions: 2 hours south-west of Washington on Route 29. 1 hour west of Richmond on I-64. The nearest airport is Charlottesville. Located in downtown Charlottesville.

Web: www.johansens.com/200southstreetinn
E-mail: southst@cstone.net
Tel: +1 434 979 0200
Fax: +1 434 979 4403
U.S./Canada Toll Free: 1 800 964 7008

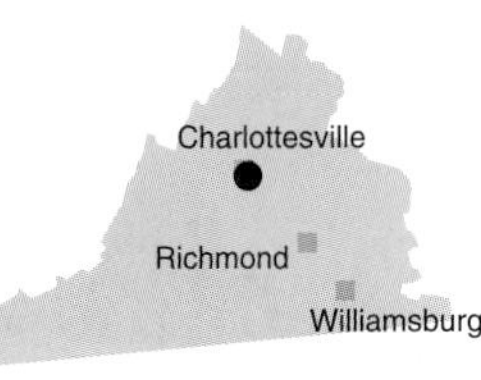

Price Guide:
rooms $150–$250
suites $235–$280

This charming hotel is the amalgamation of 2 historic 19th-century houses, set in the heart of a lively downtown. The first house was built in 1856 for a friend of Thomas Jefferson and the second some 50 years later. Careful restoration has ensured that there is still a distinct period feel to the hotel from the elegant and sweeping banister in the hallways to the wide, cool veranda. Each of the 19 bedrooms and suites is furnished in individual style, many have canopied or sleigh beds, and every room contains some charming English or Belgian antique pieces. There is a warm Virginia welcome awaiting all guests with wine and cheese on arrival, and a relaxed breakfast of home-baked breads, coffee cakes and muffins or scones can be taken on the veranda. There is plenty to entice guests away to the nearby historic downtown mall with its collection of antique shops, bookstores and restaurants but there is also a great deal of history in the region. Thomas Jefferson's house, Monticello, is only 4 miles from the hotel and Ash Lawn and Montpelier, the homes of James Monroe and James Madison are also nearby. Skyline Drive and the Blue Ridge Parkway are less than half an hour away and a definite stop for anyone wishing to walk or cycle amongst the spectacular Virginia countryside.

Our inspector loved: *The beautiful antique beds and furnishings, and the warmth of the staff.*

THE INN AT WARNER HALL

4750 WARNER HALL ROAD, GLOUCESTER, VIRGINIA 23061

Established as a plantation by George Washington's great-great grandfather in 1642, this Colonial-Revival waterfront manor house has been restored to its original grandeur and transformed into a country inn that brings Virginia's history into the modern day. A long drive to the front entrance gives the illusion of traveling back to the early days of America. Every detail has been arranged to showcase the inn's expertly restored original design. Many famous historic figures have ties to the inn, including Meriwether Lewis, General Robert E. Lee and Queen Elizabeth II. Each of the 11 rooms has period antiques and Schumacher fabrics as well as comfortable seating areas, private baths and Gilchrist Soames products. The 38 acres of grounds provide a perfect setting for special occasions. Enjoy the soothing tranquility of the Severn River at the inn's delightful boathouse. Take advantage of complimentary kayaks, canoes, fishing equipment and bicycles, and experience native wildlife and natural wonders of tidewater Virginia. A game of croquet, horseshoes or outdoor chess is the perfect way to finish the day or just laze in the hammock at sunset. Formal dining is available on weekends, while during the week, sumptuous supper baskets can be enjoyed at guests' location of choice. Area history abounds with Colonial Williamsburg, Yorktown and the Jamestown Settlement nearby.

Directions: Located on Route 629, approximately 30 minutes from Williamsburg, 1 hour from Richmond and 3 hours from Washington D.C.

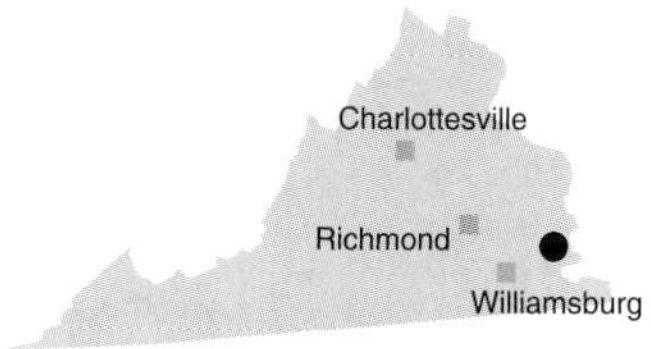

Charlottesville
Richmond
Williamsburg

Web: www.johansens.com/warnerhall
E-mail: info@warnerhall.com
Tel: +1 804 695 9565
Fax: +1 804 695 9566
U.S./Canada Toll Free: 1 800 331 2720

Price Guide:
rooms $175 - $245

Our inspector loved: *The water and estate views from the back porch.*

Hope and Glory Inn

65 TAVERN ROAD, IRVINGTON, VIRGINIA 22480

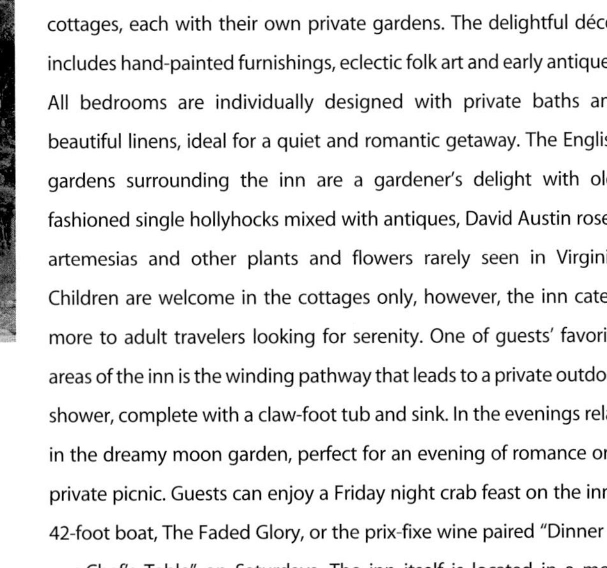

Set on the picturesque Chesapeake Bay shore, Hope and Glory Inn is a whimsical and elegantly restored schoolhouse with several guest cottages, each with their own private gardens. The delightful décor includes hand-painted furnishings, eclectic folk art and early antiques. All bedrooms are individually designed with private baths and beautiful linens, ideal for a quiet and romantic getaway. The English gardens surrounding the inn are a gardener's delight with old-fashioned single hollyhocks mixed with antiques, David Austin roses, artemesias and other plants and flowers rarely seen in Virginia. Children are welcome in the cottages only, however, the inn caters more to adult travelers looking for serenity. One of guests' favorite areas of the inn is the winding pathway that leads to a private outdoor shower, complete with a claw-foot tub and sink. In the evenings relax in the dreamy moon garden, perfect for an evening of romance or a private picnic. Guests can enjoy a Friday night crab feast on the inn's 42-foot boat, The Faded Glory, or the prix-fixe wine paired "Dinner at our Chef's Table" on Saturdays. The inn itself is located in a most charming and historic waterfront town while its elegant pool and 8 of its cottages called "tents" are located within White Fences Vineyard and Winery.

Directions: 3 hours from Washington D.C., 75 minutes from Richmond, Virginia, 90 minutes from Norfolk, Virginia, and 60 minutes from Williamsburg/Jamestown.

Web: www.johansens.com/hopeandglory
E-mail: inquiries@hopeandglory.com
Tel: +1 804 438 6053
Fax: +1 804 438 5362
U.S./Canada Toll Free: 1 800 497 8228

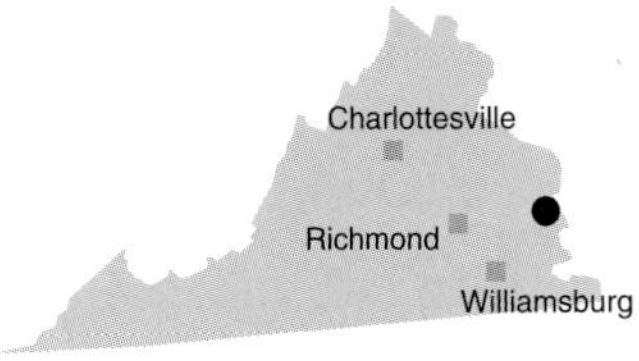

Charlottesville
Richmond
Williamsburg

Price Guide:
rooms $165-$225
cottages $220-$380

Our inspector loved: *The fun and hopelessly romantic outdoor shower.*

The Goodstone Inn & Estate

36205 Snake Hill Road, Middleburg, Virginia 20117

This superb inn is located in the heart of Virginia's famous hunt country and wine region, just 3 miles from the historic town of Middleburg. Steeped in history, Goodstone is situated on 265 acres of picturesque estate grounds, with the Blue Ridge Mountains visible in the distance. 17 individually decorated guest rooms and suites are situated in luxury residences renovated in elegant English and French country styles. Each residence has a sitting room and fully-equipped modern kitchen stocked with a variety of beverages and tempting edibles. The heart of the inn is the Carriage House where a full breakfast and afternoon tea are served daily. Guests at Goodstone enjoy complimentary recreational activities that include mountain bikes, canoes, a woodland nature trail and a round of golf at Stoneleigh Country Club, in nearby Round Hill. Relax by the beautiful heated swimming pool, at the arbors that have been preserved since the 1930s or soak in the hot tub after enjoying the sunset from a rope swing in Woodsy Garden. On-site massage and horse-trail rides in the foothills of the Blue Ridge Mountains may be arranged. A new restaurant featuring sophisticated American cuisine recently opened at the estate. Nearby Middleburg offers upscale shopping, restaurants and historic attractions.

Our inspector loved: *The gorgeous grounds and beauty surrounding this historic estate.*

Directions: From Middleburg take Route 50 west. Turn right at light onto North Madison Street then follow Foxcroft Road and turn left onto Snake Hill Road.

Web: www.johansens.com/goodstoneinn
E-mail: information@goodstone.com
Tel: +1 540 687 4645
Fax: +1 540 687 6115
U.S./Canada Toll Free: 1 877 219 4663

Price Guide:
rooms $225–$450
suites $275–$600

Frederick House

28 North New Street, Staunton, Virginia 24401

Entering these beautifully restored 19th-century houses that comprise the Frederick House collection the guest instantly steps back into a bygone age. These adjoining town houses and 2 detached houses lie in the quiet downtown of historic Staunton, which is in itself a great starting point for a tour of Virginia's historic sites, combining the intimacy of a local town with fine architecture and a wide variety of shopping and cultural activities. The earliest of the Frederick houses dates back to 1809 and is the epitome of period elegance with its Federal staircase. Each of the rooms has been painstakingly designed to incorporate period features and charm with modern facilities. Each is uniquely decorated and displays original antiques, books and pictures. Making careful use of the building's hillside setting, guests enjoy the balconies, terraces and front porches that overlook an abundance of flowering trees and culinary herbs that scent the walkways. The quiet downtown location belies the accessibility to a wealth of historic attractions: Woodrow Wilson's Pesidential Library, the Frontier Cultural Museum, Mary Baldwin College, and American Shakespeare Center's Blackfriars Playhouse, are all within easy walking distance.

Our inspector loved: *The hand-painted wall stencils in many of the rooms.*

Directions: Located in historic downtown Staunton, 20 minutes from Shenandoah Regional Airport.

Web: www.johansens.com/frederickhouse
E-mail: stay@frederickhouse.com
Tel: + 1 540 885 4220
Fax: +1 540 885 5180
U.S./Canada Toll Free: 1 800 334 5575

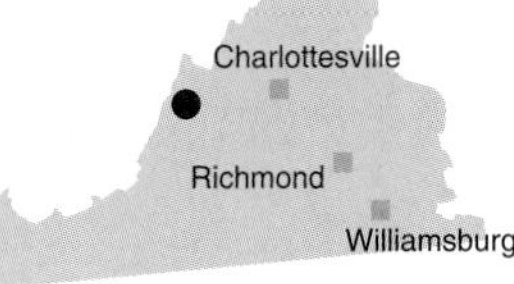

Price Guide:
rooms $95–$175
suites $140–$275

Morrison House

116 South Alfred Street, Alexandria, Virginia 22314

Nestled in historic Old Town Alexandria is a detailed work of art: Morrison House, a new member of the Kimpton Hotel & Restaurants Group. A striking reproduction of an 18th–century Federal manor house with period furnishings, the hotel features quiet sophistication without pretense. A beautiful bricked courtyard and sculpture fountain beckon guests into the marble foyer, where they are greeted in true Morrison House fashion. Upon entering, guests are escorted directly to an elegant guest room with mahogany poster bed, Italian marble bath and ultra-luxurious linens. The soul of Morrison House is superlative service. From welcoming butlers to attentive concierges, every detail is handled with impeccable care. The culinary arts are alive: acclaimed cuisine, flawless service and a comfortable atmosphere successfully combine for a memorable evening. There is also an extensive wine list featuring over 200 bottles and 16 wines by the glass. Gracious hospitality and attentive service provide the perfect combination for corporate and social events alike. The highest standards ensure that your event exceeds your expectations. This is a Mobil 4-Star and AAA 4-Diamond hotel.

Our inspector loved: *The in-room check-in, and the piano bar.*

Directions: 40 miles from Baltimore Washington Airport.

Web: www.johansens.com/morrisonhouse
E-mail: concierge@morrisonhouse.com
Tel: +1 703 838 8000
Fax: +1 703 684 6283
U.S./Canada Toll Free: 1 866 834 6628

Price Guide: (room only)
rooms $175-$329
suites $299-$399

45 25

FRIDAY HARBOR HOUSE

130 WEST STREET, FRIDAY HARBOR, WASHINGTON 98250

This delightful retreat is easily accessible from Seattle by ferry, plane or water taxi, and is the ideal place to unwind and get away from the stresses of city life. Located in the Pacific Northwest's "Banana Belt" the area is famed for averaging 245 days of sunshine a year, and the inn itself sits high on a hilltop overlooking San Juan Island. The essence of life here, where the pace is slower and the welcome is exceptionally warm, is reflected in the relaxing 23 guest rooms. Each has floor to ceiling windows that frame wonderful views of the water and the mountains, and luxurious spa baths; pretty fireplaces create a cozy ambience. The dining room has a great reputation for its ever-changing seasonal menu, and the aroma of freshly ground coffee heralds the arrival of breakfast. Friday Harbor is a delightful town with a wide variety of shops, galleries and cafés, whilst there is also a stunning range of amenities available locally. Whale watching, sailing, kayaking and scuba diving can all be arranged from the hotel. There is also a golf club nearby and some excellent biking trails.

Our inspector loved: *The great bathrooms and sweeping harbor views.*

Directions: Accessible from Seattle by ferry, plane or water taxi. A 45-minute plane trip from Seattle Sea-Tac Airport.

Web: www.johansens.com/fridayharbor
E-mail: fhhouse@rockisland.com
Tel: +1 360 378 8455
Fax: +1 360 378 8453
U.S./Canada Toll Free: 1 866 722 7356

Price Guide:
rooms $130-$300

Run of the River Inn and Refuge

9308 E. LEAVENWORTH ROAD, LEAVENWORTH, WASHINGTON 98826

Run of the River is an intimate 6 suite inn with a luxury cabin, Ravenwood, the perfect place for a romantic retreat, re-energizing getaway or celebration. The Inn and Refuge sits on a high water channel of the Icicle River, about ½ mile upriver from Leavenworth. The inn is surrounded by the Department of Wildlife bird refuge and is home to wildlife such as deer, bear and the occasional elk. Each room has a spectacular view of the mountains and river, features a king-size bed with soft linens, deluxe Jacuzzi surrounded by river rock and a romantic fireplace with fireside leather chairs. In addition, each has a spacious bathroom with invigorating rain shower, plush robes, Egyptian cotton towels and wireless Internet access. Guests wake up to an array of fresh and hearty breakfast fare served family-style each morning. During the day, guests can explore with bicycles, relax on their own private balcony swing or simply feed the birds and nature watch with personal binoculars provided by the inn. The inn even supplies guests with their own hiking gear, including daypacks and walking sticks. Run of the River is located near Leavenworth, a charming town with a Bavarian-flare. Guests can enjoy German specialties and other cuisine at one of the many restaurants in town. Skiing is nearby in the winter and summer activities include hiking, rafting, biking and golfing in the Icicle Valley.

Directions: Seattle Airport is a 2-hour drive from Run of the River.

Web: www.johansens.com/runoftheriver
E-mail: info@runoftheriver.com
Tel: +1 509 548 7171
Fax: +1 509 548 7547
U.S./Canada Toll Free: 1 800 288 6491

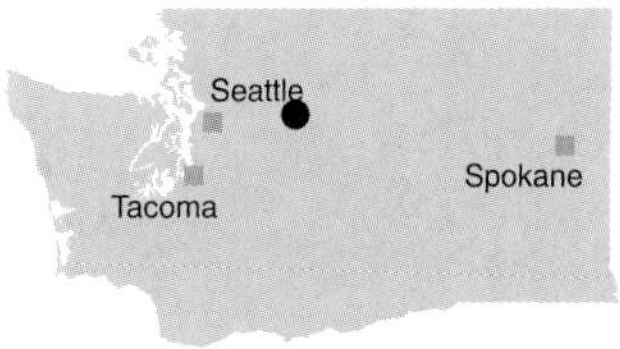

Price Guide:
rooms $220-$255
cabin $425

Our inspector loved: *The fully functional antique typewriters in each room.*

The Davenport Hotel and Tower

10 SOUTH POST STREET, SPOKANE, WASHINGTON 99201

This elegant stately hotel was established in 1914 and was carefully refurbished in 2002. Classical architecture and large formal rooms create a rather splendid atmosphere ideal for meetings, parties and weddings. With 611 spacious and well-planned guest rooms and suites the hotel's Penthouse floor houses the most spectacular collection of suites, including the vast Presidential Suite. The Venetian-inspired Hall of the Doges and the Grand Pennington Ballroom combined can accommodate 600 guests for banquets and other functions, and some of the smaller meeting rooms can easily seat 150; some feature glorious examples of oak paneling. The Peacock Room, with its unique stained-glass ceiling, is reputed as serving the best martinis. The Palm Court Grill restaurant serves a delightful selection of Northwest inspired cuisine accompanied by a fine wine selection, and the hotel's Lobby fireside is great for breakfast, tea or cocktails. The new 328-room Tower, located just across the street, will add a contemporary flavor of world travel. The Tower's Safari Room Fresh Grill and Bar Restaurant will add a spice of adventure to every guests' stay featuring seasonally inspired dishes and flavoursome flatbreads.

***Our inspector loved:** The custom-made Davenport beds wrapped in the finest linens.*

Directions: 15 minutes from Spokane Airport.

Web: www.johansens.com/davenport
E-mail: reservations@thedavenporthotel.com
Tel: +1 509 455 8888
Fax: +1 509 624 4455
U.S./Canada Toll Free: 1 800 899 1482

Price Guide: (room only)
rooms $199-$299
suites $359-$2,000

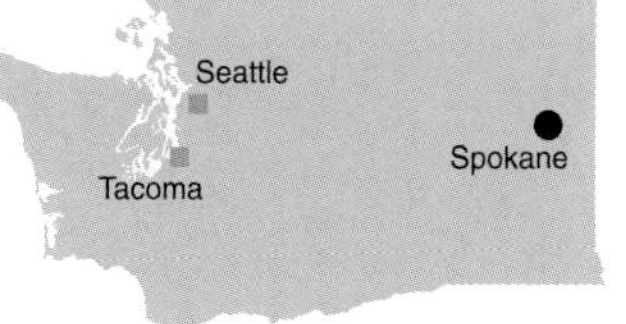

Alderbrook Resort & Spa

10 EAST ALDERBROOK DRIVE, UNION, WASHINGTON 98592

This resort's location is breathtaking; it stands just west of Seattle, on Hood Canal, a natural, glacier-carved fjord more than 60 miles long famed for its profusion of sea life, boating, fishing and abundance of oysters. Gateway to the Olympic Peninsula the site is lined by old cedar and towering evergreen trees while in the distance the snow-capped peaks of the Olympic Mountains can be seen. The special touches featured within the rooms are inspired by the beauty of the outdoors with splashes of sage green, chocolate brown and vibrant orange. Most rooms have a "window box" daybed from which guests can enjoy the views or curl up and read a good book. Accommodations vary with king or queen-size beds to 2-bedroom cottages. All rooms have every home comfort and facility and cottages offer a fireplace, porch and a community lawn on which to enjoy a barbecue. An abundance of recreational facilities include fishing, crabbing, boating, kayaking and bird watching. An indoor swimming pool is perched on the edge of Hood Canal and above the resort is a challenging par 72 golf course and tennis courts. A fitness center provides state-of-the-art exercise equipment while the spa offers a range of invigorating and rejuvenating treatments. Alderbrook has a no smoking policy.

Our Inspector Loved: *The spectacular views of Hood Canal where orcas are often spotted.*

Directions: A convenient hour's drive from Seattle Sea Tac Airport. 90 minutes by ferry/auto or 20 minutes by seaplane from Seattle.

Web: www.johansens.com/alderbrook
E-mail: mail@alderbrookresort.com
Tel: +1 360 898 2200
Fax: +1 360 898 4610
U.S./Canada Toll Free: 1 800 622 9370

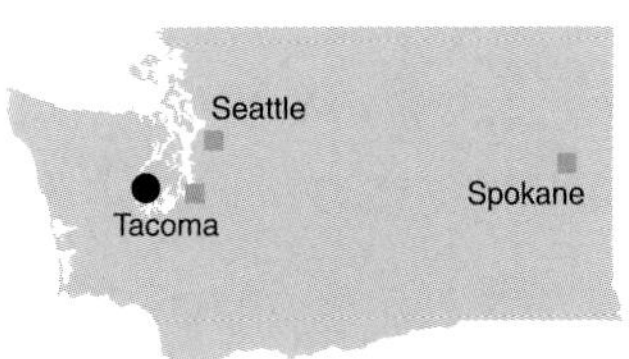

Price Guide: (room only)
rooms $235-$315
cottages $340-$500

THE HERBFARM

14590 NORTH EAST 145TH STREET, WOODINVILLE, WASHINGTON 98072

The Herbfarm is a rare treat. Visitors are enveloped by the warm and personalized hospitality of owners, husband and wife, Ron Zimmerman and Carrie Van Dyck but without a doubt the food is the centerpiece of this magnificent place. Themed dinner evenings run throughout the year with menus created just hours before service to utilize the best produce at the peak of its perfection. The majestic 9-course dinners are accompanied by a selection of 5 or 6 fine wines chosen by The Herbfarm's sommeliers. Each course is an indulgence to the senses, chef Jerry Traunfeld has won numerous awards including the James Beard award for Best American Chef from the Northwest and other well deserved accolades from prestigious organizations such as Gourmet and Zagat. The Herbfarm offers 2 luxurious suites on the property of romantic Willows Lodge; the Orchard House Suite is decorated in rich hues of red and gold embellished with paintings and sculptures, while the Herb Garden Suite displays relaxing shades of green and mauve complemented by delicate lighting. The surrounding area boasts a number of wineries and is a wonderful place for outdoor pursuits such as cycling, golf and fishing.

Our inspector loved: *Dinner at the Herbfarm restaurant; a most memorable experience!*

Directions: A 40-minute drive from Seattle's Sea-Tac Airport.

Web: www.johansens.com/herbfarm
E-mail: reservations@theherbfarm.com
Tel: +1 425 485 5300
Fax: +1 425 424 2925

Price Guide:
rooms $300-$395

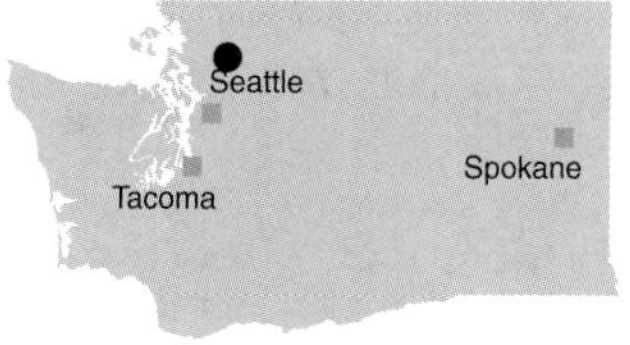

West Virginia

Hotel location shown in red with page number

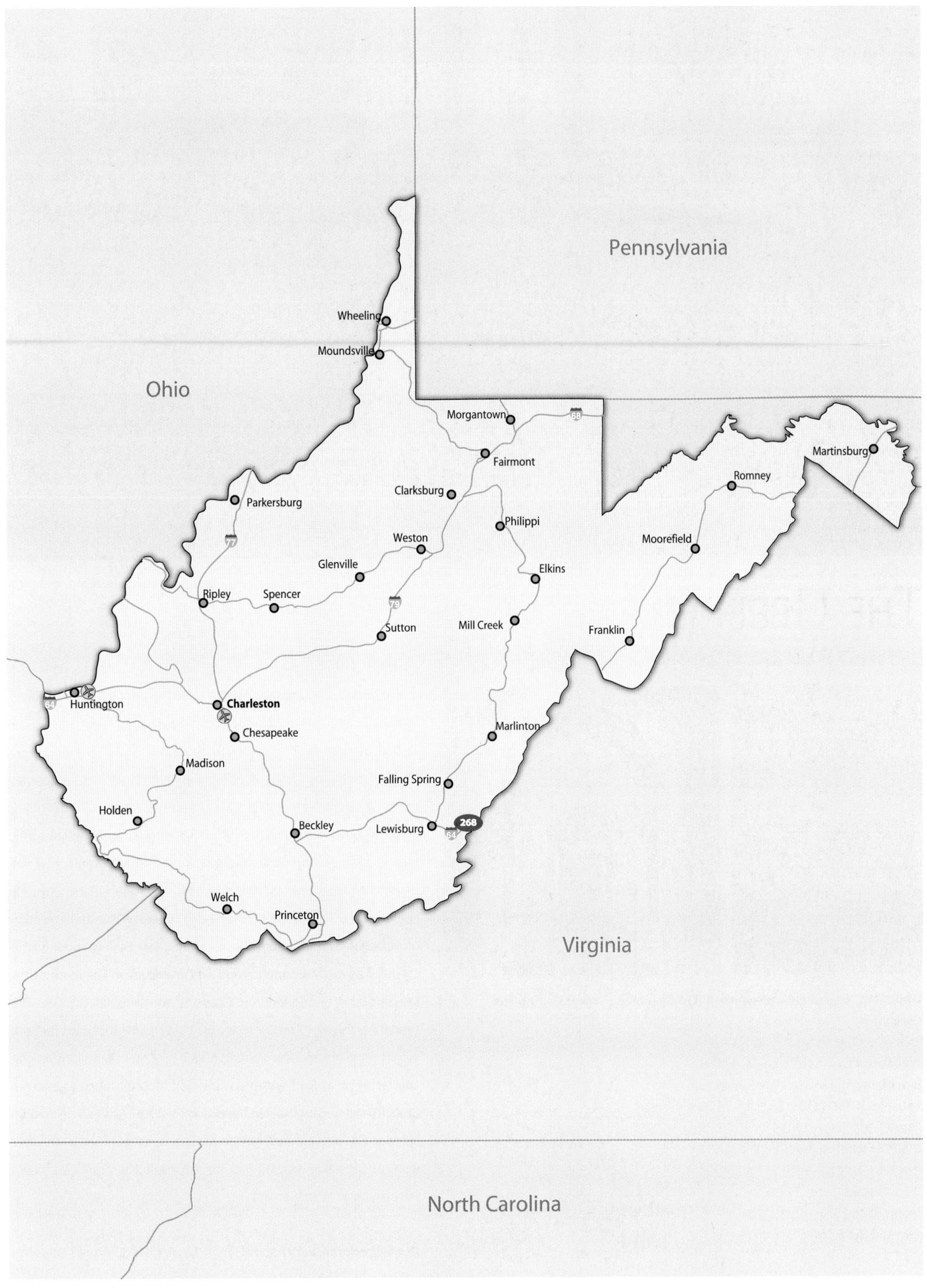

The Greenbrier

300 West Main Street, White Sulphur Springs, West Virginia 24986

A historic and beautiful estate set in 6,500 acres of the Allegheny Mountains, The Greenbrier is a National Historic Landmark with classic architecture, beautifully landscaped grounds and exquisite design. The property boasts an AAA 5 Diamond rating, 1 of only 3 properties to receive the award 30 years in a row. Over a span of 2 centuries, famous guests have included an astonishing 26 presidents, royalty, business leaders and many celebrities. The elegant Main Lobby has majestic high ceilings, cozy sitting areas in a series of lobbies, historic paintings, vibrant floral décor and a regal fireplace. There is a selection of first-class dining options including the Main Dining Room with a menu of classical, continental and American cuisine. The more casual Draper's and Rhododendron Café are also popular choices. The Greenbrier Culinary Arts Center is a hands-on center that is fun for both children and adults. After a round of golf on 1 of 3 championship golf courses, relax at Sam Snead's at the Golf Club for lunch and a cool drink. To rejuvenate the mind and body, visit the Spa with its natural Sulphur Springs famous for its healing benefits. This is an ideal getaway for active couples, families and executive retreats with over 50 recreational activities and over 30 shops located on-site.

Our inspector loved: *That this resort "has it all" including a fascinating history and world-renowned service and amenities.*

Directions: Greenbrier Valley Airport (L.W.B.) is only 15 minutes from The Greenbrier.

Web: www.johansens.com/greenbrier
E-mail: the_greenbrier@greenbrier.com
Tel: +1 304 536 1110
Fax: +1 304 536 7818
U.S./Canada Toll Free: 1 800 624 6070

Price Guide:
rooms $274-$524
suites $346-$5,369

Wisconsin

Hotel location shown in red with page number

Canoe Bay

RELAIS & CHÂTEAUX

P.O. BOX 28, CHETEK, WISCONSIN 54728

This secluded, couples only, rustic wooded retreat is tucked away in 280 acres of peaceful woodland and surrounded by 3 pristine lakes. Sheer luxury and impeccable service within this beautiful wilderness setting create a wonderfully romantic atmosphere and blissful respite whilst surrounded by every comfort and the very best of amenities. Idyllic rooms and cottages are extremely private, each with their own whirlpool tub and large cedar deck that either looks out over the woods or lakes. Fireplaces in every room create a cozy atmosphere that allows for total relaxation and peace. Sumptuous Continental breakfasts are delivered to guests' door each morning, and the gourmet picnic lunches are sublime. The hotel's glass enclosed dining room has breathtaking views over the lake and offers exceptional dinners on a daily changing set menu. All dishes are produced from local, fresh organic ingredients served with an extensive choice of fine wines. For those who wish to curl up with a good book, there are thousands to choose from in the beautiful, very current library. Outdoor enthusiasts will love kayaking, canoeing, fishing and swimming on one of the 3 picturesque lakes. During the winter the wooded hiking trails are ideal for snowshoeing, and for pure indulgence try a fireside massage. WiFi access is available.

Our inspector loved: *This ultimate luxury getaway for couples with breathtaking views and great service.*

Directions: From Minneapolis follow I-94 east to 53 north and exit at Chetek.

Web: www.johansens.com/canoebay
E-mail: mail@canoebay.com
Tel: +1 715 924 4594
Fax: +1 715 924 2078
U.S./Canada Toll Free: 1 800 568 1995

Price Guide: (room only)
rooms $325-$525
cottages $375-$1,800

The Delafield Hotel

415 Genesee Street, Delafield, Wisconsin 53018

A new American Inn, The Delafield Hotel is traditional in style with all the conveniences of a modern luxury hotel. Beyond the beautiful red brick exterior this boutique property offers oversized suites with beautiful Baker furnishings and oil paintings throughout. A highlight of the suites are the unique "spa" bathrooms with the latest in Kohler showers and baths featuring high-tech bubble massage tubs with chromatherapy. This is an ideal setting for romantic and intimate weekends and upscale business retreats alike. The restaurant, Andrew's, offers fine American cuisine by owner, Andrew Ruggeri and Chef de Cuisine, Dean Schmitz, that is perfectly matched with wines from the world-class wine cellar. The expansive cellar boasts over 2,000 wines from the finest international vineyards. Dinner guests will enjoy views of the Kettle Moraine from the lanai and serene privacy in the engagement rooms. Enjoy the sultry live music every weekend at the Jazz Bar. The hotel is conveniently located in downtown Delafield, 25 miles from Milwaukee. Downtown, there are many specialty shops, spas, coffee shops, craft stores, a winery and several restaurants. The hotel's golf course, Erin Hills, is located 20 minutes north of the hotel. The course is home to a 2008 U.S.G.A. sanctioned event, the Women's Amateur Public Links, found in the town of Erin, 17 miles north.

Directions: 25 miles from Milwaukee off I-94. Exit Highway C and go north ¼ mile and the hotel is on the left.

Web: www.johansens.com/delafield
E-mail: info@thedelafieldhotel.com
Tel: +1 262 646 1600
Fax: +1 262 646 1613
U.S./Canada Toll Free: 1 800 594 8772

Price Guide:
suites $250-$800

Our inspector loved: *The luxurious state-of-the-art "spa" bathrooms.*

Wyoming

Hotel location shown in red with page number

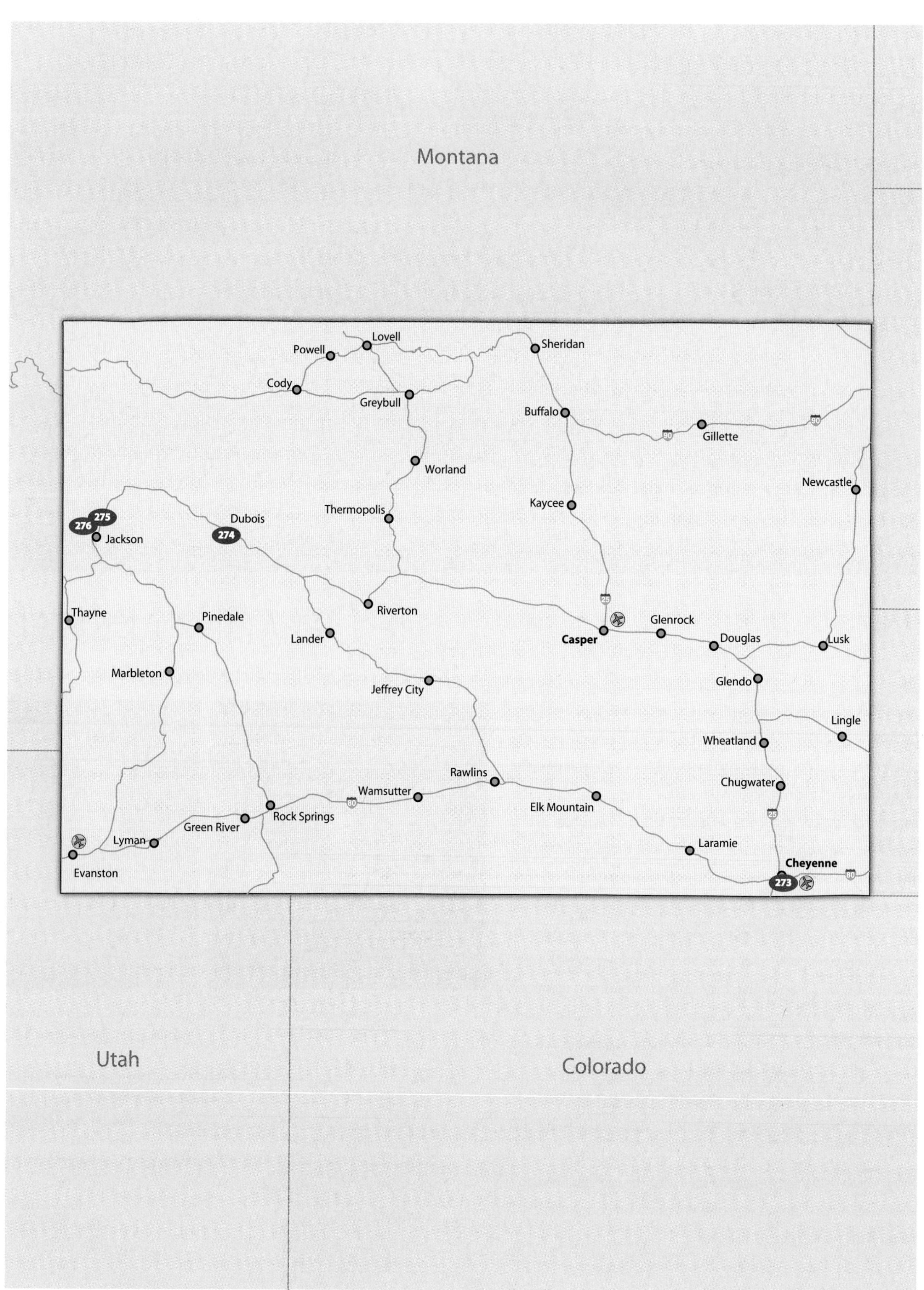

Nagle Warren Mansion

222 East 17th Street, Cheyenne, Wyoming 82001

One of Cheyenne's most stylish residences, the Nagle Warren Mansion is steeped in a rich and interesting history. Built in 1888 by Erasmus Nagle, the mansion was home to Francis E. Warren, Governor and Wyoming Senator. Set on the edge of downtown Cheyenne, the elegant Victorian décor is complemented by the fine craftsmanship of a bygone era. Vestiges of the past are evident as guests walk up the ornate wooden staircases admiring the authentic period touches. Antique furnishings abound throughout the mansion. In the 12 bedrooms, the contemporary guests' needs have been met with each room offering air conditioning, telephone and color television. The delicious breakfast includes freshly baked muffins, and special recipes by the cook are a daily treat. Guests can spend the day hiking through mountains, and afterwards the outdoor hot tub is most inviting! Set in an enclosed gazebo, it will delight guests regardless of the season. Less strenuous pastimes include shopping or exploring historic Cheyenne.

Our inspector loved: *The gourmet wine-pairing dinners served by special reservation.*

Directions: From the I-25 proceed to the I-80 east, leave at exit 362. If travelling eastbound turn left on Central, if westbound turn right.

Yellowstone National Park
Buffalo
Jackson
Cheyenne

Web: www.johansens.com/naglewarrenmansion
E-mail: jim@nwmbb.com
Tel: +1 307 637 3333
Fax: +1 307 638 6879
U.S./Canada Toll Free: 1 800 811 2610

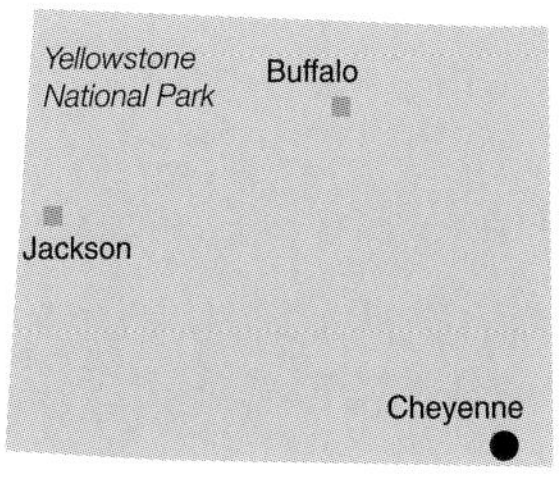

Price Guide:
rooms $108–$138
suites $138–$160

Brooks Lake Lodge

458 BROOKS LAKE ROAD, DUBOIS, WYOMING 82513

Directions: Jackson Hole Airport is a 1 hour and 30-minute drive from the lodge.

Web: www.johansens.com/brookslake
E-mail: brookslake@wyoming.com
Tel: +1 307 455 2121
Fax: +1 307 455 2221

Price Guide:
rooms $200-$350

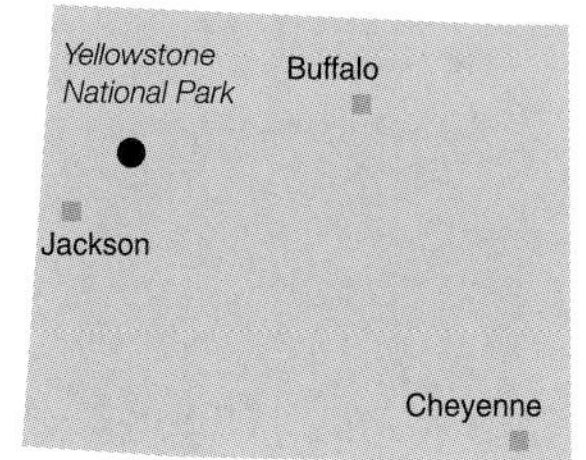

This rustic hideaway near Jackson Hole, is a gem to discover throughout the seasons. Snowmobiling adventures, cross country skiing, ice fishing, dog-sled tours and snowshoeing trails are all on offer when the powder snow falls. The warmer climate brings hiking to Austin's Peak and the Jade Lakes, fishing for rainbow trout in clear mountain lakes and horseback riding for a true adventure in the wilderness camp. After a day out in the stunning surrounds, unwind in one of the rooms in the main lodge featuring lodge-pole beds, goose down comforters and pine décor. Wood burning stoves and private patios enhance the family-sized cabins, which enjoy a spruce and pine forest backdrop and glorious views of the Pinnacle and Brooks Mountains. Descend to the grand dining hall and feast on a 3-course gourmet meal of regional fare such as grilled bison rib eye or beef tenderloin with a red/white wine demi glaze and potato duchesse. In the evenings guests enjoy postprandial drinks, visits from local musicians and artists or a game of shuffle board or foosball. If the rural activities prove too strenuous, the new spa offers massages, facials, body wraps, a dry sauna and outdoor Jacuzzi. Nearby attractions include the city of Dubois, Wyoming's shops and the legendary Yellowstone National Park.

***Our inspector loved:** The majestic views from the hot tub.*

   SPA   

Jenny Lake Lodge

INNER PARK LOOP ROAD, GRAND TETON NATIONAL PARK, WYOMING 83013

Jenny Lake Lodge is situated in the heart of Grand Teton National Park, at the foot of the Teton Mountains. This 4 Diamond lodge has been offering first-class hospitality to guests since the 1920s. The lodge has 31 single room log cabins and 6 log cabin suites. Locally handmade quilts and cozy down comforters add to the rustic ambience and the traditional Old West charm of each cabin. Many guests return time and again to stay in their favorite cabin in the woods and to wander over to the historic main lodge where they can enjoy the wonderful food, an award-winning wine list and attentive, cheerful service while gazing up at the incomparable view of the mountains. Rates include a healthy, hearty breakfast, a 5-course dinner, bicycles and horseback riding. Box lunches are available as well as an à la carte lunch in the dining room. Visitors can leave their log cabin, cross the little one-way road in front of Jenny and reach hiking trails through the Tetons. Enjoy boating and canoeing on nearby lakes and world-class fly fishing in the Snake River and numerous, nearby creeks. Alternatively, attend a talk held by the Lodge's historian, on the creation of Danny Ranch through to the present day. The town of Jackson, with its rodeo, art galleries and museums, is just 45 minutes away.

Our inspector loved: *The fascinating history of the property recounted weekly to guests by Jenny Lake's own historian.*

Directions: Jackson Airport is a 45-minute drive from the lodge.

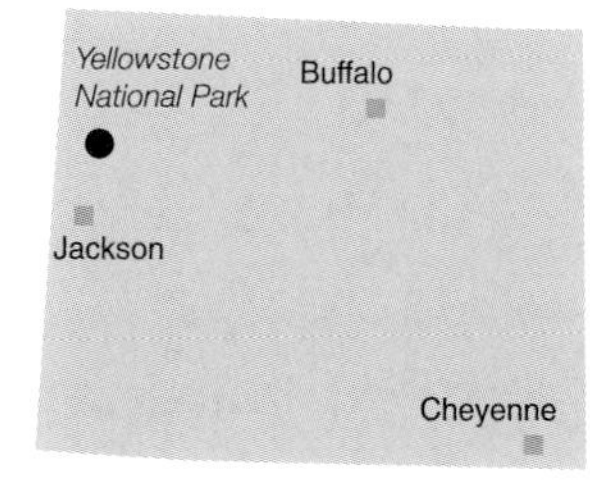

Web: www.johansens.com/jennylake
Tel: +1 307 543 3300
Fax: +1 307 543 3358
U.S./Canada Toll Free: 1 800 628 9988

Price Guide: (including breakfast, dinner, horseback riding and cycling)
rooms $495
suites $660-$715

COSTA RICA - GUANACASTE (ISLITA)

HOTEL PUNTA ISLITA

GUANACASTE

Directions: Approximately a 4-hour drive or a 40-minute flight from either San José (SJO) or Liberia (LIR) Airports. A 4-wheel drive is recommended if driving; the hotel can arrange private transfers.

Web: www.johansens.com/hotelpuntaislita
E-mail: reservas@hotelpuntaislita.com
Tel: +506 231 6122
Fax: +506 231 0715

Price Guide:
deluxe rooms U.S.$180-U.S.$240
suites U.S.$300-U.S.$385
villas U.S.$450-U.S.$660

A member of Virtuoso and Q Club, Hotel Punta Islita offers an authentic Costa Rican experience courtesy of its close ties with surrounding villages and internationally lauded responsible tourism model focusing on community, art, responsibility and environment. Spanning 35 acres, the tiered layout discreetly tucks away rooms, romantic suites and family-friendly villas offering privacy and ocean views. Many have private outdoor whirlpools or plunge pools. The 1492 Restaurant, with an open layout and native-inspired 50-foot thatched palm ceiling, serves Costa Rican fusion cuisine. The Borrancho Beach Club Restaurant provides casual poolside dining. Enjoy unique activities led by local guides such as horseback riding through the tropical dry forest and beaches, zip-lining over the forest canopy, river kayaking, A.T.V. tours, monkey safaris, nature walks, bird-watching and surfing. There is also an al fresco yoga/Pilates platform studio, an air-conditioned panoramic exercise room and a par 3, executive 9-hole golf course due to open in December 2006. The 3,700 sq. ft. Casa Spa features a generous menu of stress-reducing treatments and packages including massages, wraps, exfoliating scrubs and body polish. In the neighbor town of Islita, there is the hotel-sponsored Open Air Contemporary Art Museum, the only one of its kind in Latin America pairing Costa Rican artists with local counterparts.

Our inspector loved: *The ocean and tropical views from every location.*

Paradisus Playa Conchal

BAHÍA BRASILITO, PLAYA CONCHAL, SANTA CRUZ, GUANACASTE

Enchantment awaits at Paradisus Playa Conchal, a luxurious seaside retreat amongst green forests in Costa Rica's North-Pacific Riviera. Set amidst meandering walkways, bubbling fountains, shimmering lakes and lush tropical gardens, this is the only top-of-the-line, all-inclusive beach and golf resort in Costa Rica. Luxurious guest rooms are proportioned to feel more like home, with spacious living areas and private terraces. Personalized concierge and butler service is available for those who wish the ultimate in indulgence during their stay. Paradisus Playa Conchal invites its guests to explore their culinary fantasies in one of 7 restaurants, where the fine Italian, Caribbean and Asian fusion cuisine delight the senses. Entertainment options include nightly musical reviews, 4 bars, a casino, kids center, spa and water sports along the resort's 1½-mile white sand beach. A championship eco-golf course, Reserva Conchal Golf Club, incorporates majestic ocean vistas. Day-trippers will marvel at the closeness of prime national parks and wildlife refuges while the truly adventurous can enjoy white-water rafting, deep-sea fishing and scuba diving.

Our inspector loved: *The beautiful suites and choices of so many water sports, restaurants and nightlife activities.*

Directions: 60km from Liberia International Airport. 15 minutes from Tamarindo.

Liberia
Puerto Limón
San Jose

Web: www.johansens.com/paradisusplayaconchal
E-mail: info@paradisusplayaconchal.com
Tel: +506 654 4123
Fax: +506 654 4181
U.S./Canada Toll Free: 1 888 956 3542

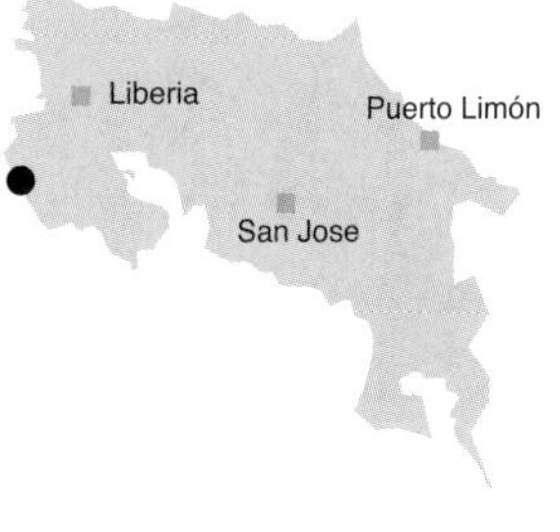

Price Guide: (all inclusive)
rooms U.S.$249-U.S.$550
suites U.S.$369-U.S.$1,800

412 400 1 SPA

Gaia Hotel & Reserve

KM 2.7 CARRETERA QUEPOS, MANUEL ANTONIO

Directions: A 10-minute drive from Quepos Airport (XQP). 20 minutes by air from San José International Airport (SJO).

Web: www.johansens.com/gaiahr
E-mail: reservations@gaiahr.com
Tel: +506 777 9797
Fax: +506 777 9126
U.S./Canada Toll Free: 1 800 226 2515

Price Guide:
rooms U.S.$250-U.S.$330
suites U.S.$350-U.S.$880

Nestled high on a hill above Costa Rica's Pacific coastline, Gaia Hotel & Reserve offers the ultimate in luxury and personal service amidst pristine wilderness. The sleek Bauhaus design is fresh, modern and uncluttered. All rooms are equipped with central air, cable, flat-screen T.V.s, portable telephones, home entertainment units, Internet connectivity, 500-thread count linens, mini-bars stocked to guests' specifications, beautiful bathrooms, Jacuzzis and amazing views of the surrounding jungle and ocean. Each room has a personal valet to cater to every need from laundry, room service, tours and transportation to personal shopping. There is a gym with personal trainer, full-service Terra Spa at Gaia, an in-room spa service menu and a spectacular 3-tiered, infinity-pool with in-water table dining. La Luna restaurant offers exceptional cuisine featuring international, local and special dietary requirements, along with a 24-hour menu of fresh salads, soups, appetizers, sandwiches and desserts. Guests can tour Gaia's 12.1 acres of nature reserve with a certified nature guide. The reserve contains a wide range of rare flora, fauna and mammals, such as the White Face and Squirrel monkeys, 3-toed sloths, coatis and red-eyed tree frogs. The resort is 10 minutes from Manuel Antonio National Park, with its pristine white sand beaches, live coral reefs, hiking trails and 346 different species.

Our inspector loved: *The view from the 3-tiered, infinity-edge pool.*

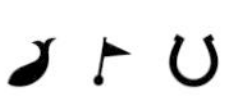

Central America - Honduras

Hotel location shown in red with page number

The Lodge at Pico Bonito

A. P. 710, LA CEIBA, ATLÁNTIDA, C. P. 31101

Directions: Fly into La Ceiba and take the lodge's 15-minute transfer bus.

Web: www.johansens.com/picobonito
E-mail: picobonito@caribe.hn
Tel: +504 440 0388
Fax: +504 440 0468
U.S./Canada Toll Free: 1 888 428 0221

Price Guide: (room only)
rooms U.S.$230-U.S.$350

There can be few locations to rival the dramatic backdrop to The Lodge at Pico Bonito. Cradled between the Caribbean Sea and Pico Bonito Mountain, which soars 8,000 feet above the jungle floor, the lodge lies in the heart of the rainforest and is surrounded by 200 acres bursting with exotic flora and fauna. Accommodation is provided in a series of enchanting secluded cabins, sympathetically designed with native hardwood floors, crisp linens and cooling ceiling fans. Each cabin has its own private veranda, which features a romantic atmosphere at night as the stars rise over the mountain, and a refreshing place to start the day when typical Honduran breakfast is served. The staff is immaculate and attentive, and English speaking guides will escort guests through the tropical jungle to see manatees, monkeys, parrots and toucans. The canoe trip into the wildlife reserve is an absolute must, and the more intrepid guest may also wish to take advantage of guided night hikes to witness the nocturnal jungle. Just-picked fruit and freshly-squeezed juices are typical cuisine and the local chef prides himself on his delicate Meso-American recipes that are served for lunch and dinner in the beautifully appointed restaurant, or one of the many outdoor decks.

Our inspector loved: *The impressive trips within the rainforest.*

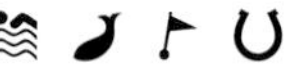

South America - Argentina

Hotel location shown in red with page number

1555 Malabia House

MALABIA 1555, C1414DME BUENOS AIRES

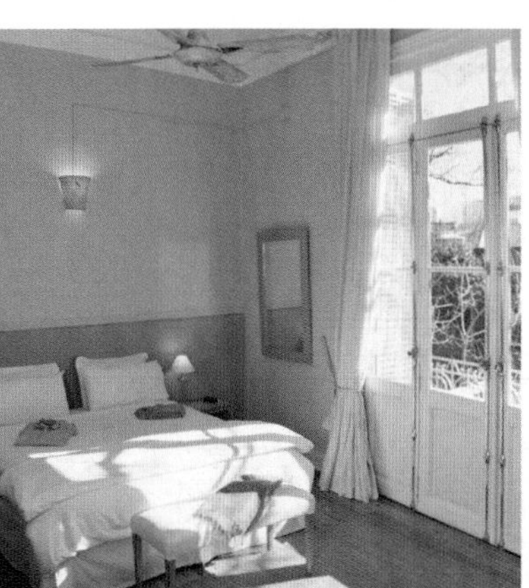

Directions: Located at Palermo Viz 50 or SE 40 Pontiño which is approximately an hour's drive from Eziza's International Airport.

Web: www.johansens.com/malabiahouse
E-mail: info@malabiahouse.com.ar
Tel: +54 11 4832 3345
Fax: +54 11 4832 3345

Price Guide:
rooms U.S.$127-U.S.$170

In the heart of Palermo Viejo, the most exclusive neighborhood in Buenos Aires, exists the first designer bed and breakfast in Argentina. A century ago, this historic house was donated by a French noblewoman to the Church of Santo Domingo as lodging for single women. Painstakingly remodeled, 1555 Malabia House today welcomes international travelers who seek an environment more relaxing than that offered by traditional hotels. Rather than windows, each room has tall doors that open to fresh breezes. The stylish, warm décor conveys a sense of home. All rooms feature a private bath, television, mini-fridge, telephone and safety deposit box. The staff is impressive and provides 24-hour concierge and room service. The central patio, library and executive lounge, with fax and Internet access, afford guests space for conversation, reflection and productivity. Each morning, a delectable buffet breakfast is served in the dining room. Guests of 1555 Malabia House, now fortified for the day's adventure, can explore the winding streets and scenic plazas of Palermo Soho. The area is renowned for designer boutiques, avant-garde art, fine cuisine and intense nightlife.

Our inspector loved: *The charming details of the décor, and the delicious breakfast.*

LoiSuites Recoleta Hotel

VICENTE LÓPEZ 1955 – C1128ACC, CIUDAD DE BUENOS AIRES

LoiSuites is a contemporary hotel with 112 well-appointed studios and suites combining style, comfort and technology in the upscale district of Recoleta. This hotel is a great choice for both business and leisure visitors. All rooms are spacious and furnished in modern style with amenities including mobile phones and Internet access. Among the hotel's facilities are an indoor heated pool, fitness center, sauna and massage. There is also meeting space and an efficient business center. Breakfast can be enjoyed on the delightful winter garden patio, and the restaurant menu offers an interesting variety of international cuisine. For those wishing to dine in, there is also a room service menu. An excellent concierge is available to help guests navigate the many offerings of Recoleta, the sophisticated cultural center of Buenos Aires. Recoleta is reminiscent of a European city with its historical parks, art galleries and restaurants. The National Fine Arts Museum contains some of the nation's greatest treasures and the National Museum of Decorative Art, housed in a magnificent French classical landmark building, has a fascinating collection of furnishings and home décor, most of which was donated by Argentina's leading families.

Our inspector loved: *The great location of this comfortable hotel.*

Directions: The hotel is a 40-minute drive from Ezeiza International Airport (E.Z.E.).

Web: www.johansens.com/loisuites
E-mail: recoleta@loisuites.com.ar
Tel: +54 11 5777 8950
Fax: +54 11 5777 8999
U.S./Canada Toll Free: 1 800 961 4643

Price Guide:
rooms U.S.$250-U.S.$400

ARGENTINA - PATAGONIA (ISLA VICTORIA)

Isla Victoria Lodge

ISLA VICTORIA, PARQUE NACIONAL NAHUEL HUAPI, C.C. 26 (R8401AKU)

Situated on a cliff overlooking the lake and forests of cohiues and cypresses, Isla Victoria Lodge is part of the Nahuel Huapi National Park, one of the most unique areas of the Argentinean Patagonia. Bilingual guides are available to lead outdoor activities including bird watching, deer sighting, photographic safari, horse riding, kayaks, trekking and mountain biking. Every activity is carefully designed to make sure that guests enjoy and learn all about the area, get closer to nature and find out the infinite world that Victoria Island offers. There are 3 living rooms, a cozy bar with fireplace, a spa-solarium and a great wine cellar with some of the best wines the area has to offer. A warm library offers a relaxing environment and the restaurant looks out to a super view while serving delightful local cuisine.

Our inspector loved: *The overwhelming natural beauty of the island, and the atmosphere of the lodge.*

Directions: From Bariloche International Airport take Ave. Ezequiel Bustillo to Km 24.5. At Hotel Tunquelén take the boat to the island.

Web: www.johansens.com/islavictoria
E-mail: maresur@maresur.com
Tel: +54 43 94 96 05
Fax: +54 11 43 94 95 99

Price Guide: (all-inclusive, 2-night stay and all transfers included)
per person U.S.$570

Correntoso Lake & River Hotel

VLA. LA ANGOSTURA, PATAGONIA

This traditional hotel, situated at the mouth of the Correntoso River where it enters Nahuel Huapi Lake at the foot of the Andes, is a great point from which to explore the charm and scenery of Patagonia. 29 elegant accommodations feature beautiful interior décor with fine woodwork, elegant, comfortable furnishings and many modern in-room amenities. The gourmet restaurant and wine bar, specializing in regional wines, fuses Mediterranean and traditional Patagonian cuisines created with local game and produce, while Puerto Correntoso serves more casual fare on a deck overlooking the lake. At tea time, a variety of homemade pastries, chocolates and special tea blends are offered. The hotel's Spirit & Adventures department provides several custom-designed excursions to explore the natural beauty of the area: trekking, boating, rafting, horseback riding, fishing, skiing, snowshoeing and zip line canopy tours are all available in season, with gourmet picnics or complete asado (Argentine barbecue) lunches included on most tours. Guests wishing to enjoy a relaxing day can indulge in a massage, spend some time in the herbal hammam, swim in the indoor/outdoor heated pool or curl up with a book in the Patagonian-themed library.

Our inspector loved: *Enjoying a superb dinner overlooking Nahuel Huapi Lake.*

Directions: Villa La Angostura is a 1-hour drive from San Carlos de Bariloche International Airport.

Web: www.johansens.com/correntoso
E-mail: info@correntoso.com
Tel: +54 11 4803 0030
Fax: +54 11 4803 0030

Price Guide:
rooms U.S.$290-U.S.$400

South America - Brazil

Hotel location shown in red with page number

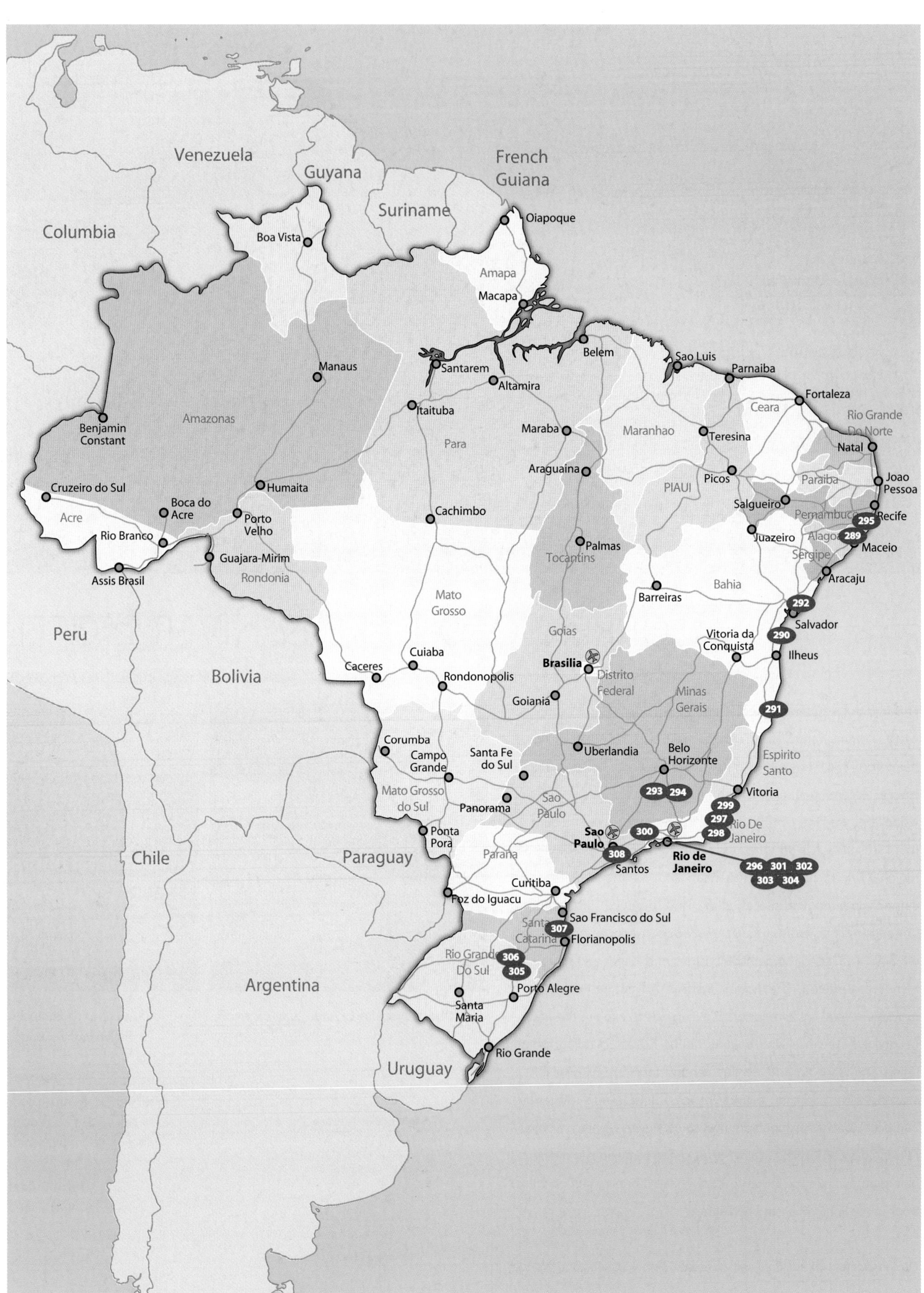

Pousada do Toque

RUA FELISBERTO DE ATAIDE, POVOADO DO TOQUE, SÃO MIGUEL DOS MILAGRES, ALAGOAS

Located amidst the Coral Coast extending to the northern shoreline of the state of Alagoas, on a private and pristine beach of Praia do Toque, this pleasant pousada has quickly become a favorite beach retreat. Combining intimacy, rusticity and charm, owners Nilo Burgarelli and his wife Gilda Peixoto have created an inspiring retreat where simplicity and comfort provides the ultimate escape. The pousada blends in beautifully with the surroundings of a coconut grove plantation. There are 13 guest rooms called chalets, which include private pools, sundecks, Jacuzzis and verandas with inviting hammocks. Nilo is a former restaurateur and uses his talents to create international cuisine including fresh local seafood and local dishes using the freshest vegetables from the garden. In addition to the delicious menu, which includes his famous scampi called "lagostins," he encourages guests to ask for special dishes not on the menu. The wine cellar also carries a wide variety of international wines. Guests can spend the day at the beachfront pool or have a relaxing massage in the small massage parlor. Rustic gazebos are situated near the lawn and there are tennis courts. From the cemetery on top of the hill above the resort, there are panoramic views of the beach and River Tatuamunha. Natural sea pools are a short drive away.

Our inspector loved: *The rusticity, coziness and comfort of all the guest rooms, in addition to the owner's attentive service.*

Directions: Aeroporto Internacional de Maceió, Zumbi dos Palmares is 90 minutes by car.

Web: www.johansens.com/pousadadotoque
E-mail: pousadadotoque@uol.com.br
Tel: +55 82 3295 1127
Fax: +55 82 3295 1127

Price Guide: (including dinner)
rooms U.S.$160-U.S.$210
suites U.S.$290-U.S.$430

Txai Resort

ROD. ILHÉUS-ITACARÉ KM 48, ITACARÉ, BAHIA 45530-000

Directions: From Ilheus-Eduardo Gomes International Airport (I.O.S.) take highway BA-001 to km 48.

Web: www.johansens.com/txairesort
E-mail: reserva@txairesort.com.br
Tel: +55 73 2101 5000
Fax: +55 73 2101 5251

Price Guide:
rooms U.S.$398-U.S.$1,000

Located on a 100-hectacre coconut plantation set along Itacarezinho beach and surrounded by unspoiled Atlantic rainforest, this sophisticated Bahia beach resort features 40 comfortable bungalows tucked amidst the coconut palms. Bungalows are built on stilts with wooden decks, palm-thatch detailing and beautiful natural vistas. Interiors have been decorated in earth tones with king beds, open-air showers, whirlpool baths and massage and relaxation beds. The restaurant, with its traditional Bahia architecture and stunning view of the ocean, serves both regional and international cuisine accompanied by a great choice of wines. A Colonial-style lounge, filled with Brazilian art and furniture and surrounded by a reflecting pool, provides an ideal spot to relax and enjoy the views or guests can take a dip in Txai's blue-tiled pool just a few yards from the beach. 2 lit tennis courts and a T.V. room with 60-inch screen are also on-site. The Txai Health Spa offers a variety of massages, treatments and classes in a beautiful hilltop location. Guests can also participate in various excursions from the property, take surfing lessons or rent bicycles. The nearby town of Itacaré was once Bahia's largest port for cacao exports and has many beautiful mansions and sites of historical interest.

Our inspector loved: *The excellent service provided by the staff, and the natural beauty of the area.*

Estrela d'Agua

ESTRADA ARRAIAL D'AJUDA, TRANCOSO S/N[A], TRANCOSO PORTO SEGURO, BAHIA 45818-000

Pousada Estrela D'Agua is located in Trancoso, a charming village founded in 1516 that has become one of the places to vacation in north-eastern Brazil. The historic square, with its carefully preserved colorful houses and exuberant atmosphere, attracts people from all over the world and has become a meeting place where artists, architects and designers come together to develop styles and ideas that are fast becoming recognized throughout Brazil. The hotel is located on the beach amidst local scenery of rivers, cliffs, natural pools and virgin beaches. Accommodations, inspired by the natural beauty of the region, are rustic yet comfortable. There are 28 suites, all of which have air conditioning and verandas with hammocks. The 6 master suites also have private pools, Jacuzzis or beachfront locations. There are 2 bars: Costa Bar on the beach, with its comfortable chairs and sofas, and the Veranda Bar, equally enjoyable day and night. Aldeia de São João Restaurant is located in the main house and offers delicious traditional and international cuisine as well as excellent wines. Guests can enjoy golf on the Terravista Golf Course at the foot of the multi-colored cliffs of Trancoso, an outdoor massage facing the ocean, horse riding or a relaxing day by the pool.

Our inspector loved: *Enjoying the excellent regional food and wine in this unique location.*

Directions: From Porto Seguro International Airport, take the ferry to the village of Arraial d'Ajuda; Trancoso is a 50-minute drive from the ferry.

Web: www.johansens.com/estreladagua
E-mail: reservas@estreladagua.com.br
Tel: +55 73 3668 1030
Fax: +55 73 3668 1030

Price Guide:
rooms U.S.$270-U.S.$690

Praia do Forte Eco Resort & Thalasso Spa

AVENIDA DO FAROL, PRAIA DO FORTE - MATA DE SÃO JOÃO, BAHIA

This resort is idyllically located on one of the most beautiful coastal regions in Brazil. Ecological reserves adjoin semi-deserted white sand beaches with calm, warm waters surrounded by natural Atlantic forests, coral reefs, lagoons, colorful and lush tropical gardens, enormous coconut groves and quiet beaches where sea turtles lay their eggs. All buildings at the resort are made from locally sourced natural materials that blend effortlessly into the environment; the intricate piaçava straw roofs were thatched by local craftsmen. Thoughtful attention to detail is evident in the spacious and peaceful bedrooms, and friendly staff create a welcoming atmosphere and provide a personal service. A feast of 115 different items on the breakfast buffet include exotic fruits, fresh breads, cakes, omelets and local specialties such as tapioca couscous and beiju. For dinner, there is a large selection of homemade, mouthwatering dishes. A prawn kiosk is popular and serves unique fish and fresh lobster as well as tropical drinks during the day. Activities include canoeing up the mangrove swamps, snorkeling, scuba diving, horse riding on the beach or forests, quadricycling, bird-watching, yoga and tai chi.

Our inspector loved: *The beauty, and wide range of services and treatments offered at both the thalasso spa and resort.*

Directions: The resort is located 55km from Salvador International Airport.

Web: www.johansens.com/praiadoforte
E-mail: reservas@ecoresort.com.br
Tel: +55 71 36 76 40 00
Fax: +55 71 36 76 11 12
Brazil Toll Free: 0800 71 88 88

Price Guide:
rooms U.S.$300-U.S.$400

Pousada dos Inconfidentes

RUA JOÃO RODRIGUES SOBRINHO 91, 36325-000, TIRADENTES, MINAS GERAIS

Located on a quiet street in the historic town of Tiradentes, Pousada dos Inconfidentes is an elegant, new Colonial-style inn with 13 nicely outfitted suites decorated by a famous Brazilian interior designer. The inn itself is named for the "Inconfidentes," 18th-century Colonial rebels against the Portuguese crown, and each suite bears the name of a different local rebellion hero. There is a lovely library where guests can enjoy a book, newspaper or magazine with a cup of tea or coffee and cookies, and beautiful gardens that are an equally pleasant spot for reading on sunny days. In the evenings, savor a drink at the cozy piano bar complete with fireplace or take advantage of the inn's home theater. There is also a fitness room, sauna, semi-Olympic outdoor swimming pool and poolside bar serving drinks, sandwiches and fresh fruit. Serenity reigns throughout this adults-only refuge, encouraging all who visit to slow their pace and relish their time at the inn. Enjoy a nice breakfast in the Café da Manhã before heading into town to explore its many beautiful churches and charming shops offering regional art and furniture.

Our inspector loved: *Reading a book in the garden as the sun sets behind the beautiful mountains.*

Directions: Tiradentes is 343 km from Rio de Janeiro-Galeão International Airport (G.I.G.). Take BR-040 toward Belo Horizonte for 293 km, then take BR-265 for the final 50 km to Tiradentes.

Web: www.johansens.com/inconfidentes
E-mail: reservas@pousadadosinconfidentes.com.br
Tel: +55 32 3355 2135
Fax: +55 32 3355 2135

Fortaleza
Brasilia
Sao Paulo
Rio de Janeiro

Price Guide:
rooms U.S.$180-U.S.$275

Solar da Ponte

PRAÇA DAS MERCÊS S/N, TIRADENTES, MINAS GERAIS 36325-000

Directions: The hotel is located at 343km from Rio de Janeiro International Airport. Take BR-040 Highway in towards Belo Horizonte and after 293km take BR-265 and drive a further 50km. The nearest local airport is 25km away at São João del Rey.

Web: www.johansens.com/solardaponte
E-mail: reservas@solardaponte.com.br
Tel: +55 32 33 55 12 55
Fax: +55 32 33 55 12 01

Price Guide:
rooms U.S.$160-U.S.$260

Solar da Ponte has been welcoming visitors to Tiradentes for more than 30 years. This is a beautiful country mansion set within peaceful shady gardens in the historical 18th-century mountain village of Tiradentes, with quaint winding streets and 8 Baroque churches. The Colonial-style architecture creates a comfortable environment, and the spacious interiors feature light color schemes complemented by traditional décor and locally made furniture. Well presented, individually decorated bedrooms provide a high degree of comfort and elegance. Healthy, light meals are served in the hotel's bar and delicious breakfasts and afternoon teas are served in a spacious room with tree-top view. Situated in the historic center of the town where local, contemporary artists display their works, there are a variety of handicrafts to admire. The many Baroque monuments and beautiful churches in the region are well worth a visit as well as the excellent restaurants nearby where guests can sample delicious local or international cuisine. Walking and horse riding in the native tropical forests is breathtaking, and the imposing São José Mountain Range, now an ecological reserve, creates an awe-inspiring backdrop where excursions for guests can be arranged by the owners.

***Our inspector loved:** The comfort of the bedrooms, and enjoying the tasty breakfast while watching little monkeys playing in nearby trees.*

Nannai Beach Resort

Rodovia PE-09, Acesso à Muro Alto, KM 3, Ipojuca, Pernambuco 55590-000

This Bali-style beach resort is tucked along the Atlantic coast of Pernambuco just north of the famous village and beaches of Porto de Galinhas. Private bungalows and terraced apartments are nestled among beautiful tropical gardens and 6000m² of pools of myriad shapes, sizes and depths. Beautiful hardwood, bright colors and light linens create a fresh, cheerful atmosphere, and privacy and personalized service make this resort an oasis of relaxation. Guests can enjoy live music while they dine on regional and international cuisine in the main restaurant overlooking the ocean or opt for the more casual atmosphere of the lounge, cybercafé or beach bar. In addition to the beach and many swimming pools, a plethora of activities including tennis, beach soccer, volleyball, water volleyball, hydro-gymnastics and dance classes are offered. Complimentary water sports include snorkeling, kayaking, laser and jangada (a Brazilian raft) and sailing; motorized water sports are available for an additional fee. For the more traditional, the resort features a fitness center, steam sauna and games room. A dedicated children's area, babysitting services and children's programs are also offered. Massages, beauty services and excursions can be arranged.

Our inspector loved: *The charming premium bungalows with private swimming pools, located right in front of Muro Alto beach.*

91

Directions: Located 59km south of Recife International Airport.

Web: www.johansens.com/nannaibeach
E-mail: reservas@nannai.com.br
Tel: +55 81 3552 0100
Fax: +55 81 3552 1474

Price Guide: (including dinner)
rooms U.S.$270-U.S.$345
suites U.S.$598-U.S.$780

Sítio do Lobo

PONTA DO LOBO, ILHA GRANDE, ANGRA DOS REIS, RIO DE JANEIRO

Directions: Located on the southern coast of Rio de Janeiro. 1 hour and 30 minutes from Rio's International Airport followed by a 15-minute boat ride from the marina to the island.

Web: www.johansens.com/sitiodolobo
E-mail: reservas@sitiodolobo.com.br
Tel: +55 21 2227 4138
Fax: +55 21 2267 7841

Price Guide: (contact the property for special packages)
rooms U.S.$350-U.S.$460
suites U.S.$425-U.S.$625

This is a blissful location. Privately owned and situated in an area of environmental protection on the 43km-long island of Ilha Grande, off the southern coast of Rio de Janeiro, Sítio do Lobo is a restful and peaceful paradise of unspoiled beauty. Reached only by boat or helicopter, it offers isolation and intimacy where guests can be as active or inactive as they wish. On the water's edge of a dense green forest, this quiet "enseada" was once a thriving coffee plantation. Once the exclusive home of José Serrado and his interior decorator wife, Julinha, they only opened the property to paying guests a few years ago. They are warm and welcoming hosts and justly proud of their hotel. The main house is an unobtrusive wooden building with a wide veranda that juts out over the rocky shore, ideal for enjoying a cool drink or quiet read. Inside, Julinha's personal touch and exquisite taste are evident in the décor and furnishing. Surrounding rustic-styled guest rooms are partially hidden by the shady foliage. Rooms range from small doubles to a lavish suite with superb ocean views. All have air conditioning and modern comforts. Facilities include a pool, volleyball court in the old plantation's slave quarters, a sauna hut next to a freshwater spring, and a small spa. Boat trips to neighboring islands can be arranged.

Our inspector loved: *The perfect integration of the rustic, beautiful décor with the amazing natural beauty surrounding the property.*

Pérola Búzios

AV. JOSÉ BENTO RIBEIRO DANTAS, 222, ARMAÇÃO DOS BÚZIOS, RIO DE JANEIRO 28950-000

Designed by Brazilian architect and plastics artist Hélio Pellegrino, Pérola Búzios offers guests a modern, artistic environment created with comfort in mind. The hotel's white, orange and dark wood décor creates a crisp, bright and cheerful ambience, accented by over 700 unique pieces of contemporary art, special lighting and music. The 7 different categories of guest rooms and apartments offer good options for singles, couples and families and feature modern amenities including high-speed Internet access and cable T.V. The Pérola restaurant serves a constantly evolving menu created from fresh local products and seafood to showcase the flavors, scents and colors of Brazilian cuisine. At breakfast, a lovely spread of fresh fruits, yogurts, natural juices, cakes, breads, cheeses and omelets is offered. Guests can also enjoy a meal at the pool bar, relax on a raised in-pool lounge bed or take advantage of the fitness center, massage service, Jacuzzi and dry and steam saunas. Pérola Negra Hall and several smaller rooms are available for conferences and special events. The many restaurants, night clubs, art galleries and stores of the Rua das Pedras and Orla Bardot are just a short walk away.

Our inspector loved: *Walking in the charming village of Búzios before enjoying a relaxed diner at Pérola's restaurant.*

 60    350     

Directions: A 2-hour drive from Rio International Airport via Lagos.

Web: www.johansens.com/perolabuzios
E-mail: reservas@perolabuzios.com
Tel: +55 22 2620 8507
Fax: +55 22 2623 9015

Fortaleza
Brasilia
Sao Paulo
Rio de Janeiro

Price Guide:
rooms U.S.$152-U.S.$440

Casas Brancas Boutique-Hotel & Spa

ALTO DO HUMAITÁ 10, ARMAÇÃO DOS BÚZIOS, RIO DE JANEIRO 28950-000

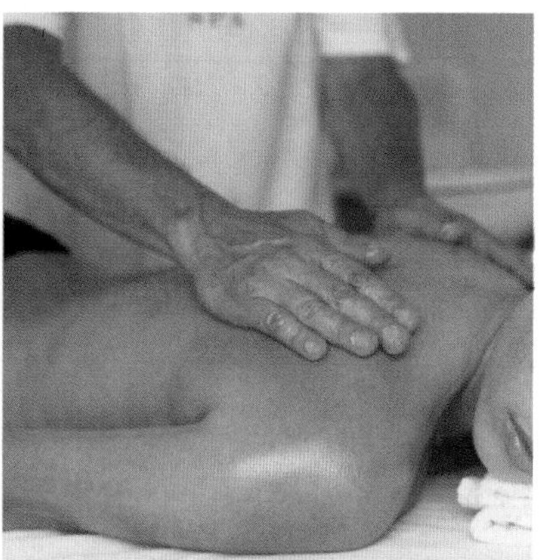

The unspoiled fishing village of Búzios became the place to visit and to be seen in following a visit by French film actress Brigitte Bardot in 1964. Situated on a peninsula protruding into the Atlantic Ocean 175km from Rio de Janeiro, it became a tropical St. Tropez. Like its equivalent in the south of France, the village has grown over the years but retains a certain charm that is emphasized by seafront vistas and a cobbled main street. Wealthy South Americans seeking luxurious relaxation view it as a fashionable beach resort. The surrounding area boasts 25 beaches where surfing, diving, sailing or simply lounging can be enjoyed. Casas Brancas Boutique-Hotel & Spa nestles in the hills overlooking the stunning Bay of Búzios, just a 5-minute stroll from Búzios's famous downtown main street where restaurants, shops, bars and musical entertainment blend harmoniously with the colorful fishing boats lining the shore. Built in a cool, Mediterranean style the hotel has an appealing, elegant, laid back atmosphere. Décor and furnishings are elegant and sophisticated; the guest rooms have sea or garden views and are well appointed. The restaurant is a dining experience to cherish: talented kitchen staff produce excellent and imaginative international cuisine as well as Brazilian delights to satisfy the most refined diner.

Our inspector loved: *Eating the great food whilst admiring the view of the charming fishing village.*

Directions: The hotel is situated 6km from the local airport and 175km from Rio's International Airport.

Web: www.johansens.com/casasbrancas
E-mail: info@casasbrancas.com.br
Tel: +55 22 2623 1458
Fax: +55 22 2623 2147

Price Guide:
rooms U.S.$180-U.S.$300

32 5      SPA   

Glenzhaus Lodge

RUA 1 - QUADRA F - LOTE 27/28, ARMAÇÃO DOS BÚZIOS, RIO DE JANEIRO 28950-000

The owner of the hotel, Cris Glenz, traveled the world for 30 years before gathering together all of her creative ideas and experiences to create Glenzhaus Lodge. This beautiful house sits on a hilltop surrounded by a tropical environment in a quiet neighborhood, yet is only 500 meters from "Rua das Pedras," the famous lively street in Búzios, brimming with popular restaurants, shops and bars. There are 11 delightful suites at the Lodge and all have queen-size beds, air conditioning, a minibar, coffee machine, and fully-equipped luxury bathroom, as well as a large terrace overlooking the bay. The décor is outstanding: from the Entrance Suite, with its huge decorative cacti, to the cool and elegant reception and junior and master suites. A full, fresh breakfast can be enjoyed al fresco. Outside is a fabulous pool surrounded by lush gardens, and a decadent gazebo for guests' private relaxation. As well as arranging transportation for guests to the center of Búzios, the Lodge offers other services including free access to a downtown fitness center, in-room massage, diving reservations, taxis, golf and tennis.

Our inspector loved: *Eating a rich breakfast by the pool, and relaxing on the guest room's large veranda.*

Directions: Búzios is 180km from Rio de Janeiro's International Airport. Drive north through Rio-Lagos Highway.

Web: www.johansens.com/glenzhaus
E-mail: glenzhaus@uol.com.br
Tel: +55 22 2623 2823
Fax: +55 22 2623 5293

Price Guide:
rooms U.S.$155-U.S.$330

Vivenda Les 4 Saisons

RUA JOÃO CORDEIRO DA COSTA E SILVA, 5, CAIXA POSTAL 127, ENGENHEIRO PAULO DE FRONTIN, RIO DE JANEIRO 26650-000

This beautiful colonial-style mansion is set in the lush Vale do Café 2,145 feet above sea level and 60 miles from Rio de Janeiro. The 7 exquisitely decorated suites draw on Brazilian, European and Oriental influences and provide the benefits of a modern hotel to achieve great style and comfort. Suites are large and airy with crisp white linens and great views. Nearby outdoor activities include trekking, horseback riding, rafting, biking and observing nature in this beautiful valley, while indoors, Dutch owner and Michelin-starred Chef du Cuisine and painter Jos P. Boomgaardt, can create something for every taste using local products including herbs from the hotel's garden. Jos' expertise includes a variety of cooking styles from Europe, Asia and Brazil and he counts the Dutch Royal Family among his most ardent admirers. Gastronomes can participate in cooking classes and periodic workshops at the Academia de Culinária Jos P. Boomgaardt with this master chef. The hotel also offers regular beginners' and advanced Portuguese workshops. The Vale do Café area has preserved many of its historical coffee fazendas or farms, which are open to visitors.

Our inspector loved: *The gourmet dinner served in this unique, charming small hotel.*

Directions: From Rio de Janeiro-Galeão International Airport (G.I.G.), take Via Dutra toward São Paulo. Take exit 212 at km 95 and follow the road to the district of Graminha in Engenheiro Paulo de Frontin.

Web: www.johansens.com/4saisons
E-mail: les4saisons@superig.com.br
Tel: +55 24 2463 2892
Fax: +55 24 2463 1395

Price Guide:
rooms U.S.$175-U.S.$350

Parador Santarém Marina

ESTRADA CORREIA DA VEIGA, 96, PETRÓPOLIS, RIO DE JANEIRO 25745-260

This boutique resort situated in the village of Itaipava, approximately 53 miles north of Rio de Janiero, is surrounded by beautiful green mountain scenery with forests and waterfalls. Suites are designed for privacy and equipped with modern amenities. In addition, Orquídeas Suites feature granite or marble bathrooms and private verandas or covered patios, Hortênsias Suites have garden views, and several of the Bromélias Suites include sofa beds, ideal for small families. The hotel facilities include a swimming pool and bar, dry and steam saunas, Jacuzzi, volleyball and basketball courts and beaten sand tennis courts. In summer, breakfast can be enjoyed by the swimming pool overlooking a small lake. The renowned good weather lends itself to the full enjoyment of outdoor on-site activities including the 9-hole golf course and nearby horse stables. The village of Itaipava, a district of Petrópolis known for its wonderful gastronomy, has an eclectic mix of shops, bars and restaurants, as well as many unique museums and sites of historical interest. A popular weekend getaway for Cariocas (Rio de Janeiro natives), Petrópolis is the Imperial city of Brazil, established when the Portuguese royal family fled to the area from Napoleon's army in 1808.

Our inspector loved: *The variety of places to relax and enjoy a good book or a glass of wine at this beautiful property.*

Directions: From Rio de Janeiro International Airport, take BR-040 to Petrópolis and then to Itaipava, approximately a 1½-hour drive.

Web: www.johansens.com/paradorsantarem
E-mail: reservas@paradorsantarem.com.br
Tel: +55 24 2222 9933
Fax: +55 24 2222 9933

Price Guide:
suites U.S.$150-U.S.$360

 14   100       

SOLAR DO IMPÉRIO

KOELER AVENUE, 376- CENTRO, PETRÓPOLIS, RIO DE JANEIRO

Located on one of the most beautiful streets of Petrópolis Historical Center, Solar do Império is a 16-room hotel that offers guests and visitors a comfortable setting in the mountain region of Rio de Janeiro. Built in a mansion and completely restored by the Solar do Império founders, the hotel is decorated in a neo-classical style with contrasting modern resources such as a covered heated swimming pool, dry and wet sauna, spa and massage area. The old stables of the mansion have been restored and modernized and can be turned into 3 adjoining large halls for events, business meetings and parties. Leopoldina, the hotel's restaurant, offers breakfast each morning. Lunch and dinner menus are created by Executive Chef Claudia Mascarenhas, featuring contemporary, international and Brazilian dishes. An extensive wine menu is available to complement the cuisine. Activities include a reading room with books and magazines, games, reservation services, sightseeing, cultural events of live classical music and poem reading. Guests can ride Vitorias: horse-drawn wagons that pick guests up from the gardens of Solar do Império for tours through the nearby historical center and the Imperial Museum.

***Our inspector loved:** The careful restoration of this 1875 mansion that transfers its guests to a feeling of total peace, and the superb cuisine.*

Directions: From Rio International Airport take BR-040 road towards Petrópolis which is approximately a 1-hour drive. The hotel is situated in the historical center.

Web: www.johansens.com/solardoimperio
E-mail: atendimento@solardoimperio.com.br
Tel: +55 24 2103 3000
Fax: +55 24 2242 0034

Price Guide:
rooms U.S.$130-U.S.$200

Tankamana EcoResort

ESTRADA JÚLIO CÁPUA, S/N VALE DO CUIABÁ, ITAIPAVA - PETRÓPOLIS, RIO DE JANEIRO 25745-050

The freshest, cleanest of air and the densest of greenery envelop this rustic mountain retreat situated 1,000m up the slopes of the beautiful Cuiabá Valley. Surrounds are lush rain forests, almost impenetrable vegetation, sparkling waterfalls and the majestic heights of the Serra dos Órgãos Range. Peace and quiet are broken only by birdsong and the squeals of small mammals, some of which are threatened by extinction. Tankamana EcoResort sprawls over 880,000m^2 of parkland, offering a unique vacation experience and the opportunity to shake off the stresses of busy, modern life. The 15 exclusive, well-spaced log cabins are the ultimate in relaxation and country-style luxury; built from Eucalyptus trunks, each boasts every 21st-century facility and has delightful décor and furnishings such as a king-size bed, fireplace, refrigerator and long deck. One cabin has a hydro-massage tub and direct access to a natural stone pool. The cabins are in perfect harmony with the environment and afford stunning views. Mouth-watering combinations of regional specialties and international cuisine are taken in the transparent, glass-floored restaurant built over trout breeding tanks. Enjoy the new fitness center, heated pool, trekking, riding the forest trails and visiting Petrópolis, Brazil's Imperial City.

Our inspector loved: *The comfort of the cabins and the overwhelming beauty of the forest that surrounds the property.*

Directions: Tankamana is situated 109km from Rio de Janeiro International Airport at Petrópolis's district of Itaipava. The resort is a 1½-hour drive from Rio through BR-040 Road.

Web: www.johansens.com/tankamana
E-mail: tankamana@tankamana.com.br
Tel: +55 24 2222 9181
Fax: +55 24 2222 9181

Price Guide:
cabins U.S.$250-U.S.$450

Hotel Marina All Suites

AV. DELFIM MOREIRA, 696, PRAIA DO LEBLON, RIO DE JANEIRO 22441-000

With its prime location directly on Leblon Beach, which is an extension of Rio's famous Ipanema Beach, and close to numerous excellent restaurants, shops and bars, Hotel Marina All Suites is a fashionable and sophisticated hotel where guests are truly made to feel at home. Built in 1999, this is the only de luxe boutique hotel in the city, and everything here is immensely stylish and aesthetically pleasing. All of the 38 individually decorated suites have ocean views and include generous living areas and some have mini-kitchens. With only 3 suites per floor, the ambience is very cozy and intimate. For a very special experience, guests may choose one of the 8 designer suites, which have been created by some of the most talented and well-known Brazilian architects and interior designers. Delicious modern French cuisine is served each night in the Bar d'Hôtel restaurant, which attracts great numbers of "the beautiful people" of Rio. The hotel's health club on the 18th floor comprises a fitness center, sauna, massage facilities and a small rooftop swimming pool offering breathtaking views across the beach. Movie lovers will be delighted with the charming air-conditioned home theater, which allows total privacy for up to 8 guests with a big screen and extremely comfortable seats.

Our inspector loved: *The comfort, the unique décor and beautiful ocean view from some of the designer suites.*

Directions: Situated at Leblon Beach, which is approximately 15 miles from Rio de Janeiro International Airport.

Web: www.johansens.com/marinaallsuites
E-mail: reservas@hotelmarina.com.br
Tel: +55 21 2172 1001
Fax: +55 21 2172 1110

Price Guide: (room only, excluding tax)
suites US$350-US$975

38   M 10       

Pousada Do Engenho

RUA ODON CAVALCANTE, 330, SÃO FRANCISCO DE PAULA 95400-000, RIO GRANDE DO SUL

This small eco-friendly lodge is nestled in the forests of southern Brazil on the border between subtropical and temperate climate zones. The result is a beautiful and unique environment abundant with diverse flora and fauna. The Pousada consists of 10 individual cabanas tucked away in the forest for complete privacy. The cabanas' rustic appearance blends with their forest surroundings and belies the modern comforts within, including Jacuzzis, wireless Internet access, cable L.C.D. T.V., C.D. and D.V.D. players. Cabanas also feature skylights and verandas with hammock swings. For recreation, the resort offers an outdoor heated swimming pool, tennis court, fitness room, sauna, steam and massage rooms. Guests can enjoy games in the lounge or venture out to try nearby trekking, rafting and horseback riding arranged by the Pousada. The cozy Casa de Babette restaurant, managed by the property's owners, offers a variety of fare from traditional Brazilian to Indian cuisine. Pousada do Engenho is located close to the famous canyons of Rio Grande do Sul and 40km from the charming Germanic village of Gramado, renowned for its chocolates.

Our inspector loved: *The exuberant nature that the comfortable cabanas evoke.*

Directions: From Salgado Filho International Airport (P.O.A.) in Porto Alegre, take BR-116 to Novo Hamburgo and RS-20 to São Francisco de Paula.

Web: www.johansens.com/pousadadoengenho
E-mail: pousadadoengenho@pousadadoengenho.com.br
Tel: +55 54 3244 1270
Fax: +55 54 3244 1270

Fortaleza
Brasilia
Sao Paulo
Rio de Janeiro

Price Guide:
cabanas U.S.$120-U.S.$240

KUROTEL

RUA NACÕES UNIDAS 533, P.O. BOX 65, GRAMADO, RIO GRANDE DO SUL 95670-000

With an international reputation for helping people achieve better health through preventive, natural medicine, Kurotel Longevity Center and Spa offers guests over 20 years of family-guided experience. Recently awarded Best Spa in South America and considered One of the 6 Best Spa's of the World by Luxury Spa Finder Magazine, this premier Latin America spa is set amid the rolling hills of southern Brazil in the charming town of Gramado. Kurotel's European-Colonial exterior is complemented by classic, richly appointed rooms and suites, and is part pampering spa and part state-of-the-art medical center. Kurotel features many innovative programs, including The Kur Plan, which focuses on lifestyle, optimum health and anti-tobacco, as well as Kinder Kur, designed exclusively for mothers and their newborn babies. On the cutting edge, the Cellular Revitalization Treatment rejuvenates the skin and aims to assist the organic functions and immunologic responses quality. This is only available in South America at Kurotel. With more than 2 staff members to attend to each client, the center provides truly personalized service and makes each guest feel at home. All programs are based on a recommended stay of 1 week and include accommodation, 7 delicious balanced meals served daily and offer more than 200 optional activities.

Our inspector loved: *The first-class service at the spa, and the restaurant.*

Directions: From Salgado Filho Airport in Porto Alegre, take RS-115 to Gravataí and RS-20 to Gramado, approximately a 1-hour and 40-minute drive.

Web: www.johansens.com/kurotel
E-mail: reservas@kurotel.com.br
Tel: +55 54 3295 9393
Fax: +55 54 3286 1203
Brazil Toll Free: 0800 90 9800

Price Guide: (all-inclusive, half week, including select number of treatments, medical consultation and assessments, excluding 10% tax) apartments and suites $1,417-$3,029

Ponta dos Ganchos

RUA EUPÍDIO ALVES DO NASCIMENTO, 104, GOVERNADOR CELSO RAMOS, SANTA CATARINA 88190-000

Clear blue water and lush green fauna surround this exclusive secluded resort on the Emerald Coast of Brazil. This adults-only Relais & Chateaux resort comprises 20 private cabanas with lounge areas where guests can escape and unwind. Cabanas feature WiFi, fireplaces and spectacular views of the sea. All meals are included in the rates, and the restaurant closes only after the last guest has retired for the evening. The gourmet kitchen highlights the regional Catarinese cuisine at lunch and international fare for dinner. Guests can also enjoy one of the private islands off the beach with an evening meal and a personal waiter. The well-stocked bars have over 200 selections of wine, fine liquors and an array of Cuban cigars. The resort has a heated, covered pool and scuba diving in the Marine Reserve can be arranged upon request. There are also diving lessons with instructors qualified by the P.A.D.I. and a tennis court with an unparalleled view of the water. A games room offers snooker, and a wide selection of D.V.D.s is available for viewing in the cinema or in your own bungalow. The new Dior Spa, which opened in the summer of 2006, uses Dior products for all its relaxation treatments. Guests can also enjoy city tours of Florianópolis, Blumenau and Governador Celso Ramos.

Our inspector loved: *The sophisticated service and food after a day at the exclusive beach.*

Directions: The hotel is located 62km from Florianopolis International Airport. Take BR-101 and then SC-410.

Web: www.johansens.com/pontadosganchos
E-mail: reservas@pontadosganchos.com.br
Tel: +55 48 3262 5000
Fax: +55 48 3262 5046

Price Guide: (all inclusive)
bungalows U.S.$580-U.S.$1,075

Hotel Frontenac

AV. DR. PAULO RIBAS, 295 CAPIVARI, CAMPOS DO JORDÃO 12460-000

This hotel is located close to the charming tourist center of Capivari, and is within walking distance of the most sophisticated stores and eateries of Campos do Jordão. Its atmosphere is warm, and the décor is classic in a European style. There are 47 guest rooms, 41 in the hotel and 6 at the Frontenac Chalet, for those requiring more privacy. Superior rooms are comfortable, with Internet access and color L.C.D. televisions, and others range from the special de luxe rooms with private balconies or indoor terraces to the Presidential Suite. The Charpentier Restaurant offers innovative and creative cuisine, with dishes such as "Shrimp in Papaya", based on the tradition and knowledge of the French culinary revival. Dining can be enjoyed on the relaxed, informal terrace or in the elegant restaurant itself. There is an extensive selection of wines from around the world. Brahm's Bar is an authentic British pub, the ideal place to meet friends, chat and play songs on the jukebox. The hotel also has a library with assorted books, a home theater with films available to rent, and a fitness center connected to an outdoor pool, patio and bar service.

Our inspector loved: *Enjoying the atmosphere of the Brahm's Bar.*

Directions: Campos do Jordão is located 180km from São Paulo. Take Highway Carvalho Pinto and then S.P.-123 at Taubaté.

Web: www.johansens.com/frontenac
E-mail: reservas@frontenac.com.br
Tel: +55 12 3669 1000
Fax: +55 12 3669 1009

Price Guide: (excluding tax)
rooms U.S.$120-U.S.$580

Hotel location shown in red with page number

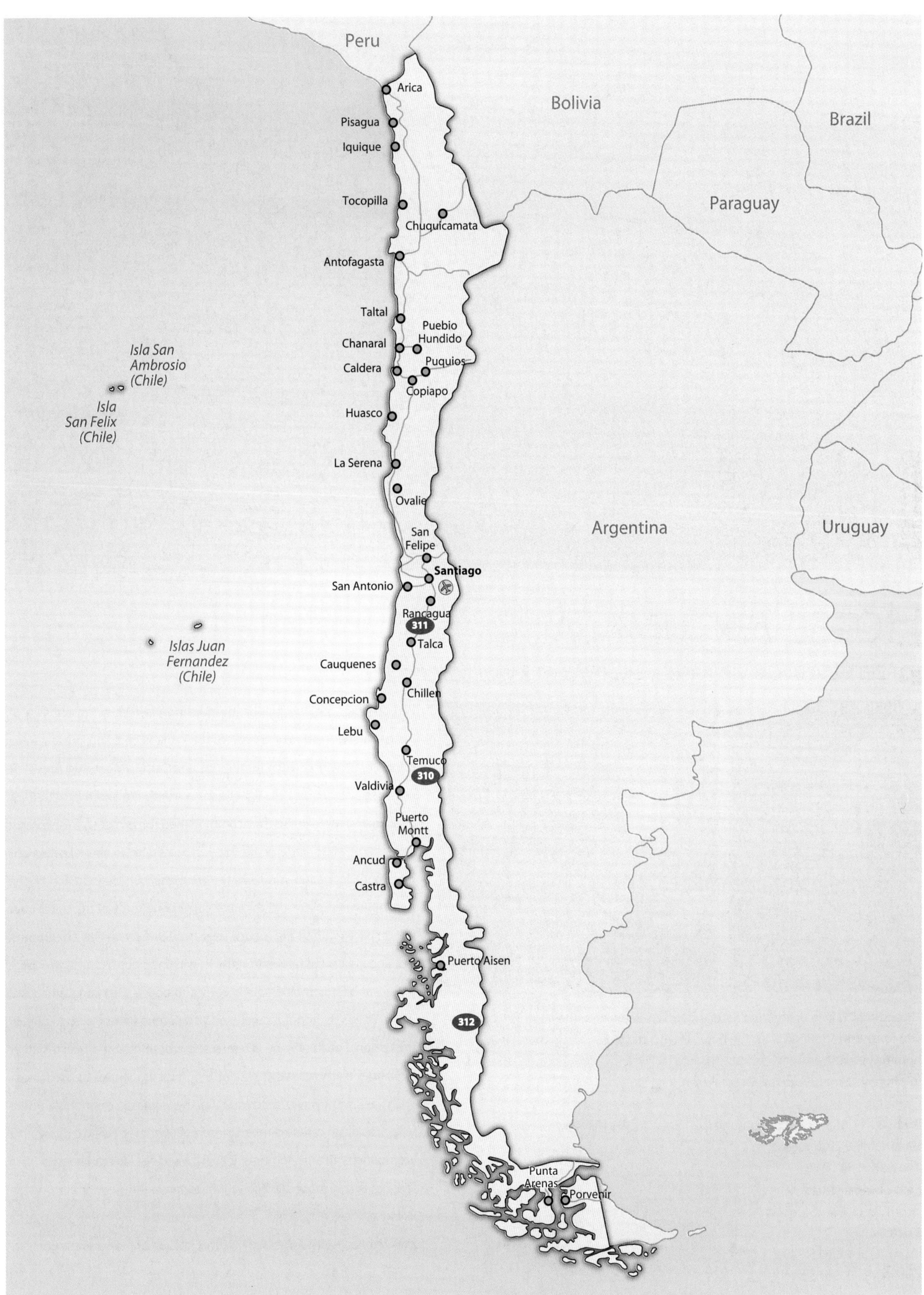

HOTEL ANTUMALAL

CARRETERA PUCON-VILLARRICA HIGHWAY AT KM 2 FROM PUCON

Perched high on the hillside overlooking Lake Villarrica within a 5-hectare park, this Frank Lloyd Wright inspired building presents airy living areas with unusual furnishings and colorful goat skin rugs. The cozy bar, with leather chairs, features a hearth fire and a large terrace overlooking the lake. Guest accommodations are simply furnished with stone floors and wooden walls. They are decorated in natural colors and have floor to ceiling windows to "bring the outside in". Each of the rooms has a fireplace and thick comforters and some of the suites offer larger spaces with sitting rooms. The Royal Suite comprises 2 bedrooms, a dining area and a huge sitting room with fabulous "picture" windows. The restaurant combines the best local produce with an international flare and has the reputation of being one of the finest places to dine in the region. Lunch may be taken on the roof terrace and guests gather for dinner in the comfortable bar before being shown to their table. There are some unique activities in this area, for example, Volcano Villarrica, which can be climbed, skied or flown over. Flying over when it is erupting is an amazing experience; the red hot lava can be seen from the air. Fishing, mountain biking, white-water rafting, swimming, water-skiing and even golf are all available nearby. Alternately, enjoy the private beach with 2 docks, the sauna, hot tub or have a massage.

Our inspector loved: *The location with its unique views and activities.*

Directions: Take a plane from Santiago to Temuco where the hotel will collect you for the 1½ hour drive to the hotel. From Satiago by car, the hotel is a 9-hour drive south of Temuco. Take the exit to Villarrica bordering the lake and the hotel is 2km before the city of Pucon.

Web: www.johansens.com/antumalal
E-mail: info@antumalal.com
Tel: +5645 441 011
Fax: +5645 441 013

Price Guide:
rooms U.S$140-U.S.$204
suites U.S.$200-U.S.$440

Hacienda Los Lingues

KM 124.5, RUTA 5 SUR + 5KM AL ORIENTE, 6A REGION, COLCHAGUA

This magnificent 17th-century, family-owned country estate is in the heart of Chile's wine region, surrounded by 9,000 acres of farmland, vineyards and rolling hills. The Hacienda is quite formal and is adorned with collector's items such as antiques, family photos and ancestral paintings. The dining room serves traditional cuisine and fine local wines. Hacienda Los Lingues® offers 5 wines: Cabernet Sauvignon Gran Reserva, Cabernet Sauvignon, Rosé (Colchagua Valley), Chardonnay and Sauvignon Blanc (Casablanca Valley) labelled as Hacienda Los Lingues®, Los Lingues®, a selection of wines from Viña Los Vascos Domaine Baron de Rothchild (Lafite). Each unique room is set around a central courtyard and has soaring ceilings with chandeliers, antique furniture and huge shutters that open out onto the grounds and hillsides. Some are warmed by wood-burning stoves and on chilly nights, guests return to their rooms to find their beds warmed by hot water bottles. Enjoy swimming in the outdoor pool, a game of tennis on one of the clay courts or a variety of games in the games room, hiking into the Andean foothills, fly-fishing, shooting, bird-watching, mountain biking and wine tasting. The Santa Cruz Museum is nearby and well-renowned for holding one of the finest South American history collections. The traditional Chilean chapel is available for weddings.

Our inspector loved: *The sophistication of this picturesque country estate.*

Directions: Comodoro A. Merino Benitez Pudahuel.

Web: www.johansens.com/loslingues
E-mail: ventas@loslingues.com
Tel: +562 431 0510
Fax: +562 431 0501

Antofagasta
Santiago
Temuco
Puerto Montt

Price Guide: (room only, excluding 15% service charge)
rooms U.S.$228
suites U.S.$228-U.S.$483

WATERLOO HOUSE

P.O. BOX H.M. 333, HAMILTON H.M. B.X.

Waterloo House is an elegant manor house with surrounding cottages dating back to 1815. The hotel stands amidst 4 acres of terraced gardens directly on Hamilton Harbor. There are 20 rooms and 10 spacious suites with views of the harbor or gardens and are appointed with antiques, French and Italian fabrics and furnishings, original paintings and en-suite bathrooms with dressing areas. The rooms are all air conditioned with hair dryers, bathrobes and slippers, safes, direct-dial telephone, T-1 Internet access, and cable T.V.; many of the rooms have whirlpool baths. Waterloo House is known around the world as one of Bermuda's best restaurants, and the Executive Chef has won numerous awards for cuisine both in North America and Europe. Guests can enjoy the exquisite cuisine at the Poinciana Terrace, on the water's edge, or in the elegant Wellington Room for dinner; popular Bermuda shorts are acceptable attire. Afternoon tea is served in the garden or flagpole terrace and a delectable tapas menu is available in Long Room Bar. Guests are encouraged to partake in the facilities of Waterloo House's sister properties, Horizons & Cottages, and the exclusive private member's club, the Coral Beach and Tennis Club. The hotel is within walking distance of many historic and cultural sites.

Our inspector loved: *The unique harborside location of this beautiful small property.*

Directions: Taxis are available from Bermuda Intenational Airport (B.D.A.).

Web: www.johansens.com/waterloohouse
E-mail: reservations@waterloohouse.bm
Tel: +1 441 295 4480
Fax: +1 441 295 2585
U.S./Canada Toll Free: 1 800 468 4100

Price Guide:
rooms U.S.$285-U.S.$480
suites U.S.$360-U.S.$780

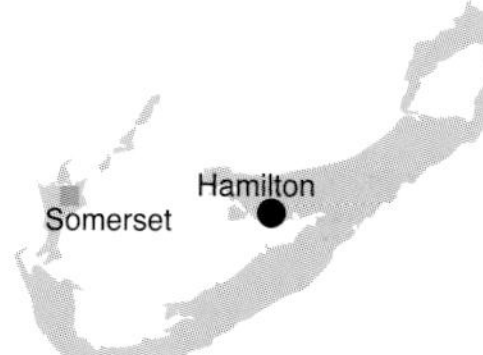

Horizons and Cottages

33 South Shore Road, Paget, P.G.04

Founded on an 18th-century plantation, Horizons and Cottages is Bermuda's oldest and most exclusive cottage colony set on a hilltop amongst 25 acres of exotic gardens. Once the home to a private family, over the years, the land surrounding it was given to such varied activities as farming, quarrying, tobacco growing, potatoes, the famous Bermuda onion, and latterly, the Bermuda Easter lilies. The 9-room main house and the 32 suites and cottages opened in 1922 and offer a classic setting. The Bermudian architecture and luxurious air-conditioned accommodations are tastefully appointed with safes and direct-dial telephone. The cottages contain from 1 to 5 bedrooms; each has a private bath and a breakfast terrace. Guests may enjoy breakfast each morning on the cottage veranda served by a personal maid or on the private room terrace overlooking the gardens and the sea. The staff can prepare canapés and snacks for guests' rooms and complimentary afternoon tea can be enjoyed on the Pool Terrace. Dinner is served on the Ocean Terrace, Barbeque Terrace or in the Middleton Room. The barmen mix favorite island cocktails and offer Cuban cigars in the resort's old-style English Pub. Golf, tennis, croquet, horticulturist tours, water sports and nature walks are available. The spa is located nearby at the Coral Beach Club.

Our inspector loved: *The "horizon" vistas from this hilltop property.*

Directions: Taxis are available from Bermuda International Airport (B.D.A.).

Web: www.johansens.com/horizonscottages
E-mail: reservations@horizons.bm
Tel: +1 441 236 0048
Fax: +1 441 236 1981
U.S./Canada Toll Free: 1 800 468 0022

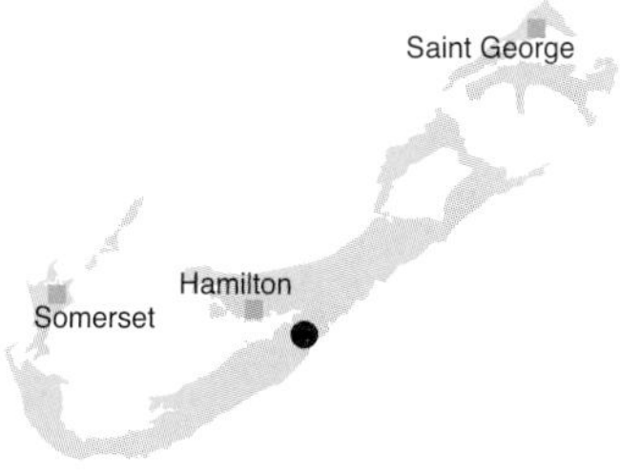

Saint George
Hamilton
Somerset

Price Guide:
rooms U.S.$330- U.S.$440
suites U.S.$450- U.S.$800

Cambridge Beaches

KINGS POINT, SOMERSET

Escape from the world and recharge at this timeless resort which was the recipient of Condé Nast Johansens "Most Excellent Spa Hotel 2006." This is the place to be in Bermuda! Set on a private 30-acre peninsula, guests enjoy spectacular sea views, charming cottage accommodations, beautiful private beaches and award-winning cuisine. For an unforgettable experience stay in any one of the incredible new water-front pool suites (the only in Bermuda) offering complete privacy and panoramic views. Dine by torchlight around the new infinity pool with terraced seating overlooking Mangrove Bay. Gourmet cuisine is still among Bermuda's best in the international Tamarisk Room or you can go casual with your toes in the sand on Long Bay Beach at the trendy beachfront bistro, Breezes. Couples enjoy private beach dinners or exclusive romantic evenings on a nearby private island. There are also endless activities for families and friends to share together. Extensive leisure facilities include a world-class spa and wellness center, snorkeling, English croquet, putting green, tennis and a private marina. Exclusive water excursions are offered daily in season, and the new Seaview Gardens offer walking trails and yoga during the summer months. Championship golf is moments away. Enquire about year-round family and reunion packages.

Our inspector loved: *The new Sothy of Paris facial at the Ocean Spa.*

Directions: A taxi will deliver guests from Bermuda International Airport.

Web: www.johansens.com/cambridgebeaches
E-mail: cambeach@ibl.bm
Tel: +1 441 234 0331
Fax: +1 441 234 3352
U.S./Canada Toll Free: 1 800 468 7300

Price Guide:
rooms $270–$795
suites $475–$900
pool suites $795-$1,650

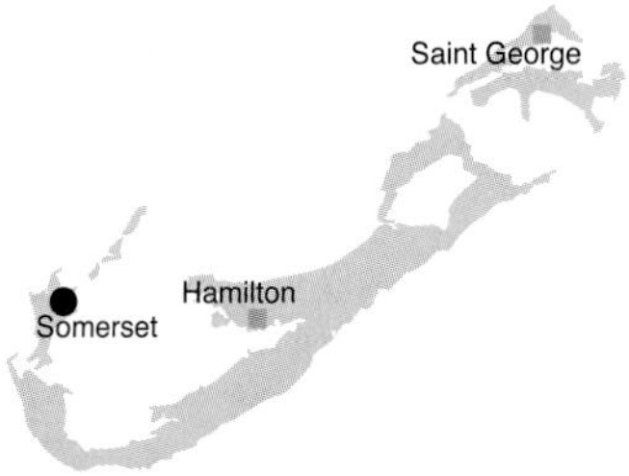

The Reefs

56 South Shore Road, Southampton

The Reefs is one of Bermuda's most picturesque resorts. Nestled along high coral cliffs and overlooking its own private beach, this intimate 65-room resort provides a relaxing atmosphere where guests can feel perfectly at ease. The Reefs was recently named in the top 3 of "The Best Resort" in all the Caribbean, Bahamas and Bermuda by Travel and Leisure Magazine and for good reason: great rooms, cuisine, and service. Every room and suite in the main resort commands sweeping ocean and sunset vistas. There are also 1, 2, and 3-bedroom Bermudian cottages popular with small groups of friends and families and each with its own private Jacuzzi. For dining guests have a choice of 3 award-winning restaurants. Grill 56, with its star-filled domed conservatory, is open year-round and its lounge is a favorite rendezvous where traditional English tea is enjoyed daily. Seasonal restaurants include Ocean Echo on the terrace above the cliffs overlooking the ocean. Coconuts dining is directly on the beach and is often described as the the best place to fall in love. Many members of the staff have been with the resort for decades and, as expected from a first-class resort, service is impeccable. Tennis courts, fitness center, spa and a boutique are available on the property. Golf, sailing and riding can be arranged.

Our inspector loved: *The "dining on the beach" option - very romantic.*

Directions: Taxis are available from Bermuda International Airport (B.D.A.).

Web: www.johansens.com/thereefs
E-mail: irr@worldnet.att.net
Tel: +1 441 238 0222
Fax: +1 441 238 8372
U.S./Canada Toll Free: 1 800 742 2008

Price Guide: (per person)
rooms U.S.$294–U.S.$544

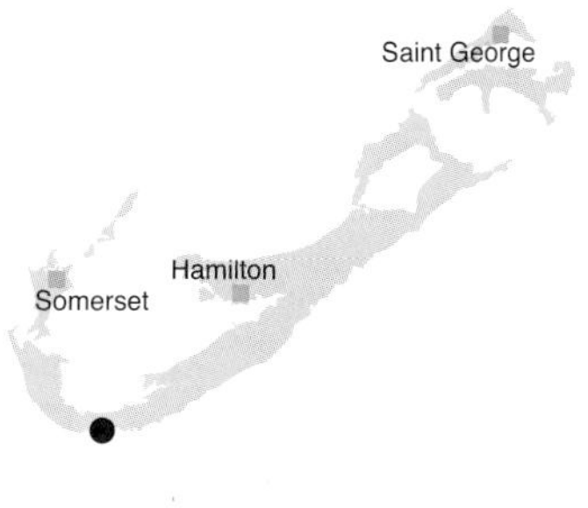

Saint George
Hamilton
Somerset

Surf Side Beach Club

90 SOUTH SHORE ROAD, WARWICK

Surf Side is a sunny, unpretentious hideaway overlooking Bermuda's unique South Shore, surrounded by 5 acres of landscaped hillside terraces and walkways above beautiful, white-sanded beaches and coves. Scattered among the colorful hibiscus blossoms, tall palms and perfect lawns are 38 newly renovated cottages, apartment-style units, penthouses and brand new 3 bedroom units. Each room has its own sea view and is designed for privacy. Guests are provided with every home comfort, from tastefully furnished bedrooms and lounges to fully-fitted kitchens and either a secluded garden patio or a wide, plant-bedecked balcony where the only sound is that of breaking waves. With a natural ambience created by the moon, soft tropical breezes and delicate scent of flowers, the Palms Restaurant and bar serves outstanding cuisine and cocktails beside the pool. The relaxed and unpretentious atmosphere is ideal for those who love to be self-sufficient and free to discover the delights of the island. Apart from sauna and Jacuzzi, Surf Side Beach Club features a beauty salon and mini-spa. Tennis, golf and riding can be arranged.

Our inspector loved: *The bird's nests, secluded sunbathing and viewing areas cut into the cliffside, overlooking the blue-green Atlantic coast.*

Directions: 3 miles south west of Hamilton.

Web: www.johansens.com/surfside
E-mail: surf@ibl.bm
Tel: +1 441 236 7100
Fax: +1 441 236 9765
U.S./Canada Toll Free: 1 800 553 9990

Price Guide:
deluxe units U.S.$295
superior suite U.S.$350
penthouse for 4 persons U.S.$500
cliffside suite for 6 persons U.S.$1,250

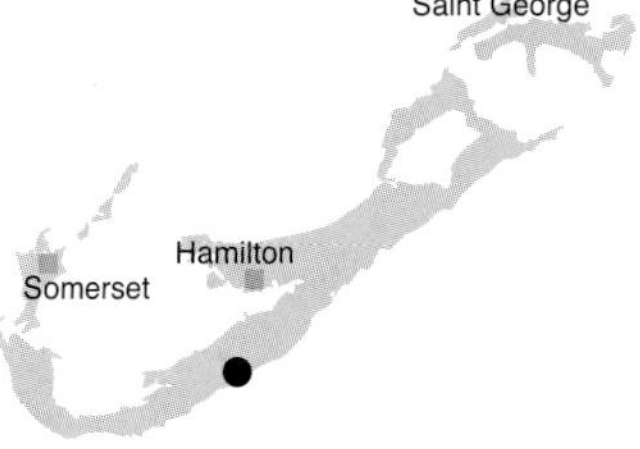

Saint George
Hamilton
Somerset

Caribbean - Anguilla

Hotel location shown in red with page number

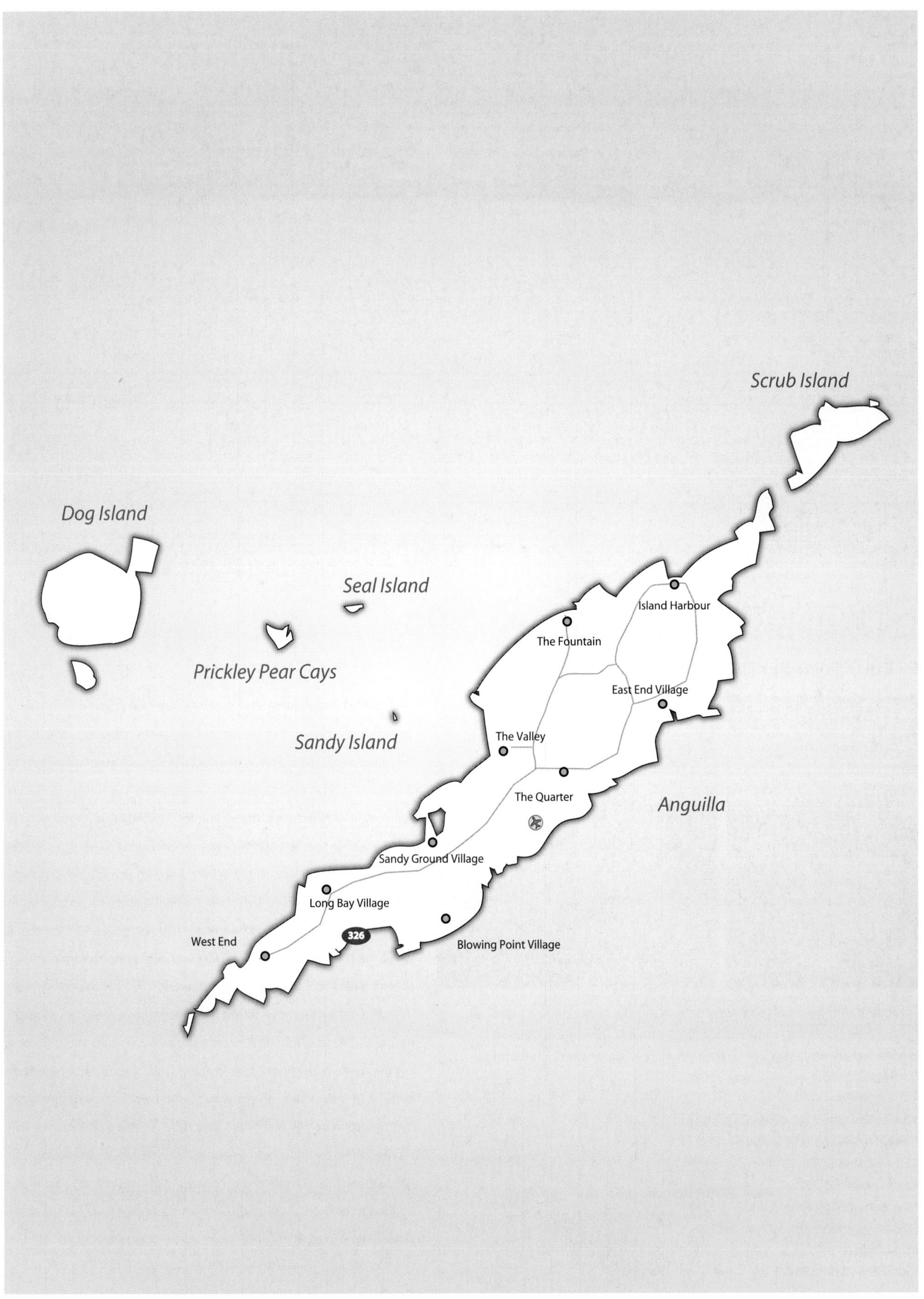

CuisinArt Resort & Spa

A member of The Leading Small Hotels of the World

P.O. BOX 2000, RENDEZVOUS BAY

The jewel of Anguilla's Rendezvous Bay, CuisinArt Resort & Spa offers a complete Caribbean experience thanks to its stunning oceanfront location, remarkable cuisine and world-class European spa. Overlooking 2 miles of powdery white sand and crystal blue waters, the gorgeous Greek-style architecture is the setting for 93 luxury guest rooms/suites and 2 penthouse suites. Each spacious room has marble baths, tropical décor and private terraces, perfect for enjoying breakfast overlooking the Caribbean Sea. Executive Chef Michael Goodman and his team create a first-class dining experience with their restaurants Santorini, which offers fine, contemporary Caribbean cuisine in a romantic setting, and Mediterraneo, a family-style restaurant. The chef's specialty fruit-infused rum can be enjoyed at the lobby bar while relaxing to Caribbean music. Guests can tour the resort's expansive hydroponic farm and organic gardens, the first of its kind at any Caribbean resort, where fresh herbs and vegetables are grown. Cucumbers harvested from the hydroponic farm are used at the Venus Spa & Fitness, the resort's full-service spa where rejuvenating treatments are enjoyed overlooking lush gardens and sea. Guests can also enjoy the resort's spectacular infinity pool, try a cooking class or spiritually connect with yoga. Great shopping can be found in St. Martin, a 25-minute ferry ride from Anguilla.

Our inspector loved: *The cooking demonstration at the Kitchen Stadium.*

Directions: The resort is 15 minutes from Wallblake Airport, Anguilla and 10 minutes from Blowing Point ferry terminal, Anguilla. 20 minutes by semi-private launch available from St. Maarten Airport lagoon and 25 minutes by ferry from Marigot Ferry Terminal, St. Martin.

Web: www.johansens.com/cuisinartresort
E-mail: reservations@cuisinart.ai
Tel: +1 264 498 2000
Fax: +1 264 498 2010
U.S./Canada Toll Free: 1 800 943 3210

Price Guide:
rooms U.S.$385-U.S.$875
suites U.S.$435-U.S.$4,510

Harbour Island
Wallblake Airport
Rendezvous Bay

Caribbean - Antigua

Hotel location shown in red with page number

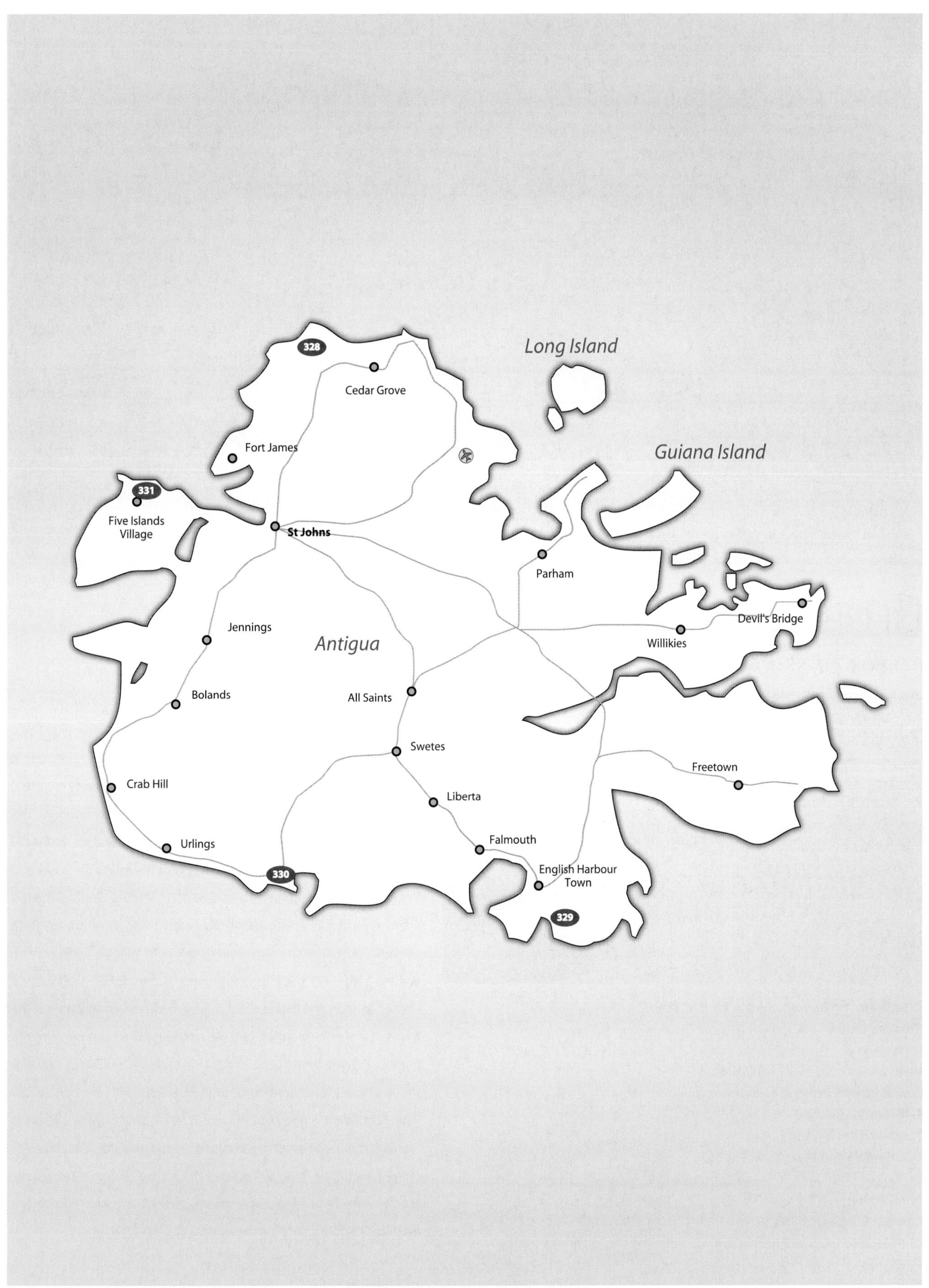

Blue Waters

P.O. BOX 257, ST. JOHN'S

This is one of Antigua's longest established and most exclusive resorts, nestling among 14 superb acres of cascading bougainvillaea, flowering hibiscus and shady palm trees on the shore of historic Soldiers Bay, and edged with 2 magnificent, white sandy beaches. Peace and tranquility abound in a luxurious tropical atmosphere. The 77 en-suite guest rooms are beautifully decorated and exceptionally appointed. Each is air conditioned, has cool terracotta tile floors and breathtaking sea or garden views. Just a 2-minute walk away there is even more luxury in the newly developed and very private Rock Cottage. Guests at the villa enjoy their own plunge pool, Jacuzzi, landing stage, 4/5 bedrooms furnished to the highest standards, a kitchen, lounge and dining room, as well as all facilities available at the resort. Excellent gourmet cuisine is beautifully presented in the friendly, fully air-conditioned and comfortable Vyviens Restaurant. For those who prefer a more outdoor dining experience the open-sided Palm Restaurant is not to be missed. Pre-dinner drinks and afternoon "coolers" can be savored in a choice of 3 attractive bars. An extensive range of sports and leisure facilities include sea and pool swimming, tennis, snorkeling, windsurfing, sailing, gymnasium, salon and golf, at a nearby 18-hole championship course, can be easily arranged.

Directions: 4 miles from the capital of St. John's. A 15-minute drive from the airport.

Web: www.johansens.com/bluewaters
E-mail: bluewaters@threesixtyhotels.com
Tel: +44 870 360 1245
Fax: +44 870 360 1246
U.S./Canada Toll Free: 1 800 557 6536

Price Guide:
rooms U.S.$369–U.S.$793
suites U.S.$575–U.S.$1,610

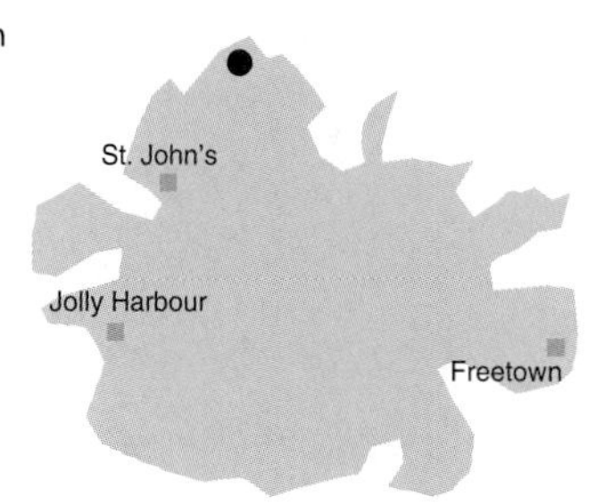

Our inspector loved: *The master suite at Rock Cottage.*

The Inn at English Harbour

ENGLISH HARBOUR

On the southern coast of Antigua's national park, in 19 acres of wooded headland and with its own white sandy beach, this charming inn boasts magnificent views over Nelson's Dockyard - reached by a complimentary day water taxi - and historic English Harbor. The new management is committed to making it the leading hotel on the island. 10 guest rooms and 24 high-standard suites are situated close to the beach and rooms are built in 3 blocks, each in a 2-story courtyard style. All are spacious and individually decorated and furnished with comfortable chairs and sofas. Special features include dark local wood ceilings, canopied and voile-draped four-poster beds and bathrooms with luxury double showers. Each has either a terrace or a veranda from where guests can sip cool drinks whilst enjoying the panoramic vista. Excellent candle-lit dinners are served in the popular Terrace Restaurant in the main part of the inn and the water-front beach restaurant offers breakfast and lunch and holds a weekly barbecue night buffet with live entertainment. Between the hotel and soft sands lie superb landscaped gardens, a swimming pool with refreshment service, tennis court and new gymnasium. Complimentary activities include sunfish-sailing, windsurfing, rowing, kayaking and snorkeling.

Our inspector loved: *The inn's location, standing at the entrance of historic English Harbour and only minutes from Nelson's Dockyard.*

Directions: 16 miles from the airport and 12 miles from the capital, St. John's.

Web: www.johansens.com/innatenglishharbour
E-mail: theinn@candw.ag
Tel: +1 268 460 1014
Fax: +1 268 460 1603
U.S./Canada Toll Free: 1 800 970 2123

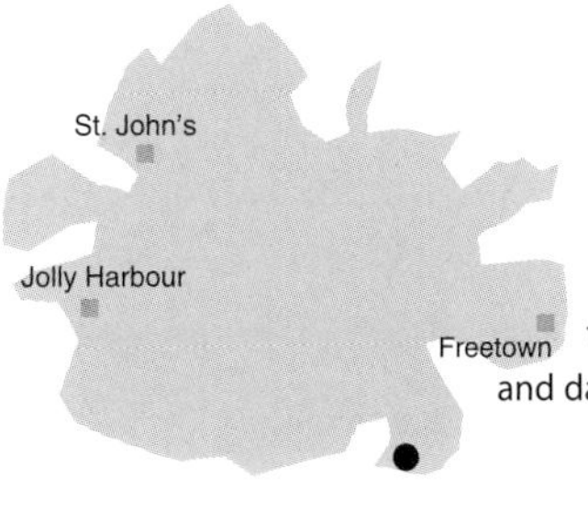

St. John's
Jolly Harbour
Freetown

Price Guide: (excludes breakfast, includes non-motorized water sports, tennis, fitness center, beach equipment and daytime water taxi to Nelson's Dockyard)
rooms U.S.$187–U.S.$480
suites U.S.$289-U.S.$698

Curtain Bluff

P.O. BOX 288, ST. JOHN'S

Directions: Approximately a 35-minute drive from the airport.

Web: www.johansens.com/curtainbluff
E-mail: curtainbluff@curtainbluff.com
Tel: +1 268 462 8400
Fax: +1 268 462 8409
U.S./Canada Toll Free: 1 888 289 9898

Price Guide: (fully inclusive)
rooms from U.S.$595

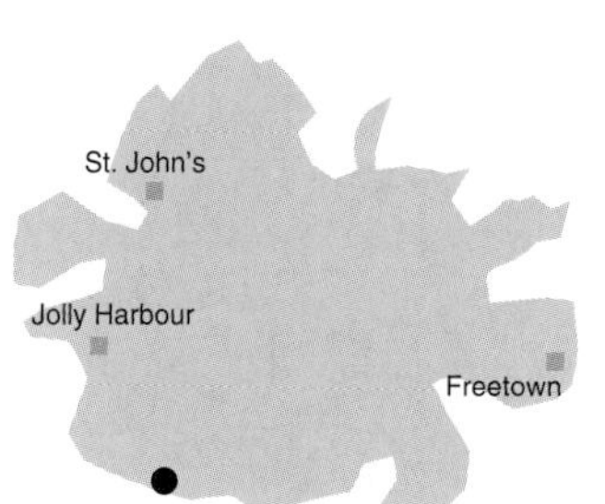

Curtain Bluff was opened by Howard W. Hulford in 1962 and celebrated its 40th anniversary in 2002. The setting is unique with smooth, lagoon-fed beach on one side and blustery windward surf on the other. This is a remarkable achievement by any standards and perfect testimony to the superb service, ability to provide only the best accommodation and a wine cellar that boasts 25,000 bottles. Attention to detail is obvious here, from the immaculately tended tropical gardens to the spacious rattan-styled bedrooms that are fitted with air conditioning, telephones and all other modern amenities. Style and culinary excellence are in the capable hands of French-born chef Christophe Blatz. Guests may dine in the garden pavilion, where the finest food is served with a view out over the lawns and dance floor. Those seeking greater informality will love the beach bar with its weekly beachfront barbecue, or total privacy can be provided by taking dinner on your balcony. Curtain Bluff is one of the sportiest hotels in the region offering a new 5,000ft. sq. spa, 5-star tennis facilities, squash and putting green; and with its private peninsula, the water sports facilities are unrivaled. There is even the opportunity of a sail on Sentio, Curtain Bluff's 49ft. Wellington ketch. Open from October 29th, 2006 to May 31st, 2007.

***Our inspector loved:** The wine cellar; a wonderful selection.*

  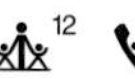    SPA    

GALLEY BAY

FIVE ISLANDS, ST. JOHN'S

Featured in Condé Nast Traveler's Gold List 2005, this Tahitian-style resort is situated on a pristine ¾-mile stretch of white sandy beach, just 10 minutes from Antigua's capital. A romantic, enchanting and exotic Caribbean hideaway, the endless sunshine and unspoiled beauty of Antigua makes this an ideal laid-back vacation destination, exclusive to adults. Thatch-roofed bungalows and oceanfront rooms are set amidst 40 acres of lush gardens and majestic coconut palms with a lagoon and bird sanctuary. Simple and stylish rattan and bamboo furniture adorns the spacious rooms, which are located directly on the beach. Ttropical flavors of Creole and Euro-Caribbean dishes are served in the Sea Grape Restaurant, or guests may choose a traditional grill whilst sipping sundowners and watching the sunset in the beachside Gauguin Restaurant. Cascading waterfalls are a feature of the freeform swimming pool and there is a well-equipped, air-conditioned fitness center overlooking the lagoon. Enjoy the beauty salon, resort boutique, library and games room or partake in non-motorized water sports such as sailing, snorkeling and windsurfing. There is tennis, bird watching and an opportunity to explore the lagoon as well as day trips to the surrounding islands. Places of interest include St. John's Harbor, Nelson's Dockyard and many ruined fortresses on the surrounding hilltops.

Our inspector loved: *Initmate oceanside dining at Gauguin Restaurant.*

Directions: 25 minutes from V.C. Bird International Airport and 10 minutes from St. John's.

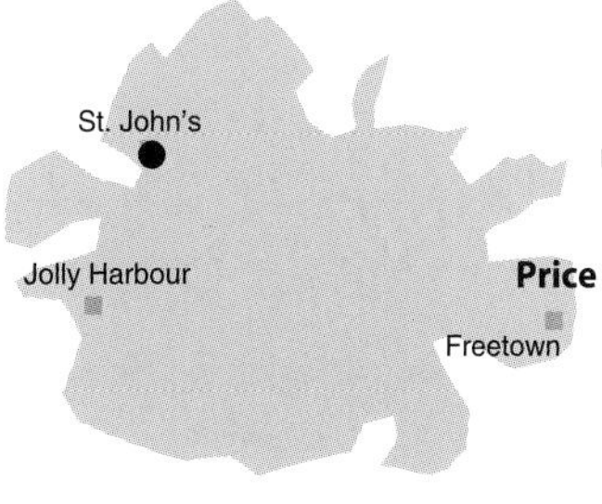

St. John's
Jolly Harbour
Freetown

Web: www.johansens.com/galleybay
E-mail: res@eliteislandresorts.com
Tel: +1 954 481 8787
Fax: +1 954 481 1661
U.S./Canada Toll Free: 1 800 858 4618

Price Guide: (including all meals, beverages, non-motorized water sports, Internet access, taxes and service charge)
rooms U.S.$625–U.S.$1,250
suites U.S.$900–U.S.$1,300

Caribbean - Barbados

Hotel location shown in red with page number

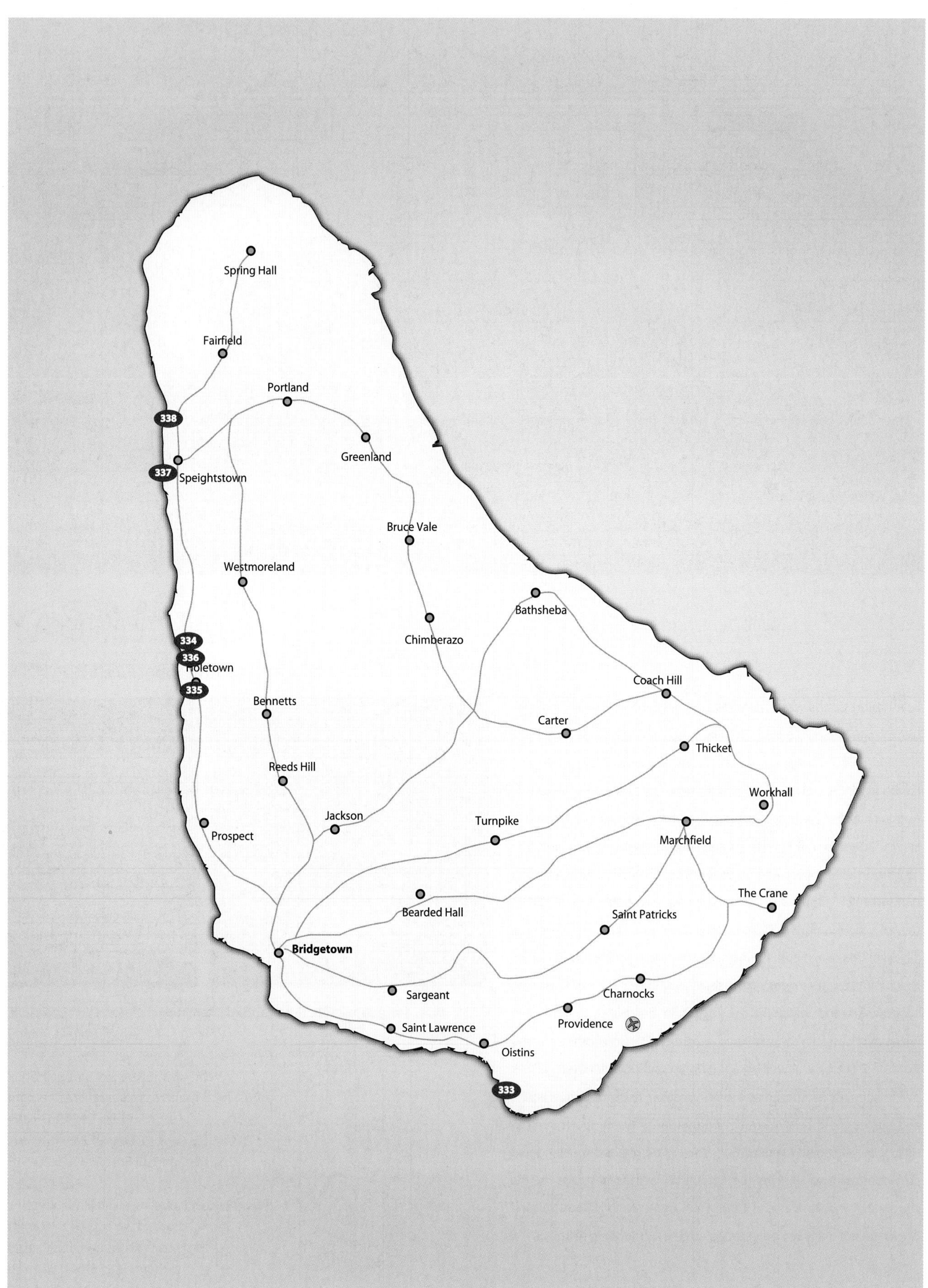

Little Arches

ENTERPRISE BEACH ROAD, CHRIST CHURCH

This delightful haven is a new addition to the island and is situated in the parish of Christ Church on the southern edge of the island. Quietly tucked away down a sleepy beachfront road, one is instantly struck by the magnificent views of the crystal blue waters below. This boutique-style hotel has just 10 rooms and suites, which lends an ambience of informality and intimacy without sacrificing that sense of Caribbean luxury. Each of the rooms is carefully appointed with cool, crisp linens and terrazzo flooring, and 2 of the suites have private plunge pools, oversized beds and dramatic views of the ocean. The al fresco dining area has an unrivaled position and guests flock here from dawn to dusk to watch the dramatic skyline – probably at its best during sunset. The hotel is proud if its 42ft. yacht, the Soul Venture, which is available for private hire and can create the most exotic and memorable of wedding venues, particularly when overnight anchorage can be arranged. Although discreetly tucked away, the hotel is well located for a stroll into the nearby town of Oistins and local shops for a true taste of Caribbean culture.

Our inspector loved: *The vivid blue of the Caribbean Sea from the magnificent Café Luna restaurant.*

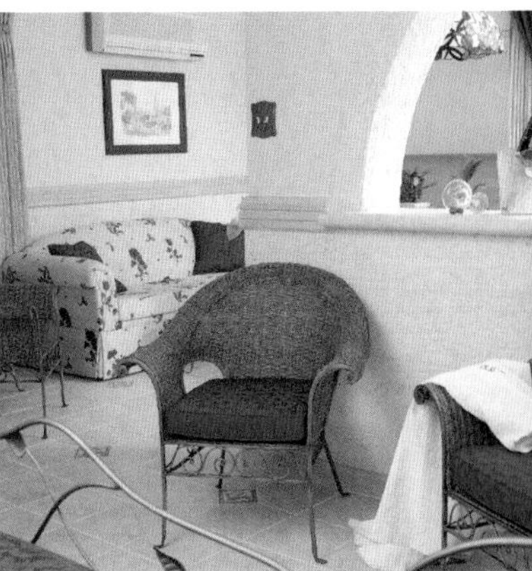

Directions: The hotel is a 10-minute taxi ride from the airport.

Web: www.johansens.com/littlearches
E-mail: paradise@littlearches.com
Tel: +1 246 420 4689
Fax: +1 246 418 0207
U.S./Canada Toll Free: 1 800 764 1000

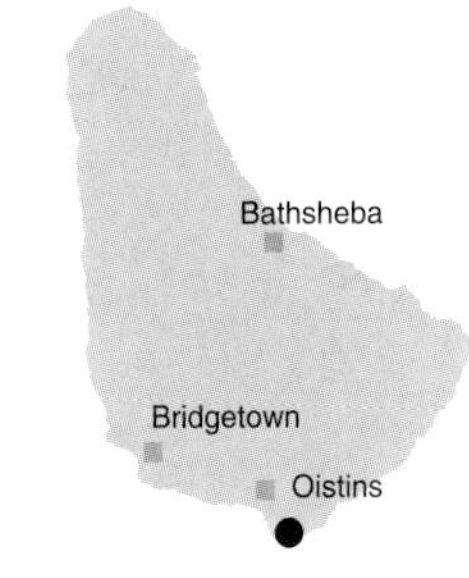

Price Guide:
(excluding 7.5% tax, including gratuity)
rooms U.S.$192-U.S.$399
suites U.S.$336-U.S.$552

Coral Reef Club

ST. JAMES

Directions: Situated on the west coast of Barbados, the hotel is 18 miles from Grantley Adams Airport and 1 mile north of Holetown.

Web: www.johansens.com/coralreefclub
E-mail: coral@caribsurf.com
Tel: +1 246 422 2372
Fax: +1 246 422 1776
U.S./Canada Toll Free: 1 800 223 1108

Price Guide:
rooms U.S.$245–U.S.$800
suites U.S.$440–U.S.$2,400

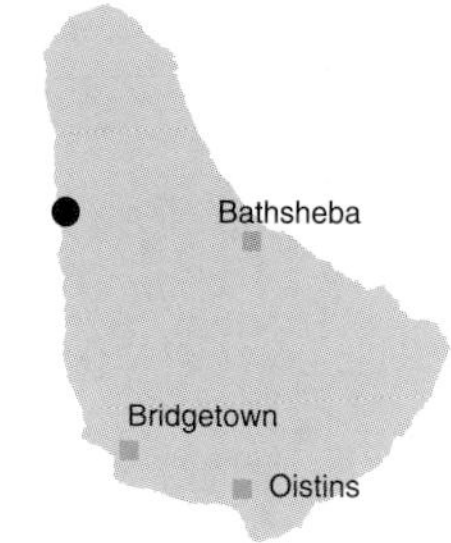

Quietly nestled in 12 acres of lush tropical gardens on Barbados's famed west coast, Coral Reef Club has been family owned and managed for almost 50 years. The O'Hara family is dedicated to providing excellence and no stone is left unturned to ensure guests' every comfort. The hotel is situated on a white sandy beach and offers a full range of complimentary water sports including waterskiing. A gymnasium is also available to guests . A quiet stroll along the coast is a relaxing way to explore the surroundings before sampling some of the excellent seafood suggestions available at the elegant ocean-front restaurant. There are just 88 rooms, cottages and junior suites named after the flowers, fruit and trees found in the grounds. All rooms are spacious and well appointed and the new luxury cottages feature a separate living room and private plunge pool. For the utmost luxury however, the 5 Plantation Suites, with their own plunge pools, are simply stunning and are the epitome of 21st-century elegance and style.

Our inspector loved: *The cocktail party for guests, hosted at the owners' family home on the property.*

Lone Star

MOUNT STANDFAST, ST. JAMES

Situated on the west coast of Barbados, boasting spectacular views, the Lone Star is a small and quaint property rapidly gaining a reputation as being an exclusive destination for the chic, discerning traveler. Originally consisting of just 4 guest suites, the property has a delightful style, reminiscent of the interior of a ship's cabin. Cool white linens, nautical blues and richly glossed woods are not only relaxing but in complete harmony with the tropical waters outside. In addition to these rooms, the hotel now includes the owner's former coral stone home, that has been beautifully converted to incorporate a further 4 ocean-front rooms. The house can be sold separately or individually but would be the most immaculate of Caribbean hideaways for a group arriving for a wedding, with its delightfully characterful Barbadian living room and well-equipped kitchen. The 2 rooms upstairs have an independent entrance affording considerable privacy from the rest of the house. The Lone Star restaurant is one of the most popular on the island, and is an ideal place for celebrity spotting; and offers breakfast overlooking the beach, light and informal lunches and romantic candle-lit dinners.

Our inspector loved: *Watching the spectacular sunsets over the Caribbean Sea from the terrace.*

Directions: The hotel is a 40-minute drive from the airport.

Web: www.johansens.com/lonestar
E-mail: wowgroupltd@sunbeach.net
Tel: +1 246 419 0599
Fax: +1 246 419 0597

Price Guide:
suites U.S.$350-U.S.$825

THE SANDPIPER

HOLETOWN, ST. JAMES

With just 47 rooms and suites The Sandpiper is a real little gem of a hotel and a true vacation hideaway on the desirable west coast of Barbados. Both discreet and elegant it has quickly become a favorite retreat for those discerning guests looking for that winning combination of intimacy, informality and privacy. Lush tropical gardens lead down to a large bay with white sands overlooking crystal blue waters, where the swimming is wonderful and the range of complimentary water sports is excellent. Each of the bedrooms and suites has its own private terrace and all are carefully appointed to be light, spacious and airy, with a touch of Caribbean color and flair. There are 2 superb new Tree Top Suites featuring their own plunge pool and sun deck, outstanding interior design and beach-front location. These suites add a new dimension of luxury to The Sandpiper. The restaurant, set in a lush garden surrounded by tranquil koi ponds, has gained a fine reputation and offers an eclectic menu with a Caribbean undertone. The attentive staff have a strong eye for detail and ensure that guests are looked after without sacrificing the relaxed atmosphere that is such a unique part of the Caribbean.

Our inspector loved: *The "South Seas" atmosphere of the hotel at night, with the flaming torches subtly lighting up the waterfalls.*

Directions: Situated on the west coast of Barbados, the hotel is 18 miles from Grantley Adams Airport and ¼ mile north of Holetown.

Web: www.johansens.com/sandpiper
E-mail: coral@caribsurf.com
Tel: +1 246 422 2251
Fax: +1 246 422 0900
U.S./Canada Toll Free: 1 800 223 1108

Price Guide:
rooms U.S.$265–U.S.$765
suites U.S.$385–U.S.$2,400

Cobblers Cove

SPEIGHTSTOWN, ST. PETER

Cobblers Cove is a classic English country house-style hotel located on the northwest coast of Barbados. Each of the 40 spacious suites has a private balcony or patio, air-conditioned bedroom, private bath with English-style toiletries, wet bar with stocked refrigerator and tea and coffee makers. The hotel boasts beautifully landscaped gardens and winding terracotta brick pathways set with hibiscus and a wide variety of tropical palms and flowers. Pathways from the suites lead down to the lounge, bar and restaurant, near the pool looking out over the sea. The award-winning open-air Terrace Restaurant is situated at the edge of the beach. Executive Chef Neil Hitchen's cuisine is a blend of classical French, British and American influences using fresh local ingredients including fish caught by the resort's own fisherman. Complimentary high tea is served each day. Enjoy an English breakfast before heading out to the white sand beach and calm ocean, excellent for swimming. The array of activities available include water skiing, windsurfing snorkeling, tennis and the air-conditioned Keep Fit Center gym. Golf enthusiasts will enjoy a round at the nearby Sandy Lane golf courses. The hotel is within walking distance of Speightstown, home to a new luxury marina, and Bridgetown is just a 10-minute drive away.

Our inspector loved: *The Friday evening fish lover's fantasy with a selection of locally caught fish and international caviar.*

Directions: 40 minutes by car from Grantley Adams International Airport.

Web: www.johansens.com/cobblerscove
E-mail: reservations@cobblerscove.com
Tel: +1 246 422 2291
Fax: +1 246 422 1460
U.S./Canada Toll Free: 1 800 890 6060

Price Guide:
rooms U.S.$460-U.S.$2,450

LITTLE GOOD HARBOUR

SHERMANS, ST. PETER

After traveling along the West Coast of Barbados through the parish of St. James and St. Peter, guests will find family-owned Little Good Harbour, an idyllic hideaway nestled within the peaceful fishing village of Shermans. 21 cottages built around the 2 swimming pools are quietly tucked away and surrounded by lush palm trees and tropical Caribbean flora. Each cottage is carefully and expertly appointed in a wistful, Colonial style with a sumptuous ambience with an emphasis on space and light; all have a private terrace or balcony. Just across a small road is a beautiful beach, which has comfortable beach chairs and gazebos. Swimming in its pristine waters is wonderful and the views, especially at sunset, are inspirational. Adjacent to the hotel is one of the island's finest restaurants, The Fish Pot, an unusual converted fort with stunning ocean views and a reputation to match. Fresh Caribbean cuisine is irresistible with mouth-watering gourmet fish dishes as its specialty. Guests will enjoy exploring the quaint craft markets and art galleries in the area, and every Friday evening there is a fish fry at the fish market nearby that is not to be missed. There are fantastic opportunities to meet local Bajans and enjoy local dining.

Our inspector loved: *The beautiful gardens surrounding each room.*

Directions: The hotel is 50 minutes from the airport.

Web: www.johansens.com/goodharbour
E-mail: info@littlegoodharbourbarbados.com
Tel: +1 246 439 3000
Fax: +1 246 439 2020
U.S./Canada Toll Free: 1 800 259 8017

Price Guide: (room only)
rooms U.S.$237-U.S.$895

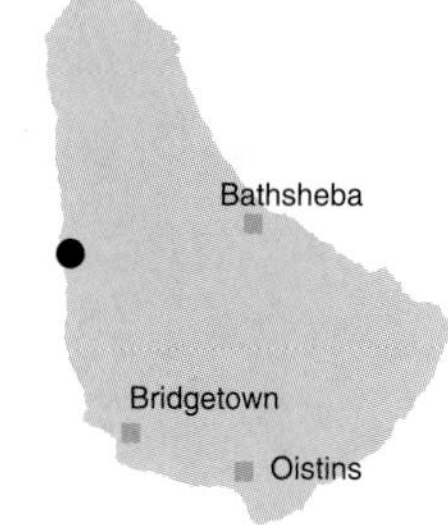

Caribbean - Bonaire

Hotel location shown in red with page number

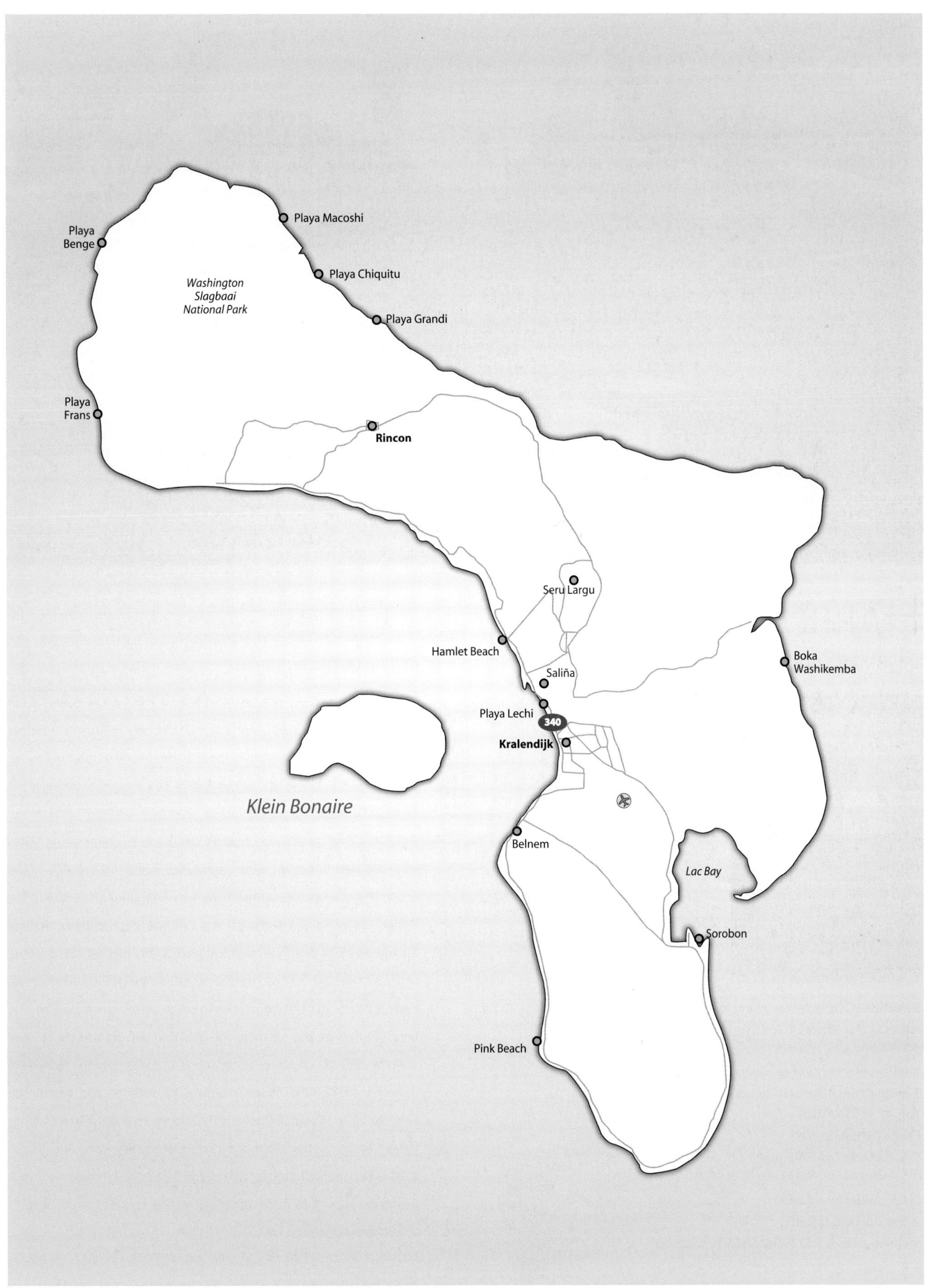

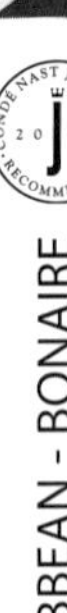

Harbour Village Beach Club

KAYA GOBERNADOR N. DEBROT NO. 71, BONAIRE, NETHERLANDS ANTILLES

Directions: The hotel provides complimentary transfers to and from Flamingo International Airport (B.O.N.).

Web: www.johansens.com/harbourvillage
E-mail: reservationsusa@harbourvillage.com
Tel: +1 305 567 9509
Fax: +1 305 648 0699
U.S./Canada Toll Free: 1 800 424 0004

Price Guide: (room only)
suites U.S.$460-U.S.$855
premier suties U.S.$2,870-U.S.$6,055 (weekly)

Located on the island of Bonaire, with rooms and suites dotted along the hotel's private beach, marina or within lush courtyards, Harbour Village Beach Club is a sunny oasis with unique opportunities for relaxing and enjoying life to the fullest. Spacious, cool interiors are beautifully appointed to create a cool and relaxing atmosphere complemented by the use of earthy tones and stunning views. Suites are extremely indulgent with double hammocks on terraces where guests may take a siesta or absorb the relaxing sounds of the waves. The design of La Balandra Beach Bar and Grill was inspired by an antique Spanish ship; the dining deck is located on a jetty that extends over the water overlooking the beach. Creative seafood specialties are irresistible and romantic candle-lit dinners on the beach are extremely popular. The Beach Club is for the exclusive use of club members and guests, and offers a fantastic choice of water sports including diving, snorkeling, kayaking, sailing, and nature programs for children and adults. The Harbour Village Tennis Center can be lit for night play whilst a state-of-the-art fitness center offers a schedule of weekly yoga and fitness classes. Bonaire is a haven for nature and a paradise for bird lovers. Pink flamingos as well as many other interesting species can be seen in several areas on the island.

Our inspector loved: *Watching the sunset while enjoying a cocktail.*

30

120

Caribbean - British Virgin Islands

Hotel location shown in red with page number

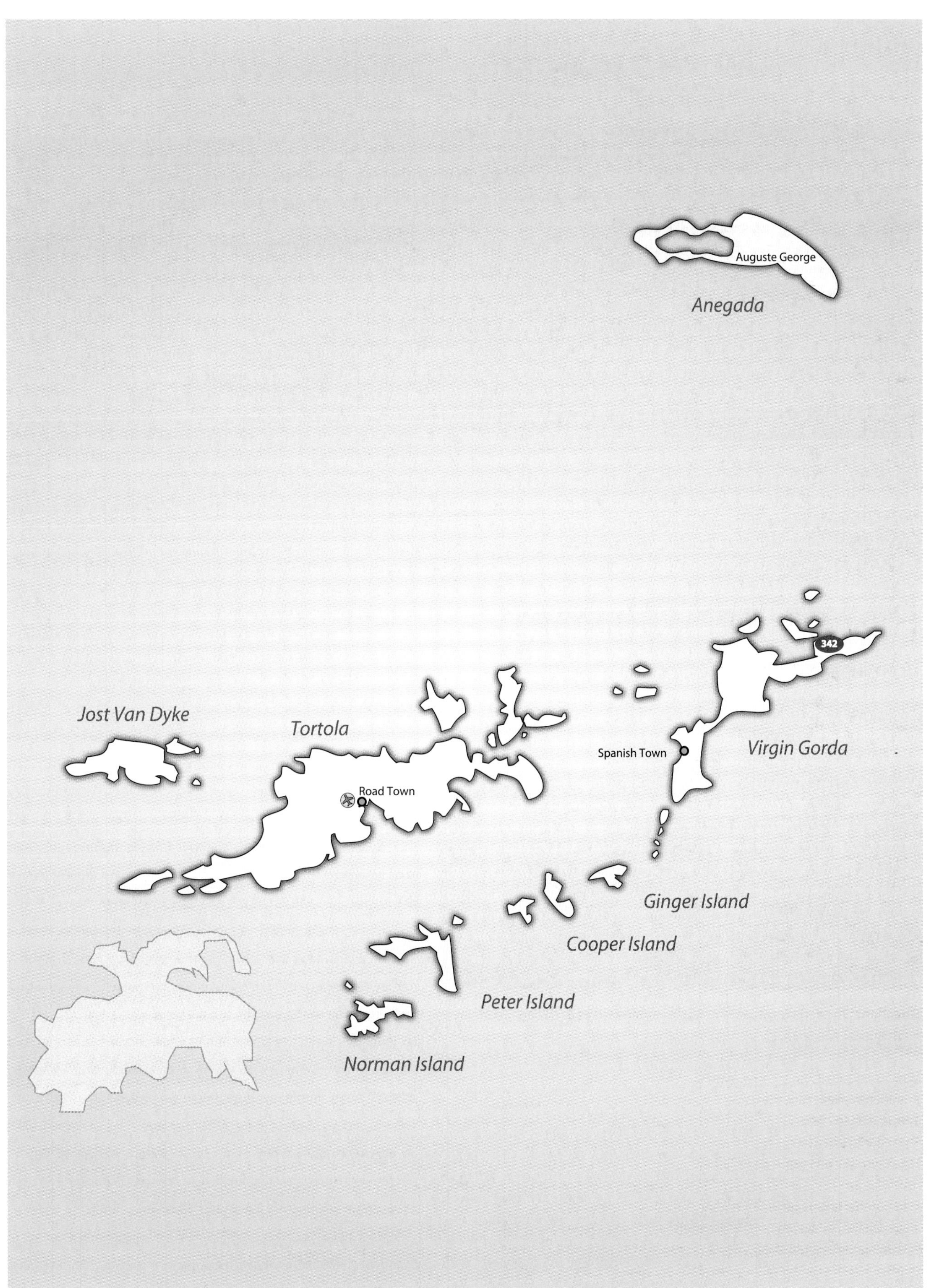

Biras Creek Resort

RELAIS & CHATEAUX

NORTH SOUND, VIRGIN GORDA

Biras Creek Resort is an elegant and rustic hideaway on a 140-acre nature reserve on Virgin Gorda. The resort is accessible only by boat, and is the perfect getaway for couples seeking to escape. The resort touches 3 bodies of water and every suite has been tropically decorated with lovely garden views or vistas of Bercher's Bay on the Atlantic shore. Central to the property is a hilltop stone castle, which accommodates the reception, main dining room and lovely terrace bar. A chess den and library are also tucked within the castle. After a day at the beach, guests can enjoy afternoon tea in the Arawak Pavilion overlooking the North Sound or play a game of snooker. A romantic evening is complete with dinner by candlelight overlooking the spectacular sunset through the airy open walls. The restaurant has an extensive wine menu and offers a selection of European and Caribbean dishes. The Spa by the Sea is the resort's new full-service seaside facility using signature Decléor aromatherapy treatments. There is also an outdoor yoga platform overlooking the ocean. Take an afternoon nap on one of the many hammocks found on the pristine white sand beaches, sail, swim or have the concierge arrange a tour of the neighboring islands by helicopter.

Our inspector loved: *Watching the sunset over the North Sound lagoon through the open walls of the resort's hilltop restaurant.*

Directions: 30 minutes by the resort's private launch from Beef Island Airport (Tortola).

Web: www.johansens.com/birascreek
E-mail: biras@biras.com
Tel: +1 310 440 4225
Fax: +1 310 440 4220
U.S./Canada Toll Free: 1 800 223 1108

Price Guide: (including breakfast, lunch, afternoon tea, dinner and airport transfers with minimum 4-night stay)
suites U.S.$675-U.S.$1,950

Anegada
Tortola
Virgin Gorda

 31  20 10    SPA      

Caribbean - Curaçao

Hotel location shown in red with page number

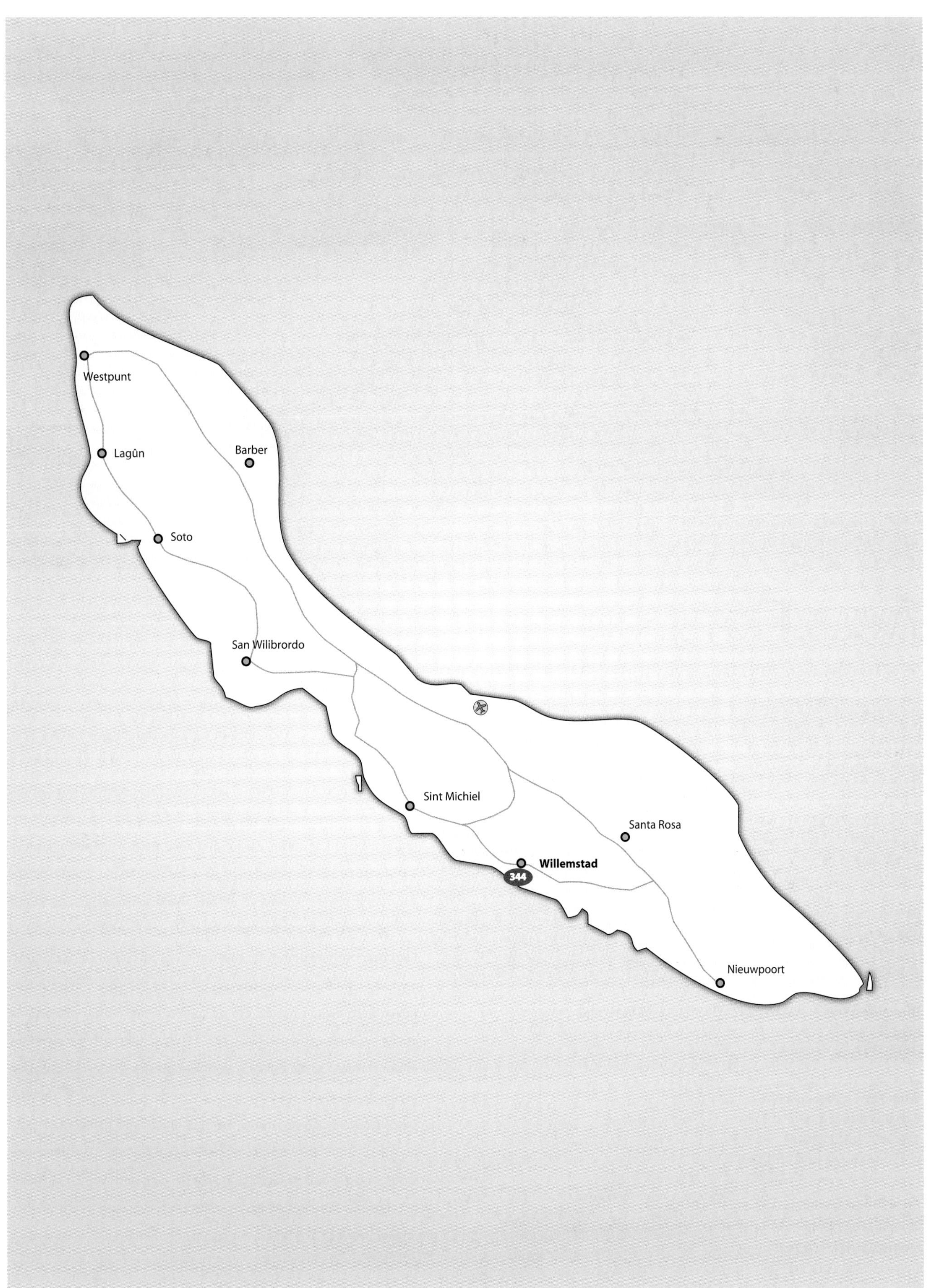

AVILA HOTEL ON THE BEACH

PENSTRAAT 130, WILLEMSTAD, CURAÇAO, NETHERLANDS ANTILLES

Originally the governor's residence the Avila Hotel is a stunning testament to Dutch-Caribbean-style architecture. Situated in Willemstad on the Dutch Antilles island of Curaçao, this refined hotel is an ideal escape. The interior is simply breathtaking: the "Blues Wing" consists of rooms with vaulted ceilings, in white and soft pastel colors and featuring Caribbean wicker and cane furniture. The furniture is stylish and comfortable, and all rooms offer a panoramic vista across the ocean and private balcony or terrace. The new deluxe Octagon Wing with spacious rooms decorated in sophisticated pastels with splashes of Caribbean colors, is due to open in Dec. 2006. This wing, with its amazing top floor Bolivar Suite, is just part of the significant upgrades being made. Renowned for its fine cuisine, diners are truly spoiled for choice with the convivial Avila Café, the elegant Belle Terrace and the informal Blues Jazz Club and Seafood Restaurant with its fantastic view of the Caribbean Sea. Wherever guests dine, the food is superbly prepared whilst making use of the fresh ingredients that abound both on and off shore. The recently opened Relax au Paradis spa offers a wide range of body and beauty treatments for men and women including outdoor massages. Alternatively, relax on the private beach or stroll around the tropical gardens, with palm trees framing the walkways.

Our inspector loved: *The spectacular ocean views.*

Directions: There are daily direct flights from Miami and daily flights (KLM) from Holland to Curaçao. Local car hire companies will provide directions or taxis are readily available.

Web: www.johansens.com/avilabeach
E-mail: info@avilahotel.com
Tel: +599 9 461 4377
Fax: +599 9 461 1493

Price Guide: (excluding 12% service charge and 7% tax, breakfast $14.11)
rooms U.S.$200–U.S.$420
suite U.S.$290–U.S.$520

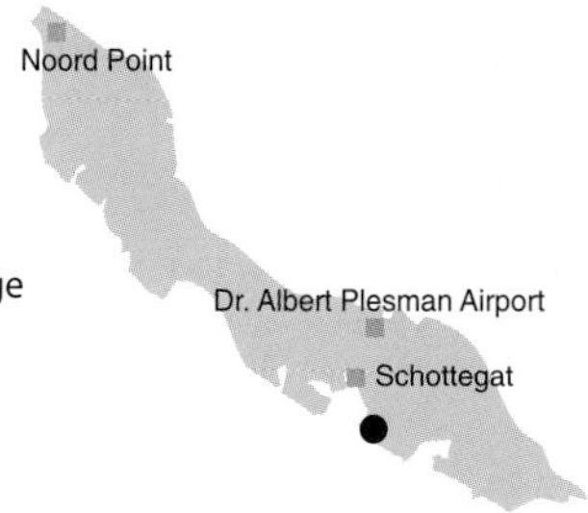

Noord Point
Dr. Albert Plesman Airport
Schottegat

     SPA   

Hotel location shown in red with page number

Casa Colonial Beach & Spa

P.O. BOX 22, PUERTO PLATA

This romantic resort is a hidden treasure that combines Old World charm and modern luxury in a beautiful beachfront setting on the northern coast of the Dominican Republic. 50 luxurious suites are tastefully decorated in a contemporary style with coralline stonework, mahogany furniture, marble floors and cathedral ceilings. Each suite has Frette linens, high-speed Internet access, in-room safe and flat-screen televisions. This family-owned resort also features a rooftop infinity pool and 4 Jacuzzis overlooking the Caribbean Sea. Dining at the 2 restaurants is a key part of the stay at Casa Colonial Beach & Spa. Lucia serves delectable Asian-fusion cuisine prepared by award-winning Chef Harald Klement in a beautiful setting with views of the mangrove jungle, and complemented by wines from the extensive wine cellar. Veranda is a more casual venue where guests can dine on the terrace or in the air-conditioned dining room. At the 12,440 square foot Bagua Spa, guests are pampered with treatments including hot stone massages and therapeutic facials in 10 indoor treatment rooms or 3 oceanfront outdoor gazebos. A full gym with personal trainers is also available. Guests have golf privileges at the nearby 18-hole Playa Dorada Golf Course and numerous restaurants, boutiques and the nightlife in Puerto Plata are nearby.

Directions: The hotel is located 9 miles from Puerto Plata International Airport, 5 minutes by helicopter or 25 minutes by car.

Web: www.johansens.com/casacolonial
E-mail: info@vhhr.com
Tel: +1 809 320 3232
Fax: +1 809 320 3131

Price Guide:
suites U.S.$350-U.S.$1,070

Our inspector loved: *The amazing spa, rooftop infinity pool and 4 Jacuzzis.*

Caribbean - Grenada

Hotel location shown in red with page number

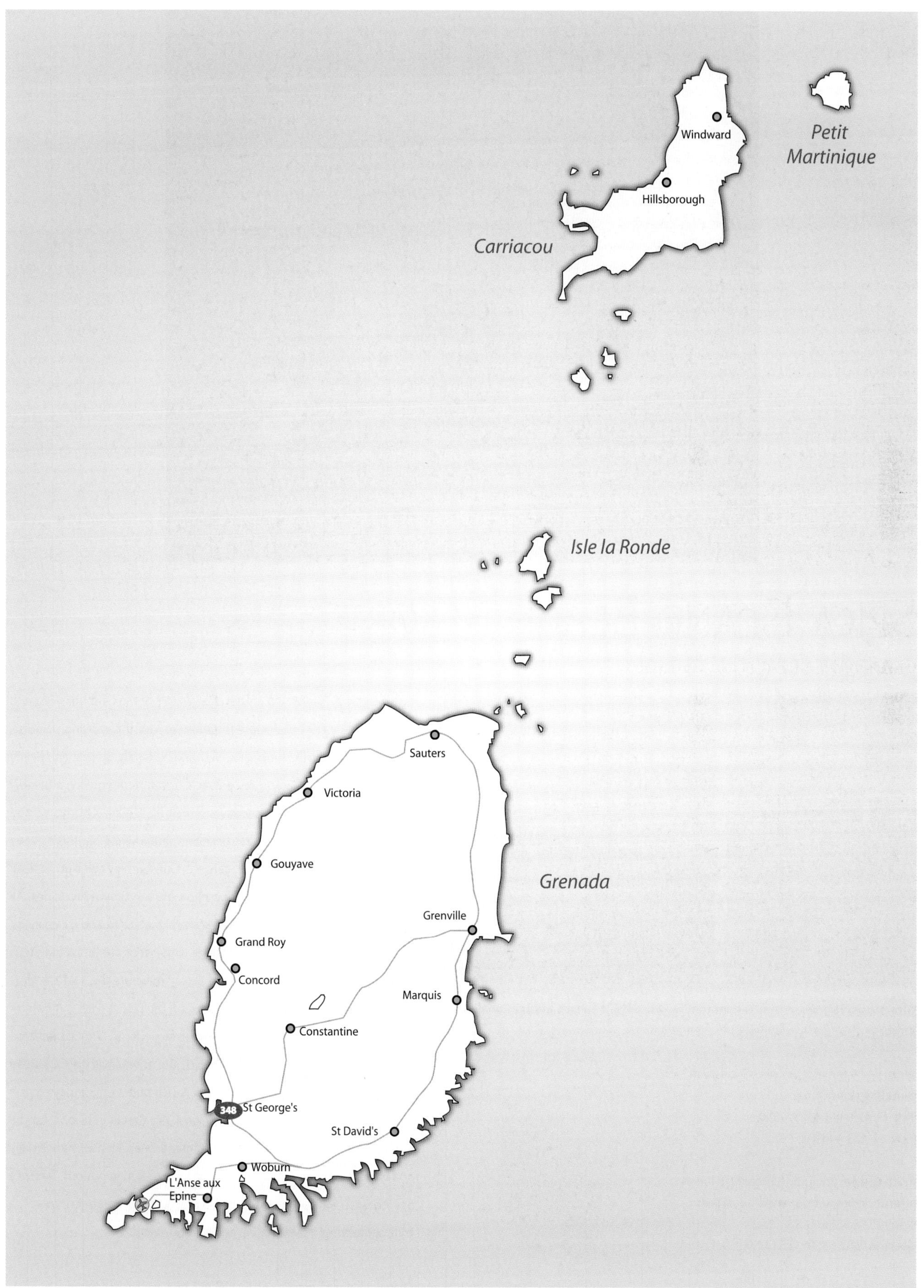

Spice Island Beach Resort

GRAND ANSE BEACH, ST. GEORGE'S

Powdery white sands, the crystal clear waters of the Caribbean Sea and the shade of palm trees create the backdrop for this relaxing paradise. Run by Sir Royston O. Hopkin, K.C.M.G. and his family, Spice Island Beach Resort is located on Grand Anse Beach. Comfort, tranquility, a friendly welcome and exceptional service are their trademark. Courtyards and terraces are filled with tropical flora and fauna while bedrooms have breathtaking views of the sea or gardens. Guests enjoy colorful, tropical-styled rooms, with fine Italian linen and Molton Brown amenities. All rooms have whirlpool tubs and flat-screen T.V.s, D.V.D. and C.D. players. The new 720sq. ft. Grape Beach Suites with patios are just a few steps from the ocean. For the ultimate in luxury there are the 1,440sq. ft. 1-bedroom Cinnamon and Saffron Suites on the beach with wet bars, 6-person dining rooms, lounges and living rooms. The oceanfront restaurant serves an excellent table d'hôte menu with a Caribbean buffet on Friday nights and a barbeque lunch buffet on Sundays. In the evenings, international cuisine, with local and Creole infusions, can be enjoyed with local entertainment 3-6 times a week. Menus change daily and include fresh seafood as well as many vegetarian options. Janissa's Spa boasts a well-equipped fitness center, 4 indoor treatment rooms, 1 outdoor treatment area, sauna and outdoor Jacuzzi.

Our inspector loved: *The new palatial 1-bedroom beach suites.*

Directions: The resort is a 10-minute drive from Point Salines International Airport.

Web: www.johansens.com/spiceisland
E-mail: spiceisl@caribsurf.com
Tel: +1 473 444 4423/4258
Fax: +1 473 444 4807

Price Guide: (including breakfast, lunch, afternoon tea, dinner and beverages)
singles U.S.$535–U.S.$1,550
doubles U.S.$635–U.S.$1,650

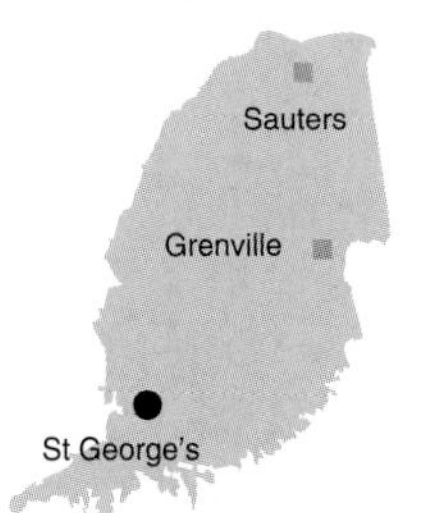

Caribbean - Jamaica

Hotel location shown in red with page number

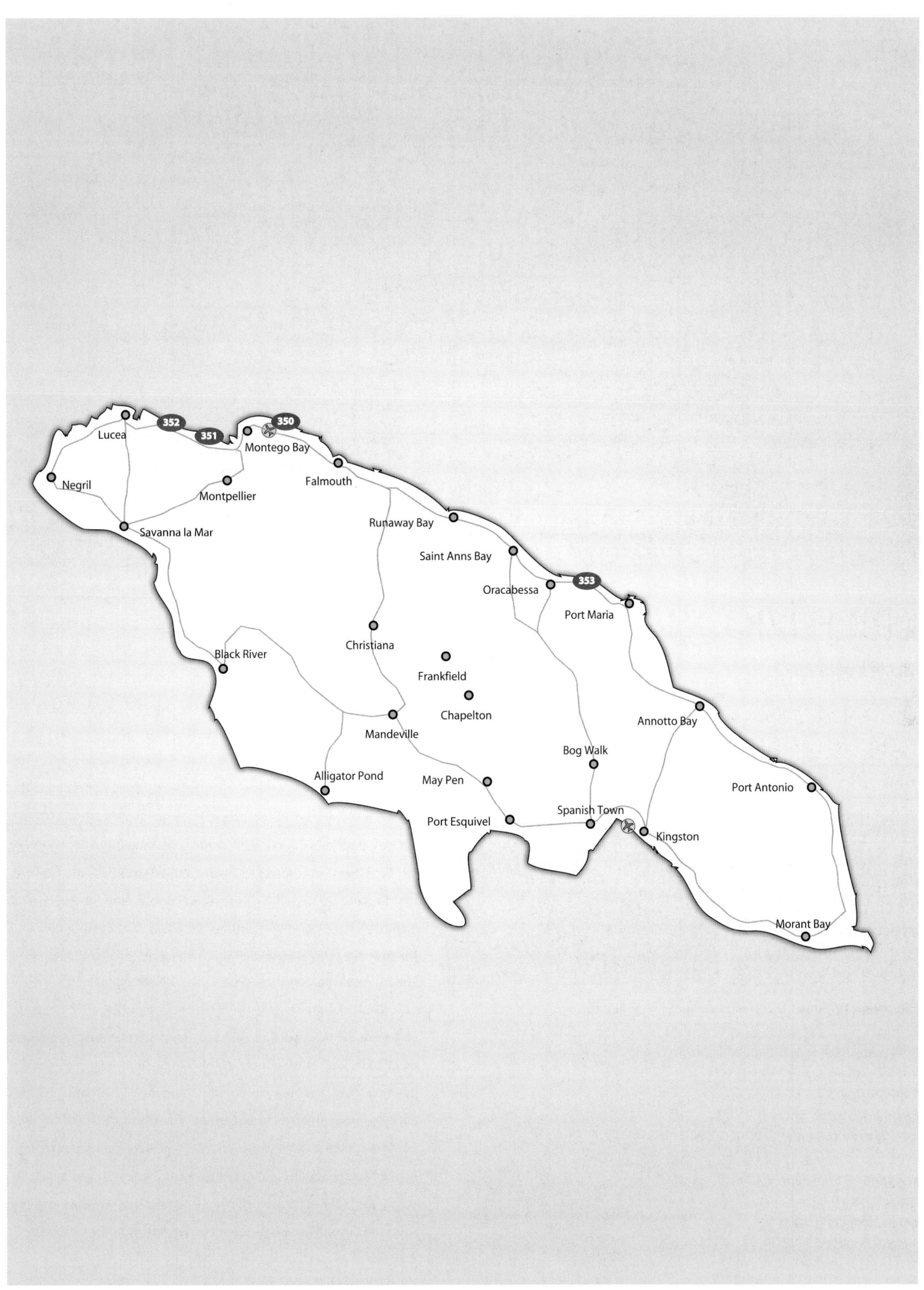

Half Moon

MONTEGO BAY

Set in 400 acres of tropical gardens edged by a crescent-shaped bay and a 2.5km white sandy beach the multi-award-winning Half Moon is one of the finest resorts in the world. This elegant, luxurious resort has recently completed a number of changes that make it even more the choice of the discerning traveler. Service and facilities are impeccable. Borne out by Royal, celebrity and business tycoon guests who have returned again and again including Her Majesty Queen Elizabeth, George Bush, Joan Collins, Paul Newman and Fidel Castro. A wide variety of accommodation includes 68 newly completed rooms and suites, all with luxurious amenities, air conditioning and stunning views. The 32 Royal Villas offer between 5, 6 and 7 luxury bedrooms, private porch and pool, the services of a butler, maid and cook. The 11 Imperial Suites are the most opulent whilst 61 Royal Suites ensure continuous pampering. Guests have a choice of 6 restaurants, ranging from the open-air Seagrape Terrace to the romantic Il Giardino and the enchanting Sugar Mill with its gourmet dinners. Leisure facilities include a swim with the dolphins experience, 13 tennis courts, 4 squash courts, 51 pools including one with a swim-up bar, 2 hot tubs and a recently upgraded 18-hole championship golf course with a just expanded pro shop and the only David Leadbetter Golf Academy in The Caribbean.

Directions: A 15-minute drive from Montego Bay Airport.

Web: www.johansens.com/halfmoongolf
E-mail: reservations@halfmoon.com
Tel: +1 876 953 2211
Fax: +1 876 953 2731
U.S./Canada Toll Free: 1 800 626 0592

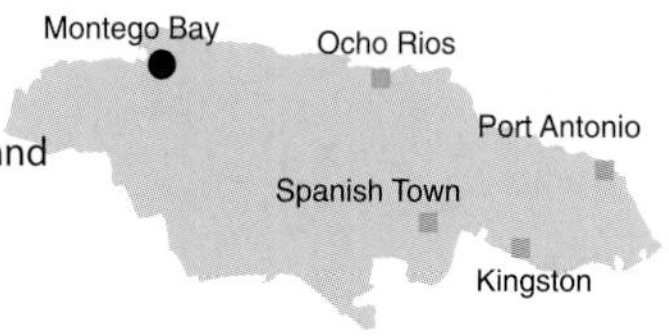

Montego Bay
Ocho Rios
Port Antonio
Spanish Town
Kingston

Price Guide: (room only, excluding tax and service charge)
rooms U.S.$250-U.S.400
suites U.S.$380–U.S.$1,520

Our inspector loved: *The Hibiscus Suites.*

Round Hill Hotel and Villas

P.O. BOX 64, MONTEGO BAY

For over 50 years Round Hill has extended a special welcome and exemplary service to the most celebrated guests whose glamorous gatherings are captured in photographs adorning the famous Piano Bar. The 36 ocean-front rooms in the Pineapple House Hotel have been newly designed by Ralph Lauren. The first and most memorable impression when entering, is the stunning view of the gardens and bay, framed by brilliant white walls, ceilings and floors. The four-poster, king-sized beds in mahogany-stained bamboo are draped in white net and feature 300 count Egyptian cotton white sheets. Nestling in luscious landscaped, subtropical hillside gardens are 27 cottages; most have a private pool and personal staff to ensure an unforgettable experience. The spa at Welcome Wharf offers a seductive choice of individualized treatments including yoga classes, hot stone massage therapy, Elemis pure aromatherapy skin care and professional therapy treatments, and of course, total relaxation after an appetizing spa lunch. Children under 12 years of age are welcome and have complimentary use of the Pineapple Kids' Club and Summer Tennis Clinic. Activities include nature walks, arts and crafts and reggae lessons. Nanny service is also available at an additional charge.

Our inspector loved: *The Ralph Lauren designed ocean-front rooms.*

Directions: 30 minutes from Donald Sangster International Airport, Montego Bay.

Montego Bay
Ocho Rios
Port Antonio
Spanish Town
Kingston

Web: www.johansens.com/roundhill
E-mail: info@roundhilljamaica.com
Tel: +1 876 956 7050
Fax: +1 876 956 7505
U.S./Canada Toll Free: 1 800 972 2159

Price Guide: (excluding breakfast)
hotel rooms U.S.$370-U.S.$590
villa suites U.S.$410-U.S.$920
villa (exclusive use) U.S.$780-U.S.$4,100

Tryall Club

P.O. BOX 1206, MONTEGO BAY

Tryall Club is immediately impressive, viewed from the main north west coast road, just 12 miles from Montego Bay. An avenue of tall, elegant coconut palms sweep up the hill through the gardens and golf course to the imposing 18th-century "Georgian Great House" and Restaurant, high above the Caribbean sea. The 73 individually designed and furnished, privately owned villas, include the intriguingly named "No Problem" and "Satisfy my Soul"! They offer from 1 to 7 bedrooms, private pools, delightful gardens and full time staff, including a cook, maid, laundress and butler. This is "home from home" on a grand estate of 2,200 acres! The 6,221-yard par-72 golf course designed by Ralph Plummer has hosted the Johnnie Walker World Championship, the Jamaica Classic and Mazda Championship. This challenging course enjoys a panorama of forest green hills, coconut palms, fruit trees, lily ponds and a full half mile along the Caribbean shore, all just a step from the luxury and comfort of your private villa. The club's facilities also include 9 "Nova-Cushion" night illuminated tennis courts, a tennis shop and International Pro. Most water sports are complimentary to guests and a rustic water's edge restaurant and bar offers relaxing hospitality. The Kids Club has a comprehensive program for even the most demanding junior guest.

Our inspector loved: *The Ralph Plummer designed golf course.*

Directions: A shuttle takes guests to and from Montego Bay Airport and Tryall Club.

Web: www.johansens.com/tryallclub
E-mail: reservation@tryallclub.com
Tel: +1 800 238 5290
Fax: +1 876 956 5673
U.S./Canada Toll Free: 1 800 361 9949

Price Guide: (per week)
villa U.S.$1,400-U.S.$19,500

GOLDENEYE

ORACABESSA, ST. MARY

Casino Royale, the first of Ian Fleming's James Bond adventures was written in the lush surroundings of Fleming's house, Goldeneye, in 1952. Other books followed from these idyllic surroundings over the next 12 years. Today, Fleming's house, with its barn like room, original writing desk, planters chairs and enormous glassless windows, perfectly convey his love of minimalism and stylish simplicity. Ian Fleming enjoyed entertaining and a steady stream of celebrities including Errol Flynn, Noel Coward, Cecil Beaton, Katherine Hepburn and Truman Capote visited Goldeneye. In 1976 the house and estate were purchased by Bob Marley and subsequently by Chris Blackwell who has developed it as part of his eclectic mix of Island Outpost resort properties. The Ian Fleming Villa has 3 bedrooms "007," "008," and "009 " a lounge, T.V. room and private pool and beach. The choice of exciting activities include deep sea fishing, windsurfing and kayaking. The restaurant serves traditional Jamaican cuisine using fresh market seasonal fruits and vegetables, fish and lobster purchased daily from local fishermen. Adjoining the Ian Fleming Villa, accessible through the gardens, are 2 additional Villas, which between them house another 3 bedrooms. All 3 villas can be exclusively hired to provide up to 6 bedrooms, ideal for a family event, groups of friends, small weddings and company retreats.

Directions: The hotel is 10 minutes from Boscobell Aerodrome and 2 hours from Montego Bay International Airport.

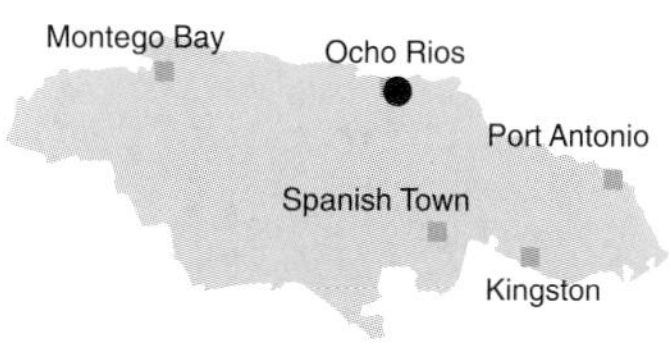

Montego Bay
Ocho Rios
Port Antonio
Spanish Town
Kingston

Web: www.johansens.com/goldeneye
E-mail: Goldeneye@cwjamaica.com and Reservations@islandoutpost.com
Tel: +1 876 975 3354
Fax: +1 876 975 3620
U.S./Canada Toll Free: 1 800 OUTPOST
U.K. Toll Free: 0800 OUTPOST 1

Price Guide: (all inclusive)
Villa U.S.$3,500 - U.S.$7,500

Our inspector loved: *The 007 bedroom.*

CARIBBEAN - MARTINIQUE

Hotel location shown in red with page number

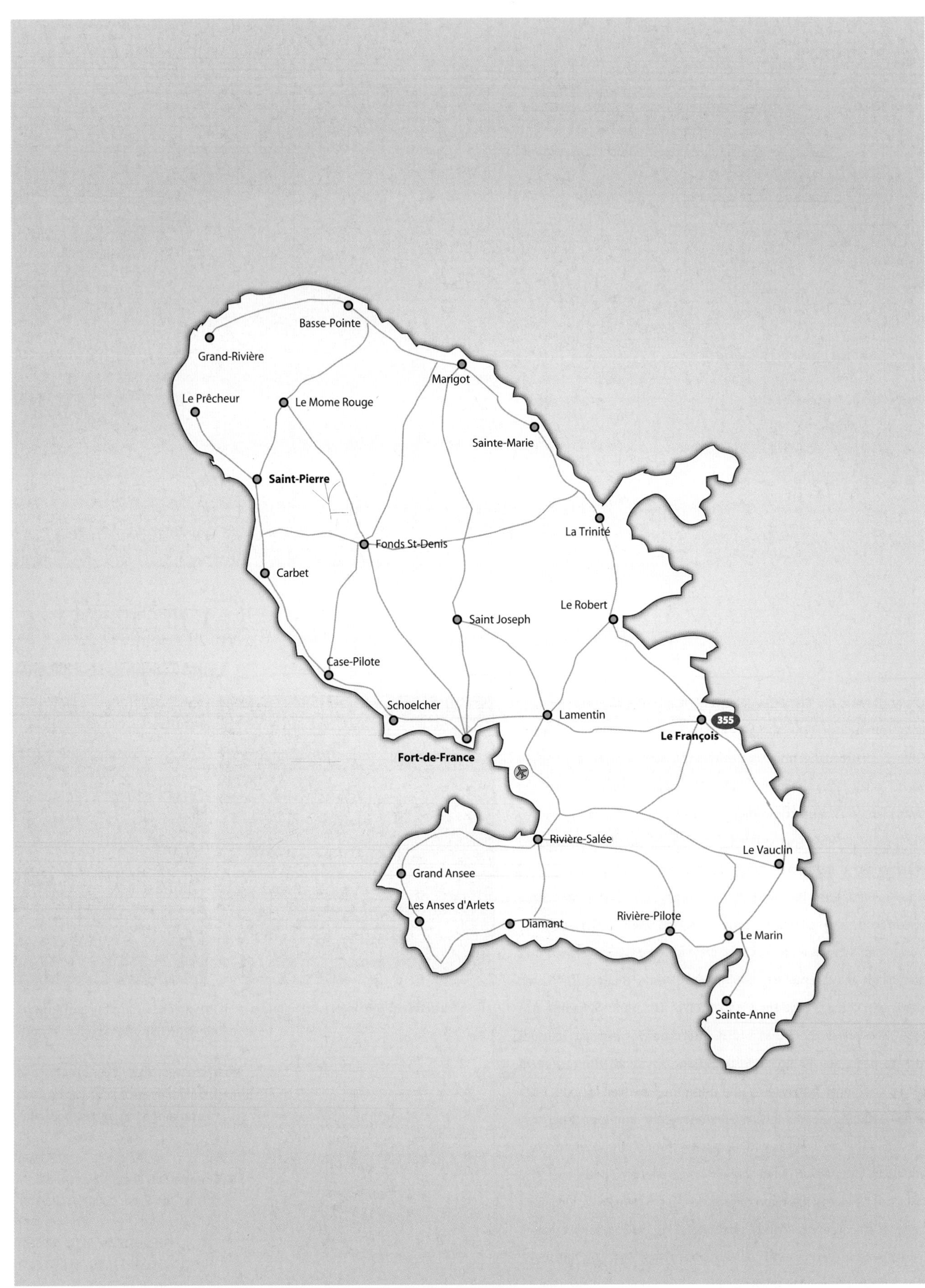

Le Cap Est Lagoon Resort & Spa

97240 LE FRANÇOIS

Crystal clear ocean, colorful coral reef barrier, soft white sand and lush tropical gardens are the backdrop to this oasis of luxury and sporting activity on Martinique's eastern coast between Francois and Vauclin. This is a stylish, relaxing resort with 50 spacious suites carefully located throughout the grounds for maximum privacy; 18 are Creole-style villas. All have ocean views, air conditioning, ceiling fans and are superbly appointed and furnished with crisp linens and cheerful prints. Home comforts include espresso and ice-making machines, loveseat and high-tech facilities such as plasma-screen televisions, D.V.D. - C.D. players and Internet connection. Many have a private pool and refreshing outdoor shower. There are 2 excellent restaurants: Le Bélem offers superb French and Creole cuisine complemented by a selection of French wines and champagne whilst the beachfront Le Campêche is popular for its fresh-from-the-tank lobsters, grilled fish and salads. More than 100 old rums can be sampled whilst enjoying the live entertainment in the lounge bar pre or post-dining. For the more active there is a large swimming pool on-site, windsurfing, kayaking, kite surfing, small catamaran day trips and motor boating. An 18-hole golf course is at nearby Trois Ilets and for relaxation, there is a spa with choice of treatment rooms.

Our inspector loved: *The ultimate, luxurious pampering at the spa, which is in exclusive partnership with Guerlain.*

Directions: Direct flights from the U.S.A. The resort is a 30-minute drive from Lamentin International Airport.

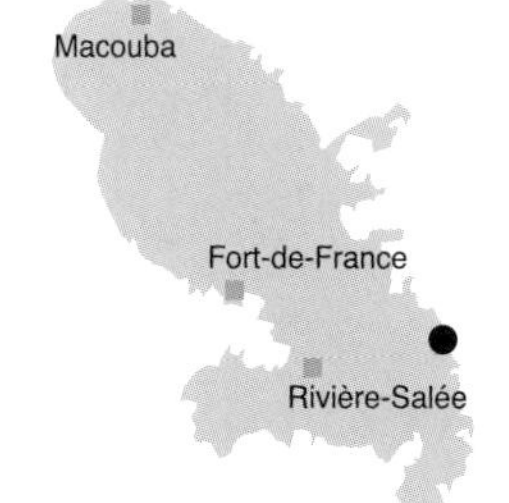

Web: www.johansens.com/capest
E-mail: info@capest.com
Tel: +596 596 54 80 80
Fax: +596 596 54 96 00

Price Guide: (including buffet breakfast, all service charges and tax)
garden suites €400-€980
deluxe suites €700-€1,280
executive suites €1,000-€1,550

Caribbean - Puerto Rico

Hotel location shown in red with page number

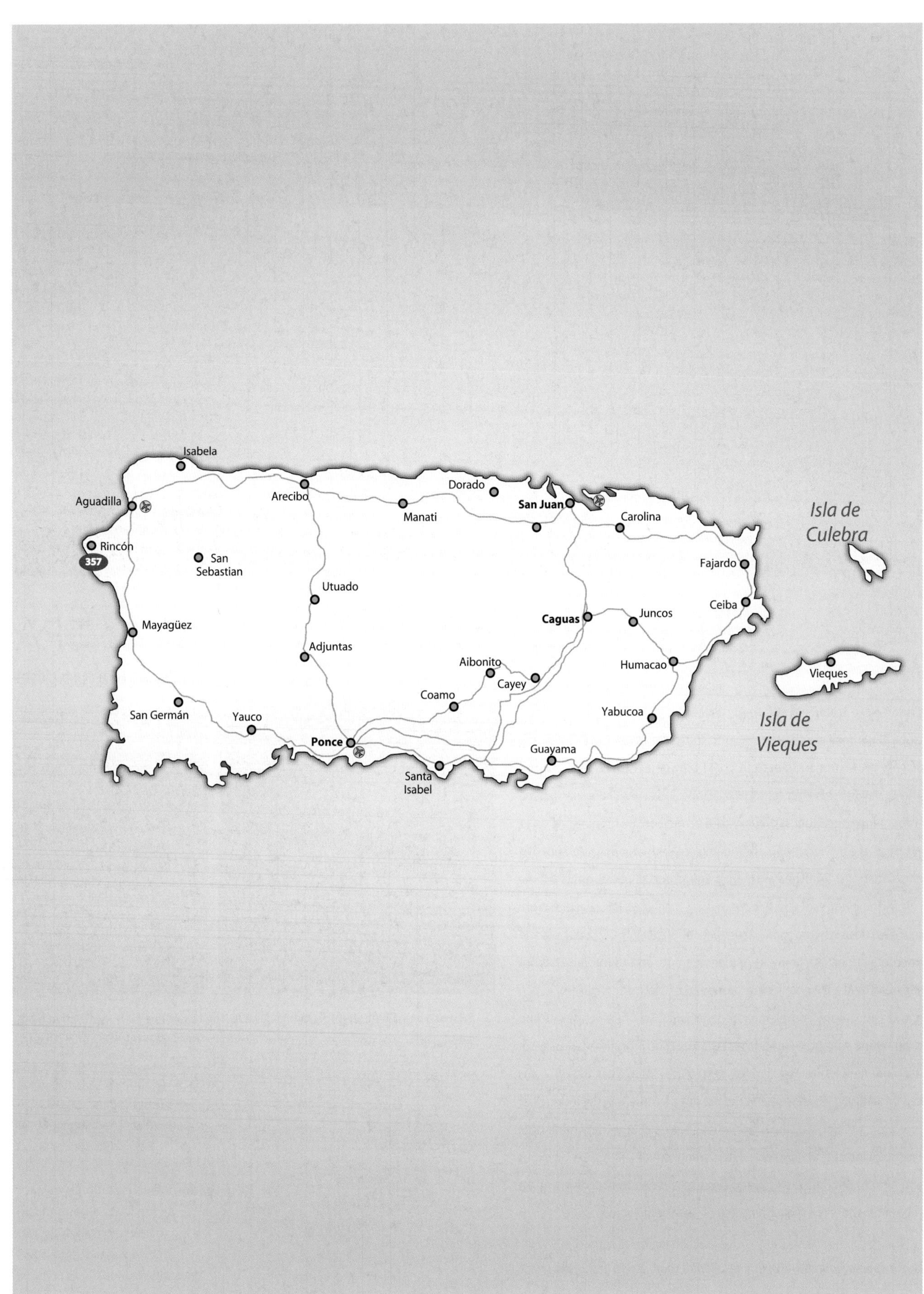

HORNED DORSET PRIMAVERA

APARTADO 1132, RINCÓN, PUERTO RICO 00677

Horned Dorset Primavera hotel, located on the western coast of Puerto Rico, is an exclusive 8-acre hillside property overlooking the Caribbean Sea. The luxurious, romantic décor features antiques, exotic woods and marble baths. The Primavera Suites, originally conceived as a small village adjoining the sea-front suites of the original hotel, are 1,400 square feet, 2-story, king-bedded town house suites with private terraces and plunge pools facing the endless horizon of the Straits of Mona. The furnishings are Spanish, Dutch, and Caribbean mahogany and teak, and the settings reach back to the 17th-century Spanish Empire of Carlos I. 17 new luxurious beachfront villas will be complete by the end of 2006 offering private dipping pools, teak mahogany furnishings, imported rugs and lamps in the Spanish Mozarabic. Gourmet cuisine at Restaurant Aaron is a selection of creative and delectable menus. Breakfast is served al fresco in The Verandah, on the terrace of the Blue Room, or in the privacy of one's suite. Room service is available for light, cold snacks throughout the day. A new wellness center with fully-equipped gymnasium, valet parking and heliport will be available by the end of 2006. Local activities in Rincón include shopping, snorkeling and diving.

Our inspector loved: *Taking breakfast al fresco on The Verandah overlooking the Caribbean Sea.*

Directions: From Mayaguez take Route 2 north then Route 115 towards Rincón. At the Anasco intersection take Route 429. 200 km from San Juan Luis Munoz Martin (Intl.), 10 km from M.E.M. de Hastos and 15 km from Aguadilla.

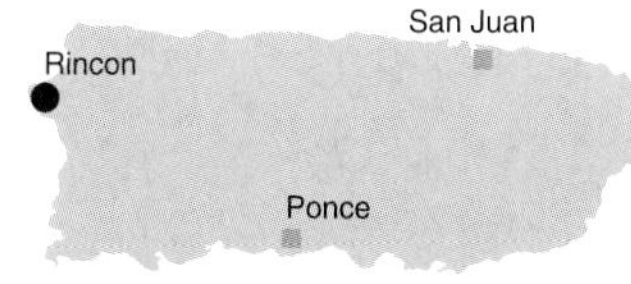

Web: www.johansens.com/horneddorset
E-mail: info@horneddorset.com
Tel: +1 787 823 4030
Fax: +1 787 823 5580
U.S./Canada Toll Free: 1 800 633 1857

Price Guide:
suites $590-$1320

Caribbean - Saint-Barthélemy

Hotel location shown in red with page number

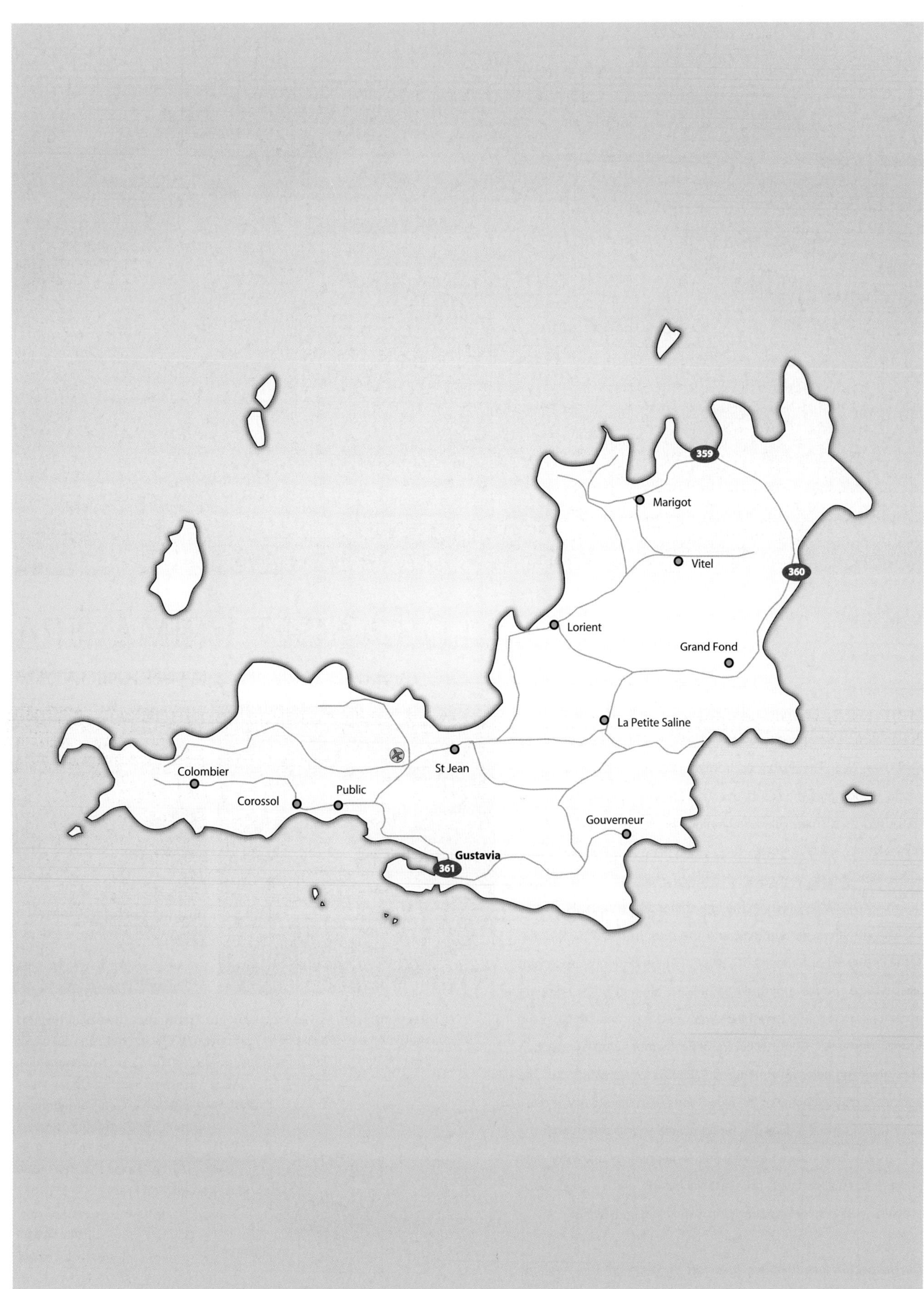

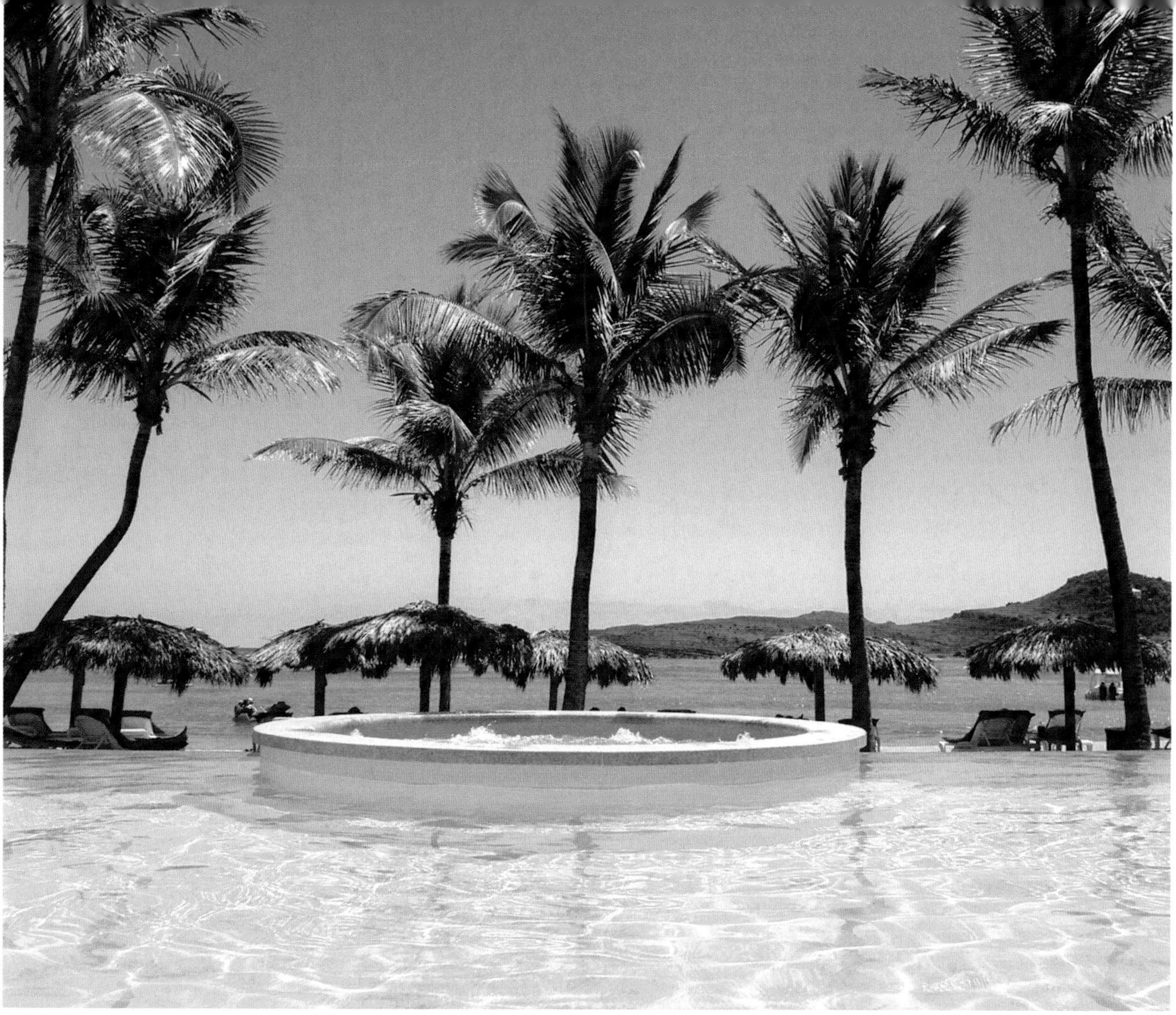

HOTEL GUANAHANI & SPA

GRAND CUL DE SAC, 97133 SAINT-BARTHÉLEMY

Hotel Guanahani & Spa is a delightful luxury resort set in a beautiful location overlooking 2 bays on a private 16-acre peninsula on the north-eastern end of St. Barts. The distinctive décor of pastel exteriors and white gingerbread trim with bright furnishings, rich mahogany floors and tropical woods create an ideal romantic honeymoon getaway. There are 35 suites and 35 deluxe rooms in bungalow style, each with terraces and private gardens; 14 have private pools. Recently completed, the open-air spa by Clarins has been decorated with a whimsical and tropical French style offering 8 treatment rooms. The spa has a pool, hammam ritual bath, beauty salon and herbal tea room. Gourmet cuisine is central to the Guanahani. Executive Chef Philippe Masseglia brings his high standards to create award-winning international cuisine with a French flair. Indigo is a casual poolside restaurant overlooking the beach and the exquisite menu at Bartolomeo is complemented by nightly jazz music. The Lounge and the beach bar, are pleasant settings for pre-dinner cocktails. This is the only hotel with its own 2 beaches perfect for snorkeling, wind-surfing and kite-surfing. Children's programs are also available. Private boat, plane and helicopter charters are available to explore the island.

Our inspector loved: *The "Wellness Suite" where guests have private key access to the spa and pool after hours.*

Directions: Free transfers to and from St. Barts' Airport or by boat from St. Maarten's Princess Julianna Airport to Gustavia Harbor can be arranged.

Web: www.johansens.com/guanahani
E-mail: guanahani@wanadoo.fr
Tel: +590 590 27 66 60
Fax: +590 590 27 70 70
U.S./Canada Toll Free: 1 800 216 3774

Price Guide: (including American breakfast, non-motorized water sports and airport transfers)
rooms €340-€1,235
suites €685-€3,350 la villa €2,475-€5,250

Le Toiny

ANSE DE TOINY, 97133 SAINT-BARTHÉLEMY

Set atop a hill on the south-eastern coast of Saint-Barthélemy overlooking the Caribbean Sea, Le Toiny's architecture is reminiscent of traditional French-Caribbean plantation houses. Suite exteriors are painted in cheerful mint, peach and lavender hues with terracotta and native gaïac wood interior décor and handmade teak and mahogany, period replica four-poster beds adding authenticity to the Old Caribbean atmosphere. Suites have been designed to catch as much natural light as possible, providing breathtaking views and architecture that harmonizes with the landscape. Each suite has top of the line sound and audio equipment including flat-screen T.V.s, D.V.D. and C.D. players as well as fully-equipped kitchenettes. Massage and beauty treatments, with the renowned spa and cosmetic company Ligne de St. Barth, are available in the privacy of guest suites. All villas have wireless Internet connection, private heated swimming pools and terraces with teak chaise lounges for relaxation. A central pool near the Main House is also available. Le Gaïac restaurant, with its 180° views of the Bay of Toiny, offers a classic French flavor with creole undertones. Custom sightseeing tours of Saint-Barthélemy can be arranged by the reception staff. Fitness equipment and a sports trainer are available on request and tennis courts are nearby.

Our inspector loved: *The privacy of each villa.*

Directions: The hotel is 15 minutes from St. Barts Airport (S.B.H.) and offers complimentary airport transfers.

Web: www.johansens.com/letoiny
E-mail: letoiny@wanadoo.fr
Tel: +590 590 27 88 88
Fax: +590 590 27 89 30 and **E-fax:** +1 617 507 0490
U.S./Canada Toll Free: 1 800 27 TOINY (86469)

Price Guide:
1-bedroom villa €800-€1,750
2-bedroom villa €1,250-€3,150
3-bedroom villa €1,500-€3,150

CARL GUSTAF HOTEL

RUE DES NORMANDS, GUSTAVIA, 97099 SAINT-BARTHÉLEMY

Voted Number 3 of Caribbean/Atlantic Hotels in Condé Nast Traveler's Reader's Choice 2005 and included on the Condé Nast Traveler's Gold List 2005, this elegant and sophisticated hotel is situated high on a hillside commanding wonderful views of the enchanting capital Gustavia, only 2 minutes from the beach. With just 14 one and 2-bedroom suites in the entire hotel, there is a true feeling of intimacy and luxury, with all rooms boasting views of the harbor and each with their own private plunge pool. The stunning views provide a magnificent backdrop to the refined, cool simplicity of the décor; watching sunsets from the hotel is a truly remarkable event. A great evening can be enjoyed by savoring a tropical cocktail followed by a French or West Indian gourmet dinner in the panoramic restaurant. The hotel has its very own 52ft. yacht, and a rare treat is to take one of the hotel's special excursions to the nearby coral reef to gaze at the tropical scenery, followed by a champagne picnic lunch on a simply beautiful beach. Windsurfing, sailing and fishing can all be arranged, whilst Gustavia has many glamorous shops selling stunning designer fashions and pieces of jewelry from France and Italy.

Our inspector loved: *Relaxing in a private plunge pool overlooking the glittering harbor of Gustavia below.*

14 24 M 20

Directions: The hotel will arrange a complimentary 10-minute roundtrip airport transfer.

Web: www.johansens.com/carlgustaf
E-mail: info@hotelcarlgustaf.com
Tel: +590 590 29 79 00
Fax: +590 590 27 82 37

Price Guide: (including welcome champagne, Continental breakfast, fitness room and sauna facilities and roundtrip airport transfer)
suites €620-€1,850

Qamea Resort & Spa

P.A. MATEI, TAVENUI

Directions: The resort's luxury 4-wheel drive will meet guests at Tavenui (Matei) Airport and a 8-minute ride in a covered boat will then take them to

Web: www.johansens.com/qamea
E-mail: qamea@connect.com.fj
Tel: +679 888 0220
Fax: +679 888 0092
U.S./Canada Toll Free: 1 866 867 2632

Price Guide: (including all meals and non-motorized activities, excluding tax)
rooms U.S.$525-U.S.$995

Set on the beautiful island of Qamea on a mile-long pristine white sandy beach, Qamea offers an authentic Fijian experience. This intimate luxury property consists of 16 spacious, air-conditioned ocean-front bures and villas nestled in 100 acres of landscaped gardens and bushland, with a stunning backdrop of jagged South Pacific mountains. Local staff are extremely welcoming and will cater for guests' every need. Strategically positioned for maximum privacy and unobstructed views of the sunset, the romantic and elegant thatched roof bures and villas were designed in traditional Fijian style, with local mahogany hardwood floors, antique Fijian art and covered decks with hammocks. A split-level honeymoon villa and 2 honeymoon bures have Jacuzzi spa pools and the 2 premium villas have private pools. 4 Fijian chefs and visiting chefs from Australia and New Zealand prepare gourmet Fijian and Continental Pacific Rim cuisine based on fresh seafood and locally grown fruits and organic vegetables, which is served in the Bure Kalau, complemented by a wide selection of Australian, New Zealand and Californian wines. Lounge the day away on the beach or by the hidden swimming pool, alternatively enjoy the great variety of activities. Some of the world's best diving and snorkeling sites can be found on the doorstep, whilst excursions to the neighboring islands can be arranged.

Our inspector loved: *The simply fabulous spa that should not be missed!*

  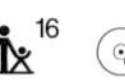   SPA   

JEAN-MICHEL COUSTEAU FIJI ISLANDS RESORT

LESIACEVA POINT, SAVUSAVU

This award-winning 5-star resort is one of the most acclaimed in the South Pacific. Recently voted No. 1 Resort on Condé Nast Traveler's Green List, the resort is set on a former 17-acre coconut plantation, reminiscent of an authentic Fijian Village. Situated on the unspoiled sunshine island of Vanua Levu it overlooks the peaceful waters of Savusavu bay. Views are stunning and the surrounding tropical gardens and coral reefs are magnificent. The 25 exclusive, colorful and spacious bures are the ultimate in relaxation and luxury. Each has a large deck, custom-made king-size bed and some have spas. Mouth-watering fusions of local and international cuisine are created by celebrated chef Dor Sami. Everything about the resort and its surroundings is a delight and the perfect combination of relaxation and discovery for the romantics, honeymooners, families and water sports enthusiasts. The variety of activities offered for all ages is exceptional; each day focuses on a shared activity including daily yoga classes, a rainforest/waterfall walk and reef snorkeling with a resident marine biologist, Fijian culture with Niumaia, the 2002 recipient of the "Cultural Tourism" honor for the "Fiji Excellence in Tourism awards." This is the Sister property to Hotel Hana Maui and Post Ranch Inn, Big Sur, California.

***Our inspector loved:** This true eco-sensitive resort combining indulgence, romance, culture and discovery.*

Directions: Daily flights from Nadi or Suva Airport to Savusavu Airport. Seaplane charters available. Free return vehicle transfers from Savusavu Airport to the resort.

Vanua Levu
Yasawa Islands
Viti Levu

Web: www.johansens.com/jean-michelcousteau
E-mail: jmcfir@alphalink.com.au
Tel: U.S.A. +1 415 788 5794,
Australia +61 3 98150379
Australia local 1300 306171
U.S./Canada Toll Free: 1 800 246 3454

Price Guide: (all inclusive, excluding alcoholic and specialty beverages and tax)
bures U.S.$575-U.S.$725

MYOLA PLANTATION

P.O. BOX 638, SIGATOKA

Directions: Luxury vehicle transfers from Nadi International Airport are provided by the resort; helicopter transfers are also available. The resort is approximately 45 minutes by car and 12 minutes by helicopter from the airport.

Web: www.johansens.com/myola
E-mail: myola@connect.com.fj
Tel: +679 652 1084
Fax: +679 652 0899

Price Guide: (including all meals)
villas FJ$2,000

Set atop a cliff on 10 acres of Viti Levu just west of Sigatoka, Myola Plantation is a secluded private estate of landscaped tropical gardens and citrus groves that offers unrivaled Pacific views across a pristine turquoise coral reef. This private villa offers 2 luxury Master Suites, each with its own spa, outdoor shower and plunge pool. A large open-plan lounge, entertainment area, dining area, fully-equipped kitchen and office complete the facilities, and sweeping balconies, luxury amenities and objets d'art complete the ambience. Discover the exotic flavours of Fijian and Western cuisine, expertly prepared by the Plantation's personal chef with only the freshest of ingredients, harvested from the nearby lush Sigatoka Valley and local seafood is plentiful. 10 personal staff, maid service and extras such as in-room massages make for a truly indulgent stay. Guests wishing to explore the area can visit the Arts Village, shop in the Sigatoka market, tour the world's second-largest soft coral reef with a personal dive master or take the old sugar plantation train from nearby Cuvu to Natadola beach. The Myola staff will prepare a barbecue lunch on the beach at Natadola before the return train ride to the Plantation.

Our inspector loved: *The exclusivity and seclusion of these stunning villas perched on a cliff overlooking the tropical reef, whales and dolphins.*

Toberua Island Resort

P.O. BOX 3332, NAUSORI

Toberua Island Resort is an emerald set in a lapis lazuli sea within 2 hectares of lush palm trees. Guests may stay in one of the 15 distinctive bures, all with en-suite bathrooms, large beds and spacious lounge areas. Each is individually appointed with traditional furnishings and weavings. Toberua (pronounced "Tomberua") means "the good life" - when staying here guests are encouraged to feel that this is their private paradise island with nothing to interrupt the reverie. Sample a pre-dinner cocktail or one of the carefully chosen imported wines before dining under the stars. The menu is a delicious mixture of international and local dishes featuring seafood, brought in by local fisherman, and the island's tropical fruits. Fishing, exploring uninhabited islands, snorkeling through the coral, observing reef life from a glass bottom boat, windsurfing, sailing or simply relaxing by the pool can fill each day. Scuba diving on the kaleidoscopic reefs is exceptional. In-keeping with the mood of Toberua Resort, there is little need for cash here; most of the activities are complimentary.

Our inspector loved: *My bure, just 10 feet from the water's edge, and the service and style of this wonderful private island.*

Directions: The resort is a 10-minute drive from Suva International Airport (Nausori). Guests may wish to take the seaplane from Nadi, then covered boat to Toberua.

Vanua Levu
Yasawa Islands
Viti Levu

Web: www.johansens.com/toberuaisland
E-mail: toberua@connect.com.fj
Tel: +679 347 2777
Fax: +679 347 2888

Price Guide:
rooms FJ$490–FJ$790
suites FJ$800–FJ$1,200

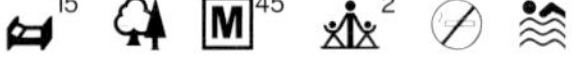

Royal Davui

P.O. BOX 3171, LAMI

Directions: By helicopter or boat transfer directly from Nadi International Airport or by luxury launch transfer from Pacific Harbour.

Web: www.johansens.com/royaldavui
E-mail: res@royaldavui.com
Tel: +679 336 1624
Fax: +679 336 1253

Price Guide: (full board)
deluxe villas U.S.$1,100
premium villas U.S.$1,270
Davui Suite U.S.$1,460

This is an idyllic and romantic exclusive retreat where island seclusion in total luxury and style can be experienced. This remote and lush green hideaway stands above a colorful barrier reef fringed by soft, pristine white sandy beaches and clear sapphire waters. Guests are freed from everyday stresses the instant they step from the helicopter or launch transportation. Friendly staff extend the warmest of welcomes ready and willing to attend to every need. 16 spacious vales (villas) nestle in the cliffs' tropical vegetation offering dramatic views over Beqa Lagoon. Each is cool with mahogany floors, thatched roof, sea grass ceiling, an open-plan layout featuring extensive glass areas and bi-folding doors that take full advantage of the stunning views. They also feature king-size beds, air conditioning, Jacuzzi, indoor and outdoor showers, 2 decks and a plunge pool. Delicious à la carte breakfast, lunch and dinner are beautifully presented in the sumptuous Banyan restaurant, which is shaded by the expansive canopy of an old Banyan tree. The menu is Pacific rim inspired with the emphasis on fruit, vegetables and seafood. Picnic hampers can be delivered to guests' rooms or to a special location. Some of the Pacific's best diving, snorkeling and fishing is on the doorstep.

Our inspector loved: *This ultimate getaway for the 3 "r"s: rest, relaxation and rejunivation. Do not miss this wonderful exclusive island experience!*

NAVUTU STARS RESORT

P.O. BOX 1838, LAUTOKA

Created as an escape from the hectic pace of modern urban living, this South Pacific barefoot paradise is the ideal place to slow down and unwind. Navutu Stars Resort is tucked away on a peaceful turquoise bay on the island of Yaqeta in the Yasawa Islands. 9 spacious, open-plan bures are decorated in a fusion of Asian-Mediterranean-Fijian styles, with South-east Asian art pieces and fabrics. Bures also feature bathrooms with double stone vanities, open-plan living rooms, wet bars, C.D. players, a selection of books and an outdoor daybed for napping under the sun or stars. The spa offers a menu of treatments based on local ingredients such as algae, coconut oil and clay. Guests can snorkel right off the Navutu Stars beach, explore the reef by scuba diving or charter a boat to go island-hopping in the Yasawa archipelago; other water sports and fishing are also available on-site. Cook up your catch in a local cuisine demonstration, take part in a yoga workshop - only available in season - or attend a Lovo night with local singing and a South Pacific Kava ceremony. Italian cuisine, with a tropical twist, featuring local seafood and produce is served on the lantern and candle-lit main veranda under the stars. Guests may choose to enjoy their meal at a table on the beach or on their own private terrace.

Our inspector loved: *The blend of Italian style and sophistication with tropical resort living in a Fijian paradise.*

 9   18   SPA   

Directions: The resort can be reached by float plane, helicopter from Nadi International Airport or by luxury catamaran from Port Denerau, Nadi.

Web: www.johansens.com/navutustars
E-mail: info@navutustarsfiji.com
Tel: +679 664 0553 and +679 664 0554
Fax: +679 666 0807

Price Guide:
beachfront bures FJ$760-FJ$808
grand bures FJ$924-FJ$981

Yasawa Island Resort & Spa

P.O. BOX 10128, NADI AIRPORT, NADI

Directions: There are daily flights from Nadi Airport to Yasawa Island airfield.

Web: www.johansens.com/yasawaisland
E-mail: reservations@yasawa.com.fj
Tel: +679 672 2266
Fax: +679 672 4456

Price Guide: (including all meals, non-alcoholic beverages and selected activities, excluding tax)
rooms U.S.$900-U.S.$1,300
honeymoon suite U.S.$1,800

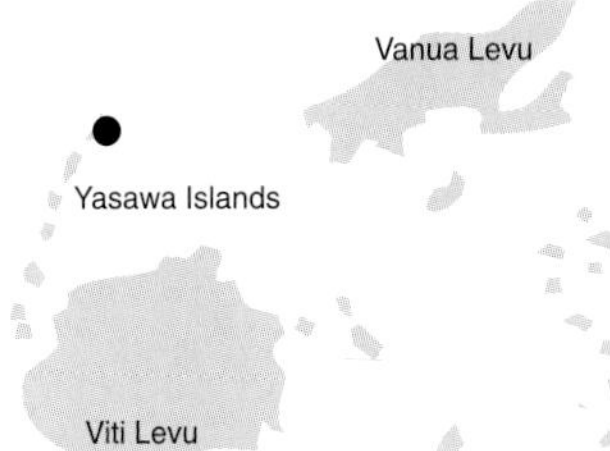

Virtually untouched and remote from the mainland, the Yasawa Islands have just 12,000 native inhabitants and are surrounded by azure blue waters, reefs and corals. Secluded and exclusive, the resort nestles on 1km of white sandy beach with a backdrop of palm trees and grass hut villages. Already established as one of the island escapes, it has recently received a $3 million upgrade, and owner Garth Downey believes it combines beauty and tranquility with the modern and romantic to offer the ultimate in luxury and pampering. Each of the air-conditioned, en-suite bures is beautifully decorated and furnished with its own separate living room and Bose system. The ultra secluded Lomalagi is recognized as the most exclusive bure in Fiji and has a private infinity lap pool and beach with an impressive split-level room. The recently opened beachfront Bavari Spa is housed beneath a thatched roof with a 180° view of the ocean and offers guests a choice of 4 different massages as well as many other treatments including bodywraps using local banana leaves. Fresh seafood is caught and served daily, with lobster available for lunch, dinner and even breakfast. With some real treasures in its cellar the resort boasts the best wine list in the Pacific. Activities include snorkeling, deep sea fishing, gourmet picnics, diving, visiting traditional villages and exploring the nearby Blue Lagoon Caves.

Our inspector loved: *The sophistication, and the new spa.*

Mini Listings Great Britain & Ireland

Condé Nast Johansens are delighted to recommend over 500 properties across Great Britain and Ireland. These properties can be found in *Recommended Hotels & Spas - GB & I 2007* and *Recommended Country Houses, Small Hotels, Inns & Restaurants - GB & I 2007.* Call TOLL FREE 1 800 564 7518 or see the Order Form on page 431 to order Guides.

Recommended Hotels & Spas Great Britain & Ireland 2007

England

The Bath Priory Hotel and Restaurant	B&NE Somerset	+44 (0)1225 331922
The Bath Spa Hotel	B&NE Somerset	+44 (0)1225 444424
Dukes Hotel	B&NE Somerset	+44 (0)1225 787960
Homewood Park	B&NE Somerset	+44 (0)1225 723731
Hunstrete House	B&NE Somerset	+44 (0)1761 490490
The Park	B&NE Somerset	+44 (0)117 937 2251
The Royal Crescent & Bath House Spa	B&NE Somerset	+44 (0)1225 823333
Moore Place Hotel	Bedfordshire	+44 (0)1908 282000
The Bear Hotel	Berkshire	+44 (0)1488 682512
Cliveden	Berkshire	+44 (0)1628 668561
The Crab at Chieveley	Berkshire	+44 (0)1635 247550
Donnington Valley Hotel & Golf Club	Berkshire	+44 (0)1635 551199
Fredrick's - Hotel Restaurant Spa	Berkshire	+44 (0)1628 581000
The French Horn	Berkshire	+44 (0)1189 692204
The Great House	Berkshire	+44 (0)118 9692277
Oakley Court Hotel	Berkshire	+44 (0)1753 609988
The Regency Park Hotel	Berkshire	+44 (0)1635 871555
The Vineyard At Stockcross	Berkshire	+44 (0)1635 528770
New Hall	Birmingham	+44 (0)121 378 2442

Danesfield House Hotel and Spa	**Buckinghamshire**	**+44 (0)1628 891010**
Hartwell House Hotel, Restaurant & Spa	Buckinghamshire	+44 (0)1296 747444
Stoke Park Club	Buckinghamshire	+44 (0)1753 717171
Hotel Felix	Cambridgeshire	+44 (0)1223 277977
The Alderley Edge Hotel	Cheshire	+44 (0)1625 583033
The Chester Grosvenor and Spa	Cheshire	+44 (0)1244 324024
Green Bough Hotel	Cheshire	+44 (0)1244 326241
Hillbark Hotel	Cheshire	+44 (0)151 625 2400
Mere Court Hotel	Cheshire	+44 (0)1565 831000
Nunsmere Hall	Cheshire	+44 (0)1606 889100
Rowton Hall Hotel, Health Club & Spa	Cheshire	+44 (0)1244 335262
Alverton Manor	Cornwall	+44 (0)1872 276633
Budock Vean - The Hotel on the River	Cornwall	+44 (0)1326 252100
Fowey Hall Hotel & Restaurant	Cornwall	+44 (0)1726 833866
The Garrack Hotel & Restaurant	Cornwall	+44 (0)1736 796199
Hell Bay	Cornwall	+44 (0)1720 422947
The Idle Rocks Hotel	Cornwall	+44 (0)1326 270771
The Lugger Hotel	Cornwall	+44 (0)1872 501322
Meudon Hotel	Cornwall	+44 (0)1326 250541
The Nare Hotel	Cornwall	+44 (0)1872 501111
The Rosevine Hotel	Cornwall	+44 (0)1872 580206
St Michael's Hotel & Spa	Cornwall	+44 (0)1326 312707
Talland Bay Hotel	Cornwall	+44 (0)1503 272667
Treglos Hotel	Cornwall	+44 (0)1841 520727
The Well House	Cornwall	+44 (0)1579 342001
Armathwaite Hall Hotel	Cumbria	+44 (0)17687 76551
Farlam Hall Hotel	Cumbria	+44 (0)16977 46234
Gilpin Lodge	Cumbria	+44 (0)15394 88818
Holbeck Ghyll Country House Hotel	Cumbria	+44 (0)15394 32375
The Inn on the Lake	Cumbria	+44 (0)17684 82444
Lakeside Hotel on Lake Windermere	Cumbria	+44 (0)15395 30001
Linthwaite House Hotel	Cumbria	+44 (0)15394 88600
The Lodore Falls Hotel	Cumbria	+44 (0)17687 77285
Lovelady Shield Country House Hotel	Cumbria	+44 (0)1434 381203
Netherwood Hotel	Cumbria	+44 (0)15395 32552
Rampsbeck Country House Hotel	Cumbria	+44 (0)17684 86442
Rothay Manor	Cumbria	+44 (0)15394 33605
Sharrow Bay Country House Hotel	Cumbria	+44 (0)17684 86301
Tufton Arms Hotel	Cumbria	+44 (0)17683 51593
Callow Hall	Derbyshire	+44 (0)1335 300900
East Lodge Country House Hotel	Derbyshire	+44 (0)1629 734474
Hassop Hall	Derbyshire	+44 (0)1629 640488
The Izaak Walton Hotel	Derbyshire	+44 (0)1335 350555
The Peacock at Rowsley	Derbyshire	+44 (0)1629 733518
Riber Hall	Derbyshire	+44 (0)1629 582795
The Arundell Arms	Devon	+44 (0)1566 784666
Bovey Castle	Devon	+44 (0)1647 445000
Buckland-Tout-Saints	Devon	+44 (0)1548 853055
Burgh Island	Devon	+44 (0)1548 810 514
Combe House Hotel & Restaurant	Devon	+44 (0)1404 540400
Gidleigh Park	Devon	+44 (0)1647 432367
The Horn of Plenty Country House Hotel & Restaurant	Devon	+44 (0)1822 832528
Hotel Riviera	Devon	+44 (0)1395 515201
Ilsington Country House Hotel	Devon	+44 (0)1364 661452
Langdon Court Hotel & Restaurant	Devon	+44 (0)1752 862358
Lewtrenchard Manor	Devon	+44 (0)1566 783222
Northcote Manor Country House Hotel	Devon	+44 (0)1769 560501
Orestone Manor & The Restaurant at Orestone Manor	Devon	+44 (0)1803 328098
The Palace Hotel	Devon	+44 (0)1803 200200
Soar Mill Cove Hotel	Devon	+44 (0)1548 561566
The Tides Reach Hotel	Devon	+44 (0)1548 843466
Watersmeet Hotel	Devon	+44 (0)1271 870333
Woolacombe Bay Hotel	Devon	+44 (0)1271 870388
Avonmouth Hotel and Restaurant	Dorset	+44 (0)1202 483434
Moonfleet Manor	Dorset	+44 (0)1305 786948
Norfolk Royale Hotel	Dorset	+44 (0)1202 551521
Plumber Manor	Dorset	+44 (0)1258 472507
The Priory Hotel	Dorset	+44 (0)1929 551666
Stock Hill Country House	Dorset	+44 (0)1747 823626
Summer Lodge Country House Hotel, Restaurant & Spa	Dorset	+44 (0)20 7589 2412
Headlam Hall	Durham	+44 (0)1325 730238
Five Lakes Hotel, Golf, Country Club & Spa	Essex	+44 (0)1621 868888
Burleigh Court	Gloucestershire	+44 (0)1453 883804
Calcot Manor Hotel & Spa	Gloucestershire	+44 (0)1666 890391
Corse Lawn House Hotel	Gloucestershire	+44 (0)1452 780479
Cotswold House Hotel	Gloucestershire	+44 (0)1386 840330
The Dial House	Gloucestershire	+44 (0)1451 822244
The Grapevine Hotel	Gloucestershire	+44 (0)1451 830344
The Greenway	Gloucestershire	+44 (0)1242 862352
The Hare and Hounds Hotel	Gloucestershire	+44 (0)1666 880233
Hotel On The Park	Gloucestershire	+44 (0)1242 518898
Lords of the Manor Hotel	Gloucestershire	+44 (0)1451 820243
Lower Slaughter Manor	Gloucestershire	+44 (0)1451 820456
The Noel Arms Hotel	Gloucestershire	+44 (0)1386 840317
The Painswick Hotel & Old Rectory Restaurant	Gloucestershire	+44 (0)1452 812160

Mini Listings Great Britain & Ireland

Condé Nast Johansens are delighted to recommend over 500 properties across Great Britain and Ireland.
These properties can be found in *Recommended Hotels & Spas - GB & I 2007* and *Recommended Country Houses, Small Hotels, Inns & Restaurants - GB & I 2007.*
Call TOLL FREE 1 800 564 7518 or see the Order Form on page 431 to order Guides.

Hotel	County	Telephone
Stonehouse Court Hotel	Gloucestershire	+44 (0)1453 794950
The Swan Hotel At Bibury	Gloucestershire	+44 (0)1285 740695
Washbourne Court Hotel	Gloucestershire	+44 (0)1451 822143
Thornbury Castle	South Gloucestershire	+44 (0)1454 281182
Audleys Wood	Hampshire	+44 (0)1256 817555
Careys Manor Hotel & Senspa	Hampshire	+44 (0)8707 512305
Chewton Glen	Hampshire	+44 (0)1425 275341
Chilworth Manor	Hampshire	+44 (0)23 8076 7333
Esseborne Manor	Hampshire	+44 (0)1264 736444
Lainston House Hotel	Hampshire	+44 (0)1962 863588
Le Poussin at Whitley Ridge	Hampshire	+44 (0)1590 622354
The Montagu Arms Hotel	Hampshire	+44 (0)1590 612324
New Park Manor & Bath House Spa	Hampshire	+44 (0)1590 623467
Passford House Hotel	Hampshire	+44 (0)1590 682398
Tylney Hall	Hampshire	+44 (0)1256 764881
Castle House	Herefordshire	+44 (0)1432 356321
Down Hall Country House Hotel	Hertfordshire	+44 (0)1279 731441
The Grove Hotel	Hertfordshire	+44 (0)1923 807807
St Michael's Manor	Hertfordshire	+44 (0)1727 864444
Sopwell House	Hertfordshire	+44 (0)1727 864477
West Lodge Park Country House Hotel	Hertfordshire	+44 (0)20 8216 3900
The Priory Bay Hotel	Isle of Wight	+44 (0)1983 613146
Eastwell Manor	Kent	+44 (0)1233 213000
The Spa	Kent	+44 (0)1892 520331
Eaves Hall	Lancashire	+44 (0)1200 425 271
The Gibbon Bridge Hotel	Lancashire	+44 (0)1995 61456
Stapleford Park Country House Hotel & Sporting Estate	Leicestershire	+44 (0)1572 787 000
41	London	+44 (0)20 7300 0041
51 Buckingham Gate	London	+44 (0)20 7769 7766
Beaufort House	London	+44 (0)20 7584 2600
Cannizaro House	London	+44 (0)208 879 1464
The Capital Hotel & Restaurant	London	+44 (0)20 7589 5171
The Cranley	London	+44 (0)20 7373 0123
Dorset Square Hotel	London	+44 (0)20 7723 7874
The Egerton House Hotel	London	+44 (0)20 7589 2412
Grim's Dyke Hotel	London	+44 (0)20 8385 3100
Hendon Hall Hotel	London	+44 (0)20 8203 3341
Jumeirah Carlton Tower	London	+44 (0)20 7235 1234
Jumeirah Lowndes Hotel	London	+44 (0)20 7823 1234
Kensington House Hotel	London	+44 (0)20 7937 2345
The Mandeville Hotel	London	+44 (0)20 7935 5599
The Mayflower Hotel	London	+44 (0)20 7370 0991
The Milestone Hotel & Apartments	London	+44 (0)20 7917 1000
The Richmond Gate Hotel and Restaurant	London	+44 (0)20 8940 0061
The Royal Park	London	+44 (0)20 7479 6600
Sofitel St James	London	+44 (0)20 7747 2200
The Sumner	London	+44 (0)20 7723 2244
Twenty Nevern Square	London	+44 (0)20 7565 9555
Etrop Grange	Greater Manchester	+44 (0)161 499 0500
Congham Hall	Norfolk	+44 (0)1485 600250
The Hoste Arms	Norfolk	+44 (0)1328 738777
Fawsley Hall	Northamptonshire	+44 (0)1327 892000
Rushton Hall	Northamptonshire	+44 (0)1536 713001
Whittlebury Hall	Northamptonshire	+44 (0)1327 857857
Marshall Meadows Country House Hotel	Northumberland	+44 (0)1289 331133
Matfen Hall	Northumberland	+44 (0)1661 886500
Tillmouth Park	Northumberland	+44 (0)1890 882255
Colwick Hall Hotel	Nottinghamshire	+44 (0)115 950 0566
Lace Market Hotel	Nottinghamshire	+44 (0)115 852 3232
Le Manoir Aux Quat' Saisons	Oxfordshire	+44 (0)1844 278881
Phyllis Court Club	Oxfordshire	+44 (0)1491 570500
The Springs Hotel & Golf Club	Oxfordshire	+44 (0)1491 836687
Weston Manor	Oxfordshire	+44 (0)1869 350621
Hambleton Hall	Rutland	+44 (0)1572 756991
Dinham Hall	Shropshire	+44 (0)1584 876464
Bindon Country House Hotel	Somerset	+44 (0)1823 400070
The Castle at Taunton	Somerset	+44 (0)1823 272671
Combe House Hotel	Somerset	+44 (0)1278 741382
Mount Somerset Country House Hotel	Somerset	+44 (0)1823 442500
Ston Easton Park	Somerset	+44 (0)1761 241631
Hoar Cross Hall Spa Resort	Staffordshire	+44 (0)1283 575671
Brudenell Hotel	Suffolk	+44 (0)1728 452071
Hintlesham Hall	Suffolk	+44 (0)1473 652334
Ravenwood Hall Country Hotel & Restaurant	Suffolk	+44 (0)1359 270345
Seckford Hall	Suffolk	+44 (0)1394 385678
The Swan Hotel	Suffolk	+44 (0)1502 722186
The Swan Hotel	Suffolk	+44 (0)1787 247477
The Westleton Crown	Suffolk	+44 (0)1728 648777
Foxhills	Surrey	+44 (0)1932 872050
Grayshott Spa	Surrey	+44 (0)1428 602020
Great Fosters	Surrey	+44 (0)1784 433822
Lythe Hill Hotel & Spa	Surrey	+44 (0)1428 651251
Pennyhill Park Hotel & The Spa	Surrey	+44 (0)1276 471774
Ashdown Park Hotel and Country Club	East Sussex	+44 (0)1342 824988
Dale Hill	East Sussex	+44 (0)1580 200112
Deans Place Hotel	East Sussex	+44 (0)1323 870248
The Grand Hotel	East Sussex	+44 (0)1323 412345
Horsted Place Country House Hotel	East Sussex	+44 (0)1825 750581
Lansdowne Place, Boutique Hotel & Spa	East Sussex	+44 (0)1273 736266
Newick Park	East Sussex	+44 (0)1825 723633
The PowderMills	East Sussex	+44 (0)1424 775511
Rye Lodge	East Sussex	+44 (0)1797 223838

▼

Hotel	County	Telephone
Amberley Castle	**West Sussex**	**+44 (0)1798 831992**
Bailiffscourt Hotel & Health Spa	West Sussex	+44 (0)1903 723511
Millstream Hotel	West Sussex	+44 (0)1243 573234
Ockenden Manor	West Sussex	+44 (0)1444 416111
The Spread Eagle Hotel & Health Spa	West Sussex	+44 (0)1730 816911
The Vermont Hotel	Tyne & Wear	+44 (0)191 233 1010
Ardencote Manor Hotel, Country Club & Spa	Warwickshire	+44 (0)1926 843111
Billesley Manor	Warwickshire	+44 (0)1789 279955
Ettington Park	Warwickshire	+44 (0)1789 450123
The Glebe at Barford	Warwickshire	+44 (0)1926 624218
Mallory Court	Warwickshire	+44 (0)1926 330214
Nailcote Hall	Warwickshire	+44 (0)2476 466174

Mini Listings Great Britain & Ireland

Condé Nast Johansens are delighted to recommend over 500 properties across Great Britain and Ireland.
These properties can be found in *Recommended Hotels & Spas - GB & I 2007* and *Recommended Country Houses, Small Hotels, Inns & Restaurants - GB & I 2007.*
Call TOLL FREE 1 800 564 7518 or see the Order Form on page 431 to order Guides.

The Shakespeare Hotel	Warwickshire	+44 (0)1789 293636
Wroxall Abbey Estate	Warwickshire	+44 (0)1926 484470
Bishopstrow House & Spa	Wiltshire	+44 (0)1985 212312
Howard's House	Wiltshire	+44 (0)1722 716392
Lucknam Park, Bath	Wiltshire	+44 (0)1225 742777
The Pear Tree At Purton	Wiltshire	+44 (0)1793 772100
Whatley Manor	Wiltshire	+44 (0)1666 822888
Woolley Grange	Wiltshire	+44 (0)1225 864705
Brockencote Hall	Worcestershire	+44 (0)1562 777876
Buckland Manor	Worcestershire	+44 (0)1386 852626
The Cottage in the Wood	Worcestershire	+44 (0)1684 575859
Dormy House	Worcestershire	+44 (0)1386 852711
The Elms	Worcestershire	+44 (0)1299 896666
The Evesham Hotel	Worcestershire	+44 (0)1386 765566
Willerby Manor Hotel	East Riding of Yorkshire	+44 (0)1482 652616
The Boar's Head Hotel	North Yorkshire	+44 (0)1423 771888
The Crown Spa Hotel	North Yorkshire	+44 (0)1723 357400
The Devonshire Arms Country House Hotel & Spa	North Yorkshire	+44 (0)1756 718111
The Feversham Arms Hotel	North Yorkshire	+44 (0)1439 770766
The Grange Hotel	North Yorkshire	+44 (0)1904 644744
Grants Hotel	North Yorkshire	+44 (0)1423 560666
Hackness Grange	North Yorkshire	+44 (0)1723 882345
Hob Green Hotel, Restaurant & Gardens	North Yorkshire	+44 (0)1423 770031
Judges Country House Hotel	North Yorkshire	+44 (0)1642 789000
Middlethorpe Hall Hotel, Restaurant & Spa	North Yorkshire	+44 (0)1904 641241
Monk Fryston Hall Hotel	North Yorkshire	+44 (0)1977 682369
The Pheasant	North Yorkshire	+44 (0)1439 771241
The Royal Hotel	North Yorkshire	+44 (0)1723 364333
Rudding Park	North Yorkshire	+44 (0)1423 871350
Simonstone Hall	North Yorkshire	+44 (0)1969 667255
The Worsley Arms Hotel	North Yorkshire	+44 (0)1653 628234
Wrea Head Country Hotel	North Yorkshire	+44 (0)1723 378211
Whitley Hall Hotel	South Yorkshire	+44 (0)114 245 4444
42 The Calls	West Yorkshire	+44 (0)113 244 0099
Holdsworth House Hotel & Restaurant	West Yorkshire	+44 (0)1422 240024

Channel Islands

The Atlantic Hotel and Ocean Restaurant	Jersey	+44 (0)1534 744101
The Club Hotel and Spa	Jersey	+44 (0)1534 876500
Longueville Manor	Jersey	+44 (0)1534 725501

Northern Ireland

Bushmills Inn Hotel	Antrim	+44 (0)28 2073 3000

Ireland

Gregans Castle	Clare	+353 65 7077005
Longueville House & Presidents' Restaurant	Cork	+353 22 47156
Harvey's Point	Donegal	+353 74 972 2208
Rathmullan House	Donegal	+353 74 915 8188
Merrion Hall Hotel	Dublin	+353 1 668 1426
The Schoolhouse Hotel	Dublin	+353 1 667 5014
Cashel House	Galway	+353 95 31001
Renvyle House Hotel	Galway	+353 95 43511
Ballygarry House	Kerry	+353 66 7123322
Cahernane House Hotel	Kerry	+353 64 31895
Park Hotel Kenmare & Sámas	Kerry	+353 64 41200
Parknasilla Hotel	Kerry	+353 1 2144800
Sheen Falls Lodge	Kerry	+353 64 41600
Killashee House Hotel & Villa Spa	Kildare	+353 45 879277
Mount Juliet Conrad	Kilkenny	+353 56 777 3000
Ashford Castle	Mayo	+353 94 95 46003
Knockranny House Hotel & Spa	Mayo	+353 98 28600
Nuremore Hotel and Country Club	Monaghan	+353 42 9661438
Marlfield House	Wexford	+353 53 94 21124

Scotland

▼

Darroch Learg	**Aberdeenshire**	**+44 (0)13397 55443**
Ardanaiseig	Argyll & Bute	+44 (0)1866 833333
Loch Melfort Hotel & Restaurant	Argyll & Bute	+44 (0)1852 200233
Kirroughtree House	Dumfries & Galloway	+44 (0)1671 402141
Channings	Edinburgh	+44 (0)131 274 7401
Le Monde Hotel	Edinburgh	+44 (0)131 270 3900
Mar Hall Hotel & Spa	Glasgow	+44 (0)141 812 9999
One Devonshire Gardens	Glasgow	+44 (0)141 3392001
Bunchrew House Hotel	Highland	+44 (0)1463 234917
Cuillin Hills Hotel	Highland	+44 (0)1478 612003
Culloden House	Highland	+44 (0)1463 790461
Drumossie Hotel	Highland	+44 (0)1463 236451
Inverlochy Castle	Highland	+44 (0)1397 702177
Loch Torridon Country House Hotel	Highland	+44 (0)1445 791242
Rocpool Reserve	Highland	+44 (0)1463 240089
Royal Marine Hotel	Highland	+44 (0)1408 621252
Dalhousie Castle and Spa	Midlothian	+44 (0)1875 820153
Ballathie House Hotel	Perth & Kinross	+44 (0)1250 883268
Cromlix House	Perth & Kinross	+44 (0)1786 822125
Kinnaird	Perth & Kinross	+44 (0)1796 482440
The Royal Hotel	Perth & Kinross	+44 (0)1764 679200
Cringletie House	Scottish Borders	+44 (0)1721 725750
Glenapp Castle	South Ayrshire	+44 (0)1465 831212

Wales

Miskin Manor Country House Hotel	Cardiff	+44 (0)1443 224204
Falcondale Mansion Hotel	Ceredigion	+44 (0)1570 422910
Bodysgallen Hall & Spa	Conwy	+44 (0)1492 584466
St Tudno Hotel & Restaurant	Conwy	+44 (0)1492 874411
Wild Pheasant Hotel	Denbighshire	+44 (0)1978 860629
Palé Hall	Gwynedd	+44 (0)1678 530285
Penmaenuchaf Hall	Gwynedd	+44 (0)1341 422129
Allt-Yr-Ynys Hotel	Monmouthshire	+44 (0)1873 890307

Mini Listings Great Britain & Ireland

Condé Nast Johansens are delighted to recommend over 500 properties across Great Britain and Ireland.
These properties can be found in *Recommended Hotels & Spas - GB & I 2007* and *Recommended Country Houses, Small Hotels, Inns & Restaurants - GB & I 2007.*
Call TOLL FREE 1 800 564 7518 or see the Order Form on page 431 to order Guides.

Property	County	Telephone
Llansantffraed Court Hotel	Monmouthshire	+44 (0)1873 840678
Lamphey Court Hotel	Pembrokeshire	+44 (0)1646 672273
Penally Abbey	Pembrokeshire	+44 (0)1834 843033
Warpool Court Hotel	Pembrokeshire	+44 (0)1437 720300
The Lake Country House and Spa	Powys	+44 (0)1591 620202
Lake Vyrnwy Hotel	Powys	+44 (0)1691 870 692
Llangoed Hall	Powys	+44 (0)1874 754525

Recommended Country Houses, Small Hotels, Inns & Restaurants Great Britain & Ireland 2007

England

Property	County	Telephone
The County Hotel	B&NE Somerset	+44 (0)1225 425003
The Ring O' Roses	B&NE Somerset	+44 (0)1761 232478
Cornfields Restaurant & Hotel	Bedfordshire	+44 (0)1234 378990
Mill House Hotel with Riverside Restaurant	Bedfordshire	+44 (0)1234 781678
Cantley House	Berkshire	+44 (0)118 978 9912
The Christopher Hotel	Berkshire	+44 (0)1753 852359
The Cottage Inn	Berkshire	+44 (0)1344 882242
The Inn on the Green, Restaurant with Rooms	Berkshire	+44 (0)1628 482638
L'ortolan Restaurant	Berkshire	+44 (0)1189 888 500
The Leatherne Bottel Riverside Restaurant	Berkshire	+44 (0)1491 872667
The Royal Oak Restaurant	Berkshire	+44 (0)1628 620541
Stirrups Country House Hotel	Berkshire	+44 (0)1344 882284
Bull & Butcher	Buckinghamshire	+44 (0)1491 638283
The Dinton Hermit	Buckinghamshire	+44 (0)1296 747473
The Ivy House	Buckinghamshire	+44 (0)1494 872184
The Tickell Arms	Cambridgeshire	+44 (0)1223 833128
Broxton Hall	Cheshire	+44 (0)1829 782321
Chandlers Waterside Apartment	Cornwall	+44 (0)1726 810800
Highland Court Lodge	Cornwall	+44 (0)1726 813320
The Hundred House Hotel & Fish in the Fountain Restaurant	Cornwall	+44 (0)1872 501336
Lower Barn	Cornwall	+44 (0)1726 844881
The Old Coastguard Hotel	Cornwall	+44 (0)1736 731222
Primrose Valley Hotel	Cornwall	+44 (0)1736 794939
Rose-In-Vale Country House Hotel	Cornwall	+44 (0)1872 552202
Tredethy House	Cornwall	+44 (0)1208 841262
Trehellas House Hotel & Restaurant	Cornwall	+44 (0)1208 72700
Trelawne Hotel - The Hutches Restaurant	Cornwall	+44 (0)1326 250226
Trevalsa Court Country House Hotel & Restaurant	Cornwall	+44 (0)1726 842468
Wisteria Lodge & Apartments	Cornwall	+44 (0)1726 810800
Broadoaks Country House	Cumbria	+44 (0)1539 445566
Crosby Lodge Country House Hotel	Cumbria	+44 (0)1228 573618
Dale Head Hall Lakeside Hotel	Cumbria	+44 (0)17687 72478
Fayrer Garden House Hotel	Cumbria	+44 (0)15394 88195
Hipping Hall	Cumbria	+44 (0)15242 71187
Lake House Hotel	Cumbria	+44 (0)15394 32360
The Leathes Head	Cumbria	+44 (0)17687 77247
Linthwaite House Hotel	Cumbria	+44 (0)15394 88600
Nent Hall Country House Hotel	Cumbria	+44 (0)1434 381584
The Pheasant	Cumbria	+44 (0)17687 76234
The Queen's Head Hotel	Cumbria	+44 (0)15394 36271
Temple Sowerby House Hotel and Restaurant	Cumbria	+44 (0)17683 61578
Underwood	Cumbria	+44 (0)1229 771116
West Vale Country House & Restaurant	Cumbria	+44 (0)1539 442 817
The Wheatsheaf @ Brigsteer	Cumbria	+44 (0)15395 68254
The Chequers Inn	Derbyshire	+44 (0)1433 630231
Dannah Farm Country House	Derbyshire	+44 (0)1773 550273
The Plough Inn	Derbyshire	+44 (0)1433 650319
The Wind in the Willows	Derbyshire	+44 (0)1457 868001
Combe House Hotel & Restaurant	Devon	+44 (0)1404 540400
Heddon's Gate Hotel	Devon	+44 (0)1598 763481
Hewitt's - Villa Spaldi	Devon	+44 (0)1598 752293
Home Farm Hotel	Devon	+44 (0)1404 831278
Ilsington Country House Hotel	Devon	+44 (0)1364 661452
Kingston House	Devon	+44 (0)1803 762 235
Lydford House	Devon	+44 (0)1822 820347
Mill End	Devon	+44 (0)1647 432282
The New Inn	Devon	+44 (0)1363 84242
Yeoldon House Hotel	Devon	+44 (0)1237 474400
The Bridge House Hotel	Dorset	+44 (0)1308 862200
The Grange at Oborne	Dorset	+44 (0)1935 813463
La Fleur de Lys	Dorset	+44 (0)1747 853717
Yalbury Cottage	Dorset	+44 (0)1305 262382
The Crown House	Essex	+44 (0)1799 530515
The Pump House Apartment	Essex	+44 (0)1277 656579
Bibury Court	Gloucestershire	+44 (0)1285 740337
Charlton Kings Hotel	Gloucestershire	+44 (0)1242 231061
Lower Brook House	Gloucestershire	+44 (0)1386 700286
Lypiatt House	Gloucestershire	+44 (0)1242 224994
The Malt House	Gloucestershire	+44 (0)1386 840295
Three Choirs Vineyards Estate	Gloucestershire	+44 (0)1531 890223
The Wild Duck Inn	Gloucestershire	+44 (0)1285 770310
Langrish House	Hampshire	+44 (0)1730 266941
The Mill At Gordleton	Hampshire	+44 (0)1590 682219
The Nurse's Cottage	Hampshire	+44 (0)1590 683402
Aylestone Court	Herefordshire	+44 (0)1432 341891
Ford Abbey	Herefordshire	+44 (0)1568 760700
Glewstone Court	Herefordshire	+44 (0)1989 770367
Moccas Court	Herefordshire	+44 (0)1981 500 019
Seven Ledbury	Herefordshire	+44 (0)1531 631317
The Swan at Hay	Herefordshire	+44 (0)1497 821188
The Verzon	Herefordshire	+44 (0)1531 670381
Wilton Court Hotel	Herefordshire	+44 (0)1989 562569
Redcoats Farmhouse Hotel and Restaurant	Hertfordshire	+44 (0)1438 729500
The White House and Lion & Lamb Bar & Restaurant	Hertfordshire	+44 (0)1279 870257
The Hambrough	Isle of Wight	+44 (0)1983 856333
Koala Cottage	Isle of Wight	+44 (0)1983 842031
Rylstone Manor	Isle of Wight	+44 (0)1983 862806
Winterbourne Country House	Isle of Wight	+44 (0)1983 852535
Little Silver Country Hotel	Kent	+44 (0)1233 850321
Romney Bay House Hotel	Kent	+44 (0)1797 364747
Wallett's Court Hotel & Spa	Kent	+44 (0)1304 852424
Ferrari's Restaurant & Hotel	Lancashire	+44 (0)1772 783148
The Inn at Whitewell	Lancashire	+44 (0)1200 448222
Springfield House Hotel	Lancashire	+44 (0)1253 790301
Tree Tops Country House Restaurant & Hotel	Lancashire	+44 (0)1704 572430
Horse & Trumpet	Leicestershire	+44 (0)1858 565000
Sysonby Knoll Hotel	Leicestershire	+44 (0)1664 563563
Bailhouse Hotel	Lincolnshire	+44 (0)1522 520883
The Crown Hotel	Lincolnshire	+44 (0)1780 763136
The Dower House Hotel	Lincolnshire	+44 (0)1526 352588
Washingborough Hall	Lincolnshire	+44 (0)1522 790340
Beechwood Hotel	Norfolk	+44 (0)1692 403231
Broom Hall Country Hotel	Norfolk	+44 (0)1953 882125
Brovey Lair	Norfolk	+44 (0)1953 882706
Elderton Lodge Hotel & Langtry Restaurant	Norfolk	+44 (0)1263 833547
The Gin Trap Inn	Norfolk	+44 (0)1485 525264
The Great Escape Holiday Company	Norfolk	+44 (0)1485 518717
Idyllic Cottages At Vere Lodge	Norfolk	+44 (0)1328 838261
The Kings Head Hotel	Norfolk	+44 (0)1485 578 265

Mini Listings Great Britain & Ireland

Condé Nast Johansens are delighted to recommend over 500 properties across Great Britain and Ireland.
These properties can be found in *Recommended Hotels & Spas - GB & I 2007* and *Recommended Country Houses, Small Hotels, Inns & Restaurants - GB & I 2007.*
Call TOLL FREE 1 800 564 7518 or see the Order Form on page 431 to order Guides.

The Neptune Inn & Restaurant	Norfolk	+44 (0)1485 532122
The Old Rectory	Norfolk	+44 (0)1603 700772
The Stower Grange	Norfolk	+44 (0)1603 860210
The Falcon Hotel	Northamptonshire	+44 (0)1604 696200
The New French Partridge	Northamptonshire	+44 (0)1604 870033
The Windmill at Badby	Northamptonshire	+44 (0)1327 702363
Waren House Hotel	Northumberland	+44 (0)1668 214581
Cockliffe Country House Hotel	Nottinghamshire	+44 (0)1159 680179
Langar Hall	Nottinghamshire	+44 (0)1949 860559
Restaurant Sat Bains with Rooms	Nottinghamshire	+44 (0)115 986 6566
Burford Lodge Hotel & Restaurant	Oxfordshire	+44 (0)1993 823354
The Dashwood Hotel & Restaurant	Oxfordshire	+44 (0)1869 352707
Duke Of Marlborough Country Inn	Oxfordshire	+44 (0)1993 811460
Fallowfields	Oxfordshire	+44 (0)1865 820416
The Feathers	Oxfordshire	+44 (0)1993 812291
The Jersey Arms	Oxfordshire	+44 (0)1869 343234
The Kings Head Inn & Restaurant	Oxfordshire	+44 (0)1608 658365
The Lamb Inn	Oxfordshire	+44 (0)1993 823155
The Plough Hotel, Game & Seafood Restaurant	Oxfordshire	+44 (0)1367 810222
The Spread Eagle Hotel	Oxfordshire	+44 (0)1844 213661
Barnsdale Lodge	Rutland	+44 (0)1572 724678
The Lake Isle Restaurant & Townhouse Hotel	Rutland	+44 (0)1572 822951
Pen-Y-Dyffryn Country Hotel	Shropshire	+44 (0)1691 653700
Soulton Hall	Shropshire	+44 (0)1939 232786
Ashwick Country House Hotel	Somerset	+44 (0)1398 323868
Bellplot House Hotel & Thomas's Restaurant	Somerset	+44 (0)1460 62600
Beryl	Somerset	+44 (0)1749 678738
Compton House	Somerset	+44 (0)1934 733944
Farthings Country House Hotel & Restaurant	Somerset	+44 (0)1823 480664
Glencot House	Somerset	+44 (0)1749 677160
Karslake Country House & Restaurant	Somerset	+44 (0)1643 851242
Three Acres Country House	Somerset	+44 (0)1398 323730
Clarice House	Suffolk	+44 (0)1284 705550
The Ickworth Hotel and Apartments	Suffolk	+44 (0)1284 735350
Chase Lodge	Surrey	+44 (0)20 8943 1862
Great Tangley Manor	Surrey	+44 (0)20 7526 4852
The Hope Anchor Hotel	East Sussex	+44 (0)1797 222216
Crouchers Country Hotel & Restaurant	West Sussex	+44 (0)1243 784995
The Mill House Hotel	West Sussex	+44 (0)1903 892426
Nuthurst Grange	Warwickshire	+44 (0)1564 783972
Beechfield House	Wiltshire	+44 (0)1225 703700
The George Inn	Wiltshire	+44 (0)1985 840396
The Lamb at Hindon	Wiltshire	+44 (0)1747 820 573
The Old Manor Hotel	Wiltshire	+44 (0)1225 777393
Stanton Manor Hotel & Gallery Restaurant	Wiltshire	+44 (0)1666 837552
Widbrook Grange	Wiltshire	+44 (0)1225 864750
The Broadway Hotel	Worcestershire	+44 (0)1386 852401
Colwall Park	Worcestershire	+44 (0)1684 540000
The Old Rectory	Worcestershire	+44 (0)1527 523000
The Peacock Inn	Worcestershire	+44 (0)1584 810506
The White Lion Hotel	Worcestershire	+44 (0)1684 592551
The Austwick Traddock	North Yorkshire	+44 (0)15242 51224
The Devonshire Fell	North Yorkshire	+44 (0)1756 729111
Dunsley Hall	North Yorkshire	+44 (0)1947 893437
Hob Green Hotel, Restaurant & Gardens	North Yorkshire	+44 (0)1423 770031
The Red Lion	North Yorkshire	+44 (0)1756 720204
Stow House Hotel	North Yorkshire	+44 (0)1969 663635
The Wensleydale Heifer	North Yorkshire	+44 (0)1969 622322
Hey Green Country House Hotel	West Yorkshire	+44 (0)1484 844235

Channel Islands

La Sablonnerie	Guernsey	+44 (0)1481 832061
The White House	Guernsey	+44 (0)1481 722159

Ireland

St Clerans Manor House	Galway	+353 91 846 555
Brook Lane Hotel	Kerry	+353 64 42077
Coopershill House	Sligo	+353 71 9165108

Scotland

Castleton House Hotel	Angus	+44 (0)1307 840340
Highland Cottage	Argyll & bute	+44 (0)1688 302030
Balcary Bay Hotel	Dumfries & Galloway	+44 (0)1556 640217
The Peat Inn	Fife	+44 (0)1334 840206
The Bridge Hotel	Highland	+44 (0)1431 821100
Corriegour Lodge Hotel	Highland	+44 (0)1397 712685

Dunain Park Hotel	**Highland**	**+44 (0)1463 230512**
Forss House Hotel	Highland	+44 (0)1847 861201
Greshornish House Hotel	Highland	+44 (0)1470 582266
Hotel Eilean Iarmain	Highland	+44 (0)1471 833332
Ruddyglow Park	Highland	+44 (0)1571 822216
The Steadings at The Grouse & Trout	Highland	+44 (0)1808 521314
Toravaig House	Highland	+44 (0)1471 833231
Knockomie Hotel	Moray	+44 (0)1309 673146
Cairn Lodge Hotel	Perth & Kinross	+44 (0)1764 662634
The Four Seasons Hotel	Perth & Kinross	+44 (0)1764 685 333
Castle Venlaw	Scottish Borders	+44 (0)1721 720384
Culzean Castle - The Eisenhower Apartment	South Ayrshire	+44 (0)1655 884455
Amhuinnsuidhe Castle	Western Isles	+44 (0)1859 560200

Wales

The Inn at the Elm Tree	Cardiff	+44 (0)1633 680225
Ty Mawr Country Hotel	Carmarthenshire	+44 (0)1267 202332
Conrah Country House Hotel	Ceredigion	+44 (0)1970 617941
Sychnant Pass House	Conwy	+44 (0)1492 596868
Tan-Y-Foel Country House	Conwy	+44 (0)1690 710507
Egerton Grey	Glamorgan	+44 (0)1446 711666
Bae Abermaw	Gwynedd	+44 (0)1341 280550
Hotel Maes-Y-Neuadd	Gwynedd	+44 (0)1766 780200
Plas Dolmelynllyn	Gwynedd	+44 (0)1341 440273
Porth Tocyn Country House Hotel	Gwynedd	+44 (0)1758 713303
The Bell At Skenfrith	Monmouthshire	+44 (0)1600 750235
The Crown At Whitebrook	Monmouthshire	+44 (0)1600 860254
Wolfscastle Country Hotel & Restaurant	Pembrokeshire	+44 (0)1437 741225
Glangrwyney Court	Powys	+44 (0)1873 811288

Historic Houses, Castles & Gardens

Incorporating Museums & Galleries

We are pleased to feature over 140 places to visit during your stay at a Condé Nast Johansens recommended hotel.

England

Bedfordshire

▼

Woburn Abbey - Woburn, Bedfordshire MK17 9WA. Tel: 01525 290333

Berkshire

Mapledurham House - The Estate Office, Mapledurham, Reading, Berkshire RG4 7TR. Tel: 01189 723350

Buckinghamshire

Doddershall Park - Quainton, Aylesbury, Buckinghamshire HP22 4DF. Tel: 01296 655238

Nether Winchendon Mill - Nr Aylesbury, Buckinghamshire HP18 0DY. Tel: 01844 290199

Stowe Landscape Gardens - Stowe, Buckingham, Buckinghamshire MK18 5EH. Tel: 01280 822850

Waddesdon Manor - Waddesdon, Nr Aylesbury, Buckinghamshire HP18 0JH. Tel: 01296 653226

Cambridgeshire

The Manor - Hemingford Grey, Huntingdon, Cambridgeshire PE28 9BN. Tel: 01480 463134

Oliver Cromwell's House - 29 St Mary's Street, Ely, Cambridgeshire CB7 4HF. Tel: 01353 662062

Cheshire

Arley Hall & Gardens - Arley, Northwich, Cheshire CW9 6NA. Tel: 01565 777353

Dorfold Hall - Nantwich, Cheshire CW5 8LD. Tel: 01270 625245

Rode Hall and Gardens - Rode Hall, Scholar Green, Cheshire ST7 3QP. Tel: 01270 873237

Co Durham

The Bowes Museum - Barnard Castle, Co Durham DL12 8NP. Tel: 01833 690606

Raby Castle - Staindrop, Darlington, Co Durham DL2 3AH. Tel: 01833 660202

Cumbria

Isel Hall - Cockermouth, Cumbria CA13 0QG.

Muncaster Castle , Gardens & Owl Centre- Ravenglass, Cumbria CA18 1RQ. Tel: 01229 717614

Derbyshire

Haddon Hall - Bakewell, Derbyshire DE45 1LA. Tel: 01629 812855

Melbourne Hall & Gardens - Melbourne, Derbyshire DE73 8EN. Tel: 01332 862502

Renishaw Hall Gardens - Renishaw, Nr Sheffield, Derbyshire S21 3WB. Tel: 01246 432310

Devon

Bowringsleigh - Kingbridge, Devon TQ7 3LL. Tel: 01548 852014

Downes Estate at Crediton - Devon EX17 3PL. Tel: 01392 439046

Dorset

Moignes Court - Moreton Road, Owermoigne, Dorchester, Dorset DT2 8HY. Tel: 01305 853 300

Essex

The Gardens of Easton Lodge - Warwick House, Easton Lodge, Gt Dumnow, Essex CM6 2BB. Tel: 01371 876979

Ingatestone Hall - Hall Lane, Ingatestone, Essex CM4 9NR. Tel: 01277 353010

Gloucestershire

Cheltenham Art Gallery & Museum - Clarence Street, Cheltenham, Gloucestershire GL50 3JT. Tel: 01242 237431

Hardwicke Court - Nr Gloucester, Gloucestershire GL2 4RS. Tel: 01452 720212

Mill Dene Garden - Blockley, Moreton-in-Marsh, Gloucestershire GL56 9HU. Tel: 01386 700 457

Sezincote - Nr Moreton-in-Marsh, Gloucestershire GL56 9AW. Tel: 01386 700444

Hampshire

Beaulieu - John Montagu Building, Beaulieu, Hampshire SO42 7ZN. Tel: 01590 612345

Beaulieu Vineyard and Estate - Beaulieu Estate, John Montagu Building, Beaulieu, Hampshire SO42 7ZN. Tel: 01590 612345

Gilbert White's House and The Oates Museum - Selborne, Nr Alton, Hampshire GU34 3JH. Tel: 01420 511275

Greywell Hill House - Greywell, Hook, Hampshire RG29 1DG. Tel: 01256 703565

Pylewell House - South Baddesley, Lymington, Hampshire SO41 5SJ. Tel: 01725 513004

Herefordshire

Kentchurch Court - Kentchurch, Nr Pontrilas, Hereford, Herefordshire HR2 0DB. Tel: 01981 240228

Hertfordshire

Ashridge - Ringshall, Berkhamsted, Hertfordshire HP4 1NS. Tel: 01442 841027

Hatfield House, Park & Gardens - Hatfield, Hertfordshire AL9 5NQ. Tel: 01707 287010

Isle of Wight

Deacons Nursery - Moor View, Godshill, Isle of Wight PO38 3HW. Tel: 01983 840750

Kent

Belmont House and Gardens - Belmont Park, Throwley, Nr Faversham, Kent ME13 0HH. Tel: 01795 890202

Cobham Hall - Cobham, Kent DA12 3BL. Tel: 01474 823371

Groombridge Place Gardens - Groombridge, Tunbridge Wells, Kent TN3 9QG. Tel: 01892 861444

Hever Castle & Gardens - Hever, Nr Edenbridge, Kent TN8 7NG. Tel: 01732 865224

Knole - Sevenoaks, Kent TN15 0RP. Tel: 01732 462100

Marle Place Gardens and Gallery - Marle Place Road, Brenchley, Nr Tonbridge, Kent TN12 7HS. Tel: 01892 722304

Mount Ephraim Gardens - Hernhill, Nr Faversham, Kent ME13 9TX. Tel: 01227 751496

The New College of Cobham - Cobhambury Road, Cobham, Nr Gravesend, Kent DA12 3BG. Tel: 01474 814280

Penshurst Place & Gardens - Penshurst, Nr Tonbridge, Kent TN11 8DG. Tel: 01892 870307

Lancashire

Stonyhurst College - Stonyhurst, Clitheroe, Lancashire BB7 9PZ. Tel: 01254 827084/826345

Townhead House - Slaidburn, Via CLitheroe, Lancashire BBY 3AG. Tel: 01772 421566

London

Dulwich Picture Gallery - Gallery Road, London SE21 7AD. Tel: 020 8299 8711

Handel House Museum - 25 Brook Street, London W1K 4HB. Tel: 020 7495 1685

Pitzhanger Manor House and Gallery - Walpole Park, Mattock Lane, Ealing, London W5 5EQ. Tel: 020 8567 1227

Sir John Soane's Museum - 13 Lincoln's Inn Fields, London WC2A 3BP. Tel: 020 7405 2107

Merseyside

Knowsley Hall - Knowsley Park, Prescot, Merseyside L32 4AG. Tel: 0151 489 4827

Historic Houses, Castles & Gardens

Incorporating Museums & Galleries

www.historichouses.co.uk

Middlesex

Syon House - Syon Park, London Road, Brentford, Middlesex TW8 8JF. Tel: 020 8560 0882

Norfolk

Fairhaven Woodland and Water Garden - School Road, South Walsham, Norwich, Norfolk NR13 6EA. Tel: 01603 270449

Walsingham Abbey Grounds - , Walsingham, Norfolk NR22 6BP. Tel: 01328 820259

Northamptonshire

Cottesbrooke Hall and Gardens - Cottesbrooke, Northampton, Northamptonshire NN6 8PF. Tel: 01604 505808

Haddonstone Show Garden - The Forge House, Church Lane, East Haddon, Northamptonshire NN6 8DB. Tel: 01604 770711

Northumberland

Chillingham Castle - Nr Wooler, Northumberland NE66 5NJ. Tel: 01668 215359

Chipchase Castle - Chipchase, Wark on Tyne, Hexham, Northumberland NE48 3NT. Tel: 01434 230203

Seaton Delaval Hall - Seaton Sluice, Whitley Bay, Northumberland NE26 4QR. Tel: 0191 237 1493 / 0786

Nottinghamshire

Newstead Abbey - Ravenshead, Nottinghamshire NG15 8NA. Tel: 01623 455 900

Oxfordshire

Blenheim Palace - Woodstock, Oxfordshire OX20 1PX. Tel: 08700 602080

Kingston Bagpuize House - Kingston Bagpuize, Abingdon, Oxfordshire OX13 5AX. Tel: 01865 820259

Sulgrave Manor - Manor Road, Sulgrave, Banbury, Oxfordshire OX17 2SD. Tel: 01295 760205

Wallingford Castle Gardens - Castle Street, Wallingford, Oxfordshire OX10 0AL. Tel: 01491 835373

Shropshire

Shipton Hall - Shipton, Much Wenlock, Shropshire TF13 6JZ. Tel: 01746 785225

Weston Park - Weston-under-Lizard, Nr Shifnal, Shropshire TF11 8LE. Tel: 01952 852100

Somerset

The American Museum in Britain - Claverton Manor, Bath, Somerset BA2 7BD. Tel: 01225 460503

Cothay Manor & Gardens - Greenham, Wellington, Somerset TA21 0JR. Tel: 01823 672283

Great House Farm - Wells Road, Theale, Wedmore, Somerset BS28 4SJ. Tel: 01934 713133

Number 1 Royal Crescent - 1 Royal Crescent, Bath, Somerset BA1 2LR. Tel: 01225 428126

Staffordshire

The Ancient High House - Greengate Street, Stafford, Staffordshire ST16 2JA. Tel: 01785 619131

Izaak Walton's Cottage - Shallowford, nr. Stafford, Staffordshire ST15 0PA. Tel: 01785 760 278

Stafford Castle - Newport Road, Stafford, Staffordshire ST16 1DJ. Tel: 01785 257 698

Whitmore Hall - Whitmore, Newcastle-under-Lyme, Staffordshire ST5 5HW. Tel: 01782 680478

Suffolk

Kentwell Hall - Long Melford, Sudbury, Suffolk CO10 9BA. Tel: 01787 310207

Newbourne Hall - Newbourne, Nr. Woodbridge, Suffolk IP12 4NP. Tel: 01473 736277

Otley Hall - Hall Lane, Otley, Suffolk IP6 9PA. Tel: 01473 890264

Surrey

Claremont House - Claremont Drive, Esher, Surrey KT10 9LY. Tel: 01372 473623

Guildford House Gallery - 155, High Street, Guildford, Surrey GU1 3AJ. Tel: 01483 444740

Loseley Park - Guildford, Surrey GU3 1HS. Tel: 01483 304440

Painshill Park - Portsmouth Road, Cobham, Surrey KT11 1JE. Tel: 01932 868113

East Sussex

Bentley Wildfowl & Motor Museum - Halland, Nr Lewes, Sussex BN8 5AF. Tel: 01825 840573

Charleston - Firle, Lewes, East Sussex BN8 6LL. Tel: 01323 811626

Firle Place - Firle, Nr Lewes, East Sussex BN8 6LP. Tel: 01273 858307

Garden and Grounds of Herstmonceux Castle - Herstmonceux Castle, Hailsham, East Sussex BN27 1RN. Tel: 01323 833816

Merriments Gardens - Hurst Green, East Sussex TN19 7RA. Tel: 01580 860666

Preston Manor - Preston Drove, Brighton, East Sussex BN1 6SD. Tel: 01273 292770

Royal Pavilion - Brighton, East Sussex BN1 1EE. Tel: 01273 290900

West Sussex

Denmans Garden - Clock House, Denmans Lane, Fontwell, West Sussex BN18 0SU. Tel: 01243 542808

Goodwood House - Goodwood, Chichester, West Sussex PO18 0PX. Tel: 01243 755000

High Beeches Gardens - High Beeches, Handcross, West Sussex RH17 6HQ. Tel: 01444 400589

Leonardslee - Lakes & Gardens - Lower Beeding, Horsham, West Sussex RH13 6PP. Tel: 01403 891212

Uppark - South Harting, Petersfield, West Sussex GU31 5QR. Tel: 01730 825415

West Dean Gardens - West Dean , Chichester, West Sussex PO18 0QZ. Tel: 01243 818210

Worthing Museum & Art Gallery - Chapel Road, Worthing, West Sussex BN11 1HP. Tel: 01903 239999

Warwickshire

Arbury Hall - Nuneaton, Warwickshire CV10 7PT. Tel: 024 7638 2804

The Shakespeare Houses - The Shakespeare Birthplace Trust, The Shakespeare Centre, Henley Street, Stratford-upon-Avon, Warwickshire CV37 6QW. Tel: 01789 201845

West Midlands

Barber Institute of Fine Arts - The University of Birmingham, Edgbaston, Birmingham, West Midlands B15 2TS. Tel: 0121 414 7333

The Birmingham Botanical Gardens and Glasshouses - Westbourne Road, Edgbaston, Birmingham, West Midlands B15 3TR. Tel: 0121 454 1860

Wiltshire

▼

Salisbury Cathedral - Visitor Services, 33 The Close, Salisbury, Wiltshire SP1 2EJ. Tel: 01722 555120

Worcestershire

Harvington Hall - Harvington, Kidderminister, Worcestershire DY10 4LR. Tel: 01562 777846

Little Malvern Court - Nr Malvern, Worcestershire WR14 4JN. Tel: 01684 892988

Spetchley Park Gardens - Spetchley, Worcester, Worcestershire WR5 1RS. Tel: 01453 810303

East Riding of Yorkshire

Burton Agnes Hall & Gardens - Burton Agnes, Driffield, East Yorkshire YO25 4NB. Tel: 01262 490324

HISTORIC HOUSES, CASTLES & GARDENS

Incorporating Museums & Galleries

www.historichouses.co.uk

North Yorkshire

Duncombe Park - Helmsley, York, North Yorkshire YO62 5EB. Tel: 01439 770213

The Forbidden Corner - Tupgill Park Estate, Coverham, Nr Middleham, North Yorkshire DL8 4TJ. Tel: 01969 640638

Fountains Abbey & Studley Royal - Ripon, North Yorkshire HG4 3DY. Tel: 01765 608888

Norton Conyers - Wath, Nr Ripon, North Yorkshire HG4 5EQ. Tel: 01765 640333

Ripley Castle - Ripley Castle Estate, Harrogate, North Yorkshire HG3 3AY. Tel: 01423 770152

Skipton Castle - Skipton, North Yorkshire BD23 1AW. Tel: 01756 792442

West Yorkshire

Bramham Park - Bramham, Wetherby, West Yorkshire LS23 6ND. Tel: 01937 846000

Harewood House - Harewood, Leeds, West Yorkshire LS17 9LG. Tel: 0113 218 1010

Ledston Hall - Hall Lane, Ledstone, Castleford, West Yorkshire WF10 2BB. Tel: 01423 523 423

Northern Ireland

Co Down

Seaforde Gardens - Seaforde, Downpatrick, Co Down BT30 8PG. Tel: 028 4481 1225

Ireland

Co Cork

Bantry House & Gardens - Bantry, Co Cork. Tel: 00 353 2 750 047

Co Dublin

Ardgillan Castle - Balbriggan, Co Dublin. Tel: 00 353 1 849 2212

Co Kildare

The Irish National Stud, Garden & House Museum - Tully, Kildare Town, Co Kildare. Tel: 00 353 45 521617

Co Offaly

Birr Castle Demesne & Ireland's Historic Science Centre - Birr, Co Offaly. Tel: 00 353 57 91 20336

Co Waterford

Lismore Castle Gardens - Lismore, Co Waterford. Tel: 00 353 58 54424

Co Wexford

Kilmokea Country Manor & Gardens - Great Island, Campile, Co Wexford. Tel: 00 353 51 388109

Co Wicklow

Mount Usher Gardens - Ashford, Co Wicklow. Tel: +353 404 40205

Scotland

Argyll

Inveraray Castle - Inveraray, Argyll PA32 8XE. Tel: 01499 302203

Ayrshire

Kelburn Castle and Country Centre - South Offices, Kelburn, Fairlie, Ayrshire KA29 0BE. Tel: 01475 568685

Dumfries

Drumlanrig Castle, Gardens and Country Park - Thornhill, Dumfries DG3 4AQ. Tel: 01848 330248

Orkney Islands

Balfour Castle - Shapinsay, Orkney Islands KW17 2DY. Tel: 01856 711282

Peebles

Traquair House - Innerleithen, Peebles EH44 6PW. Tel: 01896 830323

Perthshire

Scone Palace - Perth, Perthshire PH2 6BD. Tel: 01738 552300

Scottish Borders

Bowhill House & Country Park - Bowhill, Selkirk, Scottish Borders TD7 5ET. Tel: 01750 22204

Manderston - Duns, Berwickshire, Scottish Borders TD11 3PP. Tel: 01361 882636

Strathclyde

Mount Stuart - Isle of Bute, Strathclyde PA20 9LR. Tel: 01700 503877

West Lothian

Hopetoun House - South Queensferry, Nr Edinburgh West Lothian EH30 9SL. Tel: 0131 331 2451

Newliston - Kirkliston, West Lothian EH29 9EB. Tel: 0131 333 3231

Wigtownshire

Ardwell Estate Gardens - Ardwell House, Stranraer DG9 9LY. Tel: 01776 860227

Wales

Conway

Bodnant Garden - Tal-y-Cafn, Nr Colwyn Bay, Conway LL28 5RE. Tel: 01492 650460

Dyfed

Pembroke Castle - Pembroke, Dyfed SA71 4LA. Tel: 01646 681510

Flintshire

Golden Grove - Llanasa, Nr. Holywell, Flintshire CH8 9NA. Tel: 01745 854452

Gwynedd

Plas Brondanw Gardens - Menna Angharad, Plas Brondanw, Llanfrothen, Gwynedd LL48 6SW. Tel: 01766 770484

Monmouthshire

Usk Castle - Castle House, Monmouth Road, Usk, Monmouthshire NP15 1SD. Tel: 01291 672563

Pembrokeshire

St Davids Cathedral - The Close, St. David's, Pembrokeshire SA62 6RH. Tel: 01437 720199

France

Château de Chenonceau - Chenonceaux, 37150. Tel: 00 33 2 47 23 90 07

Château de Thoiry - Thoiry, Yvelines 78770 . Tel: 00 33 1 34 87 53 65

Mini Listings Europe

Condé Nast Johansens are delighted to recommend 435 properties across Europe & The Mediterranean.

Call 1 800 564 7518 or see the Order Form on page 431 to order Guides.

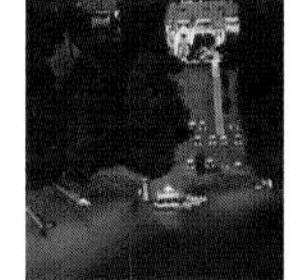

AUSTRIA / KÄRNTEN (VELDEN)

Seeschlössl Velden

Klagenfurter Strasse 34, 9220 Velden, Austria
Tel: +43 4274 2824
Fax: +43 4274 2824 44
Web: www.johansens.com/seeschlosslvelden

BELGIUM (ANTWERP)

Firean Hotel

Karel Oomsstraat 6, 2018 Antwerp, Belgium
Tel: +32 3 237 02 60
Fax: +32 3 238 11 68
Web: www.johansens.com/firean

BELGIUM (AS)

Hostellerie Mardaga

121 Stationsstraat, 3665 As, Belgium
Tel: +32 89 65 62 65
Fax: +32 8965 62 66
Web: www.johansens.com/mardaga

BELGIUM (BRUGES)

Hotel Die Swaene

1 Steenhouwersdijk (Groene Rei), 8000 Bruges, Belgium
Tel: +32 50 34 27 98
Fax: +32 50 33 66 74
Web: www.johansens.com/swaene

BELGIUM (KNOKKE~HEIST)

Romantik Hotel Manoir du Dragon

Albertlaan 73, 8300 Knokke~Heist, Belgium
Tel: +32 50 63 05 80
Fax: +32 50 63 05 90
Web: www.johansens.com/dudragon

BELGIUM (KORTRIJK)

Grand Hotel Damier

Grote Markt 41, 8500 Kortrijk, Belgium
Tel: +32 56 22 15 47
Fax: +32 56 22 86 31
Web: www.johansens.com/damier

BELGIUM (TURNHOUT)

Hostellerie Ter Driezen

18 Herentalsstraat, 2300 Turnhout, Belgium
Tel: +32 14 41 87 57
Fax: +32 14 42 03 10
Web: www.johansens.com/terdriezen

CROATIA (DUBROVNIK)

Grand Villa Argentina

Frana Supila 14, 20000 Dubrovnik, Croatia
Tel: +385 20 44 0555
Fax: +385 20 43 2524
Web: www.johansens.com/grandvillaargentina

CROATIA (TROGIR)

Villa Lavandula

Put Salduna 3, 21220 Trogir, Croatia
Tel: +385 21 798 330
Fax: +385 21 798 331
Web: www.johansens.com/lavandula

CZECH REPUBLIC (PRAGUE)

Alchymist Grand Hotel and Spa

Trziste 19, Malá Strana, 11800 Prague, Czech Republic
Tel: +420 257 286 011/016
Fax: +420 257 286 017
Web: www.johansens.com/alchymist

CZECH REPUBLIC (PRAGUE)

Aria Hotel Prague

Trziste 9, 118 00 Prague 1, Czech Republic
Tel: +420 225 334 111
Fax: +420 225 334 666
Web: www.johansens.com/aria

CZECH REPUBLIC (PRAGUE)

Art Hotel Prague

Nad Královskou Oborou 53, 170 00 Prague 7, Czech Republic
Tel: +420 233 101 331
Fax: +420 233 101 311
Web: www.johansens.com/arthotel

CZECH REPUBLIC (PRAGUE)

Bellagio Hotel Prague

U Milosrdnych 2, 110 00 Prague 1, Czech Republic
Tel: +420 221 778 999
Fax: +420 221 778 900
Web: www.johansens.com/bellagio

CZECH REPUBLIC (PRAGUE)

Golden Well Hotel

U Zlaté studne 166/4, 118 00 Prague 1, Czech Republic
Tel: +420 257 011 213
Fax: +420 257 533 320
Web: www.johansens.com/zlatestudna

CZECH REPUBLIC (PRAGUE)

Hotel Hoffmeister & Lily Wellness and Spa

Pod Bruskou 7, Malá Strana, 11800 Prague 1, Czech Republic
Tel: +420 251 017 111
Fax: +420 251 017 120
Web: www.johansens.com/hoffmeister

CZECH REPUBLIC (PRAGUE)

Nosticova Residence

Nosticova 1, Malá Strana, 11800 Prague, Czech Republic
Tel: +420 257 312 513/516
Fax: +420 257 312 517
Web: www.johansens.com/nosticova

CZECH REPUBLIC (PRAGUE)

Romantik Hotel U Raka

Cernínská 10/93, 11800 Prague 1, Czech Republic
Tel: +420 2205 111 00
Fax: +420 2333 580 41
Web: www.johansens.com/uraka

ESTONIA (PÄRNU)

Ammende Villa

Mere Pst 7, 80010 Pärnu, Estonia
Tel: +372 44 73 888
Fax: +372 44 73 887
Web: www.johansens.com/villaammende

FRANCE / ALSACE~LORRAINE (COLMAR)

Hôtel Les Têtes

19 Rue des Têtes, BP 69, 68000 Colmar, France
Tel: +33 3 89 24 43 43
Fax: +33 3 89 24 58 34
Web: www.johansens.com/lestetes

FRANCE / ALSACE~LORRAINE (COLMAR)

Romantik Hotel le Maréchal

4 Place Six Montagnes Noires, Petite Venise, 68000 Colmar, France
Tel: +33 3 89 41 60 32
Fax: +33 3 89 24 59 40
Web: www.johansens.com/marechal

FRANCE / ALSACE~LORRAINE (CONDÉ NORTHEN)

Domaine de la Grange de Condé

41 rue des Deux Nied, 57220 Condé Northen, France
Tel: +33 3 87 79 30 50
Fax: +33 3 87 79 30 51
Web: www.johansens.com/grangedeconde

FRANCE / ALSACE~LORRAINE (GÉRARDMER – VOSGES)

Hostellerie les Bas Rupts Le Chalet Fleuri

181 Route de la Bresse, 88400 Gérardmer, Vosges, France
Tel: +33 3 29 63 09 25
Fax: +33 3 29 63 00 40
Web: www.johansens.com/lesbasrupts

Mini Listings Europe

Condé Nast Johansens are delighted to recommend 435 properties across Europe & The Mediterranean.
Call 1 800 564 7518 or see the Order Form on page 431 to order Guides.

FRANCE / ALSACE~LORRAINE (GUEBWILLER)

Hostellerie St Barnabé

68530 Murbach – Buhl, Guebwiller, France
Tel: +33 3 89 62 14 14
Fax: +33 3 89 62 14 15
Web: www.johansens.com/stbarnabe

FRANCE / ALSACE~LORRAINE (JUNGHOLTZ)

Romantik Hotel les Violettes

Thierenbach, BP 69, 68500 Jungholtz, France
Tel: +33 3 89 76 91 19
Fax: +33 3 89 74 29 12
Web: www.johansens.com/lesviolettes

FRANCE / ALSACE~LORRAINE (LA WANTZENAU)

Romantik Hotel Relais de la Poste

21 rue du Général~de~Gaulle, 67610 La Wantzenau, France
Tel: +33 3 88 59 24 80
Fax: +33 3 88 59 24 89
Web: www.johansens.com/relaisposte

FRANCE / ALSACE~LORRAINE (OBERNAI)

Hotel à la Cour d'Alsace

3 Rue de Gail, 67210 Obernai, France
Tel: +33 3 88 95 07 00
Fax: +33 3 88 95 19 21
Web: www.johansens.com/couralsace

FRANCE / ALSACE~LORRAINE (ROUFFACH)

Château d'Isenbourg

68250 Rouffach, France
Tel: +33 3 89 78 58 50
Fax: +33 3 89 78 53 70
Web: www.johansens.com/isenbourg

FRANCE / ALSACE~LORRAINE (STRASBOURG – OSTWALD)

Château de L'Ile

4 Quai Heydt, 67540 Strasbourg - Ostwald, France
Tel: +33 3 88 66 85 00
Fax: +33 3 88 66 85 49
Web: www.johansens.com/chateaudelile

FRANCE / ALSACE~LORRAINE (STRASBOURG)

Romantik Hotel Beaucour-Baumann

5 Rue des Bouchers, 67000 Strasbourg, France
Tel: +33 3 88 76 72 00
Fax: +33 3 88 76 72 60
Web: www.johansens.com/beaucour

FRANCE / ALSACE~LORRAINE (THIONVILLE)

Romantik Hotel L'Horizon

50 Route du Crève~Cœur, 57100 Thionville, France
Tel: +33 3 82 88 53 65
Fax: +33 3 82 34 55 84
Web: www.johansens.com/lhorizonfrance

FRANCE / BRITTANY (BILLIERS)

Domaine de Rochevilaine

Pointe de Pen Lan, BP 69, 56190 Billiers, France
Tel: +33 2 97 41 61 61
Fax: +33 2 97 41 44 85
Web: www.johansens.com/domainederochevilaine

FRANCE / BRITTANY (DINARD)

Villa Reine Hortense

19, rue de la Malouine, 35800 Dinard, France
Tel: +33 2 99 46 54 31
Fax: +33 2 99 88 15 88
Web: www.johansens.com/villareinehortense

FRANCE / BRITTANY (LA GOUESNIÈRE - SAINT~MALO)

Château de Bonaban

35350 La Gouesnière, France
Tel: +33 2 99 58 24 50
Fax: +33 2 99 58 28 41
Web: www.johansens.com/chateaudebonaban

FRANCE / BRITTANY (MISSILLAC)

Hôtel de La Bretesche

Domaine de la Bretesche, 44780 Missillac, France
Tel: +33 2 51 76 86 96
Fax: +33 2 40 66 99 47
Web: www.johansens.com/delabretesche

FRANCE / BRITTANY (MOËLAN~SUR~MER)

Manoir de Kertalg

Route de Riec~Sur~Belon, 29350 Moëlan~sur~Mer, France
Tel: +33 2 98 39 77 77
Fax: +33 2 98 39 72 07
Web: www.johansens.com/manoirdekertalg

FRANCE / BRITTANY (NIVILLAC - LA ROCHE~BERNARD)

Domaine de Bodeuc

Route de Saint~Dolay, 56130 Nivillac, La Roche Bernard, France
Tel: +33 2 99 90 89 63
Fax: +33 2 99 90 90 32
Web: www.johansens.com/hotelbodeuc

FRANCE / BRITTANY (PERROS~GUIREC)

Hotel l'Agapa & Spa

12, Rue des Bons Enfants, 22700 Perros~Guirec, France
Tel: +33 2 96 49 01 10
Fax: +33 2 96 91 16 36
Web: www.johansens.com/lagapa

FRANCE / BRITTANY (SAINT~MALO - PLEVEN)

Manoir du Vaumadeuc

22130 Pleven, BP 69, France
Tel: +33 2 96 84 46 17
Fax: +33 2 96 84 40 16
Web: www.johansens.com/manoirduvaumadeuc

FRANCE / BRITTANY (TREBEURDEN)

Ti al Lannec

14 Allée de Mezo~Guen, 22560 Trebeurden, France
Tel: +33 2 96 15 01 01
Fax: +33 2 96 23 62 14
Web: www.johansens.com/tiallannec

FRANCE / BURGUNDY - FRANCHE~COMTÉ (AVALLON)

Château de Vault de Lugny

11 Rue du Château, 89200 Vault de Lugny, France
Tel: +33 3 86 34 07 86
Fax: +33 3 86 34 16 36
Web: www.johansens.com/vaultdelugny

FRANCE / BURGUNDY - FRANCHE~COMTÉ (CHOREY~LES~BEAUNE)

Ermitage de Corton

R.N. 74, 21200 Chorey~les~Beaune, France
Tel: +33 3 80 22 05 28
Fax: +33 3 80 24 64 51
Web: www.johansens.com/ermitagedecorton

FRANCE / BURGUNDY - FRANCHE~COMTÉ (LA BUSSIÈRE~SUR~OUCHE)

Abbaye de la Bussière

21360 La Bussière~sur~Ouche, Côte d'Or, France
Tel: +33 3 80 49 02 29
Fax: +33 3 80 49 05 23
Web: www.johansens.com/abbayedelabussiere

FRANCE / BURGUNDY - FRANCHE~COMTÉ (MONT~SAINT~JEAN)

Château les Roches

Rue de Glanot, 21320 Mont~Saint~Jean, France
Tel: +33 3 80 84 32 71
Web: www.johansens.com/lesroches

FRANCE / BURGUNDY - FRANCHE~COMTÉ (POLIGNY)

Hostellerie des Monts de Vaux

Les Monts de Vaux, 39800 Poligny, France
Tel: +33 3 84 37 12 50
Fax: +33 3 84 37 09 07
Web: www.johansens.com/montdevaux

Mini Listings Europe

Condé Nast Johansens are delighted to recommend 435 properties across Europe & The Mediterranean.
Call 1 800 564 7518 or see the Order Form on page 431 to order Guides.

FRANCE / BURGUNDY - FRANCHE~COMTÉ (VOUGEOT)

Château de Gilly

Gilly~les~Cîteaux, 21640 Vougeot, France
Tel: +33 3 80 62 89 98
Fax: +33 3 80 62 82 34
Web: www.johansens.com/gilly

FRANCE / CHAMPAGNE~ARDENNES (DOLANCOURT)

Le Moulin du Landion

5 rue Saint~Léger, 10200 Dolancourt, France
Tel: +33 3 25 27 92 17
Fax: +33 3 25 27 94 44
Web: www.johansens.com/moulindulandion

FRANCE / CHAMPAGNE~ARDENNES (ETOGES~EN~CHAMPAGNE)

Château d'Etoges

51270 Etoges~en~Champagne, France
Tel: +33 3 26 59 30 08
Fax: +33 3 26 59 35 57
Web: www.johansens.com/etoges

FRANCE / CHAMPAGNE~ARDENNES (FÈRE~EN~TARDENOIS)

Château de Fère

02130 Fère~en~Tardenois, France
Tel: +33 3 23 82 21 13
Fax: +33 3 23 82 37 81
Web: www.johansens.com/chateaudefere

FRANCE / CHAMPAGNE~ARDENNES (SAINTE~PREUVE)

Domaine du Château de Barive

02350 Sainte~Preuve, France
Tel: +33 3 23 22 15 15
Fax: +33 3 23 22 08 39
Web: www.johansens.com/barive

FRANCE / CÔTE D'AZUR (AUPS)

Bastide du Calalou

Village de Moissac-Bellevue, 83630 Aups, France
Tel: +33 4 94 70 17 91
Fax: +33 4 94 70 50 11
Web: www.johansens.com/calalou

FRANCE / CÔTE D'AZUR (ÈZE VILLAGE)

Château Eza

Rue de la Pise, 06360 Èze Village, France
Tel: +33 4 93 41 12 24
Fax: +33 4 93 41 16 64
Web: www.johansens.com/eza

FRANCE / CÔTE D'AZUR (GRASSE)

Bastide Saint~Mathieu

35 Chemin de Blumenthal, 06130 Saint~Mathieu, Grasse, France
Tel: +33 4 97 01 10 00
Fax: +33 4 97 0110 09
Web: www.johansens.com/saintmathieu

FRANCE / CÔTE D'AZUR (LE RAYOL – CANADEL~SUR~MER)

Le Bailli de Suffren

Avenue des Américains, Golfe de Saint~Tropez, 83820 Le Rayol – Canadel~Sur~Mer, France
Tel: +33 4 98 04 47 00
Fax: +33 4 98 04 47 99
Web: www.johansens.com/lebaillidesuffren

FRANCE / CÔTE D'AZUR (RAMATUELLE)

La Ferme d'Augustin

Plage de Tahiti, 83350 Ramatuelle, Near Saint~Tropez, France
Tel: +33 4 94 55 97 00
Fax: +33 4 94 97 59 76
Web: www.johansens.com/fermedaugustin

FRANCE / CÔTE D'AZUR (SAINT~PAUL~DE~VENCE)

Le Mas d'Artigny

Route de la Colle, 06570 Saint~Paul~de~Vence, France
Tel: +33 4 93 32 84 54
Fax: +33 4 93 32 95 36
Web: www.johansens.com/masdartigny

FRANCE / CÔTE D'AZUR (SAINT~RAPHAËL)

La Villa Mauresque

1792 route de la Corniche, 83700 Saint~Raphaël, France
Tel: +33 494 83 02 42
Fax: +33 494 83 02 02
Web: www.johansens.com/mauresque

FRANCE / CÔTE D'AZUR (VENCE)

Hôtel Cantemerle

258 Chemin Cantemerle, 06140 Vence, France
Tel: +33 4 93 58 08 18
Fax: +33 4 93 58 32 89
Web: www.johansens.com/hotelcantemerle

FRANCE / LOIRE VALLEY (AMBOISE)

Château de Pray

Route de Chargé, 37400 Amboise, France
Tel: +33 2 47 57 23 67
Fax: +33 2 47 57 32 50
Web: www.johansens.com/chateaudepray

FRANCE / LOIRE VALLEY (AMBOISE)

Le Choiseul

36 Quai Charles Guinot, 37400 Amboise, France
Tel: +33 2 47 30 45 45
Fax: +33 2 47 30 46 10
Web: www.johansens.com/lechoiseul

FRANCE / LOIRE VALLEY (AMBOISE)

Le Manoir les Minimes

34 Quai Charles Guinot, 37400 Amboise, France
Tel: +33 2 47 30 40 40
Fax: +33 2 47 30 40 77
Web: www.johansens.com/lemanoirlesminimes

FRANCE / LOIRE VALLEY (CHÊNEHUTTE~LES~TUFFEAUX)

Le Prieuré

49350 Chênehutte~les~Tuffeaux, France
Tel: +33 2 41 67 90 14
Fax: +33 2 41 67 92 24
Web: www.johansens.com/leprieure

FRANCE / LOIRE VALLEY (LUYNES, NEAR TOURS)

Domaine de Beauvois

Le Pont Clouet, Route de Cléré~les~Pins, 37230 Luynes, France
Tel: +33 2 47 55 50 11
Fax: +33 2 47 55 59 62
Web: www.johansens.com/domainedebeauvois

FRANCE / LOIRE VALLEY (MONTBAZON, NEAR TOURS)

Château d'Artigny

37250 Montbazon, France
Tel: +33 2 47 34 30 30
Fax: +33 2 47 34 30 39
Web: www.johansens.com/dartigny

FRANCE / LOIRE VALLEY (MONTBAZON, NEAR TOURS)

Domaine de la Tortinière

Route de Ballan~Miré, 37250 Montbazon, France
Tel: +33 2 47 34 35 00
Fax: +33 2 47 65 95 70
Web: www.johansens.com/domainetortiniere

FRANCE / LOIRE VALLEY (SAINT~CALAIS)

Château de la Barre

72120 Conflans~sur~Anille, France
Tel: +33 2 43 35 00 17
Web: www.johansens.com/delabarre

FRANCE / LOIRE VALLEY (SAINTE~MAURE~DE~TOURAINE)

Hostellerie des Hauts de

2-4 avenue du Général~de~Gaulle, 37800 Sainte~Maure~de~Touraine, France
Tel: +33 2 47 65 50 65
Fax: +33 2 47 65 60 24
Web: www.johansens.com/saintemaure

Mini Listings Europe

Condé Nast Johansens are delighted to recommend 435 properties across Europe & The Mediterranean.
Call 1 800 564 7518 or see the Order Form on page 431 to order Guides.

FRANCE / MIDI~PYRÉNÉES (CARCASSONNE~FLOURE)

Château de Floure

1, Allée Gaston Bonheur, 11800 Floure, France
Tel: +33 4 68 79 11 29
Fax: +33 4 68 79 04 61
Web: www.johansens.com/floure

FRANCE / MIDI~PYRÉNÉES (CARCASSONNE - MIREPOIX)

Relais Royal

8 Rue Maréchal Clauzel, 09500 Carcassonne - Mirepoix, France
Tel: +33 5 61 60 19 19
Fax: +33 5 61 60 14 15
Web: www.johansens.com/relaisroyal

FRANCE / NORMANDY (BAYEUX - PORT~EN~BESSIN)

Château la Chenevière

Escures-Commes, 14520 Port~en~Bessin, France
Tel: +33 2 31 51 25 25
Fax: +33 2 31 51 25 20
Web: www.johansens.com/cheneviere

FRANCE / NORMANDY (CAMBREMER)

Château les Bruyères

Route du Cadran, 14340 Cambremer, France
Tel: +33 2 31 32 22 45
Fax: +33 2 31 32 22 58
Web: www.johansens.com/lesbruyeres

FRANCE / NORMANDY (COUTANCES~MONTPINCHON)

Le Castel

50210 Montpinchon, France
Tel: +33 2 33 17 00 45
Web: www.johansens.com/lecastelnormandy

FRANCE / NORMANDY (CRICQUEBOEUF)

Manoir de la Poterie, Spa "Les Thermes"

Chemin Paul Ruel, 14113 Cricqueboeuf, France
Tel: +33 2 31 88 10 40
Fax: +33 2 31 88 10 90
Web: www.johansens.com/manoirdelapoterie

FRANCE / NORMANDY (ETRETAT)

Domaine Saint~Clair, Le Donjon

Chemin de Saint~Clair, 76790 Etretat, France
Tel: +33 2 35 27 08 23
Fax: +33 2 35 29 92 24
Web: www.johansens.com/donjon

FRANCE / NORMANDY (SAINT~CHRISTOPHE~SUR~CONDE)

Château la Thillaye

27450 Saint~Christophe~Sur~Conde, France
Tel: +33 2 32 56 07 24
Fax: +33 2 32 56 70 47
Web: www.johansens.com/thillaye

FRANCE / NORTH - PICARDY (ALBERT)

Hôtel Royal Picardie

Avenue du Général Leclerc, 80300 Albert, France
Tel: +33 3 22 75 37 00
Fax: +33 3 22 75 60 19
Web: www.johansens.com/royalpicardie

FRANCE / NORTH - PICARDY (BETHUNE - GOSNAY)

La Chartreuse du Val Saint~Esprit

62199 Gosnay, France
Tel: +33 3 21 62 80 00
Fax: +33 3 21 62 42 50
Web: www.johansens.com/lachartreuse

FRANCE / NORTH - PICARDY (CALAIS - RECQUES~SUR~HEM)

Château de Cocove

62890 Recques~sur~Hem, France
Tel: +33 3 21 82 68 29
Fax: +33 3 21 82 72 59
Web: www.johansens.com/chateaudecocove

FRANCE / NORTH - PICARDY (DOULLENS - REMAISNIL)

Château de Remaisnil

80600 Remaisnil, France
Tel: +33 3 22 77 07 47
Fax: +33 3 22 77 41 23
Web: www.johansens.com/remaisnil

FRANCE / NORTH - PICARDY (LILLE)

Carlton Hotel

Rue de Paris, 59000 Lille, France
Tel: +33 3 20 13 33 13
Fax: +33 3 20 51 48 17
Web: www.johansens.com/carltonlille

FRANCE / PARIS (CHAMPS~ELYSÉES)

Hôtel de Sers

41, Avenue Pierre 1er de Serbie, 75008 Paris, France
Tel: +33 1 53 23 75 75
Fax: +33 1 53 23 75 76
Web: www.johansens.com/hoteldesers

FRANCE / PARIS (CHAMPS~ELYSÉES)

Hôtel San Régis

12 Rue Jean Goujon, 75008 Paris, France
Tel: +33 1 44 95 16 16
Fax: +33 1 45 61 05 48
Web: www.johansens.com/sanregis

FRANCE / PARIS (CHAMPS~ELYSÉES)

La Trémoille

14 Rue de la Trémoille, 75008 Paris, France
Tel: +33 1 56 52 14 00
Fax: +33 1 40 70 01 08
Web: www.johansens.com/tremoille

FRANCE / PARIS (CONCORDE)

Hôtel de Crillon

10, Place de La Concorde, 75008 Paris, France
Tel: +33 1 44 71 15 00
Fax: +33 1 44 71 15 02
Web: www.johansens.com/crillon

FRANCE / PARIS (ÉTOILE - PORTE MAILLOT)

Hôtel Duret

30 rue Duret, 75116 Paris, France
Tel: +33 1 45 00 42 60
Fax: +33 1 45 00 55 89
Web: www.johansens.com/duret

FRANCE / PARIS (ÉTOILE - PORTE MAILLOT)

La Villa Maillot

143 Avenue de Malakoff, 75116 Paris, France
Tel: +33 1 53 64 52 52
Fax: +33 1 45 00 60 61
Web: www.johansens.com/lavillamaillot

FRANCE / PARIS (INVALIDES)

Hôtel le Tourville

16 Avenue de Tourville, 75007 Paris, France
Tel: +33 1 47 05 62 62
Fax: +33 1 47 05 43 90
Web: www.johansens.com/tourville

FRANCE / PARIS (JARDIN DU LUXEMBOURG)

Le Relais Médicis

23 Rue Racine, 75006 Paris, France
Tel: +33 1 43 26 00 60
Fax: +33 1 40 46 83 39
Web: www.johansens.com/medicis

FRANCE / PARIS (JARDIN DU LUXEMBOURG)

Le Sainte~Beuve

9 Rue Sainte~Beuve, 75006 Paris, France
Tel: +33 1 45 48 20 07
Fax: +33 1 45 48 67 52
Web: www.johansens.com/saintebeuve

Mini Listings Europe

Condé Nast Johansens are delighted to recommend 435 properties across Europe & The Mediterranean.

Call 1 800 564 7518 or see the Order Form on page 431 to order Guides.

FRANCE / PARIS (MADELEINE)

Hôtel le Lavoisier

21 rue Lavoisier, 75008 Paris, France
Tel: +33 1 53 30 06 06
Fax: +33 1 53 30 23 00
Web: www.johansens.com/lelavoisier

FRANCE / PARIS (MADELEINE)

Hôtel Opéra Richepanse

14 Rue du Chevalier de Saint~George, 75001 Paris, France
Tel: +33 1 42 60 36 00
Fax: +33 1 42 60 13 03
Web: www.johansens.com/richepanse

FRANCE / PARIS (MARAIS)

Hôtel du Petit Moulin

29-31 Rue de Poitu, 75003 Paris, France
Tel: +33 1 42 74 10 10
Fax: +33 1 42 74 10 97
Web: www.johansens.com/petitmoulin

FRANCE / PARIS (SAINT~GERMAIN)

Hôtel Duc de Saint~Simon

14 rue de Saint~Simon, 75007 Paris, France
Tel: +33 1 44 39 20 20
Fax: +33 1 45 48 68 25
Web: www.johansens.com/saintsimon

FRANCE / PARIS (SAINT~GERMAIN)

Hôtel le Saint~Grégoire

43 Rue de L'Abbé Grégoire, 75006 Paris, France
Tel: +33 1 45 48 23 23
Fax: +33 1 45 48 33 95
Web: www.johansens.com/saintgregoire

FRANCE / PARIS REGION (AUGERVILLE LA RIVIÈRE)

Château d'Augerville

Place du Château, 45330 Augerville la Riviere, France
Tel: +33 2 38 32 12 07
Fax: +33 2 38 32 12 15
Web: www.johansens.com/augerville

FRANCE / PARIS REGION (BARBIZON)

Hostellerie du Bas-Breau

22 Rue Grande, 77630 Barbizon, France
Tel: +33 1 60 66 40 05
Fax: +33 1 60 69 22 89
Web: www.johansens.com/basbreau

FRANCE / PARIS REGION (BERCHERE~SUR~VESGRES)

Château de Berchères

18 rue de Château, 28260 Berchères~sur~VesgreS, France
Tel: +33 2 37 82 28 22
Fax: +33 2 37 82 28 23
Web: www.johansens.com/bercheres

FRANCE / PARIS REGION (GRESSY~EN~FRANCE - CHANTILLY)

Le Manoir de Gressy

77410 Gressy~en~France, Chantilly, Near Roissy, Charles de Gaulle Airport, Paris, France
Tel: +33 1 60 26 68 00
Fax: +33 1 60 26 45 46
Web: www.johansens.com/manoirdegressy

FRANCE / PARIS REGION (SAINT~SYMPHORIEN~LE~CHÂTEAU)

Château d'Esclimont

28700 Saint~Symphorien~Le~Château, France
Tel: +33 2 37 31 15 15
Fax: +33 2 37 31 57 91
Web: www.johansens.com/esclimont

FRANCE / PARIS REGION (SAINT~GERMAIN~EN~LAYE)

Cazaudehore la Forestière

1 Avenue du Président Kennedy, 78100 Saint~Germain~en~Laye, France
Tel: +33 1 30 61 64 64
Fax: +33 1 30 73 73 83
Web: www.johansens.com/cazaudehore

FRANCE / POITOU-CHARENTES (CHÂTEAUBERNARD)

Château de L'Yeuse

65 Rue de Bellevue, Quartier de L'Echassier, 16100 Châteaubernard, France
Tel: +33 5 45 36 82 60
Fax: +33 5 45 35 06 32
Web: www.johansens.com/chateaudelyeuse

FRANCE / POITOU-CHARENTES (LA ROCHELLE)

Hotel "Résidence de France"

43 Rue Minage, 17000 La Rochelle, France
Tel: +33 5 46 28 06 00
Fax: +33 5 46 28 06 03
Web: www.johansens.com/residencedefrance

FRANCE / POITOU-CHARENTES (MARTHON)

Château de la Couronne

16380 Marthon, France
Tel: +33 5 45 62 29 96
Web: www.johansens.com/couronne

FRANCE / POITOU-CHARENTES (MASSIGNAC)

Domaine des Etangs

16310 Massignac, France
Tel: +33 5 45 61 85 00
Fax: +33 5 45 61 85 01
Web: www.johansens.com/etangs

FRANCE / POITOU-CHARENTES (SAINT~PREUIL)

Relais de Saint~Preuil

Lieu-dit Chez Riviere, 16130 Saint~Preuil, France
Tel: +33 5 45 80 80 08
Fax: +33 5 45 80 80 09
Web: www.johansens.com/saintpreuil

FRANCE / PROVENCE (GORDES)

Les Mas des Herbes Blanches

Joucas, 84220 Gordes, France
Tel: +33 4 90 05 79 79
Fax: +33 4 90 05 71 96
Web: www.johansens.com/herbesblanches

FRANCE / PROVENCE (LE PARADOU - LES BAUX~DE~PROVENCE)

Domaine le Hameau des Baux

Chemin de Bourgeac, 13520 Le Paradou, France
Tel: +33 4 90 54 10 30
Fax: +33 4 90 54 45 30
Web: www.johansens.com/hameaudesbaux

FRANCE / PROVENCE (LES BAUX~DE~PROVENCE)

Oustau de Baumanière

13520 Les Baux~de~Provence, France
Tel: +33 4 90 54 33 07
Fax: +33 4 90 54 40 46
Web: www.johansens.com/oustadebaumaniere

FRANCE / PROVENCE (PORT CAMARGUE)

Le Spinaker

Pointe de la Presqu'île, Port Camargue, 30240 Le Grau~du~Roi, France
Tel: +33 4 66 53 36 37
Fax: +33 4 66 53 17 47
Web: www.johansens.com/spinaker

FRANCE / PROVENCE (SABRAN - BAGNOLS~SUR~CÈZE)

Château de Montcaud

Combe, Bagnols~sur~Cèze, 30200 Sabran, Near Avignon, France
Tel: +33 4 66 89 60 60
Fax: +33 4 66 89 45 04
Web: www.johansens.com/montcaud

FRANCE / PROVENCE (SAINT~RÉMY~DE~PROVENCE)

Château des Alpilles

Route Départementale 31, Ancienne Route du Grès, 13210 Saint~Rémy~de~Provence, France
Tel: +33 4 90 92 03 33
Fax: +33 4 90 92 45 17
Web: www.johansens.com/chateaudesalpilles

Mini Listings Europe

Condé Nast Johansens are delighted to recommend 435 properties across Europe & The Mediterranean.
Call 1 800 564 7518 or see the Order Form on page 431 to order Guides.

FRANCE / PROVENCE (SAINT~SATURNIN~LES~APT)

Domaine des Andéols

84490 Saint~Saturnin~lès~Apt, France
Tel: +33 4 90 75 50 63
Fax: +33 4 90 75 43 22
Web: www.johansens.com/domainedesandeols

FRANCE / RHÔNE~ALPES (CONDRIEU)

Le Beau Rivage

2 rue du Beau-Rivage, 69420 Condrieu, France
Tel: +33 4 74 56 82 82
Fax: +33 4 74 59 59 36
Web: www.johansens.com/beaurivage

FRANCE / RHÔNE~ALPES (DIVONNE~LES~BAINS)

Château de Divonne

01220 Divonne~les~Bains, France
Tel: +33 4 50 20 00 32
Fax: +33 4 50 20 03 73
Web: www.johansens.com/chateaudedivonne

FRANCE / RHÔNE~ALPES (DIVONNE~LES~BAINS)

Domaine de Divonne

Avenue des Thermes, 01220 Divonne~les~Bains, France
Tel: +33 4 50 40 34 34
Fax: +33 4 50 40 34 24
Web: www.johansens.com/domainededivonne

FRANCE / RHÔNE~ALPES (LES GETS)

Chalet Hôtel La Marmotte

61 Rue du Chêne, 74260 Les Gets, France
Tel: +33 4 50 75 80 33
Fax: +33 4 50 75 83 26
Web: www.johansens.com/chaletlamarmotte

FRANCE / RHÔNE~ALPES (MEGÈVE)

Le Fer à Cheval

36 route du Crêt d'Arbois, 74120 Megève, France
Tel: +33 4 50 21 30 39
Fax: +33 4 50 93 07 60
Web: www.johansens.com/cheval

FRANCE / RHÔNE~ALPES (SCIEZ~SUR~LÉMAN)

Château de Coudrée

Domaine de Coudrée, Bonnatrait, 74140 Sciez~sur~Léman, France
Tel: +33 4 50 72 62 33
Fax: +33 4 50 72 57 28
Web: www.johansens.com/decoudree

FRANCE / SOUTH WEST (BIARRITZ)

Hôtel du Palais

1 Avenue de L'Impératrice, 64200 Biarritz, France
Tel: +33 5 59 41 64 00
Fax: +33 5 59 41 67 99
Web: www.johansens.com/palais

FRANCE / SOUTH WEST (RIBERAC - DORDOGNE)

Château le Mas de Montet

Petit-Bersac, 24600 Ribérac, Dordogne, France
Tel: +33 5 53 90 08 71
Fax: +33 5 53 90 66 92
Web: www.johansens.com/lemasdemontet

FRANCE / SOUTH WEST (SAINTE~RADEGONDE – SAINT~EMILION)

Château de Sanse

33350 Sainte~Radegonde, France
Tel: +33 5 57 56 41 10
Fax: +33 5 57 56 41 29
Web: www.johansens.com/chateaudesanse

FRANCE / SOUTH WEST (SOURZAC-DORDOGNE)

Le Chaufourg~en~Périgord

24400 Sourzac, Périgord, Dordogne, France
Tel: +33 5 53 81 01 56
Fax: +33 5 53 82 94 87
Web: www.johansens.com/chaufourg

FRANCE / WESTERN LOIRE (CHALLAIN~LA~POTHERIE)

Château de Challain

49440 Challain~la~Potherie, France
Tel: +33 2 41 92 74 26
Fax: +33 2 41 61 54 25
Web: www.johansens.com/challain

FRANCE / WESTERN LOIRE (CHAMPIGNÉ - ANGERS)

Château des Briottières

49330 Champigné, France
Tel: +33 2 41 42 00 02
Fax: +33 2 41 42 01 55
Web: www.johansens.com/chateaudesbriottieres

GREAT BRITAIN / ENGLAND (BERKSHIRE)

The Crab at Chieveley

Wantage Road, Newbury, Berkshire RG20 8UE, England
Tel: +44 1635 247550
Fax: +44 1635 247440
Web: www.johansens.com/crabatchieveleyeuro

GREAT BRITAIN / ENGLAND (BERKSHIRE)

The French Horn

Sonning on Thames, Berkshire, RG4 6TN, England
Tel: +44 1189 692 204
Fax: +44 1189 442 210
Web: www.johansens.com/frenchhorneuro

GREAT BRITAIN / ENGLAND (CHESHIRE)

Hillbark Hotel

Royden Park, Frankby, Wirral, CH48 1NP, England
Tel: +44 151 625 2400
Fax: +44 151 625 4040
Web: www.johansens.com/hillbarkeuro

GREAT BRITAIN / ENGLAND (DEVON)

Soar Mill Cove Hotel

Soar Mill Cove, Salcombe, South Devon TQ7 3DS
Tel: +44 1548 561566
Fax: +44 1548 561223
Web: www.johansens.com/soarmillcoveeuro

GREAT BRITAIN / ENGLAND (EAST SUSSEX)

Ashdown Park Hotel

Wych Cross, Forest Row, East Sussex, RH18 5JR, England
Tel: +44 1342 824988
Fax: +44 1342 826206
Web: www.johansens.com/ashdownparkeuro

GREAT BRITAIN / ENGLAND (EAST SUSSEX)

The Grand Hotel

King Edward's Parade, Eastbourne, East Sussex, BN21 4EQ, England
Tel: +44 1323 412345
Fax: +44 1323 412233
Web: www.johansens.com/grandeastbourneeuro

GREAT BRITAIN / ENGLAND (EAST SUSSEX)

Rye Lodge

Hilder's Cliff, Rye, East Sussex, TN31 7LD, England
Tel: +44 1797 223838
Fax: +44 1797 223585
Web: www.johansens.com/ryelodgeeuro

GREAT BRITAIN / ENGLAND (HAMPSHIRE)

Tylney Hall

Rotherwick, Hook, Hampshire, RG27 9AZ, England
Tel: +44 1256 764881
Fax: +44 1256 768141
Web: www.johansens.com/tylneyhalleuro

GREAT BRITAIN / ENGLAND (LONDON)

The Cranley

10 Bina Gardens, South Kensington, London, SW5 0LA, England
Tel: +44 20 7373 0123
Fax: +44 20 7373 9497
Web: www.johansens.com/cranleyeuro

Mini Listings Europe

Condé Nast Johansens are delighted to recommend 435 properties across Europe & The Mediterranean.
Call 1 800 564 7518 or see the Order Form on page 431 to order Guides.

GREAT BRITAIN / ENGLAND (LONDON)

Jumeirah Carlton Tower
On Cadogan Place, London, SW1X 9PY, England
Tel: +44 20 7235 1234
Fax: +44 20 7235 9129
Web: www.johansens.com/carltontowereuro

GREAT BRITAIN / ENGLAND (LONDON)

Jumeirah Lowndes Hotel
21 Lowndes Street, Knightsbridge, London, SW1X 9ES, England
Tel: +44 20 7823 1234
Fax: +44 20 7235 1154
Web: www.johansens.com/lowndeseuro

GREAT BRITAIN / ENGLAND (LONDON)

The Mayflower Hotel
26-28 Trebovir Road, London, SW5 9NJ, England
Tel: +44 20 7370 0991
Fax: +44 20 7370 0994
Web: www.johansens.com/mayflowereuro

GREAT BRITAIN / ENGLAND (LONDON)

The Royal Park
3 Westbourne Terrace, Lancaster Gate, Hyde Park, London, W2 3UL, England
Tel: +44 20 7479 6600
Fax: +44 20 7479 6601
Web: www.johansens.com/royalparkeuro

GREAT BRITAIN / ENGLAND (LONDON)

Twenty Nevern Square
20 Nevern Square, London, SW5 9PD, England
Tel: +44 20 7565 9555
Fax: +44 20 7565 9444
Web: www.johansens.com/twentynevernsquareeuro

GREAT BRITAIN / ENGLAND (OXFORDSHIRE)

Phyllis Court Club
Marlow Road, Henley-on-Thames, Oxfordshire, RG9 2HT, England
Tel: +44 1491 570 500
Fax: +44 1491 570 528
Web: www.johansens.com/phylliscourteuro

GREAT BRITAIN / ENGLAND (STAFFORDSHIRE)

Hoar Cross Hall Spa Resort
Hoar Cross, Near Yoxall, Staffordshire, DE13 8QS, England
Tel: +44 1283 575671
Fax: +44 1283 575652
Web: www.johansens.com/hoarcrosshalleuro

GREAT BRITAIN / ENGLAND (WEST SUSSEX)

Amberley Castle
Amberley, Near Arundel, West Sussex, BN18 9LT, England
Tel: +44 1798 831 992
Fax: +44 1798 831 998
Web: www.johansens.com/amberleycastleeuro

GREECE (ATHENS)

Astir Palace Vouliagmeni
40 Apollonos Street, 166 71 Vouliagmeni, Athens, Greece
Tel: +30 210 890 2000
Fax: +30 210 896 2582
Web: www.johansens.com/astirpalace

GREECE (ATHENS)

Hotel Pentelikon
66 Diligianni Street, 14562 Athens, Greece
Tel: +30 2 10 62 30 650
Fax: +30 210 62 81 400
Web: www.johansens.com/pentelikon

GREECE (CHIOS)

Argentikon
Kambos, 82100 Chios, Greece
Tel: +30 227 10 33 111
Fax: +30 227 10 31 465
Web: www.johansens.com/argentikon

GREECE (CORFU)

Villa de Loulia
Peroulades, Corfu, Greece
Tel: +30 266 30 95 394
Fax: +30 266 30 95 145
Web: www.johansens.com/villadeloulia

GREECE (CRETE)

Athina Luxury Villas
Ksamoudochori, Platanias, 73014 Chania, Crete, Greece
Tel: +30 28210 20960
Fax: +30 28210 20970
Web: www.johansens.com/athinaluxuryvillas

GREECE (CRETE)

Elounda Gulf Villas & Suites
Elounda, 72053 Crete, Greece
Tel: +30 28410 90300
Fax: +30 28410 42274
Web: www.johansens.com/eloundagulf

GREECE (CRETE)

Elounda Peninsula All Suite Hotel
72053 Elounda, Crete, Greece
Tel: +30 28410 68012
Fax: +30 28410 41889
Web: www.johansens.com/peninsulacrete

GREECE (CRETE)

Pleiades Luxurious Villas
Plakes, 72100 Aghios Nikolaos, Crete, Greece
Tel: +30 28410 90450
Fax: +30 28410 90479
Web: www.johansens.com/pleiades

GREECE (CRETE)

St Nicolas Bay Resort Hotel & Villas
PO Box 47, 72100 Aghios Nikolaos, Crete, Greece
Tel: +30 2841 025041
Fax: +30 2841 024556
Web: www.johansens.com/stnicolasbay

GREECE (KAVALA)

Imaret
30-32 Poulidou Street, 65110 Kavala, Greece
Tel: +30 2510 620 151-55
Fax: +30 2510 620 156
Web: www.johansens.com/imaret

GREECE (LEFKADA)

Pavezzo Country Retreat
Katouna, Lefkada, Greece
Tel: +30 26450 71782
Fax: +30 69450 71800
Web: www.johansens.com/pavezzo

GREECE (MYKONOS)

Apanema
Tagoo, Mykonos, Greece
Tel: +30 22890 28590
Fax: +30 22890 79250
Web: www.johansens.com/apanema

GREECE (MYKONOS)

Tharroe of Mykonos
Mykonos Town, Angelica, 84600 Mykonos, Greece
Tel: +30 22890 27370
Fax: +30 22890 27375
Web: www.johansens.com/tharroe

GREECE (RHODES)

Fashion Hotel
Medieval City, 26 Panetiou Avenue, 85100 Rhodes, Greece
Tel: +30 22410 70773/4
Fax: +30 22410 24643
Web: www.johansens.com/fashionhotel

Mini Listings Europe

Condé Nast Johansens are delighted to recommend 435 properties across Europe & The Mediterranean.
Call 1 800 564 7518 or see the Order Form on page 431 to order Guides.

GREECE (RHODES)

Melenos Lindos
Lindos, 85107 Rhodes, Greece
Tel: +30 224 40 32 222
Fax: +30 22 440 31 720
Web: www.johansens.com/melenoslindos

GREECE (SANTORINI)

Alexander's Boutique Hotel of Oia
84702 Oia, Santorini, Greece
Tel: +30 22860 71818
Fax: +30 22860 72375
Web: www.johansens.com/alexanders

GREECE (SANTORINI)

Canaves Oia
Oia, 87402 Santorini, Greece
Tel: +30 22860 71453/71128
Fax: +30 22860 71195
Web: www.johansens.com/canavesoia

GREECE (SANTORINI)

Fanari Villas
Oia, 84702 Santorini, Greece
Tel: +30 22860 71007
Fax: +30 22860 71235
Web: www.johansens.com/fanarivillas

GREECE (SPETSES, NEAR ATHENS)

Orloff Resort
Spetses Island, Old Harbour, 18050 Spetses, Greece
Tel: +30 229 807 5444/5
Fax: +30 229 807 4470
Web: www.johansens.com/orloffresort

IRELAND (DUBLIN)

Aberdeen Lodge
53-55 Park Avenue, Ballsbridge, Dublin 4, Ireland
Tel: +353 1 283 8155
Fax: +353 1 283 7877
Web: www.johansens.com/aberdeenlodge

ITALY / CAMPANIA (AMALFI COAST & NAPLES)

Furore Inn Resort & Spa
Via Dell'Amore, 84010 Furore, Amalfi Coast, Italy
Tel: +39 089 830 4711
Fax: +39 089 830 4777
Web: www.johansens.com/furoreinn

ITALY / CAMPANIA (RAVELLO)

Hotel Villa Maria
Via S. Chiara 2, 84010 Ravello (SA), Italy
Tel: +39 089 857255
Fax: +39 089 857071
Web: www.johansens.com/villamaria

ITALY / CAMPANIA (SORRENTO)

Grand Hotel Cocumella
Via Cocumella 7, 80065 Sant'Agnello, Sorrento, Italy
Tel: +39 081 878 2933
Fax: +39 081 878 3712
Web: www.johansens.com/grandcocumella

ITALY / EMILIA ROMAGNA (PARMA)

Palazzo Dalla Rosa Prati
Strada al Duomo 7, 43100 Parma, Italy
Tel: +39 0521 386 429
Fax: +39 0521 502 204
Web: www.johansens.com/palazzodallarosaprati

ITALY / EMILIA ROMAGNA (PIACENZA - BORGO DI RIVALTA)

Torre di San Martino - Historical Residence
Loc. Borgo di Rivalta, 29010 Gazzola, Piacenza, Italy
Tel: +39 0523 972002
Fax: +39 0523 972030
Web: www.johansens.com/torredisanmartino

ITALY / EMILIA ROMAGNA (REGGIO EMILIA)

Hotel Posta (Historical Residence)
Piazza del Monte, 2, 42100 Reggio Emilia, Italy
Tel: +39 05 22 43 29 44
Fax: +39 05 22 45 26 02
Web: www.johansens.com/posta

ITALY / EMILIA ROMAGNA (RICCIONE - ADRIATIC COAST)

Hotel des Nations
Lungomare Costituzione 2, 47838 Riccione (RN), Italy
Tel: +39 0541 647878
Fax: +39 0541 645154
Web: www.johansens.com/hoteldesnations

ITALY / EMILIA ROMAGNA (SAN MARINO REPUBLIC)

Hotel Titano
Contrada del Collegio 31, 47890 San Marino (RSM), San Marino Republic
Tel: +378 99 10 07
Fax: +378 99 13 75
Web: www.johansens.com/hoteltitano

ITALY / LAZIO (CIVITA CASTELLANA)

Relais Falisco
Via Don Minzoni 19, 01033 Civita Castellana (VT), Italy
Tel: +39 0761 54 98
Fax: +39 0761 59 84 32
Web: www.johansens.com/falisco

ITALY / LAZIO (ORTE)

La Locanda della Chiocciola
Loc. Seripola SNC, 01028 Orte, Italy
Tel: +39 0761 402 734
Fax: +39 0761 490 254
Web: www.johansens.com/lalocanda

ITALY / LAZIO (PALO LAZIALE – ROME)

La Posta Vecchia Hotel Spa
Palo Laziale, 00055 Ladispoli, Rome, Italy
Tel: +39 0699 49501
Fax: +39 0699 49507
Web: www.johansens.com/postavecchia

ITALY / LAZIO (ROME)

Hotel Aventino
Via San Domenico 10, 00153 Rome, Italy
Tel: +39 06 57 00 57
Fax: +39 06 5783 604
Web: www.johansens.com/aventino

ITALY / LAZIO (ROME)

Hotel dei Borgognoni
Via del Bufalo 126 (Piazza di Spagna), 00187 Rome, Italy
Tel: +39 06 6994 1505
Fax: +39 06 6994 1501
Web: www.johansens.com/borgognoni

ITALY / LAZIO (ROME)

Hotel dei Consoli
Via Varrone 2/d, 00193 Roma, Italy
Tel: +39 0668 892 972
Fax: +39 0668 212 274
Web: www.johansens.com/deiconsoli

ITALY / LAZIO (ROME)

Hotel Fenix
Viale Gorizia 5/7, 00198 Rome, Italy
Tel: +39 06 8540 741
Fax: +39 06 8543 632
Web: www.johansens.com/fenix

ITALY / LAZIO (ROME)

Villa Spalletti Trivelli
via Piacenza 4, 00184 Rome, Italy
Tel: +39 06 48907934
Fax: +39 06 4871409
Web: www.johansens.com/villaspallettitrivelli

Mini Listings Europe

Condé Nast Johansens are delighted to recommend 435 properties across Europe & The Mediterranean.

Call 1 800 564 7518 or see the Order Form on page 431 to order Guides.

ITALY / LIGURIA (FINALE LIGURE)

Hotel Punta Est

Via Aurelia 1, 17024 Finale Ligure (SV), Italy
Tel: +39 019 600611
Fax: +39 019 600611
Web: www.johansens.com/puntaest

ITALY / LIGURIA (MONEGLIA)

Abbadia San Giorgio - Historical Residence

Piazzale San Giorgio, 16030 Moneglia (GE), Italy
Tel: +39 0185 491119
Fax: +39 0185 49470
Web: www.johansens.com/abbadiasangiorgio

ITALY / LIGURIA (PORTOFINO)

Hotel San Giorgio - Portofino House

Via del Fondaco, 11, 16034 Portofino (Genova), Italy
Tel: +39 0185 26991
Fax: +39 0185 267139
Web: www.johansens.com/portofinohouse

ITALY / LIGURIA (SAN REMO COAST - DIANO MARINA)

Grand Hotel Diana Majestic

Via Oleandri 15, 18013 Diano Marina (IM), Italy
Tel: +39 0183 402 727
Fax: +39 0183 403 040
Web: www.johansens.com/dianamajestic

ITALY / LIGURIA (SANTA MARGHERITA - PORTOFINO COAST)

Grand Hotel Miramare

Via Milite Ignoto, 30, 16038 Santa Margherita Ligure - Genova, Liguria, Italy
Tel: +39 0185 287013
Fax: +39 0185 284651
Web: www.johansens.com/grandmiramare

ITALY / LIGURIA (SESTRI LEVANTE)

Hotel Vis à Vis

Via della Chiusa 28, 16039 Sestri Levante (GE), Italy
Tel: +39 0185 42661
Fax: +39 0185 480853
Web: www.johansens.com/visavis

ITALY / LOMBARDY (BELLAGIO - LAKE COMO)

Grand Hotel Villa Serbelloni

Via Roma 1, 22021 Bellagio, Lake Como, Italy
Tel: +39 031 950 216 or +39 031 956 450
Fax: +39 031 951 529
Web: www.johansens.com/serbelloni

ITALY / LOMBARDY (BORMIO - BAGNI NUOVI - VALTELLINA)

Bagni di Bormio Spa Resort

Località Bagni Nuovi, 23038 Valdidentro (Sondrio), Italy
Tel: +39 0342 901890
Fax: +39 0342 913511
Web: www.johansens.com/bagnidibormio

ITALY / LOMBARDY (CANTELLO - VARESE)

Albergo Madonnina

Largo Lanfranco da Ligurno 1, 21050 Cantello - Varese, Italy
Tel: +39 0332 417 731
Fax: +39 0332 418 402
Web: www.johansens.com/madonnina

ITALY / LOMBARDY (ISEO HILLS - LAKE ISEO)

I Due Roccoli Relais

Via Silvio Bonomelli, Strada per Polaveno, 25049 Iseo (Brescia), Italy
Tel: +39 030 9822 977/8
Fax: +39 030 9822980
Web: www.johansens.com/idueroccoli

ITALY / LOMBARDY (LAKE GARDA - GARDONE RIVIERA)

Grand Hotel Gardone Riviera

Via Zanardelli 84, 25083 Gardone Riviera (BS), Lake Garda, Italy
Tel: +39 0365 20261
Fax: +39 0365 22695
Web: www.johansens.com/gardoneriviera

ITALY / LOMBARDY (LAKE GARDA - SALÒ)

Hotel Bellerive

Via Pietro da Salò 11, 25087 Salò (BS), Italy
Tel: +39 0365 520 410
Fax: +39 0365 290 709
Web: www.johansens.com/bellerive

ITALY / LOMBARDY (LIVIGNO - VALTELLINA)

Hotel Marzia

Via Pedrana 388, 23030 Livigno (SO), Italy
Tel: +39 0342 996 020
Fax: +39 0342 971 070
Web: www.johansens.com/marziahotel

ITALY / LOMBARDY (MILAN - FRANCIACORTA)

L'Albereta

Via Vittorio Emanuele II, no 23, 25030 Erbusco (Bs), Italy
Tel: +39 030 7760 550
Fax: +39 030 7760 573
Web: www.johansens.com/albereta

ITALY / LOMBARDY (MILAN - MONZA)

Hotel de la Ville

Viale Regina Margherita 15, 20052 Monza (MI), Italy
Tel: +39 039 3942 1
Fax: +39 039 367 647
Web: www.johansens.com/hoteldelaville

ITALY / LOMBARDY (MILAN)

Petit Palais maison de charme

Via Molino delle Armi 1, 20123 Milan, Italy
Tel: +39 02 584 891
Fax: +39 02 584 40732
Web: www.johansens.com/petitpalais

ITALY / MARCHE (CASTEL DI LUCO - ACQUASANTA TERME)

Castel di Luco

Acquasanta Terme, Frazione Castel di Luco, 63041 (AP), Italy
Tel: +39 0736 802319
Fax: +39 0736 802319
Web: www.johansens.com/casteldiluco

ITALY / PIEMONTE (ALAGNA - MONTE ROSA)

Hotel Cristallo

Piazza degli Alberghi, 13021 Alagna (VC), Italy
Tel: +39 0163 922 822/23
Fax: +39 0163 922 821
Web: www.johansens.com/cristallo

ITALY / PIEMONTE (CLAVIÈRE)

Hotel Bes

Via Nazionale 18, 10050 Clavière (TO), Italy
Tel: +39 0122 878735
Fax: +39 0122 444502
Web: www.johansens.com/hotelbes

ITALY / PIEMONTE (GAVI)

Albergo L'Ostelliere

Frazione Monterotondo 56, 15065 Gavi (AL), Piedmont, Italy
Tel: +39 0143 607 801
Fax: +39 0143 607 811
Web: www.johansens.com/ostelliere

ITALY / PIEMONTE (LAKE MAGGIORE - BELGIRATE)

Villa dal Pozzo d'Annone

Strada Statale del Sempione 5, 28832 Belgirate (VB), Lake Maggiore, Italy
Tel: +39 0322 7255
Fax: +39 0322 772021
Web: www.johansens.com/dalpozzodannone

ITALY / PIEMONTE (LAKE MAGGIORE - CANNOBIO)

Hotel Pironi

Via Marconi 35, 28822 Cannobio, Lake Maggiore (VB), Italy
Tel: +39 0323 70624
Fax: +39 0323 72184
Web: www.johansens.com/hotelpironi

Mini Listings Europe

Condé Nast Johansens are delighted to recommend 435 properties across Europe & The Mediterranean.
Call 1 800 564 7518 or see the Order Form on page 431 to order Guides.

ITALY / PIEMONTE (LAKE MAGGIORE - STRESA)

Hotel Villa Aminta

Via Sempione Nord 123, 28838 Stresa (VB), Italy
Tel: +39 0323 933 818
Fax: +39 0323 933 955
Web: www.johansens.com/aminta

ITALY / PIEMONTE (PENANGO - ASTI - MONFERRATO)

Relais Il Borgo

Via Biletta 60, 14030 Penango (AT), Italy
Tel: +39 0141 921272
Fax: +39 0141 923067
Web: www.johansens.com/relaisilborgo

ITALY / PUGLIA (MARTINA FRANCA)

Relais Villa San Martino

Via Taranto, Zona G - 59, 74015 Martina Franca (TA), Italy
Tel: +39 080 480 5152
Fax: +39 080 485 77 19
Web: www.johansens.com/martino

ITALY / SARDINIA (ALGHERO)

Villa Las Tronas

Lungomare Valencia 1, 07041 Alghero (SS), Italy
Tel: +39 079 981 818
Fax: +39 079 981 044
Web: www.johansens.com/lastronas

ITALY / SARDINIA (PORTO CERVO - COSTA SMERALDA)

Grand Hotel in Porto Cervo

Località Cala Granu, 07020 Porto Cervo (SS), Italy
Tel: +39 0789 91533
Fax: +39 0789 91508
Web: www.johansens.com/portocervo

ITALY / SARDINIA (SANTA MARGHERITA DI PULA - CAGLIARI)

Villa del Parco and Spa at Forte Village

SS 195, Km 39.600, Santa Margherita di Pula, 09010 Cagliari, Italy
Tel: +39 070 92171
Fax: +39 070 921246
Web: www.johansens.com/villadelparco

ITALY / SICILY (AEOLIAN ISLANDS - LIPARI)

Grand Hotel Arciduca

Via G Franza, 98055 Lipari (ME), Isole Eolie, Italy
Tel: +39 090 9812 136
Fax: +39 090 9811 387
Web: www.johansens.com/arciduca

ITALY / SICILY (AEOLIAN ISLANDS - SALINA)

Hotel Signum

Via Scalo 15, 98050 Salina~Malfa, Italy
Tel: +39 090 9844 222
Fax: +39 090 9844 102
Web: www.johansens.com/signum

ITALY / SICILY (CALATABIANO)

Castello di San Marco

Via San Marco 40, 95011 Calatabiano, Taormina (CT), Italy
Tel: +39 095 641 181
Fax: +39 095 642 635
Web: www.johansens.com/castellodisanmarco

ITALY / SICILY (MODICA)

Palazzo Failla Hotel

Via Blandini 5, 97010 Modica (RG), Italy
Tel: +39 0932 941 059
Fax: +39 0932 941 059
Web: www.johansens.com/plalazzopfailla

ITALY / SICILY (RAGUSA IBLA)

Locanda Don Serafino

Via XI Febbraio, 15 Ragusa Ibla, Italy
Tel: +39 0932 220 065
Fax: +39 0932 663 186
Web: www.johansens.com/serafino

ITALY / SICILY (TAORMINA MARE)

Grand Hotel Atlantis Bay

Via Nazionale 161, Taormina Mare (ME), Italy
Tel: +39 0942 618 011
Fax: +39 0942 23 194
Web: www.johansens.com/atlantis

ITALY / SICILY (TAORMINA MARE)

Grand Hotel Mazzarò Sea Palace

Via Nazionale 147, 98030 Taormina (ME), Italy
Tel: +39 0942 612 111
Fax: +39 0942 626 237
Web: www.johansens.com/mazzaroseapalace

ITALY / SICILY (TAORMINA RIVIERA – MARINA D'AGRO)

Baia Taormina Hotel - Resort & Spa

Statale dello Ionio, Km 39, 98030 Marina d'Agro, Taormina Riviera (ME), Italy
Tel: +39 0942 756 292
Fax: +39 0942 756 603
Web: www.johansens.com/baiataormina

ITALY / TRENTINO - ALTO ADIGE / DOLOMITES (BOLZANO - FIÈ ALLO SCILIAR)

Romantik Hotel Turm

Piazza della Chiesa 9, 39050 Fiè Allo Sciliar (Bz), Italy
Tel: +39 0471 725014
Fax: +39 0471 725474
Web: www.johansens.com/turm

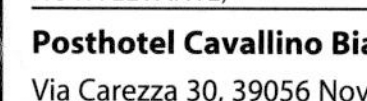

ITALY / TRENTINO - ALTO ADIGE / DOLOMITES (BOLZANO - NOVA LEVANTE)

Posthotel Cavallino Bianco

Via Carezza 30, 39056 Nova Levante (Bz), Dolomites, Italy
Tel: +39 0471 613113
Fax: +39 0471 613390
Web: www.johansens.com/weissesrossl

ITALY / TRENTINO - ALTO ADIGE / DOLOMITES (COLFOSCO - CORVARA)

Romantik Hotel Art Hotel Cappella

Str. Pecei 17, Alta Badia - Dolomites, 39030 Colfosco - Corvara (BZ), Italy
Tel: +39 0471 836183
Fax: +39 0471 836561
Web: www.johansens.com/cappella

ITALY / TRENTINO - ALTO ADIGE / DOLOMITES (MERANO)

Castel Fragsburg

Via Fragsburg 3, 39012 Merano, Italy
Tel: +39 0473 244071
Fax: +39 0473 244493
Web: www.johansens.com/fragsburg

ITALY / ?TRENTINO - ALTO ADIGE - DOLOMITES (VAL BADIA)

Hotel Gardena Grödnerhof

Str. Vidalong 3, 39046 Ortisei, Italy
Tel: +39 0471 796 315
Fax: +39 0471 796 513
Web: www.johansens.com/gardena

ITALY / TUSCANY (AMBRA - CHIANTI ARETINO)

Le Case Del Borgo - Tuscan Luxury Living

Loc. Duddova, 52020 Ambra (Arezzo), Italy
Tel: +39 055 991 871
Fax: +39 055 991 872/87
Web: www.johansens.com/lecasedelborgo

ITALY / TUSCANY (CASTAGNETO CARDUCCI - MARINA)

Tombolo Talasso Resort

Via del Corallo 3, 57024 Marina di Castagneto Carducci (LI), Italy
Tel: +39 0565 74530
Fax: +39 0565 744052
Web: www.johansens.com/tombolo

ITALY / TUSCANY (CORTONA)

Villa Marsili

Viale Cesare Battisti 13, 52044 Cortona (Arezzo), Italy
Tel: +39 0575 605 252
Fax: +39 0575 605 618
Web: www.johansens.com/villamarsili

Mini Listings Europe

Condé Nast Johansens are delighted to recommend 435 properties across Europe & The Mediterranean.
Call 1 800 564 7518 or see the Order Form on page 431 to order Guides.

ITALY / TUSCANY (ELBA ISLAND - PORTOFERRAIO)

Hotel Villa Ottone

Loc. Ottone, 57037 Portoferraio (LI), Isola d'Elba, Italy
Tel: +39 0565 933 042
Fax: +39 0565 933 257
Web: www.johansens.com/ottone

ITALY / TUSCANY (FLORENCE - BORGO SAN LORENZO)

Monsignor Della Casa Country Resort

Via di Mucciano 16, 50032 Borgo San Lorenzo, Florence, Italy
Tel: +39 055 840 821
Fax: +39 055 840 8240
Web: www.johansens.com/monsignor

ITALY / TUSCANY (FLORENCE)

Casa Howard

18 via della Scala, Piazza Santa Maria Novella, Florence, Italy
Tel: +39 066 992 4555
Fax: +39 066 794 644
Web: www.johansens.com/casahoward

ITALY / TUSCANY (FLORENCE)

Hotel Lorenzo Il Magnifico

Via Lorenzo Il Magnifico 25, 50129 Florence, Italy
Tel: +39 055 463 0878
Fax: +39 055 486 168
Web: www.johansens.com/lorenzomagnifico

ITALY / TUSCANY (FLORENCE)

Marignolle Relais & Charme

Via di S Quirichino a Marignolle 16, 50124 Florence, Italy
Tel: +39 055 228 6910
Fax: +39 055 204 7396
Web: www.johansens.com/marignolle

ITALY / TUSCANY (FLORENCE)

Relais Piazza Signoria

Via Vacchereccia 3, 50122 Florence, Italy
Tel: +39 055 3987239
Fax: +39 055 286306
Web: www.johansens.com/piazzasignoria

ITALY / TUSCANY (FLORENCE)

Relais Santa Croce

Via Ghibellina 15, 50122 Florence, Italy
Tel: +39 055 2342230
Fax: +39 055 2341195
Web: www.johansens.com/santacroce

ITALY / TUSCANY (FLORENCE)

Residenza del Moro

Via del Moro 15, 50123 Florence, Italy
Tel: +39 055 290884
Fax: +39 055 2648494
Web: www.johansens.com/delmoro

ITALY / TUSCANY (FLORENCE)

Villa Montartino

Via Gherardo Silvani 151, 50125 Florence, Italy
Tel: +39 055 223520
Fax: +39 055 223495
Web: www.johansens.com/villamontartino

ITALY / TUSCANY (FORTE DEI MARMI)

Hotel Byron

Viale A Morin 46, 55042 Forte dei Marmi (LU), Italy
Tel: +39 0584 787 052
Fax: +39 0584 787 152
Web: www.johansens.com/byron

ITALY / TUSCANY (LORO CIUFFENNA - AREZZO)

Relais Villa Belpoggio (Historical House)

Via Setteponti Ponente 40, 52024 Loro Ciuffenna, Arezzo, Italy
Tel: +39 055 9694411
Fax: +39 055 9694411
Web: www.johansens.com/villabelpoggio

ITALY / TUSCANY (LUCCA - PIETRASANTA)

Albergo Pietrasanta - Palazzo Barsanti Bonetti

Via Garibaldi 35, 55045 Pietrasanta (Lucca), Italy
Tel: +39 0584 793 727
Fax: +39 0584 793 728
Web: www.johansens.com/pietrasanta

ITALY / TUSCANY (LUCCA - SAN LORENZO A VACCOLI)

Albergo Villa Marta

Via del Ponte Guasperini 873, San Lorenzo a Vaccoli, 55100 Lucca, Italy
Tel: +39 0583 37 01 01
Fax: +39 0583 37 99 99
Web: www.johansens.com/villamarta

ITALY / TUSCANY (MONTEBENICHI - CHIANTI AREA)

Country House Casa Cornacchi

Loc. Montebenichi, 52021 Arezzo, Tuscany, Italy
Tel: +39 055 998229
Fax: +39 055 9983863
Web: www.johansens.com/cornacchi

ITALY / TUSCANY (PISA)

Hotel Relais Dell'Orologio

Via della Faggiola 12/14, 56126 Pisa, Italy
Tel: +39 050 830 361
Fax: +39 050 551 869
Web: www.johansens.com/relaisorologio

ITALY / TUSCANY (POGGI DEL SASSO - MAREMMA)

Castello di Vicarello

Loc. Vicarello, 58044 Poggi del Sasso (GR), Italy
Tel: +39 0564 990 718
Fax: +39 0564 990 718
Web: www.johansens.com/vicarello

ITALY / TUSCANY (PORTO ERCOLE - ARGENTARIO)

Il Pellicano Hotel & Spa

Loc. Sbarcatello, 58018 Porto Ercole (Gr), Tuscany, Italy
Tel: +39 0564 858111
Fax: +39 0564 833418
Web: www.johansens.com/ilpellicano

ITALY / TUSCANY (ROCCATEDERIGHI - GROSSETO)

Pieve di Caminino (Historical Residence)

Via Prov. di Peruzzo, 58028 Roccatederighi - Grosseto, Italy
Tel: +39 0564 569 736/7 or +39 3933 356 605
Fax: +39 0564 568 756
Web: www.johansens.com/caminino

ITALY / TUSCANY (SIENA - ASCIANO)

Hotel Borgo CasaBianca

Località Casabianca, 53041 Asciano (SI), Italy
Tel: +39 0577 704 362
Fax: +39 0577 704 622
Web: www.johansens.com/casabianca

ITALY / TUSCANY (SIENA - LOCALITA BAGNAIA)

Borgo La Bagnaia Resort, Spa and Events Venue

Strada Statale 223 Km 12, 53016 Localita Bagnaia - Siena, Italy
Tel: +39 0577 813000
Fax: +39 0577 817464
Web: www.johansens.com/labagnaia

ITALY / TUSCANY (SIENA - MONTEPULCIANO)

Relais Dionora

Via Vicinale di Poggiano, 53040 Montepulciano (Siena), Italy
Tel: +39 0578 717 496
Fax: +39 0578 717 498
Web: www.johansens.com/dionora

ITALY / TUSCANY (SIENA - MONTEPULCIANO)

Villa di Poggiano

Via di Poggiano 7, 53045 Montepulciano (Siena), Tuscany, Italy
Tel: +39 0578 758292
Fax: +39 0578 715635
Web: www.johansens.com/villadipoggiano

Mini Listings Europe

Condé Nast Johansens are delighted to recommend 435 properties across Europe & The Mediterranean.
Call 1 800 564 7518 or see the Order Form on page 431 to order Guides.

ITALY / TUSCANY (SIENA - MONTERIGGIONI – STROVE)

Castel Pietraio

Strada di Strove 33, 53035 Monteriggioni, Italy
Tel: +39 0577 300020
Fax: +39 0577 300977
Web: www.johansens.com/castelpietraio

ITALY / TUSCANY (SIENA - PIEVESCOLA)

Relais la Suvera (Dimora Storica)

53030 Pievescola – Siena, Italy
Tel: +39 0577 960 300
Fax: +39 0577 960 220
Web: www.johansens.com/relaislasuvera

ITALY / TUSCANY (VIAREGGIO)

Hotel Plaza e de Russie

Piazza d'Azeglio 1, 55049 Viareggio (LU), Italy
Tel: +39 0584 44449
Fax: +39 0584 44031
Web: www.johansens.com/russie

ITALY / UMBRIA (ASSISI - ARMENZANO)

Romantik Hotel le Silve di Armenzano

06081 Loc. Armenzano, Assisi (PG), Italy
Tel: +39 075 801 9000
Fax: +39 075 801 9005
Web: www.johansens.com/silvediarmenzano

ITALY / UMBRIA (ASSISI - TORDANDREA)

San Crispino Resort & Spa

Loc Tordandrea - Assisi, Tordandrea (PG), Italy
Tel: +39 075 804 3257
Fax: +39 075 804 3257
Web: www.johansens.com/sancrispinoresortspa

ITALY / UMBRIA (CORTONA - PETRIGNANO)

Relais Alla Corte del Sole

Loc. I Giorgi, 06061 Petrignano del Lago (PG), Italy
Tel: +39 075 9689008
Fax: +39 075 9689070
Web: www.johansens.com/cortedelsole

ITALY / UMBRIA (GUBBIO)

Castello di Petroia

Località Scritto di Gubbio, Petroia, 06020 Gubbio (Pg), Italy
Tel: +39 075 92 02 87
Fax: +39 075 92 01 08
Web: www.johansens.com/castellodipetroia

ITALY / UMBRIA (ORVIETO - ALLERONA)

I Casali di Monticchio

Vocabolo Monticchio 34, 05011 Allerona, Orvieto (TR), Italy
Tel: +39 0763 62 83 65
Fax: +39 0763 62 83 65
Web: www.johansens.com/monticchio

ITALY / UMBRIA (PERUGIA - DERUTA)

L'Antico Forziere

Via della Rocca 2, 06051 Casalina Deruta (PG), Italy
Tel: +39 075 972 4314
Fax: +39 075 972 9392
Web: www.johansens.com/lanticoforziere

ITALY / UMBRIA (PERUGIA - PIEVE SAN QUIRICO)

Le Torri di Bagnara (Medieval Historical Residences)

Strada della Bruna 8, 06080 Pieve San Quirico, Perugia, Italy
Tel: +39 075 579 2001 and +39 335 6408 549
Fax: +39 075 579 3001
Web: www.johansens.com/bagnara

ITALY / UMBRIA (PERUGIA - SAN MARTINO)

Alla Posta dei Donini

Via Deruta 43, 06079 San Martino in Campo (PG), Italy
Tel: +39 075 609 132
Fax: +39 075 609 132
Web: www.johansens.com/postadonini

ITALY / UMBRIA (UMBERTIDE - CALZOLARO)

La Preghiera

Via del Refari, 06018 (PG), Calzolaro, Umbertide, Italy
Tel: +39 075 9302428
Fax: +39 075 9302428
Web: www.johansens.com/lapreghiera

ITALY / VALLE D'AOSTA (COURMAYEUR - MONT BLANC)

Mont Blanc Hotel Village

Localita La Croisette 36, 11015 La Salle (AO), Valle d'Aosta, Italy
Tel: +39 0165 864 111
Fax: +39 0165 864 119
Web: www.johansens.com/montblanc

ITALY / VALLE D'AOSTA (GRESSONEY~LA~TRINITE)

Hotel Jolanda Sport

Loc. Edelboden 31, Gressoney~La~Trinite, 11020 Gressoney La Trinita (Aosta), Italy
Tel: +39 0125 366 140
Fax: +39 0125 366 202
Web: www.johansens.com/jolandasport

ITALY / VENETO (BASSANO DEL GRAPPA)

Hotel Villa Ca' Sette

Via Cunizza da Romano 4, 36061 Bassano del Grappa, Italy
Tel: +39 0424 383 350
Fax: +39 0424 393 287
Web: www.johansens.com/ca-sette

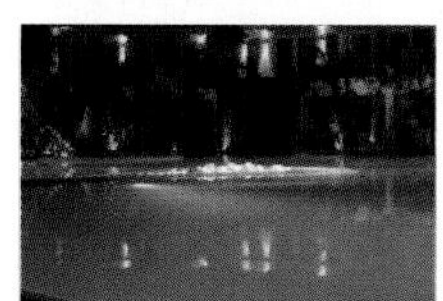

ITALY / VENETO (LAKE GARDA - VERONA - BARDOLINO)

Color Hotel

Via Santa Cristina 5, 37011 Bardolino (VR), Italy
Tel: +39 045 621 0857
Fax: +39 045 621 2697
Web: www.johansens.com/color

ITALY / VENETO (LAKE GARDA - VERONA - PESCHIERA DEL GARDA)

Ai Capitani Hotel

Via Castelletto 2/4, Peschiera del Garda (VR), Italy
Tel: +39 045 6400782 or 7553071
Fax: +39 045 6401571 or 7552885
Web: www.johansens.com/aicapitani

ITALY / VENETO (LAKE GARDA - VERONA - SAN VIGILIO)

Locanda San Vigilio

Località San Vigilio, 37016 Garda (VR), Italy
Tel: +39 045 725 66 88
Fax: +39 045 627 81 82
Web: www.johansens.com/sanvigilio

ITALY / VENETO (LIDO DI JESOLO)

Park Hotel Brasilia

Via Levantina, 30017 Lido di Jesolo, Italy
Tel: +39 0421 380851
Fax: +39 0421 92244
Web: www.johansens.com/parkhotelbrasilia

ITALY / VENETO (ROLLE DI CISON DI VALMARINO)

Relais Duca di Dolle

Via Piai Orientale 5, 31030 Rolle di Cison di Valmarino (TV), Italy
Tel: +39 0438 975 809
Fax: +39 0438 975 792
Web: www.johansens.com/foresteriabisol

ITALY / VENETO (TREVISO - ASOLO)

Albergo Al Sole

Via Collegio 33, 31011 Asolo, Treviso, Italy
Tel: +39 0423 951 332
Fax: +39 0423 951 007
Web: www.johansens.com/alsole

ITALY / VENETO (VENICE – LIDO)

Albergo Quattro Fontane - Residenza d'Epoca

Via Quattro Fontane 16, 30126 Lido di Venezia, Venice, Italy
Tel: +39 041 526 0227
Fax: +39 041 526 0726
Web: www.johansens.com/albergoquattrofontane

Mini Listings Europe

Condé Nast Johansens are delighted to recommend 435 properties across Europe & The Mediterranean.
Call 1 800 564 7518 or see the Order Form on page 431 to order Guides.

ITALY / VENETO (VENICE)

Ca Maria Adele

Dorsoduro 111, 30123 Venice, Italy
Tel: +39 041 52 03 078
Fax: +39 041 52 89 013
Web: www.johansens.com/camariaadele

ITALY / VENETO (VENICE)

Hotel Flora

San Marco 2283/A, 30124 Venice, Italy
Tel: +39 041 52 05 844
Fax: +39 041 52 28 217
Web: www.johansens.com/hotelflora

ITALY / VENETO (VENICE)

Hotel Giorgione

SS Apostoli 4587, 30131 Venice, Italy
Tel: +39 041 522 5810
Fax: +39 041 523 9092
Web: www.johansens.com/giorgione

ITALY / VENETO (VENICE)

Hotel Sant' Elena Venezia

Calle Buccari 10, Sant' Elena, 30132 Venice, Italy
Tel: +39 041 27 17 811
Fax: +39 041 27 71 569
Web: www.johansens.com/santelena

ITALY / VENETO (VENICE)

Londra Palace

Riva degli Schiavoni, 4171, 30122 Venice, Italy
Tel: +39 041 5200533
Fax: +39 041 5225032
Web: www.johansens.com/londrapalace

ITALY / VENETO (VENICE)

Novecento Boutique Hotel

San Marco 2684, 30124 Venice, Italy
Tel: +39 041 24 13 765
Fax: +39 041 52 12 145
Web: www.johansens.com/novecento

ITALY / VENETO (VERONA - COSTERMANO)

Locanda San Verolo

Località San Verolo, 37010 Costermano (VR), Italy
Tel: +39 045 720 09 30
Fax: +39 045 620 11 66
Web: www.johansens.com/sanverolo

ITALY / VENETO (VERONA - SAN PIETRO IN CARIANO)

Villa Giona

Via Cengia 8, 37029 San Pietro in Cariano (VR), Italy
Tel: +39 045 685 50 11
Fax: +39 045 685 50 10
Web: www.johansens.com/villagiona

ITALY / VENETO (VERONA - VALPOLICELLA)

Relais la Magioca

Via Moron 3, 37024 Negrar - Valpolicella (VR), Italy
Tel: +39 045 600 0167
Fax: +39 045 600 0840
Web: www.johansens.com/lamagioca

ITALY / VENETO (VERONA)

Hotel Gabbia d'Oro (Historical Residence)

Corso Porta Borsari 4A, 37121 Verona, Italy
Tel: +39 045 8003060
Fax: +39 045 590293
Web: www.johansens.com/gabbiadoro

LATVIA (JURMALA)

TB Palace Hotel & Spa

Pilsonu Street 8, Jurmala, LV-2015, Latvia
Tel: +371 714 7094
Fax: +371 714 7097
Web: www.johansens.com/tbpalace

LATVIA (RIGA)

Hotel Bergs

Bergs Bazaar, Elizabetes Street 83/85, LV-1050, Riga, Latvia
Tel: +371 777 09 00
Fax: +371 777 09 40
Web: www.johansens.com/bergs

LITHUANIA (VILNIUS)

Grotthuss Hotel

Ligoninès 7, 01134 Vilnius, Lithuania
Tel: +370 5 266 0322
Fax: +370 5 266 0323
Web: www.johansens.com/grotthusshotel

LITHUANIA (VILNIUS)

The Narutis Hotel

24 Pilies Street, 01123 Vilnius, Lithuania
Tel: +370 5 2122 894
Fax: +370 5 2622 882
Web: www.johansens.com/narutis

LUXEMBOURG (REMICH)

Hotel Saint~Nicolas

31 Esplanade, 5533 Remich, Luxembourg
Tel: +35 226 663
Fax: +35 226 663 666
Web: www.johansens.com/saintnicolas

MONTENEGRO (ST. STEFAN)

Villa Montenegro

2 Vukice Mitrovic Str, 86312 St. Stefan, Montenegro
Tel: +381 86 468 802
Fax: +381 86 468 809
Web: www.johansens.com/villamontenegro

THE NETHERLANDS (AMSTERDAM)

Ambassade Hotel

Herengracht 341, 1016 Amsterdam, The Netherlands
Tel: +31 20 5550222
Fax: +31 20 5550277
Web: www.johansens.com/ambassade

THE NETHERLANDS (NOORD BRABANT - BREDA)

Bliss Hotel

Torenstraat 9, 4811 XV Breda, The Netherlands
Tel: +31 076 533 5980
Fax: +31 076 533 5981
Web: www.johansens.com/bliishotel

THE NETHERLANDS (SANTPOORT - AMSTERDAM)

Duin & Kruidberg Country Estate

Duin en Kruidbergerweg 60, 2071 Santpoort, Amsterdam, The Netherlands
Tel: +31 23 512 1800
Fax: +31 23 512 1888
Web: www.johansens.com/duinkruidberg

THE NETHERLANDS (VREELAND)

Hotel Restaurant de Nederlanden

Duinkerken 3, 3633 EM, Vreeland aan de Vecht, The Netherlands
Tel: +31 294 232 326
Fax: +31 294 231 407
Web: www.johansens.com/denederlanden

THE NETHERLANDS (ZEELAND - VEERE)

Auberge de Campveerse Toren

Kaai 2, 4351 AA Veere, The Netherlands
Tel: +31 0118 501 291
Fax: +31 0118 501 695
Web: www.johansens.com/campveersetoren

POLAND

Hotel Copernicus

ul. Kanonicza 16, 31-002 Kraków, Poland
Tel: +48 12 424 34 00/1/2
Fax: +48 12 424 34 05
Web: www.johansens.com/copernicus

Mini Listings Europe

Condé Nast Johansens are delighted to recommend 435 properties across Europe & The Mediterranean.
Call 1 800 564 7518 or see the Order Form on page 431 to order Guides.

PORTUGAL / ALENTEJO (BORBA)

Casa do Terreiro do Poço

Largo dos Combatentes da Grande Guerra 12, 7150-152 Borba, Portugal
Tel: +351 917 256077
Fax: +351 268 083624
Web: www.johansens.com/casadoterreiro

PORTUGAL / ALENTEJO (BORBA - ESTREMOZ)

Monte da Fornalha

Borba - Estremoz, Portugal
Tel: +351 268 840 314
Fax: +351 268 891 885
Web: www.johansens.com/montedafornalha

PORTUGAL / ALENTEJO (ÉVORA)

Convento do Espinheiro Heritage Hotel & Spa

Canaviais, 7005-839 Évora, Portugal
Tel: +351 266 788 200
Fax: +351 266 788 229
Web: www.johansens.com/espinheiro

PORTUGAL / ALENTEJO (MÉRTOLA)

Estalagem São Domingos

Rua Dr Vargas, Mina de São Domingos, 7750-171 Mértola, Portugal
Tel: +351 286 640 000
Fax: +351 286 640 009
Web: www.johansens.com/saodomingos

PORTUGAL / ALENTEJO (MONTEMOR~O~NOVO)

Monte do Chora Cascas

Apt 296, 7050-013 Montemor~o~Novo, Portugal
Tel: +351 266 899 690
Fax: +351 266 899 690
Web: www.johansens.com/montechoracascas

PORTUGAL / ALENTEJO (REDONDO)

Convento de São Paulo

Aldeia da Serra, 7170-120 Redondo, Portugal
Tel: +351 266 989 160
Fax: +351 266 989 167
Web: www.johansens.com/conventodesaopaulo

PORTUGAL / ALGARVE (ALMANCIL)

Hotel Quinta do Lago

8135-024 Almancil, Algarve, Portugal
Tel: +351 289 350 350
Fax: +351 289 396 393
Web: www.johansens.com/quintadolago

PORTUGAL / ALGARVE (GARRÃO)

Quinta Jacintina

Garrão de Cima, 8135-025 Almancil, Portugal
Tel: +351 289 350 090
Fax: +351 289 350 099
Web: www.johansens.com/jacintina

PORTUGAL / ALGARVE (LAGOS)

Villa Esmeralda

Porto de Mós, 8600 Lagos, Portugal
Tel: +351 282 760 430
Fax: +351 282 760 433
Web: www.johansens.com/esmeralda

PORTUGAL / BEIRAS (MARIALVA - MÊDA)

Casas do Côro

Marialvamed Turismo Histórico e Lazer Lda, Largo do Côro, 6430-081 Marialva, Mêda, Portugal
Tel: +351 91 755 2020
Fax: +351 27 159 0003
Web: www.johansens.com/casasdocoro

PORTUGAL / LISBON & TAGUS VALLEY (CASCAIS)

Albatroz Palace, Luxury Suites

Rua Frederico Arouca 100, 2750-353 Cascais, Lisbon, Portugal
Tel: +351 21 484 73 80
Fax: +351 21 484 48 27
Web: www.johansens.com/albatroz

PORTUGAL / LISBON & TAGUS VALLEY (CASCAIS)

Hotel Cascais Mirage

Av. Marginal, No 8554, 2754-536 Cascais, Portugal
Tel: +351 210 060 600
Fax: +351 210 060 601
Web: www.johansens.com/cascaismirage

PORTUGAL / LISBON & TAGUS VALLEY (CASCAIS)

Senhora da Guia

Estrada do Guincho, 2750-642 Cascais, Portugal
Tel: +351 214 869 239
Fax: +351 214 869 227
Web: www.johansens.com/senhoradaguia

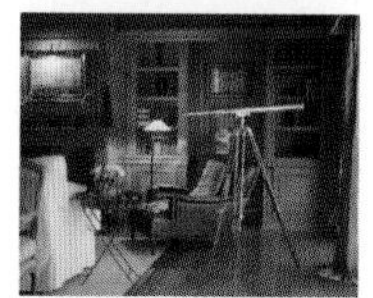

PORTUGAL / LISBON & TAGUS VALLEY (LISBON)

As Janelas Verdes

Rua das Janelas Verdes 47, 1200-690 Lisbon, Portugal
Tel: +351 21 39 68 143
Fax: +351 21 39 68 144
Web: www.johansens.com/janelasverdes

PORTUGAL / LISBON & TAGUS VALLEY (LISBON)

Heritage Av Liberdade

Avenida da Liberdade 28, 1250-145 Lisbon, Portugal
Tel: +351 213 404 040
Fax: +351 213 404 044
Web: www.johansens.com/liberdade

PORTUGAL / LISBON & TAGUS VALLEY (LISBON)

Hotel Britania

Rua Rodrigues Sampaio 17, 1150-278 Lisbon, Portugal
Tel: +351 21 31 55 016
Fax: +351 21 31 55 021
Web: www.johansens.com/britania

PORTUGAL / MADEIRA (FUNCHAL)

Quinta da Bela Vista

Caminho do Avista Navios 4, 9000 Funchal, Madeira, Portugal
Tel: +351 291 706 400
Fax: +351 291 706 401
Web: www.johansens.com/quintadabelavista

PORTUGAL / MADEIRA (PONTA DO SOL)

Estalagem da Ponta do Sol

Quinta da Rochinha, 9360 Ponta do Sol, Madeira, Portugal
Tel: +351 291 970 200
Fax: +351 291 970 209
Web: www.johansens.com/pontadosol

PORTUGAL / OPORTO & NORTHERN PORTUGAL (ERVEDOSA DO DOURO)

Quinta de San José

5130-123 Ervedosa do Douro, Portugal
Tel: +351 254 420000 or +351 917 220450
Fax: +351 254 420009
Web: www.johansens.com/quintasanjose

PORTUGAL / OPORTO & NORTHERN PORTUGAL (PINHÃO)

Vintage House

Lugar da Ponte, 5085-034 Pinhão, Portugal
Tel: +351 254 730 230
Fax: +351 254 730 238
Web: www.johansens.com/vintagehouse

PORTUGAL / OPORTO & NORTHERN PORTUGAL (VIANA DO CASTELO)

Casa da Torre das Neves

Lugar de Neves, Vila de Punhe 4905-653, Viana do Castelo, Portugal
Tel: +351 932 032 980 and +351 258 771 300
Fax: +351 226 178 854
Web: www.johansens.com/torredasneves

PORTUGAL / OPORTO & NORTHERN PORTUGAL (VIDAGO)

Vidago Palace Hotel & Golf

Parque de Vidago, 5425-307 Vidago, Portugal
Tel: +351 276 990 900
Fax: +351 276 907 359
Web: www.johansens.com/vidago

Mini Listings Europe

Condé Nast Johansens are delighted to recommend 435 properties across Europe & The Mediterranean.
Call 1 800 564 7518 or see the Order Form on page 431 to order Guides.

SLOVAKIA (SALGOVCE - PIESTANY)

The Château
Salgovce 28, 95606 Slovakia
Tel: +421 385 395 155
Fax: +44 7005 961 845
Web: www.johansens.com/thechateausk

SLOVENIA (BLED)

Hotel Golf
Cankarjeva 4, 4260 Bled, Slovenia
Tel: +386 4579 1700
Fax: +386 45791701
Web: www.johansens.com/hotelgolfsi

SPAIN / ANDALUCÍA (ANTEQUERA - LA JOYA)

Hotel La Fuente del Sol
Paraje Rosas Bajas, 29260 La Joya, Antequera, Spain
Tel: +34 95 12 39 823
Fax: +34 95 12 32 090
Web: www.johansens.com/fuentedelsol

SPAIN / ANDALUCÍA (ARCOS DE LA FRONTERA)

Hacienda el Santiscal
Avda. El Santiscal 129 (Lago de Arcos), 11638 Arcos de La Frontera, Spain
Tel: +34 956 70 83 13
Fax: +34 956 70 82 68
Web: www.johansens.com/haciendaelsantiscal

SPAIN / ANDALUCÍA (ARCOS DE LA FRONTERA)

Hotel Cortijo Faín
Carretera de Algar Km 3, 11630 Arcos de la Frontera, Cádiz, Spain
Tel: +34 956 704 131
Fax: +34 956 717 932
Web: www.johansens.com/cortijofain

SPAIN / ANDALUCÍA (BENAHAVÍS - MARBELLA)

Gran Hotel Benahavís
Huerta de Rufino s/n, 29679 Benahavís, Málaga, Spain
Tel: +34 902 504 862
Fax: +34 902 504 861
Web: www.johansens.com/hotelbenahavis

SPAIN / ANDALUCÍA (CORDOBA)

Hospes Palacio del Bailío
Ramirez de las Casas Deza 10-12, 14001 Cordoba, Spain
Tel: +34 957 498 993
Fax: +34 957 498 994
Web: www.johansens.com/hospesbailio

SPAIN / ANDALUCÍA (ESTEPONA)

Gran Hotel Elba Estepona & Thalasso Spa
Urb. Arena Beach, Ctra. Estepona-Cádiz 151, 29680 Estepona, Spain
Tel: +34 952 809 200
Fax: +34 952 809 201
Web: www.johansens.com/elbaestepona

SPAIN / ANDALUCÍA (GAUCIN)

Hotel Casablanca
Calla Teodoro de Molina, No 12, 29480 Gaucin, Málaga, Spain
Tel: +34 952 151 019
Fax: +34 952 151 495
Web: www.johansens.com/hotelcasablanca

SPAIN / ANDALUCÍA (GRANADA - COSTA TROPICAL)

Casa de los Bates
Carretera Nacional 340 Málaga - Almeria, Km 329, 5 Salobreña - Motril, Provincia de Granada, Spain
Tel: +34 958 349 495
Fax: +34 958 834 131
Web: www.johansens.com/casadelosbates

SPAIN / ANDALUCÍA (GRANADA)

Barceló la Bobadilla *** GL**
Finca La Bobadilla, Apto. 144, 18300 Loja, Granada, Spain
Tel: +34 958 32 18 61
Fax: +34 958 32 18 10
Web: www.johansens.com/bobadilla

SPAIN / ANDALUCÍA (GRANADA)

El Ladrón de Agua
Carrera del Darro 13, 18010 Granada, Spain
Tel: +34 958 21 50 40
Fax: +34 958 22 43 45
Web: www.johansens.com/ladrondeagua

SPAIN / ANDALUCÍA (GRANADA)

Hospes Palacio de los Patos
C/ Solarillo de Gracia 1, 18002 Granada, Andalucía, Spain
Tel: +34 958 535 790
Fax: +34 958 536 968
Web: www.johansens.com/lospatos

SPAIN / ANDALUCÍA (GRANADA)

Hotel Casa Morisca
Cuesta de la Victoria 9, 18010 Granada, Spain
Tel: +34 958 221 100
Fax: +34 958 215 796
Web: www.johansens.com/morisca

SPAIN / ANDALUCÍA (GRANADA)

Hotel Palacio de Santa Inés
Cuesta de Santa Inés 9, 18010 Granada, Spain
Tel: +34 958 22 23 62
Fax: +34 958 22 24 65
Web: www.johansens.com/sanaines

SPAIN / ANDALUCÍA (GRANADA)

Palacio de los Navas
Calle Navas 1, 18009 Granada, Spain
Tel: +34 958 21 57 60
Fax: +34 958 21 57 60
Web: www.johansens.com/palaciodelosnavas

SPAIN / ANDALUCÍA (GRANADA)

Santa Isabel la Real
Santa Isabel La Real 19, 18010 Granada, Spain
Tel: +34 958 294 658
Fax: +34 958 294 645
Web: www.johansens.com/santaisabel

SPAIN / ANDALUCÍA (JEREZ DE LA FRONTERA)

Casa Viña de Alcantara
Ctra. de Arcos Km 7.8, Jerez (Cádiz), Spain
Tel: +34 956 393 010
Fax: +34 956 393 011
Web: www.johansens.com/vinadealcantara

SPAIN / ANDALUCÍA (MÁLAGA)

El Molino de Santillán
Ctra. de Macharaviaya, Km 3, 29730 Rincón de la Victoria, Málaga, Spain
Tel: +34 952 40 09 49
Fax: +34 952 40 09 50
Web: www.johansens.com/molinodesantillan

SPAIN / ANDALUCÍA (MÁLAGA)

Hotel Molina Lario
Molina Lario 22, 29015 Málaga, Spain
Tel: +34 952 06 002
Fax: +34 952 06 001
Web: www.johansens.com/hotelmolina

SPAIN / ANDALUCÍA (MARBELLA)

Gran Hotel Guadalpin Banús
c/ Edgar Neville, s/n 29660 Nueva Andalucía, Marbella, Málaga, Spain
Tel: +34 952 89 94 04 or +34 952 89 97 00
Fax: +34 952 86 81 72 or +34 952 89 97 01
Web: www.johansens.com/granhotelguadalpinbanus

SPAIN / ANDALUCÍA (MARBELLA)

Gran Hotel Guadalpin Marbella
Blvd. Príncipe Alfonso de Hohenlohe, 29600 Marbella, Málaga, Spain
Tel: +34 952 89 94 04 and +34 952 89 94 00
Fax: +34 952 86 81 72 and +34 952 89 94 01
Web: www.johansens.com/granhotelguadalpinmarbella

Mini Listings Europe

Condé Nast Johansens are delighted to recommend 435 properties across Europe & The Mediterranean.
Call 1 800 564 7518 or see the Order Form on page 431 to order Guides.

SPAIN / ANDALUCÍA (MARBELLA)

Vasari Resort & Spa

Urb. La Alzambra, Edif. Vasari Center, 29660 Marbella, Málaga, Spain
Tel: +34 952 907 806
Fax: +34 952 906 798
Web: www.johansens.com/vasari

SPAIN / ANDALUCÍA (MIJAS~COSTA)

Gran Hotel Guadalpin Byblos

Urbanización Mijas Golf, 29650 Mijas, Málaga, Spain
Tel: +34 952 89 94 04 or +34 952 89 94 03
Fax: +34 952 86 81 72 or +34 952 89 94 01
Web: www.johansens.com/granhotelguadalpinbyblos

SPAIN / ANDALUCÍA (RONDA)

Hotel Molino del Arco

Partido de los Frontones s/n, 29400 Ronda, Málaga, Spain
Tel: +34 952 114 017
Fax: +34 952 11 44 57
Web: www.johansens.com/molinodelarco

SPAIN / ANDALUCÍA (SEVILLA - CAZALLA DE LA SIERRA)

Palacio de San Benito

c/San Benito S/N, 41370 Cazalla de La Sierra, Sevilla, Spain
Tel: +34 954 88 33 36
Fax: +34 954 88 31 62
Web: www.johansens.com/palaciodesanbenito

SPAIN / ANDALUCÍA (SEVILLA - ÉCIJA)

Hotel Palacio de Los Granados

Emilio Castelar 42, 41400 Écija, Sevilla, Spain
Tel: +34 955 905 344
Fax: +34 955 901 412
Web: www.johansens.com/granados

SPAIN / ANDALUCÍA (SEVILLA - GUILLENA)

Hotel Cortijo Águila Real

Ctra. Guillena–Burguillos Km 4, 41210 Guillena, Sevilla, Spain
Tel: +34 955 78 50 06
Fax: +34 955 78 43 30
Web: www.johansens.com/cortijoaguilareal

SPAIN / ANDALUCÍA (SEVILLA - LAS CABEZAS)

Cortijo Soto Real

Ctra. Las Cabezas Villamartin Km 13, 41730 - Las Cabezas (Sevilla), Spain
Tel: +34 955 869 200
Fax: +34 955 869 202
Web: www.johansens.com/sotoreal

SPAIN / ANDALUCÍA (SEVILLA - OSUNA)

Palacio Marqués de la Gomera

C/ San Pedro 20, 41640 Osuna, Sevilla, Spain
Tel: +34 95 4 81 22 23
Fax: +34 95 4 81 02 00
Web: www.johansens.com/palaciomarquesdelagomera

SPAIN / ANDALUCÍA (SEVILLA - SANLÚCAR LA MAYOR)

Hacienda Benazuza el Bulli Hotel

C/Virgin de las Nieves S/N, 41800 Sanlúcar La Mayor, Seville, Spain
Tel: +34 955 70 33 44
Fax: +34 955 70 34 10
Web: www.johansens.com/haciendabenazuza

SPAIN / ANDALUCÍA (SEVILLA)

Casa No 7

Calle Virgenes No 7, 41004 Sevilla, Spain
Tel: +34 954 221 581
Fax: +34 954 214 527
Web: www.johansens.com/casanumero7

SPAIN / ANDALUCÍA (SEVILLA)

Hospes las Casas del Rey de Baeza

C/Santiago, Plaza Jesús de la Redención 2, 41003 Sevilla, Spain
Tel: +34 954 561 496
Fax: +34 954 561 441
Web: www.johansens.com/casasdelrey

SPAIN / ANDALUCÍA (SOTOGRANDE)

Hotel Almenara

A-7 (National Road), 11310 Sotogrande, Spain
Tel: +34 956 58 20 00 or +34 902 18 18 36
Fax: +34 956 58 20 01
Web: www.johansens.com/almenara

SPAIN / ANDALUCÍA (ÚBEDA)

Palacio de la Rambla

Plaza del Marqués 1, 23400 Úbeda~Jaén, Spain
Tel: +34 953 75 01 96
Fax: +34 953 75 02 67
Web: www.johansens.com/rambla

SPAIN / ARAGÓN (TRAMACASTILLA DE TENA)

Hotel el Privilegio de Tena

Plaza Mayor, 22663 Tramacastilla de Tena, Aragón, Spain
Tel: +34 974 487 206
Fax: +34 974 487 270
Web: www.johansens.com/elprivilegiodetena

SPAIN / ARAGÓN (VALDERROBRES)

La Torre del Visco

44587 Fuentespalda, Teruel, Spain
Tel: +34 978 76 90 15
Fax: +34 978 76 90 16
Web: www.johansens.com/torredelvisco

SPAIN / ASTURIAS (CANGAS DE ONÍS)

Hotel La Cepada

Avenida Contranquil s/n, 33550 Cangas de Onís, Spain
Tel: +34 985 84 94 45
Fax: +34 985 84 95 66
Web: www.johansens.com/cepada

SPAIN / ASTURIAS (VILLAMAYOR)

Palacio de Cutre

La Goleta S/N, Villamayor, 33583 Infiesto, Asturias, Spain
Tel: +34 985 70 80 72
Fax: +34 985 70 80 19
Web: www.johansens.com/palaciodecutre

SPAIN / BALEARIC ISLANDS (IBIZA)

Atzaró Agroturismo

Ctra. San Juan, Km 15, 07840 Santa Eulalia, Ibiza, Balearic Islands
Tel: +34 971 33 88 38
Fax: +34 971 33 16 50
Web: www.johansens.com/atzaroagroturismo

SPAIN / BALEARIC ISLANDS (IBIZA)

Can Lluc

Crta. Santa Inés, km 2, 07816 San Rafael, Ibiza, Balearic Islands
Tel: +34 971 198 673
Fax: +34 971 198 547
Web: www.johansens.com/canlluc

SPAIN / BALEARIC ISLANDS (IBIZA)

Cas Gasi

Camino Viejo de Sant Mateu s/n, PO Box 117, 07814 Santa Gertrudis, Ibiza, Balearic Islands
Tel: +34 971 197 700
Fax: +34 971 197 899
Web: www.johansens.com/casgasi

SPAIN / BALEARIC ISLANDS (MALLORCA)

Blau Porto Petro Beach Resort & Spa

Avenida des Far 12, 07691 Porto Petro (Santanyi), Mallorca, Balearic Islands
Tel: +34 971 648 282
Fax: +34 971 648 283
Web: www.johansens.com/blaupivilege

SPAIN / BALEARIC ISLANDS (MALLORCA)

Ca's Xorc

Carretera de Deià, Km 56.1, 07100 Sóller, Mallorca, Balearic Islands
Tel: +34 971 63 82 80
Fax: +34 971 63 29 49
Web: www.johansens.com/casxorc

Mini Listings Europe

Condé Nast Johansens are delighted to recommend 435 properties across Europe & The Mediterranean.
Call 1 800 564 7518 or see the Order Form on page 431 to order Guides.

SPAIN / BALEARIC ISLANDS (MALLORCA)

Can Simoneta

Ctra. de Artá a Canyamel km 8, Finca Torre de Canyamel, 07580 Capdepera, Mallorca, Balearic Islands
Tel: +34 971 816 110
Fax: +34 971 816 111
Web: www.johansens.com/simoneta

SPAIN / BALEARIC ISLANDS (MALLORCA)

Hospes Maricel

Carretera d'Andratx 11, 07181 Cas Català, (Calvià) Mallorca, Balearic Islands
Tel: +34 971 707 744
Fax: +34 971 707 745
Web: www.johansens.com/maricel

SPAIN / BALEARIC ISLANDS (MALLORCA)

Hotel Aimia

Santa Maria del Camí, 1 07108 Port de Sóller, Mallorca, Spain
Tel: +34 971 631 200
Fax: +34 971 638 040
Web: www.johansens.com/aimia

SPAIN / BALEARIC ISLANDS (MALLORCA)

Hotel Cala Sant Vicenç

c/Maressers 2, Cala Sant Vicenç, 07469 Pollença, Mallorca, Spain
Tel: +34 971 53 02 50
Fax: +34 971 53 20 84
Web: www.johansens.com/hotelcala

SPAIN / BALEARIC ISLANDS (MALLORCA)

Hotel Dalt Murada

C/ Almudaina 6-A, 07001 Palma de Mallorca, Mallorca, Balearic Islands
Tel: +34 971 425 300
Fax: +34 971 719 708
Web: www.johansens.com/daltmurada

SPAIN / BALEARIC ISLANDS (MALLORCA)

Hotel Migjorn

Poligono 18, Parcela 477, Campos, Mallorca, Spain
Tel: +34 971 650 668
Fax: +34 971 651 418
Web: www.johansens.com/hotelmigjorn

SPAIN / BALEARIC ISLANDS (MALLORCA)

Hotel Tres

C/ Apuntadores 3, 07012 Palma de Mallorca, Balearic Islands, Spain
Tel: +34 971 717 333
Fax: +34 971 717 372
Web: www.johansens.com/hoteltres

SPAIN / BALEARIC ISLANDS (MALLORCA)

La Reserva Rotana

Cami de Sa Vall, Km 3, Apart. Correos 69, 07500 Manacor, Mallorca, Spain
Tel: +34 971 84 56 85
Fax: +34 971 55 52 58
Web: www.johansens.com/reservarotana

SPAIN / BALEARIC ISLANDS (MALLORCA)

Palacio Ca Sa Galesa

Carrer de Miramar 8, 07001 Palma de Mallorca, Balearic Islands
Tel: +34 971 715 400
Fax: +34 971 721 579
Web: www.johansens.com/casagalesa

SPAIN / BALEARIC ISLANDS (MALLORCA)

Read's Hotel & Vespasian Spa

Carretera Viejo de Alaro S/n, Santa María 07320, Mallorca, Balearic Islands
Tel: +34 971 14 02 61
Fax: +34 971 14 07 62
Web: www.johansens.com/reads

SPAIN / BALEARIC ISLANDS (MALLORCA)

Son Brull Hotel & Spa

Ctra. Palma - Pollença, MA 2200 - Km 49.8, 07460 Pollença, Mallorca, Spain
Tel: +34 971 53 53 53
Fax: +34 971 53 10 68
Web: www.johansens.com/sonbrull

SPAIN / BALEARIC ISLANDS (MALLORCA)

Valldemossa Hotel & Restaurant

Ctra. Vieja de Valldemossa s/n, 07170 Valldemossa, Mallorca, Balearic Islands
Tel: +34 971 61 26 26
Fax: +34 971 61 26 25
Web: www.johansens.com/valldemossa

SPAIN / CANARY ISLANDS (FUERTEVENTURA)

Hotel Elba Palace Golf

Urb. Fuerteventura Golf Club, Ctra. de Jandia, km11, 35610 Antigua, Fuerteventura, Canary Islands
Tel: +34 928 16 39 22
Fax: +34 928 16 39 23
Web: www.johansens.com/elbapalacegolfhotel

SPAIN / CANARY ISLANDS (FUERTEVENTURA)

Kempinski Atlantis Bahía Real

Avenida Grandes Playas s/n, 35660 Corralejo, Fuerteventura, Canary Islands
Tel: +34 928 53 64 44
Fax: +34 928 53 75 75
Web: www.johansens.com/atlantisbahiareal

SPAIN / CANARY ISLANDS (GRAN CANARIA)

Gran Hotel Lopesan Costa Meloneras

C/Mar Mediterráneo 1, 35100 Maspalomas, Gran Canaria, Canary Islands
Tel: +34 928 12 81 00
Fax: +34 928 12 81 22
Web: www.johansens.com/costameloneras

SPAIN / CANARY ISLANDS (GRAN CANARIA)

Gran Hotel Lopesan Villa del Conde

C/Mar Mediterráneo 7, Urbanización Costa Meloneras, 35100 Maspalomas, Gran Canaria, Canary Islands
Tel: +34 928 563 200
Fax: +34 928 563 222
Web: www.johansens.com/lopesanconde

SPAIN / CANARY ISLANDS (LANZAROTE)

Caserío de Mozaga

Mozaga 8, 35562 San Bartolomé, Lanzarote, Canary Islands
Tel: +34 928 520 060
Fax: +34 928 522 029
Web: www.johansens.com/caseriodemozaga

SPAIN / CANARY ISLANDS (LANZAROTE)

Princesa Yaiza Suite Hotel Resort

Avenida Papagayo s/n, 35570 Playa Blanca, Yaiza, Lanzarote, Canary Islands
Tel: +34 928 519 222
Fax: +34 928 519 179
Web: www.johansens.com/yaiza

SPAIN / CANARY ISLANDS (TENERIFE)

Abama

Carretera General TF-47, Km 9, 38687 Guía de Isora, Tenerife, Canary Islands
Tel: +34 922 126 000
Fax: +34 922 126 100
Web: www.johansens.com/abama

SPAIN / CANARY ISLANDS (TENERIFE)

Hotel Jardín Tropical

Calle Gran Bretaña, 38670 Costa Adeje, Tenerife, Canary Islands
Tel: +34 922 74 60 00
Fax: +34 922 74 60 60
Web: www.johansens.com/jardintropical

SPAIN / CANARY ISLANDS (TENERIFE)

Gran Hotel Bahía del Duque Resort *** G.Lujo**

C/Alcalde Walter Paetzmann, s/n, 38660 Costa Adeje, Tenerife, Canary Islands
Tel: +34 922 74 69 00
Fax: +34 922 74 69 16
Web: www.johansens.com/granhotelbahiadelduque

SPAIN / CANARY ISLANDS (TENERIFE)

Hotel las Madrigueras

Golf Las Américas, 38660 Playa de Las Américas, Tenerife, Canary Islands
Tel: +34 922 77 78 18
Fax: +34 922 77 78 19
Web: www.johansens.com/madrigueras

Mini Listings Europe

Condé Nast Johansens are delighted to recommend 435 properties across Europe & The Mediterranean.
Call 1 800 564 7518 or see the Order Form on page 431 to order Guides.

SPAIN / CANARY ISLANDS (TENERIFE)

Jardín de la Paz

Calle de Acentejo 48-52, 38370 La Matanza, Tenerife, Canary Islands
Tel: +34 922 578 818
Fax: +34 922 578 436
Web: www.johansens.com/jardindelapaz

SPAIN / CASTILLA LA MANCHA (BELVÍS DE LA JARA)

Finca Canturias

Ctra. Alcaudete - Calera, Km 12, 45660 Belvís de la Jara, Toledo, Spain
Tel: +34 925 59 41 08
Fax: +34 925 59 4107
Web: www.johansens.com/canturias

SPAIN / CASTILLA Y LEÓN (SALAMANCA)

Hotel Rector

c/Rector Esperabé 10–Apartado 399, 37008 Salamanca, Spain
Tel: +34 923 21 84 82
Fax: +34 923 21 40 08
Web: www.johansens.com/rector

SPAIN / CASTILLA Y LEÓN (SALAMANCA - TOPAS)

Castillo de Buen Amor

Carretera National 630 Km 317.6, 37799 Topas, Salamanca, Spain
Tel: +34 923 355 002
Fax: +34 923 355 112
Web: www.johansens.com/buenamor

SPAIN / CASTILLA Y LEÓN (SALAMANCA - VALDERÓN)

Hacienda Zorita

Carretera Salamanca-Ledesma, Km 8.7, 37115 Valderón, Salamanca, Spain
Tel: +34 923 129 400
Fax: +34 923 129 401
Web: www.johansens.com/haciendazorita

SPAIN / CATALUÑA (ALCANAR)

Tancat de Codorniu

Ctra. N340, Km 1059, 43530 Alcanar, Spain
Tel: +34 977 737 194
Fax: +34 977 737 231
Web: www.johansens.com/tancat

SPAIN / CATALUÑA (BARCELONA)

Gallery Hotel

C/ Rosselló 249, 08008 Barcelona, Spain
Tel: +34 934 15 99 11
Fax: +34 934 15 91 84
Web: www.johansens.com/gallery

SPAIN / CATALUÑA (BARCELONA)

Grand Hotel Central

Via Laietana 30, 08003 Barcelona, Spain
Tel: +34 93 295 79 00
Fax: +34 93 268 12 15
Web: www.johansens.com/grandhotelcentral

SPAIN / CATALUÑA (BARCELONA)

Hotel Casa Fuster

Passeig de Gràcia 132, 08008 Barcelona, Spain
Tel: +34 93 255 30 00
Fax: +34 93 255 30 02
Web: www.johansens.com/fuster

SPAIN / CATALUÑA (BARCELONA)

Hotel Claris

Pau Claris 150, 08009 Barcelona, Spain
Tel: +34 93 487 62 62
Fax: +34 93 215 79 70
Web: www.johansens.com/claris

SPAIN / CATALUÑA (BARCELONA)

Hotel Cram

C/ Aribau 54, 8011 Barcelona, Spain
Tel: +34 93 216 77 00
Fax: +34 93 216 77 07
Web: www.johansens.com/hotelcram

SPAIN / CATALUÑA (BARCELONA)

Hotel Duquesa de Cardona

Paseo Colon 12, 08002 Barcelona, Spain
Tel: +34 93 268 90 90
Fax: +34 93 268 29 31
Web: www.johansens.com/duquesadecardona

SPAIN / CATALUÑA (BARCELONA)

Hotel Gran Derby

Calle Loreto 28, 08029 Barcelona, Spain
Tel: +34 93 445 2544
Fax: +34 93 419 6820
Web: www.johansens.com/granderby

SPAIN / CATALUÑA (BARCELONA)

Hotel Granados 83

c/ Enric Granados 83, 08008 Barcelona, Spain
Tel: +34 93 492 96 70
Fax: +34 93 492 96 90
Web: www.johansens.com/granados83

SPAIN / CATALUÑA (BARCELONA)

Hotel Omm

Rosselló 265, 08008 Barcelona, Spain
Tel: +34 93 445 40 00
Fax: +34 93 445 40 04
Web: www.johansens.com/hotelomm

SPAIN / CATALUÑA (BARCELONA)

Hotel Pulitzer

C/Bergara 8, 08002 Barcelona, Spain
Tel: +34 93 481 67 67
Fax: +34 93 481 64 64
Web: www.johansens.com/pulitzer

SPAIN / CATALUÑA (BEGUR)

El Convent Begur

c/del Racó 2, sa Riera, 17255 Begur, Spain
Tel: +34 972 62 30 91
Fax: +34 972 62 31 04
Web: www.johansens.com/conventbegur

SPAIN / CATALUÑA (BOLVIR DE CERDANYA)

Torre del Remei

Camí Reial s/n, 17539 Bolvir de Cerdanya, Gerona, Spain
Tel: +34 972 140 182
Fax: +34 972 140 449
Web: www.johansens.com/torredelremei

SPAIN / CATALUÑA (COSTA BRAVA)

Hotel Rigat

Av. America 1, Playa de Fenals, 17310 Lloret de Mar, Costa Brava, Gerona, Spain
Tel: +34 972 36 52 00
Fax: +34 972 37 04 11
Web: www.johansens.com/rigatpark

SPAIN / CATALUÑA (COSTA BRAVA)

Hotel Santa Marta

Playa de Santa Cristina, 17310 Lloret de Mar, Spain
Tel: +34 972 364 904
Fax: +34 972 369 280
Web: www.johansens.com/santamarta

SPAIN / CATALUÑA (LA GARRIGA)

Gran Hotel Balneario Blancafort

Mina 7, 08530 La Garriga (Barcelona), Spain
Tel: +34 93 860 56 00
Fax: +34 93 861 23 90
Web: www.johansens.com/blancafort

SPAIN / CATALUÑA (LA SELVA DEL CAMP)

Mas Passamaner

Camí de la Serra 52, 43470 La Selva del Camp (Tarragona), Spain
Tel: +34 977 766 333
Fax: +34 977 766 336
Web: www.johansens.com/passamaner

Mini Listings Europe

Condé Nast Johansens are delighted to recommend 435 properties across Europe & The Mediterranean.
Call 1 800 564 7518 or see the Order Form on page 431 to order Guides.

SPAIN / CATALUÑA (ROSES)

Romantic Villa - Hotel Vistabella
Cala Canyelles Petites, PO Box 3, 17480 Roses (Gerona), Spain
Tel: +34 972 25 62 00
Fax: +34 972 25 32 13
Web: www.johansens.com/vistabella

SPAIN / CATALUÑA (SITGES)

Dolce Sitges Hotel
Av. Cami de Miralpeix 12, Sitges 08870, Spain
Tel: +34 938 109 000
Fax: +34 938 109 001
Web: www.johansens.com/doclesitges

SPAIN / CATALUÑA (SITGES)

San Sebastian Playa Hotel
Calle Port Alegre 53, 08870 Sitges (Barcelona), Spain
Tel: +34 93 894 86 76
Fax: +34 93 894 04 30
Web: www.johansens.com/sebastian

SPAIN / EXTREMADURA (BADAJOZ - ZAFRA)

Casa Palacio Conde de la Corte
Plaza Pilar Redondo 2, 06300 Zafra (Badajoz), Spain
Tel: +34 924 563 311
Fax: +34 924 563 072
Web: www.johansens.com/condedelacorte

SPAIN / EXTREMADURA (JERTE - CÁCERES)

Tunel del Hada Hotel & Spa
Travesía de la Fuente Nueva 2, 10612 Jerte (Cáceres), Spain
Tel: +34 927 470 000
Fax: +34 927 470 021
Web: www.johansens.com/tuneldelhada

SPAIN / MADRID (MADRID)

Antiguo Convento
C/ de Las Monjas, s/n Boadilla del Monte, 28660 Madrid, Spain
Tel: +34 91 632 22 20
Fax: +34 91 633 15 12
Web: www.johansens.com/elconvento

SPAIN / MADRID (MADRID)

Gran Meliá Fénix
Hermosilla 2, 28001 Madrid, Spain
Tel: +34 91 431 67 00
Fax: +34 91 576 06 61
Web: www.johansens.com/granmeliafenix

SPAIN / MADRID (MADRID)

Hotel Orfila
C/Orfila, No 6, 28010 Madrid, Spain
Tel: +34 91 702 77 70
Fax: +34 91 702 77 72
Web: www.johansens.com/orfila

SPAIN / MADRID (MADRID)

Hotel Quinta de los Cedros
C/Allendesalazar 4, 28043 Madrid, Spain
Tel: +34 91 515 2200
Fax: +34 91 415 2050
Web: www.johansens.com/loscedros

SPAIN / MADRID (MADRID)

Hotel Urban
Carrera de San Jerónimo 34, 28014 Madrid, Spain
Tel: +34 91 787 77 70
Fax: +34 91 787 77 99
Web: www.johansens.com/urban

SPAIN / MADRID (MADRID)

Hotel Villa Real
Plaza de las Cortes 10, 28014 Madrid, Spain
Tel: +34 914 20 37 67
Fax: +34 914 20 25 47
Web: www.johansens.com/villareal

SPAIN / PAIS VASCO (ARMINTZA)

Hotel Arresi
Portugane 7, 48620 Armintza, Spain
Tel: +34 94 68 79 208
Fax: +34 94 68 79 310
Web: www.johansens.com/arresi

SPAIN / VALENCIA (ALICANTE)

Hospes Amérigo
C/ Rafael Altamira 7, 03002 Alicante, Spain
Tel: +34 965 14 65 70
Fax: +34 965 14 65 71
Web: www.johansens.com/amerigo

SPAIN / VALENCIA (ALICANTE)

Hotel Sidi San Juan & Spa
Playa de San Juan, 03540 Alicante, Spain
Tel: +34 96 516 13 00
Fax: +34 96 516 33 46
Web: www.johansens.com/sanjuan

SPAIN / VALENCIA (ALQUERIAS - CASTELLÓN)

Torre la Mina
C/ La Regenta 1, 12539 Alquerias-Castellón, Spain
Tel: +34 964 57 1746/0180
Fax: +34 964 57 0199
Web: www.johansens.com/torrelamina

SPAIN / VALENCIA (BENICÀSSIM)

Hotel Termas Marinas el Palasiet
Partida Cantallops s/n, 12560 Benicàssim, Castellón, Costa del Azahar, Spain
Tel: +34 964 300 250
Fax: +34 964 302 236
Web: www.johansens.com/termasmarinas

SPAIN / VALENCIA (DÉNIA)

La Posada del Mar
Plaça de les Drassanes, 1-2 03700 Dénia, Spain
Tel: +34 96 643 29 66
Fax: +34 96 642 01 55
Web: www.johansens.com/posadadelmar

SPAIN / VALENCIA (JÁTIVA - XÀTIVA)

Hotel Mont Sant
Subida Al Castillo, s/n Játiva - Xàtiva, 46800 Valencia, Spain
Tel: +34 962 27 50 81
Fax: +34 962 28 19 05
Web: www.johansens.com/montsant

SPAIN / VALENCIA (TÁRBENA)

Casa Lehmi
El Buscarró 1-3, E-03518 Tárbena, Alicante, Spain
Tel: +34 96 588 4018
Fax: +34 96 588 4106
Web: www.johansens.com/casalehmi

SPAIN / VALENCIA (VALENCIA)

Hospes Palau de la Mar
Navarro Reverter 14, 46004 Valencia, Spain
Tel: +34 96 316 2884
Fax: +34 96 316 2885
Web: www.johansens.com/palaudelamar

SPAIN / VALENCIA (VALENCIA)

Hotel Sidi Saler & Spa
Playa el Saler, 46012 Valencia, Spain
Tel: +34 961 61 04 11
Fax: +34 961 61 08 38
Web: www.johansens.com/saler

SPAIN / VALENCIA (VILAMARXANT)

Mas de Canicattí
Ctra. de Pedralba, Km 2.9, 46191 Vilamarxant, Valencia, Spain
Tel: +34 96 165 05 34
Fax: +34 96 165 05 35
Web: www.johansens.com/canicatti

Mini Listings Europe

Condé Nast Johansens are delighted to recommend 435 properties across Europe & The Mediterranean.
Call 1 800 564 7518 or see the Order Form on page 431 to order Guides.

SWITZERLAND (LUGANO)

Villa Sassa - Hotel & Spa
Via Tesserete 10, 6900 Lugano, Switzerland
Tel: +41 91 911 41 11
Fax: +41 91 922 05 45
Web: www.johansens.com/villasassa

SWITZERLAND (WEGGIS - LAKE LUCERNE)

Park Hotel Weggis
Hertensteinstrasse 34, 6353 Weggis, Switzerland
Tel: +41 41 392 05 05
Fax: +41 41 392 05 28
Web: www.johansens.com/weggis

SWITZERLAND (ZÜRICH)

Alden Hotel Splügenschloss
Splügenstrasse 2, Genferstrasse, 8002 Zürich, Switzerland
Tel: +41 44 289 99 99
Fax: +41 44 289 99 98
Web: www.johansens.com/aldenhotel

TURKEY (ANTALYA)

The Marmara Antalya
Eski Lara Yolu No 136, Sirinyali, Antalya, Turkey
Tel: +90 242 249 36 00
Fax: +90 242 316 81 04
Web: www.johansens.com/marmaraantalya

TURKEY (BODRUM PENINSULA - MUGLA)

Divan Bodrum Palmira
Kelesharim Caddesi 6, Göltürkbükü, Mugla, 48483 Bodrum, Turkey
Tel: +90 252 377 5601
Fax: +90 252 377 5952
Web: www.johansens.com/divanpalmira

TURKEY (BODRUM)

The Marmara Bodrum
Suluhasan Caddesi, Yokusbasi, Mahallesi No 18, PO Box 199, 48400 Bodrum, Turkey
Tel: +90 252 313 8130
Fax: +90 252 313 8131
Web: www.johansens.com/marmarabodrum

TURKEY (ÇESME - IZMIR)

Degirmen Otel
Degirmen Sok 3, Alaçati, Çesme, Izmir, Turkey
Tel: +90 232 716 6714
Fax: +90 232 716 8936
Web: www.johansens.com/degirmen

TURKEY (GÖREME – CAPPADOCIA)

Cappadocia Cave Suites
Gafferli Mahallesi, unlü Sokak, 50180 Göreme - Nevsehir, Turkey
Tel: +90 384 271 2800
Fax: +90 384 271 27 99
Web: www.johansens.com/cappadociacaves

TURKEY (ISTANBUL)

Ajia Hotel
Ahmet Rasim Pasa Yalisi, Çubuklu Caddesi, No 27, Kanlica, Istanbul, Turkey
Tel: +90 216 413 9300
Fax: +90 216 413 9355
Web: www.johansens.com/aijahotel

TURKEY (ISTANBUL)

The Marmara Istanbul
Taksim Meydani, Taksim, 34437 Istanbul, Turkey
Tel: +90 212 251 4696
Fax: +90 212 244 0509
Web: www.johansens.com/maramaraistanbul

TURKEY (ISTANBUL)

The Marmara Pera
Mesrutiyet Caddesi, Tepebasi, 34430 Istanbul, Turkey
Tel: +90 212 251 4646
Fax: +90 212 249 8033
Web: www.johansens.com/marmarapera

TURKEY (ISTANBUL)

Sumahan On The Water
Kulelí Caddesi No 51, Çengelköy, 34684 Istanbul, Turkey
Tel: +90 216 422 8000
Fax: +90 216 422 8008
Web: www.johansens.com/sumahan

TURKEY (KALEIÇI - ANTALYA)

Tuvana Residence
Tuzcular Mahallesi, Karanlik Sokak 7, 07100 Kaleiçi - Antalya, Turkey
Tel: +90 242 247 60 15
Fax: +90 242 241 19 81
Web: www.johansens.com/tuvanaresidence

TURKEY (KALKAN - ANTALYA)

Villa Mahal
PO Box 4 Kalkan, 07960 Antalya, Turkey
Tel: +90 242 844 32 68
Fax: +90 242 844 21 22
Web: www.johansens.com/villamahal

TURKEY (KAS - ANTALYA)

Villa Hotel Tamara
Çururbag Yarimadasi, Kas, Antalya, Turkey
Tel: +90 242 836 3273
Fax: +90 242 836 2112
Web: www.johansens.com/villahoteltamara

TURKEY (SAPANCA - ADAPAZARI)

Richmond Nua Wellness - Spa
Sahilyolu, 54600 Sapanca, Adapazari, Turkey
Tel: +90 264 582 2100
Fax: +90 264 582 2101
Web: www.johansens.com/richmondnua

TURKEY (ÜRGÜP - CAPPADOCIA)

Sacred House
Karahandere Mahallesi, Barbaros Hayrettin Sokak, No 25, 50400 Ürgüp, Turkey
Tel: +90 384 341 7102
Fax: +90 384 341 6986
Web: www.johansens.com/sacredhouse

Index by Property

0-9

A

B

C

D

E

Index by Property

Index by Property

K

L

M

N

O

P

Index by Property

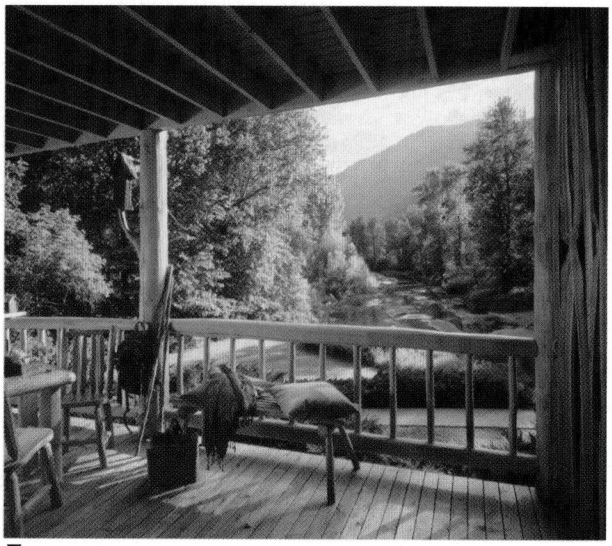

Index by Location

North America

Canada

Mexico

The United States of America

Index by Location

Index by Location

Central America

South America

Index by Location

Atlantic

The Caribbean

Pacific

INDEX BY ACTIVITY

SPA Dedicated Spa

Canada

Mexico

The United States of America

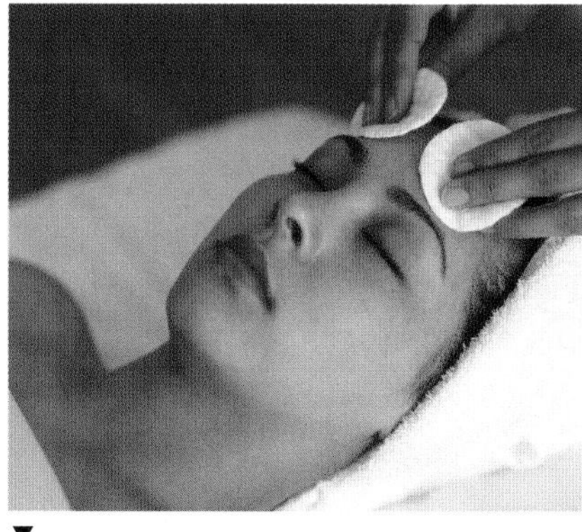

Central America

South America

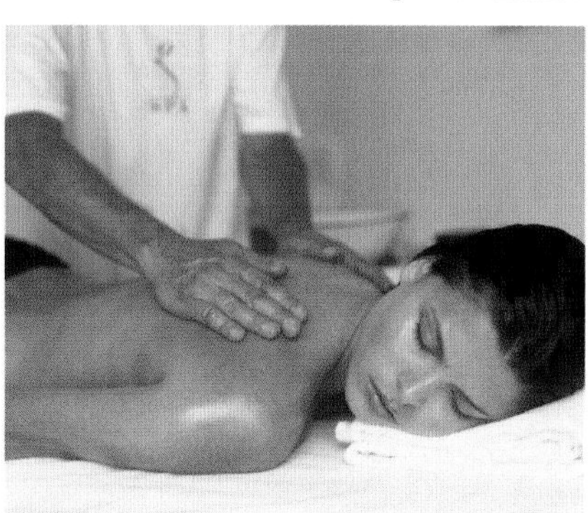

Atlantic

Caribbean

Pacific

Index by Activity

Located in a Ski Resort

Canada

The United States of America

Fishing on-site

Canada

Mexico

The United States of America

Central America

South America

Atlantic

Caribbean

Pacific

Golf course on-site

Mexico

The United States of America

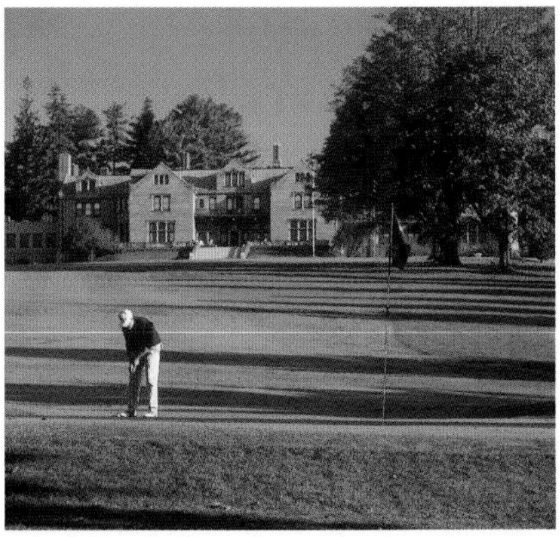

▼

Cranwell Resort, Spa & Golf Club ... Massachusetts ... 166

Central America

South America

Atlantic

Caribbean

Index by Activity

Atlantic

Water sports on-site

Canada

Mexico

The United States of America

South America

Atlantic

Caribbean

Atlantic

▼ **Toberua Island Resort ...... Fiji Islands 385**

Scuba diving on-site

Mexico

The United States of America

South America

Atlantic

Caribbean

Atlantic

NR HP National Register of Historic Places

The United States of America

▼ **Monmouth Plantation ...... Mississippi 170**

Index by Activity / Consortium

M Conference facilities for 130 delegates or more

Canada

Mexico

The United States of America

Central America

South America

Caribbean

Classic Inns of the South

The United States of America

The Leading Hotels of the World

Mexico

The United States of America

Central America

Caribbean

INDEX BY CONSORTIUM

Loews Hotels

The United States of America

Mexico Boutique Hotels

Mexico

▼

Preferred Hotels

The United States of America

Caribbean

Relais & Châteaux

Canada

The United States of America

▼

South America

Atlantic

Caribbean

Small Luxury Hotels

Canada

Mexico

The United States of America

Central America

Atlantic

Caribbean

Pacific

With over 1,300 Recommendations across The Americas, the UK and Europe, our website is a great reference point to source a property that fits the experience you're after, be it a luxury hotel, a coastal hideaway, a traditional inn, country house or resort. Each one is annually inspected and you can feel confident that we have taken care in helping you to select a place to stay.

You can search for a place by location, see what special breaks are on offer and send an enquiry. The on-line Bookshop offers great gift ideas - Guides and gift certificates to use in any of our worldwide destinations. You can also register on-line to receive our monthly Newsletter.

For a great source of inspiration...

johansens.com

From top, left to right: Cliveden, England; One & Only Palmilla, Mexico; Lake Vyrnwy Hotel, Wales; Fawsley Hall, England; Sorrel River Ranch Resort & Spa, U.S.A.; Elounda Peninsula All Suite Hotel, Greece; Dalhousie Castle and Spa, Scotland; Lainston House Hotel, England; Qamea Resort & Spa; Fiji Islands.

GUIDE ORDER FORM

Save up to $30 when you order multiple Guides...

Order 4 Guides get $30 off, 3 Guides get $15 off, 2 Guides $8 off

Hotels & Spas
Great Britain & Ireland
$35

QUANTITY | $

Country Houses, Small Hotels
Inns & Restaurants, Great
Britain & Ireland - $30

QUANTITY | $

Hotels & Spas
Europe & Mediterranean
$35

QUANTITY | $

Hotels, Inns, Resorts & Spas
The Americas, Atlantic,
Caribbean, Pacific - $30

QUANTITY | $

Business Venues
(published Feb 2007)
$38.00

QUANTITY | $

Save $98 when you order the **The International Collection...**

The International Collection
$100.00

QUANTITY | $

a boxed presentation set of the 4 leisure Guides,

PLUS the Recommended Venues Guide,

PLUS our exclusive silver plated luggage tag.

A great offer for only $100

DISCOUNT - Discount does not apply to The International Collection 2 Guides = $8 off ☐ 3 Guides = $15 off ☐ 4 Guides = $30 off ☐

SHIPPING & HANDLING - Add $6 per Guide or $38 for The International Collection $

GRAND TOTAL - Don't forget to deduct your discount $

☐ Please charge my Visa/Mastercard ☐ I enclose a check payable to Condé Nast Johansens

Card No.: Exp. Date: Card Security Code:

The **Card Security Code** is the last 3 digits of the number shown above the signature strip on the reverse side of the credit card.
For Amex, the 4 digit code is printed on the front of the card just above and to the right of your main credit card number.

Name: Signature:

Address:

Zipcode: Tel: E-mail:

Please check if you would like to receive information or offers from The Condé Nast Publications Ltd. by telephone☐ or SMS☐ or E-mail☐
Please check if you would like to receive information or offers from other selected companies by telephone☐ or SMS☐ or E-mail☐
Please check if you prefer not to receive direct mail from The Condé Nast Publications Ltd. ☐ and other reputable companies ☐

Mail to Condé Nast Johansens, 1317 Third Avenue, Suite 100, New York, NY 10021
or register on-line at www.cnjguides.co.uk quoting reference K009

CALL OUR HOTLINE NOW: U.S. TOLL FREE 1 800 564 7518
OR ORDER ONLINE AT www.cnjguides.co.uk ref: K009

GUEST SURVEY REPORT

Evaluate your stay in a Condé Nast Johansens Recommendation

Following your stay in a Condé Nast Johansens Recommendation, please spare a moment to complete this Guest Survey Report. This is an important source of information for Condé Nast Johansens, in order to maintain the highest standards for our Recommendations and to support our team of Inspectors. It is also the prime source of nominations for Condé Nast Johansens Awards for Excellence, which are held annually and include properties from all over the world that represent the finest standards and best value for money in luxury, independent travel.

Your details

Name: ________________

Address: ________________

Zip: ________

Telephone: ________________

E-mail: ________________

Your rating of the hotel

	Excellent	Good	Disappointing	Poor
Bedrooms	❍	❍	❍	❍
Public Rooms	❍	❍	❍	❍
Food/Restaurant	❍	❍	❍	❍
Service	❍	❍	❍	❍
Welcome/Friendliness	❍	❍	❍	❍
Value For Money	❍	❍	❍	❍

Hotel details

Name of hotel: ________________

Location: ________________

Date of visit: ________________

Any other comments

If you wish to make additional comments, please write separately to the Publisher, Condé Nast Johansens, 6-8 Old Bond Street, London W1S 4PH, Great Britain

Please tick if you would like to receive information or offers from The Condé Nast Publications Ltd by telephone ☐ or SMS ☐ or E-mail ☐
Please tick if you would like to receive information or offers from other selected companies by telephone ☐ or SMS ☐ or E-mail ☐

Please fax your completed survey to +44 (0) 207 152 3566
or go to www.johansens.com (E-Club) where you can complete the survey online

GUEST SURVEY REPORT

Evaluate your stay in a Condé Nast Johansens Recommendation

Following your stay in a Condé Nast Johansens Recommendation, please spare a moment to complete this Guest Survey Report. This is an important source of information for Condé Nast Johansens, in order to maintain the highest standards for our Recommendations and to support our team of Inspectors. It is also the prime source of nominations for Condé Nast Johansens Awards for Excellence, which are held annually and include properties from all over the world that represent the finest standards and best value for money in luxury, independent travel.

Your details

Name: ________________

Address: ________________

Zip: ________

Telephone: ________________

E-mail: ________________

Your rating of the hotel

	Excellent	Good	Disappointing	Poor
Bedrooms	❍	❍	❍	❍
Public Rooms	❍	❍	❍	❍
Food/Restaurant	❍	❍	❍	❍
Service	❍	❍	❍	❍
Welcome/Friendliness	❍	❍	❍	❍
Value For Money	❍	❍	❍	❍

Hotel details

Name of hotel: ________________

Location: ________________

Date of visit: ________________

Any other comments

If you wish to make additional comments, please write separately to the Publisher, Condé Nast Johansens, 6-8 Old Bond Street, London W1S 4PH, Great Britain

Please tick if you would like to receive information or offers from The Condé Nast Publications Ltd by telephone ☐ or SMS ☐ or E-mail ☐
Please tick if you would like to receive information or offers from other selected companies by telephone ☐ or SMS ☐ or E-mail ☐

Please fax your completed survey to +44 (0) 207 152 3566
or go to www.johansens.com (E-Club) where you can complete the survey online